ABAP/4

The SAP® Series

Edited by Bernhard Hochlehnert, SAP AG.
Other titles in Addison-Wesley's SAP® Series include:

Marcus Geiss and Roland Soltysiak
Dynamic Implementation of SAP R/3
(2000, ISBN: 0-201-67483-1)

Greg Spence
SAP R/3 & Oracle: Backup & Recovery
(1999, ISBN: 0-201-59622-9)

Norbert Welti
Successful SAP R/3 Implementation: Practical Management of ERP Projects
(1999, ISBN: 0-201-39824-9)

Rüdiger Buck-Emden
SAP R/3: An introduction to ERP and business software technology
(2000, ISBN: 0-201-59617-2)

Erich Draeger
Project Management with SAP R/3
(2000, ISBN: 0-201-39835-4)

Stefan Huth, Robert Kolbinger and Hanns-Martin Meyer
SAP on Windows NT
(1999, ISBN: 0-201-39837-0)

Gerhard Keller
SAP R/3 Process Oriented Implementation
(1998, ISBN: 0-201-92470-6)

Mario Perez, Alexander Hildenbrand, Bernd Matzke and Peter Zencke
The SAP R/3 System on the Internet
(1999, ISBN: 0-201-34303-7)

Liane Will, Christiane Hienger, Frank Strassenburg and Rocco Himmes
SAP R/3 Administration
(1998, ISBN: 0-201-92469-2)

ABAP/4

Programming the SAP R/3 System

Bernd Matzke

Addison-Wesley

An imprint of **Pearson Education**

Harlow, England · London · New York · Reading, Massachusetts · San Francisco
Toronto · Don Mills, Ontario · Sydney · Tokyo · Singapore · Hong Kong · Seoul
Taipei · Cape Town · Madrid · Mexico City · Amsterdam · Munich · Paris · Milan

PEARSON EDUCATION LIMITED

Head Office:
Edinburgh Gate
Harlow CM20 2JE
Tel: +44 (0)1279 623623
Fax: +44 (0)1279 431059

London Office:
128 Long Acre
London WC2E 9AN
Tel: +44 (0)20 7447 2000
Fax: +44 (0)20 7240 5771

Website: www.aw.com/cseng

_____

First published in Great Britain in 2001

English translation © Pearson Education Limited 2001
Copyright © 1999 by Pearson Education Deutschland GmbH. All rights reserved.

First published in the German language under the title
ABAP/4 by Pearson Education Deutschland GmbH, Munich.

The right of Bernd Matzke to be identified as Author of this Work has been asserted by him in
accordance with the Copyright, Designs and Patents Act 1988.

ISBN 0-201-67515-3

British Library Cataloguing-in-Publication Data
A CIP catalogue record for this book can be obtained from the British Library

Library of Congress Cataloging-in-Publication Data
Applied for.

The programs in this book have been included for their instructional value. The publisher does not
offer any warranties or representations in respect of their fitness for a particular purpose,
nor does the publisher accept any liability for any loss or damage arising from their use.

Many of the designations used by manufacturers and sellers to distinguish their
products are claimed as trademarks. Pearson Education Limited has made every
attempt to supply trademark information about manufacturers and their products mentioned
in this book.

10 9 8 7 6 5 4 3 2 1

Translated by Transcript Alba Ltd.
Typeset by Pantek Arts Ltd
Printed and bound in the United States of America.

The Publishers' policy is to use paper manufactured from sustainable forests.

Foreword to the 2nd edition

Release 4.6 of SAP's R/3 System saw the introduction of many new features. Some, like the completely redesigned user interface, are immediately apparent. However, the user interface conceals a large number of enhancements and additions. This is particularly true of the programming language of the R/3 System, whose functionality has been extended considerably. The additions to the scope of the ABAP language alone are enough to justify a new edition of this book.

For this edition, it was necessary to focus on essentials, primarily because only limited time was available to me, but also because of the broad scope that the book needed to cover. As a result, apart from a few exceptions, the book focuses on providing a description of the ABAP commands and of the main principles of programming. For these reasons, although many readers have requested it, I am unfortunately not able in this book to include topics that go beyond the bounds of a pure description of the language. Such topics would for example include workflow programming, batch input and the new interface controls.

I would like to thank everyone who assisted me, directly or indirectly, with my work on this book. Above all, I would like to mention the companies SAP, Addison-Wesley and IXOS, without whose generous support it would have been impossible to write this book. My special thanks go to the SAP employees who patiently gave their time to provide detailed answers to my questions, and in doing so made it much easier for me to learn and understand SAP R/3 and ABAP.

Bernd Matzke
Delitzsch, October 17, 1999

Contents

1 Introduction

The ABAP programming language is a fully integrated component of the SAP R/3 System. Apart from the system kernel, which is programmed in C, the entire R/3 System, with its development tools and applications, consists of ABAP programs. This ensures that programmers can develop software that is independent of the operating system. All the same, programmers who work with the ABAP language need to get used to some of its specific characteristics, which makes for some considerable difficulties when learning ABAP.

The ABAP language has its origins in the R/2 System. There, ABAP was a simple programming language designed for generating lists for printing. (The German abbreviation 'ABAP' translates as *general report preparation processor*.) This language, which was primarily used for reporting, gradually grew into a full-featured application development tool. This also prompted the present name *Advanced Business Application Programming*.

The ABAP programming language was not designed by a single person or a small circle of experts sitting round a table. Starting from the first version in the R/2 System, the language has been, and is, undergoing constant development. This development is being carried out by a sizeable team, in which work on individual areas (such as type concept, database connection and user interface design) is done relatively independently of the other areas. As a result, new features are introduced into the language from one version to the next. To retain compatibility with earlier releases, it is impossible, or only rarely possible, to remove obsolete elements. Inevitably, the scope of the language continues to grow and the tool itself becomes ever more powerful, but also less easy to learn and understand.

Unlike C or Java, ABAP is not one of the universally used programming languages. The R/2 and R/3 Systems use specific techniques to create programs. One example is the dynamic screen program, which is also widely known by its German name of 'dynpro', from 'dynamic program'. This imposes a relatively tight definition of the structure of an application. The components of the programming language are structured according to this concept. Thus, ABAP consists of statements that were designed for a specific program type, with predefined functionality and structure. With time, the programming language has become more flexible, above all when a graphical user interface and a client/server architecture were implemented. New commands have been created around the existing commands, or existing commands have had new options added to them, giving some commands an entirely new functionality. Often, an option for a command says more about that command's purpose than its actual name. Some of the command variants created in this way perform a very specific, often low-level, task. These commands can only be used by specialists, and will therefore not necessarily be of interest to all readers.

The ABAP language has not been set down in a standard. The language is its own standard, which changes from version to version. This is why it is neither possible nor sensible to give a comprehensive introduction to the syntax of this language. The language itself is subordinate to a programming concept, which you need to know about to understand the meaning of many commands. As a result, any introduction to ABAP programming must start with the programming concepts.

You should not view this book as an alternative to the many different sources of documentation available for the system or to the training courses offered by SAP. In the course of my own work, I discovered that beginners find it relatively difficult to sort out the vast range of facts about the R/3 System or the programming language and to filter out the points relevant for their own work. That is why I consider it difficult to learn R/3 programming without programming experience. I have actually attempted to close the gap between general introduction and the very specialised system documentation that is available. This book is primarily intended to help users with prior experience in IT to quickly learn how to program with ABAP. It is especially aimed at SAP System administrators and at people intending to develop applications using ABAP. It is not a training manual for novice programmers, because the broad scope of the material means it is impossible for me to provide a general introduction to programming in addition to the introduction to ABAP. It is therefore assumed that readers already possess a basic knowledge of programming, as well as of the structure and function of relational databases.

1.1   About the contents of this book

With regard to the concept on which it is based, the third edition of this book naturally builds on the two previous editions. All the same, R/3 Release 4.0 saw the introduction of a series of new concepts, which have had a considerable effect on the development environment and program development. That is why this book has been completely rewritten. It is based primarily on the current R/3 Release 4.6. Older versions are now mentioned only in exceptional cases.

The development environment comprises a series of components and defines some terms. It is essential that you know about them before you can understand the overall system. Chapter 2 presents the main components of the development environment and the frequently used terms. This chapter does not go into the technical details. It simply provides explanations of the basic tasks of the elements.

Chapter 3 investigates the different program types and their characteristics. In it you will find a description of the ABAP statements for these program types. This chapter does not primarily aim to provide a complete description of the various commands. Instead, it focuses on demonstrating the tasks of each of the ABAP statements within a particular program. Despite these constraints, you will find enough information on the ABAP commands to let you analyze existing standard applications and start writing new programs yourself. Chapter 3 begins with a short tutorial that shows you how to use the most important development tools. This includes a section that describes global concepts and widely used commands. That is followed by a description of the *interface*, which, for example, contains an application's menus. In the sections that follow, you will find details of one of the two fundamental program types: the report. Finally, there is a section on dialog programming.

Both programming models can also be linked with each other. After the section explaining dialog programming, you will find notes on that subject.

This is followed by a section that describes the function modules. These modules allow program code to be used from within several other applications. The SAP System provides a wide range of modules for you to use in your own applications. The final two sections demonstrate how to use SAP-specific function modules. They focus on using SAPscript for processing forms.

In addition to programming, it is also necessary to create database tables. These tables are known as Data Dictionary elements, which are covered in Chapter 5.

Chapter 6 provides more details on some resources used for programming, in particular, the transport management system, which is used for transferring applications and documenting changes. This leads on to a description of the online debugger.

While Chapter 3 primarily concentrates on the programming concepts, Chapter 7 describes how to create a simple application. Here you can see how working applications can be created from the individual components.

Chapter 8 deals with some tips, tricks and traps. Although you need some previous knowledge to analyze these tips, they will deepen your understanding of how some ABAP commands work.

The book ends with a short reference section that covers the ABAP commands in the current R/3 Release 4.6B. This reference does not give details of obsolete commands that have been superseded by others. This section also omits some commands that are only intended to be used internally at SAP itself.

Now, a few words on the programming examples. The R/3 System uses a relational database to store data. Almost all of the examples use database tables. To save the reader the trouble of having to create tables and fill them with data, before doing the actual programming, I have mainly used tables that already exist in the standard R/3 System. I have deliberately not provided a variation of the same example in the programming chapters. The ABAP programming language is so complex and diverse that a step-by-step example intended to demonstrate all the facets of ABAP programming would very quickly become just as complex as the language itself. Examples that have been specially tailored and developed to suit particular topics are easier to understand and provide a good way to illustrate specific characteristics of the programming language.

1.2 Exercises

The best way to learn a programming language is to analyze existing programs and to practise on your own. For this reason, you will find exercises in many places in this book. In sections where the scope of the information presented is still small, the exercises are located at the end of the section. Their primary purpose is to reinforce the information presented in the section. In later parts of the book, the exercises are distributed throughout the text. Examples of how to use new statements are sometimes quite complex, so there is not always room to print them in their entirety in this book. In such cases it will be your job, building on your current knowledge and the available programs, to write a test environment for the new statements or objects. In this way, you will reinforce your knowledge from previous sections and at the same time gain more confidence and experience in using the development environment. Even if it does not specifically say so in the text, you should write and test your own programs for all the programming code extracts printed in this book.

1.3   Naming conventions

There are several different ways to configure the R/3 System. A distinction is made between SAP development systems (only found internally at SAP), the development systems of SAP's partner companies and customer systems. For example, these systems use different permitted naming ranges for development objects (programs, tables, etc.). All the examples in this book were created in a customer system. If you try to follow these examples in a system that is configured differently, you will sometimes get system messages warning you of infringements of naming conventions. Usually, the required objects will be created anyway after you confirm that you have seen the warning. In the case of more serious difficulties, you should contact your system administrators. They will be able to give you information about the type of R/3 System you are working with and the related effects concerning naming conventions. In many cases, the online help which you can access from the warning messages by choosing the Help button will also provide further assistance.

2 The Elements of the Development Environment

An application written with ABAP consists of several elements of different types. These are known as *development objects*. The actual source code is one such development object. Other elements such as menus or input masks are also development objects. These objects each fulfil special tasks and there are diverse relationships between them. Other than in some exceptional cases, several types of development objects are also necessary for each application. Consequently, even simple applications need relatively extensive preparation, including generating various different development objects, which are configured to work with each other. For this reason, programming with ABAP differs considerably from programming with the conventional third-generation programming languages, such as C or Pascal. That is why, before discussing the elements of an ABAP application in detail, it makes sense to start by giving a quick description of the tasks of the different objects and their characteristics and relationships with each other, without going into the ABAP programming language in detail.

2.1 The Data Dictionary

A computer program generates and processes data. This data may be temporary data, but more often the data needs to be stored permanently, including during times when the hardware is not in operation. One of the most important tasks of an operating system is to administer disk storage capacity, which usually consists of one or more hard disks. Inevitably, the way users work with a system's disk capacity is largely determined by the operating system. The user is compelled to work with file and directory names, for which different conventions need to be applied for different systems. There are further differences for example concerning the structure of the file system, special file characteristics, and access procedures. Independently of this, different relational database systems organize their own specially reserved areas on the storage medium. Each system enforces its own strategy to control these areas. Data stored in these areas can only be accessed using the database system. All these circumstances make it difficult to create non-operating system-specific applications or to develop tools to create applications that are not dependent on one particular operating system.

The R/3 System does not directly use the operating system services to store data. Instead, it uses a relational database system. The database system is used to store all information in tables. This includes not only the actual business data, but also programs, screen programs ('dynpros'), menus and other elements. In order to overcome the problems of dependence on a specific system (mentioned briefly above), the R/3 System must provide an interface to the data that is universal and independent of any specific operating system. This interface is the *Data Dictionary*.

The Data Dictionary is used to save all information, completely independently of the platform. The applications, as well as the programmers, no longer need to be concerned about such issues as where the data will be stored or the drive and directory names. These more physical data management criteria are replaced by logical criteria such as assignment to an application, to a superordinate object in the hierarchy or to a table.

The Data Dictionary is a virtual database, whose functionality extends beyond that of a normal relational database system. In particular, it performs the following tasks:

- creates a common interface to the database system;

- provides metadata through the actual database tables;

- provides common tools for data processing.

The Data Dictionary comprises different elements that are used in different places in an application. These elements are usually maintained separately from each other, taking into account certain dependencies. The next section describes the most important of these elements in more detail.

2.1.1 Tables

The central element of a database-oriented application is the data records, which are stored in tables. One or more fields form a data record (also known as a *tupel*), which describes the characteristics of a real object (an *entity*). Any number of data records of the same type form a table.

When relational database systems are used, information is processed in such a way that, as far as possible, no redundant data is saved. This calls for suitable data modelling, which normally defines several tables that are logically related. The term 'database' is used to describe a set of related tables that are stored on the system's storage media. A relational database system, which normally works with the SQL query language, is used to administer these tables.

In R/3, with few exceptions, the database system and the database tables can only be accessed through the Data Dictionary interface. The Data Dictionary is able to store the data to be processed in a different format than the format available to users through the user interface. The real reason for this conversion is the fact that the database systems are subject to certain restrictions concerning the number of tables and the number of fields in the tables. The Data Dictionary uses special storage methods to resolve these problems. The price paid for that is different table types, which the programmer cannot always handle in exactly the same way.

The Data Dictionary provides a completely transparent interface to the database for the vast majority of tables. This means that every field in a table in the Data Dictionary corresponds to a field in the real database table. In this way, the data structure visible in the Data Dictionary completely matches the structure of the table created by the database system. That is why these tables are known as transparent tables.

In addition to these transparent tables, the Data Dictionary also knows some other table types, which have become much less important than they were. These table types should not be used when new software is developed. As already mentioned, it is sometimes necessary to combine several tables into one, due to the capacity restrictions of the various database systems. This can be done in two different ways. Different tables that are not linked with each other through a shared key will be included in what is known as a *table pool*. Tables contained in this pool are called *pooled tables*. A table pool is stored in the database as one single table. The actual key of a record, the name of the pool table and the record content are stored in separate fields of the records in this table. In this way, several logical tables are combined into a single real database table. When data is written to the table pool, the data structure of a data record is lost, but is restored when the data record is read through the Data Dictionary. To achieve this, the Data Dictionary requires the metadata mentioned above.

Occasionally there are several tables that are linked with each other through a shared key. The Data Dictionary can also be used to combine these tables into a single table. One record in the real table, in the database, contains one key and one single field in that record contains several records from the next table for the key. Here too, when data is read or written, the Data Dictionary has to process the data, as the data structure of the database table differs from the structure stored in the Data Dictionary. The elements generated in this way are called clusters, and the tables are therefore called *cluster tables*.

Both table pools and table clusters are stored as tables in the database. As the actual information has to be first processed by the Data Dictionary when it is accessed, these tables are not at first transparent tables. In the Data Dictionary, only the structures of the pool tables and cluster tables are defined, and they only represent a logical view of the data. The data is actually stored on disk with a different structure. The Data Dictionary automatically makes any necessary adjustments.

Finally, the Data Dictionary also stores structures. In the Data Dictionary, structures appear to be similar to a table, but have no records in the database. The only thing of significance is the structure of the object, that is the fields contained in it, and their attributes. In ABAP programs, a structure has a similar function to type definitions in conventional programming languages.

Apart from the table types which are handled differently by the Data Dictionary, there is another special form of transparent tables. These are tables that can work together with special ABAP statements to store what are known as data clusters. A data cluster is a group of data objects. Data clusters with different structures can be stored in the same table. Tables containing data clusters are created in the Data Dictionary as transparent tables with a predefined structure. You should not confuse data clusters, and the tables intended for use with them, with the cluster tables mentioned above.

2.1.2   Fields, data elements and domains

A database system stores the attributes of a real object (entity) in the fields of data records. These attributes can be described in more detail, with regard to their logical meaning for the user, and also with regard to their technical characteristics (data type, length and similar information).

Ensuring system independence requires, first of all, a general data description that is independent of any specific database system. It is possible for different database systems to have a set of different data types, and to map and process them internally in completely different ways. These differences can, for example, concern the number range that can be mapped or even the way in which more complex data, such as images, is stored.

The Data Dictionary stores a range of administrative information, known as metadata, about the individual table fields. This includes both technical details and application-specific information. In some cases, different attributes of one entity have similar technical attributes. On the other hand, different entities can have identical attributes. For example, both the master data record of a particular employee and a work order can contain the personnel number of that employee. Both fields have an identical format and the same meaning, despite being used in different tables. It could now be possible that a field with the same format exists, but that it contains an item reference. Bearing in mind the complexity of the R/3 System, it is preferable to store information of this kind along with the actual data it belongs to, rather than storing it separately, for example, in an item of documentation.

That is why, in the R/3 System, much more information is maintained about the characteristics of fields than the relational database system requires to process the tables. In addition to technical and application-specific data, this includes permitted value ranges for each field or a reference to a check table. Field descriptions of this kind are maintained separately from database tables because they may possibly be used many times. This has the advantage that detailed descriptions of fields, with their characteristics, can be created, independently of how they are used later. This description is then available at different locations, for example, during table maintenance or when a programmer is writing data entry programs.

A field description always needs two different elements. The most basic elements of field descriptions are *domains*. A domain describes the technical structure of a field, that is its size and its data type. Domains are given unique names. The data elements build on the domains. They contain the reference to a domain in order to define the technical attributes, and add the logical meaning of the data element to this technical information. A domain can be used in several data elements, and these in turn can be used in different database fields.

As data elements and domains exist independently of the actual table, they can be used in several tables. Before a table can be generated in the Data Dictionary, it must assemble or generate all the data fields necessary for its data elements.

In addition to the attributes that can be assigned to a table field through the data element, there are some other attributes that need to be maintained individually for each table field. These attributes are *foreign keys* or when mapping information for fields that refer to currencies or units of measurement.

However, practical applications also contain data for which the time-consuming maintenance of domains and data elements cannot be justified. That is why, from R/3 Release 3.0, there is the option of creating table fields directly without a data element and domain, with direct reference to a data type. However, fields of this kind do not have the full range of functions available to the fields that reference a data element, and that is why they are significant only in special cases.

The following example should clarify how the elements interact. Let us assume there is a domain with the name NUM4, which is four characters long and has the data type NUMC (numeric). It can therefore accept a text that consists of only four digits.

This domain can be used for the technical description of different data elements. Before the post codes were reorganized in the Federal Republic of Germany, it might have been possible, building on this domain, to define a data element called PCD which was used to describe a post code. This meaning is defined by a descriptive short text within the data element. Independently of this, the domain NUM4 could also be used in another data element, for example PNR, which is used to describe a personnel number.

When a table is created, the data element PCD would first be assigned to a field called KPCD, which is intended to include a customer's post code, as a description. In that way, all the attributes of this field would be defined in one go.

The PCD data element could also be used in other tables to describe a field which should also include a post code. These fields could (but need not) have different names from KPCD.

The advantage is obvious: at the time the post codes in Germany were actually reorganized from four to five characters, the changeover was very time consuming. However, reorganization using the method described above would not necessitate changing a large number of field descriptions in different tables. Instead, it would only be necessary to generate a new domain called NUM5 (five characters long, data type NUMC) and to enter the new domain in the description of the PCD data element. The Data Dictionary supports a where-used list for the different objects (domains, fields, tables, etc.). From a list generated by the Data Dictionary, it would now be possible to find out which tables have fields that used the PCD data element. It would then only be necessary to change the contents of these tables by entering the new post code with a conversion program.

In this way, the domain roughly corresponds to the type declarations of different programming languages (typedef in C/C++ or TYPE in Pascal). Conventional programming languages do not have features that resemble the data element to any great extent.

In addition to using domains to describe field attributes, you can use them to automate some standard checks in applications. For example, you can enter the name of a check table or a list containing fixed values in a domain's description. When the system processes a record that contains a field based on the domain, it uses a variety of system mechanisms to automatically check whether the value of the table field concerned matches a value from the check table or the fixed values list. If the value does not match, the record is rejected. These checks take place automatically, so there is no need for programmers to generate any additional code for that purpose.

2.1.3   Views

As already mentioned, when relational database systems are used, the data to be stored is distributed among several tables, so as to reduce redundancy. Unique key fields are used to connect the data records that belong together. This connection can only be achieved by using statements such as multilevel accesses in tables that logically belong together.

To make processing easier, you can create a virtual table, which links the fields from one or more tables with each other and presents them to the user as a single table. As this is not a new table that really exists, but only a special display format, it is called a view. Within the R/3 System there are different view types which are used in different application areas. The database and the customizing views are of particular interest for your own applications. Views are not only created manually by the programmer, but also generated automatically by the system. This occurs, for example, when a maintenance interface is generated for tables.

Database views

Database views are created to provide real views of the database system. Therefore, they can only include transparent tables. They provide a summary of tables. If they contain fields from more than one table, they cannot be edited. Views of this kind are especially suitable for providing a simple way of filling tables with data, without the need for writing special programs for that purpose.

Customizing views

Customizing views can be used to allow users to edit data records, even if several tables are included in the view. When views of this kind are created, the system generates maintenance programs which can be executed by using a special transaction. As the name suggests, customizing views are particularly useful for customizing. Customizing is a process in which the application can be modified to meet specific user requirements by entering default values in selected tables.

Tick mark views

Tick mark views offer a view of a single table in which fields that are not of interest are hidden (deleted from view).

Help views

Help views were created to provide a means of displaying special help information. They are used only within the help system.

Entity views

Entity views are relevant only in the context of the Enterprise Data Model.

2.1.4 Lock objects

Usually, while someone is working with a database, the database should be locked to prevent it being accessed by other users. If several applications were able to write data to the same database table at the same time, this might in some circumstances result in the data having an undefined status.

While a table is being processed, several functions can be called to lock individual records, or groups of records, against external accesses, and also to release them again. The R/3 System uses what are known as *lock objects* to make it easier to apply these lock functions, and to make changes when there are changes to the underlying database table.

These lock objects are maintained separately from any actual application. No extra programming work is necessary to generate them. The programmer enters all the necessary information in some screen templates. Once the lock object has been completely defined, the system defines two function modules, which execute all the activities necessary to lock or unlock (release) the tables or selected data records involved. These function modules can be called by all applications that want to process the table.

If there is a change to the operating conditions of the lock request, simply change the lock object and then regenerate the function modules. There is usually no need to make changes to the source code of the applications that use the lock object or the function modules. If it turns out that changes are necessary after all, they are also supported by a where-used list that you can generate by selecting an option from the menu.

2.1.5 Type groups

The type concept was updated in Release 3 of the R/3 software. Freely definable data types can be used to describe the characteristics of data fields. These data types are independent of the data elements that have already been described, and not identical to them. Definitions of this kind can be stored in globally available type groups and used by each program. As these type definitions are also used to provide information about data, the Data Dictionary also manages type groups.

2.2   Authorizations

Usually, several users from different specialist fields, with different tasks, work on one R/3 System. This makes it necessary to install effective mechanisms to prevent unauthorized access. For that purpose, the R/3 System provides a very flexible method, which is primarily based on explicit authorization checks within an application. Before a user performs an action, such as running a program, the system checks that user's authorizations. With a few exceptions, this does not happen automatically, but requires special statements in the program code. This means that this procedure is fundamentally different from implicit authorization checks, such as the ones that are known in network or multi-user operating systems. There it is usually only access to files which is monitored, using access authorizations such as read, write, execute or delete. However, you can use SAP authorizations to protect not only tables or individual fields, but also other objects or actions such as programs, reports and program branching. In doing so you can, for example, make processing or displaying data just as dependent on existing authorizations as the processing of a program itself. Applications can even branch and perform different activities, depending on the user's existing authorizations, without them even noticing.

This flexibility is primarily due to the fact that authorizations are created and administered independently of the object that is to be protected. The relationship to the object must be created explicitly within the application by testing an authorization. The system itself merely makes resources available for managing some elements, and these resources can be used to define the user's authorizations.

However, there is also a disadvantage in not using implicit authorization checks. Each programmer is capable of writing programs that have unrestricted access to nearly all system tables, and reading or even manipulating them unhindered. Furthermore, the authorization to execute programs in debugging mode can also be misused to overwrite the authorization check return value and, in this way, make the check ineffective. In production systems, this consequently makes each user who has system administration or program development authorization into a potential security risk. That is why you should use these authorizations very cautiously. All the same, some more progressive concepts are now available, in which the kernel of the R/3 System itself checks some authorizations.

The authorization check is based on a simple principle. Each user is assigned a set of *authorizations*. An authorization is a complex object that contains several authorization fields. A value is entered in each of these authorization fields. The authorizations are stored in the user's master record. In the program, a special ABAP statement is then used to check whether a particular field in the user's authorization contains a particular value or not. The result of this check is explicitly evaluated within the program. However, the check itself still does not affect the execution of the program. It is only when the program evaluates the check result that it determines what will actually be authorized. Only at that stage is the relationship between the authorization and the object that is to be protected created. That is why it is also possible to protect several actions or data objects simultaneously, with one authorization. Equally, different authorizations can allow access to one and the same object.

In practice, this type of authorization check requires the use of many similar fields, if really flexible checks are necessary, as a unique authorization field may be necessary for each object to be protected. That is why the fields and authorizations are not individually assigned to the user. Instead, there is a multilevel hierarchy of elements, with which authorizations are administered and assigned to the user.

First, the required elements are defined independently of the user. Then an *authorization object* is generated, which contains one or more fields (up to a maximum of ten). The authorization objects are then stored in authorization classes, in which the objects belonging to an application or task area are grouped. The objects generated in this way initially consist only of general descriptions, which can be roughly compared with the type definitions used in procedural programming languages such as C or Pascal. So far, no values are assigned to the fields in the authorization object.

In order to grant a user authorization for a specific task, the first step, which is performed entirely independently of the user, is to derive the authorizations from an authorization object. The fields within that authorization then contain actual values. An authorization has a unique name. Any number of authorizations, which differ from each other due to their different field values, can be derived from one authorization object. Compared with conventional programming languages, authorizations resemble the instances of a type (for the authorization object).

Now, several authorizations are combined into what are known as profiles. Several similar profiles can be combined to form a composite profile. Profiles and composite profiles logically group together authorizations that belong together. Consequently, they identify authorizations for a particular task area such as the authorizations for an asset accountant or a member of staff in the human resources department.

All authorization profiles that are intended to be made available to a user are entered in the user master record. This then means that the user has authorization fields with values available to them (through the interim levels composite profile, profile and authorization). These values can include simple Yes/No information. However, it is also possible to use the field values to pass on detailed information. For example, in the authorizations already present in the R/3 System, the value of a field is used to define whether a user is permitted to view, change or delete a table. A key figure is available for each of these activities. The actual meaning of each key figure in turn is only determined through the authorization check in the program. To make it easier to document the system, you can save descriptions for the possible field values.

When an explicit authorization check is used incorrectly, a security gap can open up. As a result, additional checks have been implemented in the system as an interim measure. Admittedly, these measures are based on the existing authorization concept. The R/3 System itself calls the check, so there is no need to program it separately. It performs these automatic checks each time a transaction is started and when particular objects such as programs are accessed. This means that a special authorization needs to be assigned to a user for each calling transaction, so that the user can start it.

The extended authorization check functions also include the authorization group. Authorization groups are descriptors that are created in a special table. You can assign various objects, such as programs or transactions, for table maintenance to an authorization group of this kind. A user can then access one of these objects only if the name of the authorization group is contained in that user's profile with a special authorization.

2.3   Number ranges

In many applications, the key of a table is made up from a sequential number, such as a document or personnel number. It is essential to ensure that this number is unique in each case, even when several applications want to assign a number of this kind simultaneously. That is why it is not the task of each application to determine this number itself. The system makes available what are known as number ranges. An application makes a request (by calling special function modules). A number range then transfers the next released number to that application. Several number ranges can be present in the system itself. That is why they are given a unique name by which they can be addressed in programs.

2.4   Transactions

Transactions form the core of R/3 program processing. For the user, they are the smallest directly executable unit. They encapsulate the actual program like a shell. The user will only be able to access executable applications if a transaction has been generated for those applications. Each transaction is identified by a four-digit transaction code. The name can consist of letters and numbers. This transaction code can either be entered directly in the command field, in the user interface or stored in the menus.

The transaction is executed through the internal control logic, which neither users nor programmers can access. In this way, the control logic monitors the application completely and, for example, also intercepts runtime errors, removes database locks under certain circumstances or automatically saves changes to databases.

For the user, a transaction in the R/3 System appears to be what you would generally think of as a program. The R/3 System includes only a few different program types. Each program type also has a special transaction type.

2.4.1 Dialog transactions

A dialog transaction is the most frequently used transaction. It is used for the execution of a dialog-oriented application. An application of this kind is based on one or more screen templates, which in SAP applications are called *screen programs* (or also 'dynpros', from 'dynamic program'). The term 'dynpro' is being used less and less frequently. Screen programs are the only way to enter into a true dialog with a program user.

2.4.2 Report transactions

In addition to the dialog-oriented applications, there is a second significant application type: the report. These run independently of the user – at least in their basic form. They produce an analysis list. To ensure that reports of this kind can be run without error from the menu, a special transaction also needs to be created for them. This links the transaction code with a particular report.

2.4.3 Parameter transactions

The dialog transactions that have already been mentioned start a dialog-oriented application. The user enters all the data. Often, dialog programs are created in such a way that the user enters some values in the first screen program. The system then uses these values to select an object for processing. All further screen programs are then used to process this object.

For example, there is the transaction SM30, with which the views mentioned above are processed. In the start screen program of this transaction, the user must enter the name of the view and select a processing type. In the subsequent screen program, the system displays the view's fields, and the user can process the data.

.   Among other things, it is a good idea to make it easier for the user to work with the application or to restrict the user's access to particular objects. To achieve this, the values that the user actually enters manually in the start screen program are transferred automatically. The application then immediately starts in the subsequent screen program, in which the user can process a view. This range of functions requires an additional transaction type, the parameter transaction. A parameter transaction starts a dialog-oriented application and transfers default values to it.

For each parameter transaction, the user enters the transaction code of the application to be started and the parameters to be transferred. If a particular application needs to be started with different parameters, then different parameter transactions are required.

2.4.4   Variant transactions

In dialog-oriented applications, communication with the user is handled by the screen programs (input templates). Admittedly, the screen programs have a static structure, but it is possible to modify the appearance of the screen programs in different ways, such as by using program statements to hide fields at runtime. Another way to tailor a screen program is to use variant transactions. You can use them to create variants of existing dialog transactions. In these variants, screen program fields can be hidden or filled with standard default values.

2.4.5   Area menu

There are two ways to call the different transactions. You can enter the four-digit transaction code directly in the command field in the user interface. This method is the quickest way of accessing an application, if you know its transaction code.

More elegantly, you can call transactions from the menus. This makes better use of the possibilities of the graphic user interface. Within an application (a transaction), menus are stored in what is known as the *interface*. From these menus, the user calls the subfunctions of an application. This method cannot be used for cross-application menus, including those from which complete transactions are called. In this case, *area menus* are used. An area menu can be described as a special transaction type, whose only task is to make a menu available to the user. That is why an area menu has a transaction code that you can use to call it. The individual menu options in the area menu have transaction codes assigned to them. If the user selects a menu option, the system executes the corresponding transaction. This can be one of the transactions for executing an application, as already mentioned, or another area menu.

2.5   Reports

Reports are the second big program group, besides dialog-oriented applications. In their basic form, reports access one or more database tables, process their contents and then display the results in the form of a list. This list can be viewed on screen or printed out. In contrast to dialog-oriented transactions, reports can be processed in the development environment, without the need to generate additional elements such as screen programs or interfaces for that purpose. That is why they are also called *online applications*. For that reason, reports are also used as resources for program development and system maintenance. If you want an end user to be able to execute a report, you should include this in an application or a report transaction, as mentioned above.

In principle, almost all ABAP statements can be used to practical ends in a report, and it is even possible to interact with the user. However, this requires some relatively time-consuming programming, which demands the use of special statements and the inclusion of dialog-oriented elements. The programming method then differs considerably from the simpler reports that do not have such interactive elements. For that reason, reports are divided into standard reports and interactive reports. Overall, reports correspond to the programs of other programming languages. As they are simpler to generate than dialog-oriented applications, I have used them in Chapter 3 to present the ABAP programming language.

2.5.1 Selections and parameters

R/3 tables and therefore analysis lists can be very extensive. That is why it is advantageous for a user to be able to restrict the amount of data to be processed, before executing a report. Before the actual report starts, it can display a selection screen, in which the user can enter values.

A selection screen is an automatically generated screen program. Each report has no more than one selection screen. The values transferred to the report via the selection screen must be evaluated in the report. Two basic types of elements can be included in the selection screen by using special statements in the report. These are called *selections* and *parameters*. Using selections, the user can define complex subareas, for example, From-To ranges or a group of individual values. However, if they use a parameter they can only transfer an individual value.

To make the work easier, different sets of values can be allocated to the selection screen as variants of the report and saved. Subsequent users of the report can also do this on their own responsibility. No additional programming is necessary. The variants are given a unique name. They can be executed at any time.

2.5.2 Logical databases

The primary key is used to create relationships between tables in relational databases. This results in a multilevel hierarchy of tables. When the data in a report is evaluated, it is usually necessary for the system to read the contents of several logically interdependent tables. To achieve that, the report must explicitly create the relationship between the tables by using appropriately formulated queries. If several reports access one particular dataset, this must also be done in each report. This requires a lot of effort and maintenance, and causes changes to the data structure. Help is available from logical databases. These are special programs that can work together with several reports. They read data from several tables, and take into account the hierarchy and the relationships. Special statements can be used to make the read data records available to the report. Then, it is only necessary to evaluate these data records and if required display them. A report can access only one logical database, but a database of this kind can be used by several reports. The real database tables can be included in any number of logical databases.

A logical database is created using a pseudo-graphical screen, in which the multilevel relationships between the individual tables are visible. An ABAP program is then generated from the logical hierarchy that is predefined in this way. It only remains for the developer to work on it further with the program editor.

2.6 Dialog-oriented applications

Interactive data processing is performed in dialog-oriented applications, which are based on the processing of screen programs. The term 'screen program' is now superseding the SAP term 'dynpro', the abbreviation for 'dynamic program', which has its origins in the R/2 System. A screen program is basically a screen template, and is sometimes also called a *'mask'*. A screen program differs considerably from the screen templates used by operating systems with a graphical user interface. A screen program is a combination of an input template and program code that belongs with this input template. The user can enter data in the input template, and the program code processes this data. A dialog application consists of one or more screen programs that are called and processed one after another. Screen programs and the program code belonging to them are combined into a special program. Screen programs are given a unique name, consisting of a four-digit number, within a program.

A screen program is processed in several phases. First of all, statements for the initialization of the screen program are executed. Then, the screen program is represented on the screen, where the user can enter data in the screen program. When the user has finished entering the data, a second group of statements is processed. The primary tasks of these statements are to process the data that the user has entered, and to control the subsequent flow of the application. The initialization phase is called the PROCESS BEFORE OUTPUT (PBO) phase. The phase after the user has finished entering the data is called the PROCESS AFTER INPUT (PAI) phase. You can program *modules* to define the actions executed during this phase. As the program code of a dialog application primarily consists of modules of this kind, it is therefore called a *module pool*. It resembles a program library.

The individual modules of the module pool have to be assigned to the screen programs. When you assign them, you need to define both the screen program and the correct processing phase (PBO or PAI). The flow logic is responsible for this task. It is available to each screen program. The flow logic is a short piece of source code in which the modules of the module pool are called. Strictly speaking, the flow logic is not an ABAP program. It uses different statements from standard ABAP programs.

It is only possible to call a dialog application through a dialog transaction. This dialog transaction needs to know both the name of the executing program and the point when it starts. As the call of screen programs is always responsible for the flow of a dialog application, the dialog transaction needs to be made aware of a screen program which acts as a start screen program.

In addition to the screen programs mentioned above, a dialog application has other elements available to it. The screen programs merely provide elements for data input and output. The menus and buttons (pushbuttons) needed for interaction with the user are contained in the interface, not in the screen programs.

2.7 Object-oriented extensions to ABAP

In many cases, object-oriented methods have been implemented for modelling and programming complex applications. This results in the combining of the data, and the functions necessary for processing it, into one element, the *object*. An object of this kind conceals its internal functions behind an interface. The only way for the user of an object to access its data and functions is through the elements of this interface. When an application is run, several objects of the same type can be present, each containing different data.

One advantage of object-oriented programming is that the programmer can work on developing the internal functions of an object relatively independently of the interface. During the design phase, the interface is primarily defined from logical viewpoints. Technical details can be implemented and taken into account later.

This logical and design-oriented view of objects makes it easier to modularize large applications, thus reducing their complexity. There are other advantages in the case of programming event-driven applications such as, for example, graphical interfaces.

Release 4.0 of the R/3 System offers the first object-oriented extension to the ABAP language. This has been continually extended up to the current Release 4.6. The descriptions and examples in this book relate to Release 4.6.

Within the R/3 System, the object-oriented language extension can be used on two different levels. First of all, it is possible to program local objects that are known and valid only within their own application. In this case, the programming consists solely of writing source code. The real advantages of object orientation are gained only when objects or their description are available globally. For this reason, a *Class Builder* exists. With its user dialog interface you can define global objects. These classes are then available throughout the whole system.

2.7.1 Classes

A class describes an object. It can be compared with a type description for a data type. However, it is more complex, as both the data and the interface are declared. In a program, objects (instances) can be generated from a class, just as such data fields can be generated by referring to a data type.

A class always consists of two parts: a declaration section and an implementation section.

2.7.2 Interfaces

An *interface* describes the interface for a class. Similarly to a class, it also has a declaration section, but no implementation section. Any number of interfaces can be included in a class declaration. The methods are then implemented in the implementation section of the class. In this way it is possible for several classes to have identical or similar interfaces.

2.7.3 Objects

An object is the real instance of a class within an application. Their relationship approximately corresponds to the relationship of a data field to its data type. Normally, actions are always only performed with the instances of a class, that is the objects. All the same, you can structure classes in such a way that elements of the class can also be accessed without the need to generate an instance.

2.7.4 Inheritance

Within a class declaration you can create a reference to an existing class. As a result, all the data and functions of the higher level class will automatically be available to your new class. You can now create your own data and functions or replace existing functions. In this way, you use existing functions and do not have to implement them again. Your newly created class is type-compatible with the old class.

This process is called inheritance. The class from which you inherit is the superclass of the new class you have generated.

2.7.5 Events

'Events' are available within the OO (object-oriented) extension of ABAP. An event is a message that is sent by objects, or can be received by them. This makes possible both targeted communication between known transmitters and recipients and also broadcasting.

Events have a unique name. Optionally, they can be provided with additional data, in order to define the triggering reactions in more detail.

2.8   User interface

The computers used as the front end for the R/3 System all work with graphical interfaces, such as Windows or Motif. These interface systems broadly comply with the CUA standard. That is why the R/3 System operates relatively independently of the front end operating system.

From the point of view of the application programmer, the current R/3 System consists of two main parts. One part is the R/3 System, in the narrower sense. This includes the internal control logic and the ABAP interpreter. The functions of this part of the R/3 System are predefined, and the application programmer cannot change them. The second part is the application written in ABAP (an 'ABAP task') that is being executed. When an ABAP task runs, it is always under the complete control of the R/3 System kernel. That is why, if the task fails to function correctly, this does not endanger the functional ability of the overall system.

This division of the R/3 System into two parts, and its assignment to a lower level under the front end operating system, is reflected in the structure of the R/3 System's visual interface. First of all, the R/3 System makes some resources available. These consist of the system's own window with some control elements, such as the system menu or buttons for resizing the window. The programmer has absolutely no influence on these elements: their functions are fixed by the system. Some additional input elements are made available and evaluated directly by the R/3 System kernel. The programmer also has no, or very limited, means of processing or evaluating these elements. They include, for example, the status bar or the functions of the command field. However, other elements are available to an ABAP task. Figure 2.1 shows the window for a task of this kind, and the names of the different areas of that window. The actual appearance of the user interface depends on both the operating system of the front end computer and on the current version of the SAP front end software, the SAPGUI. However, if there are any differences, they are only visual and not functional.

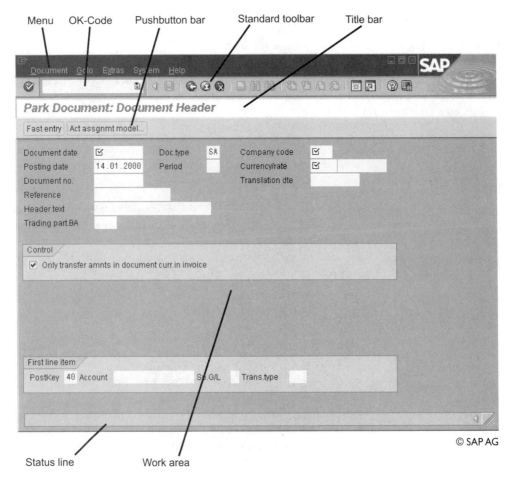

Figure 2.1   User interface of an R/3 task

The control elements provided by the operating system primarily allow the user to move the window or resize it. When a user communicates with the R/3 System core, this is processed using the icon bar. The icon bar contains some icons that have the same meaning throughout the whole system. The icon bar also contains the command field, which is sometimes also referred to as the OK Code field. The ABAP task can only activate or deactivate the icons. It is not possible to create new icons, or delete the existing icons. The function codes invoked with these icons are used directly or indirectly to control the current ABAP task. The corresponding function codes are either processed by the system (example: scrolling a list) or passed directly to the ABAP task and evaluated there, depending on the task.

The user can enter commands into the command field at any time. Any data that the user enters will be evaluated directly by the system kernel. For example, it is possible to use special commands to cancel running ABAP tasks, call tasks, generate new sessions

Table 2.1 Important commands that can be entered in the command field

Input	Effect
xxxx	Call transaction xxxx , if no transaction is currently active. If a transaction is currently active, then the system evaluates the entry xxxx as a function code within that transaction
/nxxxx	Terminate the current transaction and start transaction xxxx
/oxxxx	Generate a new session (a new window) and start transaction xxxx in this window
/n	Terminate the current transaction
/i	Delete the current session
/o	Generate a session list
/h	Switch on debugger mode
/$sync	Reset all buffers
/nend	Log off

(windows) or trigger some low-level functions. If you click on an icon in the input field, the system displays a list box with the last entries in the command field. Table 2.1 shows the most important commands.

The status bar is located at the bottom of an R/3 window. This bar contains some fields that display some system-specific information. The first field, which is empty in Figure 2.1, is especially important. The system displays the short texts for system messages in this field. If you double-click on a message in this field, the system displays a popup containing the long text of that message.

Apart from the icon and status bars and the elements of the operating system, the programmer can work with all other elements as desired. These elements form the actual interface of a transaction. This consists of two parts: the work area, which is managed by the screen program or a list output control function, and the actual control elements, which are the menu, the application toolbar and the keyboard function key assignments. You can work on these elements independently of each other.

An application's control elements are called the interface. Variants of the interface can exist within a program. These variants are known as statuses. Within the PBO module, an ABAP command can be used to set the current status. Each status is given a unique name within an ABAP program. In this way, the current version of the user interface is uniquely identified by the program name and the status name. A status includes the following elements:

- menu;

- pushbutton assignment;

- function key assignment;

- title bar.

The elements in a status give the user a means of controlling the way the program runs. As a result, before a status can be processed, it should be clear what is actually meant to happen in the program, that is, which functions are to be triggered by the control elements, for example, calls to different subsequent screen programs, depending on the menu option that the user selects or the status of some radio buttons.

Function codes provide resources for communication between the user interface and the program. A function code is a four-digit character string. Apart from exceptions such as the title or the command field, a function code of this kind is assigned to each control element. If the user activates a control element, the system stores the function code belonging to it in a special variable, where it can be evaluated within the program.

In some cases, it may be necessary to be able to completely control the application by using the keyboard. To allow that, it is important to ensure that the user can choose a menu option to select all the function codes available in a status. The most important function codes can be assigned to the function keys. They will then be immediately available. The user can right-click the mouse button to display the most important function key assignments in a popup window. In this popup, the user can trigger these function keys or the function codes belonging to them by clicking on them again with the mouse. From Release 3.0C, more key combinations are available (up to a theoretical total of 99), which can have function codes assigned to them. For some function keys, standard defaults exist throughout the system. Function keys of this kind are mostly linked with the icons in the icon bar. Some of the function codes assigned to function keys can be assigned to additional pushbuttons. These appear below the icon bar and with them, the user can access the functions quickly using the mouse. From Release 3.0, pushbuttons can also be represented as icons.

2.9   Functional modules and dialog modules

The current R/3 applications are fairly complex. This complexity gives rise to the need for powerful methods to modularize an application. As a result, cross-application resources are also necessary. These resources include, for example, functions for generating calendars or screen programs for displaying or entering standard data, such as addresses.

As mentioned, an application can be structured using modules and subroutines. In addition to this, two modules are available for cross-application use. These are functional modules and dialog modules. They can be designed and tested independently of a real application. However, they cannot run separately, like a program, but instead must be called from other applications. They have a precisely defined interface for data exchange, but have no other means of transferring data. In this way, undesirable side effects are prevented.

These dialog and function modules require more maintenance effort by the system. That is why, in the past, they were not used very frequently in the interest of an application's performance. However, the use of function modules also brings considerable advantages, so they are being used more and more often. As a result, function modules play a decisive role in the context of connecting external, third-party products to the R/3 System. However, object-related programming can be achieved by splitting the functions of an application into function modules. At times, this object-related programming comes very close to object-oriented programming. This programming method can have a very beneficial effect on an application by making it easier to understand and by making it easier to extend the application's functions later.

2.9.1 Dialog modules

Similarly to dialog transactions, dialog modules include a module pool, screen programs and an interface. The modules have a start screen program and can access a status. For that reason, dialog modules are programmed in a similar way to dialog transactions. They are used much less frequently than function modules.

2.9.2 Function modules

Function modules provide the programmer with general or cross-application functions. They are not subject to any restrictions with regard to their internal functions. Although suitable dialog modules exist for executing dialogs, screen programs can also be called up in functional modules. As a result of this, they can also offer the functions of dialog modules.

Function modules do not exist independently of their environment. Just like other elements in SAP applications, they are also included in a hierarchy. Several function modules that logically belong together are grouped into a function pool. A function pool remotely resembles a module pool. In some ways, the function modules can be compared with the individual modules. Function pools contain global data for all the function modules present in them. This data is not visible from outside. It can only be accessed through the function modules. The current values are retained after a module is left!

As the function modules can only communicate with the calling program through the defined interface, a special exceptions mechanism handles any error statuses that might possibly occur. This is also part of the interface.

Function modules can be tested independently of a calling program. Test values can be stored during these tests, and later extracted for comparisons.

2.10 Error handling and message concept

When a program is being processed, unexpected events can occur that require a response from the user. For this reason, an ABAP task can issue individual error messages, which in the R/3 System are called messages. Special options within the statement that causes a message can have a small influence on the way the message is represented in the application and the reaction necessary from the user.

Displaying messages has an influence on the program flow. That is why it does not necessarily make sense to trigger messages immediately after a special event occurs. This can, for example, be the case if an error is recognized within a function module. The function modules do not usually cause error messages. Instead they create what is known as an *exception*, which terminates the function module and passes an error code to the calling program for it to evaluate.

2.10.1 Messages

Error messages to the user are particularly necessary when the entries in the PAI modules are being checked, and errors are recognized. Then they can warn users if they enter incorrect data, and prompt them to correct it.

Users will also need to be notified in other situations. In R/3, messages are used to notify users. A screen program's flow logic, on which the programmer has only limited influence, can also influence the triggering of messages. Three parameters are necessary to trigger a message.

R/3 messages are predefined text elements. They consist of a single short text and an optional, multiline long text. A three-digit number is used to identify each message. The message text can be translated. The system always displays the messages in the language in which the user logs on to the system.

As the total of 999 messages is far too few for the R/3 System, the individual messages are assigned to what are known as message classes. A message class is identified by its two-digit name. It usually contains the messages necessary for one or more related applications. There are no functional differences between the message classes.

In addition to the message number and message class, a third piece of data is necessary to trigger a message. This is the message type. This value has no influence on the text of the message, but merely defines the way it is displayed and how it affects the flow control of the screen program.

Messages can be displayed in four different ways. The differences are both in the type of display and in the subsequent reaction of the application. For example, the system may display a short text in the status bar. Another option is to display the message in a separate window, which the user can only close by clicking a pushbutton. The user can also click an additional button in this window to display a more detailed help window that contains the long text for the message. After the user closes the window, the program continues.

2.10.2 Exceptions

Function modules use exceptions to signal error states to the calling program. These may not necessarily be genuine runtime errors. Exceptions can also be triggered in other situations, for example when a function module cannot find a data record. Only one exception type exists, and that has no variants, such as those possible in the case of the other messages. However, there can be any number of exceptions. The exact way that an application reacts to an exception depends as much on the command with which the exception is generated as on the place in which the command is being processed.

When a function module is generated, its interface is defined exactly. This interface definition also includes the descriptor for the exceptions that are to be generated within the function module. When an exception is generated, the exception's descriptor is passed to the triggering command as a parameter. However, if the exception is handled by the function module, the function module's name is displayed in the error text.

If exceptions are to be handled outside a function module, the calling program must explicitly inform the module of this when it calls the function module. For this purpose, numerical values are assigned to the descriptors of the possible exceptions. When an exception is generated, the system's control logic stores the numerical value belonging to the exception in a system variable. The calling program can now use the content of this variable to determine whether an exception has been triggered and if so which one.

2.11 Help and possible entries

Due to the complex structure of the R/3 System, and the multitude of possible entries, help on input in a field is essential. Within selected screen program fields, the user can press function key (F4), select the magnifying glass icon from the icon bar or place the mouse pointer near an input field to call input help. For preference, two kinds of help are implemented: a list of predefined values (for example, units of measurement), which the user can select, and a function for searching for values that are not known exactly, or for which only incidental information is known. This includes, for example, a search for the personnel number based on an employee's name. Both kinds of help are supported, using these three main methods:

1. The first is the use of a search help function. It is usually used to find out the key of a data record for which only lower level or non-key values are known. Search help does not require an ABAP program, as it can be generated in the dialog with special tools provided by the Data Dictionary.

2. The second method consists of using the PROCESS ON VALUE REQUEST (POV). This resembles PAI processing and requires the generation of an ABAP program. It can be used to implement customized input help.

3. The last method is accessing a value table or the fixed value of a domain. A foreign key can be defined for the fields in a table. The foreign key refers to a field in another table. The field for which the foreign key has been defined is only allowed to contain values that are contained in the other table field, which has been referred to via the foreign key. The system can automatically provide input help for a foreign key of this kind. The same input help is also activated if fixed values were defined in the domain instead of a value table. These can also be displayed without references to foreign keys.

Besides the value help, the user can press the (F1) function key to call up general help text. This is based on a long text, which can be created for many elements in the development environment alongside the short description. Alternatively, specific PROCESS ON HELP REQUEST (POH) processing can be defined. It displays a custom help text for an element.

2.11.1 Matchcodes and search help

In the relational database model, the term 'key' is of central importance. Individual tables are linked with each other through the contents of key fields. A key must normally identify a data record uniquely. In many input templates, the user enters a key value in order to then select a data record for processing. Once in a while, this value (which is often a numerical string) is not known, but other attributes of the data record that is to be processed are. However, they may not be unique. For example, someone in the Human Resources department will not know all personnel numbers by heart, so they will want to use an employee's name to find their record. For search processes of this kind, matchcodes were available up to Release 3.1x and after that search help has been available from Release 4.0. Search help is a more general implementation of the matchcode. It offers rather more functional scope. Different types of matchcodes existed, but in contrast, there is only one type of search help.

From the point of view of the user, search help is a query program that executes predefined searches within a predefined dataset, and returns one or more values from the record found. Within the search help, the user can define several subqueries, which each search for the requested search term in different ways. Referring to the example above, 'Searching for a personnel number', this could for example be determined by using an employee's name, their job, work location or salary class. From the view of the programmer, search help is a special view of the dataset. It is generated independently of the later application and can be used in several applications.

When the user activates search help in an application (usually by pressing the (F4) function key or by choosing an icon in the input field), the system displays a list containing the available search options. The user must select one. The system then displays an input template in which the user enters the search term. The user can enter wildcard characters if desired. Then the query is started. If the system finds data records that match the search criteria, it displays them in a list. The user then selects the required data record from the list, and with it selects the value to be transferred.

It is very simple to arrange access to search help from screen programs. You simply need to enter search help as an attribute for an input field. In a complete screen program, the system marks an input field to which search help has been assigned with a small triangle in the upper right-hand corner of the input field, as long as that particular field does not have the input focus.

2.11.2 The POV point in time

As an alternative to the matchcode, you can program PROCESS ON VALUE REQUEST processing within the flow logic for input fields. Just like the PBO and PAI processing, this processing phase is (optionally) part of the flow logic. Within the POV section, a special statement is used to assign individual fields of the screen program to modules. In a particular module, any number of statements can be executed, which finally place a value in the corresponding screen program field. An interactive report is often called.

2.11.3 The POH point in time

Similar to the input help created by the programmer, a module or a field supplement can be assigned to a field in the PROCESS ON HELP REQUEST (POH) processing section. This displays help information for a particular field. This processing type is used relatively rarely, as context-sensitive help information can also be made available in other ways.

2.12 System tables and system fields

ABAP programs are executed by the internal flow logic. This monitors the program and controls some actions automatically. The flow logic stores the information necessary for that purpose in some system variables and tables, which the programmer can access. This information can for example be used to control the program flow. One of these variables, SYSUBRC, supplies information about the success of the last ABAP command or a function call. This is important if you want to analyze the success or failure of database selections. Other fields contain the number of the current data record of an internal table, or the number of data records selected during a search process. System variables are predefined. They are automatically available in all applications, so there is no need to define them again.

When working with screen programs, the internal control logic generates internal tables that contain the data for each particular screen program or some of its elements. For example, there is a predefined internal table called SCREEN, which contains some attributes for each screen program field. If this table is processed at the PBO event, that is, before the screen program is displayed, the modifications have an effect on the screen program's input fields. In this way, the programmer can influence the screen program dynamically, by hiding fields or transforming them into pure display fields. This option is used very frequently.

3 The Path to the Program

Knowledge of the ABAP programming language is a very important requirement for successfully programming your own applications within the R/3 System, although it is by no means the only one. ABAP is not universally applicable like C or Pascal, even though in practice it has proved very flexible. Instead, ABAP was specifically designed for the R/3 System. The language is undergoing constant development and modification to adapt it to new requirements. From one release to the next, it may see the introduction of extensive additions. Some language elements are tailored solely to selected elements of the development environment or to SAP's philosophy. As a result, the ABAP language elements can only be sensibly described in the context of the development environment. That is why there is little point in considering specific individual aspects of the programming language without referring to the rest of the R/3 environment. It is more beneficial to start by providing basic information about the different components of an R/3 application, rather than a detailed description of all the statements, some of which have dozens of parameters and options that you can call. That is why this chapter does not set out to give a comprehensive description of all the ABAP statements. Instead, it describes a selection of the most important statements and, using some very simple examples, demonstrates how you can put them to practical use. It also shows their effect when they are combined with other elements of the development environment, and in this way also reveals the program structure of an application. Therefore, this chapter should not be seen as a complete reference for the programming language, but as a practical step-by-step introduction to programming in the R/3 environment. For that reason, you will find this chapter more useful if you work through it sequentially, rather than using it for looking up particular items of information.

The structure of this chapter is also intended to help achieve this goal. Before you can create your own programs, you have to know about the development environment and its various tools. In the first subsection, you will get to know the basic characteristics of the development environment by generating a very easy program. The section that follows describes basic statements, or statements that can be used in all program types. Almost all of these statements can be used throughout all of the system. Knowing about these statements is imperative for understanding all the ABAP applications. Although these applications may use *online* report-type programs, these programs are not fully fledged reports in the real sense of the word. Instead, they merely serve as resources for providing a practical demonstration of the first statements.

An R/3 application consists not only of the source code but also other elements, including the *interface*. This term is applied to all the menus that are used for controlling an application. You must use your own menus in almost all dialog applications and also in many reports. The third section describes the characteristics of these menus, as well as the tool used to maintain them.

The fourth subsection focuses on genuine reports, with their special attributes and statements. Some ABAP statements can only be used in reports. In addition to that, reports have a special program structure. Apart from describing these special statements, this section consolidates the previously presented information about the general statements.

The rigid generation procedure of the classic report can be made more flexible by using interactive language elements. The fifth subsection deals especially with these extensions, which can for example be used for links in sublists.

Logical databases make data selection in reports easier, and make it possible for source code to be reused. Reports can access a logical database, but do not necessarily have to. The sixth section describes the processing and use of logical databases.

The seventh subsection explains the concept of the 'screen program' (formerly known as the 'dynpro') in more detail. It begins by describing the structure of a dialog-oriented application. It then introduces the statements that are used to create this program structure.

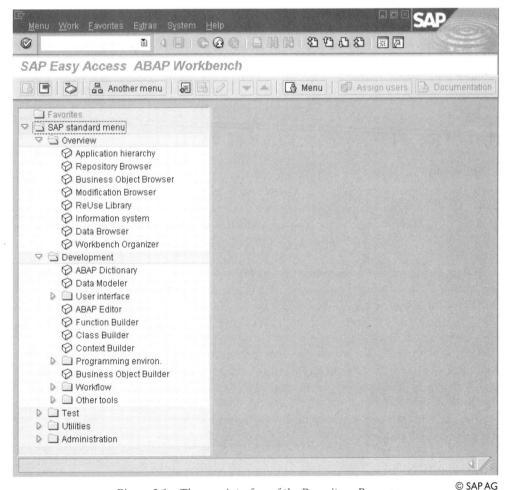

Figure 3.1   The new interface of the Repository Browser

The next section describes the relationship between lists and dialog processing.

Function and dialog modules are an important resource for providing cross-application functionality and for modularizing applications. A stand-alone programming method is also necessary for these modules. The system provides a number of preprogrammed function modules for general use. The next section of this chapter explains how these modules are processed, and the next uses some examples to describe the function modules that the system provides.

Finally, another note about the interface. From Release 4.6, the R/3 System has a completely new interface, in addition to the usual interface. This interface has a new structure, based on screen program controls, and bears similarities to tools already familiar from the world of Microsoft Windows. Figure 3.1 shows you what the *Repository Browser* looks like in the new interface.

Although the new interface makes navigation between the individual tools simpler and faster, it still does not offer the user any new processing tools, apart from a new editor. The new interface still uses the existing tools, which are also used by the old version of the development interface, for processing the various elements. In many cases, the new interface is still not being used to ensure that the users of older systems can also access the system. If the new interface is already activated on your system, and you encounter problems when using it, you will find information on how to activate the old version in Section 3.1.2.

3.1   The development tools

An R/3 application consists of different elements. It can become very complex. Special tools are available for processing each of these elements. To make the programmer's work easier, the Repository Browser provides an overview of all the elements in an application and access to all necessary administration tools from one single interface. In Release 3.x, the Repository Browser was called the Object Browser. Please note that the name varies according to the R/3 Release.

The first program will be a simple report. The term report has already been mentioned in Chapter 2. Reports are programs that generate analysis lists, display them on screen and print them if required. In its basic form, a report is not dialog oriented. Generally speaking, after a report has been started, it can generate output on the screen without further user intervention.

Because reports are not interactive, they do not require either screen programs, or an interface, or flow logic. In the simplest case, a report consists merely of a single source text with a very simple structure. In addition, reports are the only type of program that can be processed straight from the development environment. Reports are therefore the obvious choice for your first steps into programming and for demonstrating the most important ABAP statements.

3.1.1 The first program: Hello World!

Almost all programming manuals start with the same program. Its task is to output a single line of text on the screen. Usually, this reads 'Hello World!'. Naturally, this kind of program and what it can teach you about the language is of limited practical use. Instead, the important point about this method of getting started is that it gives you your first contact with the development environment or the programming tools. As these are rather complex in the R/3 System, this is an ideal way to begin.

Generating a program

All the tools necessary for application development are grouped in a *Workbench*. The user accesses it through an area menu. In older versions of the R/3 software, users could call this area menu by choosing Tools l ABAP Workbench from the main R/3 menu, or from any other location by entering transaction code S001. Figure 3.2 shows you this area menu.

From the Workbench you access the Repository Browser by clicking a pushbutton or by choosing Overview l Repository Browser from the menu. In more recent systems, however, you have to use transaction code SEU or navigate through the menu shown in Figure 3.1.

The Repository Browser's initial screen (*see* Figure 3.3) contains two subareas with some input fields, each of which you have to select by clicking an additional radio button. The upper area, the Object list, is of special interest. There you will find the PROGRAM input field and the Display pushbutton.

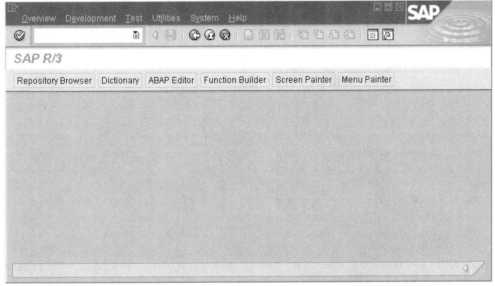

© SAP AG

Figure 3.2   Workbench in Release 4.0B

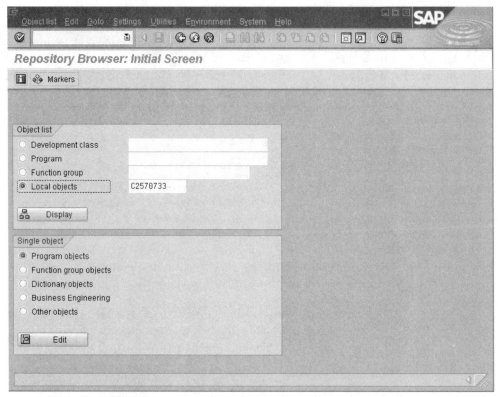

Figure 3.3   Initial screen of the Repository Browser

To generate a new program, enter the desired name in the corresponding input field. Then select the radio button to the left of the name. Figure 3.3 shows you the initial screen of the Repository Browser with the corresponding entries.

At this point, you have to take special care that you use the correct program names. In many places, the R/3 System automatically generates programs whose names are created in accordance with strict rules. The development environment also differentiates between SAP's own development systems and customer systems. Both types of system have different defaults for usable name ranges. The development environment checks some naming conventions for all elements, and not just reports. On customer systems, the names of new programs may only start with the character Y or Z. In this way, the programs developed by the customer can be clearly distinguished from SAP's programs. Accordingly, no objects beginning with these two letters can be created directly in SAP's development systems (at least not without express warning). An optional prefix can be inserted before the actual name if further distinct identification is required. This prefix identifies a naming range.

The length of the names has been increased considerably since Release 4.0. This applies both to programs and to other elements. To ensure that you can also follow the examples on older systems, this book avoids using longer name strings as much as possible.

You should take note of some conventions so you can avoid conflicts with the automatically generated names, and to allow several users on your system to run the demo programs. The examples in this book use the format Yiikknnm. For ii please enter your own unique initials. This ensures that several users can follow these examples on a single system. In this book, the two characters Z3 will be used as initials. The character string kk acts as a placeholder for the chapter number (the second structural level). nn is a consecutive number within the chapter. In some of the programs, you can or should create your own modifications. The last digit of the name is used to distinguish these variants of the program from each other. The original version is always given the character 0. Therefore the first program is given the name YZ331010.

After you have entered the program name in the initial screen of the Editor, click the Display pushbutton. If the desired program already exists, you will then see that program's object list. However, as the program does not yet exist, the development environment creates the program. To do so, it requires some additional data, which you will be prompted to enter in the screen programs described below.

First of all, a dialog box appears, in which you have to confirm that you want to create a program (Figure 3.4).

After you have confirmed this query by clicking the Yes pushbutton, you see another dialog box. In it, you have to decide (Figure 3.5) if the new program should be created as an individual file or as a framework program for *includes*.

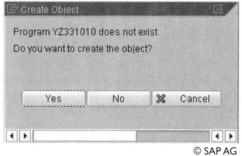

© SAP AG

Figure 3.4   Confirming that you want to create a program

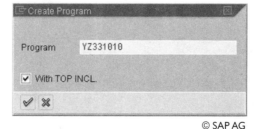

© SAP AG

Figure 3.5   Querying the user about the program structure

You can split up large programs into several subfiles (includes). The development environment supports this programming method by automatically creating a framework program that only consists of include statements. However, you do not need this complex program structure yet, so you should deselect the With TOP INCL flag. Then you can exit this dialog box by pressing the (Enter) key or by clicking the corresponding icon.

You now see a new input template (Figure 3.6), in which you define the important attributes of the new application. Many elements of an application, and also of a simple report, have some administration information. Three fields, which always require input, are of special importance here. A question mark in the input fields indicates that you must enter data. These three fields are a short description of the program, the program type and the application group to which this program will be assigned.

The more recent versions of the R/3 software automatically enter a default short description in the Title field. You can overwrite this default at any time, for example with 'Hello World!'. This short description is indispensable in practice: it is the only thing that gives a genuine indication of the program's function. This is due to the fact that some program names are created automatically, and their length is limited, and because there are a large number of programs in the R/3 System. Incidentally, the title also appears in the automatically generated default headers of the list generated by the report.

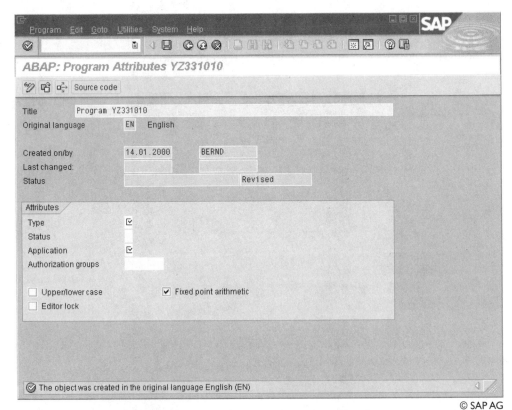

Figure 3.6   Defining a program's attributes

Different program types such as module pools, or the reports used here, have already been mentioned in Chapter 2. The program type is specifically defined in the Type field. This type definition is mandatory. Reports are always type 1 (online report). Only programs of this type can be processed immediately! With the tool used here, you can also create program types other than online reports, by selecting the type you want. Figure 3.7 shows the program types available in version 4.6, displayed in an input help screen.

The APPLICATION input field is mandatory. It is necessary for the logical assignment of the program to one of the big application groups. It does not influence the way the program works, but primarily supports a variety of search processes. As the test programs created here are not assigned to any of these groups, the asterisk (*) can be used here as a marker for cross-application reports. You can find the possible entries in the input help shown in Figure 3.8.

All other input fields are optional and used for information. You can accept the system defaults. After entering the attributes for the program, you have to save these values. You can do this by pressing function key (F11), by clicking the folder icon in the icon bar or by choosing Program | Save from the menu. When you save a new object for the first time, the system displays a correction and transport dialog box (Figure 3.9) and prompts you to enter the name of a *development class*.

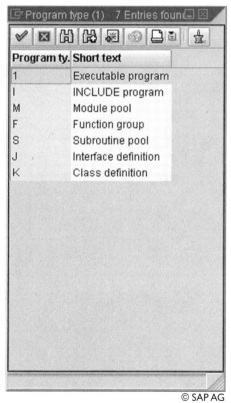

© SAP AG

Figure 3.7   Program type input help

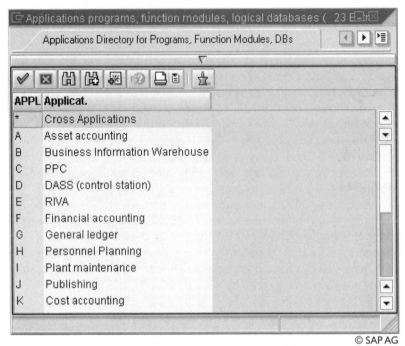

Figure 3.8   Application area input help

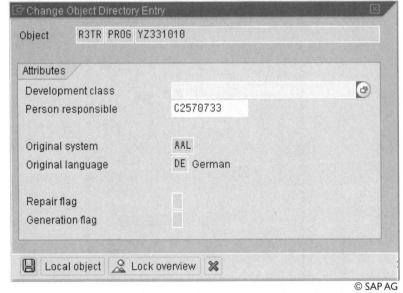

Figure 3.9   Transport management system (correction and transport)

Development classes are used to group the different development objects within the R/3 System. Elements that logically belong together are assigned to a common development class. This development class also defines whether objects can be transported out of the current system into other systems or not. Normally, in the R/3 System, programs are developed in an autonomous test system. After they have been developed and tested, the programs are then transferred to the desired target system, using the transport management system's correction and transport class. Consequently, the correct maintenance of the development classes and the assignment of the applications to these classes are of the utmost importance for the subsequent transfer of applications to other systems. You will find more details about this in Chapter 6.

Development objects can also be marked as *local objects*. This is useful if you want to avoid including every single small test or utility program in the 'official' program development. In the dialog box shown, you can click a special pushbutton to mark development objects as local objects. Local objects will not be registered in the transport class; that is why they cannot be transferred into other systems. All demo programs should be created as local objects. You will then be able to exit the dialog box without having to enter any more data by clicking the Local Object button. The function of this button is the same as when you enter the development class $TMP in the corresponding input field.

During programming, this dialog box will be displayed for each new object. You should always deal with it as explained here. From now on, this step will no longer be mentioned in this book.

After defining the development class, you will be returned to the screen for attribute maintenance. The system has added a few input fields (Figure 3.10). Apart from the general attributes, each program type has additional attributes necessary only for that type. However, at this point no further data needs to be entered for our small demo program.

In this screen you can click the Source code button or choose the Goto | Source code menu option to jump to the actual Editor (Figure 3.11). It shows the program, which currently consists only of a single genuine statement and a few comment lines. In the case of online reports, the system automatically generates a program line, consisting of the report keyword and the program name.

At this point, you can enter the program. To do so, you only have to add one single line:

```
REPORT YZZ31010.
WRITE 'Hello world!'.
```

With one simple mouse click you can position the mouse pointer on the line below the REPORT statement. Then, you enter the additional statement. Within the Editor, you can press the (Enter) key to add line breaks. Although the arrow keys work, they do not allow you to scroll in the source code. To do so you have to use the (PgUp) or (PgDn) keys or the scroll bar at the edge of the screen. You will find more information on the Editor's functions in Section 3.1.3.

The first line uses the REPORT keyword to instruct the system that the following statements are actually an individual program. Incidentally, the alternative PROGRAM statement is identical to the REPORT statement. The second line writes text to the output window.

When you enter ABAP statements, you do not have to comply with any particular format; they can be several lines long or indented. This makes it necessary to clearly mark

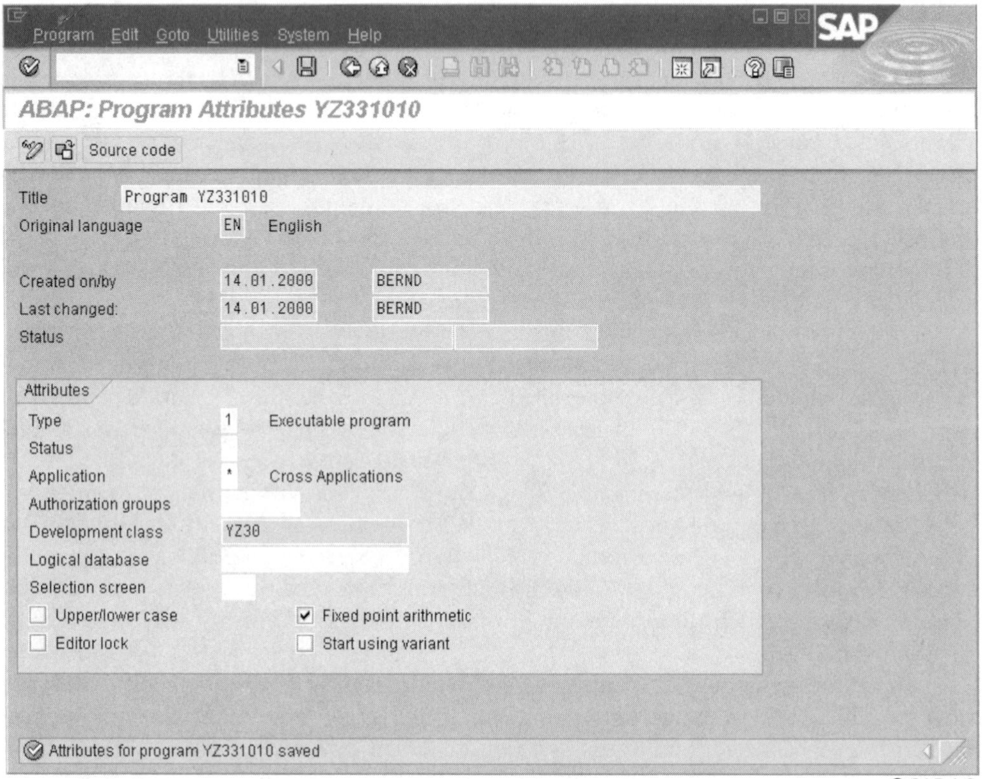

© SAP AG

Figure 3.10   Extended attributes screen for reports

the end of an ABAP statement. In ABAP, you use a full stop, also known as a period, for this purpose.

Now you can execute the application directly from the Editor. To do this, choose the Program | Execute from the menu or press function key (F8). If there are no typing errors, the Editor screen program will be replaced by the program output screen. You should now see the result displayed in Figure 3.12. The reports do not generate the screen output directly to the window. Instead, a report writes its output to a buffer, which will only be displayed in the output window after the report has completed processing. In the case of a more complex report, this can take some time!

The system can buffer the output, making it possible to scroll longer lists on screen after they have been created. In addition, you can print the buffer contents and the output list without the report needing to contain further special statements.

Next to the expected display of 'Hello world!', you will also find the report's title and a page number in the output. These elements will be automatically generated by the system, as they are standard items on each printing list. You can return to the Editor from the report output window by pressing the (F3) function key or by choosing the icon with the green arrow.

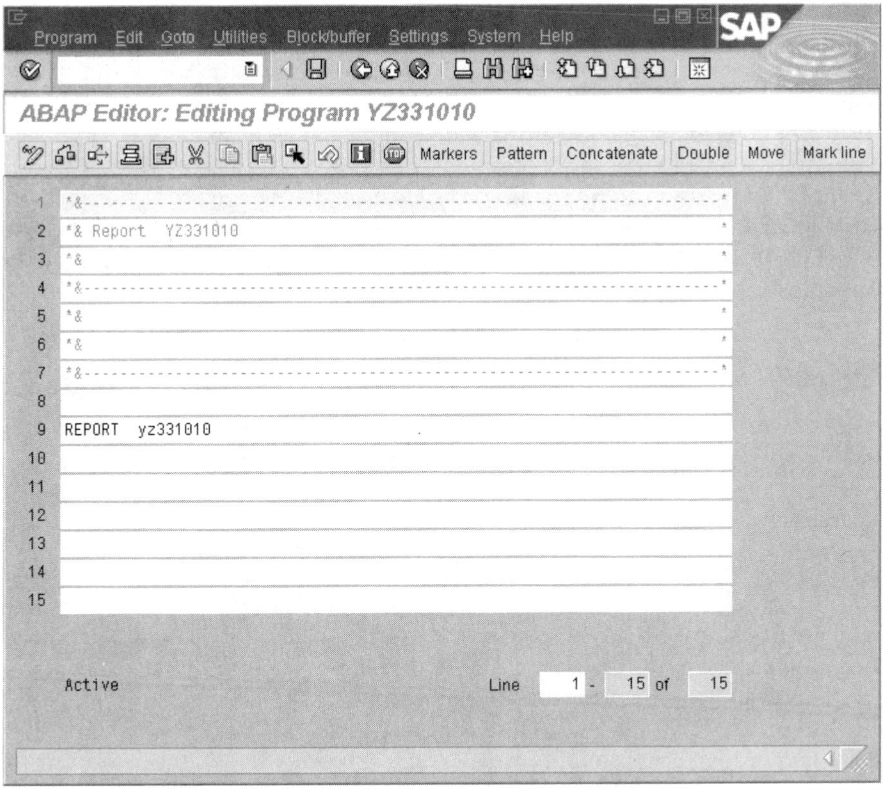

© SAP AG

Figure 3.11 Editor with program header

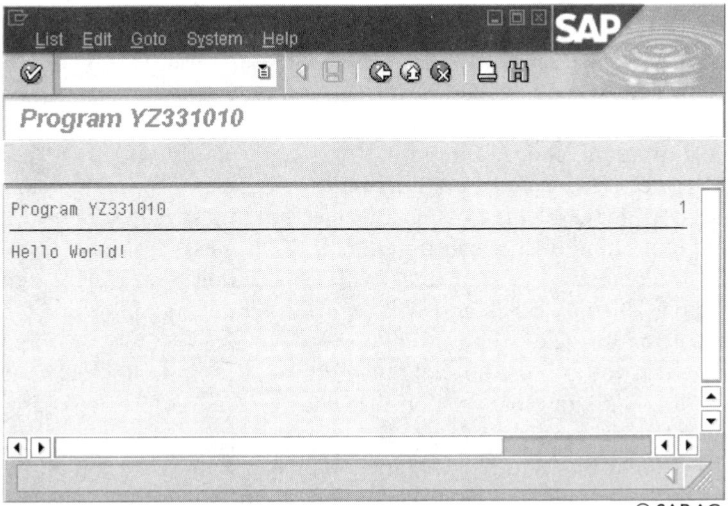

© SAP AG

Figure 3.12 The first program, displayed on screen

The REPORT or PROGRAM statement can be provided with some additional data, which will affect the appearance of the generated list. You can first try adding the NO STANDARD PAGE HEADING setting. This setting switches off the automatically generated list header.

Long and complex programs can be made easy to understand by adding comments. In ABAP, two options are available for marking comments: you can enter an asterisk in the first column of a line containing a comment, but this is rather conspicuous. Comments that are not supposed to start in the first column, but after it, such as the ones that are in the same line as an ABAP statement, should begin with quotation marks. The example below demonstrates the changes described so far. Inserting the additional characters is good practice for working with the Editor.

```
*&------------------------------------------------------------------*
*& REPORT YZ331010     *
*&               *
*&------------------------------------------------------------------*
*& This program creates a short text  *
*&          *
*&------------------------------------------------------------------*
REPORT YZZ31010 NO STANDARD PAGE HEADING.
WRITE 'Hello world!'. " text output
```

If you are working with an R/3 System up to and including Release 4.0, you have now finished creating the application. For later R/3 Releases, an additional step is necessary. This is the activation of the program. When the system is processing existing programs, it often has to process several elements (screen programs, includes, etc.). As a result, inconsistent states might occur temporarily, which would prevent the execution of the application. This is why, from Release 4.5A onwards, all changes are first saved in an inactive form, and are activated only after development has been completed. As a result, all changes will become effective at the same time. Until the new version is activated, the previous version of the application remains active. Therefore, if you test a program without first activating the new version, this would merely execute the old version of the application. An exception is the call from the Editor, as used here, which immediately accesses the new source code. However, this applies only to the program currently in the Editor and therefore applies neither to its includes nor to other elements!

To activate a program, choose Program | Activate from the menu or press (Ctrl)(F3). Alternatively, you can click a corresponding button in the application toolbar.

If, as in this case, there is only one inactive element, the system will immediately activate it without requesting further confirmation. If there are several inactive elements, you have to select the objects you want to activate in a dialog box. During activation, the system carries out a syntax check and will report potential syntax errors. Depending on the type of the error, this takes the form of a simple message in the screen program, or a dialog box in which you can use special pushbuttons to jump to the location of the error. If you are working with an older version that does not yet require activation, the syntax check will run when the application is started.

Do not mistake activation for the generation of an application. Activation lets you define which source text version applies. However, in the case of generation, the system generates an intermediate code from the active source code, which can be executed much more quickly.

Outputting a line of text

Many ABAP statements can be called with several parameters. In the case of the only statement used so far, the `WRITE` statement, this means that several character strings and a statement can be simultaneously output to the output list. However, this requires a small addition to the syntax. If you add a colon immediately after the actual keyword, this calls the list of parameters. You have to separate the individual parameters from each other with commas.

```
WRITE: 'These','are','several','character strings'.
```

The colon is also used in many other statements, and not only in `WRITE`. Unfortunately, the official syntax descriptions do not state which statements actually support the use of the colon in this way.

Of course, it makes little sense to make several hard-coded texts into individual parameters. However, if you execute this example, it will show you that, when the system outputs several parameters, it automatically separates them all from each other by inserting a space between them. The parameters that the `WRITE` statement can use only become more interesting when you add arguments for formatting the output. This especially applies to arguments for defining the target position of the character strings that are to be output on a line. The system outputs the parameter in the defined column, to a field whose length is entered in brackets, using prefixed numerical values that have this format:

```
column(length)parameter
```

Both entries are optional. A leading slash produces a new line. For example:

```
WRITE:/'These',/7'are',/11(4)'several',/(5)'character strings'.
```

Apart from defining the position, additional options provide you with a very powerful way of processing the output values. For example, you can use a mask to format them or align them within a column. To describe these options at this point would be more likely to create confusion than to be of any use. You will find further information in the section on report programming (Chapter 3.4.4).

Data fields and expressions

Naturally, the ability to output simple character strings is not sufficient for a fully fledged application. To that end, it is essential to know how to handle data and how to control the program flow. The sections that follow provide you with details of the statements necessary for this purpose. The program below, which displays the multiplication tables under ten, serves as a brief introduction. Later in this section, this program is also used as a test program for the Debugger.

```
REPORT yz331030 NO STANDARD PAGE HEADING.
DATA:
  row TYPE i VALUE 1,
  col TYPE i,
  res TYPE i.
```

```
DO 10 TIMES.
  IF row = 1.
    WRITE: (5) space.
    col = 1.
    DO 10 TIMES.
      WRITE: (5) col.
      col = col + 1.
    ENDDO.
    WRITE: / sy-uline(80).
  ENDIF.
  col = 1.
  WRITE: /(5) row.
  DO 10 TIMES.
    res = col * row.
    WRITE: (5) res.
    col = col + 1.
  ENDDO.
  row = row + 1.
ENDDO.
```

This program uses the DATA statement to declare the three data fields col, row and res. All three fields are of the type INTEGER. The VALUE extension is used to preset the value for ROW to 1.

The DO 10 TIMES statement opens a loop, which is executed exactly ten times. The ENDDO statement at the end of the program ends this loop.

During the first run through this loop, the system starts by outputting a table header. This is marked by the value for row, which is 1 during the first run. The statement IF checks this status. This statement checks a logical expression (row = 1). If this expression is true, the statements between IF and ENDIF are executed. This entry will output a five-digit empty field for the creation of the table header:

```
WRITE: (5) space.
```

In the other lines below this field, you will find the descriptors of the table rows. Then, col is assigned the value 1 for the first column. In a second loop, the value for col is output in a five-character output field and is then increased by 1. After all 10 column names have been output, a line break is inserted and an unbroken line is printed to separate the table header from the body table. This statement is used:

```
WRITE: / sy-uline(80).
```

The sy-uline field is one of the predefined system fields. It contains the character to generate a horizontal separating line.

All subsequent statements are executed through the outer loop for each run. The value for col is again set to 1. Following that, the line number is output in a five-character field. The '/' character in the WRITE statement ensures that this output always begins at the start of a new line.

This is again followed by a DO loop in which the total number of lines and columns is calculated, then this result is output. The character '/' is missing here because all outputs are meant to be on one line. It is necessary to use the res utility field because the WRITE statement cannot process expressions as parameters. Before finishing with ENDDO, the line number is increased by 1.

Exercises

1. Add comments to the first program.

2. Create your own programs in order to test the described variants of the WRITE statement.

3. Test the 1×1 program.

3.1.2 The Repository Browser

The previous section described all the steps for creating a simple application with the aid of the Repository Browser. This section begins by making you a bit better acquainted with the development environment before you generate more programs in which the various ABAP statements will be described in more detail.

Object lists

Although the currently used Repository Browser represents the core of the screen program concept, there are other important tools beside it. That is why you are not introduced to program development using the Repository Browser, but using the Workbench area menu, which has already been mentioned. The Repository Browser itself is another collection of development tools. It has a special place within the screen program concept. While the other tools each process a particular type of element, the Repository Browser provides an overview of all parts of an application. As a result, it can be used, indirectly, to access almost all other tools. Therefore, in practice, this tool is almost always used to start learning R/3 programming. It can be started directly, with a call to transaction SEU or SE80, as well as from the Workbench menus. In Figure 3.13, you can see the Repository Browser initial screen again.

The input fields in this screen program have been combined into two groups. If you click the Display button when you are pointing to one of the fields in the OBJECT LIST group, this will take you to a tree-like list where you can get an overview of a complex object or group of objects within the development environment. In this overview you can edit an application's subobjects. If you point to one of the fields in the second, Single object group, and click the DISPLAY button, this activates direct access to a single development object and its tools. The Repository Browser is the preferred tool for providing an introduction to object lists, as these tools can also be started in another way, but the object list is only available in the Repository Browser.

You can display an object list by selecting one of the check boxes within the first frame and by entering the name of the object you want to display in the input field beside it. Then, click the DISPLAY pushbutton. If the object exists, the Repository Browser displays

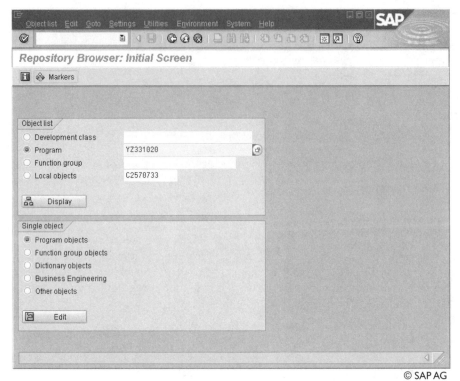

Figure 3.13   Initial screen of the Repository Browser with typical values

its object structure. If not, the system prompts you to create the object. You already used this option when creating the first example.

As already mentioned, the elements of the development environment are assigned to *development classes*. A development class records all the objects that belong to a project or complex application. These may well involve several programs and additional objects. The development class is the highest level in the development objects hierarchy. Figure 3.14 shows you an example of the structure of SAP's own SBF_WEB development class. The actual Repository Browser object list distinguishes between elements and object groups. An object group is not a real individual object, but comprises several elements. In turn, elements are the actual components of an application. They are also called development objects. The various object groups will be introduced to you step by step and will not be described in detail at this point.

You can open or close individual branches of the object hierarchy, simply by clicking on the folder icon in front of the object group's name, with the mouse. In the case of some groups, such as programs or function groups, the next level contains a list of the particular elements involved. Other groups, such as those with DDIC objects, are further subdivided.

With the exception of programs and function groups, you can double-click on an element in the object list to start its editing tool. In the case of programs and function groups, you do not immediately access the source text editor when you double-click on

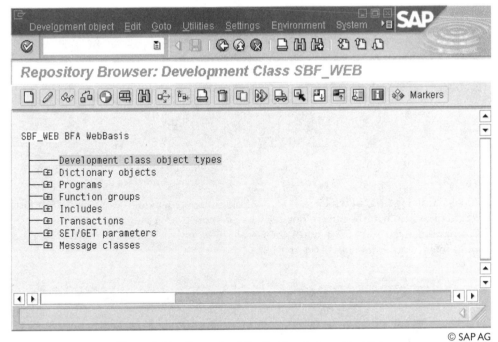

© SAP AG

Figure 3.14   Example of the first level of an object list

them. Instead, you see a second object list that contains only the subelements of the
selected program or function group. As programs and function groups are themselves
very complex objects, this display method ensures an improved overview.

You can also display the object list of a function group or program directly from the
Repository Browser initial screen. To do so, you can enter its name in one of two input
fields, one for a function group name and one for a program name.

The lower input field in the initial screen refers to the local private objects. When you
select this object list, the Repository Browser searches for all objects assigned to the $TMP
development class and belonging to the user whose login name you have entered in the
input field. By default, your identification is entered there.

You will find the input fields described above in all releases of the R/3 System, even
very old ones. However, there has been a new addition, the object list for classes. This is
part of the object-oriented extension to ABAP.

Creating new elements

The Repository Browser has a very wide range of functions. Frequently, there are several
different ways to achieve the same result. In this way, you also can create new objects
within the object lists. To do so, you position the mouse pointer on an element or an
object group and click the CREATE icon or choose DEVELOPMENT OBJECT | CREATE from the
menu. The Repository Browser evaluates the object on which the mouse pointer is positioned. If it is able to determine the type of the new element on the basis of that object, it

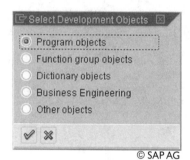

© SAP AG

Figure 3.15   Dialog box for the creation of program objects

displays a dialog box, in which you can define the new element or subelement in more detail. For example, if the mouse pointer was positioned on a program or the object class for programs (*see* Figure 3.14) when the Create function was called, then the dialog box would refer to program objects (Figure 3.15).

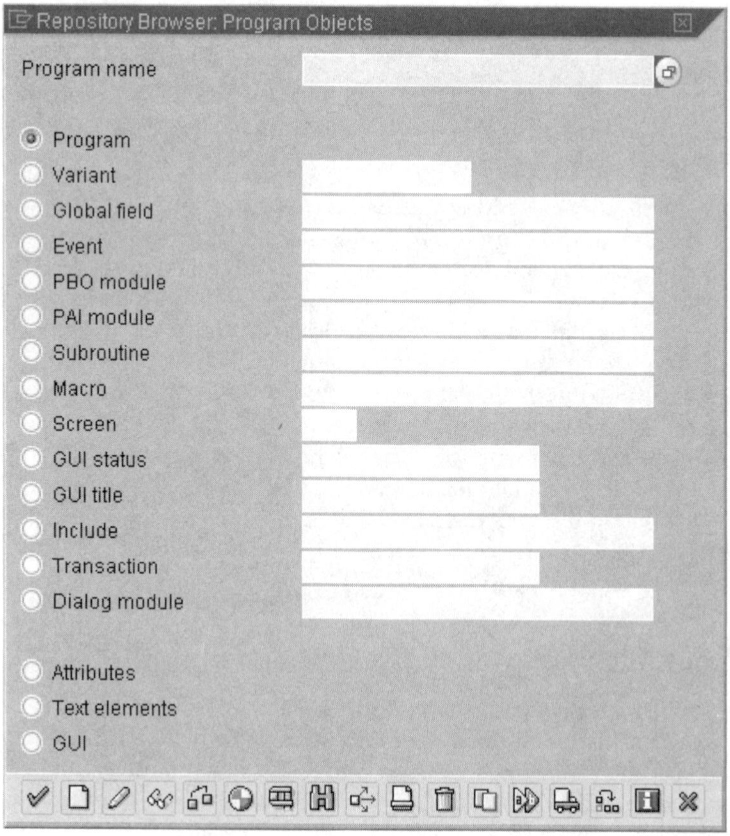

© SAP AG

Figure 3.16   Selecting the object class when creating new objects

In this dialog box, you have to select one of the elements in the check box and enter the required names in the input field, which is then displayed. Then, you click the CREATE pushbutton in the dialog box. This will take you to the initial screen of the tool that you use to create the element.

If the Repository Browser is unable to define the necessary object class while attempting to create a new object, it displays a smaller image (Figure 3.16) in front of the actual CREATE dialog box, in which you first have to select the required object class.

Basic settings

You can choose SETTINGS | WORKBENCH OR SETTINGS | EDITOR MODE from the menu in the REPOSITORY BROWSER, and also in many other tools. Regardless of where you call it from, each menu path will always take you to a dialog box containing several tabs, each with different information. These tabs may also be subdivided in turn.

Figure 3.17 shows you the settings for the source code Editor. You will find a detailed description of it in the next section. The WORKBENCH (GENERAL) tab, shown in Figure 3.18, is particularly important. You can select the check box in this tab to set the characteristics of the development interface.

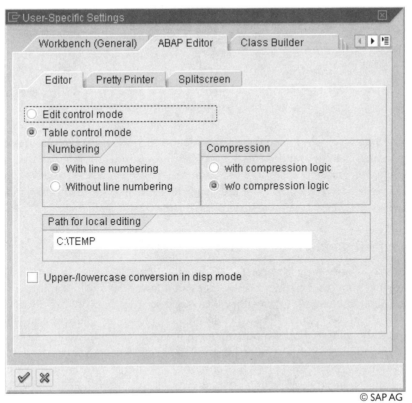

© SAP AG

Figure 3.17   Basic settings for the development environment

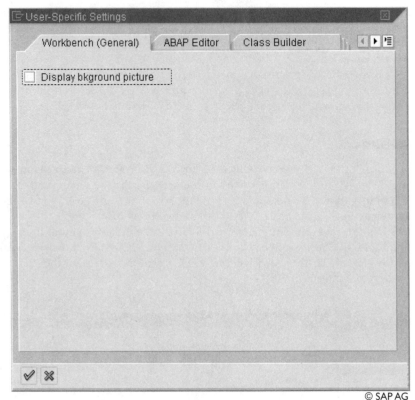

Figure 3.18   Activating the new interface

With the setting shown above, you can force the system to use the old version of the interface, which is based on the previous screen program technology. If you select the check box in this tab, you activate a new interface based on the use of screen program controls. This is only possible if you are using R/3 Release 4.6x or higher and a corresponding SAPGUI, and if the necessary controls have been installed.

Applying functions to elements

Within the Repository Browser object list, you can apply a variety of functions to an element. However, not every function that is available can be applied to every element. Apart from that, the way the Repository Browser responds does not only depend on the selected function, but also on the particular element. To apply a function to an element, you position the mouse pointer on the name of the object and choose the required menu option. There are details of how to create and change objects above. In addition, you can delete, rename or copy them. When you copy or rename an object, the Repository Browser displays one or more dialog boxes depending on the type of element selected. In them you can enter the name of the subelements to be copied and the target names.

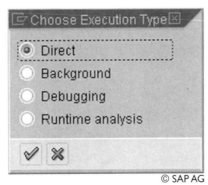

© SAP AG

Figure 3.19   Selecting the run type for a program

Apart from the actual editing tools, a series of help tools is also available. They include activate, transport, check and transport.

You can also test the named objects. This is more important than the functions mentioned above. To test an object, choose DEVELOPMENT OBJECT | TEST/EXECUTE from the menu option. The Repository Browser responds to this function in different ways, depending on the selected element. For example, when you apply the function to tables, this calls the Data Browser, which prompts you to analyze the contents of the table. When you are testing an executable program, you are prompted to select its run type in a small dialog box (Figure 3.19). Then the system runs the program.

The *direct* execution type transfers control to the program to be tested. It runs immediately, in the foreground. You can work with the program in the usual way. The *background* execution type also executes the program immediately, but it runs in the background as a batch job. This execution type is only suitable for reports. During program development, the *debugging* execution type is of major importance. It causes the executing program to be loaded into the Debugger and to be executed under its control. You can find out more about how the Debugger procedure operates in Section 3.1.4. Last but not least comes the *runtime analysis* run type, which is rarely used. It works in a similar way to direct execution, but generates a protocol containing runtime information, which can provide valuable information on performance improvements.

3.1.3 The Editor

The following information only applies to the previous version of the interface. The new version, based on controls, uses a new Editor, which operates in the same way as standard Windows programs.

From Release 3.0 on, the Editor can be run in different modes, which differ in their screen display and sometimes their function key assignments. Occasionally, some function key assignments even vary between R/3 Releases, despite being in the same Editor mode.

The previous section described how you select Editor modes. Even within the Editor, you can choose the menu option SETTINGS | EDITOR mode to change the current mode. Although EDIT CONTROL MODE offers some advantages to the experienced user, PC mode with line numbering is more suitable for PC users.

Just like many other system tools, the Editor (Figure 3.20) is an ABAP program, so the Editor's interface is a screen program. Currently, ABAP only provides single-line input fields in screen programs; the Editor works line by line. However, it makes full use of all options provided by the screen programs. Therefore, the functions of the R/3 Editor generally resemble those of modern, page-orientated editors.

The actual work area consists of several lines. Each line is identified by a line number. The system automatically assigns this numbering. The length of the input in each line is restricted to the visible length (72 characters). There are no automatic line breaks. Each input line is edited individually.

If the Editor is in Change mode, the lines that are ready for input are highlighted in colour, similar to the fields ready for input in a screen program (default: black text on white background). However, in Display mode the text is displayed in the same way as the key fields of a screen program (default: black text on grey background).

In the lower right-hand corner of the window, the current line numbers are displayed. To jump directly to a particular line, you can enter the line number in the input field and then press (Enter).

The status bar displays status information. For example, it is important to see whether the Editor is in insert or overwrite mode.

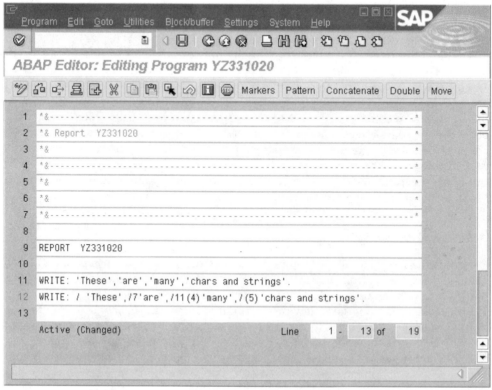

Figure 3.20   The R/3 Editor

If you click on the status bar with the right mouse button, it displays a menu showing the current function key assignments. You can click on one of the entries with the mouse to select it. Alternatively, you can press the relevant function key. The R/3 System supports up to 24 function keys. Due to the fact that most PC keyboards provide only 12 function keys, you can simulate the function keys from (F13) onward by combining each function key with the Shift key. For example, the combination (Shift)(F1) corresponds to (F13). Instead of pressing a function key, you can also enter its two-digit number while holding down the Control key (Ctrl). In this way, you can access additional functions in systems that use Release 3.0 and higher. You can also select some of the most important functions by clicking on their icon in the application toolbar.

You can position the mouse pointer either with the mouse or with the direction keys. In this case, the text does not scroll vertically. Instead, the mouse pointer jumps from the last to the first line. You can press (Tab) or (Shift)(Tab) to toggle between the input elements of the Editor (the source text fields and line number field). To edit the program text, you can use the keys shown in Table 3.1 below:

Table 3.1   *Important Editor keys and functions*

Taste	Function
Insert	Toggles between insert and overwrite mode
Delete	Deletes the character to the right of the mouse pointer
<-	Deletes the character to the left of the mouse pointer
(Enter)	Splits the line in which the mouse pointer is positioned or inserts a new line
Ctrl-63	Deletes the line in which the mouse pointer is positioned
F5	Duplicates the line in which the mouse pointer is positioned or the selected block
F7	Joins the current and the next line if there is sufficient space
F9	Selects a line or block

You can choose PROGRAM | SAVE | SAVE WITHOUT CHECKING from the menu or click the Save icon to save a program. However, the PROGRAM | CHECK function checks a program for syntax errors. You should always run this type of check before saving a program. Programs which contain syntax errors should never be saved! This type of error may not be a problem for the demo programs discussed here, but if you save real applications containing syntax errors this can, in unfavourable circumstances, lead to the functional breakdown of whole application groups.

You can call help for ABAP statements either by pressing (F1) to display context-sensitive help or by choosing UTILITIES | HELP ON... from the menu.

ABAP programs do not distinguish between lower-case and upper-case (capitals) letters. When you save a program, the system converts all the letters that are not part of character string constants or comments into upper-case letters. In the Editor they can be displayed either in upper-case or lower-case letters. You select the character display mode in the same dialog box as you select the Editor mode. In some R/3 Releases, you

can also choose between upper-case letters for ABAP key words and lower-case letters
for all other statements.

The compression logic function is another very interesting function. If this function is
switched on, a small icon (*see* Figure 3.21) is displayed to the right of all statements that
introduce a statement block. By clicking on one of these icons, you can display or hide its
associated statement block. In this way, you can hide parts of a program that are not relevant, and only display in detail the parts of the source code that are currently relevant. As
the first and last line of the statement block (often an IF, CASE, LOOP or SELECT statement) will always be displayed, this can give you a very good overview of the structure
of an application. You can then further improve its transparency by adding a comment in
front of such statements, describing the tasks of the following statement block.

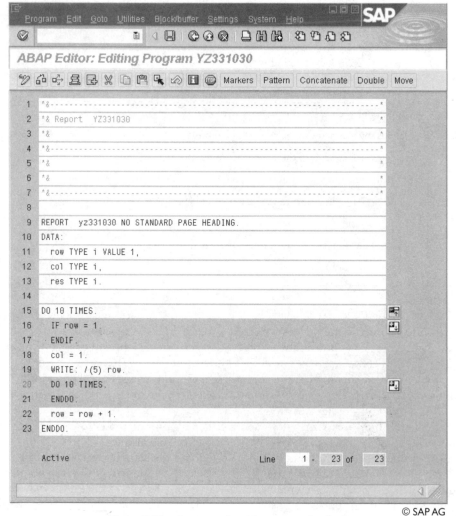

Figure 3.21   Source code with compression logic

3.1.4 The Debugger

The use of a Debugger during program development makes troubleshooting a lot easier. Naturally, the ABAP development environment provides this kind of tool. You can use it to process an application step by step at source text level.

Starting the Debugger

You can use various statements to start the Debugger. To call it directly, you can choose the corresponding screen program menu options as well as using static and dynamic breakpoints.

When you use the Repository Browser to run an application, the system offers you different execution types. One of them starts the program to be executed in the Debugger.

Occasionally, it is not necessary to debug the application right from the start. A screen program's behaviour is of particular interest in the case of dialog applications. In this case, you can also start the Debugger later. To do so, enter the statement /h in the statement field. After you press (Enter), a message in the status row above tells you that debug mode has been switched on. The Debugger starts after the next action that leads to the processing of a statement, i.e. each action that completes user input into the screen program and executes the PAI part. Instead of the next screen program, the interface of the Debugger appears.

Function modules have their own test environment in which different run types can be selected. One of these is a debug mode.

You can also use the '/h' statement in reports. However, in that case you should only do so in the selection screen or after displaying a sublist in the interactive report, because simple reports only display the list after processing the complete program.

Neither of the two methods for calling the Debugger mentioned above allow you to precisely select the starting point. However, you can do so by directly placing one or more breakpoints in the program. There are several ways to define a breakpoint. First of all, you can enter the following statement in the program:

BREAK-POINT.

On reaching this statement, the system activates the Debugger. Naturally, this statement must not be present in production applications, and is only suitable for use in the development phase. A slightly less powerful variant of this statement is:

BREAK user.

This breakpoint is only effective if the name of the current user matches the one defined in the BREAK statement argument. All other users can execute the program without interruption. These two statements can be used as often as required.

You do not have to set breakpoints with hard-coded statements. You can also do so dynamically, within the Editor or the Debugger. In the Editor, you will find the UTILITIES | BREAKPOINTS | SET menu option. Some Editor modes also offer a corresponding pushbutton. It places a breakpoint in the line in which the mouse pointer is located. You can also use this function as often as required. However, the breakpoints set in this way remain active only during the current user session.

Within the Debugger, you can set or delete breakpoints by double-clicking before the first character of a program line. In Release 3.0 and higher, they are highlighted by an icon (stop character). Older releases use the lower-case letter 'b' for this purpose.

Some special types of breakpoint are evaluated dynamically. They are not dependent on special line numbers, but are linked to events. Examples of triggering events are a jump to a subprogram, reaching a selected statement, a change to the value in a data field or a value for SY-SUBRC that is not 0. The only way to define the settings for these special types of breakpoint is to select the menu option BREAKPOINT | BREAKPOINT AT in the Debugger.

Operating the Debugger

When you jump to the Debugger, you first of all see its default mode (Figure 3.22), which is used to display individual field contents.

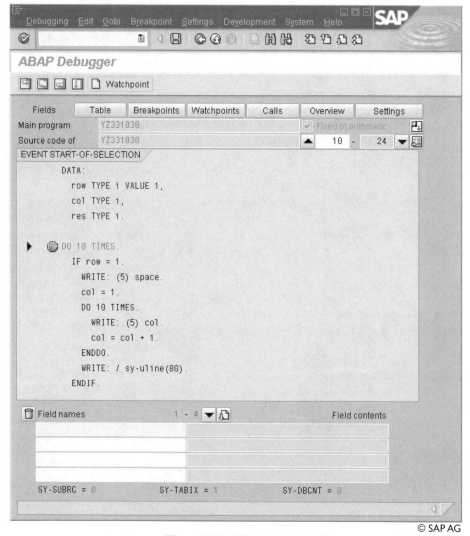

Figure 3.22   The Debugger

When you are working with this mode, an extract from the executed program is displayed in the centre of the screen. The statement that is to be executed next is marked with a black triangle that points to the right. In the first line of the work area, i.e. immediately under the application toolbar, a few buttons are displayed. You can use them to toggle between the different Debugger modes. Below the line containing the buttons, you will find two lines containing status information. Underneath the area containing the program code, you see a table containing four rows in which the field contents are output. Finally, underneath these four lines, you see three important system fields.

The Debugger can work in different display modes. In these modes, the statements used for further program processing are almost identical. The main differences between the Debugger modes concern the program-specific information that is displayed. The default mode, which is active when you open the Debugger, is the mode that provides a display option for data fields.

Before describing the different Debugger display modes, we first need to describe the statements that are available in all modes. With a few exceptions, you can call them by clicking on pushbuttons in the application toolbar or by pressing function keys, which makes them easy to use. All keys also have menu options associated with them. The most efficient way to work is to use the pushbuttons or function keys. The functions described below are also available in earlier releases, but are sometimes called something different there.

The SINGLE STEP key, (F5), processes the statement marked with a black triangle that points to the right, mentioned above. This links to subroutines or function modules, which can also be processed statement by statement. The EXECUTE key, (F6), executes the highlighted statement without branching to modularization units. To stop step-by-step processing, press CONTINUE, (F8). The program runs on to the next breakpoint, to where the mouse pointer is positioned or to the end of the program. In each case, the first breakpoint reached applies. PRESS RETURN, (F7), to end the processing of a subroutine or of a function module. The Debugger completely processes the subroutine and then pauses in the higher level program, i.e. at the statement directly following the call to the subroutine.

The second key shown in Figure 3.22, Table, (Ctrl)(F4), switches the display mode so that internal tables are displayed. This display mode is the most frequently used, besides the default mode. Other display modes contain the Fields pushbutton, (F12), which returns you to the default mode.

Frequently, test data is created for testing an application, which will be changed by the application. Because each screen change in an application triggers a *Commit Work*, which results in the saving of database changes, the test data would therefore have to be recreated after each Debugger run. To avoid this, you can trigger a rollback of the database by choosing the DEBUGGING | DATABASE | ROLLBACK menu option.

On the outer right-hand edge of the first status row, you will find another small pushbutton, displayed only as an icon, showing either a green plus character or a red minus character. This key either enlarges the source code display area to fill the whole screen program area or returns to the normal state (source code with additional information, depending on display mode).

In total, approximately a dozen display modes are available. You can activate the seven most important of them by clicking the pushbutton in the first line of the screen program. You can also activate all display modes by choosing their menu option. The different modes occasionally offer additional functions. Below you will find a description of the most important display modes, together with their special functions.

Fields mode

This mode is the default mode, as already mentioned. Apart from the source code, it displays a table containing four pairs of cells. This is used to display the contents of data fields (single fields or structures, i.e. also table header rows). In each left-hand cell you enter the name of the data field, and the system displays the current contents of that field in the right-hand cell. Structures are interpreted as a field of the type C. The contents of the display field are updated during PAI processing of the Debugger screen program. Therefore, if you enter a field name in a cell in the left-hand column manually, you must press (Enter) before the system displays the field contents. You can also select the fields to be displayed by double-clicking in the source code. The system automatically copies them into the next free field in the display area. This enables you to easily monitor more than four fields. In this case, you can click the icons above the small table to scroll through the list of the monitored fields.

This mode enables you not only to evaluate field contents, but also to permanently change them. To do so, you enter the new value in the cell in the right-hand column and then click the Change pushbutton (with the pencil icon) next to the input field pushbutton with the pencil icon next to the input field.

Tables mode

This display mode is probably used most frequently after the default mode. It displays the contents of an internal table. In this mode, only a few lines are available for the source code (*see* Figure 3.23). That is why it is less suitable for monitoring the program flow.

In the first line below the source code display area, you can see two input fields. In one you input the name of the internal table that you want to be displayed. In the other you set the display mode (*see* Table 3.2). In an output field between the two input fields you can see information on the internal table type. You can click on an icon on the outer right-hand edge to enlarge or reduce the table contents display area. It appears either as a green plus character or as a red minus character.

Table 3.2   Debugger display types for internal tables

Display type	Function
C	Table line displayed as unstructured character field
E	Tables displayed in columns
X	Hexadecimal display

The second line also consists of two input fields. In the first one you can enter the record number to which you wish to jump. The second field of this line records the column headings. By overwriting the column name, you can change the sequence in which the columns are displayed.

The table contents display begins in the third line. It contains the header row of the internal table. This is highlighted with an icon that looks like a hat. The other lines, each marked with a line number, record the contents of the internal table.

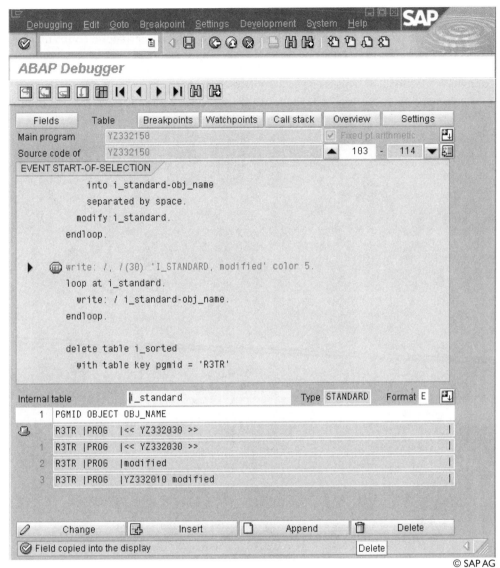

Figure 3.23   Internal tables display in the Debugger

You can use the four pushbuttons underneath the table display area to add new columns, delete existing ones or change individual field values.

Similar to the individual fields display, the table display also offers alternatives for recording the table name. If the display mode for tables is already active, you only have to double-click the table name in the source code display area. Otherwise, position the mouse pointer on the table name and then switch to this mode by clicking the TABLE button.

Individual field mode

In this mode, the Debugger supplies information on a field or a structure. For elementary fields, it displays the data type, the defined and output length, as well as the number of decimal points. In the case of structures, the Debugger generates a table containing the contents of all subfields. This is especially interesting, for example, for the structure SYST. If you select that structure, the system outputs the contents of all system fields (Figure 3.24).

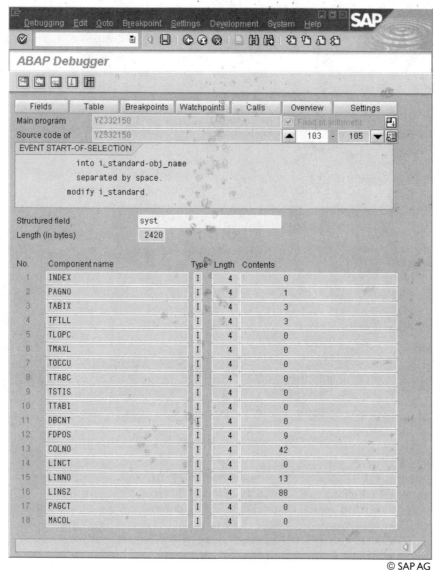

© SAP AG

Figure 3.24   Structures display in individual field mode

Overview mode

In this mode, the Debugger shows the structure of the current program with its modules, events and subroutines.

Requests mode

This mode displays the request sequence of the various subroutines, function modules, and their events.

Settings mode

This mode supplies no information on the current program, but enables you to modify the Debugger's settings.

Watchpoints mode

This mode is relatively new. You can use it to define watchpoints. These are used to constantly compare field contents with a predefined template and to interrupt the program flow if a predefined condition occurs. You create watchpoints by clicking on a button in the application toolbar or an icon within the Watchpoints area (*see* Figure 3.25).

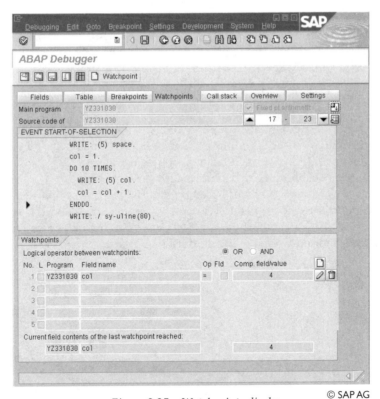

Figure 3.25   Watchpoints display

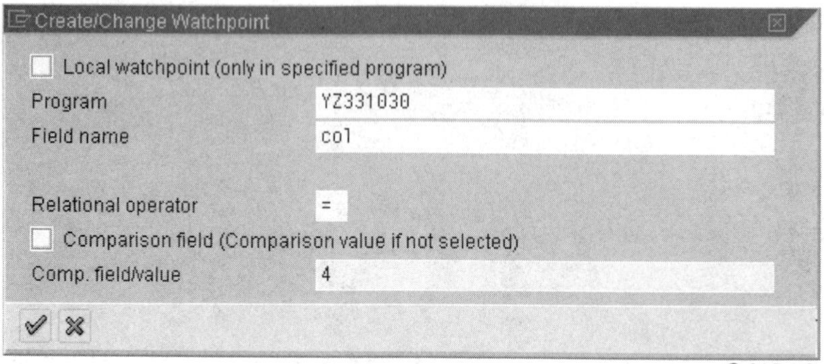

© SAP AG

Figure 3.26   Creating watchpoints

You enter the data that is necessary to create a watchpoint in a small dialog box (Figure 3.26). The system inserts the program name. In the field below, you enter the name of the field that is to be monitored. Then, you specify the comparison operator. Finally, in the COMP. FIELD/VALUE input field, enter the name of the template with which an actual value or field contents are to be compared. If you want field content to be compared, you must also select the COMPARISON FIELD checkbox.

3.1.5 Naming ranges

Up to R/3 Release 3.x, the element names of the development environment were subject to limitations on their length and, to some extent, their structure. These limitations prevented, for example, the assignment of descriptive names to applications. Apart from that, SAP customers had to remain strictly within their customer-specific naming range when developing their own software in order to avoid data loss after SAP upgrades.

A new concept for assigning descriptors should eliminate most of these problems. The basis of this concept is longer descriptors for most of the elements in the development environment, and more convenient assignment of naming ranges.

Table 3.3 contains details of the maximum length of descriptors.

The names can be given a prefix enclosed by a slash '/'. For example: /IXOS/TEST-PROG1. These prefixes represent the descriptor of a naming range which is administered by SAP and can be assigned to third-party developers. This eliminates naming conflicts in customer systems and subsequent problems during upgrades.

Table 3.3   Maximum length of descriptors in Release 4.0

Element	Length in characters
DDIC table	30
Data element	30
Domain	30
Program	40
Function modules	30
Function group	26
Development class	30
Logical database	20
Get/Set parameters	20
Module name	30
Subroutine name	30
Search help	30
Area menu	20
Transaction	20

3.2   Basic statements

In this section, you will be introduced to statements which can be used for almost every program type (report or dialog application). Simple reports are used for demonstrating these statements because, as already shown, they can be generated and processed with little effort.

3.2.1   Text symbols and headings

The language elements described in this subsection are not ABAP statements as such, but reserved descriptors which are maintained through special transactions and are used in many applications. This shows that programming in the R/3 System requires more knowledge than merely being acquainted with the various statements.

Please note here that the elements described below, just like the actual source code, must be activated after changes are made so that the new version becomes effective.

Text symbols

A piece of modern standard software must be able to transcend language barriers. This means among other things that it must be easy to translate displays, error messages, field names in screen programs, etc. into other languages. That is why it is not usual to enter character strings directly in the ABAP program. Instead, ABAP provides *text symbols* which are assigned to a program. The text symbols are given a three-digit descriptor. The system identifies text symbols by means of this descriptor and the logon language. During logon, the user selects the logon language and, from this point on, the system stores it in a system variable. The text symbols can be translated into different target languages totally independently of actual program development. In previous versions of the R/3 software, text symbols were described as numbered text elements, because only numbers were allowed as identifiers.

In the program, text symbols are defined by the keyword `text` and a three-digit descriptor. The text symbols (and some other translation-specific elements) are maintained in a separate transaction, SE32. You can choose DEVELOPMENT | PROGRAMMING ENVIRONMENT | TEXT ELEMENTS from the menu to call it from the development environment area menu. When you call it in this way, you must specify the name of the program for which you want to maintain the text elements in the transaction initial screen (Figure 3.27). If you click the Analysis pushbutton you generate a work list, which you can then process by clicking the CHANGE pushbutton. Within the Editor, you can choose GOTO | TEXT ELEMENTS | TEXT SYMBOLS from the menu to access this tool.

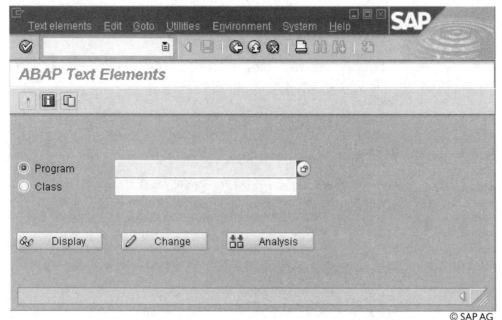

© SAP AG

Figure 3.27   Initial screen of transaction SE32 for maintaining text symbols

During program development it is usually rather a nuisance to leave the Editor, call another transaction in which you maintain the text element, and then have to return to the Editor. Now this is no longer necessary. The development environment has a powerful navigation feature which allows you to maintain many elements directly from the Editor. In the source code, you can simply double-click on the texts to maintain them. You can also position the mouse pointer on a text element and then press function key (F2). The Editor responds in different ways according to the text element selected. When you click on existing elements such as data fields, subprogram names, etc., you either jump to the place in the source code where this element has been defined or to the tools with which you maintain this element. If a selected element does not yet exist, the system displays tools with which you can create this element. The navigation function also works between programs!

For a practical demonstration, you should now generate the following program:

```
REPORT yz332010.
SET TITLEBAR 'T01'.
WRITE / TEXT-001.
WRITE / TEXT-002.
WRITE / TEXT-ABC.
```

Save the program and then double-click on the character string TEXT-001 with the mouse. As this text symbol does not yet exist, you must first confirm in a dialog box that you really wish to create this text symbol. This calls transaction SE32 in which you maintain text elements (*see* Figure 3.28). Here, the initial screen is skipped and you immediately jump to the screen where you maintain text symbols. In it you specify the maximum length of the text in the mLen column. Then you can enter a text for this element. Here you should take into consideration that if the text is translated, the translation may be longer than the original. Afterwards, press (F11) to store your input or click the Save icon. Then press (F11) or click the Back icon (green arrow) to return to the Editor. Repeat this step for the other two texts, and check the result by executing the program. You can enter any text.

You must also activate text symbols. To do so you can click an icon in the application toolbar or choose TEXT ELEMENTS | ACTIVATE from the menu in the maintenance transaction. The system text always searches for symbols/icons in the logon language. If no translation is available in this language, the system will not output any text. Such errors should be avoided, if possible. In the program you can define a default value for a text symbol by typing:

```
string(identifier).
```

This default value takes effect only if the text symbol is not available in the current language. In a program, a statement of this kind could read as follows:

```
WRITE / 'Date:'(017).
```

Text symbols are not mentioned any more in this introduction. In the printed program examples we have chosen to enter directly the individual texts because it makes the source code easier to understand, even though this does not conform to the conventions for R/3 applications.

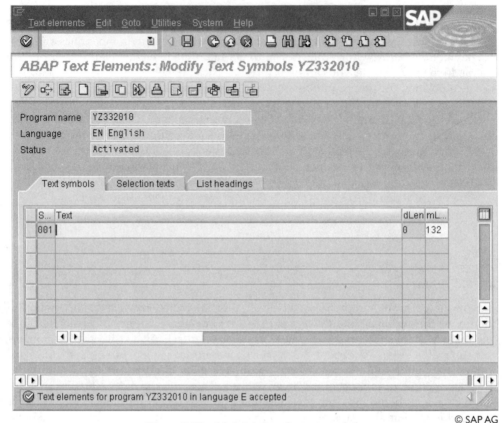

Figure 3.28   Maintaining the text symbols

© SAP AG

Headings

Beside text symbols, which can be used both in reports and in dialog applications, there are additional elements which are only useful for reports. These are the headings for the entire list and for the columns. You also maintain these elements in transaction SE32. There you simply click the List headings tab or select the element you want to maintain when you call the transaction through a menu option in the Editor.

The list heading is output in the first line. The column heading, which is highlighted in colour, appears underneath.

Selection texts

There are two statements for reports, SELECT-OPTIONS and PARAMETERS, which you can use to enable selection value input by users. These statements generate a screen program with input fields. You will find details in Section 3.4.3. To maintain the descriptive names of these input fields, use the Selection texts function in the text element maintenance system. Here, you can only input data in these fields if your report contains the statements mentioned above.

Title

In the ABAP program, you can also set the contents of a window's header row, beside the texts that you can access within the work area. To do so you use this statement:

SET TITLEBAR *title* [**OF PROGRAM** *program*] [**WITH** *g1 g2 ... gn*].

If you do not set a title, the system will enter the short text defined in the program attributes. Titles are similar to numbered texts, but are processed with completely different tools. The title is identified by a three-digit character string. To maintain titles you can either use Workbench functions or double-click on them, as described for text elements. This is easiest. Enter a syntactically correct SET TITLEBAR statement in the source code, such as

SET TITLEBAR 'T01'.

Then position the mouse pointer on the line and click function key (F2) or double-click on the title identifier with the mouse. The system may then carry out a security check. It will in any case open a dialog box (Figure 3.29) in which you maintain the title. These titles can be translated just like the numbered texts, i.e. they are available in each valid logon language.

The titles need to be activated just like the program text so they can take effect. To do so, you click the Maintain all pushbutton in the maintenance dialog box. The screen program which appears lists all the titles in the program. To activate the titles, choose the USER INTERFACE | GENERATE MENU option or click the appropriate icon in the application toolbar.

The titles activated here have nothing to do with the text element maintenance function title. They are totally separate elements which can be used as an alternative to the default title. The title identifier can be transferred to the SET TITLEBAR statement either as an actual value, as shown above, or as field contents.

The title may contain the dummy values '&1' up to '&9'. You use the WITH option to supply these dummies with values. If you would like to get the title from a different program, instead of from the texts stored for the current program, you can define the name of that program by using the OF PROGRAM addition. This is necessary, or at least desirable, if, for example, you call a screen program in a function module that has been created for general use, and would like to use the title of the current main program in this screen program.

If your application has its own interface, you can also use the Screen Painter to maintain titles.

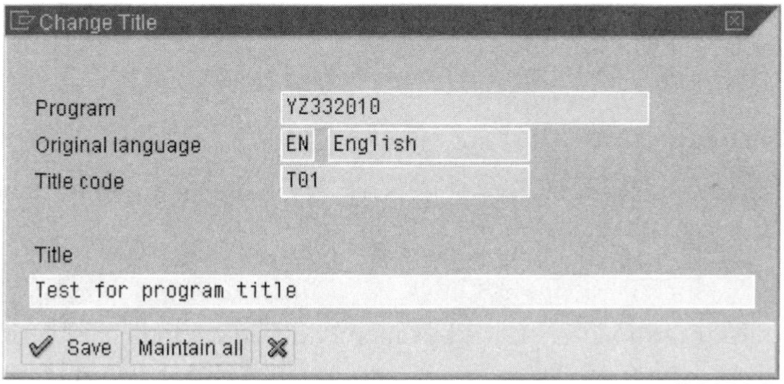

© SAP AG

Figure 3.29   Processing a title

Exercises

1. Create the program YZ332010 and the three text symbols.

2. Maintain a list heading and a column heading for this program.

3. Maintain and define a program title.

3.2.2 Data objects and data types

The ABAP programs we have seen so far have served as an initial introduction to program development. Of course, a serious programming language has to be able to do more than merely output texts. It needs to handle data of very different types flexibly, and process this data in a wide variety of ways. Just like any other programming language, ABAP is also fully competent in working with variables. In ABAP, the term data field or short *field* was frequently used for variables. Even today, these names are still valid. However, different types of variable, and a sophisticated type concept, have come into being in the meantime, so it is generally preferable to speak of data types and data objects. Data objects are the instances of data types. Therefore, data types describe the characteristics of data objects. Only data objects are used for saving data.

In the R/3 System there are three types of data object:

1. individual field;

2. structures;

3. internal tables.

Individual fields are based directly or indirectly on the data types predefined in the R/3 System. Each can contain a value. The term *structures* is equivalent to the term *data record*. A structure groups several other data objects into a new, complex object. Data types that define structures are often called *linetypes*. Internal tables group several similar individual fields or structures into a table. However, this table does not exist in the database, only in the computer's RAM. Data types that describe tables are also called *table types*.

In this section you will first of all find an explanation of the terms *definition* and *declaration*. After this, the predefined data types are introduced. The main part of this section describes the three data object groups mentioned. In it, the definition and declaration are each dealt with in context.

Definition and declaration

In the context of data types and data objects, two statements are important. To define a data type you use this statement:

```
TYPES datatype typedefinition.
```

A data type itself cannot store data, but merely describes the characteristics of a data object. The type definition can be very complex, as table types especially can have a multitude of characteristics which can be defined in the definition.

In order to generate a data object, you use the DATA statement. This declaration reserves memory. This is the only way to create a data object in which you can store data. The syntax of this statement is:

DATA *dataobject* **TYPE** *datatype.*

You can use a rather more complex form of the DATA statement to avoid having to define a data type in the case of complex data objects. The declaration contains the name of the data object and also the type definition. This type of declaration was used before the TYPES statement was introduced. It cannot be used for all data objects. The syntax of this statement is:

DATA *dataobject datadefinition.*

Although this form of the declaration is still supported, you are recommended to use a separate data type. In this way, you keep a clearer view of what is going on, and you can precisely define the parameters of subroutines and function modules.

Apart from directly defining data types in a program, you can also generate so-called *type pools*. These are source texts that may only contain type definitions and constant declarations. To add them to applications, use this statement:

TYPE-POOLS *type_group.*

You create type pools in the dictionary maintenance function (transaction SE11).

Predefined data types

ABAP contains a few predefined data types. Table 3.4 lists them. A data type primarily defines how the system will interpret information saved in a particular field. In addition, a data field's default length and its initial value are dependent on its data type.

Table 3.4   Predefined data types

Data type	Standard length	Possible length	Default value	Description
C	1	1 to 65 535	Blank	Text (character string)
N	1	1 to 65 535	'0...0'	Numerical character string
T	6	6	'000000'	Point in time (HHMMSS)
D	8	8	'00000000'	Date (YYYYMMDD)
F	8	8	'0.0'	Floating point number
I	4	4	0	Integer
P	8	1 to 16	0	Packed number
X	1	1 to 65535	X'00'	Hexadecimal
STRING	0	Any	Null string	Variable-length character field
XSTRING	0	Any	Null	Variable-length hexadecimal

From Release 4.0, you can also use dictionary elements (tables and data elements) as data types. Here, data elements serve as a single type and tables define a line type. However, to ensure definitions are unique, dictionary tables and data elements must be located in the same naming range. From Release 4.0 onwards, data elements with the same name as a table are no longer allowed. If you still develop under Release 3.x, you should make sure you include this condition to avoid errors when you upgrade your applications to Release 4.x.

Character string (type C)

Character strings can contain any character. They record general information such as names, descriptions, etc. Each character is saved in a place in the data field.

Numerical character string (type N)

A numerical character string resembles the character string described above. However, it only contains numbers. Other characters cannot be assigned to a numerical character string. The value is entered right-aligned and empty spaces are filled with '0'. Numerical character strings are usually used as a key value; for example, order, material or personnel number, etc.

Point in time (type T)

This data type records a point in time defined in hours, minutes and seconds (HHMMSS). Two places are available for each value. No separators are necessary between these elements. A T-type field consequently has a fixed length of six characters. This display format is used without separators both when assigning values and when outputting them with WRITE. If you want to use other formats for output, these require special additional parameters for the WRITE statement. When using the point in time data type, you must bear in mind one particular characteristic: if the value exceeds 24 hours, there will not be a runtime error. Nor will any other warning be generated. Instead, counting will simply begin again from the start.

Date (type D)

A date field contains the date defined in years, months and days (YYYYMMDD). No separators are necessary between these subvalues. You can display a date in different ways by using special formatting parameters, and applying them, for example to the WRITE statement. If you use WRITE to display a date without defining additional parameters, the date's subvalues are redistributed in accordance with the date style set in the user profile. This is usually country specific. Date fields are always eight digits long, so they can contain all the necessary information. Longer date fields would be unnecessary and shorter ones could not contain a correct value.

Floating point number (type F)

A floating point number is saved as a binary value which cannot be directly displayed. In it the value is split into an exponent and mantissa which, naturally, is based on the dual number system. This data type therefore corresponds approximately to the `float` data type in the C programming language. The length of eight digits indirectly influences the possible number of digits and accuracy of the value. In ABAP, the representable value ranges run from -1E307 up to +1E307. The resolution (smallest representable absolute value) is 1E-307. The accuracy is approximately 15 digits.

When floating point numbers are output, the system uses exponential representation by default. However, you can assign them using a different format, provided the value is always enclosed in apostrophes. Numbers with fractional values use a decimal point, as is generally the case in other programming languages. Possible values are for example:

```
'1'
'1.2'
'1.23E2'
'-123E-5'.
```

Floating point numbers are used for calculations requiring a large value range, and in which absolute accuracy is not essential.

Integers (type I)

Integers are also saved as binary values, which means that the length of the field does not correspond directly to the number of digits in the value. This data type roughly corresponds to the `longint` data type in the C programming language. The system hardware that is usually used can represented a value range from -2**31 to +2**31 (-2,147,483,648 up to +2,147,483,647). Data type I is the preferred data type for counter variables, indexes, etc.

Packed numbers (type P)

This data type is used to store fixed point numbers. You can use the optional parameter `DECIMALS n` in the `DATA` statement to define the number of the digits after the decimal point for a particular data field. The default value for `DECIMALS` is 0! In packed fields, two numbers of the value will be saved in a digit (in a byte). This also takes into account a number which records the number digits after the decimal point. A P-type data field with length L can therefore include values with L * 2 minus 1 digit, independent of the prefix operator. Here, the digits after the decimal point, and possibly also a prefix operator, have to be included in counting! As in the case of the floating point number, a decimal point is used in the value as a separator between the integer part and the decimal place digits. The exponential style is not used to assign values to this data type.

To work effectively with packed numbers, you must mark the FIXED POINT ARITHMETIC flag in the program's attributes. Then the number of digits can automatically be taken into account both for calculations and for output. Normally, when you generate a new program, this flag is set by default (*see also* Figure 3.2).

Packed numbers will be used where values with a constant number of digits after the decimal point occur. Examples include prices, quantities, etc. Fields using this data type often relate to a currency or a unit of quantity. The `WRITE` statement therefore contains special extensions for P-type fields. These can be used to process the contents of such a field according to the currency or the unit of measure.

Hexadecimal fields (type X)

In hexadecimal fields, one digit in the data element takes up two hexadecimal characters, as is the case with packed fields. To assign a value to a hexadecimal field, you must mark it with an X, for example, X'0D0A'. Usually, such fields are used only in special circumstances.

Variable-length character strings (type STRING)

This data type resembles C-type character strings. However, it has a variable length that you do not have to define when declaring it. The real length is dynamically defined by the system at application runtime, which uses less memory than character strings of fixed length.

Currently you cannot use strings in screen programs or dictionary elements.

Variable-length hexadecimal fields (type XSTRING)

The XSTRING data type stores hexadecimal values. Its required length is defined dynamically, similar to the length of the STRING data type, so that the length is not assigned when the XSTRING value is being defined.

Data object names

The names of data objects can be up to 30 characters long. In the case of multipart names (i.e. in the fields present in structures) this applies to the whole name and not only to one element. You can use any character, including numbers, apart from the special characters '(', ')', '+', '.', ',' and ':'. However, the name must not consist solely of numbers. Furthermore, you should not use hyphens, '-', even though they are one of the permitted characters. In structures they are used to separate the individual parts of a name. If you used hyphens in the names of data objects that were also part of the structures, this would make the names confusing. If you have to split the individual words in the name of a field, you can use the underscore, '_'. These are examples of permitted field names:

```
number
M1
M123
PURCHASE ORDER_NUMMER
STOCK_QUANTITY_OLD
STOCK_QUANTITY_NEW.
```

The system defines some fields itself. The names of these fields are also reserved, so you must not use them as field names either. This especially concerns the field name SPACE and the actual system variables, which all start with SY- or SYST-.

Different ABAP statements have a variety of parameters and options. The names of these additions can be used as field names, but in some circumstances this can make the statements confusing. Examples include the descriptors TO, INTO and FROM.

The system administers data types and data objects independently of each other. This means that there may be a type and a data object with identical names, simultaneously. This can result in misunderstandings because both data types and data objects can be used to name other data objects in declarations. That is why you should always ensure that you use unique names. You can do so, for example, by adding a prefix such as 'T_' in front of the type name.

In complex applications, it is always recommended that you mark the various types and objects by systematically using name prefixes. Table 3.5 contains guidelines with recommended prefixes for the names of data objects. These prefixes describe the type of each data object or its scope of validity.

Table 3.5 Data object type and scope of validity

Prefix	Meaning
C	Constant
G	Global data object (declared in the top include)
L	Local data object (within subroutines or function modules)
P	Parameter
T	Data type

If necessary, prefixes can be expanded with a second letter from Table 3.6. This second letter identifies the structure of the data object. Under certain circumstances, the corresponding letter can also be used on its own.

Table 3.6 Prefixes to identify the structure of data objects

Prefix	Meaning
F	Field symbol
I	Internal table
R	Record (structure)

Finally, you can define the parameters of subroutines or function modules in more detail. The data in Table 3.7 is meant for use as an addition to prefix P.

Table 3.7 Additional values for prefix P (function module or subroutine parameters)

Prefix	Meaning
C	Changing parameter
E	Export parameter
I	Internal table
V	Value parameter

Table 3.8 contains some examples of descriptors:

Table 3.8   Name creation examples

Descriptor	Meaning
ti_tadir	Internal table type identifier (table type)
tr_e70	Data record type identifier (line type)
t_line	Elemental field type identifier
c_yes	Constant
i_tadir	Internal table
g_fcode	Global field
lr_e071	Local structure
p_line	Parameter
pv_line	Value parameter
pi_tadir	Internal table used as parameter

3.2.3   Simple data fields

Each simple data field records a single value of a particular data type. You can use four different methods to declare a simple data field. First, you can derive a simple data field directly from one of the predefined data types. In some data types you can also define a length:

```
DATA field[(length)] [ TYPE predefined_type].
```

If you enter nothing else when declaring a simple data field, ABAP generates a C-type data field with the length 1. The simplest variant of the DATA statement therefore reads:

```
DATA field.
```

Length specifications are only permitted for data types C, I, N, P and X. In these cases, if you specify a length, it is enclosed in round brackets and follows directly after the field name (no space between them). For example:

```
DATA name(10).
```

The third method of declaring a simple data field is to use a reference to a type definition. The third method is to use a reference to a Data Dictionary data element. In this case, you do not specify the field's length because the length is already predefined both in the type definition and through the data element.

```
DATA field TYPE datatype.
```

```
DATA field TYPE dataelement.
```

The fourth method is to declare a field whose attributes are the same as those of a field that is already present in the current program, or in the Data Dictionary (table field). To do so, use the following statement:

DATA *field* **LIKE** *field_2*.

This method ensures that a data field always has the same attributes as another field (usually a table field). This means that, if changes are made to the data structure in the Data Dictionary, no changes are required in the program. If the control field is a table field, and is used only in the declaration, the corresponding table does not have to be declared before being used in the field declaration.

You can use VALUE to set an initial value for all kinds of declaration. In this case, the value must be enclosed in single quotation marks:

DATA ... **VALUE** '*<value>*'.

Unless you use this format to enter the statement, the system fills the field with the default value defined for the particular data type.

The DATA statement supports the use of colon notation so that several parameters can be transferred:

DATA: *field_1* [**TYPE** | **LIKE** ...], ... *field_n* [**TYPE** | **LIKE** ...].

The type definitions that are possible for simple data types resemble the declaration instruction. You can create a complete type definition by referring to one of the predefined data types and by defining a length if required:

TYPE *datatype*[*(length)*] [**TYPE** *predefined_type*].

If the data type reference is missing, the system automatically uses data type C, as was the case for declarations. If you want to generate a data type that has the same attributes as an existing data field, you can also use LIKE in the TYPES statement to create a reference to the field that actually exists:

TYPE *datatype* **LIKE** *field*.

You can also use the two other methods, i.e. defining another data type and/or data element, but in practice this makes little sense because the two objects concerned are already data types.

TYPE *datatype* **TYPE** *datatype*.

TYPE *datatype* **TYPE** *dataelement*.

Examples of definitions and declarations:

```
TYPES:

  t_name(30) TYPE C,
  t_custno TYPE custno
  t_accnt LIKE aca1-accnt.
```

```
DATA:

 is_changed,
 name(10),
 matno(8) TYPE N,
 c_yes VALUE 'Y',
 ok_code LIKE sy-tcode,
 fname TYPE t_name 'IXOS'.
```

Constants

You use the statement below to create constants:

CONSTANTS *constant* [**TYPE** | **LIKE** ...] **VALUE** [*value* | **IS INITIAL**].

This is similar to the method you use to create the fields mentioned above. The same conventions apply to the names of CONSTANTS as of DATA. You can also use LIKE or TYPE to define the attributes of constants (type, length, etc.) or use () to define a specific length. You can also use () to simultaneously declare several constants, by splitting them with colons.

When you declare constants, it is essential to set a default value. As a result, the VALUE parameter is not optional when you use the CONSTANTS statement. If you want to create a constant with the same initial value as the current data type, you can use the IS INITIAL parameter instead of an explicit value.

Examples:

```
CONSTANTS:
 c_yes VALUE 'X',
 c_no VALUE IS_INITIAL.
```

Special data type-dependent features of output with WRITE

The WRITE statement processes the different predefined data types and any simple fields derived from them by you in different ways during output. When you are formatting a list you should take these special features into consideration. The differences involve the predefined field width during output and the alignment of the value within the output field. Table 3.9 shows the typical characteristics.

In many cases the output length is of secondary importance because the default values generally create quite satisfactory results. The output length is usually set in these three cases:

1. Character string fields can sometimes be rather long if they are explanatory or verbal descriptions. These fields will very frequently be shortened.

2. In date and time fields, it is usual to always set a bigger output length (10 or 8) for the output to ensure that the separators will also be output correctly. If date and time fields

Table 3.9   Default output formats using WRITE

Type	Default output length	Alignment
C	Field length	Left-justified
D	8	Left-justified
F	22	Right-justified
I	11	Right-justified
N	Field length	Left-justified
P	2* field length or 2* field length +1	Right-justified
T	6	Left-justified
X	2* field length	Left-justified

have the default output length, they do not have enough space for these characters. Therefore only the eight or six numbers would be output. In this context, please note the demo program for type conversion and the exercises at the end of this section.

3. In floating point numbers, the length is very often limited, and this is combined with additional formatting of the output in order to cut off unnecessary digits after the decimal point.

Assigning values

If a data field is to receive a value, this can only be achieved by assigning it. The use of the VALUE clause for this purpose, when the data field is being defined, has already been mentioned. Apart from this, there are other methods. The information below only concerns the assignments that fill individual data fields with values. You can use different methods for assigning values to structures and tables.

The most universal and descriptive assignment operator is the equals sign. Value assignments marked with it are very similar to the value assignments in other programming languages. The syntax of an assignment is as follows:

```
field = expression.
```

In this case, expression can be a direct value, a field or a complex expression. The value of the expression is assigned to the selected field. Here, implicit type conversions usually take place if the fields concerned are of different data types. Naturally, the length of the target field is also taken into account: the number of digits transferred is limited to the maximum that the target field is able to record. In assignments that use the equals sign, you can also define multiple assignments, using this syntax:

```
field_1 = field_2 = expression.
```

These are then processed from right to left. The only place where an expression is permitted instead of a field is on the extreme right-hand side. The MOVE statement is functionally identical to the equals sign in the way it assigns values. It resembles Assembler programming, which plays a big role in the mainframe-based SAP R/2 System.

```
MOVE field_1 TO field_2.
```

You can use this statement to assign the value of another field, or a value that is hard-coded in the program, to a field. You cannot use an expression instead of field_1. When you are assigning values to fields of different types, the system automatically carries out type conversions. The interesting feature of this method is the fact that you can use the colon to define multiple assignments:

```
MOVE:      a TO b,
           c TO d,
           e TO f.
```

The final WRITE statement parameter is a special clause with which you can divert the output of one field into another field. Here, the target field must be of a C-type field.

```
WRITE field_1 TO field_2.
```

In this kind of assignment, the system carries out output processing which corresponds to the processing which outputs the values in a list. This processing is not identical to the implicit type conversion that takes place when MOVE is used. Here is a small example, to make the difference clearer:

```
REPORT yz332020
DATA:
 d TYPE D,
 s(10).
d = sy-date.
MOVE d TO s.
WRITE: / s.
WRITE d TO s.
WRITE: / s.
```

In contrast to MOVE, this form of the WRITE statement also allows you to indirectly specify the name of the source field. This is then not present directly in the statement, but in a third field which must be enclosed in round brackets in the WRITE statement.

```
WRITE (field_1) TO field_2.
```

Here is another small example:

```
REPORT yz332030
DATA:
 name(10),
 s1(10) VALUE 'A',
 s2(10).
```

```
name = 'S1'.
WRITE (name) TO s2.
WRITE / s2.
```

You can use the CLEAR statement to reset fields to their initial value, through the colon function. For example:

```
CLEAR: name, s1, s2.
```

Defining an offset and length

The introduction to the WRITE statement showed that you can limit the output length of fields. This does not only apply to output, but also for other field uses. However, it does not apply to fields that have the data types P, F and I, as they are limited by their internal representation and you cannot use them to access the value as a whole.

If you enter a numerical value in round brackets directly behind a field name, this specifies a number of digits, and restricts access to that number of digits. You can also define an offset. If you do so, the system does not access the field value from the first digit in that field, but offsets it by the specified number of digits. Consequently, an offset of 0 addresses the first digit of the data field, an offset of 1 addresses the second digit, etc. If you interpret the offset as an index, this begins with 0, within the data field.

You also define the offset after the field name, but in front of the length specification. You mark the offset with a leading plus character, +. There must be no spaces between the individual elements! The following syntax is used:

```
field+offset(length)
```

The data mentioned is applied both when the system reads data fields and also when values are assigned to them. In the case of assignments, both the offset and the length can be set dynamically, i.e. specified as the contents of a field, instead of as constant values. This form of dynamic offset and length specification does not exist in other cases, such as output with WRITE.

The following programming example illustrates the definition, assignments and the offset and length specifications:

```
REPORT YZ332040.
DATA: s1(4),
  s2(20) VALUE 'In aqua ',
  s3(20) VALUE 'vino veritas.',
  three TYPE I VALUE 3,
  four TYPE I VALUE 4.

* During assignments the system checks the length of the data
* fields and truncates values that are too long.
s1 = s3.
WRITE / s1.
WRITE /.
```

```
* You can enter position specifications both in the source
* and in the target.
s2+8 = s3+5.
WRITE / s2.
WRITE /.

* You can use a length specification to precisely define the range
* to be replaced.
s2+three(four) = s1.
WRITE / s2.
WRITE /.

* This is because assignments whose length is unlimited
* overwrite from the start position to the end.
s2+3 = s1.
WRITE / s2.
```

The STRLEN function supports the use of character strings. For example, in Releases before 3.0, this function is needed to allow character strings to be linked with each other. From Release 3.0 on, special statements support the use of character strings (*see* Table 3.10).

Table 3.10   Statements for string processing

Statement	Function
CONCATENATE	Links several character strings
CONDENSE	Eliminates spaces
REPLACE	Replaces character by character
SHIFT	Moves character by character
SPLIT	Splits a character string
TRANSLATE	Changes the type of writing and exchanges characters

The following program shows an example of how to work with STRLEN:

```
REPORT yz332050.
DATA: s1(30) VALUE 'This is',
      s2(30) VALUE 'a linked sentence.',
      len TYPE I.

* STRLEN finds the last character which is not a space.
* The important features are the spaces between brackets and
* parameters.
len = STRLEN( s1 ).
```

```
WRITE: / s1.
WRITE: / 'LEN:', AT len '^', /.

* The addition of 1 to len, due to hyphenation
* S1+LEN+1, causes a syntax error!
ADD 1 TO len.
s1+len = s2.
WRITE: / s1, /.

* All the positions of a C field within the length specification
* are always available. Outputs use the full length.
s1 = ' '.
WRITE: / s1, '<'.
s1+15 = s2.
WRITE: / s1, '<'.
```

This example demonstrates another important feature of the character data fields, besides the use of the STRLEN function. Although the S1 field contains only six characters, you can use the assignment S1+LEN to address the 8th place in the field. In some other programming languages, if you attempted to address a location outside the current length of the string, this would cause a runtime error. However, ABAP permits all assignments, as long as they lie within the field length, independent of the current contents of a field. Output uses the defined field length as the default instead of the length of the current value.

Operations

ABAP distinguishes between operations that are executed by operational characters and those for which special *operational statements* are available.

It is preferable to represent arithmetical operations with operational characters. The characters +, − , * and / are available for basic arithmetic calculations. You can use ** to perform exponentiation. Use DIV for division with integers and MOD to determine the result of division.

In complex expressions, you can use brackets to define the processing sequence. As a general rule, the processing sequence is as follows: functions, then exponentiation, followed by multiplication and division (including DIV and MOD) and finally addition and subtraction. It is important to ensure that you always separate operational characters and operators from each other with a space. Below are some examples using expressions:

```
a = 1 + 3.
c = 8 / ( 3 + 1 ).
b = a - c
d = c+3. "Warning! Not a numerical expression!
```

ABAP also supports the functions shown in Table 3.11.

Table 3.11   Arithmetic functions

Name	Description	Permitted data types
EXP	Exponential function	F
LOG	Natural logarithm	F
SIN	Sine function	F
COS	Cosine function	F
SQRT	Square root	F
DIV	Integer division	F
MOD	Returns the remainder	F
ACOS	Arc-Cosine	F
ASIN	Arc-Sine	F
TAN	Tangent	F
COSH	Hyperbolic cosine	F
SINH	Hyperbolic sine	F
TANH	Hyperbolic tangent	F
LOG10	Base 10 logarithm	F
ABS	Absolute value	F, I, P
SIGN	Prefix operator (-1, 0, 1)	F, I, P
CEIL	Smallest integer value >=x	F, I, P
FLOOR	Largest integer value <= x	F, I, P
TRUNC	Integer part	F, I, P
FRAC	Fraction	F, I, P

Assignments using the equals sign are a simplified, special form of ABAP assignment, as all statements usually start with a keyword. That is why there are also long-form versions of the described assignments. These are introduced by a keyword. Consequently, the complete syntax for assignments actually reads as follows:

COMPUTE *field = expression.*

In this syntax, the COMPUTE keyword is optional so it is hardly used in practice. The operational statements ADD TO, SUBTRACT FROM, MULTIPLY BY and DIVIDE BY are alternatives to the operational characters. Below is an example of how these statements can be applied:

ADD value TO sum.

The keywords must be followed by a constant or a field. Otherwise the expression will not be processed and an error message will be generated during the syntax check. A few additional special types exist for the statements mentioned. These special types are only used in exceptional cases, such as when structures are involved.

Type conversions

Currently there are already 10 predefined data types. Therefore, there are 100 different ways of using assignments to combine these different types, and so there are theoretically 100 different rules for type conversion. ABAP automatically supports almost all imaginable conversions. It is not possible to describe all the rules here. They are described in detail in the R/3 System online help. The following basic rules are of central importance:

- The source field must have a value that can be converted into a value of the target field type. If, for example, the source field is of type C and the target field is of type F, then the source field must contain the representation of a floating point number.

- There are various ways of handling an insufficient number of digits in the target field. These range from simply truncating the contents, to completely deleting them (the system fills the target field with the character *), to a runtime error.

- Under certain conditions, date and time entries will be converted into time periods (in days or seconds) starting from a particular reference point in time. Conversion in the opposite direction (time period into date) may also occur. This makes date calculations of the following type easier:

```
date = date + integer_value.
```

The example below shows the effects of some type conversions. It can serve as a basis for your own experiments. You should note that ABAP applications mostly use the data types C, N, D and P, so the type conversions involving them are of special interest.

```
REPORT yz332060.
DATA: s(20),
      n TYPE I,
      d TYPE D,
      x TYPE F.

s = '123'.
n = s.
WRITE: / '1. CHAR -> INT ', 25(10) s, (20) n.

n = s + 1.
WRITE: / '2. CHAR -> INT ', 25(10) s, (20) n.

n = s+1.
WRITE: / '3. CHAR -> INT ', 25(10) s, (20) n.
WRITE /.
```

```
s = '123.789'.
x = s.
WRITE: /   '4. CHAR -> FLOAT', 25(10)  s,
           (20)  x DECIMALS 5 EXPONENT 0.


n = x.
WRITE: /   '5. FLOAT-> INT ',
           25(10)  x DECIMALS 5 EXPONENT 0,  (20)n.
WRITE /.
WRITE /.


s = '19900601'.
d = s.
WRITE: /  '6. CHAR -> DATUM, 25(10)  s,  (10)  d.


s = '900601'.
d = s.
WRITE: /  '7. CHAR -> DATUM, 25(10)  s,  (10)  d.
WRITE /.


d = '19991231'.
s = d.
WRITE: /  '8. DATUM -> CHAR', 25(10)  d,  (10)  s.


n = d.
WRITE: /  '9. DATUM -> INT', 25(10)  d,  (10)  n.
```

This short program, in which 'DATUM' means 'DATE', generates the output shown in Figure 3.30.

The first three lines demonstrate the assignment of character strings to numerical fields. First of all, the unchanged character string is assigned to an I-type field. As expected, it is correctly converted into a number. The next assignment demonstrates the use of a character string in a numerical expression. As above, it is correctly converted into a number, with the number being subsequently used for evaluating the expression.

The use of character strings in numerical expressions can create a rather insidious trap for the programmer. The syntax of the third assignment is correct, but is not a numerical expression, despite being identical to the previous expression, with the exception of the spaces. Here, the contents of the character string, from offset 1 onward (i.e. from the second places), are used to assign the value of the numerical field. Therefore, this does not receive the value 124, but merely 23. And here, the spaces take on considerable importance. This kind of logical error will never be found by a syntax check, and occasionally such assignments are even intended by the programmer. However, in such cases it would be useful to add an explanatory comment, emphasizing the accuracy and the purpose of the statement.

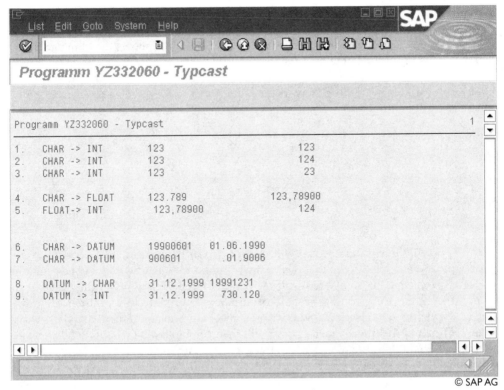

Figure 3.30   Type conversions

In assignment 4, a fractional number, represented as a character string, is assigned to a floating point field. The different delimiters between the digits before and after the comma/point are important here. When the floating point value is output with WRITE, it uses a real comma, but it must be replaced with a point in the character string representation of the value. This entry results in a runtime error, because the character string cannot be interpreted as a number:

```
s = '123,789'.
x = s.
```

When a floating point number is assigned to an integer field, the system rounds off the digits after the comma/point.

A special entry type is required for assigning character strings to date fields (6). This must also be used if a value is assigned to a date field with a hard-coded constant instead of a character string field. The date entry format must always be YYYYMMDD. Here, too, the formats used for assignment and for output with WRITE differ from each other. If characters are missing during assignment, invalid date values will result, as demonstrated in screen line 7. Similar conditions apply to time entries (type T).

The last two assignments demonstrate once again how date values are converted into character strings or integer values. The assignment of a character string results in the well-known YYYYMMDD format. The integer value, however, shows the number of days that have passed since starting the time counter (01.01.0001).

The implicit type conversion in expressions and assignments hides some pitfalls, as the final result can depend on the conversion sequence. The following extract from a program shows this:

```
REPORT yz332070.
DATA d TYPE D.
d = '19991225' + 7.
WRITE / d.
d = '19991225'.
d = d + 7.
WRITE / d.
```

If you execute this program, you will receive two different results, although the executed operations appear to be identical. This is because, while the system is calculating the expressions, the intermediate results are of a different data type. In the first expression, a character string consisting only of numbers is linked with a numerical value. Within the expression it is not known that, at a later stage, an assignment to a date field is to take place and that the character string will then contain a date. Therefore, the character string is first of all converted into an integer value and increased by 7. Only then will it be converted into a date. However, on the right-hand side of the assignment, you will now see an integer value and not a character string. That is why the date field is assigned a date which is 19.991.232 days after the 1.1.0001. This produces an invalid entry which leads to the assignment of 0 to the date field.

In the second part of the program, the assignment and expression have been split into two lines. The assignment to the date field now produces the correct result, because the runtime system can clearly define the data types of the source value and the target field. The subsequent operation is clear with regard to the data types, and therefore the result is 1.1.2000.

Apart from the implicit type conversion in expressions and assignments, you can also execute explicit type conversions with the help of some variants of the ASSIGN statement, described in Section 3.2.5.

Exercises

1. Test the statements discussed so far. Generate your own framework programs for the incomplete examples shown.

2. Test the type conversions between different data types. Analyze the behaviour in case of violations of the value range.

3. Create a program which enters values into the fields of all predefined types and displays them. Change the output length to values smaller and larger than the default length and then evaluate the results.

4. Practise working with packed numbers. Pay special attention to how the system rounds off numbers and the calculation accuracy in the case of intermediate results.

5. Test date computation, especially addition and subtraction among date fields and between date and integer fields. Assign the result both to date and to integer fields.

6. Test the output from date and time fields with and without explicitly defining an output length that is sufficient for the representation of the value with delimiters.

3.2.4 Structures

Relational database systems combine several individual fields into one *record*. No general program language can do without such records, which are also known as *structures*. Naturally, ABAP also has comparable elements called *structures*. Data types defining this kind of structure are also described as *line types*.

Structures can be generated in two different ways. One method automatically creates a structure for each database table used in a program. This structure is then used for exchanging data between an ABAP application and database system.

In the second method, the DATA or TYPES statements are used to explicitly declare structures or structure types. Here, various options are available for defining the structure of the structure. First of all, you can use BEGIN OF and END OF to define the structure directly, independently of other elements:

```
DATA: BEGIN OF record,
  declarations
END OF record.
```

or

```
TYPES: BEGIN OF record,
  declarations
END OF record.
```

You use DATA to introduce all the declarations between BEGIN OF and END OF, and not only the declarations already described above. This means that a structure may itself contain other structures or even internal tables. This is an example of how a structure type might be defined in a program:

```
TYPES: BEGIN OF t_address,
  name(20),
  street(30),
  city(20),
  zipcode(6),
END OF t_address.
```

In structure declarations and definitions, as in the basic form of DATA for individual fields, you can use LIKE or TYPE respectively to refer to an existing element (field or structure) or type. There are no constraints on the structure of the added element. Consequently, structures themselves can contain other structures:

```
DATA: BEGIN OF invoice,
  customer TYPE t_address,
  value TYPE P DECIMALS 2,
END OF invoice.
```

Within the DATA and the TYPES statement, there are two new ways in which you can refer to internal tables. You can use these statements to generate a structure whose structure corresponds to the structure of the table line displayed after LINE OF.

[**DATA** | **type**] *record* **TYPE LINE OF** *itabtype*.

or

[**DATA** | **type**] *record* **LIKE LINE OF** *itab*.

This is useful, for example, in subroutines, if you want to generate a work area for internal tables without a header row. You will find more details on internal tables in Section 3.2.7.

You can use a similar syntax to generate structures or corresponding types whose structure corresponds to that of a Data Dictionary table:

[**DATA** | **type**] *record* **LIKE** *database_table*.

The LINE OF addition is not required here.

When accessing structures, you have to distinguish between access to the structure as a whole or access to individual fields. When a field, which is a component of a structure, is used, its name comprises the name of the structure and the name of the actual field. Both names will be separated by a hyphen. If a structure contains other structures, the name consists of more than two parts. For example, the following field names would be valid for the declarations above:

```
invoice-value
invoice-customer-city
```

The second access option is rather risky, although it is almost impossible to do without it sometimes. In ABAP, a structure is an individual C-type field, whose length is defined by the fields it contains. Here, the length of the structure can exceed the total length of the individual fields, as characters might have been automatically added to them, to adjust them to word limits. That is why you can use offset and length specifications to access a structure without regard to its internal structure. Indirectly, this also provides you with a way of accessing fields that can otherwise not be processed using offset and length specifications. This feature also enables you to assign a structure to a character string, which is then distributed among the subfields according to the number of characters it contains. Here is an example:

```
REPORT yz332080.
DATA: BEGIN OF f1,
  c1(2) VALUE '##',
  c2(2) VALUE '##',
  n TYPE I,
END OF f1.
```

```
WRITE: / f1-c1, / f1-c2, / f1-n.
f1 = 'ABCDEFGH'.
WRITE: / f1-c1, / f1-c2, / f1-n.
```

In this statement, you enter new values into all three fields of structure f1. While there is no problem assigning values to fields c1 and c2, (splitting a field into subfields), field n on the other hand is also given a value depending on how the assigned bit sample is interpreted. This depends on the data type. Assignments of this kind are definitely undesirable.

You can even use a whole structure when assigning a structure to another structure or a structure to a single field. With these assignments, the system transfers the individual characters without type conversion from the source to the target, where they may be reinterpreted. The length of the target field, which is always taken into consideration, is the only constraint on using structures in this way. Therefore, assignments between structures only achieve a correct result if both structures have the same structure. However, ABAP applications very often require the transfer of the values in several fields with identical names between structures with different structures. The following program, for example, copies order data and an item description into a third structure. To avoid having to write an individual assignment for each subfield, this statement is used:

MOVE-CORRESPONDING *source_record* **TO** *target_record*.

This statement transfers the contents between fields with identical names in two structures:

```
REPORT yz332090.
TYPES t_wert TYPE P DECIMALS 2.

DATA: BEGIN OF mat,
   matno(10) TYPE N VALUE '1234567890',
   matnm(20) VALUE 'Writing desk lamp',
   price TYPE t_wert VALUE '123.45',
END OF mat.

DATA: BEGIN OF ordr,
   matno LIKE mat-matno,
   item TYPE I VALUE '2',
   total TYPE t_wert,
END OF ordr.

DATA: BEGIN OF invc,
   matno LIKE mat-matno,
   matnm LIKE mat-matnm,
   item LIKE ordr-item,
   price LIKE mat-price,
   total LIKE ordr-total,
END OF invc.
```

```
MOVE-CORRESPONDING ordr TO invc.
MOVE-CORRESPONDING mat TO invc.
invc-total = invc-item * invc-price.

WRITE: /  invc-matno, invc-matnm, invc-price,
           invc-item, invc-total.
```

The type concept is not available in R/3 Release 3.0 or earlier. Neither is it possible to use LIKE to refer to internal tables or Data Dictionary tables. Therefore, the options for creating structures are extremely restricted. Here, you can only use this statement to integrate substructures:

INCLUDE STRUCTURE *structure*.

The INCLUDE statement is a stand-alone statement that must end with a full stop. Consequently, it cannot simply be added to the parameter list of the DATA statement. Instead, BEGIN OF and END OF require their own DATA statement as is shown in the following example:

```
DATA: BEGIN OF invoice.
  INCLUDE STRUCTURE adr.
DATA: value TYPE P DECIMALS 2,
END OF invoice.
```

Here, adr must either be a Data Dictionary structure or a structure defined with DATA in the program (structure or internal table). The INCLUDE statement adds the elements of the structure as individual fields, i.e. it breaks up the adr structure. As a result, structures in previous releases cannot be multiply nested: there is only one field level.

The syntax of the declaration statement shown above is correct, although somewhat confusing. The reason for this is that two DATA statements seemingly have to generate the structure independently of each other. The BEGIN and END keywords, which are decisive in defining the data structure, are located in the centre of the statement and are easily overlooked, especially in more complex declaration statements. The reason for such constructions is that the syntax of ABAP was extended retrospectively. It is impossible to create a completely new design as compatibility with previous releases is absolutely essential. When the language is extended, while guaranteeing full compatibility with previous Releases, complicated, and occasionally misleading syntax, is often the price that has to be paid. To minimize the consequences of such complicated syntax, you should arrange your code clearly, and use indents. The statement below is completely compatible with the previous example, despite an additional (redundant) DATA statement. The keywords BEGIN OF and END OF are the decisive factors in the declaration of structures, and not the DATA statements. In fact, you can use almost any number of DATA statements, even for each individual subfield of the structure.

```
DATA: BEGIN OF invoice.
  INCLUDE STRUCTURE adr.
  DATA value TYPE P DECIMALS 2.
DATA: END OF invoice.
```

You can use the `INCLUDE` statement in another way, which allows you to include the type definition of a structure instead of an existing structure or table, thereby breaking it up. In this case, the statement is as follows:

INCLUDE TYPE *type*.

The same notes apply for its use as for `INCLUDE STRUCTURE`.

Although you read above that `INCLUDE` leads to a break-up of the structure, Release 4.6 and higher offer you the option of continuing to handle the added elements as a unique object. Here, a few syntactical subtleties emerge which require more detailed explanation.

You can use this addition to name the added structure:

AS *name*

Although the structure does get broken up, you can access the element with the assigned name, as if *name* were a unique substructure. In addition, you can specify a character string that is automatically added to the names of the added fields when adding a component. By using this method, you can repeatedly add substructures and still assign them unique field names. To do so, use this addition with the `INCLUDE` statement:

RENAMING WITH SUFFIX *suffix*.

The following program clarifies the effect of the two new options. As it was included afterwards, the name assignment function deviates somewhat from the general scheme.

```
 1 REPORT yz332095 NO STANDARD PAGE HEADING.
 2 TYPES: BEGIN OF trec1,
 3 f11,
 4 f12,
 5 f13,
 6 END OF trec1.
 7
 8 TYPE: BEGIN OF trec2,
 9 f21,
10 f22,
11 f23,
12 END OF trec2.
13
14 DATA: BEGIN OF rec1.
15 INCLUDE TYPE trec1 AS a.
16 INCLUDE TYPE trec2 AS b.
17 DATA: END OF rec1.
18
19 DATA: BEGIN OF rec2.
20 INCLUDE TYPE trec1 AS a RENAMING WITH SUFFIX low.
21 INCLUDE TYPE trec1 AS b RENAMING WITH SUFFIX high.
22 DATA: END OF rec2.
```

```
23
24 rec1-f11 = '1'.
25 rec1-f21 = '4'.
26 rec1-a-f12 = '2'.
27 rec1-b-f22 = '5'.
28 WRITE: / '1. ', rec1.
29 WRITE: / '2. ', rec1-a.
30 WRITE: / '3. ', rec1-b.
31
32 rec2-f11low = 'A'.
33 rec2-f13low = 'C'.
34 rec2-f11high = 'D'.
35 rec2-f13high = 'F'.
36 rec2-a-f12 = 'B'.
37 rec2-b-f12 = 'E'.
38 WRITE: / '4. ', rec2.
39
40 CLEAR rec2.
41 MOVE-CORRESPONDING rec1 TO rec2.
42 WRITE: / '5. ', rec2.
43
44 CLEAR rec2.
45 MOVE-CORRESPONDING rec1 TO rec2-a.
46 MOVE-CORRESPONDING rec1 TO rec2-b.
47 WRITE: / '6. ', rec2.
```

Two short structure types are defined at the start of the program. Lines 14 to 17 show how these two types are used within the declaration of structure rec1, and how they are given a structure name (here a and b). In lines 19 to 22, a second structure is declared, which includes the structure trec1 twice. The RENAMING addition ensures that unique field names are still assigned, by adding the character strings low and high.

The next part of the program shows the different access options for the subfields. The statements in lines 24 and 25 are identical to the usual means of accessing flat structures. They prove that the INCLUDE statement produces a flat structure. In lines 26 and 27, the name of the substructure is used as an additional parameter to access the subfields. At this point, this does not offer any advantages, but merely demonstrates the necessary convention. The two structure names a and b simply provide access to the three fields of each substructure. This statement would consequently cause a syntax error, although the subfield f22 is contained in rec1:

```
rec1 a f22 = 'X'.
```

The subsequent WRITE statements show a possible use of the substructure name. It provides a simple way of accessing a subset of the structure.

In lines 32 to 35, the RENAMING addition creates a flat structure that clearly shows the names of the subfields. However, if the structure names are used to access the subfields, then the old names without suffix (*see* lines 36 and 37) are valid. You should take this feature into consideration, for example, in the case of assignments using MOVE CORRESPONDING, as the field names are then relevant. In line 41, rec1 is assigned to rec2. The MOVE-CORRESPONDING statement uses the flat structure because only the name of the actual structure is used. In this view, the names of the subfields are naturally different, due to the addition of the suffixes in rec2 and the field contents are not transferred. This however changes with the substructure names, making the original field names visible. This is the case in lines 45 and 46. Now it is possible to assign subfields f11 to f13.

3.2.5 Field symbols

Although the assignments and access procedures described above allow for fairly flexible data handling, they still have their limitations when low-level problems need to be solved. This is the case in dynamic data access. Some subroutines have to work with differently structured data, i.e. they cannot use hard-coded field names. ABAP provides *field symbols* to solving these special problems. A field symbol is distantly related to a pointer in the C programming language, and has the reference to an existing field assigned to it. You can then work with the field symbol as if it were the original field.

Basic form

To declare field symbols, use the following statement:

FIELD-SYMBOLS *<field_symbol>*.

The pointed brackets are part of the field symbol's name. The ASSIGN statement is responsible for assigning a field to a field symbol. Its structure approximately corresponds to that of the MOVE statement:

ASSIGN *field[+offset[(length)]]* **TO** *<field_symbol>*.

In this type of assignment, the field symbol takes on the data type of the source field. If you assign several fields of different types to a field symbol in succession, the data type of the field symbol changes accordingly. The field symbol also takes on other attributes of the source field such as its length, unless you are working with an explicit length specification. If the reference field is accessed with an offset during assignment, it is highly probable that this will result in other data being overwritten when you do not want it to be. You can prevent this by defining the length specification '(*)'. In assignments, this addition prevents the field limits from being exceeded.

```
REPORT yz332100.
FIELD-SYMBOLS <fs>.

DATA: BEGIN OF f,
   c1(3),
   c2(2),
   c3(10),
END OF f.
```

```
ASSIGN f-c1+2 TO <fs>.
<fs> = '12345'.
WRITE: / 'Field symbol :', <fs>.
WRITE: / 'Assignment without * :', f-c1, f-c2, f-c3.

CLEAR f.
ASSIGN f-c1+2(*) TO <fs>.
<fs> = '12345'.
WRITE: / 'Assignment with * :', f-c1, f-c2, f-c3.
```

In this example, a field symbol is derived from the field f-c1. As this field is only three digits long, the system will only take into account these three digits when assigning the field symbol. The first WRITE statement illustrates this. However, as the field symbol does not start at the first digit of field c1, the assignments also apply to field c2 as demonstrated in the second output. If, during derivation of the field symbol, the (*) addition is used, the system calculates the space available in c1 and then assigns this length to the field symbol. The last output instruction illustrates this quite clearly.

You can use offset and length specifications when using field symbols, as well as when linking field symbols with fields. Here too, the system only checks the validity of these values if field length monitoring has been activated with '(*)'. This is shown in the following example:

```
REPORT yz332110.
FIELD-SYMBOLS <fs>.

DATA: BEGIN OF f,
  c1(3) VALUE 'ABC',
  c2(2) VALUE 'DE',
  c3(5) VALUE 'FGHIJ',
END OF f.

ASSIGN f-c1+2 TO <fs>.
<fs>+2 = '12345'.
WRITE: / f-c1 , f-c2, f-c3.

ASSIGN f-c1+2(*) TO <fs>.
* Now comment out the next code line.
* This causes a runtime error, as <fs> is outside the field
*<fs>+2 = '12345'.
```

In this programming example, values are entered in the structure's fields during definition, to enable you to quickly recognize the effects of subsequent assignments. As shown in the previous example, the field symbol is placed in the last position of field c1. During assignment, an offset of 2 is entered again. This results in an offset of 4, so the target of the assignment is consequently the last digit of c2. When you use ASSIGN to assign field symbols, the system recognizes that, due to the offsets in the ASSIGN statement, only one character may be transferred. However, this one transferred character is then inserted as the last digit of c2 due to the second offset in <fs>+2. The number of characters to be transferred is calculated correctly, but the target position lies outside the selected target field, c1. Occasionally, this behaviour can be desirable. However, the effects of the assignments are now rather difficult to foresee as two offsets have been specified. If you want to ensure that no other fields apart from the one specified in the ASSIGN statement will be overwritten, it is essential to add (*) to the ASSIGN statement. When attempting to carry out assignment, the system recognizes that the target position is located outside the actual target field C1. In this case, the system generates a runtime error. To be able to test the first part of the program, you must comment out the last assignment.

You can use additional options to extend the basic form of the ASSIGN statement, which is currently in use, in two ways. These additional options are typing and dynamic definition of the source field. They allow you to carry out explicit type conversions, and to construct generic statements able to deal with any data structure. The options are described below. They can usually be combined with each other. Please see your system documentation for more detailed information.

Typing

In the basic form of assignment using ASSIGN, the field symbol's data type changes to the data type of the reference field. You can deviate from this default in different ways. First, you can create a typed field symbol:

FIELD-SYMBOL <*field_symbol*> **TYPE** type.

When the system is executing an ASSIGN statement for a typed field symbol, it checks whether the data type and other attributes of the reference field, such as its length, are suited to the data type of the field symbol. If not, the program check generates a syntax error. Therefore, the type checks already take place before the application is processed. This precise check is possible as all type information is available at this point in time. The checks executed here are at times far stricter than in other assignments. In this type of check, data type C is incompatible with data type N, although it is sometimes possible to create assignments between the two types without problems.

Further typing options are available at runtime when executing the ASSIGN statement. Here you can define the required field symbol type:

ASSIGN field **TO** <*field_symbol*> **TYPE** type.

This type of statement first of all assigns a field symbol and only afterwards sets its type. Therefore, the type checks are at this point not as strict as when the type is defined statically. However, the lengths of the fields concerned are of considerable importance. In addition, the contents of the reference field must be suitable for conversion into a value of the selected data type. Unlike during definition, the target type is transferred as a character string or as a field. The following statement types would therefore be correct:

```
DATA:
  field(3) TYPE c,
  fs_type VALUE 'C'.
```

```
FIELD-SYMBOLS:
  <fs>

ASSIGN field TO <fs> TYPE 'N'.
ASSIGN field TO <fs> TYPE fs_type.
```

You use the methods mentioned above to define the field symbol's type. You can also force the system to interpret the reference field according to a predefined data type, if the field symbol's type has been determined. To do so you use the CASTING addition. The basic form is:

ASSIGN *field* **TO** *<field_symbol>* **CASTING**.

Here, the source field is treated as a data field with the same type as the field symbol, regardless of its actual type. For this to happen, the system must be able to interpret the source field according to the specified type. In this case, the field symbol must already have been declared as a typified field symbol.

The following statement variants link the interpretation of the reference field with the assignment of a new data type to a field symbol. Here, it is also possible to dynamically assign the new field symbol type.

ASSIGN *field* **TO** *<field_symbol>* **CASTING TYPE** *type.*
ASSIGN *field* **TO** *<field_symbol>* **CASTING TYPE** *(typename).*
ASSIGN *field* **TO** *<field_symbol>* **CASTING LIKE** *typefield.*

The example below is a modified version of an example from above. Below, it demonstrates the effect of typing:

```
REPORT yz332120.
DATA:
  d TYPE D,
  s(8).
FIELD-SYMBOLS
  <fd> TYPE D.

s = '19991225'.
ASSIGN s TO <fd> CASTING.
d = <fd> + 7.
WRITE /(10) d.
d = '19991225'.
d = d + 7.
WRITE /(10) d.
```

The field symbol is of the data type D. Because the system is forced to interpret it as a date during assignment of the source field, the field symbol is assigned a correct value as its contents. Therefore, the subsequent expression works with a date that achieves the desired result in both calculations.

Here is another program to demonstrate the differences between the various typing options:

```
 1: REPORT yz332130.
 2: DATA:
 3: fc(8) VALUE '19991225'.
 4:
 5: FIELD-SYMBOLS:
 6: <d> TYPE D,
 7: <f>.
 8:
 9: ASSIGN fc TO <f>. 'ok
10: WRITE: /(10) <f>.
11:
12: *ASSIGN fc TO <d>. 'Not OK, as fc and <d> are of different types
13: ASSIGN fc TO <d> CASTING.
14: WRITE: /(10) <d>.
15:
16: ASSIGN fc TO <f> TYPE 'D'.
17: WRITE: /(10) <f>.
```

First you create a character string field, fc, and enter a valid date value in it. Then, you declare two field symbols. One of them is of data type D, and no type is set for the other one.

The character string is assigned to the untyped field symbol in line 9, where the field symbol assumes the data type of the source field. The subsequent output instruction then writes the unmodified character string to the monitor.

It is not possible to assign the character string field to the typed field symbol <d> (line 12), as the data types of the two elements are not identical. This statement, which is commented out in the example, therefore causes a syntax error. You now have two ways to output the character string field as a date value using a field symbol. The statement in line 13 shows how to correctly assign it to a D-type field symbol. Using the CASTING addition, the source field is interpreted as a date field and assigned to the typified field symbol. As a result, the subsequent WRITE statement is able to output a correct date value.

Another method would be to assign the character string value to an untyped field symbol, and in doing so to force a field symbol type that is different from the source field type. Line 16 shows the statement used to do this. Here, the assignment is carried out first, and then the field symbol type is defined. That is why there will be no problems during the type check. The subsequent output also generates a correct date value in this case.

Dynamic field mapping

So far, we have always specified the reference field directly, but it can also be assigned indirectly or dynamically. The system can derive the name of the reference field from another field:

```
ASSIGN (field) TO <field_symbol>.
```

The name of the reference field is enclosed in round brackets. No spaces are permitted between the brackets and field name. Alternatively, you can address a subfield of a structure (structure) by using an index or name:

```
ASSIGN COMPONENT [idx | name] OF STRUCTURE struc TO <fs>.
```

You can process and output the contents of any database table, according to specific types, by linking the typing of a field symbol to the runtime. The statements in the examples below, which are new to you, will be described in the sections that follow.

```
REPORT yz332140.
DATA:
  tabname TYPE tabname VALUE 'E070',
  record(2048).
FIELD-SYMBOLS:
  <rec>,
  <field>.

SELECT * FROM (tabname) INTO record UP TO 100 ROWS.
  ASSIGN record TO <rec> CASTING TYPE (tabname).
  DO.
    ASSIGN COMPONENT sy-index OF STRUCTURE <rec> TO <field>.
    IF sy-subrc <> 0.
      EXIT.
    ENDIF.
    WRITE: /(3) sy-index, <field>.
  ENDDO.
ENDSELECT.
```

The SELECT statement reads data from a database table. In the example above, the name of the table to be read is dynamically transferred in the tabname field. The name of the table used here is particularly suitable as it contains date and time entries, as well as simple character strings. In this way, you can ensure the output format is correct. You can enter other values, instead of tabname, to read other tables. For this purpose you should always use table names like TADIR, T000 or USR01, as these tables always contain data.

Additional options in the SELECT statement ensure that each record that is read is stored in the unstructured record field and that a maximum of 100 records will be read.

The first ASSIGN statement positions a field symbol on the record field, thereby setting the field symbol type. Again, the table name is used to set the type that is indirectly transferred in the tabname field. This is possible because Data Dictionary elements can be used as type identifiers too. In the subsequent loop you will find a second ASSIGN statement, with which you successively position a second field symbol on each of the individual fields within a record. In this type of assignment, the field symbol takes on the data type of the reference field. The subsequent WRITE statement can therefore execute type-specific output conversion.

Deleting assignments

You can use this statement to undo the assignment made with `ASSIGN`:

UNASSIGN `<field_symbol>`.

The field symbol then no longer refers to valid data. This logical expression now outputs a space as the icon for 'incorrect':

... `<field_symbol>` **IS ASSIGNED**.

3.2.6 Determining field attributes

Data fields have attributes that are determined and evaluated at runtime. Within certain conditions, you can use the `IS` operator to determine selected states of data fields. These statements check whether the contents of a field consist of a space or whether the field's initial value has been set:

... *field* **IS SPACE**

   or

... *field* `IS` **INITIAL**.

You can use this statement to test whether the field symbol `field_symbol` has been assigned to a field:

... `<field_symbol>` **IS ASSIGNED** ....

Within function modules, you can test the condition

... *parameter* **IS REQUESTED** ....

The comparison is considered true if the formal parameter was assigned a current parameter when the function module was called.

Besides evaluating the status, you can use the `DESCRIBE` statement to determine a series of additional attributes. Use this syntax to call the statement:

DESCRIBE `field option result`.

Here, *field* is the name of the field to be evaluated. Table 3.12 lists the possible descriptors for *option*. Each result will be stored in the *result* field, whose data type must correspond with the expected result. Some of the values are only available for fields with Data Dictionary references.

Not only does the statement return the descriptors of the eight predefined data types for the data type, but it may also return the values listed in Table 3.13.

Table 3.12   DESCRIBE statement options

Option	Description
LENGTH	Defines length
Type	Data type
TYPE type **COMPONENTS** count	type specifies a complex data type
	count specifies a number of components
OUTPUT LENGTH	Output length
DECIMALS	Number of decimal places
EDIT MASK	Output mask
HELP ID	ID of the help text

Table 3.13   Additional IDs for data types

Alternative Data Type	Description
h	Internal table
r	Object reference
s	2-byte integer with prefix operator
b	1-byte integer without prefix operator
u	Structure without internal table
v	Structure containing at least one internal table

3.2.7   Internal tables

Apart from the tables administered by the Data Dictionary, there is a second type of table, the internal table. This does not exist in the database but only in the computer's RAM. It is therefore not intended for the permanent storage of information, but instead for temporarily storing and processing data within an application. Apart from a few exceptions, you always have to use internal tables with ABAP if you want to combine several records with identical structures into one joint data object. The term *arrays*, known from other programming languages, does not exist in ABAP. In compensation, and in addition to the table-oriented access options, ABAP offers some additional statements for the internal tables, which you can use to access internal tables through an index. This is similar to accessing an array.

Internal tables are used for the most varied reasons. Very often they buffer the result of a SELECT statement within an application, and therefore improve the application's run-time behaviour. Internal tables are also useful for exchanging data with subroutines or function modules. Furthermore, they allow you to sort and condense temporary datasets by different criteria.

When exchanging data between an internal table and application, you should take note of a special feature. The actual contents of the table mostly stay hidden from the program. Generally, they can only be accessed through a structure called the *header row* or *work area*. Special statements read one of the records in the internal table and then make it available in the work area. Others paste the contents of the work area into the internal table. For internal tables, the work area is the only interface between the dataset and application. Depending on the table type, the work area may be any field, as long as it offers sufficient space for entering a record, or it may be a structure with the same name as the internal table. In the latter case this is called a *header row*.

Release 4.0 has considerably expanded the concept of internal tables. There are now different types of internal table that differ from each other in the way they handle a key for the records. In this context, extensive extensions to the syntax have been implemented. The three new groups are:

1. standard table (STANDARD TABLE);

2. sorted table (SORTED TABLE);

3. hash table (HASHED TABLE).

The STANDARD TABLE type table resembles the basic form known from previous Releases of the R/3 software, in many of its attributes. Strictly speaking, the usual internal tables are a subset of the STANDARD TABLE-type table. Internal tables that have been generated with statements which would have already been available before Release 4.0 then automatically use the table type STANDARD TABLE. However, the new variants of the declaration allow you to specify additional attributes for this table type. That is why the new table type is able to replace the previous basic type without any problems. From now on, when we mention STANDARD TABLE-type tables or, in short, standard tables, this will apply both to tables to which this table type was explicitly assigned, and to the usual internal tables.

The system accesses standard tables sequentially or through the record number, both for reading and for writing. There is no automatic index management based on a table key. Therefore, the table may contain many records with identical contents. The table does not sort the records. Instead, if you want the records to be in a particular sequence, you must set that up explicitly. Apart from a few exceptions, the system searches for a particular record by time-consuming, sequential reading of the dataset.

The next variant of internal tables is sorted tables. They are given the description SORTED TABLE. When new records are being added, the R/3 System always keeps the contents of these tables in a sorted state. You therefore automatically receive the sorted records because the system carries out a LOOP through the table. Search functions execute a binary search. You can also enter index criteria to access the records of this table type, both to reading them and to writing to them, while taking into account the sorting sequence. Sorted additions require extra effort from the runtime system which in turn results in increased processing time. Sorted tables are used mainly if the dataset in a loop needs to be processed in sequence.

The last variant is tables whose key is administered by the R/3 System using the hash process. These are described as HASHED TABLES. Due to the administration method, it is

not possible to use a record number to access them. The records in this table are not physically sorted. New records will always be added at the end of the table. Within a LOOP
through the dataset you therefore receive the records in the sequence in which they have
been added to the table. However, the system administers an index according to the key
definition. You can use this key to access records in the internal table (statement READ
TABLE ... WITH TABLE KEY ...). This kind of table has the advantage that the time
taken to find a record is not determined by the position of the record within the table.
Furthermore, it is not necessary to resort the whole table when you add a new record.
Instead, only the index information is updated, so that the time spent on adding network
records is less than in sorted tables. Therefore, hash tables are particularly suitable as
tables that have to be frequently searched for a record.

With the DATA statement you can create real data objects for the above mentioned table
types. Here, you can describe the attributes of the table either directly in the DATA statement or indirectly through a table type. However, you should note that internal tables
that have been declared using a table type, or with the new syntax variants, only have a
header row if it has been explicitly generated during declaration.

Tables of the types SORTED TABLE and HASHED TABLE can only be transferred to
subroutines as USING or CHANGING parameters, and no longer as TABLES parameters.
This requires a new form of subroutine parameter typing. Therefore, a user-defined data
type should always be available for internal tables if possible.

Beside the three table types described, there are two more table names that are only
used for typing subroutine parameters. They are INDEX TABLE, which acts as the
common descriptor for standard and sorted tables, and ANY TABLE, which applies to all
three table groups. Tables based on these table types cannot be used for declaring internal
tables in a DATA statement.

At this point it is useful to emphasize again that line types can contain complex data
objects, as well as single fields. Therefore, a field in an internal table can contain structures or even additional internal tables.

Definition

From Release 4.6, you can define internal tables in the Data Dictionary. These definitions
will then be available as data types, just like Data Dictionary tables or data elements. In
addition, you can define internal table types within your application. Use the following
statement:

```
TYPES itabtype
   [ TYPE | LIKE ]
   [ STANDARD TABLE |
     SORTED TABLE |
     HASHED TABLE |
     INDEX  TABLE |
     ANY   TABLE ]
  OF
```

```
[ linetype | lineobject ]
[ WITH [ UNIQUE | NON-UNIQUE ]
       [ KEY fieldlist |
         KEY TABLE LINE |
         DEFAULT KEY | ] ]
[ INITIAL SIZE n ].
```

Immediately after TYPES you enter the name of the table type to be created. Then, you define the table type. To do so you can use all five table types mentioned above. However, you can only declare data objects with the table types STANDARD TABLE, SORTED TABLE or HASHED TABLE. You can use the other two table types only for typing subroutine parameters.

After the table type, you have to define the structure of the internal table. To do so, you either specify a line type, or a data object that is similar to a line. This definition must correspond with the LIKE or TYPE statement. For example, at the start, you might have defined that you wish to describe the structure of the table with a line type, by entering:

TYPES ... TYPE.

Now, you have to specify a line type after OF. However, you might use this statement to create a reference to an existing record:

TYPES ... LIKE.

Now, you have to enter the name of a structure or Data Dictionary structure after OF. Here you could also use an unstructured data type. In this case, you would define an internal table that only has one column with the attributes of the unstructured element. This kind of table is required when dynamically transferring selection criteria to the SELECT statement, for example. In a table generated in this way, no column names are available. The only way to access the table is through its name. There is an example below of how such tables are declared and used.

After this, you define whether the internal table should be given a key or not and whether this key is unique. This is not appropriate for all table types. If you attempt to assign a unique key to a standard table, you will receive an error during the syntax check. For standard tables, a non-unique key has been set as default, so you do not have to specify the key type in these tables. This also applies to sorted tables, but here the result is a generic table type that can only be used for typing subroutine parameters, and not for declaring data objects. You must enter one of the two key types to complete the definition of a data type for sorted tables. You must also define a key type for hash tables, but in this case it must be a unique key. The structure of the key is described with one of these parameters:

- **KEY** *fieldlist*;

- **KEY TABLE LINE**;

- **DEFAULT KEY**.

You can use the first parameter to explicitly name the key fields. You can use the second to define the entire table line as a key. The third parameter selects the standard method of key generation (all elementary non-number fields).

It is useful to explain the last parameter in more detail. Before the creation of the new table types, internal tables did not possess a genuine key with which a record could be identified. To ensure that it was still possible to search for a record in an internal table, all individual fields that were not number fields (type F, I and P) were by definition key fields of the table. This key was primarily used by a variant of the READ statement.

With the final parameter, INITIAL SIZE, you define the size of a buffer area in RAM. If the value is 0, the system will calculate the size of the buffer. Normally, this setting is sufficient.

If the declaration of the key is missing or if one of the table types INDEX TABLE or ANY TABLE is involved, we are dealing with a generic type. You can only use a generic data type for typing subroutine parameters. Using generic data types within the DATA statement will result in a syntax error.

You can use the following statement to summarize the definition of a type for a standard table:

type *itabtype* [**TYPE** *linetype* | **LIKE** *lineobject*] **OCCURS** *n*.

This statement corresponds to the statement known from previous R/3 Releases. Here, the effect of the OCCURS parameter is identical to the effect of INITIAL SIZE.

Please note here that you always have to base your definition of a table type on a structure that already exists, or a line type that is already present. You cannot define the structure of an internal table directly within the definition of the internal table (for example, with BEGIN OF and END OF). You must define this line type separately as already described in the section dealing with structures.

Below, you will find some examples of how internal tables are defined. The statements shown here form the first part of a program, which you will enhance with additional statements in the course of this section.

```
REPORT yz332150.
TABLES: tadir.
TYPES:
  t_line(72),

  BEGIN OF tr_tadir,
    pgmid(4),
    object LIKE tadir-object,
    obj_name TYPE sobj_name,
  END OF tr_tadir,

  ti_standard
    TYPE STANDARD TABLE OF tr_tadir
    INITIAL SIZE 0,

  ti_sorted
    TYPE SORTED TABLE OF tr_tadir
    WITH UNIQUE DEFAULT KEY
    INITIAL SIZE 0,
```

```
ti_hashed
  TYPE HASHED TABLE OF tr_tadir
  WITH UNIQUE KEY pgmid object obj_name
  INITIAL SIZE 0,

ti_flat
  TYPE STANDARD TABLE OF t_line
  INITIAL SIZE 0,

ti_old
  TYPE tr_tadir OCCURS 0.
```

The first two data types are not data types for internal tables, but instead are an elementary type and a structure. These two elements will be required as resources when the internal tables are defined. The first table type is `ti_standard`. It is created for a default table that is supposed to have the same structure as `ti_tadir`. There are no entries for the key.

The definition of `ti_sorted` is somewhat more time consuming. Here, you use an additional option to define that this table should have a unique key whose structure uses the default (all elementary non-number fields).

The third table type, `ti_hashed`, also requires you to define a key. Here the key field is named explicitly to practically demonstrate this variant of the statement.

The type `ti_flat` describes a standard table consisting only of one column. Additional data concerning the key can be omitted. The last definition for `ti_old` uses a variant of the `TYPES` statement for internal tables that already existed in Release 3.x.

Declaration

Due to the universal type concept, internal tables are declared in a similar way to other data objects. The basic form of the declaration is as follows:

DATA *itab* **TYPE** *itabtype* [**WITH HEADER LINE**] .

You can use the `WITH HEADER LINE` addition to generate an internal table with a header row. If this addition is missing, a separate work area has to be used for data exchange between the application and internal table.

When declaring internal tables, it is also possible to do without a separate table type definition. However, if you do so, you then have to add the options necessary for the definition to the declaration. This results in the following statement:

```
DATA itabtype
  [ TYPE  | LIKE ]
  [ STANDARD TABLE |
    SORTED    TABLE |
    HASHED    TABLE ]
  OF
```

```
[ linetype | lineobject ]
[ WITH [ UNIQUE | NON-UNIQUE ]
       [ KEY fieldlist    |
         KEY TABLE LINE   |
         DEFAULT KEY      | ] ]
[ INITIAL SIZE n]
[ WITH HEADER LINE].
```

This statement must not contain data which would cause the definition of a generic type. This means that the table types INDEX TABLE and ANY TABLE are not permitted. Apart from that, you must enter a correct key type (UNIQUE or NON-UNIQUE) for both the table types SORTED TABLE and HASHED TABLE. With the exception of WITH HEADER LINE, which again forces a header row, the remaining parameters are the same as those used in the TYPES statement.

There is also a short form for declaring a STANDARD TABLE-type table with the default key. This reads as follows:

DATA *itab* [**TYPE TABLE OF** *linetype* | **LIKE TABLE OF** *lineobj*].

Here, an entry for the memory size (parameter INITIAL SIZE) is missing. The system will automatically enter 0, because the TABLE OF addition defines that an internal table is to be generated, and not a structure. This statement is rather similar:

DATA *itab* [**TYPE** *linetype* | **LIKE** *lineobj*] **OCCURS** *n* [**WITH HEADER LINE**].

Here, too, a STANDARD TABLE-type is being generated. This statement has been available since Release 3.x.

For standard tables, it is possible to further compress the declaration. You can directly define the structure of the table in the declaration without reference to a line type. You are consequently not dependent on an explicitly existing data type. In this case, the syntax of the declaration statement reads as follows:

DATA:
    BEGIN OF *itab* **OCCURS** *n*,
    declarations,
    END OF *itab*.

With the exception of the OCCURS parameter, this is identical to a structure declaration. This means that, even here, the special features described in the structures section can occur in the context of the INCLUDE STRUCTURE statement. Internal tables that have been created in this way always have a header row.

Below are some examples of declaration where the previously created table types are used.

```
DATA:
   r_tadir TYPE tr_tadir,
   i_standard TYPE tr_tadir OCCURS 0 WITH HEADER LINE,
   i_sorted TYPE SORTED TABLE OF tr_tadir
     WITH UNIQUE KEY pgmid object obj_name
     INITIAL SIZE 0,
   i_hashed TYPE ti_hashed,
   i_condition TYPE ti_flat WITH HEADER LINE.
```

The first statement declares a structure that later acts as a work area for the different internal tables. The second statement generates a standard table. To do so, it uses the declaration variant that was already available in Release 3.x. This is made especially clear by the use of the OCCURS parameter. The table type defined earlier is not used here, but only the line type `tr_tadir`. The declaration of the sorted table `i_sorted` also makes no reference to the existing table type. In contrast to the table type `ti_sorted`, the key is defined here by listing the key fields. Because the `with header row` addition is missing here, this table has no header row.

While the two previous declarations require quite a lot of typing, the table type is used to declare an internal table, making this much easier. It is no more time consuming to declare the hash table than an elementary data field. In this case, once again, a table without a header row is generated, as the corresponding addition is missing. However, it can also be used in this type of declaration, as is demonstrated in the last statement for the `i_condition` table.

Accessing internal tables

The statements for working with internal tables can be split into two groups:

1. commands for modifying the table contents;

2. commands for reading records.

Each of these statement groups contains various statements that may not always be applied to all table types. Furthermore, some statements work generically and can consequently be used for all table types, and some are used only for standard and sorted tables. The generic statement types can often be recognized by their keyword TABLE within the statement.

Adding records

You can use the APPEND statement to add new records at the end of an internal table. You cannot use this statement for hash tables. If you use APPEND to add a record to a table of the type SORTED TABLE, the table still has to have the status 'sorted' even after the data has been added, otherwise a runtime error will be triggered. Therefore, this statement is almost exclusively used for STANDARD TABLE-type internal tables. The syntax of this statement is:

APPEND [*record* **TO** | **INITIAL LINE TO**] *itab*.

The shortest possible form of the statement is therefore:

APPEND itab.

In this case, the record to be appended is extracted from the header row of the internal table itab and added there. If you are working with tables without a header row, or if you want to extract the data from a different record than the header row, you will have to use the **TO** option:

APPEND *record* **TO** *itab*.

You can use the INITIAL LINE TO option to add an empty record to the table. You will find examples of the APPEND statement at the end of the following section, which is about the INSERT statement.

Inserting records

Inserting new records with the INSERT statement is somewhat more complicated than simply adding them at the end of the table. The reason for this is that various methods have to be used to define the position of the record to be added. The universally valid, generic version of the statement is:

INSERT [**record INTO** | **INITIAL LINE INTO**] **TABLE** *itab*.

You can use this statement for all table types. The statements in the APPEND statement apply, with reference to the provision of data in the header row or in a separate record. In sorted tables, this statement ensures that the new record is added according to the defined key. In hash tables, the record is added at the end, but the internal key table is updated. If the key has been defined as unique (UNIQUE), duplicates will trigger a return code 4 in the SY-SUBRC field.

In tables without automatic sorting function, i.e. STANDARD TABLE-type tables, the generic INSERT TABLE statement works like the APPEND statement and adds the record at the end of the table. If you do not want this, you can use a non-generic form of the INSERT statement to insert a record at an exactly defined place in the table:

INSERT [*record* **INTO** | **INITIAL LINE INTO**] *itab* [**INDEX** *index*].

If the sorting sequence of a sorted table is violated due to additions, a runtime error will occur. Note here that this statement differs from the previous variant, because this statement does not contain the TABLE keyword. As this statement does not work generically, it cannot be used for hash tables.

You can also use this statement without defining an index, but only within a LOOP through the internal table to which a record is to be added. In this case, the new record is added at the current position of the record pointer. A missing index outside of LOOPs normally causes a runtime error. During the syntax check, this error is not recognized.

Both forms of the INSERT statement have a variant which you can use to copy several records out of one table into another. To do so you restrict the source area by making two optional index entries. If the index entries are missing, reading starts at the first and finishes at the last line.

The generally applicable form of the statement is as follows:

INSERT LINES OF *itab_source* [**FROM** *index1*] [**TO** *index2*]
  INTO TABLE *itab_target*.

In this case, it is also true that an APPEND actually takes place for standard tables. In all other tables, apart from hash tables, you can therefore use a second form of the statement to define the position at which the target table of the new record is to be added.

```
INSERT LINES OF itab_source [ FROM index1 ] [ TO index2 ]
  INTO itab_target [ INDEX index3 ].
```

Below are some examples of how to add and insert a record into internal tables.

```
i_standard-pgmid = 'R3TR'.
i_standard-object = 'PROG'.
i_standard-obj_name = 'YZ332020'.
APPEND i_standard.
r_tadir = i_standard.
APPEND r_tadir TO i_sorted.

i_standard-obj_name = 'YZ332030'.
INSERT i_standard INDEX 1.

r_tadir = i_standard.
INSERT r_tadir INTO TABLE i_sorted.
INSERT r_tadir INTO TABLE i_hashed.

r_tadir-obj_name = 'YZ332010'.
INSERT r_tadir INTO TABLE i_standard.
INSERT r_tadir INTO TABLE i_sorted.
INSERT r_tadir INTO TABLE i_hashed.
```

The i_standard table has a header row. The first three statements enter values into this header row. The statement in the fourth line appends the header row to the internal table with the same name. The two other tables (i_sorted and i_hashed) do not possess a header row. To exchange data with these tables, a separate field is required as a work area. In the fifth line, values from the header row of the i_standard table are entered into this work area, which is then added to the sorted table. As this table is empty, no problems can occur concerning the sorting sequence. The statements that follow demonstrate how to use an explicit index to insert records into a standard table, and how to use the generic variant of the INSERT statement.

Modifying records

You use the MODIFY statement to modify existing records in an internal table. This statement also has a generic variant that you can use for all table types, as well as a non-generic form which you cannot use for hash tables. The generally applicable statement has the following syntax:

```
MODIFY TABLE itab [ FROM record ] [ TRANSPORTING field_1 ...
field_n ].
```

The data required by the statement is either located in the table's header row or in a separate work area record. The statement first extracts the key from the record and then searches the internal table for the first record that corresponds with this key. The structure of the key, i.e. which fields must be evaluated, was specified when the table was being defined. The search process depends on the type of the table. For example, standard tables are searched sequentially. This can result in considerable performance problems when the system is repeatedly accessing large tables.

If a suitable entry is found, the system replaces its data with the data in the header row or the work area. If necessary, you can use the TRANSPORTING option to restrict the number of fields transferred. The field list can also contain dynamic data for this purpose. To achieve this, you have to make an entry in a simple data field containing the name of the table field to be transferred. In the field list, the name of the reference field has to be enclosed in oval brackets. It is not possible to alter the key of a record with this statement.

Occasionally, you need to modify entries in several records, with the modification being dependent on one condition. You can use a variant of the MODIFY statement for this purpose:

```
MODIFY itab [ FROM record ] TRANSPORTING field_1 ... field_n
 WHERE condition.
```

You can apply this statement to all table types. Within the WHERE condition you must insert a field from the internal table on the left-hand side of each individual comparison expression.

Besides the variants of the MODIFY statement described above, there is also a non-generic variant that provides you with a means of indexed access to records. Like the INSERT statement, this statement cannot be used for hash tables:

```
MODIFY itab [ FROM record ] [ INDEX index ]
 [ TRANSPORTING field_1 ... field_n ].
```

The way this statement provides the data and indexes the record to be modified is identical to the INSERT statement. In addition, you can specify the fields to be modified here. As with the INSERT statement, in the non-generic variant of the MODIFY statement you do not need to specify an index if the MODIFY statement is located within a LOOP through the internal table. In this case, the current record will be modified.

Below is an example of each indexed access and of modification within a LOOP.

```
i_standard-pgmid = 'R3TR'
i_standard-object = 'PROG'
i_standard-obj_name = 'modified'.
MODIFY i_standard INDEX 2.

LOOP AT i_standard WHERE obj_name NS 'modified'.
  CONCATENATE '<<' i_standard-obj_name '>>'
    INTO i_standard-obj_name
    SEPARATED BY SPACE.
  MODIFY i_standard.
ENDLOOP.
```

In the first part of the example, new values are entered into the header row of the standard table. Then, the second record in the table is overwritten with the new values. The subsequent LOOP reads all records apart from the one that has just been modified. For this purpose, a WHERE clause is used to extend the loop. Within the loop, the obj_name field has new contents assigned to it. Subsequently, the MODIFY statement, which has no index entry here, writes the other record back into the internal table.

Deleting records

You use the DELETE statement to delete data records in internal tables. There are generic variants of this statement which work with all table types, as well as other variants that are not suited for hash tables. First of all, the generic variants:

DELETE TABLE *itab* [**FROM** *record*] **.**

This statement completely conforms with the principle we already know. The key fields are extracted from the header row or the separate work area. Following that, the record is searched and deleted. This form of the statement always uses the key predefined during the definition of the table, so you do not have to take its structure into consideration when you use the statement. It is also possible to use other fields to identify the record to be deleted. To do so, you can use a second generic statement which allows for the free definition of the key, independent of the key definition in the table type:

DELETE TABLE *itab*
 WITH TABLE KEY { [*table_field* | (*pointer_field*)] = *pattern* } **.**

You must insert a field from the internal table on the left-hand side of each subkey. Alternatively, this field can be transferred dynamically.

Another DELETE statement which you could use for all table types, but which has certain limitations, is:

DELETE *itab* **WHERE** *condition* [**FROM** *index1*] [**TO** *index2*] **.**

This statement deletes all the records that fulfil the specified condition. The compare conditions correspond with those of the MODIFY-WHERE statement. For all index-type tables (i.e. all tables apart from the hash tables), you can restrict the area to be deleted. To do so you make two optional index entries. For hash tables, neither of the two indexes may be used.

All other DELETE statements do not work generically and consequently cannot be used for hash tables. You can delete a specific, individual record by specifying an index:

DELETE *itab* [**INDEX** *index*] **.**

The index can be omitted in a loop through the table concerned. In this case, the current record is deleted. You can delete a larger range with this statement:

DELETE *itab* [**FROM** *index1*] [**TO** *index2*] **.**

Here, you have to define at least one of the index criteria. If the value for FROM is missing, the system will start deleting from the first record. If the value for TO is missing, the system will extend the range to be deleted up to the last record in the table.

The following statement was created especially for tables without a unique key:

DELETE ADJACENT DUPLICATES FROM *itab*
 [**COMPARING** [*fieldlist* | **ALL FIELDS**]] **.**

It allows you to delete duplicated entries from a table. The table has to be sorted according to the applicable key. With the COMPARING option you can deviate from the standard key. You use this parameter either with a field list or with the ALL FIELDS descriptor, which allows you to force a check of all fields and not only of the key fields that may have been defined.

The following example uses the DELETE TABLE statement to delete a record from an internal table:

```
DELETE TABLE i_sorted
    WITH TABLE KEY pgmid = 'R3TR'
                   object = 'PROG'
                   obj_name = 'YZ332020'.
```

Reading records sequentially

Two main methods are available for reading the records in an internal table. You can work through the table sequentially, in a loop, or you can access individual records.

You use the LOOP statement for sequential reading.

```
LOOP AT itab.
...
ENDLOOP.
```

The system runs the LOOP statements once for each record. Each time, the data is made available in the header record. You can use certain additions to restrict the range of records to be processed. You can use FROM and TO to define an index range. You can use WHERE to specify selection according to one or more search terms. The LOOP statement is then as follows:

```
LOOP AT itab FROM first TO last.
...
ENDLOOP.
```

or

```
LOOP AT itab
WHERE condition.
...
ENDLOOP.
```

If you are using READ or LOOP to process internal tables without their own header rows, you have to access the tables through a specified work area. In both statements, you use this addition to specify it:

```
... INTO workarea.
```

Another addition enhances performance by suppressing copy actions. Instead, a field symbol is directly assigned to the record in the internal table. Consequently, changes made using the field symbol immediately take effect in the internal table, so it is no longer necessary to use a MODIFY statement.

```
LOOP AT itab ASSIGNING <field_symbol>.
```

If the key fields are modified, this might disrupt the sorting sequence in tables of the types SORTED TABLE and HASHED TABLE, and so modifications are therefore prohibited. The runtime system monitors this kind of access and triggers a runtime error in the case of violations.

Below are some additional examples of the different variants of the LOOP statement.

```
FIELD-SYMBOLS:
  <f_tadir> TYPE tr_tadir.

LOOP AT i_standard.
  WRITE: / i_standard-obj_name.
ENDLOOP.

LOOP AT i_sorted ASSIGNING <f_tadir>.
  WRITE: / <f_tadir>-obj_name.
ENDLOOP.

LOOP AT i_hashed INTO r_tadir.
  WRITE: / s_tadir-obj_name.
ENDLOOP.
```

Finding records

You use the READ statement to search for an individual record. There are two main variants of this statement. First, READ can search for a record in the internal table by using one or several search terms. In addition, it can use an index entry to access a record. As in the case of the other statements, READ also has generic and non-generic variants. However, SAP has explicitly declared all non-generic statements obsolete. Therefore, they should no longer be used in the interests of compatibility. The new generic variants will take over all the tasks of the obsolete statements.

In all variants of this statement, the system enters the record number of the corresponding record into the SY-TABIX system field, if one was found. In this case, the SY-SUBRC field contains the value 0. The value in SY-TABIX can later be used in a MODIFY statement to re-enter the record into the internal table after it has been modified.

To search for a record, you must define the valid search term for the READ statement. The easiest way is to use this statement:

```
READ TABLE itab FROM record.
```

The system extracts the search term from the selected record. The fields that are included depend on the definition of each table's particular key. The key fields can also be provided with values individually:

```
READ TABLE itab

  WITH TABLE KEY { [ table_field | (pointer_field)] = pattern }.
```

Here, the name of the key fields in the internal table can also be transferred dynamically. In this case, each field name concerned is contained in a field whose name, in turn, has to be enclosed in oval brackets in the statement. In this variant of the statement, it is important that, even here, the fields are accessed using the key defined for the table. In the following variant of the statement, however, this is not the case:

READ TABLE *itab*

WITH KEY { [*table_field* | (*pointer_field*)] = *pattern* } [**BINARY SEARCH**].

Here you can use any fields for the search. Note here that the only way this statement differs from the previous statement is that the word TABLE is missing between WITH and KEY. This statement normally searches the table sequentially. If a standard table is sorted according to the search fields, you can use the BINARY SEARCH addition to force a fast binary search. The system will make a binary search in SORTED TABLE-type tables, if the selected search fields correspond with the key, or at least with the start of the key.

To use an index to directly access data records, use this syntax:

READ TABLE *itab* **INDEX** *index*.

You can use additions to call all the statements discussed so far. You can use this statement to write the record that has been read into a separate work area:

... **INTO** *record*.

In tables without a header row this is essential. Just as when reading sequentially, you can also position a field symbol on the record to be searched:

... **ASSIGNING** <*field_symbol*>.

As this field symbol points directly to the data area of the internal table, any modifications made using the field symbol take immediate effect on the contents of the internal table, so it is no longer necessary to use a MODIFY statement. Of course, you must not modify the key fields of tables of the types SORTED TABLE or HASHED TABLE.

Occasionally, you should only test whether or not a record with a particular key exists in an internal table. In this case, it is not necessary to transport data from the internal table into the work area. Working without data transport will save some processing time. Use this addition to avoid copying data into the work area:

... **TRANSPORTING NO FIELDS**.

If you require only certain information from the internal table, you can use this addition to select the field data to be transported:

... **TRANSPORTING** *fieldlist*.

The field names can also be dynamically transferred.

The following example searches for a record in an internal table and modifies it if it finds it:

```
READ TABLE i_sorted INTO r_tadir
   WITH TABLE KEY pgmid = 'R3TR'
                  object = 'PROG'
                  obj_name = 'YZ332010'
IF sy-subrc = 0.
   CONCATENATE '::' r_tadir-obj_name '::'
     INTO r_tadir-obj_name
     SEPARATED BY SPACE.
   MODIFY i_sorted FROM r_tadir INDEX sy-tabix.
ENDIF.
```

Sorting and grouping

In addition to the statements described above, there are still a few more unique state-ments or variants of the statements already described that affect the sequence in which the records are stored in the internal table. If you would like to sort by a different field or a list of fields, you have to use the SORT statement. You must specify the name of an internal table. You can use the BY addition to name the fields that are to be used as sort-ing criteria. You use the ASCENDING or DESCENDING parameters to define the sorting sequence. If you use BY to define that you do not wish to use a structure, the SORT state-ment will form the key from all the alphanumerical fields of the record. When sorting the contents of text fields, you can use the AS TEXT addition to influence the sorting sequence of special characters (such as German and other accented characters). In this case, the system sorts records in accordance with a predefined text.

During sorting, several records may be found to have identical sort criteria. This may be the case when the system has sorted several different fields, one after the other. The basic form of the SORT statement cannot ensure that, after sorting, these records will still be in exactly the same sequence as before sorting. If you want to retain their sort sequence, you must use the STABLE addition to explicitly force this.

Therefore, the complete syntax of the SORT statement is as follows:

```
SORT itab
   [ BY { field [ ASCENDING | DESCENDING ] [ AS TEXT ] } ]
   [ STABLE ].
```

The subsequent sorting of an internal table is relatively time consuming and is there-fore only rarely carried out. In R/3 Releases from 4.0 on, it is possible to use a sorted table (SORTED TABLE) right from the start. In previous Releases, it is recommended that you create the desired sort sequence for the records when you are entering data in an internal table. You can do this, for example, by carrying out a binary search for a record and by using an index for insertion, as shown in the following example:

```
REPORT yz332160.
TABLES tadir.
DATA:
   itadir LIKE tadir OCCURS 50,
   ftadir LIKE tadir.
```

```
SELECT * FROM tadir
WHERE author = sy-uname.

* Determine index for new record
* READ should only be used to set SY-TABIX,
* therefore it is not necessary to transport field contents
  READ TABLE itadir
    WITH KEY obj_name = tadir-obj_name
             object   = tadir-object
             pgmid    = tadir-pgmid
  BINARY SEARCH
  TRANSPORTING NO FIELDS.

* Insert TADIR entry into internal table
  IF sy-subrc <> 0.
    INSERT tadir INTO itadir INDEX sy-tabix.
  ENDIF.
  ENDSELECT.

* Test listing of the table contents
LOOP AT itadir INTO ftadir.
  WRITE: / ftadir-obj_name, ftadir-object.
ENDLOOP.
```

In this example, the program again reads the TADIR table. The SELECT statement finds all objects generated by the current user. For each object, the program looks for another identical object in the ITADIR internal table. This search will always be unsuccessful because the three fields used for the search are key fields of the TADIR table, but only one record with this key is allowed to exist. However, apart from the actual search result (SY-SUBRC), the READ statement also shows the index of the next larger record in the sy-tabix field. This value can now be used to insert the new record into the internal table in accordance with the desired sorting sequence.

The APPEND statement has a SORTED BY addition. Not only does this ensure a defined sequence when new records are inserted, but it also has two special features:

1. The internal table is sorted in descending (!) order according to the selected field.

2. Only the number of records defined in the OCCURS parameter are retained in the table. In this special case, the OCCURS parameter therefore represents a true dimension.

This statement is only of practical use if all records are written to the internal table in this way.

There is also a statement, the COLLECT statement, which automatically combines several records. This is a bit more special and therefore rarely to be found. It checks for the existence of a record whose alphanumerical fields all have the same contents as the record to be added. If this is the case, the numerical fields of both records will be added together and the existing record will be updated accordingly. If no such record exists, the new record will be added. Here is a simple example:

```
REPORT yz332170.
TABLES tadir.
DATA:
  BEGIN OF it_object OCCURS 0,
    object TYPE trobjtype,
    count TYPE I,
  END OF it_object.

SELECT * FROM tadir WHERE author = sy-uname.
  it_object-object = tadir-object.
  it_object-count = 1.
  COLLECT it_object.
ENDSELECT.

LOOP AT it_object.
WRITE: / it_object-object, it_object-count.
ENDLOOP.
```

In a SELECT loop through the TADIR table, the program reads all the administration entries to the current user's objects. It copies the name of the object group into the internal table header row. In addition, it sets the counter field to the value 1. The subsequent COL-LECT statement now either adds a new record to the internal table IT_OBJECT or adds the value 1 to an existing record in the COUNT field. After selection is complete, the COUNT field of each record displays the number of the corresponding objects.

Special features

To copy internal tables you can use a special convention that has been defined for the assignments operator. To copy the contents of an internal table into another table, use this statement:

```
itab_body_target = itab_body_source.
```

However, if you only enter the table name, that is not enough. In internal tables with a header row, the table name represents the header row in assignments. It does not represent the table's data area. This is indicated by two square brackets directly behind the table name. However, in tables without a header row, you only need to enter the table name.

Examples of how internal tables are used

The examples below again demonstrate how the new table types are used, in context. First of all, the examples above are shown in a complete program. This program contains an example of internal tables without an internal structure, apart from the statements discussed above.

```
REPORT yz332150.
TABLES: tadir.
TYPES:
  t_line(72),

  BEGIN OF tr_tadir,
  pgmid(4),
  object LIKE tadir-object,
  obj_name TYPE sobj_name,

  END OF tr_tadir,

ti_standard
  TYPE STANDARD TABLE OF tr_tadir
  INITIAL SIZE 0,
ti_sorted
  TYPE SORTED TABLE OF tr_tadir
  WITH UNIQUE DEFAULT KEY
  INITIAL SIZE 0,
ti_hashed
  TYPE HASHED TABLE OF tr_tadir
  WITH UNIQUE KEY pgmid object obj_name
  INITIAL SIZE 0,

ti_flat
  TYPE STANDARD TABLE OF t_line
  INITIAL SIZE 0,

ti_old
  TYPE tr_tadir OCCURS 0.

DATA:
  r_tadir TYPE tr_tadir,
  i_standard TYPE tr_tadir OCCURS 0 WITH HEADER LINE,
  i_sorted TYPE SORTED TABLE OF tr_tadir
    WITH UNIQUE KEY pgmid object obj_name
    INITIAL SIZE 0,
  i_hashed TYPE ti_hashed,
  i_condition TYPE ti_flat WITH HEADER LINE.
FIELD-SYMBOLS:
  <f_tadir> TYPE tr_tadir.

i_standard-pgmid     = 'R3TR'.
i_standard-object    = 'PROG'.
i_standard-obj_name  = 'YZ332020'.
```

```
APPEND i_standard.
r_tadir = i_standard.
APPEND r_tadir TO i_sorted.

i_standard-obj_name = 'YZ332030'.
INSERT i_standard INDEX 1.

r_tadir = i_standard.
INSERT r_tadir INTO TABLE i_sorted.
INSERT r_tadir INTO TABLE i_hashed.

r_tadir-obj_name = 'YZ332010'.
INSERT r_tadir INTO TABLE i_standard.
INSERT r_tadir INTO TABLE i_sorted.
INSERT r_tadir INTO TABLE i_hashed.

WRITE: /(30) 'I_STANDARD' COLOR 5.

LOOP AT i_standard.
  WRITE: / i_standard-obj_name.
ENDLOOP.

WRITE: /, /(30) 'I_SORTED' COLOR 5.
LOOP AT i_sorted ASSIGNING <f_tadir>.
  WRITE: / <f_tadir>-obj_name.
ENDLOOP.

WRITE: /, /(30) 'I_HASHED' COLOR 5.
LOOP AT i_hashed INTO r_tadir.
  WRITE: / r_tadir-obj_name.
ENDLOOP.

i_standard-pgmid = 'R3TR'.
i_standard-object = 'PROG'.
i_standard-obj_name = 'modified'.
MODIFY i_standard INDEX 2.

READ TABLE i_standard
  WITH TABLE KEY pgmid = 'R3TR'
          object = 'PROG'
          obj_name = 'YZ332010'.
IF sy-subrc = 0.
  CONCATENATE i_standard-obj_name 'modified'
    INTO i_standard-obj_name
    SEPARATED BY SPACE.
```

```
  MODIFY i_standard INDEX sy-tabix.
ENDIF.

LOOP AT i_standard WHERE obj_name NS 'modified'.
  CONCATENATE '<<' i_standard-obj_name '>>'
    INTO i_standard-obj_name
    SEPARATED BY SPACE.
  MODIFY i_standard.
ENDLOOP.

WRITE: /, /(30) 'I_STANDARD, modified' COLOR 5.
LOOP AT i_standard.
  WRITE: / i_standard-obj_name.
ENDLOOP.

DELETE TABLE i_sorted
  WITH TABLE KEY pgmid = 'R3TR'
                 object = 'PROG'
                 obj_name = 'YZ332020'.

WRITE: /, /(30) 'I_SORTED, modified and deleted' COLOR 5.
LOOP AT i_sorted ASSIGNING <f_tadir>.
  WRITE: / <f_tadir>-obj_name.
ENDLOOP.

i_condition = 'OBJ_NAME LIKE ''YZ%'' '.
  APPEND i_condition.

WRITE: /, /(30) 'I_CONDITION' COLOR 5.
SELECT * FROM tadir
  WHERE (i_condition).
  WRITE: / tadir-obj_name.
ENDSELECT.
```

The second example explains how internal tables are transferred to subroutines. In the program, the FILL_ITAB subroutine takes on the role of entering test data into the internal table. It is therefore transferred as a parameter.

The TABLES option in the FORM or PERFORM statement can only handle the usual internal tables, and not the new table types. You must use the options USING or CHANGING to transfer these new tables subroutines, like simple parameters. Furthermore, you must use TYPE or LIKE to assign a type to them. When data is transferred in this way, it may result in an existing header line of the internal table being lost. Therefore, you can only access individual fields in the internal table, within the subroutine, if you declare a corresponding work area. Below is the application's listing.

```
REPORT yz332180.
TYPES:
  BEGIN OF tr_rec,
    number(6) TYPE n,
    price TYPE p DECIMALS 2,
  END OF tr_rec,

ti_sort
  TYPE SORTED TABLE OF tr_rec
  WITH UNIQUE KEY number
  INITIAL SIZE 5.

DATA:
  i_rec TYPE ti_sort WITH HEADER LINE.

PERFORM fill1 USING i_rec[].
PERFORM fill2 USING i_rec[].
PERFORM fill3 USING i_rec[].

READ TABLE i_rec WITH TABLE KEY number = '000112'.
WRITE: / i_rec-number, i_rec-price.

WRITE: /.
LOOP AT i_rec.
  WRITE: / i_rec-number, i_rec-price.
ENDLOOP.

FORM fill1 USING pi LIKE i_rec[].
DATA l LIKE LINE OF pi.
  l-number = '000112'.
  l-price = '3.95'.
  INSERT l INTO TABLE pi.
ENDFORM.

FORM fill2 USING pi TYPE SORTED TABLE.
DATA l TYPE tr_rec.
  l-number = '300111'.
  l-price = '432.00'.
  INSERT l INTO TABLE pi.
ENDFORM.

FORM fill3 USING pi TYPE ti_sort.
DATA l TYPE tr_rec.
  l-number = '000111'.
  l-price = '123.45'.
  INSERT l INTO TABLE pi.
ENDFORM.
```

At the start of the program, an internal table's record type and type reference are declared. An internal table is then generated using the table type, but this time with a header line. This is why a separate work area can be dispensed with in the main program.

The table that has been created is transferred to three subroutines as a parameter. Because the `ti_rec` table has a header line and the `USING` addition is used only for the transfer of the table, you have to enter square brackets after the table name to show that you would like to use the internal table, and not the header line, as a parameter. This is not necessary if the internal table does not have a header line.

The three subroutines `FILL1` to `FILL3` illustrate different ways of typing. In the first subroutine, the `ps` parameter is derived from the `i_rec` table through a similarity relationship. You again have to enter two square brackets to show that you are referring to the `i_rec` table and not to the `i_rec` header line. Because you can only transfer a data object with `USING`, the header line of `i_rec` will be lost and only the body of the table will remain. However, within the subroutine you can use the structure of the `ps` parameter to declare a work area, by referring to a line in the parameter.

In the second subroutine, a generic table type is defined. This form of type definition only defines that the transferred parameter is a `SORTED TABLE`-type table. Here, you can transfer tables of any structure. Within the subroutine, another work area is declared. However, there is no way of checking that the table and work area are compatible, apart from automatically monitoring the length of table lines and the work area.

The third subroutine describes the parameter by referencing the `ti_sort`-type declaration. Because the data type already defines that a table is involved, no square brackets are necessary.

The remaining part of the program resembles the others. The generic `READ` statement can also handle this table type. As standard tables are not sorted, and do not have a unique key, the `INSERT` statement is correct in this example. The output in the loop shows you that the records in the table are not sorted.

3.2.8 Control statements

Up to now, only relatively simple statements for data processing have been mentioned. These are processed sequentially and you cannot use them to influence the program flow. ABAP also has some statements with which you can create program links or cyclical repeats. This basic principle is fairly well known, so no more details are provided on it.

IF

When a complex condition is evaluated, an IF statement splits into a YES (`IF`) branch or an optional NO (`ELSE`) branch, according to the results of evaluation. These conditions are described in a separate section, as they are also used in some other statements. The two alternative program sections are formed with the statements `IF` and `ELSE` or `ELSE` and `ENDIF`.

You can use an additional `IF` statement to link the `ELSE` branch of an `IF` statement to an `ELSEIF` statement. Examples:

```
IF a < b.
  WRITE / 'A is smaller than B'.
ELSEIF a > b.
  WRITE / 'A is greater than B'.
ELSE.
  WRITE / 'A equals B'.
ENDIF.
```

WHILE

The WHILE statement forms loops which will run as long as a condition is fulfilled. The complete syntax of the WHILE statement is as follows:

```
WHILE condition.
  statements
ENDWHILE.
```

The following listing shows a real example of how the WHILE statement can be used:

```
WHILE n < 10.
  WRITE: / n.
  n = n + 1.
ENDWHILE.
```

CASE

The CASE statement compares the contents of a field with several patterns. Each pattern is assigned statements that will be executed if the field and pattern correspond. An optional alternative branch will be executed if the field contents do not correspond with any pattern. The syntax of the CASE statement is:

```
CASE field.
  WHEN pattern_1.
    statement_block_1.
  WHEN pattern_ 2.
    statement_ block_2.
  WHEN pattern _x.
    statement_block_x.
  WHEN OTHERS.
    alternative statement_block.
ENDCASE.
```

In the CASE statement, only one WHEN OTHERS branch may be present. If a statement block should be executed for several values of *field*, you can link the control patterns with each other via an OR operator:

```
CASE field.
  WHEN pattern_1 { OR pattern_x }.
    statements.
```

The following example is taken from a real-life application:

```
CASE okcode.
  WHEN 'OPC+'.
    result = value1 + value2.
    op = '+'.
    LEAVE TO SCREEN 200.
  WHEN 'OPC-'.
    result = value1 - value2.
    op = '-'.
    LEAVE TO SCREEN 200.
  WHEN 'OPC*'.
    result = value1 * value2.
    op = '*'.
    LEAVE TO SCREEN 200.
  WHEN 'OPC/'.
    result = value1 / value2.
    op = '/'.
    LEAVE TO SCREEN 200.
  WHEN '/NEX'.
    LEAVE PROGRAM.
  WHEN OTHERS.
    MESSAGE E137.
ENDCASE.
```

DO

There are two variants of the DO statement. The first one forms an endless loop that has to be explicitly quitted with an EXIT, STOP or REJECT statement. The EXIT statement is used most frequently:

```
DO.
  statements
ENDDO.
```

In the second variant, the DO loop can serve as a simple replacement for the FOR loop, which does not exist in ABAP. A parameter determines how often the loop should be executed:

```
DO n TIMES.
  statements
ENDDO.
```

Within the DO loop, you can extract the number of loops that are actually executed from the SY-INDEX system variables.

```
DO 6 TIMES.
  WRITE: / sy-index.
ENDDO.
```

EXIT, CONTINUE and CHECK

It has already been mentioned that DO loops have to be explicitly quitted with EXIT. Within a loop (i.e. in the case of LOOP, WHILE, SELECT), this statement causes the loop to terminate. However, if you call this statement outside of loops, but within a modularization unit (FORM, modules, FUNCTION, AT), this will exit that unit.

Frequently, no subordinate modularization units exist in reports. In this case, if you enter EXIT, this will terminate report generation and output the list.

You should only use the CONTINUE statement within loops. This statement merely terminates the current loop run and causes a jump to the beginning of the loop. There, the loop condition is evaluated again and the loop is run again. This statement sequence terminates one loop run and begins the next:

```
IF NOT condition.
  CONTINUE.
ENDIF.
```

There is an abbreviated form of this statement:

```
CHECK condition.
```

This statement is very frequently used in SELECT loops within reports to analyze *selections*:

```
DO 10 TIMES.
  ADD 1 TO i.
  WRITE: / i.
  CHECK i < 6.
  WRITE: '<'.
ENDDO.
```

Conditions

In the statements that are used for flow control you must specify conditions, also called *logical expressions*. These expressions are divided into different groups. Some of the expressions are permitted only for special data types.

The simplest way to create conditions is to compare a field with a value or another field. The operators used here (*see* Table 3.14) can be used to compare numerical values, and also fields of all other data types. You can also compare values of different types. However, if you do so, type conversions are executed and you must take their effects into consideration when formulating the statement!

During comparisons, the different data types are dealt with individually. Character strings are compared in a lexicographical sequence. The two character strings are compared with each other character by character, and the first character that is different determines the result of the comparison. In date fields, the later date is the greater one, while in time entries, the later time entry is the greater value.

Table 3.14   Comparison operators

Operator	Alternative writing convention	Description
>	GT	Greater
>=		
=>	GE	Greater than or equal to
=	EQ	Equal
<=		
=<	LE	Smaller than or equal to
<	LT	Smaller
<>, ><	NE	Not equal

Some additional comparison operators, shown in Table 3.15, are available for character strings. Use this input format for these comparison operators:

```
string1 operator string2
```

Table 3.15 describes the functions available, and shows the sequence of operators you must use.

With regard to the patterns for the operators CP and NP, note that you should use the '*' character for any pattern, and the '+' character for any character. This convention is different from the one that applies to other ABAP statements.

Table 3.16 shows additional options. Some of them have already been described in the context of the WHERE clause.

You can also compare hexadecimal fields, whose length is 1, bit by bit. These comparisons are slightly different from the usual bit comparisons made in other programming languages. You must apply the following format to the operators used:

```
f1 operator f2.
```

Here, f1 is the field to be checked and f2 is the bit mask. Table 3.17 shows the three possible bit operators.

Table 3.15   Operators for string comparison

Operator	Description
CO	Contains only
	String1 contains only characters from String2.
CN	Contains not only
	String1 not only contains characters from String2.
CA	Contains any
	String1 contains at least one character from String2.
NA	Not any
	String1 does not contain any character from String2.
CS	Contains string
	String1 contains String2.
NS	No string
	S1 does not contain S2.
CP	Contains pattern
	S1 corresponds to pattern in S2.
NP	Not pattern
	S1 does not correspond to pattern in S2.

Table 3.16   More comparison operators

Function	Description
BETWEEN ... AND	Range definition
IS INITIAL	Field equals initial value
IS SPACE	Field equals SPACE
IS ASSIGNED	Field symbol has been assigned
IS REQUESTED	A function module's formal parameter is assigned a value in the calling program
IN	Contained in the selection table

Table 3.17   Bit operators

Operator	Description
O (One)	True, if the positions that, in f1, are filled with 1, also contain 1 in f2.
Z (Zero)	True, if the positions that, in f1, are filled with 0, also contain 0 in f2.
M (Mixed)	True, if f1 contains 1, in at least one of the positions marked in f2, and contains 0 in at least one position.

The following program shows some options for using the IF statement:

```
REPORT yz332190.
data:
  s1(10) VALUE 'ABCDEFGHIJ',
  s2(3) VALUE 'XFH',
  s3(5) VALUE '*DEF*'.

IF s1 CA s2.
  WRITE: / s1, 'contains any', s2, sy-fdpos.
ELSE.
  WRITE: / s1, 'contains no', s2.
Endif.

IF s1 CP s3.
  WRITE: / s1, 'contains pattern', s3, sy-fdpos.
ELSE.
  WRITE: / s1, 'does not contain', s3.
ENDIF.

IF s1 CO s2.
  WRITE: / s1, 'CO', s2, sy-fdpos.
ELSE.
  WRITE: / s1, 'contains not only', s2.
ENDIF.
```

3.2.9 Processing Data Dictionary tables

The real task of reports is to evaluate tables. This section concentrates on that topic. You need to be familiar with the knowledge contained in the previous parts of this book before you can work with database tables.

The TABLES statement

Like all other data objects, tables have to be declared before they can be used in programs. To do so, use this statement:

TABLES `table`.

Alternatively, you can use this colon notation:

TABLES: `table_1, table_2, ..., table_n.`

You cannot use `TABLES` to declare a table unless that table is actively contained in the Data Dictionary. Otherwise, when the system carries out a syntax check before processing a program, this will result in an error. Besides using views to read tables, in the narrower sense, you can also read data with them. However, in views there are only limited functions for maintaining data.

The system stores some administration information internally. This includes the position and contents of the current record, with a reference to the name of the table. Due to this administration method, it is impossible to simultaneously access several records in a table. As this kind of access is often necessary in practice, a second work area with separate administration information can be generated for each database. Furthermore, each table is assigned a pseudonym that consists of the table's name with an asterisk in front. This second work area can be used completely independently of the first declaration type. This is an example of a declaration of this kind:

TABLES: TADIR, *TADIR.

Accessing tables

After declaring a table you can use different statements to process its contents. First, the contents of a record have to be transferred from the table to fields within a program or in the opposite direction, from fields to the table. To do this, standard programming languages have a file concept that uses explicit read and write statements. It is necessary to declare both file descriptors, as well as variables for storing the values, and these have to be used in the statements. Files have to be opened and closed and, during reading and writing, the source and the target must be specified.

In ABAP, it is a lot simpler to access tables. When you use `TABLES` to declare a table, this does not only make the program aware of the table, it also creates a structure containing the name of the table. This automatically uses the structure that was defined in the Data Dictionary for this particular table. You can use the previously described statements for data fields and structures to access this structure. This kind of structure only ever contains one record out of the table. In ABAP language usage, this structure assigned to a table is also called a *header line, work area* or table work area.

When you use `TABLES` to declare a table, you therefore create two different objects that have the same name. In fact, this occasionally gets forgotten because the relatively simple ABAP statements almost always achieve the desired results, even when used intuitively. All the same, there are statements that are only used for editing the database table. Others only affect the header line, without producing any changes to the database table. The contents of the work area are automatically updated if a record in the database table is read. Changes in the work area, i.e. through assignment, will however not be automatically transferred into the database table. This must be triggered by the appropriate statements.

Database queries with SELECT

The R/3 System uses database systems based on SQL. For accessing the datasets, ABAP provides some statements that can be generally grouped under the term *Open-SQL*. These statements correspond to the default SQL statements, which often have identical names, but they sometimes differ considerably where their implemented functionality is concerned. The functional scope of the Open-SQL statements depends to a large extent on the R/3 System Release. Full compliance with the SQL standards is not achieved because of the requirement for system independence. This forces a restriction to the lowest common denominator of all database systems that can be supported by the R/3 System.

To read records, you use the SELECT statement to execute a database query. Up to Release 2.2, the SELECT statement used some clauses from the default SQL statement suite, but did not offer even a fraction of its functions. From Release 3.0, these SQL clauses were much better supported. The current Release, 4.x, includes another extension to the functionality. The SELECT statement consists of several clauses, some of which are optional. As the syntax of this statement is very complex, it is impossible to clearly illustrate the whole statement in just one syntax description. For the time being, we will have to use the following simplified overview as a starting point:

```
SELECT what
   [ INTO target]
     FROM source
   [ WHERE  condition]
   [ GROUP BY fieldlist
   [ HAVING condition]]
   [ ORDER BY fieldlist]
[ENDSELECT] .
```

When a SELECT statement has the correct syntax, it consists of the SELECT clause and FROM clause, at least. The SELECT clause defines the values to be read in more detail. For example, it defines how many fields are to be read. Here, the result fields can also be the results of functions that will be applied to the individual values that are read.

In the FROM clause you specify which tables should be read. Up to Release 3.x, only one table could be evaluated at a time. Release 4.x and higher now offer the option of using joins to link several tables with each other.

In practice, you also need to use the WHERE clause to specify search conditions. Although the SELECT statement is syntactically correct without a WHERE clause, it will then return all records contained in the table concerned.

Use the INTO clause to store the results in other fields than the header line of the table. In some cases it is optional, and in others absolutely essential, depending on the structure of the SELECT clause and the structures of the other clauses.

You can use the ORDER BY clause to force the sort order of the results.

Use the GROUP BY clause to condense groups of records with identical attributes into one line of the results. When you use GROUP BY, the HAVING clause can contain conditions that will be taken into account when the group is created.

The SELECT statement can be either a simple statement or a loop statement. This depends on the type of processing you set for the selected records. You can define this in more detail with several options, which are available for various clauses. You have to use the SELECT statement as a simple statement in two cases. They are: if the SELECT statement can only return a single record, when you are using different options (i.e. SELECT SINGLE or COUNT(*)), or if you are using INTO to divert the entire results into an internal table. In all other cases, however, you use the SELECT statement as a loop statement, which you must terminate with ENDSELECT.

The subsections that follow deal with the individual clauses of the SELECT statement in more detail. They begin with a simple example. Note here that the TADIR table is an extremely important system table which you can read, but which you cannot modify under any circumstances. This table is the development environment's 'table of contents'. For example, it contains an entry for each program. It is precisely these entries (the current user's programs) that need to be determined.

```
PROGRAM yz332200.
TABLES
   tadir.

SELECT * FROM tadir
   WHERE author = sy-uname
   AND object = 'PROG'.

     WRITE: / tadir-pgmid,
              tadir-object,
              tadir-obj_name,
              tadir-author.
ENDSELECT.
```

The example above uses two compare statements linked with AND. Both are really self-explanatory. They check whether the owner of the program corresponds is the same as the currently registered user, and they also use the OBJECT field to filter out all programs.

Like all other Open-SQL statements, SELECT sets the SY-SUBRC system variable to a predefined value. By doing so it signals whether the statement was successful or whether it failed. Table 3.18 shows possible values and their meaning.

Table 3.18   Values for SY-SUBRC after SELECT

SY-SUBRC	Meaning
0	Search was successful, at least one record found.
4	No record found.
8	Only applies to SELECT SINGLE. The search term was ambiguous, a random record included in the results is returned.

The SELECT statement uses SY-SUBRC to set other system variables over. Frequently, SY-DBCNT is evaluated in programs. This field contains the number of records found.

The SELECT clause

You use the SELECT keyword to introduce the SELECT clause. It uses a field list to define in which table fields the returned data volume should be contained. This field list consists of a list of individual fields or an asterisk, which represents all table fields. If you use the asterisk, the selected records can be stored in the table's header line. You can use the INTO clause to divert the results to other destinations (structure, internal table). The INTO clause is certainly necessary if you select a field or use aggregate expressions in the SELECT clause. Program YZ332210 shows an example of how a field selection is applied. It fulfils the same task as program YZ332200.

```
PROGRAM yz332210.
TABLES
  tadir.
DATA:
  pid LIKE tadir-pgmid,
  obj LIKE tadir-object,
  nam LIKE tadir-obj_name,
  aut LIKE tadir-author.

SELECT pgmid object obj_name author
  INTO (pid, obj, nam, aut)
  FROM tadir
  WHERE author = sy-uname
    AND object = 'PROG'.

  WRITE: / pid, obj, nam, aut.
ENDSELECT.
```

Some other options of the SELECT clause force direct processing of the selected sets by the SELECT statement. This normally involves the condensing of several records on the basis of various criteria.

In each of these processing options, you can use the DISTINCT addition to combine identical output lines. Identical output lines can occur if the SELECT statement does not read all the fields in the table, but uses a field list to select individual fields. If one or more of the table's key fields are missing here, output lines with identical contents can certainly appear. The program below lists all object types generated by the current user, but not the individual objects. Because DISTINCT is only useful in combination with a field list in the SELECT clause, it inevitably becomes necessary to also use the INTO clause to transfer the contents of the selected table fields to fields within the program.

```
REPORT yz332220.
TABLES
  tadir.
DATA:
  obj LIKE tadir-object.

SELECT DISTINCT object
  INTO obj
  FROM tadir
  WHERE author = sy-uname.

    WRITE: / obj.
ENDSELECT.
```

Another way to evaluate the selected records would be to use aggregate functions. An aggregate function evaluates the contents of a (usually numerical) table field in all selected records. It makes one single value available as a result. Table 3.19 shows the available aggregate functions.

Table 3.19   Aggregate functions

Aggregate function	Description
AVG (field)	Average
COUNT (DISTINCT field)	Number of different values
COUNT (*)	Number of selected records
MAX (field)	Maximum value
MIN (field)	Minimum value
SUM (field)	Sum of the field contents

The program below uses an aggregate function to determine the number of objects belonging to the current user.

```
REPORT yz332230.
TABLES
  tadir.
DATA:
  qty TYPE I.

SELECT COUNT( * )
  INTO qty
  FROM tadir
  WHERE author = sy-uname.

WRITE: / qty.
```

Aggregate functions are a special form of field selection. When you use them, you must use the INTO clause to transfer the result of the function to a data field within the program. In practice, aggregate functions are mostly used in combination with the GROUP BY clause.

Because tables are given a unique key in the SAP System, you can address a specific individual record by formulating the WHERE clause accordingly. In this case, you do not need to use a SELECT-ENDSELECT loop. You can add a SINGLE keyword to the SELECT statement to instruct it to find and return one specific record:

SELECT SINGLE * ...

In this case, the WHERE clause must test the complete table key. In individual comparisons, only a similarity check is permitted and therefore only one record can be found (provided the key is unambiguous). In this case, the SELECT clause can trigger a temporary record lock protecting the selected record from being overwritten by other users. To do so, use this addition:

... FOR UPDATE.

The FROM clause

You must specify the table to be evaluated in the obligatory FROM clause. In it, the name can be transferred either as a character string or in a data field. In the latter case, you must enclose the field name in oval brackets:

... FROM *dbtab* [**AS** *alias*]
... FROM (*dbtabname*).

You only assign an alias name for tables if you are working with joins and have to uniquely define the field names there. In such cases, a shorter alias saves typing effort and gives a better overview. As joins are such a complex topic, a separate subsection is dedicated to them. Below you will find a description of just some of the FROM clause's options.

The whole R/3 System is a client/server application. In practice, this means that several hierarchically linked computers can connect to the database. A table's data might be buffered in the memory of *application servers*, if this is permitted for that particular table. Therefore, the database is not always accessed directly. In datasets that are frequently modified, or in especially critical queries, this can lead to differences between the result of the SELECT statement and the real dataset. You can add this addition to the FROM clause, to force a program to read the database directly, avoiding all buffers:

... BYPASSING BUFFER

Direct database access has a negative effect on system performance so you should only use this statement when really necessary.

In certain situations there is no need to return absolutely every record that is found using the selection criterion. In such cases you can use this addition to set the maximum number of records to be returned:

... UP TO n **ROWS.**

You can add this addition to switch off the system's automatic client handling:

... `CLIENT SPECIFIED`.

You can also use this addition with other Open-SQL statements. When you use it, the system has to supply the client field in client-dependent tables with a valid value, as well as supplying a value to other key fields. This provides you with a client-independent means of processing client-dependent tables! You only access tables in this way in special circumstances, and so common application software does not access tables in this way.

The INTO clause

The `INTO` clause is always necessary if the results either cannot, or should not, be stored in the table's header line. If the `SELECT` clause supplies the whole record (field list *), the `INTO` clause is optional. After `INTO`, you can specify a structure or internal table in which the selected records will be stored, depending on the size of the results:

... `INTO` *record*.

This form of the `INTO` clause writes the record that has been read to an alternative work area, `RECORD`, and not to the database table header line. This has no effect on the way the `SELECT` statement actually functions. In particular, if an `ENDSELECT` statement is present, this does not become redundant. Naturally, the structure of `RECORD` must correspond with the structure of the database table, so that the read data can be evaluated correctly. If the structure of `RECORD` differs from that of the database table, you can use this addition to define that only fields with identical names are to be transferred from the database table to the record:

... `INTO CORRESPONDING FIELDS OF` *record*.

In practice, this is necessary when you want to read data from several dependent tables and to combine them into one record. Here is an example of how to achieve this:

```
REPORT yz332240.
TABLES:
  dd02l, 'Tables
  dd02t. 'Texts for tables
DATA:
  BEGIN OF f_tabinfo,
    tabname TYPE tabname,
    ddtext TYPE as4text,
  END OF f_tabinfo.

SELECT SINGLE *
  FROM dd02l
  INTO CORRESPONDING FIELDS OF f_tabinfo
  WHERE tabname = 'TADIR'.
```

```
SELECT SINGLE *
  FROM dd02t
  INTO CORRESPONDING FIELDS OF f_tabinfo
  WHERE tabname = f_tabinfo-tabname
    AND ddlanguage = sy-langu.
```

```
WRITE: / f_tabinfo.
```

Similarly, you can use INTO to divert the results into an internal table. Here, you also have the option of using an internal table that has the same structure as the database table's, or only assigning fields with identical names:

... **INTO TABLE** *itab*
... **INTO CORRESPONDING FIELDS OF TABLE** *itab.*

The internal table specified as the target will be completely overwritten each time, which means that all previous contents will be lost. You can avoid this by substituting APPENDING for INTO:

... **APPENDING TABLE** *itab*
... **APPENDING CORRESPONDING FIELDS OF TABLE** *itab.*

Although this form of the statement no longer contains the INTO keyword, it is still an INTO clause in terms of the Open-SQL syntax. It has the same effect as the INTO TABLE statement, except that the existing contents of the internal table remain intact, and the newly read records are appended to it.

If the SELECT clause contains a field list consisting of individual fields, or uses aggregate expressions, you have to use the INTO clause to name a separate data field to hold the results for each field listed in the SELECT clause, or each aggregate expression. If the field list in the INTO clause contains more than one field, it has to be enclosed in oval brackets. In this case, the field names have to be separated by commas. There are examples above. The general syntax is:

... **INTO** *field*
... **INTO** (*field_1, ..., field_n*).

The ORDER BY clause

Use the ORDER BY clause to sort the output. To sort in ascending order according to the key fields or a field list, you can use the PRIMARY KEY addition. You can enter the field list details directly, or they can be transferred in an internal table:

ORDER BY [**PRIMARY KEY** | *fieldlist* | (*itab*)].

The GROUP BY clause

Use the GROUP BY clause in a SELECT statement to combine records into groups. A group consists of records that have identical values in selected fields. The SELECT statement generates one single output record for each group. If aggregate functions are used in the SELECT clause, their results will be determined and output for one group at a time.

The fields responsible for generating groups are shown in the GROUP BY clause's field list. This clause also requires you to use a field list in the SELECT clause that lists all the fields used for generating groups. In addition, the structure must contain fields to record the results of any aggregate functions that may be present. There is no point in using the SELECT clause for reading database fields that are not used to generate groups, because it will not show any valid value, due to the combination of records. Therefore, apart from the aggregate functions, the SELECT clause and GROUP BY clause field lists are identical. However, these aggregate functions can only relate to fields that will not be used to differentiate between record groups. Below is an example of how the GROUP BY clause is used:

```
REPORT yz332250.
TABLES
  tadir.
DATA:
  obj LIKE tadir-object,
  qty TYPE I.

SELECT OBJECT COUNT( DISTINCT obj_name )
  INTO (obj, no.)
  FROM tadir
  WHERE author = sy-uname
  GROUP BY object .

    WRITE: / obj, no.
ENDSELECT.
```

This short program finds all the development objects created by the current user (programs, transactions, screen programs, etc.), but does not list them individually. Instead, it totals the number of elements per object type, for each group, and only outputs that number on screen.

The HAVING clause

You can use the HAVING clause to define additional conditions for evaluating the record groups generated with GROUP BY. These conditions usually concern information about a record group, i.e. the number of records or the values of aggregate functions. This is demonstrated in the slightly modified program to the GROUP BY example below:

```
REPORT yzz31150.
TABLES
  tadir.
DATA:
  obj LIKE tadir-object,
  qty TYPE I.
```

```
SELECT OBJECT COUNT( DISTINCT obj_name )
  INTO (obj, qty)
  FROM tadir
  WHERE author = sy-uname
  GROUP BY object
  HAVING count ( * ) > 1 .

    WRITE: / obj, qty.
ENDSELECT.
```

In this example, the HAVING clause ensures that only the object groups which contain more than one object will be listed. Here, the count (*) expression does not refer to the total number of records determined with SELECT, but to each individual group generated with GROUP BY.

The WHERE clause

The WHERE clause in the SELECT statement can contain one or more comparisons which you can link with the AND and OR operators. In each comparison, the system checks a field in the table to see whether it fulfils a condition or not. Different types of comparison are possible. These include numerical comparisons, string or pattern checks, and checks against a selection table. Similar comparisons are also used in some control statements (i.e. IF, WHILE or CHECK). However, there are differences between the WHERE clause's possible expressions and those of other statements.

In the Open-SQL statements, the WHERE clause is the most important clause, because it defines what database records are to be selected. It processes a number of different expressions that are described in this section. The WHERE clause defines the selection condition. It can evaluate different subexpressions, which can be grouped using brackets and the operators AND and OR. In addition, you can use the NOT operator to negate a subexpression. The following selection criteria are available:

- Compare a database field with a value or a field.

- Check a database field against a number of values or fields.

- Check a database field against a pattern.

- Check a database field against a range (lower and upper limit).

- Check a database field against a specially structured internal table (selection).

- Check against the fields of any internal table (only for the SELECT statement).

- Dynamic declaration of the condition (only for the SELECT statement).

When a field is being directly compared with another field (or value), the usual comparison operators are available. These can either be specified as a symbol or as a two-digit operator. Table 3.20 shows the available operators.

Table 3.20   Comparison operators

Operator	Icon	Meaning
EQ	=	Equals
NE	<> ><	Not equal to
LT	<	Less than
LE	<=, =<	Less than or equal
GT	>	Greater than
GE	>=, =>	Greater than or equal

The examples below show expressions in WHERE clauses. They refer to the TADIR table, so you can test them after modifying program YZ231110. Here, the user name test should remain in the WHERE clause, as otherwise thousands of results lines might possibly appear in the list. Please remember to replace the two characters Z3 with your initials in all examples where program names are used in the search term, so that the system only searches for programs generated by you.

A selection expression listing all objects, whose version number is lower than 3, could read as follows:

```
WHERE ... versid < 3.
```

If you do not want to check for an individual value, but for a match with an element from a larger unit, you can use the IN statement. Here, you define the quantity in oval brackets.

```
WHERE ... object IN ('PROG', 'TABL', 'DOMA').
```

Use the LIKE statement to check against a pattern. Two characters can act as wildcards (pattern character, joker) in the pattern. The underscore, '_', represents any character, while the percent character, '%', represents any character string (including an empty one). However, this check is only possible for alphanumeric values. The statement would therefore read:

```
WHERE ... obj_name LIKE 'YZ3%'.
```

Sometimes you need to search for one of the two characters '%' or '_'. To do so, you need to switch off their special function in the pattern. You can use the ESCAPE statement to specify a character with which you disable the effect of the two wildcards in the pattern. You can specify any character for this purpose, which allows you to overcome the most difficult situations. When testing the example below, the WHERE clause should only contain a single expression for a change. The search criterion is sufficiently restrictive to keep the length of the results list within reasonable limits. An additional test against the user name would reduce the number of the records found to 0, as there is a high possibility that you have not yet created any object matching the following search pattern:

```
WHERE obj_name LIKE 'V\_T%' ESCAPE '\'.
```

If you want to check a range with an upper and lower limit, you have to use the `BETWEEN` statement. The upper and lower limits are separated from each other with AND. The limit values can be strings or numerical values.

```
WHERE obj_name BETWEEN 'YZ332030' AND 'YZ332100'.
```

You may want to select several records with completely different keys, or by dynamically selecting a subset of the selection criteria. As a result, the other selection criteria cannot be used. In this case you have to use a *selection table* that has a special structure. The user can interactively enter data in a report's selection screen. A subsequent section contains more details on selection tables. You can check against a selection table simply by entering the name of the selection after the `IN` statement:

```
WHERE NAME IN selection.
```

Selection tables are not processed by the database, but are split into individual statements by the SAP control logic. This is why the selection table must not be too extensive, as the database systems limit the size of SQL statements. There is a related check, which is exclusive to the `SELECT` statement, and uses the `FOR ALL ENTRIES` statement to check any internal table, regardless of its structure. This checks each record in the database table against all the entries of an internal table. In addition, you naturally have to specify which fields are to be compared. If you do not do so, the `WHERE` clause checks all fields with identical names. An extract from a `WHERE` clause could therefore have the following appearance:

```
FOR ALL ENTRIES IN icondition WHERE name = icondition-name.
```

This statement is only available in Release 3.0 and higher.

As the examples demonstrate, you only have to enter the field name in the `WHERE` clause. You do not have to enter the table name, as this is already apparent from the `FROM` clause. However, you can store the value used for checking a table field in the table's header line. This results in the following statement, which is rather unclear:

```
tadir-obj_name = 'YZZ%'.
SELECT * FROM tadir
WHERE obj_name LIKE tadir-obj_name.
```

The only way to understand this statement is to remember that the table and header line are two different objects. First of all, a value is made available in the header line. The R/3 System internal control logic processes the `SELECT` statement, and the statement is then sent to the database server. This receives a statement similar to the following one:

```
SELECT * FROM tadir
WHERE obj_name LIKE 'YZZ%'.
```

Contrary to what you would expect from the original statement, at first glance, the system does not check each record read in the table against the `obj_name` field in the `tadir` table (i.e. against itself), but against a value which was stored in the `TADIR` structure.

Parameter transfer in internal tables

The parameters of the various clauses do not have to be hard-coded in the program. With the exception of INTO, it is possible to transfer the necessary parameters to all clauses in an internal table. This must have a special structure (only one field, type C, length 72 characters). In the various clauses, you then only have to enter the name of the particular internal table, enclosed in round brackets:

```
... SELECT [SINGLE [FOR UPDATE] | DISTINCT] (itab_s)
... FROM (itab_f)
... WHERE (itab_w)
... GROUP BY (itab_g)
... HAVING (itab_h)
... ORDER BY (itab_o).
```

By transferring parameters in internal tables, you can generally formulate the SELECT statement at runtime. This makes it much easier to program generic applications that can modify themselves to suit different record structures or queries at runtime.

```
REPORT yz332270.
TABLES:
  tadir.
TYPES:
  t_line(72).
DATA:
  i_where TYPE t_line OCCURS 0 WITH HEADER LINE,
  i_to LIKE tadir OCCURS 0 WITH HEADER LINE,
  tabname LIKE dd02l-tabname.

i_where = 'OBJ_NAME LIKE ''YZ%'' '.
APPEND i_where.
tabname = 'TADIR'.
SELECT * FROM (tabname)
  UP TO 100 ROWS
  INTO TABLE i_to
  WHERE (i_where).

LOOP AT i_to.
  WRITE: / i_to-obj_name.
ENDLOOP.
```

Alias names

In the previous examples, we have always used the SELECT statement to access just one table at a time. Consequently, all field entries in the SELECT statement were automatically unambiguous. Now we can use the new JOIN clause to address more than one table in a SELECT statement. If two table fields with identical names are present, you first have to make them unique by placing the table name before the field name. To reduce effort, when entering code you can use the FROM clause to assign appropriate alias names to the tables. In the subsequent clauses, you can then use the aliases as an alternative to the table names. You will find further examples of this in the next section, which deals with the JOIN clause.

Joins

One of the design aims in using relational data structures is to generally reduce redundancies. Here, data that logically belongs together is saved in different tables, which are joined using unique keys. Therefore, it is often necessary to combine records from several tables with each other, within an application. For example, when creating an invoice, you do not just have to read the individual invoice items, but also determine the invoice recipient's source data. Up to now, in the R/3 System, you had to use a variety of resources or tricks such as logical databases with nested SELECT statements, or temporary interim memory buffers (internal tables, extract datasets) in order to process tasks of this kind. The SQL standard provides the JOIN clause for solving problems of this kind. The conditions contained in a JOIN clause define how records from two or more tables are to be linked with each other.

The SQL standard distinguishes between an INNER JOIN and an OUTER JOIN. In the case of an INNER JOIN, the database system first locates all the record pairs fulfilling the JOIN condition. It then applies the remaining clauses of the SQL statement, especially the SELECT clause, to this data volume. That is why only records that fulfil the conditions of the SELECT clause, as well as those of the JOIN clause, will appear in the results. As the conditions in both clauses are linked with AND, it does not matter, in the results, which clause contains a selection criterion.

In the case of an OUTER JOIN, all records in a primary table that fulfil the JOIN condition are first assigned to the records of a secondary table. All the other records in the primary table are linked with an empty record. The data volume found in this intermediate step therefore contains all the records in the primary table. Then, the SELECT clause is again applied to this data volume. Contrary to the INNER JOIN, the result of an OUTER JOIN depends on the clause that contains a particular condition. It would therefore seem a good idea to use this method to determine all the primary table records that do not fulfil the JOIN expression by simply testing a field of the secondary table for the value NULL in the WHERE clause. Unfortunately, this is not possible because the actual SELECT clause is only allowed to contain fields from the primary table.

The JOIN clause is entered in the FROM clause. For an INNER JOIN, the syntax of the statement is as follows:

... **FROM** *primary_table* [**INNER**] **JOIN** *secondary_table* **ON** {*condition*}.

An OUTER JOIN is not identified with the keyword OUTER, but with LEFT. Therefore, its syntax is as follows:

... **FROM** *primary_table* **LEFT** [**OUTER**] **JOIN** *secondary_table* **ON** {*condition*}.

The database systems supported by the R/3 Systems differ from the SQL standard with regard to their compatibility. That is why you should note these constraints when using the JOIN clause:

- Joins cannot be nested. Therefore, only a table name or view name is allowed to stand to the right of the JOIN keyword. An additional JOIN statement is not permitted.

- The conditions in a Join can only be linked with each other with AND.

- Each JOIN condition must contain a field from the secondary table.

For an OUTER JOIN, the following additional constraints apply:

- The WHERE clause must not contain fields from the secondary table.

- In the JOIN clause's conditions, only EQ (=) is allowed.

- The JOIN condition must contain at least one field from the primary table.

Examples

The examples below demonstrate the JOIN clause by means of some simple selections. To make these selections, you access tables that are part of the Transport Management System. Just like the frequently used TADIR table, you should only access these tables to read them.

The Transport Management System saves the header lines of all tasks and jobs in table E070. Table E071 contains the elements belonging to the tasks or jobs. By evaluating these tables you can determine which programmer has processed a particular object and when.

The first example program is designed to output the names of all programmers who have modified objects, and to list those objects. As the number of entries can be very large, a parameter can limit the selection to specific programmers. Without the JOIN statement, two nested SELECT statements would be necessary. The first would read table E070 and determine all jobs, sorted according to their programmer's name. A second SELECT statement would read table E071 to find all objects belonging to the particular jobs. However, this simple approach has one disadvantage. If a user repeatedly processes the same object, that object will also appear repeatedly in the results. Therefore, the correct solution to this task would also require the use of an internal table to eliminate duplicate entries.

The JOIN statement greatly simplifies programming. Within the JOIN clause, the two tables, E070 and E071, are linked with each other. This link is created using a field that exists in both tables, so an alias must be created for each of the two tables. In this case, the aliases are A and B. In the link condition, these two aliases then ensure unique field names. It is not possible to achieve unique field names by simply placing the table name in front.

Due to the task set, only the AS4USER, PGMID, OBJECT and OBJ_NAME fields in the results are of any interest. These will be displayed in the SELECT statement's field list. As these fields are contained in only one table at a time, no alias is necessary. You should already be familiar with the subsequent clauses of the SELECT statement from previous examples, which is why no further explanation is necessary here.

```
REPORT yz332280.
TABLES:
  e070,
  e071.


PARAMETERS p_user LIKE e070-as4user.
TRANSLATE p_user USING '*%?_'.
SELECT DISTINCT as4user pgmid object obj_name
  INTO (e070-as4user, e071-pgmid, e071-object, e071-obj_name)
  FROM e070 as a LEFT JOIN e071 as b ON a~trkorr = b~trkorr
  WHERE as4user LIKE p_user
  ORDER BY as4user pgmid object obj_name.
    WRITE: / e070-as4user, e071-pgmid, e071-object, e071-
obj_name(30).
ENDSELECT.
```

As already mentioned, the right-hand part of a JOIN clause must not contain any further clause of this kind. In contrast, the left-hand section can. This gives you the option to link more than two tables with each other, as the next example demonstrates. This expands on the previous example. In addition, the SELECT statement determines the development class belonging to each particular object:

```
REPORT yz332290.
TABLES:
  e070,
  e071,
  tadir.


PARAMETERS p_user LIKE e070-as4user.
PARAMETERS p_devc LIKE tadir-devclass.
TRANSLATE p_user USING '*%?_'.
TRANSLATE p_devc USING '*%?_'.


SELECT DISTINCT as4user b~pgmid b~object b~obj_name devclass
  INTO ( e070-as4user, e071-pgmid, e071-object,
         e071-obj_name, tadir-devclass)
  FROM e070 as a JOIN e071 as b ON a~trkorr = b~trkorr
  JOIN tadir as c ON
    b~pgmid = c~pgmid AND
    b~object = c~object AND
    b~obj_name = c~obj_name
  WHERE as4user LIKE p_user
    AND devclass LIKE p_devc
  ORDER BY as4user b~pgmid b~object b~obj_name.
  WRITE: / e070-as4user, e071-pgmid, e071-object,
         e071-obj_name(30),tadir-devclass.
ENDSELECT.
```

The third example demonstrates an Outer Join. A SELECT statement has the task of determining all users existing in the current client, as well as the Transport Management System tasks or jobs which they might have created. The solution resembles the first example, where the LEFT JOIN statement also makes all users without entries in the Transport Management System appear in the output.

```
REPORT yz332300.
TABLES:
  usr01,
  e070.


PARAMETERS p_user LIKE e070-as4user.
TRANSLATE p_user USING '*%?_'.

SELECT DISTINCT a~bname b~trkorr
  INTO (usr01-bname, e070-trkorr)
  FROM usr01 as a LEFT JOIN e070 as b ON a~bname = b~as4user
  WHERE bname LIKE p_user
  ORDER BY a~bname.
    WRITE: / usr01-bname, e070-trkorr.
ENDSELECT.
```

Modifying, adding and deleting records

Records have to be written to a table before they can be read in it. Additional statements are necessary for modifying or deleting records. Use this statement to add new records to a table:

INSERT *table.*

This statement writes the contents of the specified work area to the specified table. Then, the SY-SUBRC field again informs you whether the statement has been processed successfully. A value of 0 means that the new record was successfully added. Values greater than 0 indicate an error. In the case of INSERT, an error will occur if, for example, a record with an identical key already exists. Therefore, you cannot use INSERT to change the contents of records that already exist. To do this, use this statement:

UPDATE *table.*

This statement completely overwrites an existing record with the contents of the work area. Contrary to INSERT, the record to be overwritten must already exist. This statement also influences the contents of the SY-SUBRC field. Again, the key for identifying the record is derived from the work area.

Similar to the SQL UPDATE statement, the ABAP statement also has a variant that lets you modify one or more fields of records that correspond to a predefined pattern. In this case, the syntax is as follows:

```
UPDATE table
SET expression
WHERE condition.
```

In this example, the defined assignments will be executed in all records that fulfil the condition. It is not always possible to differentiate between inserting and modifying. In this case you can use this statement:

```
MODIFY table.
```

This statement automatically recognizes if a new record should be inserted into the table or if an existing record should be modified. However, this luxury comes at the price of poorer performance.

All previously discussed statements, with the exception of the mass update, work in conjunction with the table's header line, from which they derive the key for the record to be processed. This is also possible when deleting records. To delete the record identified by the key in the work area, you simply need this statement:

```
DELETE table.
```

This version of the delete statement is useful, for example, if you want to delete some of the read records within a SELECT loop. However, similarly to mass modification, an UPDATE can also trigger a mass deletion if the records to be deleted are selected using a WHERE clause:

```
DELETE FROM table
WHERE condition.
```

Here, the conditions of the WHERE clause correspond with those of the SELECT statement, just like in the case of the UPDATE statement.

The statements discussed have some additional variants and options whose exact syntax you will find in the quick reference guide. These options primarily serve to disable automatic client handling (CLIENT SPECIFIED) and to derive the field to be modified from a structure or an internal table.

After the statements for database modification have been executed, the modifications to the database are still not completely committed. You can undo them at any time by using this statement:

```
ROLLBACK WORK.
```

This can become necessary, for example when writing to several logically independent tables, one of the write statements ends in an error. To ensure the data is consistent, the changes in all tables have to be undone in this case. As a counterpart to ROLLBACK WORK, there is also a statement to confirm the modifications. This statement is:

```
COMMIT WORK.
```

When this statement is executed, all modifications are finally committed. The R/3 System offers a special feature here. After each screen change, i.e. each time a screen program finishes, the internal control logic automatically executes a COMMIT WORK. Apart from committing the modifications, this statement deletes the internal cursor (record pointer), for example, of a SELECT statement. This is why you must not change screen programs between the SELECT and ENDSELECT statements. Therefore, it is not always possible to sequentially process the read records in a screen program within such a loop.

In ABAP tasks, the statements described above for updating datasets are very often transferred into special program sections whose only task is to write information to the database, i.e. updating. As entry functions of this type are primarily used in dialog programs, you will find further details on updating in Section 3.2.17.

In the following short program, a table is filled with a few records that will be required as test data for some other programs in this book. Do not execute this program if you have already entered data as instructed in the example in Chapter 7! At the start of this program, any existing table contents will be deleted!

Before you can execute this program, you must first generate the table. It is not part of the standard R/3 System. The section dealing with the maintenance of Data Dictionary elements in Chapter 5 describes how to create data elements, domains and tables.

```
REPORT yz332310.
TABLES yz3stock.

DELETE FROM yz3stock WHERE wkz LIKE '%'.

yz3stock-wkz = '123456'.
yz3stock-name = 'SAP'.
INSERT yz3stock.

yz3stock-wkz = '654321'.
yz3stock-name = 'IXOS'.
INSERT yz3stock.

yz3stock-wkz = '888888'.
yz3stock-name = 'NAGEL & CO'.
INSERT yz3stock.
COMMIT WORK.

WRITE: / 'Contents after insertion'.
SELECT * FROM yz3stock.
  WRITE: / yz3stock-wkz, yz3stock-name, yz3stock-branch.
ENDSELECT.

UPDATE yz3stock
SET branch = 'S'
WHERE name = 'SAP' OR name = 'IXOS'.

WRITE: /, /, 'Contents after update'.
SELECT * FROM yz3stock.
  WRITE: / yz3stock-wkz, yz3stock-name, yz3stock-branch.
ENDSELECT.
```

```
DELETE FROM yz3stock
WHERE branch <> 'S'.

WRITE: /, /, 'Contents after deletion.
SELECT * FROM yz3stock.
  WRITE: / yz3stock-wkz, yz3stock-name, yz3stock-branch.
ENDSELECT.
```

3.2.10 Data context

The R/3 System contains some tables which have a core function. Almost all the applications in a business management module access these tables. Frequently, only a few records will be read across different application and user platforms. Examples include the data for accountancy cycles or currencies. Other records, i.e. catalogue data, are relatively static in character. They only change over long periods of time. In both cases, each application rereads the data and consequently places considerable load on the system.

To avoid unnecessary data selection, SAP uses the concept of the *data context*. A data context is a buffer created on an application server, whose contents are available to all applications and users working on that application server. In the data context, records from one or more tables that logically belong together are saved. When a record is accessed for the first time, it is read from the database table and stored in the context, where it is then made available to all users and applications. If another application would like to read the same record, that record does not have to be extracted from the database again: it is made available straight from the context. The resulting system performance is only slightly inferior to that of a MOVE-CORRESPONDING statement.

In the program, a context has to be declared in a similar way to a data type. To do so, use this statement:

CONTEXTS contextname.

You can use colon notation with this statement to declare several contexts simultaneously.

When you declare a context, the system automatically generates several data types. One of the data types is given the description CONTEXT_contextname. You have to use this data type to declare instances of a context with the DATA statement. The other data types describe the fields in the context. They are given descriptions that use this format: CONTEXT_T_contextname-contextfield.

The only way to access a context is to use an instance created with DATA. You can create several instances of a context to access different records at the same time:

DATA context **TYPE** contexttype.

After a context has been declared, the keywords required for selection have to be transferred to an instance of that context. To do so, use the following statement:

SUPPLY { parameter = value } **TO CONTEXT** context.

In the further course of the application, the corresponding data fields will then be read with the DEMAND statement:

DEMAND { *parameter* = *value* } **FROM CONTEXT** *context.*

The system will only search for the corresponding data in the context when executing the DEMAND statement. If necessary, it will carry out a database selection. When a context is being processed, error messages can emerge. You can use the following statement suffix to divert these messages into an internal table:

... **MESSAGES INTO** *itab.*

This table must have the same structure as SYMSG.

Context example

The example below shows how to define and use a context that determines the development class of a specified object, and returns the person responsible for this development class.

Before you can use a data context in a program, you must first of all define it with transaction SE33. In this definition you specify the tables involved, their relationships with each other and the fields that are of interest. Some of these fields are the key fields used to select a record, while others are the data fields that are to be read, and make up the actual contents of the record.

In the initial screen of transaction SE33 you only have to enter the name of the context, and click a pushbutton to select the corresponding function (*see* Figure 3.31).

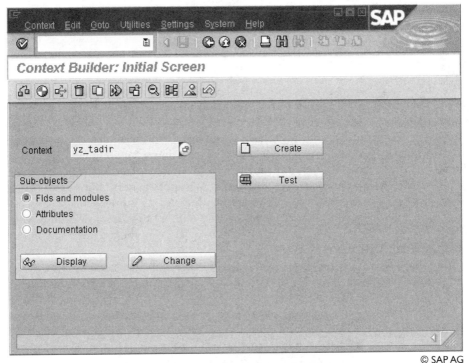

Figure 3.31   Context Builder: initial screen

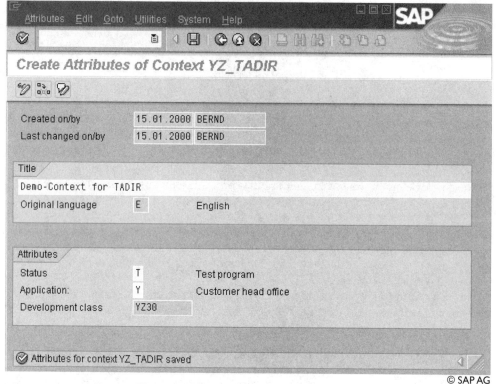

Figure 3.32   Entering a context's attributes

When creating a new context, you enter its description and an abbreviation for the application group in a screen program that will be displayed after the initial screen (Figure 3.32).

In that screen program, you can select Goto | Fields and modules from the menu or press function key (F6) to jump to the actual context editing screen (Figure 3.33). If you are editing an existing context, you jump directly from the initial screen to the editing screen.

The context maintenance screen program consists of several table views. The R/3 System adjusts their size to fit the size of the window. All the same, even on large monitors there is still not sufficient area to work easily with all the views. Therefore you can enlarge each table view to the size of the window by clicking the magnifying glass in the upper-left corner of that table view.

First, you must enter the tables (TADIR and TDEVC) in the *Modules* table view (*see* Figure 3.34). Here, you might also have to use the Insert icon, to the left of the table view, to generate new entry lines.

The system transfers the fields in these tables into a second table view called *Parameter*. It is located at the bottom right-hand side of the overview screen program (Figure 3.33). If you select a table in the *Module* table view by double-clicking on it, this table view displays all the fields in it (Figure 3.35). The arrow in the I/O column defines whether each

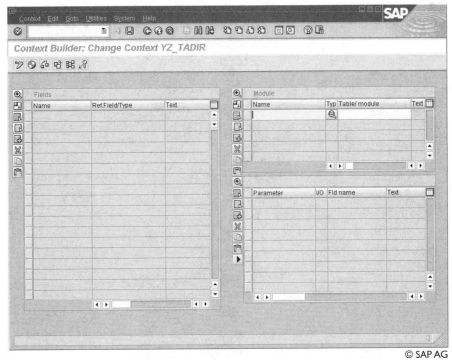

© SAP AG

Figure 3.33   Maintaining the features of a context

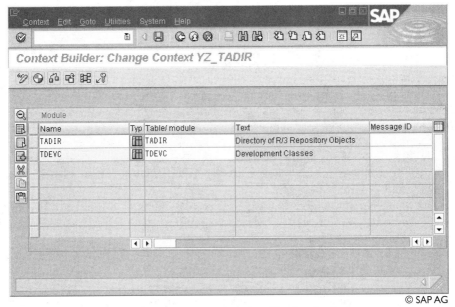

© SAP AG

Figure 3.34   Entering the tables involved

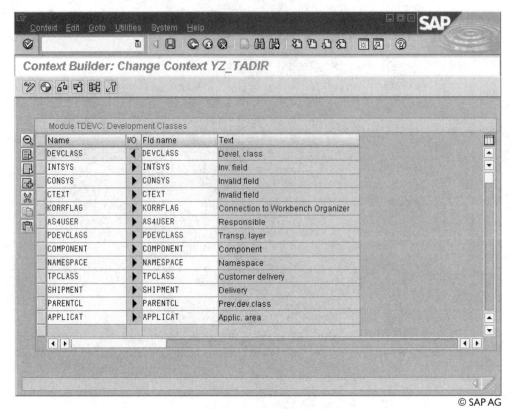

Figure 3.35   Defining import and export parameters

field is an import or export field. You can toggle the setting by double-clicking on it. You can use the SUPPLY statement to enter search conditions in the import fields. The DEMAND statement, however, reads the contents of export fields and makes their values available to the calling program. The current settings are already correct, as all key fields are preset as import fields and all others as export fields by default.

To execute a selection in several tables, you must either enter the appropriate values in the import fields or create a field link. When you create a field link, a table field is automatically filled with the value of the field in another table that is linked to it. The system creates such links automatically between foreign key fields. Here, this is the case for the DEVCLASS field in both tables.

Should the system be unable to create direct relationships, you have to create them manually. To do so, you have to select the corresponding field in the *Fields* table view and choose CONTEXT | LINK FIELDS.

Before this, you might first have to choose CONTEXT | FOREIGN KEY TABLE to copy the foreign key tables to be evaluated into the context.

The R/3 System uses the data field domains to determine possible relationships. By clicking on the table icon at the beginning of each line, you can activate one of the proposed relationships. Figure 3.36 shows you the corresponding screen program.

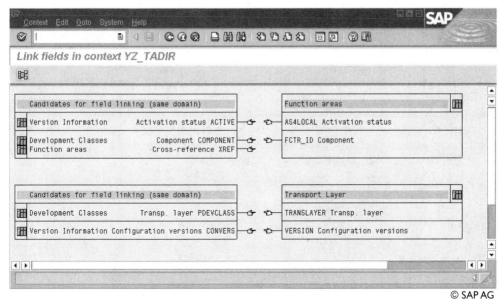

Figure 3.36   Creating field links

After you have created the field relationships, choose Context | Generate from the menu to generate the context. Then you can use it in a program.

```
REPORT yz332320.
CONTEXTS yz_tadir.
DATA: c1 TYPE context_yz_tadir,
      user TYPE context_t_yz_tadir-as4user.

PARAMETERS:  p_pgm LIKE tadir-pgmid DEFAULT 'R3TR',
             p_obj LIKE tadir-object DEFAULT 'PROG',
             p_nam LIKE tadir-obj_name.

SUPPLY   pgmid = p_pgm
         object = p_obj
         obj_name = p_nam
  TO CONTEXT c1.

DEMAND as4user = user FROM CONTEXT c1.

WRITE: / user.
```

3.2.11 Processing persistent data clusters

Information is not always structured clearly enough to be stored without problems in records in tables. In a program, it often becomes necessary to use several data objects which, although they logically belong together, have a completely different structure or size.

Apart from the usual database tables, special tables are also available. Data clusters can be saved permanently in these tables. The term data clusters is used to describe one or more fields or internal tables that logically belong together, and can be saved with a common key in a database table. When internal tables are being stored, the header lines are not considered; only the data saved in the internal table will be written to the data cluster.

The database table used for storing data clusters must have a special structure. According to the structure of the table used for storing the clusters, you can create either client-dependent or client-independent data cluster stores. Chapter 5, Section 5.1.4 (tables for data clusters) contains further details of the structure of these tables.

To write data to the database table, use this statement:

EXPORT *elements* **TO DATABASE** *table(area)* **ID** *key.*

`elements` is the list of objects to be stored. In `table` you enter the name of the database table where the data will be stored. Each table contains different areas (`area`), which use a two-digit descriptor. When calling a statement, this descriptor must always be entered as a direct value. Within an area, the unique key `key` is used to distinguish between the individual entries. The key is transferred as an individual field. The EXPORT statement is used to split it into the key fields of the database table.

You can read the data in a data cluster with the following statement:

IMPORT *elements* **FROM DATABASE** *table(area)* **ID** *key.*

The parameters are the same as those of the EXPORT statement. In the basic form of this statement, the names of the elements to be read have to be the same as those of the written elements. This means that the data is stored in exactly the fields from which it has previously been read. You can deactivate this constraint with the following options:

`...` **FROM** source `....`

or

`...` **TO** *target* `....`

If you do so, you have to code these options separately for each element.

The IMPORT and EXPORT statements only fill the table's key fields and the actual data cluster. A table intended for data clusters can also have other fields. You can process these fields with the statements used for database tables (SELECT, UPDATE, etc.).

The directly accessible fields of a table used for data clusters do not give you any information about the actual contents. Although it is possible to read the keys of all data clusters by reading the key fields of the table, the only way to determine the names of the objects in the cluster is to use this special statement:

```
IMPORT DIRECTORY
  INTO itab
  FROM DATABASE table(area) ID key.
```

This statement writes the information on all elements in a specified cluster to an internal table. This table must have the same Data Dictionary structure as CDIR.

Because the elements in a data cluster can be of any length and type, data clusters are, among other things, especially suited for the simple storage of binary data, regardless of origin. For example, a front end system could use the Upload function to write this kind of data to the system. In Section 3.10.3, you will find an example of how data can be uploaded and downloaded, and of how you use data clusters.

3.2.12 Subroutines

Very large programs force you to use a modular approach. With this approach, not only can you make the source code easier to understand, but you can also reuse parts of programs many times. The simplest way to split up a program is to use subroutines. The subroutines used in ABAP are broadly similar to the procedures used in Pascal. They can accept parameters, but do not return a function value.

Definition

The following statement defines a subroutine:

```
FORM subroutine_name [parameters].
  statements
ENDFORM.
```

Due to the name of the statements, such subroutines are also known as *FORM routines, or forms* for short, in ABAP. The name can be up to 30 characters long. It can start with numbers and even special characters. However, in practice you should apply the same naming conventions as those valid for field names. Subroutine names should therefore start with a letter, be as self-explanatory as possible and only use the underscore as a special character.

When you have used FORM to define a subroutine, this is followed by the subroutine's statements, and concluded with the ENDFORM statement. FORM routines can generally contain all statements that are also permitted in the main program. However, you should note these constraints, which concern further modularization: FORM routines must not contain additional statements for modularizing the program, i.e. no timing instructions and no further declarations of subroutines. However, there is no problem in declaring local data within subroutines.

When subroutines are being declared in reports, a nasty trap awaits the unwary programmer. Apart from the subroutines, there are additional statements that are used for modularization, such as *timing instructions*. The statement block belonging to these statements does not explicitly conclude with a special statement. Instead, it ends at another modularization statement or even at the end of the program. A FORM statement might therefore complete the statement block of a previous timing instruction. These connections are easily overlooked. The trap consists in the fact that the PROGRAM or REPORT statements work in a similar way to the START-OF-SELECTION timing instruction that is described later. The statements in a report will be executed only if they come after a START-OF-SELECTION statement or immediately follow a PROGRAM or REPORT statement. If a subroutine is defined at the beginning of a report, the report statements after ENDFORM will be executed only if ENDFORM is followed by a START-OF-SELECTION statement. In simple reports, subroutines should therefore be defined at the end of the program. Larger programs, however, frequently relocate subroutines and declarations into INCLUDE files, which are included at the start of the program. In such cases, the 'main program' should be launched with a START-OF-SELECTION statement. You will find more information on the function of timing instructions, and how to use them, in the section dealing with report programming.

Calling subroutines

To call subroutines, use this statement:

PERFORM *subroutine_name* ... .

In it you can enter fields or tables in the current program as current parameters. This has to be highlighted by two additional keywords. If you want to specify basic internal tables, you need to use the TABLES statement:

PERFORM *subroutine_name* **TABLES** *itab1 itab2* ... .

However, to transfer elementary fields, structures and internal tables of the three new table types, use the USING statement:

PERFORM *subroutine_name* **USING** *param_1 param_2* ... .

You can even call subroutines from outside the program. This is called an external call or, in the SAP environment, external performs. For this type of call, you have to enter the name of the external program or module pool in oval brackets after the name of the FORM routine:

PERFORM *subroutine_name(program)* ... .

You can also use the IN PROGRAM addition with the PERFORM statement to enable the dynamic transfer of routines and program names. You can either enter both names directly in the statement, or they can be contained in fields that have to be enclosed in round brackets in the statement. For example:

PERFORM *subroutine_name* **IN PROGRAM** *program* ... .

or

PERFORM (*subroutine_name*) **IN PROGRAM** (*program*) ... .

Parameters

You can transfer parameters to subroutines. If you do so, the system carries out a type check. The extent of this check depends both on which Release of the R/3 System you are using, and on certain options in the program. You can use all previously explained data types, apart from database tables, i.e. individual fields, structures and internal tables, as parameters. In addition, when transferring the parameters, you can define if they are to act as value or reference parameters. The latter enable values to be returned to the calling program.

Now a concrete explanation of the syntax; in the FORM statement, you enter a list of the formal parameters after the USING keyword. This contains the names of fields that are only available within the FORM routine. You can only use blank spaces to separate the formal parameters from each other.

FORM *subroutine_name* **USING** *formal_par_1 formal_par_2 ...*
formal_par_n.

When you call a subroutine with PERFORM, you specify the current parameters that are assigned to the formal parameters according to the sort sequence in the parameter list. All formal parameters, which have only been defined with USING, are reference parameters. This means that any changes to the values of the formal parameters are also applied to the current parameters of the calling program. The formal parameter refers to the same memory block as the current parameter.

Transfers of values of this kind can result in undesirable side effects if values are assigned to formal parameters, although the current parameters should not actually be changed. This may not necessarily occur in the same routine. A subroutine often calls additional subroutines while transferring formal parameters. This makes it rather difficult to determine the origin of a formal parameter, and side effects can no longer be foreseen. That is why value parameters, which are copies of the current parameters, are used in addition to the reference parameters. If values are assigned to formal parameters, they will take effect there, but not in the current parameter. The syntax for a call of this kind is rather more complex:

FORM *subroutine_name* **USING VALUE** (*formal_par_1*) **VALUE** (*formal_par_1*)
. . . .

Finally, there is still a somewhat inconsistent mixture between value and reference parameters that might be unique in this form. The syntax resembles the syntax for defining value parameters:

FORM *subroutine_name* **CHANGING VALUE** (*formal_par_1*) . . . .

These parameters are essentially reference parameters. Consequently, they enable you to transfer values to the current parameters. However, the values are only transferred if the ENDFORM statement is reached. If the subroutine terminates with an error message (MESSAGE statement), the contents of the current parameter will not be changed. However, subroutine terminations with EXIT jump to the ENDFORM statement, as a result of which the value transfer will be executed.

Apart from fields and structures, FORM routines can also accept internal tables as parameters. However, no distinction is made between value and reference parameters: internal tables will always be transferred as reference. Changes to the table contents consequently remain intact even after the subroutine is left. From Release 4.0 on, you must take into account the particular table type when transferring tables as parameters. A formal parameter for a basic table is marked with the TABLES keyword:

FORM *subroutine_name* **TABLES** *itab1 itab2 ... .*

Here, the TABLES statement must be positioned before the USING or CHANGING statements. From Release 3.0 on, internal tables without header lines exist. If a table of this kind
is transferred to a subroutine as a parameter, the ABAP interpreter generates a header line
for this table within the subroutine, which considerably simplifies its processing.

As yet it is only possible to transfer the new tables available from Release 4.0 on as a
CHANGING parameter.

If structured data types, i.e. structures or internal tables, are transferred to a subroutine, the structure information will be lost. Within the subroutine, structures and header
lines in internal tables will be dealt with as simple, unstructured CHAR fields. The correct
data type will only be transmitted internally to the subroutine for simple fields. To illustrate this, a first example:

```
REPORT yz332330.
DATA: BEGIN OF f1,
   n TYPE I,
   c(10),
END OF f1.

DATA i TYPE I.

f1-n = 123.
f1-c = 'abc'.
i = 12345.

PERFORM x USING f1 i.

FORM x USING f1 f2.
DATA: t,
      l TYPE I.

  WRITE f1-n. "Leads to a syntax error!
              "Delete after first syntax check!

  WRITE / f1 .
  DESCRIBE FIELD f1 TYPE t.
  DESCRIBE FIELD f1 LENGTH l.
  WRITE: / t , l, / .

  WRITE / f2.
  DESCRIBE FIELD f2 TYPE t.
  DESCRIBE FIELD f2 LENGTH l.
  WRITE: / t , l .
ENDFORM.
```

The data type of the second parameter, i.e. a simple field, can be determined correctly. However, the structure of the structure is not known within the FORM routine. The attempt to access an element of the structure causes an error message to be generated during the syntax check. Therefore, the corresponding statement must be commented out or deleted. The DESCRIBE statement merely specifies the data type C for f1.

As an additional statement of the subroutine shows, the structure can be accessed as a whole. On the other hand, this can lead to an undesirable result: the (binary) contents of an integer field are interpreted and output as a character string. You can of course avoid the problems demonstrated here. You can use various options to send detailed information on parameter attributes to subroutines. This was possible since before Release 3.0, but it was only in Release 3.0 that some additional options were introduced for the FORM statement, which you can use to transfer detailed information on a parameter's data type to the subroutines. To some extent, the more stringent checks connected with this are not compatible with those of Release 2.2.

Below you will find a description of the procedure commonly used in Release 2.2. Here you can use the optional STRUCTURE keyword to transfer some information on the structure of structures and internal tables. You enter the structure statement after the parameter:

FORM ... *formal_param* **STRUCTURE** *structure*.

In Release 2.2 you can use the name of a Data Dictionary structure (table or structure), an internal table or a structure, as a structure statement. However, the system does not check whether the formal parameter really has this structure, because it is precisely this information that is not available. If it was, the STRUCTURE statement would not be required. The system only checks the length of the formal parameter and the length of the structure. The parameters must have at least the same length as the structure. Otherwise it would be possible to use elements of the structure to access data areas which are no longer part of the formal parameters. The FORM routine in the last example could therefore be expanded as follows, to enable access to individual elements of the structure:

```
FORM x USING f1 STRUCTURE f1 f2.
...
WRITE: / f1-n, f1-c.
```

The ABAP interpreter's syntax check recognizes incorrect field lengths in structure statements. This error is recognized during a program check in the development environment or before processing for the first time. When structures are being defined, the control logic occasionally inserts filler fields to fill fields to word limits. These filler fields are taken into consideration during the length check. Occasionally, the sum of a structure's field lengths can exceed the sum of the field lengths of the actual components of the formal parameter. It is not the sum of the field lengths that gets checked, but instead the actual memory requirements in RAM, due to the possible filling of the subfields up to word limits.

As already mentioned, Release 3.0 has seen the introduction of more extensive parameter checks. The STRUCTURE keyword is now only retained for compatibility reasons. It can only be used to describe a formal parameter, which has to be a structure. The descriptive structure itself can also only be a structure: internal or database tables are no longer permitted.

From Release 3.0 on, you should use LIKE and TYPE, together with some other options, to describe a parameter in more detail, instead of the STRUCTURE statement. Besides structured parameters such as structures or internal tables, simple fields can also be checked. Which options you use depends on the type of reference object. If you want to use a data type as a descriptive object for the parameter, you must use TYPE:

```
FORM ... formal_param TYPE data_type.
```

By defining the type, you can carry out some further data checks whose scope depends on the type of the descriptive type. If the type description refers to one of the predefined types such as C or I, the system merely checks if the formal parameter matches the corresponding data type. It does not check the length. Therefore this is also called a generic type check. However, if you enter a user-defined data type after TYPE, the control logic checks whether the length and elementary data type of each component of a formal parameter corresponds with the particular element of the type description. On the other hand, it does not check whether the names match with the names of the components. Complex data types are only identical if all components are also identical. To illustrate this, here is another example:

```
REPORT yz332340.
TYPES:
   BEGIN OF t1,
      a,b,c,
   END OF t1,

   BEGIN OF t2,
      e,f,g,
   END OF t2,

   BEGIN OF t3,
      h(3),
   END OF t3.

DATA
   a TYPE t1.

PERFORM f1 USING a.  'OK
PERFORM f2 USING a.  'OK
PERFORM f3 USING a.  'Typo, commented out after syntax check

FORM f1 USING f TYPE t1.
ENDFORM.

FORM f2 USING f TYPE t2.
ENDFORM.

FORM f3 USING f TYPE t3.
ENDFORM.
```

The whole program consists only of declarations, and it has no functionality whatsoever. Therefore, it does not have to be processed either. Only the program's syntax check
is of interest. All three declared types have the same overall length. If the three subroutines were to use the STRUCTURE statement instead of TYPE, the program's syntax would
be correct. However, the more detailed check launched by the type definition recognizes
that the first component in the FORM routine F3 has an incorrect length, and triggers a
syntax error.

Naturally, you can use structure descriptions for internal tables, as well as for structures.
The following example illustrates how the TYPES option is used for a basic internal table:

```
REPORT yz332350.
TYPES:
  BEGIN OF t_line,
    number TYPE I,
  END OF t_line,

  t_tab TYPE t_line OCCURS 10.

DATA:
  fl TYPE t_line,
  itab TYPE t_tab.

PERFORM filltab TABLES itab USING 3.

LOOP AT itab INTO fl.
  WRITE / fl-number.
ENDLOOP.

FORM filltab TABLES p_tab TYPE t_tab
             USING VALUE(p_number) TYPE i.
  DO 10 TIMES.
    p_tab-number = p_number.
    APPEND p_tab.
    p_number = p_number + 1.
  ENDDO.
ENDFORM.
```

If you would like to use an object created with DATA instead of a data type, to describe
the parameter, you must replace the TYPE keyword with the LIKE keyword. The system
will carry out the same checks. In this case, the FORM statement from the example above
could also read as follows:

```
FORM filltab TABLES p_tab LIKE itab ....
```

For one of the new types of table, the program will have to be structured somewhat
differently. Note, especially, that the new types of table can no longer be transferred after

the TABLES keyword. Instead, tables will now be listed after USING, just like simple parameters. There they have to be assigned a correct table type.

```
REPORT yz332360.
TYPES:
  BEGIN OF t_line,
    number TYPE i,
  END OF t_line,
  t_tab TYPE HASHED TABLE OF t_line WITH UNIQUE KEY number INITIAL
  SIZE 0.

DATA: fl TYPE t_line,
      itab TYPE t_tab.

PERFORM filltab USING itab 3.

LOOP AT itab INTO fl.
  WRITE / fl-number.
ENDLOOP.

FORM filltab USING p_tab TYPE t_tab
                   VALUE(p_number) TYPE I.
DATA fl TYPE LINE OF t_tab.
  DO 10 TIMES.
    fl-number = p_number.
    INSERT fl INTO TABLE p_tab.
    p_number = p_number + 1.
  ENDDO.
ENDFORM.
```

From Release 3.0, the type checks are so strict that you even have to differentiate
between structures and internal tables. It is now no longer possible to use a structure to
describe an internal table that was transferred as a parameter and vice versa.
Consequently, these two statements are not correct, and will be rejected during the program's syntax check:

```
FORM filltab TABLES p_tab TYPE t_line ....
```

   or

```
FORM filltab TABLES p_tab LIKE fl ....
```

During day-to-day operation it is occasionally necessary to transfer an individual
record from an internal table to a subroutine. If there is no designated structure type
available for this record, you can use these options to describe a structure through an
internal table or a corresponding table type instead:

```
... formal_param TYPE LINE OF table_type.
```

or

... *formal_param* **LIKE LINE OF** *itab*.

If necessary, you can, in exceptional cases, use this statement to switch off the type check:

... **TYPE ANY**.

Following this, any parameter type is permitted. In a similar way, you can use this statement to simply check if the parameter is an internal table or not:

... **Type TABLE**.

In both cases, no additional information will be available on what the structure of the parameter might be.

Local data

In subroutines, you can declare local data objects and local data types. To do so you can use all the statements described earlier (DATA, TYPE, FIELD-SYMBOLS, CONSTANTS). If you do so, the elements you create in this way are only valid within this particular subroutine. If a field, which also exists globally with the same name, has to be created in a subroutine, the local field is valid within that subroutine. The global field is not affected by the actions in the subroutine. All global fields, that are not obscured by local fields with identical names, can still be accessed from out of the subroutine. The contents of the local fields created with DATA or CONSTANTS will be lost if you leave the routine. Each time you call the routine, these fields will be created again and initialized. In addition to complete local data declarations, you can use this statement to protect a global field from being changed by mistake:

LOCAL *field*.

or

LOCAL: *field_1*, *field_2*, ... *field_n*.

This statement is only useful after a FORM statement. It causes the contents of the field(s) to be saved immediately after the routine is launched, and causes the contents to be recovered after the routine concludes. As more powerful options have now become available for generating local data, the LOCAL statement has become obsolete.

Release 3.0 introduces another declaration statement which can be used to generate fields that are locally visible, but have static validity in subroutines. These fields will be generated and initialized when a routine is first launched, but remain intact after the routine is left. Access to these fields is only possible within the subroutine. You create fields of this kind with this statement:

STATICS *field*.

Just like with DATA, you can create fields, structures and internal tables. The following example demonstrates the difference between normal and static fields:

```
REPORT yz332370.

DO 10 TIMES.
  PERFORM fstat.
ENDDO.

FORM fstat.
DATA n1 TYPE I.
STATICS n2 TYPE I.
  WRITE: / n1, n2.
  ADD 1 TO n1.
  ADD 1 TO n2.
ENDFORM.
```

3.2.13 Macros

Some of the statements described above, especially the internal table declarations, etc., require a lot of typing. You can reduce this to some extent by using macros. A macro is a statement block with a name that can contain some placeholders (dummy data). In the program, the macros will be called, during which current parameters will be passed. During the generation of an application, the system will resolve macros and consequently replace the macro calls with the complete source code. You use these statements to define a macro:

```
DEFINE macro.
  statements
END-OF-DEFINITION.
```

In the statements, the characters &1 up to &9 can be used as placeholders. This is an example of a macro and how it is used:

```
DEFINE decl_st_tab.
  DATA: BEGIN OF &1 OCCURS 0.
    INCLUDE STRUCTURE &2.
  DATA: END OF &1.
END-OF-DEFINITION.

...
DEFITAB i_shares yzzshr.
DEFITAB i_forex yzzfex.
```

The DEFITAB macro makes it easier to declare the original kind of internal table, which is derived from a Data Dictionary table or a Data Dictionary structure. When using the macro, you will now only have to type the two variable parameters in the source code.

3.2.14 Data exchange between applications

In ABAP, each application, i.e. each transaction and each of the function groups (which are described later), has its own data area in RAM. The data stored there is not immediately accessible by other applications. In many cases it is however desirable for applications to jointly use data. For example, this is useful if help routines from other reports are used via external subroutine calls. Therefore, when programming applications, the programmer can choose between three ways of using data stored in RAM outside a program. The one they choose depends on the program type and the relationship between the applications involved.

Common Part

A special variant of the DATA statement is used to generate a *common part* data area. This is used for data exchange between applications which are linked with each other through external subprogram calls. A common part can contain any data declarations. A program can contain several common parts, but they must then each be given a unique name. If you only use one common part, you do not have to define a name for it.

```
DATA: BEGIN OF COMMON PART [name],
 declaration
END OF COMMON PART.
```

In both programs, the common part data area must be generated with the same name and structure. This is easiest if the declaration to create the common part is stored in a separate file. It is assigned program type I for *Include program*. Use this statement to include it in all applications involved:

```
INCLUDE filename.
```

GET/SET parameters

The GET/SET parameters are intended to store individual values across application borders and, above all, to automatically transfer them into screen program input fields. The GET/SET parameters are given a three-digit descriptor. These descriptors are defined in the TPARA system table. You can use transaction SM31 to maintain this table. In a program, you can use the following statement to assign a value to a parameter:

```
SET parameter ID parameter field field.
```

This value is usually taken from the contents of a field. The parameter's contents remain intact, even across application borders, until the user logs off from the system. Now, you can use this statement to read the contents of the parameter from RAM and assign them to a field:

```
GET parameter ID parameter field field.
```

In addition, when designing a screen program, you can also assign a parameter of this kind to the individual fields and activate the Get and/or Set mechanism independently from each other. Values will then be transferred automatically. The section dealing with dialog-oriented applications describes this approach in more detail.

Global Memory

From a report or a dialog-oriented application, you can use the CALL statement to call different elements (transactions, and functional or dialog modules). These will then be run like a subroutine. Within an application chain of this kind, launched with CALL, you can use this statement to place field contents or internal tables in a global memory area:

EXPORT { *field* | *itab* } | (*itab*) **TO MEMORY**.

Here you can also omit a hard-coded list of elements, and instead transfer the names of the elements to be transferred in an internal table.

You can use this statement to read the data from the memory area:

IMPORT { *field* | *itab* } | (*itab*) **FROM MEMORY**.

The statement EXPORT is an overwriting statement, which means there will be no additions to the contents of the memory. You can avoid this constraint by using this addition to assign names to the elements placed in the memory area:

`...` **ID** *name*.

You can use ID without a name or specify names, at the same time. The memory area is released if you leave the top-level element of the applications linked with CALL.

Cross-transaction application buffer

Apart from the cross-application data context, there is another buffer that can be used by all applications of an application server. This is a further development of these statements: EXPORT TO DATABASE and IMPORT FROM DATABASE. The new statements and the applicable options correspond with those of the DATABASE-specific functions. The only difference is that the SHARED BUFFER keyword is used, instead of DATABASE. Consequently, the syntax of these statements is as follows:

EXPORT { *field* | *itab* } | (*itab*)
   TO SHARED BUFFER *table(area)* `....`
IMPORT { *field* | *itab* } | (*itab*)
   FROM SHARED BUFFER *table(area)* `....`
DELETE { *field* | *itab* } | (*itab*)
   FROM SHARED BUFFER *table(area)* `....`

Although entries are made in RAM, a table, `table`, with a predefined structure, must be present. Its structure has already been described in the DATABASE-specific functions.

3.2.15 Authorizations check

In many cases, not every user should be allowed to execute all the available applications or all the functions of a particular application. Very often, each user is assigned different data access authorizations. Often, only a much smaller user group is permitted to modify data than to display it. Permission to access data and programs must be achieved through explicit authorization checks. *'Authorizations'* are stored in the user master record. These authorizations consist of versions of an authorization object.

Chapter 6, Section 6.2, which deals with the authorization concept, also describes how to create authorization objects and authorizations. To make the checks easier to understand, let us just say this, for now: an authorization object is a template or type description for the authorization. An authorization object contains up to ten authorization fields. You can derive any number of authorizations from an authorization object, and assign individual values to their fields. The system then stores the authorizations, with their defined field values, in a user master record. During the authorization check, you must remember to specify which authorization object the system is to check. The system will then determine which actual authorizations, derived from this object, have been assigned to the current user, and checks against the field values contained in this authorization. Therefore, when you are programming the authorization check, you only need to know the authorization objects and the fields that they contain. If new authorization objects are required for an application, it is the programmer's responsibility to create and document these authorization objects. Without this documentation, the system administrator will not be able to create authorizations for the user. The system administrator has to know which objects fields have to be taken from, and what values have to be assigned to those fields, to permit access to particular data or program branches.

In a program, you can use the following statement to check authorization:

```
AUTHORITY-CHECK OBJECT authorization_object
  ID authorizationfield_1 FIELD value_1
  ...
  ID authorizationfield_x DUMMY
  ...
  ID authorizationfield_10 FIELD value_10.
```

All values can either be transferred as a direct value enclosed in simple quotation marks, or as a field with the corresponding contents. First, the statement determines the current user's authorization on the basis of the specified authorization object. This authorization contains one or more authorization fields whose names are each entered after the ID addition. These fields contain one or more values or range statements. Then, the system checks whether the check value entered in the statement (field or constant) is contained in the authorization field. If an authorization object contains several fields, the individual check results will be linked with AND. It is possible that a user possesses several authorizations that have been derived from the same object. In this case, the check results will be linked per field with OR. If an authorization field should not be checked, the DUMMY addition will be used instead of the FIELD addition.

The AUTHORITY-CHECK statement returns the check result in the SY-SUBRC system field. There are different check results. Table 3.21 shows the possible return codes.

Table 3.21   Authorization check return values

Return code	Meaning
0	Authorization present
4	Authorization not present
8	Number of parameters too large
12	No features (authorization) for the desired object present in the user master record
24	Authorization fields not present in the authorization object
28, 32, 36	Authorizations in the user master record are corrupted

It is the programmer's responsibility to analyze the check result. The statement merely supplies a return code. If the check results are negative, it does not automatically trigger the closing of a program, etc. Because the application's reaction to a non-existing authorization is left to the programmer to decide, this type of authorization check is extremely flexible.

A brief example below provides you with a bit more detail on how the authorization check is applied. Let us assume that, in one of its screen programs, an application provides a function for displaying additional information on a record that has just been modified. This could be done, for example, through a dialog box which the user calls by clicking a pushbutton. In the OK-CODE module, statements similar to the ones listed below would then be displayed:

```
CASE ok-code.
  WHEN 'DETA'.
    CALL SCREEN 210.
  ...
ENDCASE.
```

The authorization check ought to be executed before the dialog box is called. To do so, an authorization object is necessary: its field(s) are used to assign the actual authorizations. This object should be named Y_ZZDEMO and should contain the YPOPUP field. If an authorization check is now executed before the CALL SCREEN statement, it could look like this:

```
CASE ok-code.
  WHEN 'DETA'.
    AUTHORITY-CHECK OBJECT 'Y_ZZDEMO'
      ID 'YPOPUP' FIELD 'X'.
    IF sy-subrc = 0.
      CALL SCREEN 210.
    ELSE.
      MESSAGE E999.
*       You have no authorization for this function!
    ENDIF.
  ...
ENDCASE.
```

The authorization check only returns the return code 0 if the YPOPUP field, in the authorization derived from Y_ZZDEMO, contains a value or pattern that corresponds with the check value. As the authorization only contains a Yes/No item of information, there is also the option of using the letter 'X' as a release value.

However, it is rather time consuming to maintain an individual authorization for each user and to either set or delete the flag in this authorization. So there is a different way of carrying out the authorization check. Using this alternative method, you could, for example, also enter the names of the users who are authorized to call the additional function in the authorization field. In this case, there would only be one, easily maintained, authorization for all potential users. All the same, the number of users whose names you would have to enter in the authorization field does limit the practical application of this type of authorization check. As a result, this type of authorization check is only suitable for a small group of users. Only slight modifications are needed to the check in the program:

```
CASE ok-code.
  WHEN 'DETA'.
    AUTHORITY-CHECK OBJECT 'Y_ZZDEMO'
      ID 'POPUP' FIELD SY-NAME.
    IF sy-subrc = 0.
      CALL SCREEN 210.
    ELSE.
      MESSAGE E999.
* You have no authorization for this function!
    ENDIF.
  ...
ENDCASE.
```

If you use this type of authorization check and enter an asterisk in the authorization field, you assign all users the necessary authorization, because the asterisk acts as a pattern character (wildcard).

3.2.16 Messages

Messages have a dual function. In almost all cases they influence program flow, mostly by relaunching the processing of the current screen program or selection screen from the start. In addition, they supply the user with a message which points out an error.

Messages are essentially specially numbered text elements. They can be identified through two fields: the message class (twenty-digit, alpha-numeric) and the message number (three-digit, numeric). For each message, an extensive long text can be entered beside the one-line short text. The message text can contain up to four & placeholder characters that are handled in a similar way to the title elements described previously. The placeholder characters in messages can also be indexed (&1 up to &4).

Creating messages

To maintain messages you use transaction SE91 or choose DEVELOPMENT | PROGRAMMING ENVIRONMENT | MESSAGES. When you select this menu option, you access the initial screen of the maintenance transaction for message classes (Figure 3.37):

In this dialog, you can create both a new message and process individual messages within a class. You click on one of two check boxes to select the object to be processed.

First, we are going to create a new message class. Enter the name of the new class to the input field. Then click on the Create button. In this case, the two check boxes in the subobjects window have no effect. You then access a second screen program (Figure 3.38), in which you enter the name of the person responsible together with a short text about the message class. Save your entries.

To access the maintenance screen for the individual messages, click on the Messages button or select the GOTO | MESSAGES menu option. There is another way to access the maintenance screen in the initial screen: enter the name of an existing message class in the MESSAGE CLASS input field. Then click on the MESSAGES check box and then click on the Change button. The third way to access the maintenance screen for individual messages is to navigate to it.

Initially the maintenance screen for individual messages is in display mode. When you double-click one of the message numbers (here 000), you can access and maintain the text of this message (*see* Figure 3.39).

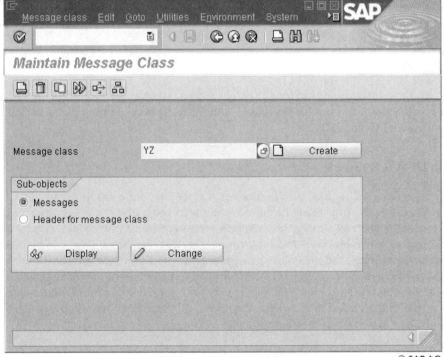

© SAP AG

Figure 3.37   Creating a message class

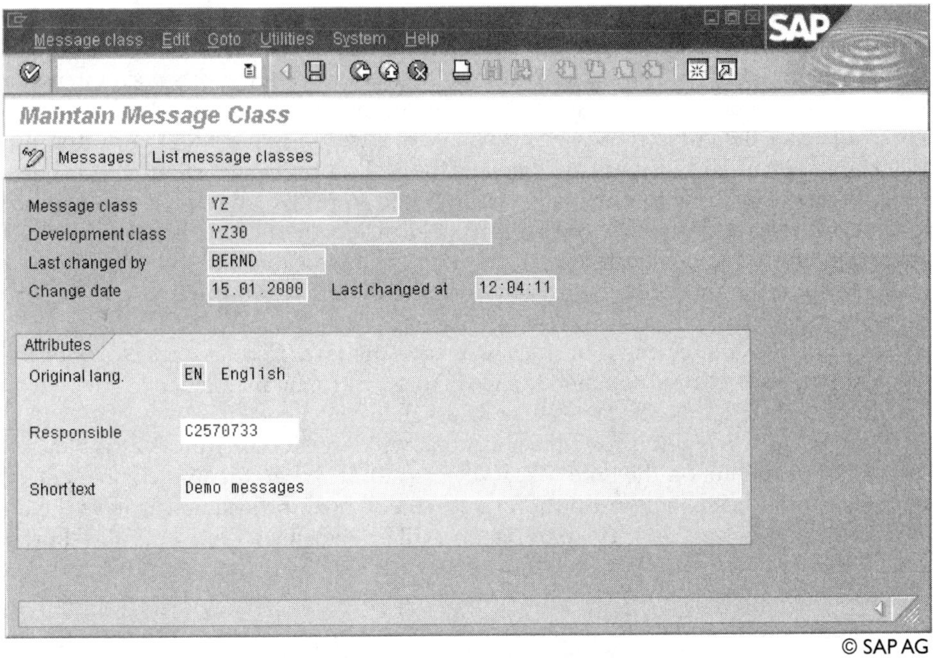

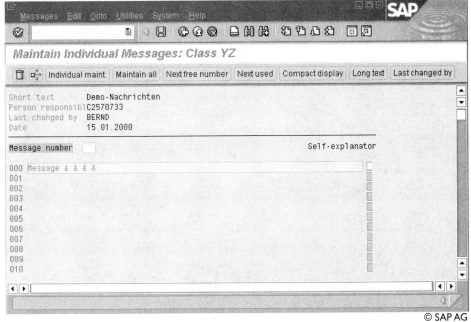

Figure 3.38   Maintenance of administration data of a message class

Figure 3.39   Maintaining an individual message

Enter the text shown in the screenshot. This message can be used as a placeholder to display any text. The SELF-EXPLANATORY flag at the end of the message defines if a long text can be entered for the message. This long text describes the errors encountered, and provides troubleshooting information. This type of long text is entered fairly frequently. First of all, save the entered message text. Then, click on the LONG TEXT button in the application toolbar. The system now displays the SAPscript Editor (Figure 3.40). You will find more details on how to use this Editor in Section 3.11, which deals with the processing of forms. At the moment, you simply need to enter the four lines visible in the screenshot. Should you require new lines, you can insert them easily by pressing the (Enter) key. For the time being, you can omit the descriptor in the first column of the screen program.

After you have entered the four lines, you save the text. To do so, select DOCUMENT | SAVE | ACTIVE VERSION from the menu, and then return to the maintenance screen for the individual messages. This completes the processing of the message.

If the message is triggered later, the short text will appear either in a status bar or in a dialog box, depending on the type of call selected for it. When the user double-clicks on the status bar or clicks on a pushbutton in the dialog box, the system displays the associated long text (Figure 3.41). The parameters will be transferred into both the short and the long text.

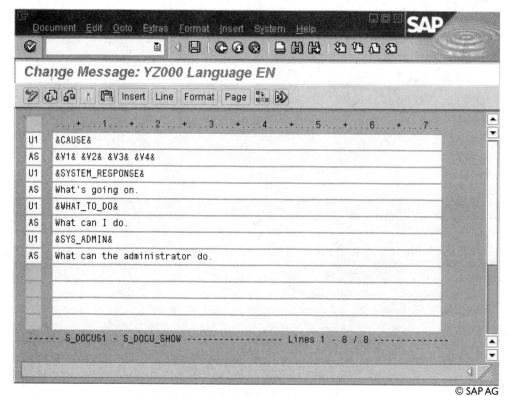

© SAP AG

Figure 3.40   Maintaining a message's long text

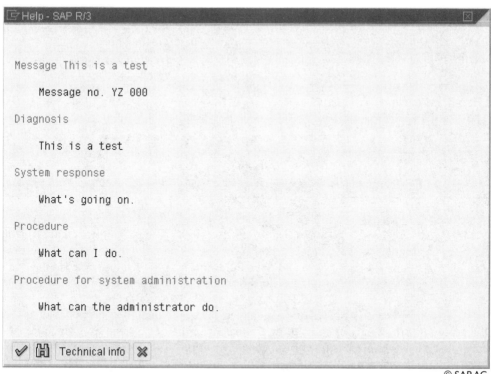

Figure 3.41   Message long text in an application

Using messages

In an application, you can use this statement to send a message:

MESSAGE ID *class* **TYPE** *type* **NUMBER** *number*.

   All three parameters must be enclosed in single quotation marks. Apart from the message class and the message number, you also have to define the message type in this statement. There are some system defaults for this type. Contrary to the message text and the message class, you do not have to maintain it. It is not an attribute of special messages, as you can for example assign a function type to the function codes. Instead, this message type is more like a code character that defines how the system is to deal with the message. The message type influences the program flow and the way that the message is displayed. Table 3.22 shows the possible message types.

   Message type E is the most frequently used type. It displays the short text of the message in the status bar and triggers repeated processing of the screen program. It is used to highlight incorrect entries in a screen program. Within dialog applications, a message is always triggered in a module or in subroutines that are called from within a module. If this module has been linked with explicitly specified fields, using the FIELD statement or a CHAIN, only these fields will become ready for input when this message triggers the reprocessing of a screen program.

Table 3.22   Message types

Type	Description	Display in	Effect
I	Info	Dialog box	Program will be continued after confirmation (user presses pushbutton or (Enter))
W	Warning	Status bar	Processing will be continued after user presses (Enter)
E	Error	Status bar	Repeated processing of the screen program
A	Abnormal end	Dialog box	Transaction will be terminated
S	Success	Status bar	Text display only

Message type W is a bit less severe in its effects. Similar to type E, it points to an error, in the status bar. However, it allows the processing of the screen program to continue after the user has pressed (Enter) to confirm the warning. Type I works in a similar fashion, but does not display the message in the status bar. Instead it displays it in its own dialog box.

Message type S only displays one message in the status bar. As it has no influence on the program flow, it only appears in the status bar of the next screen program, after the current screen program has been processed. The application usually uses S-type messages to inform the user about the successful execution of a task. They have texts like 'Record saved successfully'.

Message type A is completely different from those described above: it terminates the current transaction. This message type is used to stop all further processing tasks in the case of serious problems, such as inconsistencies in the dataset. The short text of the message is again displayed in the status bar.

If a message short text is displayed in the status bar, you can display its long text in a dialog box by simply double-clicking on the short text. Message type I also offers you a pushbutton in the dialog box.

Apart from the long form of the MESSAGE statement, there is also a short form which is slightly easier to work with. This is as follows:

MESSAGE *tnnn(kk)*.

Here, t represents the message type, nnn the number and kk the message class. The type and number have no delimiter and no quotation marks. The message class must be enclosed in oval brackets, and also stands after the message number without a delimiter. In the PROGRAM or REPORT statement, you can use this addition to set a default message class for the whole application:

... **MESSAGE-ID** *kk*.

If you do so, you do not have to enter the individual message class. Here, the message class name must not be enclosed in quotation marks. In the program, you only have to enter the message class if you want to replace the default with a different class.

If you want to replace the message placeholders with values at runtime, you have to use this addition to transfer them to the MESSAGE statement:

```
... WITH value_1 value_2 value_3 value_4.
```

There are additional options for the MESSAGE statement when it is used with function modules. There, you can use the MESSAGE statement to trigger *exceptions*. These exceptions do not always result in the events described above, such as the restarting of the screen program. Instead, they merely terminate the processing of the function module. The calling program is informed of the error condition and can decide for itself how to react. For example, it could send out the necessary message by itself. To set this up, you call the MESSAGE statement and enter the message class in the SY-MSGID system fields, the message type into SY-MSGTY, the message number into SY-MSGNO and various parameters into SY-MSGV1 to SY-MSGV4. The calling program can then access these fields.

Intercepting runtime errors

If an error occurs, many statements trigger runtime errors that terminate an application with a short dump. From Release 4, selected runtime errors can be intercepted. This enables the application to independently determine how it reacts to an error.

To intercept runtime errors in a sequence of statements, these statements must be included in a block which begins with this statement:

```
CATCH SYSTEM-EXCEPTIONS ....
```

It must end with

```
ENDCATCH.
```

The runtime errors to be intercepted must be listed in the CATCH statement's parameter list. To do so, list the particular runtime error and assign it a return code. If a runtime error occurs, the system interrupts the current processing and executes the statement after ENDCATCH instead. Before this, the return code assigned at runtime error is placed in the SY-SUBRC system variable. This procedure therefore resembles the way exceptions are handled in function modules. The CATCH-ENDCATCH blocks may be nested at any depth.

The complete syntax of the CATCH statement therefore reads:

```
CATCH SYSTEM-EXCEPTIONS {runtime_error = return_code}.
```

There are three different methods for defining runtime errors. First of all, there are error classes. An error class contains several errors, sorted by topic. If you enter the name of an error class of this kind in runtime_error, then the return code specified with return_code will be returned for all the errors in this error class if they occur. Therefore this method cannot be used to determine the actual runtime error. If you need to do so, you can enter the name of an individual runtime error in runtime_error instead. However, if you do so, none of the other errors of the same class as this runtime error will be caught. Third, you can use the OTHERS descriptor to specify all existing runtime errors.

When using the CATCH statement, you should be aware of a few constraints. Runtime errors will only be caught at the current call level. The CATCH statement has no effect on

runtime errors that occur within subroutines or function modules that are called within a
`CATCH-ENDCATCH` block. In addition, there is a set of runtime errors that can be caught
for each ABAP statement. `CATCH` will not handle other runtime errors. You can find the
runtime errors that can be caught in the online documentation for the keywords.

It is entirely possible for several return codes to match one runtime error. This can be
the case, for example, if a runtime error is contained in several error classes, or if both an
individual runtime error and the whole error class have been assigned in the `CATCH` statement. In this case, the `SY-SUBRC` system field only returns the first matching return code.

3.2.17 Lock and update concept

An SAP application is a multiuser application. This means that at a certain point in time,
several users might want to access the same record simultaneously. Read-only access
poses no problems. However, to ensure the consistency of the data, you have to prevent
several users processing a record simultaneously. That is why individual records or
whole groups of records can be protected against access from third parties in an application. In practice, a record would be locked immediately after being read and would only
be released again after having been updated in the source database. If other users
attempted to relock or overwrite a record that was already locked, their statements would
lead to an error being displayed through the `SY-SUBRC` system field.

Records are not locked and released (unlocked) directly, using special ABAP statements, but by calling automatically generated function modules. These function modules
are based on the definition of a *lock object*. This is one of the Data Dictionary objects, and it
is described in Chapter 5, Section 5.5. However, the way these function modules are
called, and the way the system evaluates the return codes, are typical of the statements
for dialog-oriented applications discussed in this section. The following extract from a
real program shows the statement for locking a group of records:

```
...
CALL FUNCTION 'ENQUEUE_EFMHICTR'
  EXPORTING
    fikrs = g_fikrs
  EXCEPTIONS
    foreign_lock = 1
    system_failure = 2.

CASE sy-subrc.
  WHEN 1.
    MESSAGE E645. ' Already locked
  WHEN 2.
    MESSAGE A523. ' System error during lock request
ENDCASE.
```

To actually write data to records, you use the statements already described in the section on working with databases (Chapter 3.2). They include `MODIFY` or `UPDATE`.

However, there are some procedures that primarily aim to improve performance and make a program easier to understand. For example, it is possible to move write processes into subroutines, and then use this addition to call them:

`... ON COMMIT.`

Subroutines called in this way will only be executed if the application calls the `COMMIT WORK` statement, which confirms the database changes. However, it is not possible to transfer parameters to the subroutine. Therefore, the data to be written must be globally available.

You can make function module calls or execution dependent on the `COMMIT WORK` statement. The function module is provided with this addition for that purpose:

`... IN UPDATE TASK.`

The function modules that have this addition must have special attributes. These attributes control the execution type. For example, very extensive updates can also be executed asynchronously to the program flow. You will find more details on using this call type for a function module in Section 3.9.

Update modules will be executed if the program processes this statement:

`COMMIT WORK.`

In the case of an implicit commit being executed automatically during each screen change, the system does not process the update modules.

3.3 The interface

Each application, regardless of whether it is a report or a dialog application, has an interface that contains the control elements for the user (menu, application toolbar, etc.). An interface groups together several *statuses*. Each status is a separate version of the interface. The different statuses have different menu structures and functions available. Within a status, the control elements are linked with function codes. Function codes are descriptors that are passed to an application and evaluated by it. To process the interface or the status, you use Menu Painter. This tool is available from the development environment main menu (DEVELOPMENT | USER INTERFACE | MENU PAINTER), from the object list in the Object Browser and through the program editor navigation function. As with other elements, you simply need to enter a status name in a program and then double-click on it. This loads Menu Painter with the selected status. The transaction code for Menu Painter is `SE41`.

An interface or status can contain the following elements:

- menu;

- icon bar;

- application toolbar;

- function key setting;

- title.

The first four elements are genuine control elements. The title plays only a passive role. There are different interface types, in some of which it is not always possible to use all elements. During interface maintenance, you can choose a *status-oriented* or *element-oriented* way of working. Status-oriented means that all the elements that form a status (menu, pushbuttons, function keys, etc.) are simultaneously available in an interface. During element-oriented work, you can simultaneously display and process the menus or the function key settings of all an interface's statuses. In addition, some elements within the interface are global elements (the function codes and title), but you can also maintain them from each status's interface.

3.3.1 The interface types

A status does not exist on its own, but is always accessed and used from a screen program or report. When creating a new status, you must therefore specify a status type. Currently, there are three basic status types, and an additional attribute.

Screen program

This status type provides a full-screen interface for normal screen programs. It contains all the control element groups already mentioned, i.e. a menu, the icon bar, the function key settings and pushbuttons. Unlike in previous Releases of the R/3 software, there is no longer any difference between the status for dialog applications and the status for lists.

Dialog box

Dialog box-type screen programs can be executed rather like a dialog box, but are not dialog boxes. They do not have a menu and can only be controlled using the function keys and pushbuttons. You must create a dialog box-type status for dialog box-type screen programs. As above, there is no longer any difference between the status for dialog applications and lists.

Context menu

You can display context menus by clicking the right mouse button. Normally, this displays a list of the function codes of the current status, which are linked with function keys. When using special controls in the screen program and object-oriented programming, you can also generate special context menus with precisely defined contents. They play no part within the usual programming models.

Interfaces for lists

Reports have an interface too. If an interface has not been specified, the system will use a default interface that contains the special function codes necessary for list processing. If you would like to set your own interface for a report, you can use a special flag to mark that the status has been reserved for a list, and not for a dialog application. Menu Painter then inserts some special, list-specific icons into the interface. This flag is available for the screen program- and dialog box-type interfaces.

3.3.2 Function codes

The term *function code* is somewhat confusing because it is used to refer to a complex element with several features. A function code is assigned to a control element (menu option, button, function key). The control element then takes on some attributes of the function code, such as the text to be displayed. When you use the control element, the function code's descriptor is passed to the application. The type of transfer is different for reports and dialog applications.

The function codes for all interface statuses are contained in a shared list. To prevent every function code from being triggered in every status, you can activate or deactivate a function code separately in each status. If the function code that is assigned to a menu option or a pushbutton is deactivated, the associated element still appears in the interface, but users cannot activate it. Deactivated elements are displayed with grey text instead of black.

The maximum length of a function code's name is 20 characters. At present only 10 characters can be maintained in Menu Painter. You can define function code descriptors to suit your own requirements. However, you should avoid using function codes that are used by the system itself. These are, for example, function codes that start with '%' or the function codes P+, P++, P- and P—.

A function code has different attributes. The most significant are the *function type, text type, text* and 'FASTPATH'. The function type defines how the system handles the function code. Table 3.23 shows the available function types. The text type and the text influence how the function text is displayed in menu options and pushbuttons. In each status, you can assign a different text to a function code. The Fastpath defines a key with which you can select the function code directly in an open pull-down menu. The easiest way to process all the attributes is in the function list.

Table 3.23   Function types

Function type	Meaning
Blank	Default, normal function code
E	Exit statement (evaluated by an AT EXIT COMMAND module)
H	Internal usage
P	Local GUI function
S	System function
T	Used to start a transaction

Standard function codes are used to terminate input in a screen program and to start its PAI section. The exit function codes operate in a similar way. They are the only ones that use the AT EXIT COMMAND addition to process PAI modules. In this case, no automatic screen program checks are carried out (i.e. for mandatory input fields). You will find more details about this in Section 3.7.

Use function type T to trigger a direct jump to another transaction. The system evaluates the function code as a descriptor to determine the transaction you want to start. Here, too, no checks are carried out. Function type S is really only of use in an application's test phase. It triggers system functions. For example, it activates the Debugging tool. Function type S uses the system function's code letter as a function code. Function type H triggers the event ON HELP REQUEST. Function type P is not processed by the screen program flow logic, but instead is processed directly by a screen program control (currently, only the tab strip). In practical applications, only the function types for normal and exit functions are of real importance.

You can define two texts for each function code. One of these texts is used in the menu and, in some cases, for labelling function keys and pushbuttons. The other text is only used for pushbuttons. It appears in a separate small dialog box if the user positions the mouse pointer over the button for a short while. Apart from using a text, you can also define an icon and an optional additional text for function codes that have been assigned to a button.

All these settings are static. If required, you can also modify a function code's text dynamically, at runtime. To do so, you first have to change the function code's text type. You then only see a single input field, in which you enter the name of a data field. This data field must contain the description of the function code at runtime.

In a status you can define up to 35 pushbuttons. However, there will be no room for them all in the application toolbar, if they are filled with text. Therefore, you can represent them as icons, which enables you to display icons in the pushbuttons instead of text.

If a dynamic text has been specified for a pushbutton, the associated data field can also contain the identifier for an icon at runtime. This icon will then appear instead of, or together with, the actual pushbutton text. This dynamic assignment of icons has one disadvantage: the system only evaluates the icon identifier when displaying the pushbutton, and not when displaying menu options. Therefore, if you define that a function code containing a dynamic text should be used both in the menu and in the application toolbar, this overrides any icon you may have assigned: the icon will only be correctly displayed in the pushbutton.

You can also use the keyboard to operate the actual menu. To speed up selection, individual letters in the menu options are marked with an underscore. You can select a menu option by pressing the key combination (ALT) + 'character key', where 'character key' is the letter marked with an underscore in the menu option. In Menu Painter you can use the Fastpath function to define which letters are to be used for the shortcuts in each menu.

3.3.3 Using Menu Painter

You trigger the function codes by clicking on one of the interface control elements. You can assign the control elements to one of four groups:

1. menu

2 application toolbar

3. icon bar

4. function keys.

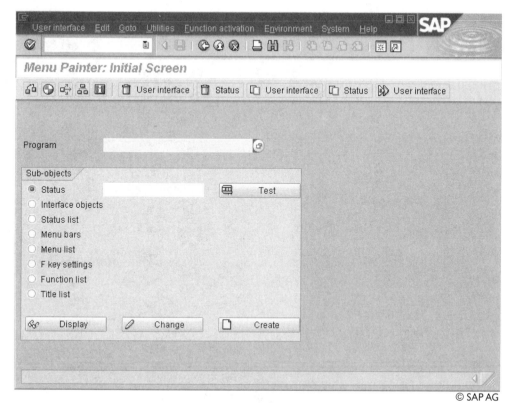

© SAP AG

Figure 3.42   Menu Painter initial screen

The contents of the icon bar are predefined, so you cannot modify them. However, you can activate or deactivate all the icons, apart from the (Enter) key, as required. To do this, you assign function codes to special function keys or assign them directly to the icons. The actual method depends on which SAP release you are using.

You can call Menu Painter in different ways. The initial screen of transaction SE41 (Figure 3.42) is similar to the interface of other maintenance programs in the development environment:

In an input field, you enter the name of the program whose interface you want to process. You select the actual interface element from a range of selection fields. The status is the only one of these elements that has several attributes, which is why you also have to enter its name if you want to jump directly to a particular status. You activate the actual action (display, change, create) by clicking on a pushbutton in the screen program.

If you are in the Repository Browser and want to create the status, you have two options. The first option is to position the cursor on the program name in an application's object list and call the Create function. In a dialog box window (Figure 3.43) click in a selection box to select the element you want to create. Enter the name of the status you want to create in the input field next to the selection box, and then activate the Create function again in the dialog box.

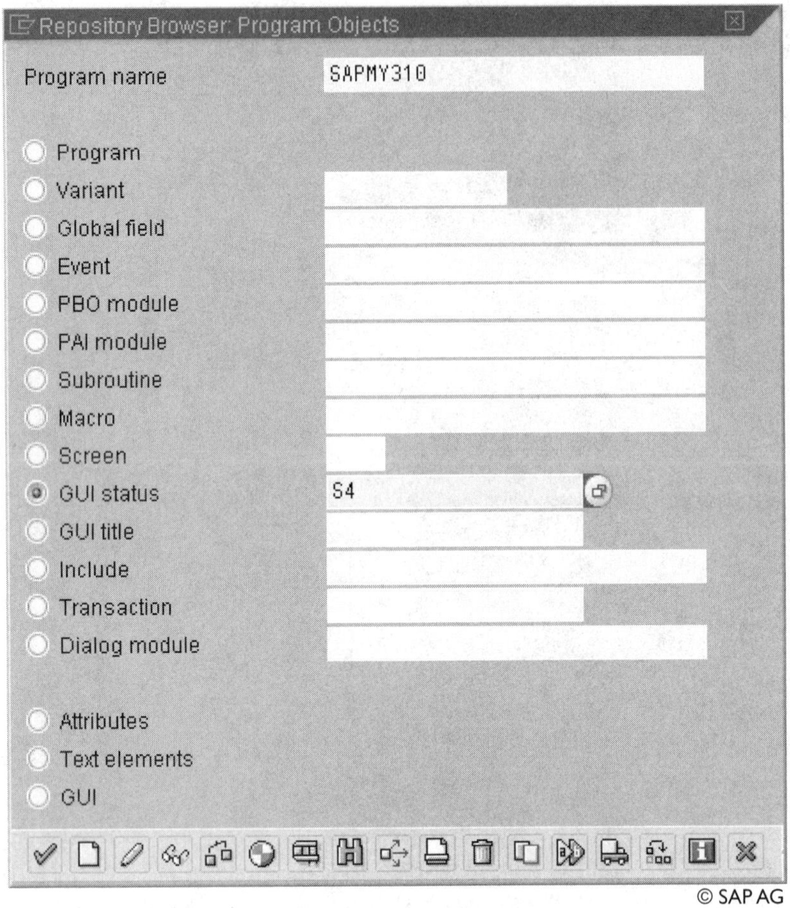

© SAP AG

Figure 3.43   Creating a status from the Repository Browser

If at least one status exists already, the object list contains a GUI status entry. If you position the cursor on this entry before calling the Create function, the selection dialog box does not appear. Instead, you will see a smaller dialog box (Figure 3.44) where you enter the name of the new status.

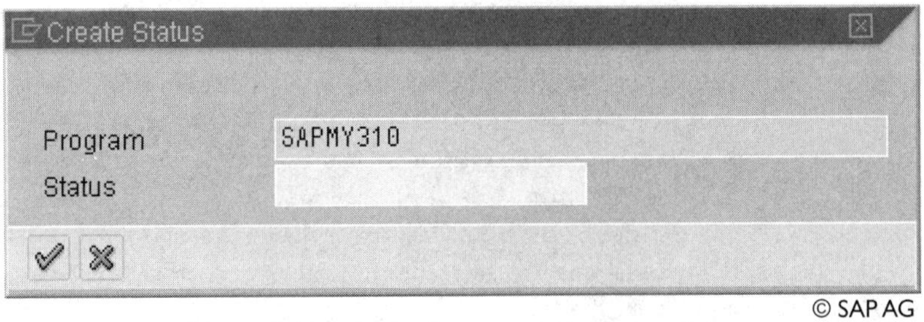

© SAP AG

Figure 3.44   Assigning a name to a new status

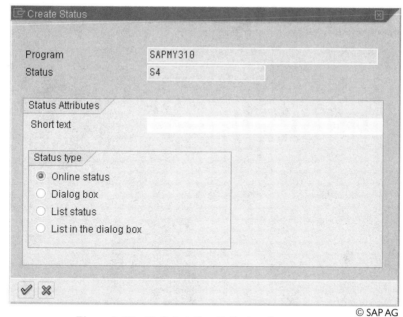

© SAP AG

Figure 3.45   Defining the attributes of a status

The second option is to use the development environment's navigation function. Then simply double-click to generate a status.

No matter what type of entry you use, a second dialog box window (Figure 3.45) appears. In it the system prompts you to enter a short text and to define the status type.

After you click the OK button to confirm this dialog box, you will finally access the actual Menu Painter maintenance interface, as shown in Figure 3.46:

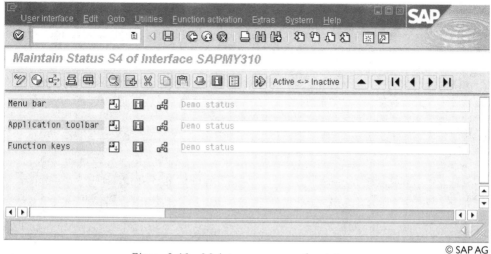

© SAP AG

Figure 3.46   Maintenance screen for statuses

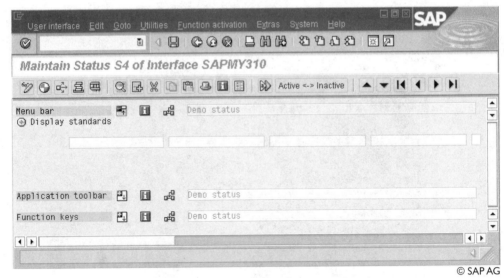

Figure 3.47   Status with an empty menu area

You can access this screen program from every point in the application by selecting the GOTO | CURRENT status menu option or by pressing function key (F6). You can display and hide the different individual subelements so you can clearly see what is happening in the screen. To open a subarea, click on the square icon with the green plus symbol with the mouse. Figure 3.47 shows you the open work area for menus.

In the final version of the application, the R/3 System automatically adds the two entries SYSTEM and HELP to the menu. You cannot modify the contents of these two pull-down menus.

Menus

A newly created status does not contain any menu options at first. All the input fields are empty. By clicking on the circular icon with the green plus symbol and the label 'Display standards', you can display the menu setup that is recommended for dialog applications. This default complies with the SAP style guide. If possible, you should always use the recommended menu setup as a guide when developing your own programs. Figure 3.48 shows Menu Painter with the inserted menu options and an open pull-down menu. You can open and close pull-down menus by double-clicking on the name of the submenu concerned.

In this view you see three different types of input field. The first line of the work area contains the pull-down menu entries. Each of the fields displayed here contains the name of one of these menus. This entry is only a descriptor. You cannot use these entries to activate a function code. You can modify the descriptors as required. You must modify the first entry, <OBJECT>, shown here. The character strings enclosed in

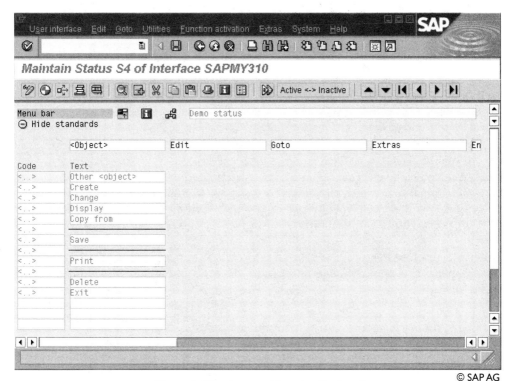

Figure 3.48   Status with menu displayed

pointed brackets are placeholders which you must replace with actual data. A dialog application usually references a business management object, such as an invoice or an order. According to the SAP Style Guide, the first pull-down menu must contain the basic functions used to process an object, as you can see in the pull-down menu displayed above. That is why you must select this submenu's description to suit the object to be processed. If necessary, you can insert additional pull-down menus. To do this, choose EDIT | INSERT | ENTRY from the menu.

Underneath the descriptor you can display the associated menu. In the Menu Painter, this type of menu consists of a table with two columns. In the first column, you enter the function code descriptor. In the second, you enter the menu option text. When you insert the template, the system adds some menu options, but does not assign a function code. The character string <..> for the function code is a placeholder. This function code, and therefore all the menu options with this function code, will not appear in the menu in the final version of the application. You can now activate the menu options that are already displayed by entering a real function code. Alternatively, you can create and add your own function codes with your own text. If you enter a function code that does not yet exist in the function list, the system creates it automatically. If you are using one function code in several statuses, you can assign different texts to it in each status.

Because the Menu Painter interface is also a screen program, the entries are not evaluated until the system executes the PAI part of the current screen program, in this case the Menu Painter. This happens after you press (Enter), choose a menu option or press a function key. Once you do this, any existing descriptions in the function list are added to all the newly created function codes. If a new function code does not have a description yet, the Menu Painter prompts you to enter the appropriate text in a dialog box.

Choose EDIT | INSERT | SEPARATOR LINE from the menu to insert a horizontal separator line in a pull-down menu. If a menu option is designed to activate a subordinate pull-down menu instead of a function code, the function code column remains empty. You simply enter the new menu description in the second column. Double-click on this entry to open the new menu. When the program is running, the entries in pull-down menus that reference other menus are highlighted with a small triangle that points to the right. You can delete menu elements by choosing EDIT | ENTRY | DELETE from the menu, by clicking an icon in the application toolbar or by pressing the key combination (Ctrl) + (F9).

Other important menu options you use to process a menu option are the functions used to insert new menu elements (*see* Table 3.24). You will find all of them in the EDIT | INSERT menu.

Table 3.24   Menu options for inserting new menu elements

Function	Description
Entry	Inserts a new entry in front of the current cursor position
Separator line	Inserts a separator line in front of the cursor position
Include menu	Dynamically inserts a menu from another status
Menu with dynamic text	Inserts a pull-down menu whose text can be set dynamically
Function with dynamic text	Inserts a menu option whose text can be set dynamically

Application toolbar

Underneath the menu's work area, you see the area where you maintain pushbuttons (Figure 3.49). In the screen program's application toolbar, pushbuttons appear either as a button with text or as an icon.

To transfer an entry into the status's application toolbar, enter that entry's function code in one of the input fields. In this example, a pushbutton appears in the application toolbar, with the text that was assigned to the function code. Alternatively, you can assign an icon. The simplest way of doing this is by maintaining the function list. This procedure is described in its own section. Please note that you can only create pushbuttons for function codes that have been linked with a function key.

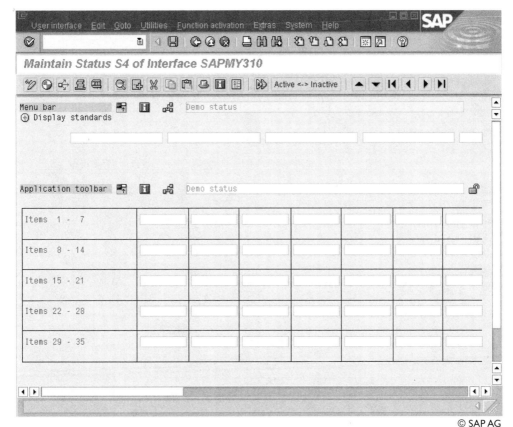

Figure 3.49   Status with open application toolbar

Function keys

Function keys have been provided to make it faster and easier to select important functions. In SAP's terminology, the term function key refers not only to the special function keys on the keyboard (mostly (F1) to (F12)), but to any key that can trigger a function code. These may be single keys (i.e. function keys (F1) to (F12) on the keyboard) or key combinations (i.e. control keys + alphanumeric keys) that can be used to directly trigger function codes.

The function keys are divided into four groups. The first group contains function keys with a system-wide, predefined meaning. These keys ((F1), (F4) and (F10)) are recognized and evaluated by the system. Therefore they do not require a function code and are always active.

The second group contains keys that correspond to specific icons in the icon bar. The keys in this group are also designed to trigger system-wide, uniform functions. However, if you want them to do so, you have to assign a function code and implement the real functions. The assignment of icons to keys is predefined. This is why the Menu Painter does not provide specific function keys for separate processing. Instead, it provides an

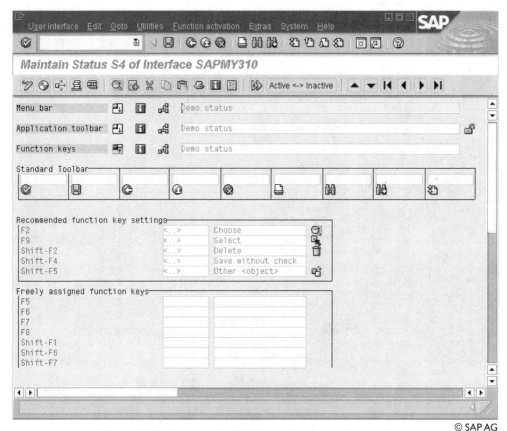

Figure 3.50   Status with fields for maintaining function keys

additional icon bar that you can use to process hard-coded functions that you cannot modify. In this icon bar, the functions are assigned a function code. Therefore this function code is also immediately assigned to one of the hard-coded keys. You activate these function keys by assigning a function code to the corresponding icon (see also Figure 3.50). When you do this, use the input help to ensure that you pick the correct function codes from those available.

Table 3.25 shows the keys in the two groups mentioned above and their usual assignments.

The third group contains function keys for which SAP recommends a particular use, such as deleting or selecting data. The function code is assigned directly to each of these function keys. There is no space in the icon bar for these function keys. However, some of the keys have a predefined icon that appears in the application toolbar if the function code has been assigned to a pushbutton.

The last group contains function keys that you can use anywhere. You process these keys in the same way as the function keys in the third group. A further 36 function keys are provided in this group. When you click the right-hand mouse button in the final version of the application, a menu is displayed in a dialog box. In it, the available function keys are displayed. To select them, click on them with the mouse.

Table 3.25   Function keys with their predefined meaning

Function key	Icon	Meaning	Function code required
F1	Question mark	Context-sensitive help	No
F3	Green arrow	Back	Yes
F4	Magnifying glass	Input help	No
F10, ALT	No icon	Activate menu bar	No
F11	Yellow folder icon	Save	Yes
F12	Red cross	Cancel	Yes
F15	Yellow arrow	Exit	Yes
F21, Ctrl PgUp	Double arrow pointing upwards	Back to the first page	Sometimes
F22, PgUp	Single arrow pointing upwards	Back one page	Sometimes
F23, PgDn	Single arrow pointing downwards	Forward one page	Sometimes
F24, Ctrl PgDn	Double arrow pointing downwards	Forward to the last page	Sometimes

You process all the function keys that can, or must, be provided with a function code in the same way as menu options. When you assign function codes, you should ensure that you only use those function codes that are also available in the function key menu. Users should always be able to control an entire application by using the menu.

You can use the default settings to automatically assign function codes to some of the function keys. A large number of function codes are used that are evaluated by the system itself, especially in the statuses for lists. Although you can change these default settings, this would only have the disadvantage that users would find it harder to process lists.

Function list

The maintenance screen described above is the core of Menu Painter. In addition to this maintenance screen, the *function list* is of crucial importance. You use these two maintenance screens to execute almost all tasks when you maintain the interface. To access the function list, choose GOTO | OBJECT LISTS | FUNCTION LIST from the menu. Figure 3.51 shows the function list.

The list contains all the function codes used in the different statuses of the interface, and shows all the function code attributes. If one function code has several text entries, you will also see several rows in this table containing lines of text.

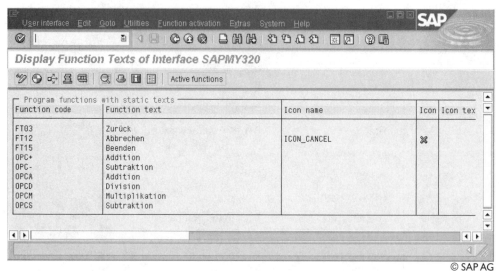

© SAP AG

Figure 3.51   List of function codes

As you already know, function codes can contain both static and dynamic text. If the function code contains dynamic text, you cannot assign an icon to the function code. The function list therefore consists of two parts. The first part displays the function codes that contain static text, and the second displays those that contain dynamic text.

You can maintain all of a function code's attributes in a dialog box. You activate this dialog box by double-clicking on the relevant function code line. Figure 3.52 shows this dialog box.

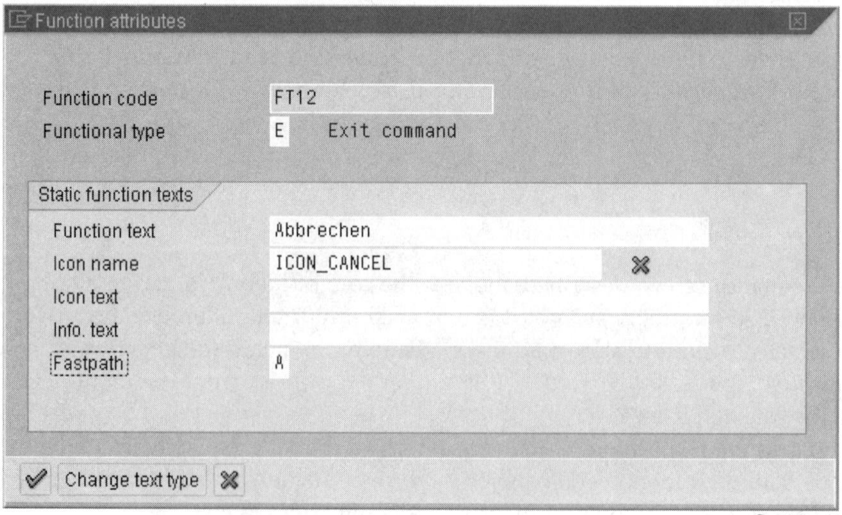

© SAP AG

Figure 3.52   Maintaining function code attributes

You use three input fields in this dialog box to maintain the text entries. The FUNC-TION TEXT field contains the menu option text. This text also appears in the pushbutton if the function code has not had an icon assigned to it. In the ICON TEXT field, you maintain an optional text which appears in the pushbutton together with the icon. The Info text field also contains an optional text which appears in a small yellow window when you hold the mouse pointer over a pushbutton. In the Fastpath field, you enter a keyboard character that you can then use as a shortcut to call the function in an open pull-down menu.

The role of the function types has already been described. Input help is available because the values for this field are predefined (Figure 3.53).

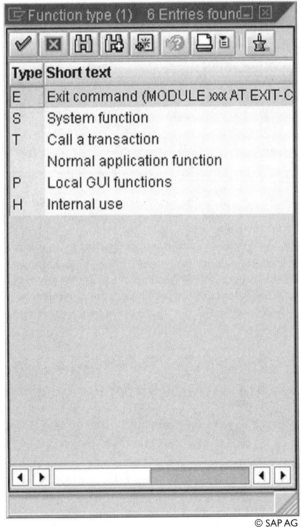

Figure 3.53   Input help for function types

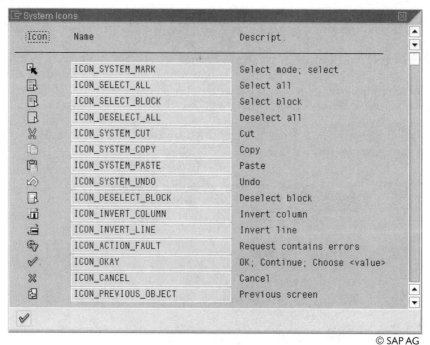

© SAP AG

Figure 3.54   Input help for icons

If you want to assign an icon to the function code, you should use the corresponding input help (Figure 3.54). The number of icons available, and to some extent their appearance, depends on which R/3 Release you are using.

You use the CHANGE TEXT TYPE pushbutton in the Attributes dialog box to toggle between static and dynamic text assignment. When you click this pushbutton, the structure of the dialog box changes. This is because, for function codes whose text is assigned dynamically, you can only maintain the field name for text transfer and the function type (Figure 3.55).

This dialog box also contains a button that you can click to change the text type. Here, of course, it changes from dynamic to static text assignment.

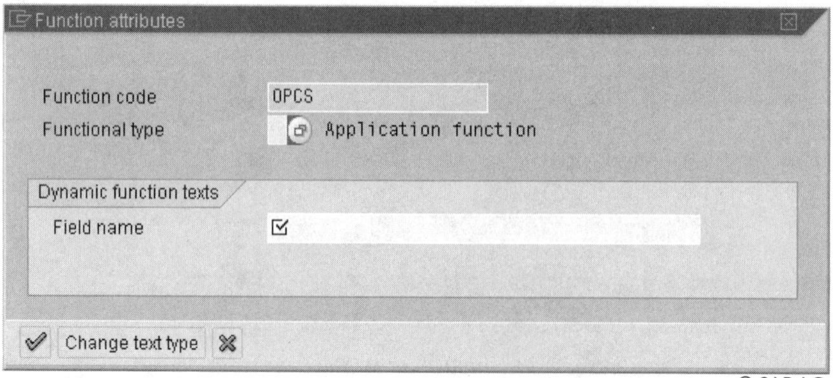

© SAP AG

Figure 3.55   Attributes dialog box for function codes with dynamic text entry

Templates

The various application types (dialog application, report) operate in different ways. In addition to this, there are reports that have special functions. An example is interactive reports with a hierarchical display (i.e. Repository Browser). Each of these applications has particular functions (i.e. list printing, opening nodes in a hierarchy display or browsing in the output list), which the runtime system should evaluate directly. They should not be evaluated by an application that you have written yourself. You must activate predefined function codes for these functions. To make your work easier, you therefore have the option of entering predefined function codes in your status. To do this, select the EXTRAS | ADJUST TEMPLATES menu option (Figure 3.56).

In this dialog box, you can either choose a predefined status or reference an existing status in any other program.

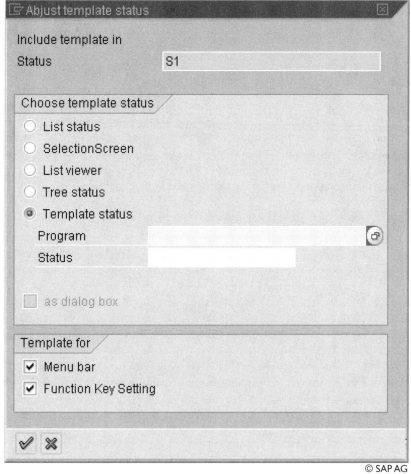

© SAP AG

Figure 3.56   Selecting the template for the status

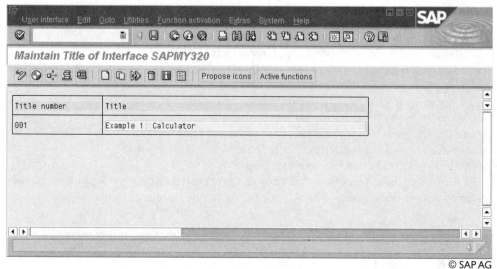

Figure 3.57   Title bar

Title list

A title list exists alongside the actual interface. This is why the Repository Browser has a separate category called *GUI Title*. A title is one line of text that can be placed in a window's title line at program runtime. One interface may contain several titles. They are identified by their ten-character descriptor. When you maintain an interface, you can choose GOTO | OBJECT LISTS | TITLE LIST from the menu to switch to the title maintenance functions. Figure 3.57 gives you an impression of what the maintenance interface looks like.

3.3.4 The interface for lists

For reports, the R/3 System automatically provides an interface with its own statuses. Depending on the report's status (selection screen processing, list output), the system automatically sets an appropriate status unless you use your own status. The system automatically evaluates the function codes that are generated in the various default statuses. Tables 3.26 to 3.28 show all the function codes processed by the system, listed by their logical function type. Not all these function codes are available in all statuses. The function codes are first evaluated by the system. The system processes point-in-time statements for some function codes, which then allow you to make an individual evaluation. You will find more details about transferring and evaluating function codes in reports in Section 3.4.3.

Table 3.26   Function codes for list processing: jumping to other program parts

Function code	Function	Designated function key
%CH	Header maintenance	
%EX	Exit	F15
%GD	Graphic	
%PC	Save the list on front end system	
%SC	Search for character string	
%SL	Jump to the Office menu	
%ST	Reporting hierarchy	
BACK	Back	F3
FSET	Values	
RSET	Variants	
LEAV	Leave	
ONLI	Program start (from the selection screen)	
RW	Back one list step	F12

Table 3.27   Function codes for list processing: moving around in the list

Function code	Function	Designated function key	Point-in-time statement
P	First page		
P+	Forward one page	F23	
P++	Jump to the end of the list	F24	
P-	Back one page	F22	
P—	Jump to the start of the list	F21	
PFnn	Function key Fnn pressed (SAP abbreviates 'function key' to 'PF')	Fn	AT PFnn
PICK	Line selected	F2	AT LINE SELECTION
PL++	Jump to the last line of the current section		
PL+n	Jump n lines forward		
PL—	Jump to the first line of the current section		
PL-n	Jump n lines backwards		

Table 3.27   Continued

Function code	Function	Designated function key	Point-in-time statement
PP+(n)	Jump one (n) section(s) forward		
PP++	Jump to the start of the last page		
PP-(n)	Jump one (n) section(s) forward		
PP—	Jump to the start of the list		
PPn	Jump to the start of section n		
PRI	Print list	F13	
PS++	Jump to the last column of the list		
PS+n	Jump n columns to the right		
PS—	Jump to the first column of the list		
PS-n	Jump n columns to the left		
PSnn	Jump to column n		

Table 3.28   Function codes for list processing: selection screen

Function code	Function	Designated function key
ALLS	All selections	Ctrl + B
DBAC	Back	
DCAN	Cancel	
DELA	Delete entire selection	
DELS	Delete an entry in the selection	F14, Ctrl +14
DSAV	Accept	
DYNS	Dynamic selection	F16
E	Back	F3
ECAN	Cancel	F12
ENDE	End	F15, Ctrl + 15
FC01	User function 1	F19
FC02	User function 2	F20
FEWS	Selected selections	Ctrl + D
FSET	Complex limit	

Table 3.28   Continued

Function code	Function	Designated function key
GET	Get variant	F17
GOON	Continue	
JOBS	Set in job	
NFIE	Select new field	
ONLI	Execute	F8
OPTI	Selection options	F2
PRIN	Execute + print	F13, Ctrl + 13
SAVE	Save as variant	
SCRH	Help selection screen	
SJOB	Execute in the background	F9
SPOS	Save as variant	F11
VATT	Attributes	
VBAC	Back	

Before you can use your own functions in reports, you must include them in a status. When you run the report, you must then set the status by using the SET PF-STATUS statement. If you have to set a new status for a report, you must assign it to the report. To do this, create a new status with Menu Painter and select a suitable template. You can then complete the status with your own function codes. If necessary, you can also delete existing function codes to prevent the end user from executing certain functions. However, when you do this you must ensure that the basic list of processing functions (scrolling, exit) are safeguarded at all times.

3.3.5   Title and interface statements

Setting the interface

In almost all cases, a screen program must be linked with an interface's status before the user can trigger program activities. You use the following statement to do this:

`SET PF-STATUS` *status*.

The status name can be up to 20 characters long. It must be written in capitals and enclosed in inverted commas. Once a status has been set, it remains active until you set a new status or you use this statement to call a default status:

`SET PF-STATUS SPACE`.

This default status is also active if you do not set a status. You can change a status as often as required in one application, even within the same screen program. The name of each current status is displayed in the SY-PFKEY system field.

Occasionally you may have to temporarily deactivate some of the function codes in a status. If, for example, a screen program allows users to browse through a dataset, record by record, using the Next page and Previous page functions, it would be a good idea to switch off one of these two functions at the start or at the end of the dataset. Also, if authorizations for special functions (i.e. delete) are missing, you should deactivate them to ensure that unauthorized users are not even able to access them. Of course, you could use various different statuses to solve this problem, but this may force you to spend more time and energy in programming and administration. You can, therefore, deactivate function codes in a status at runtime, without having to change the entire status. The menu options of the deactivated function codes still appear in the menu, but are now shown in grey and users can no longer select them.

You use the SET PF-STATUS statement's EXCLUDING parameter to deactivate function codes. This addition can be followed by a single function code or an internal table that can contain any number of function codes. This table must have the following structure:

```
DATA: BEGIN OF FCODE_TAB OCCURS 5,
  FCODE LIKE SY-UCOMM,
END OF FCODE_TAB.
```

These are examples of how to call the extended statement:

```
SET PF-STATUS 'STAT1' EXCLUDING 'FNC1'.
```

and

```
REFRESH FCODE_TAB.
FCODE_TAB-FCODE = 'FNC1'.
APPEND FCODE_TAB.
FCODE_TAB-FCODE = 'FNC2'.
APPEND FCODE_TAB.
SET PF-STATUS 'STAT1' EXCLUDING FCODE_TAB.
```

In the last example, you must create the internal FCODE_TAB table in the module pool's global data. A status is usually set at the PBO time point. In rare cases, it may be a good idea to set a new status or modify an existing status in the PAI part, depending on the current function code. You should only do this in exceptional cases because it has an impact on the clarity of the data.

Setting the title

Each window has a title bar. This title is also set at the PBO time point. The title is set with the following statement:

```
SET TITLEBAR title.
```

You enter the title here with a three-character identifier. In the program, you must enclose the identifier in inverted commas. This is why it can easily be mistaken for a direct value. If no title is present when a statement is being processed, the system will use a default.

You maintain these titles in Menu Painter. However, when you are programming the source code, it is easier to use the navigation function to call the tool used to maintain the title. To do this, you must first code the correct descriptor and then double-click on this descriptor.

A title can contain up to nine placeholders for parameters. These placeholders consist of the following: only the character &, or the character & and a sequential number from 1 to 9. When you set the title, use the `WITH` addition to pass the values that are to be inserted.

SET TITLEBAR *title* **WITH** *parameter_1 ... parameter_9*.

Numbered placeholders are replaced with the parameter at the corresponding place in the statement. However, placeholders without numbers are assigned sequentially to the `SET` statement's parameters, starting from the left. If no placeholder is available for a parameter, it is filled with a blank. If the title is to contain a & character, you must enter this twice when you maintain the title (`&&`).

The system not only displays the final title in the window, but also in the `SY-TITLE` system field.

3.4   Default reports

The online programs described above have enabled you to try out some ABAP statements. Although you have already had an opportunity to read a database table, these examples are still not complete reports in the real sense. In the R/3 System, the term report describes a special program type with a precisely defined task. Reports are designed to read, process and display data from one or more tables. The ABAP programming language was not designed as a universal language, but as a tool for developing the R/3 System. That is why it contains some statements whose functions have been tailored to meet the requirements of list programming. The effective use of these statements, and the support for list generation provided by the internal logic of the R/3 System, naturally require a programming method that specifically complies with the characteristics of that internal logic. Now that previous sections have introduced some of the globally significant statements, the next section will deal with the actual requirements of report programming, and the statements you will require to implement it. We shall continue to follow the format of this book which is to first discuss the concepts and relationships of the ABAP programming language. Therefore, this section begins with a description of the statements that will help you understand the structure and working methods of a report. At the end of this section, you will find a list of additional statements which, although helpful, are not absolutely necessary for a report's functions.

The R/3 System and the ABAP programming language are undergoing continued development. As part of this, reports, which originally were not capable of dialog, have been updated by the addition of some very specialized statements. These statements allow programmers to identify some of a user's actions (i.e. pressing function keys) within a report and to respond by providing the user with individual program functions. As a result, reports are now interactive to some extent. This is why reports are often divided into non-interactive (default) reports and interactive reports. Although interactive reports are merely a special form of non-interactive reports, they are described in a separate section. This is because new statements have been added to them and the programming method has changed as a result.

3.4.1 Formatting data

Usually intermediate headers and subtotals are used to structure large-scale lists. It often happens that one list receives data that flows into it from several tables, which are linked together by key fields. In some situations, you may have to carry out different actions with this data, depending on each record or record group. ABAP provides some functions that help you program typical data formatting functions quickly and easily.

Forming groups

You use a LOOP to process an internal table or an extract dataset (which will be described in Section 3.5). When you do so, you can make program activities dependent on changes to the contents of a table field. However, you cannot use the LOOP statement's WHERE addition for this purpose. The statements described in this subsection are not restricted to reports. You could also use them in dialog applications. However, you will have to use these statements in dialog applications on some rare occasions and for this reason, they are described here.

Different records, in which one or several fields have a constant value, are gathered into groups. Statements are executed that apply to all records in a group. You can execute group-specific program parts before and after a group. You use the following statements to carry out group-specific processing:

AT NEW *field.*

. . .

ENDAT.

or

AT END OF *field.*

. . .

ENDAT.

The statements within the AT-ENDAT block are executed if the specified field, or a field that is positioned further to the left in the structure, changes its value. Here, you can use the NEW or END OF options to define whether the statement block is to be executed when the system reads the first or last record of a corresponding group. The LOOP statement recognizes the name of the table to be processed. That is why you only need to code the actual field names (without a table name) in the AT statements in the LOOP. Therefore you can only apply the AT statement to the table named in the LOOP statement. The following statements work independently of field names:

AT FIRST.

. . .

ENDAT.

  and

AT LAST.

. . .

ENDAT.

They allow you to execute statements immediately at the start of the first, or after the end of the last, LOOP run.

Although these group-forming statements have a similar syntax to point-in-time statements, they are not in fact point-in-time statements (which will be described in Section 3.5). They do not create logical jump targets for the internal control logic, to which you can jump at a particular point in time. They merely act as a symbol for more complex operations. You could create the same effect as these statements by using an IF statement to carry out an interim save on a record and comparing it with the current record. The statements for forming groups are therefore not called with the control logic, but are integrated into the sequential flow of the statements within the LOOP. You must take this into account when you position the statements in relationship to output instructions. You should also note that you may well have to sort the dataset if you do not use automatically sorted tables. The statements used to form groups can only work correctly if all the records that are to appear in a group in the list are also read sequentially.

The descriptions of the two programs below include more details on the statements used to form groups and their attributes. The first program outputs all the records for an item of turnover statistics information, and creates a subgroup of records for each employee. In this case, you must enter the data required for this operation directly in the internal table. In practice this data would, of course, be read from a database table.

```
REPORT yz334010.

* Internal table for demo
DATA: BEGIN OF sales OCCURS 10,
  name(20),
  date TYPE d,
  turnover TYPE i,
END OF sales.

* Fill the table with 6 records
sales-name = 'SMITH'.
sales-date = '19950703'.
sales-turnover = 300.
APPEND sales.
```

```
sales-name = 'SMITH'.
sales-date = '19950703'.
sales-turnover = 200.
APPEND sales.

sales-name = 'SMITH'.
sales-date = '19950704'.
sales-turnover = 100.
APPEND sales.

sales-name = 'JONES'.
sales-date = '19950704'.
sales-turnover = 110.
APPEND sales.

sales-name = 'JONES'.
sales-date = '19950704'.
sales-turnover = 220.
APPEND sales.

sales-name = 'JONES'.
sales-date = '19950705'.
sales-turnover = 330.
APPEND sales.

* Loop through internal table
LOOP AT sales.

*   Output a header in the first loop run
  AT FIRST.
    WRITE: / 'date', 19 'Turnover', / .
  ENDAT.

*   Intermediate header if a new name occurs
  AT NEW name.
    WRITE: / sales-name.
    WRITE: / '============================='.
  ENDAT.

*   Output a record
  WRITE: /(10) sales-date, sales-turnover.
```

```
*    Output sub-total
   AT END OF name.
     SUM.
     WRITE: / '=============================='.
     WRITE: / 'Sub-total:', 12 sales-turnover, /.
   ENDAT.

*    In the last loop run, final total
   AT LAST.
     SUM.
     WRITE: /, /, 'Total:' , 12 sales-turnover.
     WRITE: /, /10 '*** END ***'.
   ENDAT.

ENDLOOP.
```

The demo program processes the internal table that you previously created and filled with data in a loop. In the first loop run, called AT FIRST, the application generates a modest table header. This is only used to demonstrate the AT FIRST statement. In complete reports, the table and page headers are generated in a different way. After the AT FIRST statement, AT NEW NAME evaluates any group change that may have occurred and generates an intermediate header that consists of the sales person's name. After that, the system can output the contents of the record that you require.

You must ensure that the AT and WRITE statements are in the correct sequence. The intermediate header must be generated before the actual record is output. If the AT FIRST and WRITE statements in the example shown above were swapped round, the record would appear first in the list, followed by the intermediate header.

A new statement, SUM, appears in the AT END OF statement. This statement adds together all the numerical fields of all the records in each particular group and provides them for use in the table's header line. After the SUM statement, the sales-turnover field therefore contains the total for all sales made by a particular sales person. The AT END OF statement also depends on the sequence of the statements in the program. This statement may only be positioned after the record output statement. Figure 3.58 shows the list created by the program.

If the field contents change, it is not only the field named in the AT statement, but also all fields to the left of it, that trigger a group change. You can test this in the first demo program for forming groups, by grouping the data according to the DATE field instead of the NAME field. Although the date in the third and fourth record is the same, the NAME field triggers a group change because it is now further to the left in the data structure. For this reason, both the structure and sorting of the internal table must be tailored to suit the analysis you require. This is particularly important if you want to interlace different AT statements. Here is another short example: you want to sort the data by their names and group records that have the same date. The listing below only shows the new LOOP. You do not need to modify the rest of the program. You can therefore copy YZ334010 and then make a few modifications to the LOOP statement:

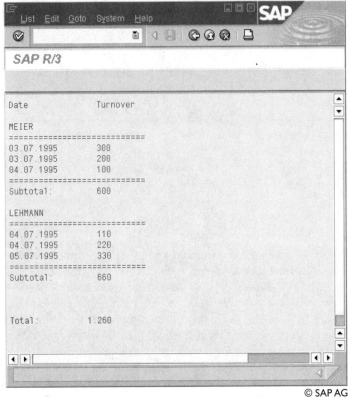

Figure 3.58   Output from the YZ334010 demo program

```
REPORT YZ334020.
...
LOOP AT sales.
  AT NEW date.
    AT NEW name.
      WRITE: / sales-name.
      WRITE: / '==============================='.
    ENDAT.
  ENDAT.

  AT END OF date.
    SUM.
    WRITE: /(10) sales-date, sales-turnover.
    AT END OF name.
      SUM.
      WRITE: / '==============================='.
      WRITE: / 'Total:', 12 sales-turnover, /.
    ENDAT.
  ENDAT.

ENDLOOP.
```

The outer AT statements must refer to the field with the lowest value. In this case, this is the DATE field, so that you can identify each group change. Within the date group change function itself, the system can determine whether there has also been an additional group change in the NAME field. If you were to use the name as the criterion for a group change in the outer AT statement, the system would only check for a date change if the name changed. In this case, therefore, the system would not group the records with identical dates.

Individual records are not output because only one summary record is displayed for each date. The WRITE statement that follows the AT END OF date statement does not refer to an actual record in the table. Instead, the program uses the header that is processed by the SUM statement. However, because the SUM statement only processes numerical fields, the contents of the date field are correct. Figure 3.59 shows the output from the modified program.

This example is of special interest for two reasons: the nested AT statements and the way the SUM statement is used. After the AT END OF date statement it summarizes all sales that took place on a specific date, without you having to enter any additional data. It also takes all the sales made by a particular sales person into account after the AT END OF NAME statement. The SUM statement is closely related to the AT statement. This example also indirectly illustrates that SUM is a very complex statement and that it can only tell which records are to be summarized from the source code and the AT statements.

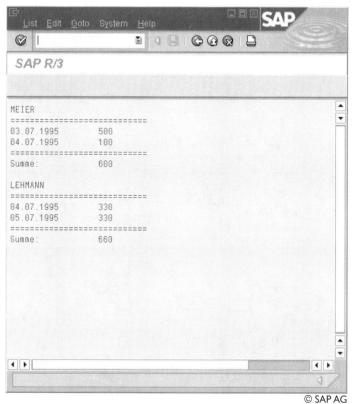

Figure 3.59   List with summarized records

EXTRACT datasets

It often happens that data from several tables is output in a report. In such cases, the individual output lines frequently appear in a different sequence than was predefined in the primary keys of these tables. Here is another (slightly simplified) real-life example of this: all invoices from a particular period are to be displayed in a list, containing the invoice headers and all individual items, sorted according to supplier and invoice number. You want the list to contain an intermediate header and subtotals for each supplier and invoice. At this point, it is still relatively easy to determine what data is required. First, the program searches the document header table for invoices that occur in the selected period. The invoice number is used to find the individual invoice line items, and the creditor number is used to find the supplier information. In the list, the supplier is used as the highest level sorting criterion, but the data structure predefines the invoice number as the main attribute. For this reason, you cannot output the selected list immediately; you must first use an internal table to process it. You could use the following process, formulated as pseudo-code:

```
DATA: ITAB OCCURS 1000,
   VENDORNUM,
   VENDORNAME,
   INVNUM,
   INVDATE,
   TYPENUM,
   TYPENAME,
   QTY,
   INDIVPR,
   TOTAL,
END OF ITAB.

SELECT * FROM INVHEAD WHERE DATE IN Period.
   SELECT SINGLE * FROM VENDOR WHERE VENDORNUM = INVHEAD-VENDORNUM.
   SELECT * FROM INVLINE WHERE INVNUM = INVHEAD-INVNUM.
      MOVE ... . " Fill the internal table.
   ENDSELECT.
ENDSELECT.

SORT ITAB.

LOOP AT ITAB.

   AT NEW VENDORNUM.
      " Output data about the vendor
      AT NEW INVNUM.
        " Output invoice header
      ENDAT.
   ENDAT.
```

```
" Output invoice line item

AT END OF ... .
    ...
ENDAT.
```

```
ENDLOOP.
```

In addition to using internal tables, ABAP provides one more method of combining data in this way. This is called EXTRACT datasets. You may well need some time to get used to working with EXTRACT datasets. They also require more detailed explanation.

Each report can manage just one of this type of dataset. For this reason, the dataset is not given a name, but is used implicitly when you execute special statements. You must work through the following steps:

1. First, nominate one or more field groups that are to be included in the dataset. Here, you only need to declare the field group names. You can use any name you want as long as it complies with the predefined constraints for descriptors. Although the system does not automatically generate a HEADER field group, that still has a predefined meaning if it is created in a report. This predefined meaning means that it is usually always included.

2. Then you assign the data fields or table fields to the field groups. This makes a field group the symbol for one or more fields. It can now no longer be compared with a structure, and you can no longer access elements in the field group (or attempts to access them do not succeed as expected).

3. This is followed by data evaluation. If all the fields in a field group have been filled with correct values, the field group, and all its assigned fields, can be written to the EXTRACT data area. Here, the contents of the fields in the HEADER field group are also automatically written to the dataset. This is why all the key fields are usually included in this field group.

4. After the dataset has been created, you can sort it. This process includes all the fields in the HEADER field group. After the fields have been sorted, you cannot add any more values to the dataset.

5. After the data has been sorted, the system carries out the final evaluation. This process is similar to that for an internal table, in particular because the group-forming statements described earlier are available. Once the data has been sorted and/or evaluated you cannot add any further values to the dataset.

New statements, or variants of statements that have already been described, are available for carrying out each step. These statements are listed and arranged in the sequence of the steps to which they apply.

Declaring field groups

When you declare the field groups, you must first make their names known to the system. The statement you use to do this is quite simple:

FIELD-GROUPS: *fieldgroup_1, fieldgroup_2, ... fieldgroup_n.*

The syntax description shows how you can enter a colon in the statement to introduce several field groups. It is possible to declare an individual field group, but this is not usually a good idea. You can, of course, use the statement without a colon to declare an individual field group.

Assigning fields to field groups

To assign fields to a field group, you use a special variant of the INSERT statement:

INSERT *fieldlist* **INTO** *fieldgroup.*

The field list contains and lists all the fields that are to be included in the field group. The individual field names are separated from each other by a blank. You can also enter a colon in the INSERT statement to make assignments to several field groups within one INSERT statement:

INSERT: *fieldlist_1* **INTO** *fieldgroup_1,*
          fieldlist_2 **INTO** *fieldgroup_2,*
          ...
          fieldlist_n **INTO** *fieldgroup_n.*

Although the INSERT statement is used here, this is still not data manipulation. You are merely inserting references to the fields or field names in the field group. You are not inserting data!

Filling a dataset

You use this statement to transfer the current contents of the fields, that you assigned to the field group using INSERT, into the EXTRACT dataset:

EXTRACT *fieldgroup.*

If a HEADER field group is present, the contents of its fields are automatically transferred as well. An EXTRACT statement generates a record in the dataset. Here, the fields of the field groups that are not processed in the EXTRACT statement remain empty.

Like many other statements, EXTRACT can also process several parameters if you use a colon to introduce them:

EXTRACT: *fieldgroup_1, fieldgroup_2, ... fieldgroup_n.*

Sorting the dataset

The following statement is the simplest version of the statement for sorting the dataset:

`SORT.`

If you do not enter a name, this statement automatically processes the `EXTRACT` dataset. You can use a range of options to influence the sorting sequence and the fields used for sorting. The fields you select must all belong to the `HEADER` field group.

If the fields that are to be used for sorting are empty, these fields or records are sorted first. If records have identical sorting definitions, their sequence is random!

Evaluating the dataset

An `EXTRACT` dataset is processed by a `LOOP-ENDLOOP`:

```
LOOP.
 statements
ENDLOOP.
```

As with `SORT`, a name is also missing here after `LOOP`. This is to show that the internal dataset is to be processed. The fields sent to the dataset with `EXTRACT` are prepared one after the other in the loop. The contents of each particular record in the `EXTRACT` dataset are transferred back to the original fields and can be evaluated there. However, the program only changes those fields for which data is present in the `EXTRACT` dataset. All other field contents remain unchanged! This feature means you have to use special statements to test the validity of data. To test the data, use the same statements that you used to determine the field group.

Forming groups and field group reference

To form groups you can use the usual statements described above, such as `AT FIRST` or `AT NEW`. They refer to the data fields. You use this statement to make the processing of statements within the block dependent on whether the current record was generated with an `EXTRACT` statement for this specific field group:

```
AT fieldgroup.
. . .
ENDAT.
```

You can use an alternative version of the statement to make execution dependent on whether the record that follows the current record matches a precisely defined second field group.

```
AT fieldgroup_1 WITH fieldgroup_2.
. . .
ENDAT.
```

You can, for example, use this to hide header records without subsequent records.

The example provides a clear way to understand these rather theoretical explanations. In contrast to other demo programs, the line numbers are also printed here to make them easier to refer to. The dataset used for the evaluation is generated in the example and made available in internal tables.

In this respect, the example differs from the pseudo-code described above. This example focuses on evaluating table data with the aid of an EXTRACT. It does not cover the reading of data from tables.

```
 1 REPORT YZ334030.
 2
 3 DATA NUM TYPE I.
 4
 5 DATA: BEGIN OF DELI OCCURS 10,
 6    LNUM(4) TYPE N,
 7    NAME(20),
 8 END OF DELI.
 9
10 DATA: BEGIN OF INVO OCCURS 10,
11    INVONO(4) TYPE N,
12    LNUM LIKE DELI-LNUM,
13 END OF INVO.
14
15 DATA: BEGIN OF INVOLINE OCCURS 10,
16    INVONO LIKE INVO-INVONO,
17    ARTICLE(20),
18 END OF INVOLINE.
19
20 DELI-LNUM = '1'. DELI-NAME = 'iXOS'. APPEND DELI.
21
22 DELI-LNUM = '2'. DELI-NAME = 'SAP'. APPEND DELI.
23
24 INVO-INVONO = '123'. INVO-LNUM = '1'. APPEND INVO.
25
26 INVO-INVONO = '234'. INVO-LNUM = '2'. APPEND INVO.
27
28 INVO-INVONO = '345'. INVO-LNUM = '1'. APPEND INVO.
29
30 INVOLINE-INVONO = '234'. INVOLINE-ARTICLE = 'SAP R/3'.
31 APPEND INVOLINE.
32
33 INVOLINE-INVONO = '123'. INVOLINE-ARTICLE = 'Development'.
34 APPEND INVOLINE.
35
36 INVOLINE-INVONO = '123'. INVOLINE-ARTICLE = 'iXOS Archive'.
```

```
37 APPEND INVOLINE.
38
39 INVOLINE-INVONO = '123'. INVOLINE-ARTICLE = 'Project ABC'.
40 APPEND INVOLINE.
41
42 INVOLINE-INVONO = '345'. INVOLINE-ARTICLE = 'iXOS Archive'.
43 APPEND INVOLINE.
44
45 FIELD-GROUPS: HEADER, VENDOR, ARTICLE.
46
47 INSERT: DELI-LNUM INVO-INVONO NUM  INTO HEADER,
48         DELI-NAME                  INTO VENDOR,
49         INVOLINE-ARTICLE           INTO ARTICLE.
50
51 LOOP AT INVO.
52
53   MOVE SPACE TO DELI.
54   DELI-LNUM = INVO-LNUM.
55   READ TABLE DELI.
56   IF SY-SUBRC = 0.
57
58     EXTRACT VENDOR.
59     LOOP AT INVOLINE WHERE INVONO = INVO-INVONO.
60       EXTRACT ARTICLE.
61       ADD 1 TO NUM.
62     ENDLOOP.
63
64   ENDIF.
65
66 ENDLOOP.
67
68 CLEAR: DELI, INVO, INVOLINE, NUM.
69
70 LOOP.
71   WRITE: /  DELI-LNUM, INVO-INVONO,
72            NUM, DELI-NAME,
73            INVOLINE-ARTICLE.
74
75 CLEAR: DELI, INVO, INVOLINE, NUM.
76
77 ENDLOOP.
78
79 SORT.
80
81 LOOP.
```

```
82
83   AT VENDOR WITH ARTICLE.
84     AT NEW DELI-LNUM.
85       WRITE: /, 'Vendor:', DELI-NAME.
86     ENDAT.
87   ENDAT.
88
89   AT NEW INVO-INVONO.
90     WRITE: / INVO-INVONO.
91   ENDAT.
92
93   WRITE: /5 INVOLINE-ARTICLE.
94
95   AT END OF INVO-INVONO.
96     WRITE: /.
97   ENDAT.
98
99 CLEAR: DELI-LNUM, INVO-INVONO,
100         DELI-NAME, INVOLINE-ARTICLE.
101
102 ENDLOOP.
```

In the first part of this example, lines 3 to 43, all the fields and internal tables are declared and filled with appropriate data. This section of the program does not introduce any unfamiliar statements. In line 45, the three field groups HEADER, VENDOR and ARTI-CLE are declared and linked with data or table fields in lines 47 to 49. The HEADER field group, whose contents are necessary for sorting the record, contains the fields for the vendor number and the invoice number. In addition, it contains a sequential number that ensures that the individual records in the list are sorted correctly.

After this preparatory work, you can now structure the data. In lines 51 to 66, two nested LOOPS and a READ statement simulate the SELECT statements in the pseudo-code. The outer loop processes all invoice header lines. It uses a READ statement to search for the vendor data for each invoice header. If this data exists, the contents of the fields that form the VENDOR field group are copied into the EXTRACT in line 58. The fields that form the HEADER field group are automatically transferred as well. The statements in lines 59 to 62 read the individual item lines of each invoice and also copy them into the EXTRACT as separate records.

Lines 68 to 77 define the structure of the EXTRACT and the contents of the individual records. First, the data fields are initialized. Then, the data is read with a LOOP and the contents of the relevant fields are output. In the LOOP, only the fields that are actually con-tained in the data can be updated, so the data fields will be initialised each time the loop runs. This is the only way to see which data is contained in each record in the EXTRACT. The only purpose of this section of the program is to show what data is present.

The actual evaluation of the data starts in line 79 with the sorting of the records. Lines 81 to 103 define a more extensive loop in which the sorted data is finally listed. Line 83 contains an AT statement that defines that only vendor records, followed by an ARTICLE record, will be processed. In this case, the subsequent AT statement checks whether it is necessary to output a header line for the vendor and generates it if required. All the statements that follow are easy to understand. New invoice numbers will also be displayed. Following each new invoice, all the item lines in that invoice will be listed. At the end of each invoice the report generates an empty separator line.

Exercises

1. Create and execute your own report for the second group change example.

2. In the first group change example report, change the sequence of the AT FIRST and WRITE statements. Execute the report and analyze the result.

3. Modify the first example so that the date is used to form the group instead of the name.

4. In the second example, change the sequence of the AT statements. Analyze the result.

5. In the EXTRACT statement example, delete the NUM field from line 47 in the field group declaration. Compare the result with that of the unchanged program.

6. In the EXTRACT statement example, delete the CLEAR statement in the first loop (line 75). Compare the contents of the structure with its contents when you executed this statement with CLEAR.

7. In the EXTRACT statement example, delete line 26. This creates a vendor without a delivery. What happens next?

3.4.2 The events concept in standard reporting

The ABAP programming language is an event-driven programming language. When the system processes a program, a report or a dialog-oriented application, its internal flow logic differentiates between various events, such as when the user has finished entering data in a screen program. It can also recognize special events, such as when a list reaches the end of a page. There is a range of events of different types. Programmers can assign special program code to the events, if they want to. The basic elements for controlling events are used in a similar way to when programming using graphic interfaces such as Windows. However, on closer inspection, there are considerable differences in the way events control is implemented. Any existing experience from the Windows environment is of little use here.

Event statements are used to link an event with its program code. If an event occurs in an application, the control logic will search in the program for an event statement associated with this event and process the program code following this statement. Here, the end of the instruction block is generated by the program end, another event statement or the definition of a subprogram, i.e. the FORM statement.

The SAP documentation describes the statements for forming groups in the context of genuine event statements. Although the syntax is almost identical, there are important differences in their functions. For this reason, the two statement types are dealt with separately.

Event statements can be very precisely assigned to particular sections or parts of an application. In standard reporting, some events are available that are mainly addressed using special events during output to a list and selection screen processing. The simplest and most frequently used events are:

`TOP-OF-PAGE.`

and

`END-OF-PAGE.`

As their name suggests, these events, or their associated statements, are executed when a new page is started or a page is finished. In this way, you can insert headers or footer lines in the list.

A report can work in conjunction with *logical databases*. These databases have functions which allow them to acquire data from one or more tables while taking into account links between the tables. They then transfer the read data into the actual report in a defined order. The report as such then only evaluates and displays the data that has been made available by the logical database. Due to the complexity of this topic, logical databases are discussed in a separate subsection. The reports used in previous R/3 System Releases did not use a logical database. In these Releases, this event is triggered right at the start of a program and before the first record is read from logical database:

`START-OF-SELECTION.`

After the last record is read, this event is triggered:

`END-OF-SELECTION.`

If the report does not work with a logical database, the `START-OF-SELECTION` event if explicitly specified is identical to the start of the actual main section of the report. If the `START-OF-SELECTION` event statement exists in an application, the system executes the statements starting with `REPORT` or `PROGRAM` first. Then it executes the statements after the explicit `START` statement. The main reason for using a `START-OF-SELECTION` statement in programs that do not use a logical database is to delimit the 'main program' from the statements for additional events such as `TOP-OF-PAGE`.

3.4.3 Selections and parameters

The R/3 System is designed for processing very large volumes of data. The number of records in a table can easily exceed a million. Lists with such a large number of entries are practically useless on their own, which means that resources for selecting specific records are essential. The actual selection tool, i.e. the `SELECT` statement, has already been introduced. However, this statement requires parameters in the `WHERE` clause, which the report cannot simply request from the user because no dialog functions are available for this purpose. One solution is the selection screen. This is an automatically generated input template in which users can enter their own selection criteria. Figure 3.60 shows an example selection screen for the development environment info system.

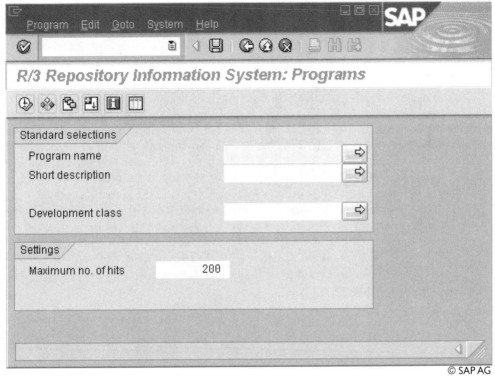

Figure 3.60   Selection screen program for a report

The programmer uses two special statements in the report's source code to define which input fields should appear in the selection screen. The internal control logic of the system then generates the selection screen program without any further input by the programmer, and processes it before executing the report. Within certain limits, you can modify the appearance of the selection screen, using special statements. If necessary, you can combine them with event statements.

Up to Release 3.x, selection screens were reserved for reports. From Release 4.0 you can now define and use selection screens for all program types. This has no impact on the statements described below. However, some new statements have been added for defining and calling the selection screens. These are described at the end of this section.

Here are some notes on how to use the selection screen. You first enter the appropriate search terms in the various input fields. To give the current contents of the selection screen a unique name, and save them as a *variant*, choose GOTO | VARIANTS | SAVE AS VARIANT from the menu. Later you can access all variants saved in this way by selecting GOTO | VARIANTS | GET or by clicking the pushbutton with the same name (if it is active).

The reports are only processed if the system receives a statement that explicitly instructs it to do so. This statement can be one of the following three menu options PROGRAM | EXECUTE, PROGRAM | EXECUTE AND PRINT and PROGRAM | EXECUTE IN BACKGROUND and a pushbutton in the application toolbar.

Parameters

The simplest way of transferring a value to a report is to use *parameters*. You generate a parameter in the report with this statement:

PARAMETERS *parameter.*

You can declare several parameters at the same time by separating them with colons in the statement. A parameter appears in the selection screen as a single input field in which a value can be entered (*see* Figure 3.60, MAXIMUM NO. OF HITS). When you name a parameter, you must meet the same criteria as the criteria for naming a data field. In addition, a parameter may contain a maximum of eight characters. Within the report, a parameter can be used like a simple data field. In other words, a parameter is a data field into which the report's user can enter a value in an input template before the report is executed.

As already described, a field has specific characteristics such as type and length. Naturally, a parameter must also have these characteristics, as it too is only a data field in the report. To define these characteristics, use various additions to the PARAMETERS statement. If you do not, the system will create a C-type data parameter with length 1, like in the case of DATA. The simplest and most frequently used method is to use LIKE to refer to an existing field, as follows:

PARAMETERS *parameter* **LIKE** *field.*

A table field often serves as a reference field. This ensures that it is easy to evaluate the parameter later. If *foreign key references* have been maintained for the table field, the system automatically provides the user with input help, if they press (F4), and it also carries out a value check. Apart from LIKE, parameters can also refer to a predefined or even user-defined data type:

PARAMETERS *parameter* **TYPE** *type.*

There are no constraints concerning the data type, except in the case of data type P, for packed numbers. Here, it is necessary to define the number of digits after the decimal point. There is a special addition which you can use for this purpose:

PARAMETERS *parameter* **TYPE P DECIMALS** *decimal_places.*

It can be a good idea to set default values for some parameters. When a parameter is declared, the default values are transferred with the DEFAULT addition:

PARAMETERS *parameter* **DEFAULT** *default_value.*

If a parameter field requires mandatory input from the user, you can force the user to enter data, by setting the OBLIGATORY addition:

PARAMETERS *parameter* **OBLIGATORY.**

Apart from alphanumeric input fields, graphic interfaces also use check boxes and radio buttons. Check boxes are fields that the user can select (check) independently from each other, so you can use them to select several entries in a list, etc. Radio buttons differ because they are grouped. In a group you can only select one of the radio buttons, so you can only use them to select one object from a number of objects.

Check boxes and radio buttons can also be generated in selection screens. To generate a check box, enter the following statement:

PARAMETERS *parameter* **AS CHECKBOX**.

To generate a radio button, enter the following statement:

PARAMETERS *parameter* **RADIOBUTTON GROUP** *group*.

In the second example, an identical group name has to be entered for all fields that belong together. After input in a selection screen, the selected fields have the content 'X' and the others contain a space. The example below demonstrates some parameter declarations. This example can be executed. After the start, the parameter screen appears. In it you can now enter values. Then, you have to select PROGRAM | EXECUTE from the menu. This ends input in the parameter screen and processes the actual report, which shows the contents of all parameters.

```
REPORT YZ334030 NO STANDARD PAGE HEADING.
TABLES: tadir.
DATA m_field.

PARAMETERS p_ins.
PARAMETERS p_field LIKE tadir-author.
PARAMETERS p_course TYPE p DECIMALS 2.
PARAMETERS p_obl LIKE m_field OBLIGATORY.

PARAMETERS: c1 AS CHECKBOX,
            c2 AS CHECKBOX,
            c3 AS CHECKBOX.

PARAMETERS: r1 RADIOBUTTON GROUP g1,
            r2 RADIOBUTTON GROUP g1,
            r3 RADIOBUTTON GROUP g1.

START-OF-SELECTION.
  WRITE: / 'P_INS:', p_ins.
  WRITE: / 'P_FIELD:', p_field.
  WRITE: / 'P_COURSE:', p_course.
  WRITE: / 'P_OBL :', p_obl.
  WRITE: /.
  WRITE: / 'Checkbox :', c1, c2, c3.

  WRITE: /.
  WRITE: / 'Radiobutton:', r1, r2, r3.
```

Apart from the PARAMETERS statement options mentioned above, additional ones are available. The number of options depends on the R/3 System Release. Table 3.29 contains a list of the additions available in Release 4.6B. Some of the options can, or must, be combined with each other. Apart from that, using some of the options requires additional programming.

Table 3.29   PARAMETERS statement options

Option	Description
DEFAULT value	Set default value
TYPE type	Parameters with defined data type
DECIMALS dec	Set number of decimal points for data type P
LIKE field	Describe parameters through other field
MEMORY ID pid	Link parameter with GET/SET parameter
MATCHCODE OBJECT mobj	Input help through matchcode
MODIF ID id	Define modification group
NO-DISPLAY	No display on selection screen, but data transfer possible in the case of SUBMIT
LOWER CASE	Toggle upper/lower-case typing
OBLIGATORY	Obligatory input
AS CHECKBOX	Representation as check box
RADIOBUTTON GROUP radi	Representation as radio button
FOR TABLE dbtab	Parameter for database table
FOR NODE node	Parameter for node of a logical database
AS SEARCH PATTERN	Parameter entered into search help-table
VALUE REQUEST	User can press (F4) to display value help
HELP REQUEST	User can press (F1) to display general help
VISIBLE LENGTH len	Set output length
VALUE CHECK	Check field contents against a table field's value range
LIKE (g)	Dynamically describe parameter attributes
USER-COMMAND ucom	Call subroutine in the case of change

Selections

Apart from the simple parameters, ABAP offers *selection tables*. Selection tables are primarily internal tables with a predefined structure (*see* Table 3.30).

Table 3.30   Structure of selection tables

Field	Task	Field length
SIGN	Marks whether selected records are part of the results volume (I) or are to be excluded from it (E).	1
option	Reference operator (EQ, NE, CP, NP, GE, LT, LE, GT)	2
LOW	Pattern or lower value limit of a range	Like data field
HIGH	Upper limit of a range	Like data field

You enter one or several individual patterns or range statements in the selection table on the selection screen. The functions needed are made available by the internal control logic, so no extra programming is necessary. In the selection screen, the system only displays two input fields for a selection table. You click the button next to the second input field. Then the system either displays a dialog box or an additional screen program, which varies according to the R/3 System Release. You can enter additional records for the selection table in the dialog box. Figure 3.61 shows the dialog box for the selection screen of transaction `SE16` (Data Browser). In the dialog box you can enter the search terms in separate index cards as individual values or range statements. Beside creating a search for a match (green label on the index card), you can also define exclusion criteria (red label). The values you enter here can be found again later in the `LOW` (individual value or lower limit) and `HIGH` (upper limit) columns, in the selection table. The entries that are checked for a match are given the value 'I' in the `SIGN` field, in the selection table. Exclusion criteria are marked with an 'E' in the `SIGN` field.

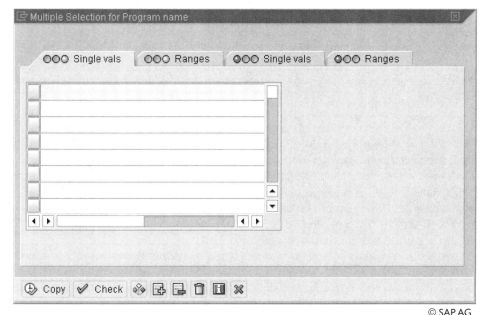

© SAP AG

Figure 3.61   Inserting values in a selection table

Figure 3.62   Selecting the reference operator

If you click the selection icon in a table line or the SELECTION OPTIONS button, you jump to a second dialog box (Figure 3.62), in which you can select a reference operator for the current line.

The reference operators are stored as a two-digit abbreviation in the selection table's Option field.

Selections are generated in a similar way to parameters. For selections, the declaration statement reads:

SELECT-OPTIONS *selection* **FOR** *field* | *(field)*.

The maximum length permitted for the names of selections is, once again, eight characters. The declaration statement includes an obligatory reference to a data or table field. This defines some attributes of the LOW and HIGH fields in the selection table and consequently the attributes of the input fields in the selection screen, such as the length field. If the database field has a length of three characters, then the input field on the selection screen will also be only three characters long. The field for which a selection is to be created can be transferred directly or dynamically.

When the system is confirming the input, it checks whether the values or pattern correspond with the data type of the referenced field. For example, in selections that have been linked with a type-N field (numerical character string), you can only enter the permitted numerical characters (digits). If you enter any other characters, this will cause the system to display an error message. In addition, the CHECK statement, which is described shortly, provides an abbreviated notation method for evaluating a selection table, in which the field from the declaration statement will always be checked.

The SELECT-OPTIONS statement also has a series of options, some of which are explained in more detail below.

... **DEFAULT** *value_low* [**TO** *value_high*] [**OPTION** *op*] [**SIGN** *s*] .

You can set a default value for a selection. Because a line in the selection table consists of four individual fields, the corresponding option also offers up to four parameters. To force an entry for the lower limit of the selection, you can use this statement:

... **OBLIGATORY**

Table 3.31 contains the other options for the SELECT-OPTIONS statement.

Table 3.31   SELECT-OPTIONS statement options

Option	Description
DEFAULT v_low [TO v_high] [OPTION op] [SIGN s]	Set default values
MEMORY ID pid	Link selection with GET/SET parameter
MATCHCODE OBJECT mobj	Link selection with matchcode
MODIF ID id	Assign modification group
NO-DISPLAY	No display on selection screen, but values transfer possible in the case of SUBMIT
LOWER CASE	Enable uppercase / lower-case type
OBLIGATORY	Obligatory input
NO-EXTENSION	Only one line can be entered
NO INTERVALS	Only the LOW field appears in the first selection screen. All additional entries are made in the second selection screen
NO DATABASE SELECTION	No user-definable delimiter in the logical database
VALUE REQUEST [FOR LOW | HIGH]	User can press (F4) to display value help
HELP REQUEST [FOR LOW | HIGH]	User can press (F4) to display general help
VISIBLE LENGTH len	Set output length

It is not always possible, or even advisable, to let users make entries in selection tables. For example, the performance of SELECT statements can be optimized by selection tables, because selection tables allow for fairly detailed definition of the records through the database. Therefore, even within an application, selection tables can be generated and filled by the program itself without the need for a selection screen. To declare a selection table, use the following statement:

RANGES *table* **FOR** *field*.

It generates a selection table with the predefined structure. In these tables you enter the usual statements for internal tables, i.e. mainly APPEND.

From Release 4.x, an additional statement has become available for creating selection tables. Its syntax conforms better with the general data concept because it is a variant of the DATA statement:

DATA *seltab* (**TYPE** | **LIKE**) **RANGE OF** (*type* | *field*)
[**INITIAL SIZE** *n*]
[**WITH HEADER LINE**].

Similarly, in Release 4.x and later, you can also generate type definitions for selection tables. To do so, you use this statement:

TYPES *seltab_type* (**TYPE** | **LIKE**) **RANGE OF** (*type* | *field*)
[**INITIAL SIZE** *n*].

Evaluation of parameters and selections

The preferred reason for using selections and parameters is to transfer search terms to a report. These must naturally be evaluated in the report when records are being selected. To evaluate search terms, you can choose between two methods:

1. inclusion in the WHERE clause;

2. use in the CHECK statement.

The CHECK statement has already been mentioned. It enables you to analyze parameters or selections within any loop. These loops can be SELECT-ENDSELECT loops, but do not necessarily have to be. However, it is a lot better for system performance to select records by structuring the SELECT statement in a suitable way instead of using CHECK in the loop.

If a selection has been derived from a database field, using LIKE, you can use an abbreviated form of notation for the condition. This statement automatically creates the reference to the database field in a SELECT loop:

CHECK *selection*.

It corresponds to the long form:

CHECK *table_field* **IN** *selection*.

Parameters can be used in a direct comparison. There, different reference operators can be used (see *IF* statement):

CHECK `table_field = parameter.`

Parameters can also be present in a WHERE clause. There they are used like other fields or directly coded constants. Because search patterns that can also contain sample characters are usually entered in parameters, only the LIKE statement can, in many cases, be a serious contender for use as a reference operator. This statement expects the two characters '%' or '_' as sample characters. However, the sample characters normally used by the operator are the asterisk, '*', and the plus character, '+'. Before using a parameter in the WHERE clause, you therefore have to replace the sample characters '*' and '+' with '%' and '_' respectively. You can use ABAP's TRANSLATE statement for this purpose. The syntax of this statement is as follows:

TRANSLATE `string` **USING** `pattern.`

In a character string, the TRANSLATE statement replaces characters in the way defined in the sample character string. The sample character string contains pairs of characters, that are to be replaced with their new characters, one behind the other. To exchange the sample characters in a parameter, you need the following statement:

TRANSLATE `parameter` **USING** `'*%+_'.`

This kind of transformation is not necessary for the sample characters in the selection table, as these can be checked with the IN statement in the WHERE clause. When using selection tables, you should take into account one of the system's limitations: the system's internal flow logic uses the contents of the selection table to structure a genuine SQL SELECT statement consisting of several individual terms. This statement must not exceed a certain size (currently approximately 8 KB). That is why the number of records in a selection table is limited, at least theoretically. All the same, if you use selection tables as opposed to running checks with CHECK within a SELECT-ENDSELECT loop, this offers considerable improvements in system performance because fewer records are selected in the database and have to be transferred over the network. The following example demonstrates the two most important options for analyzing parameters or selections:

```
PROGRAM YZ334050.
TABLES tadir.

PARAMETERS p_autor LIKE tadir-author OBLIGATORY.
SELECT-OPTIONS s_name FOR tadir-obj_name.

TRANSLATE p_autor USING '*%+_'.

SELECT * FROM tadir
  WHERE author LIKE p_autor.
    CHECK s_name.
    WRITE: / tadir-pgmid, tadir-obj_name.
ENDSELECT.
```

This program uses the SELECT statement first of all, to determine all programs created by the programmers whose names match the pattern in the P_AUTOR parameter. It then checks them individually if they are located within the name range defined by the selection table. Note that a user entry is mandatory in the names parameter. If this field remains empty, the SELECT statement cannot find any records. It would therefore be practical to mark the parameter as OBLIGATORY or use DEFAULT to define a default value for it.

You can of course place both checks in the SELECT statement or perform them with CHECK. This has often a considerable effect on system performance at runtime. In addition, the compare conditions must also be re-formulated. The following listing shows a second variant of the same program:

```
PROGRAM YZ334060.
TABLES TADIR.


PARAMETERS p_autor LIKE tadir-author.
SELECT-OPTIONS s_name FOR tadir-obj_name.

SELECT * FROM tadir
  WHERE obj_name IN s_name.
    CHECK tadir-author CP p_autor.
    WRITE: / tadir-pgmid, tadir-obj_name.
ENDSELECT.
```

Beside the alphanumeric entries, parameters can also provide radio buttons and check boxes. The parameters then contain either a blank or an 'X'. Naturally, these kinds of parameter cannot be used directly for database selection. Instead, they are evaluated in control statements such as IF or CASE for the purpose of modifying the program run.

Editing the selection screen

The examples above clearly show that the individual parameters and selections each appear in an individual line in the selection screen in the sequence in which they are declared. In each case, the parameter's or selection's name in the program code serves as a descriptor.

Some statements allow you to modify the appearance of the selection screen. For example, you can use transaction SE32 to assign descriptive text to the selections and parameters. This is the same transaction as you use to enter the numbered text elements. One way to call transaction SE32, from the Editor, is to choose GOTO | TEXT ELEMENTS | SELECTION TEXTS from the menu. This enables you to enter text while processing the program. The text entered in this way can also be translated, creating a multilingual selection screen as a result.

Additional statements allow you to modify the sequence in which the fields are displayed in the screen. You use different variants of the SELECTION-SCREEN statement to structure the selection screen. These two statements form a statement block in which the line feed has been switched off:

```
SELECTION-SCREEN BEGIN OF LINE.
. . .
SELECTION-SCREEN END OF LINE.
```

All parameters declared in this block appear in one line. Selections must not be declared in a block of this kind. In the block mentioned above, you must use this statement to horizontally adjust the input fields within a line:

```
SELECTION-SCREEN POSITION position.
```

This sets the output position for a parameter declaration that follows it. It therefore is essential to declare a parameter immediately after such a statement. In this form of positioning, however, the descriptors will be lost. Another variant of the SELECTION-SCREEN statement therefore allows text to be positioned in selection screens. The statement for this is:

```
SELECTION-SCREEN COMMENT format text.
```

There are two ways to set the format. The first is similar to the length and output column definition already discussed in the WRITE statement. Alternatively, you can use the POS_LOW and POS_HIGH icons for the positions in which the LOW and the HIGH fields of a selection will be displayed. You can also use them for SELECTION-SCREEN POSITION.

There are also two different ways to define the text. First, the text can be represented by a text element (which cannot be selection text!). You use the method described above to maintain it. The text is static and cannot be modified at runtime. Alternatively, you can specify a field name, but its length is restricted to a maximum of eight characters at this location. This field is automatically declared by the SELECTION-SCREEN statement! At runtime, the user must enter a value in the text field before the system displays the selection screen. This is only possible by using selection screen-specific event statements (i.e. INITIALIZATION). That is why this type of statement is only demonstrated in the next section.

Extensive selection screens can be subdivided by inserting empty lines or separators. You can use this statement to insert *n* empty lines:

```
SELECTION-SCREEN SKIP n.
```

If you do not define a number of empty lines, the system will enter 1 empty line by default. This statement inserts a separator:

```
SELECTION-SCREEN ULINE format.
```

The format definition is the same as the one used in *SELECTION-SCREEN COMMENT*. The example below demonstrates some simple statements for structuring the selection screen. It has no functions whatsoever and consequently does not generate an output list.

```
REPORT YZ334070.
SELECTION-SCREEN SKIP.

SELECTION-SCREEN BEGIN OF LINE.
  SELECTION-SCREEN COMMENT 5(10) t1.
  SELECTION-SCREEN POSITION 20.
  PARAMETERS c1 AS CHECKBOX.
```

```
  SELECTION-SCREEN POSITION 40.
  PARAMETERS c2 AS CHECKBOX.

  SELECTION-SCREEN POSITION 60.
  PARAMETERS c3 AS CHECKBOX.
SELECTION-SCREEN END OF LINE.

SELECTION-SCREEN ULINE.

SELECTION-SCREEN BEGIN OF LINE.
  SELECTION-SCREEN COMMENT 5(15) t2.
  SELECTION-SCREEN POSITION pos_low.
  PARAMETERS r1 RADIOBUTTON GROUP g1.

  SELECTION-SCREEN POSITION pos_high.
  PARAMETERS r2 RADIOBUTTON GROUP g1.
SELECTION-SCREEN END OF LINE.

INITIALIZATION.
  t1 = 'Checkbox'.
  t2 = 'Radio Button'.
```

Another option would be to gather fields into groups. These groups can be separated from each other with a frame. Groups and frames can be nested together: currently up to five levels of nesting are possible. The system automatically defines the dimensions of the frames. The creation of groups provides selection screens with a clearer structure. In addition, you can use special event statements to execute program activities specially for a group of parameters or selections (see Chapter 4). To create groups you use the following statements:

SELECTION-SCREEN BEGIN OF BLOCK *block*.

and

SELECTION-SCREEN END OF BLOCK *block*.

These two statements simply group the parameters or selections involved. To generate a frame, enter this addition immediately after the BEGIN OF BLOCK statement:

... WITH FRAME.

Finally, enter this addition to insert a title:

... WITH TITLE *title*.

Here, the title is generated in the same way as a comment, i.e. either from a numbered text element or an automatically generated data element. The next listing shows a simple example of this.

```
REPORT yz334080 NO STANDARD PAGE HEADING.
SELECTION-SCREEN BEGIN OF BLOCK a WITH FRAME.

  SELECTION-SCREEN BEGIN OF BLOCK b WITH FRAME TITLE t1.
     PARAMETERS p1.
  SELECTION-SCREEN END OF BLOCK b.

  SELECTION-SCREEN BEGIN OF BLOCK c WITH FRAME TITLE t2.
     PARAMETERS: r1 RADIOBUTTON GROUP g1,
                 r2 RADIOBUTTON GROUP g1.
  SELECTION-SCREEN END OF BLOCK c.


SELECTION-SCREEN END OF BLOCK a.

INITIALIZATION.
  t1 = 'Group B'.
  t2 = 'Group C'.
```

Beside the usual input elements, a selection screen can also contain pushbuttons. You can use special event statements to determine which pushbutton has been pressed in the selection screen. With the pushbuttons you can then execute alternative program branches within the report. For example, many repair programs allow a test run in which the changes to be implemented are only displayed, but not yet executed. The selection screen provides the two pushbuttons CHECK and UPDATE for this purpose.

There are two ways to generate pushbuttons. You can insert up to two additional push-buttons into the actual application toolbar with this statement:

SELECTION-SCREEN FUNCTION KEY *n*.

In this statement, *n* represents the numbers 1 or 2. When the user presses one of these buttons, they generate the function code FC01 or FC02. The next section demonstrates how to evaluate the function code. When working with additional function codes and their evaluation, you have to declare a Data Dictionary structure in the report:

TABLES SSCRFIELDS.

This structure is used by the selection screen to communicate with the program that contains it. In the case of the pushbuttons, the text that the two pushbuttons should contain is entered in the two fields SSCRFIELDS-FUNCTXT_01 and SSCRFIELDS-FUNCTXT_02 in the initialization part (INITIALIZATION event).

Alternatively, you can use the following statement to generate any number of pushbut-tons within the selection screen:

SELECTION-SCREEN PUSHBUTTON *format name* **USER-COMMAND** *function_code*.

The format corresponds to the one already described in the COMMENT addition. This defines the position and width of the pushbutton. The parameter *name* specifies the text of the pushbutton. The procedure already described for COMMENT also applies here.

Consequently, you either use a numbered text element or a data element assigned at the initialization event. The function code to be triggered by the pushbutton is a four-digit, alphanumerical descriptor. It is transferred to the statement as the parameter function_code. Do not enter it in quotation marks.

The example below shows how both types of pushbuttons are generated. The obligatory parameter serves to display the function codes initiated when the user clicks the pushbutton. The example also introduces the problem of the event statements for selection screens, two of which have already been used without detailed explanation.

```
REPORT yz334090 NO STANDARD PAGE HEADING.
TABLES sscrfields.


PARAMETERS p1 LIKE sscrfields-ucomm.


SELECTION-SCREEN SKIP 3.


SELECTION-SCREEN FUNCTION KEY 1.
SELECTION-SCREEN FUNCTION KEY 2.
SELECTION-SCREEN PUSHBUTTON 5(15) pb1 USER-COMMAND 0001.
SELECTION-SCREEN PUSHBUTTON 25(15) pb2 USER-COMMAND 0002.
SELECTION-SCREEN PUSHBUTTON 45(15) pb3 USER-COMMAND 0003.


INITIALIZATION.
  sscrfields-functxt_01 = 'Button 1'.
  sscrfields-functxt_02 = 'Button 2'.
  pb1 = 'Button 3'.
  pb2 = 'Button 4'.
  pb3 = 'Button 5'.


AT SELECTION-SCREEN.
  p1 = sscrfields-ucomm.
```

Events for selection screens

The selection screens above were processed by the system's control logic. The control logic ensures, for example, that the default values in the parameters and selections saved in a variant will be transferred if the user calls a report from that variant. The programmer is able to intervene in this process. During the generation and processing of the selection screen, the system processes three events that enable the execution of individual statements with the help of corresponding event statements. These events are INITIALIZATION, AT SELECTION-SCREEN OUTPUT and AT SELECTION-SCREEN.

The INITIALIZATION event is the very first event to be processed when a report starts. This occurs after the selection screen has been created and filled with default values from the PARAMETERS statements. Consequently, these default values can be overwritten here. The transfer of values from variants occurs only after INITIALIZATION, which consequently would overwrite defaults. The INITIALIZATION event is triggered only once during each program call.

Immediately before the selection screen is displayed, the AT SELECTION-SCREEN OUTPUT event is triggered. The control logic makes no further modifications to the selection screen between this event and the processing of the selection screen by the user. That is why values can again be overwritten or other modifications of the selection screen can be executed at this time, such as the hiding of fields, etc. The AT SELECTION-SCREEN OUTPUT event is inseparably linked with the processing of the selection screen. It is always processed before the selection screen is ready for processing. It is not possible to display the selection screen without triggering this event.

After the user has finished processing the selection screen, the control logic will process the AT SELECTION-SCREEN event. Within the corresponding statements you can for example test whether input values are appropriate. If the MESSAGE statement triggers an error message during this event, the system processes the selection screen again and makes the selections and parameters available for input again. Naturally, the AT SELECTION-SCREEN OUTPUT event will be processed beforehand.

There are a number of variants of the AT SELECTION-SCREEN statement with which you can refer to selected input fields in the selection screen or the groups mentioned earlier. In addition, you can use variants of this statement to call input help for fields or display help information. However, programming this context-sensitive help or creating input help requires some knowledge of dialog programming, which will only be taught in the next section. In all cases, the system will recommence processing of the selection screens after executing the statements. The example below, YZ334100, is based on the program for defining blocks, YZ334080. The program below has simply been extended with the following statements:

```
AT SELECTION-SCREEN ON P1.
  IF P1 > 'H'.
    MESSAGE ID 'YZ' TYPE 'E' NUMBER '000'.
  ENDIF.

AT SELECTION-SCREEN ON BLOCK C.
  IF R2 <> 'X'.
    MESSAGE ID 'YZ' TYPE 'E' NUMBER '000'.
  ENDIF.

START-OF-SELECTION.
  WRITE: / 'Parameter :', P1.
  WRITE: / 'Radiobutton 1:', R1.
  WRITE: / 'Radiobutton 2:', R2.
```

The MESSAGE statement triggers a message. The message concept is described in more detail in Section 3.7. It is worth mentioning here that the MESSAGE statement can terminate the processing of programs or dialogs. Apart from that, it places a text in the status line. The example uses a randomly selected message to cancel the processing of the selection screen. Any information in the status line does not actually relate to the example, but is purely coincidental. There is a high probability that only *E:EYZ000* will be displayed.

The two checks in the example serve only to demonstrate the principle, and do not fulfil any practical purpose. The first event statement checks whether a value greater than the letter 'H' was entered in the P1 parameter. If so, the system executes the MESSAGE statement and reprocesses the selection screen. However, only the parameter is available for input from the user: the two radio buttons appear dimmed and the user cannot select them. Apart from during the initial processing of the selection screen, one of the two radio buttons can only be selected if a character that appears before 'H' in the alphabet has been entered in parameter P1. The second event statement concerns block C, which is the block containing the two radio buttons. The user must select the second button, otherwise the system will not continue processing the program. In the selection screen, only the two radio buttons are available for input: the parameter field is inactive. This restriction is caused by the link between the event statement and the block.

Function codes in the selection screen

In the selection screen, there are only a few reasons to trigger a non-standard function code created by the programmer. One reason could be to set special values for the parameters with one push of the button, and another would be to modify the selection screen (dynamic display of additional input fields, etc.). Another reason would be to set options for structuring the list or for executing the program. Many low-level reports do not primarily serve to display information, but to execute data-specific actions such as to repair discrepancies in data or to check records for consistency. Many of these reports run in two different modes: a test mode only showing errors, and a repair mode which also corrects errors. For reports of this kind, you could define two pushbuttons called Check and Repair and set a flag that will be evaluated in the report depending on the function code. All the same, it is not good programming style to use individual function codes to link from the selection screen into completely different lists.

As the programmer, you have already seen how to generate and evaluate your own function codes using additional pushbuttons in a selection screen. A more general, but also more time-consuming option consists of setting your own status for the selection screen. This can be done at one of these events: INITIALIZATION or AT SELECTION-SCREEN OUTPUT. You should always base each of your individually defined statuses on the default status for lists to ensure that all important function codes remain unchanged. It is easiest to generate such a status by inserting a corresponding template in Menu Painter. In addition, also see Section 3.3.3 for details of how to maintain the interface.

Naturally, all individually programmed function codes must also be processed. The AT SELECTION-SCREEN event contains the current function code in the field SSCRFIELDS-UCOMM, independent of whether the function code was generated from a menu or from pushbuttons in the selection screen.

The system handles all function codes generated by the default status of the selection screen. After it has finished processing a particular function code, the selection screen will again be active if the report is not terminated and processing has not jumped to the execution of the report. Function codes that are not processed by the system will also cause the system to repeat the processing of the selection screen. From a technical programming point of view, the selection screen is the actual core of the program, and all other functions, even the one for generating the actual list, are merely subroutines in the final analysis. The ONLI function code is used to generate and output the list from the selection screen. If you want your own custom function code to start the list generation, you can only achieve this with a little trick that is shown in the following example:

```
REPORT YZ334110 NO STANDARD PAGE HEADING.

TABLES SSCRFIELDS.
DATA G_UCOMM LIKE SSCRFIELDS-UCOMM.

* PARAMETERS P1. 'Only necessary in older R/3 Releases

SELECTION-SCREEN SKIP 3.

SELECTION-SCREEN FUNCTION KEY 1.
SELECTION-SCREEN FUNCTION KEY 2.

SELECTION-SCREEN PUSHBUTTON 5(15) PB1 USER-COMMAND 0001.
SELECTION-SCREEN PUSHBUTTON 25(15) PB2 USER-COMMAND 0002.
SELECTION-SCREEN PUSHBUTTON 45(15) PB3 USER-COMMAND 0003.

INITIALIZATION.
  SSCRFIELDS-FUNCTXT_01 = 'Key 1'.
  SSCRFIELDS-FUNCTXT_02 = 'Key 2'.
  PB1 = 'Key 3'.
  PB2 = 'Key 4'.
  PB3 = 'Key 5'.

AT SELECTION-SCREEN.
  G_UCOMM = SSCRFIELDS-UCOMM.
  SSCRFIELDS-UCOMM = 'ONLI'.

START-OF-SELECTION.
  WRITE: / 'The following key was initiated: '.
  CASE G_UCOMM.
    WHEN 'FC01'.
      WRITE '1'.
    WHEN 'FC02'.
      WRITE '2'.
    WHEN '0001'.
      WRITE '3'.
    WHEN '0002'.
      WRITE '4'.
    WHEN '0003'.
      WRITE '5'.
  ENDCASE.
```

The function code that has actually been triggered is temporarily stored in a data field within the program, and evaluated in the actual report. The list generation is started when the function code ONLI is entered in the SSCRFIELDS-UCOMM field. The P1 parameter is only required in earlier Releases of the R/3 System software, because these earlier Releases only display a selection screen if it contains at least one parameter or selection.

General information on using selection screens

From Release 4.0, you can use selection screens with any program type. You can call selection screens with this statement:

CALL SELECTION-SCREEN *screen.*

In this statement, screen is a numerical value.

Within an application, you have to declare a selection screen of this kind with these statements:

SELECTION-SCREEN BEGIN OF SCREEN *screen.*

and

SELECTION-SCREEN END OF SCREEN *screen.*

Between these two statements are the usual statements that define the structure of selection screens. The example below contains two of these selection screens, as well as a default selection screen. When the user clicks on one of the two pushbuttons, this calls one of the two additional selection screens. For better control, the report lists the contents of both parameters.

```
REPORT YZ334120.
TABLES sscrfields.
SELECTION-SCREEN PUSHBUTTON 5(15) pb1 USER-COMMAND 0001.
SELECTION-SCREEN PUSHBUTTON 25(15) pb2 USER-COMMAND 0002.

SELECTION-SCREEN BEGIN OF SCREEN 1.
   PARAMETERS a(20).
SELECTION-SCREEN END OF SCREEN 1.

SELECTION-SCREEN BEGIN OF SCREEN 2.
   PARAMETERS b(20).
SELECTION-SCREEN END OF SCREEN 2.

INITIALIZATION.
   pb1 = 'Screen 1'.
   pb2 = 'Screen 2'.
```

```
AT SELECTION-SCREEN.
  CASE sscrfields-ucomm.
    WHEN '0001'.
      CLEAR: a, b.
      CASE SELECTION-SCREEN 1.
      sscrfields-ucomm = 'ONLI'.
    WHEN '0002'.
      CLEAR: a, b.
      CASE SELECTION-SCREEN 2.
sscrfields-ucomm = 'ONLI'.
  ENDCASE.

START-OF-SELECTION.
  WRITE: / 'Parameter A:', a.
  WRITE: / 'Parameter B:', b.
```

These universally applicable selection screens also have variants. In addition, they fit seamlessly into the programming concept. Not only can you call these new selection screens within an application, but you can also use them with the SUBMIT statement or when creating a report transaction. For this purpose, the functional scope of some existing statements has been extended.

To set a variant as the standard value when calling a selection screen, use this statement:

CALL SELECTION-SCREEN *screen* **USING SELECTION-SET** *variant*.

When calling a report with SUBMIT, you can use the following statement to choose the selection screen:

SUBMIT *report* **USING SELECTION-SCREEN** *screen*.

Tabstrips in selection screens

From Release 4.0, *tabstrips* have been introduced into screen programs. A tabstrip consists of an area within an input template and some pushbuttons arranged above this area. If a user clicks on one of these keys, the system displays an input template belonging to that key in the tabstrip area. This input template is a screen program that must be defined as a *sub-screen*.

In the Windows environment, the individual input templates are also known as *index cards* and the pushbuttons are known as *tabs*. The corresponding elements are not only available in screen programs, but also in selection screens. Figure 3.63 shows the selection screen of an example program with a tabstrip:

To provide a selection screen with tabstrips, you need to use two different statements. First of all, you use this statement to reserve an area 1in lines long for the tabstrip:

SELECTION-SCREEN BEGIN OF TABBED BLOCK *block* **FOR** *1in* **LINES**.

The system simultaneously creates a structure which has the same name as the block. This structure contains the three fields PROG, DYNNR and ACTIVETAB.

Then you use this statement to define the individual tabs or card indexes:

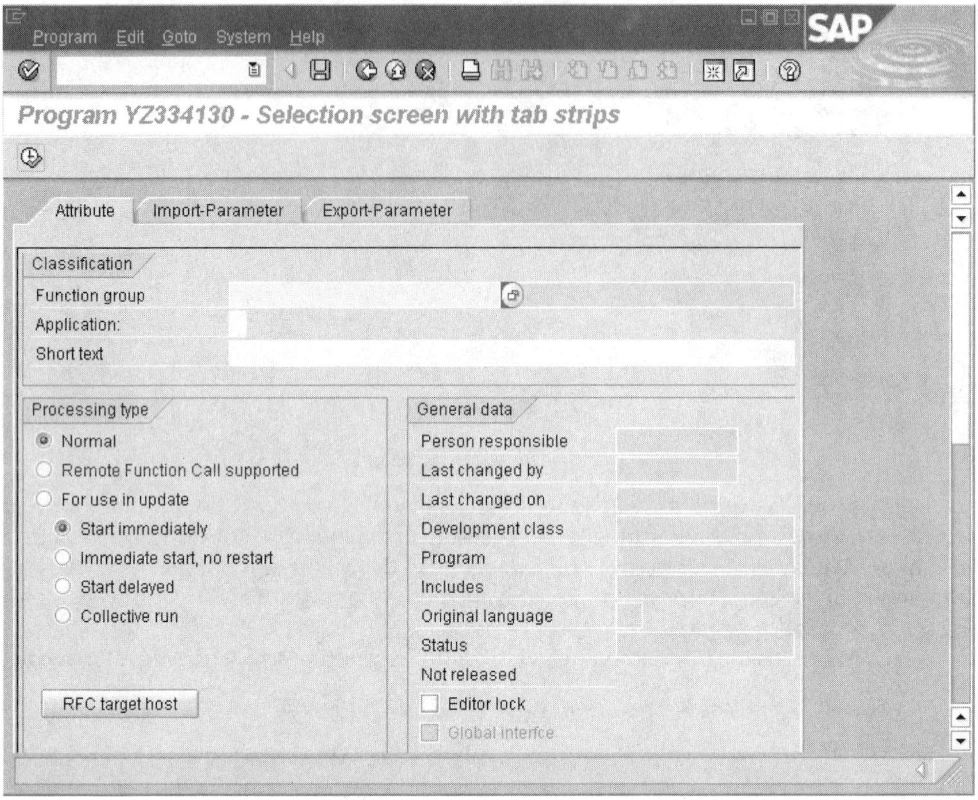

Figure 3.63   Selection screen with tabstrip

© SAP AG

```
SELECTION-SCREEN TAB (length) tabstrip_card USER-COMMAND fcode
 [ DEFAULT [ PROGRAM program ] SCREEN screen ].
```

Here you also need to enter a descriptive text for each index. The tabstrip_card parameter actually represents the name of one of the index cards. In the program, it can be used like a data field into which the system inserts the description of the tabs (index cards) at the INITIALIZATION event. The procedure resembles the one for assigning text to function keys or pushbuttons. In order for the individual tabs to be displayed with a predefined width (i.e. all with the same width), you have to specify the width of the tab with the length parameter. This parameter is mandatory. Enclose the value in oval brackets. You can use the fcode parameter to specify which function code the system should issue if a user activates the tab. To conclude a tabstrip block, use this statement, just like for a normal block:

```
SELECTION-SCREEN END OF BLOCK block.
```

Once a tab has been activated, you usually want to display the matching input template in the tabstrip area. There are two ways to achieve this. In the statement above you can use additional parameters to enter the names of the program and the screen program.

Alternatively, you can also evaluate the initiated function code at the AT SELECTION-SCREEN event and then fill the tabstrip block fields which have already been mentioned, at runtime.

A short example follows below. It uses existing R/3 System screen programs to save you from having to create your own selection screens. These include a few subscreens that are used for processing function modules. These subscreens do not process any of the values entered. You therefore do not have to be afraid of undesirable side effects. Here is the listing, first of all:

```
 1 REPORT YZ334130.
 2 SELECTION-SCREEN BEGIN OF TABBED BLOCK tstrip FOR 40 LINES.
 3   SELECTION-SCREEN TAB (79) card_1 USER-COMMAND comm1
 4                         DEFAULT program SAPMS38L SCREEN 3030.
 5   SELECTION-SCREEN TAB (79) card_2 USER-COMMAND comm2
 6                         DEFAULT program SAPMS38L SCREEN 3050.
 7   SELECTION-SCREEN TAB (79) card_3 USER-COMMAND comm3.
 8 *                       DEFAULT program SAPMS38L SCREEN 3052.
 9 SELECTION-SCREEN END OF BLOCK tstrip.
10
11 INITIALIZATION.
12   card_1 = 'Attributes'.
13   card_2 = 'Import parameters'.
14   card_3 = 'Export parameters'.
15
16 AT SELECTION-SCREEN.
17   IF SY-UCOMM = 'COMM3'.
18     tstrip-prog = 'SAPMS38L'.
19     tstrip-dynnr = 3052.
20     tstrip-activetab = 'CARD_3'.
21   ENDIF.
```

The selection screen contains a tabstrip area with three different tabs. The two statements in lines 2 and 9 define a block to create this. The statements in lines 3 and 5 each define an input page, while the subscreens to be inserted are defined statically in the statement. In line 7 this definition is omitted. Therefore the tabstrip has to be dynamically provided with the necessary data at the AT SELECTION-SCREEN event. Naturally, the function code initiated when the user clicks the tab has to be analyzed here. The function codes initiated by the tabstrip are stored in the SY-UCOMM field. When you use the SELECTION-SCREEN statement to define the tabstrip, the system creates a complex, data object with the same name. This contains the subfields PROG, DYNNR and ACTIVETAB. You enter the name of the program, from which the screen program to be inserted should be derived and the screen program number, in the first two fields. In ACTIVETAB, you enter the name of the tabstrip's tab that is to be selected. Lines 12 to 14 contain statements that will be executed once during the initialization of the selection screen. In them you define the text of the individual tabs in the tabstrip. However, unlike in this example, in real-life applications this should not be done using hard-coded texts, but instead with easily translated text icons.

Exercises

1. Modify program YZ334050 or YZ334060 in such a way that the two checks are both created in the SELECT statement or with the CHECK statement. Keep an eye on the system behaviour at runtime.

2. In the programs used for building field groups, change the sequence of the statements for creating groups and analyze the results.

3. Enter your own texts for parameters and selections.

4. First create program YZ334100 by modifying YZ3342080, and then make the changes described in the text (parameter-specific AT SELECTION-SCREEN ON statements). Test the program. Modify the program again by replacing the parameter-specific AT SELECTION-SCREEN ON statements with a joint check at the general AT SELECTION-SCREEN event. Analyze the result.

3.4.4 Output formatting

In earlier examples some data has already been displayed on the screen and formatted to a modest extent. In full-blown reports and their output lists, additional statements are available for editing both individual lines and entire pages. These statements not only simplify programming, but also enable you to use coloured editing elements to make the screen output easier to understand. The WRITE and FORMAT statements are responsible for the output lines. Besides defining the appearance of individual lines, other statements also set global defaults, such as page length or width, as well as various headers. All these statements are of minor importance for the actual functions of a report. However, they are indispensable if you want to create an output list with a clear, professional appearance. Create a new program for testing the statements below.

Page layout parameters

Initially, the system uses default values to define the dimensions of a list (length and width of a page). The width of the list depends on the current width of the window. The page length is unlimited, which means the list consists only of one page. It is, however, possible to define individual defaults. For this, you generally use two options of the REPORT statement:

```
...  LINE-SIZE columns ....
...  LINE-COUNT lines(footer) ....
```

The LINE-COUNT option can be assigned an optional definition of the number of footer lines to be kept empty. If this definition is missing, the system applies the default value 0. Enter these numbers as direct values, i.e. without surrounding quotation marks. When the system is outputting the list on the screen or to a printer, it always displays or prints the header and the list header at the upper margin of the page, regardless of the page length set. Therefore, a correct page header always appears, even in a list where no individual page length has been defined. For this reason, the definition of the page length primarily affects the correct page numbering. In the case of an endless page length, all printed pages are given the same page number. You can avoid this disadvantage by setting page breaks manually. To do so, use this statement:

```
NEW-PAGE.
```

Some options of this statement allow you to change the length and width of the new page, as well as allowing you to activate and deactivate titles and headers generated by default. That is why, within the same report, individual pages can have a very different layout from others.

Individual page header

Besides the use of standard elements, you can also use the `TOP-OF-PAGE` event statements to generate an individual page header in a report. Both the header line and column headers must be output in this page header. If you generate a separate header with this event statement, the default page header output must naturally be switched off. There are two ways to do this: the following statement, or the one after it, which is even simpler:

NEW-PAGE NO-TITLE NO-HEADING.

or

REPORT *name* **NO STANDARD PAGE HEADING.**

Within a report you can easily use the `NEW-PAGE` statement, with appropriate options, to change the defaults in the `REPORT` statement. The `NEW-PAGE` statement only inserts a page break if there has been genuine output to the page beforehand. That is why it is not possible to use `NEW-PAGE` to generate empty pages. However, the options (i.e. `NO-TITLE`) become effective in any case.

Margin and anchoring

Lists that are to be output on a printer often require a margin. A printer does not necessarily generate the margin all by itself, depending on the actual printer and its specific settings. You can therefore use this statement to specify the position at which printing starts:

SET MARGIN *column row.*

The line (row) definition is optional. You can enter both values either as a direct value or as a field reference.

Lists can be up to 255 characters wide. To view such lists on the screen, you have to scroll them horizontally with the Windows window scroll bar. You can make it easier for the user to identify where they are in the display by leaving particular help values, such as a line number, the sorting order number or a keyword, at the left margin. To set up column anchoring, use this statement:

SET LEFT SCROLL-BOUNDARY.

It anchors the columns at the current cursor position. When the user scrolls the screen horizontally, the columns will not be moved but remain at the left edge of the image. You can therefore use the following addition to define the number of columns to be anchored, independent of the cursor position:

SET LEFT SCROLL-BOUNDARY COLUMN *column*.

It is also possible to anchor individual lines such as the lines of the table header. To do so, use this statement:

NEW-LINE NO SCROLLING.

It ensures that the next output line will not be scrolled horizontally. The default list header is automatically output with this option.

Positioning

The first demo programs have already introduced an option for the targeted positioning of the screen output. There are some other statements that can be used as alternatives to WRITE in combination with format options. Below you will find a detailed description of the WRITE statement, followed by information on these alternative statements.

You can assign each output field some formatting data, which consists of a maximum of three parts: one character for line feed, one output position and one output length. You enter this formatting data in this format:

```
/position(length).
```

It stands before the value to be output. The slash is the line feed character. All three elements in the format option are optional. The values that set the position and length can be passed either as direct values or as field references. However, if you use field references, you must enter the AT prefix before the whole construct. The following extract from a program shows some correct statements:

```
. . .
DATA: P TYPE I.

WRITE: 'ABC'.
WRITE: / 'DEF'.
WRITE: /4 'GHI'.
WRITE: 8(2) 'JKL'.

P = 8.
WRITE: AT /P 'MNO'.
. . .
```

If an output length is missing, the system uses the default output length for the particular data type. The line feed character will have no effect if the output field is empty, as the following example demonstrates:

```
. . .
DATA: C.

WRITE:  /  'Start'.
WRITE:  /  C.
WRITE:  /  C.
WRITE:  /  'End'.
```

However, this special feature only occurs if the line feed character in a format option represents a field. When it is used as an independent character, i.e. without defining a field in a separate WRITE statement, or at least as an independent element in such a statement, it always generates a line feed:

```
DATA: C.

WRITE:  /  'Start'.
WRITE:  /.
WRITE:  /, C.
WRITE:  /  'End'.
```

If you want to force the output of empty lines even if the output field is empty, you can do so using this statement:

SET BLANK LINES ON.

This statement remains in effect until you switch it off again with this statement:

SET BLANK LINES OFF.

This statement is a safe way to generate empty lines:

SKIP.

As shown above, it inserts an empty line into the text. With an additional parameter you can specify the number of empty lines to be inserted:

SKIP *lines*.

Finally, you can use the following variant of the WRITE statement to position the cursor on a particular line of the page while retaining the option of jumping forward and backward within the current page length. The line count starts with 1:

SKIP TO LINE *line_number*.

Within a line, you can use this statement to set the position for later output with WRITE to a specified column:

POSITION *column*.

In lists, values should normally be positioned exactly after the column headers or, in multiline lists, after another data field. Changes in the headlines consequently require that all other position settings be edited. It is much simpler to use an additional option of the WRITE statement, with which you position the value to be output exactly in the column in which the field was output:

WRITE *value* **UNDER** *field*.

Here, you have to enter the field name in exactly the same way as for its own output. This is especially important if you refer to text elements with default values. The program below, which is a modification of YZZ32050, shows some variants of the UNDER option.

```
REPORT yz334140 NO STANDARD PAGE HEADING.
TABLES tadir.

PARAMETERS p_author LIKE tadir-author DEFAULT '*'.
SELECT-OPTIONS s_name FOR tadir-obj_name.

WRITE: 'Objecttype', 20 'Name), 40 text-002.
* create text-002 with text 'Author'!

SELECT * FROM tadir
WHERE obj_name IN s_name.
  CHECK tadir-author CP p_author.

  WRITE: / tadir-pgmid UNDER 'Objecttype',
           tadir-obj_name UNDER 'Name),
           tadir-author UNDER text-002.

ENDSELECT.
```

The UNDER addition merely sets positioning within the line and does not trigger a line feed. If the line feed is missing, the texts that are being referred to or previous output will, if necessary, be overwritten with the new values because the output occurs in the same line.

The following statements also belong indirectly to the positioning options:

BACK.

and

RESERVE *n* **LINES**.

The BACK statement sets the output position either to the first line of a page or, after the RESERVE statement has been used, on the first output line after RESERVE.

The last statement causes a page break unless at least *n* lines are empty on the current page. This statement usually stands before connected output consisting of several lines, or before the output of an intermediate header. Indirectly, it ensures that a few more data lines follow after a headline on the current page.

Formatting

The WRITE statement is not only responsible for outputting and positioning values, but also for formatting. Some options are available for formatting, which have not yet been discussed. You enter them after the output value. Consequently, the WRITE statement has the following syntax:

WRITE *format value option.*

The majority of the editing options can be described very quickly (*see* Table 3.32), but more detailed descriptions are necessary for a few options.

Table 3.32   Formatting options for WRITE

Option	Effect
NO-ZERO	Leading zeros before numbers will be replaced with spaces. If the contents equal 0, only the spaces will be output
NO-SIGN	No prefix operator will be output
NO-GAP	No separating space will be output after the value
NO-GROUPING	Suppress thousands delimiter in the case of type P and I
DD/MM/YYYY	Date field will be processed and output according to the
MM/DD/YYYY	date format template
DD/MM/YY	
MM/DD/YY	
DDMMYY	
MMDDYY	
CURRENCY curr	The field will be processed according to the settings for the currency. These settings will be defined during customizing. The TCURX table is primary
DECIMALS n	Output with n decimal points
ROUND n	Only for data type P. The decimal character will be moved n digits to the left ($r > 0$) or to the right ($n < 0$). Then the value will be output without digits after the decimal point
UNIT	Similar to CURRENCY: the value is processed according to the data in units table T006
TIME ZONE *timezone*	Processing of a time entry in UTC using the format of the specified timezone
EXPONENT n	Only for floating-point numbers. The number is output in exponential display with the specified exponents
USING EDIT MASK *mask*	The value is processed according to a mask
USING NO EDIT MASK	The conversion defined in the Data Dictionary will not be executed
UNDER *field*	Output exactly under another field
LEFT-JUSTIFIED	Aligns value to the left in the output field
CENTERED	Centres value in the output field
RIGHT-JUSTIFIED	Aligns value to the right in the output field
AS icon	Interprets the field contents as an icon name and outputs them
attributes	Controls the attributes (colour, intensity) for a field with the same statements as in FORMAT

The two USING options primarily require further explanation. A mask is predefined for the first variant (USING EDIT MASK), whose characters are mixed with those of the value to be output. The mask may contain the wildcard characters shown in Table 3.33. The actual mask has to be defined as a character string, i.e. has to be enclosed in quotation marks.

Table 3.33   Characters in output masks

Wildcard character	Effect
_ (underscore)	Each underscore represents one character of the value to be output
V	Prefix operator
LL (at the start of the mask)	Enter left-aligned
RR (at the start of the mask)	Transfer right-aligned
==xxxxx	Conversion of the value with routine CONVERSION_EXIT_xxxxx_OUTPUT
All other characters	Delimiter, will be mixed with the characters of the value

The effects of the individual wildcard characters are shown below in some examples. To make the examples clearer, you will find each generated output shown as a comment under the output statement in the program below.

```
REPORT yz334150 NO STANDARD PAGE HEADING.
DATA: w1(4)      VALUE 'ABCD',
      w2(8)      VALUE '12345678',
      w3 TYPE i VALUE '-12345'.

WRITE /(20) w1 USING EDIT MASK 'LL:_____:'.
*  :ABCD          :

WRITE /(20) w1 USING EDIT MASK 'RR:_____:'.
*  :           ABCD :

WRITE /(20) w2 USING EDIT MASK ':__-__-__-____:'.
*  :12-34-56-78  :

WRITE /(20) w2 USING EDIT MASK 'RR:__-__-__-____:'.
*  :-12-34-5678  :

WRITE /(20) w3 USING EDIT MASK 'RR:V_____:'.
*  :-12345       :
```

In the Data Dictionary you can define the five-digit name of a conversion routine, also called a *conversion exit*, for all domains. The system uses this descriptor to form the names of two function modules called CONVERSION_EXIT_xxxxx_OUTPUT and

CONVERSION_EXIT_xxxxx_INPUT. During the passing of a value from an input field in a screen program to the actual data field, the system automatically calls a routine called CONVERSION_EXIT_xxxxx_INPUT, while outputting the field CONVERSION_EXIT_xxxxx_OUTPUT. In these routines, the field contents can be converted as necessary. The wildcard characters ==xxxxx call any conversion tool for the value. This can be useful if the field to be output was not derived from a Data Dictionary field, but contains comparable contents.

If the Data Dictionary already contains a conversion function for the domain on which the field is based, you can also switch off conversion with the USING NO EDIT MASK option.

The R/3 System contains tables for currencies and units in which some information is stored during customizing. This includes the number of digits after the decimal point, conversion factors, etc. The CURRENCY and UNIT options process the values to be output, according to the data in these tables.

Screen attributes

You can give lists a much clearer structure, by visually highlighting important elements. In the R/3 System you can achieve this by using a different level of intensity (brightness) or colour. You can use a maximum of eight colours in lists, and address them using a number or predefined descriptor. The SAP Style Guide recommends certain colours for particular elements in a list. The names of the predefined descriptors are also based on its recommendations (*see* Table 3.34). It is therefore advisable to comply with these recommendations. They only fulfil their purpose if all lists in the system are structured in as uniform a way as possible, in accordance with guidelines.

Table 3.34   Colours in lists (line background)

Number	Descriptor	Used for	Colour
OFF	COL_BACKGROUND	Background	GUI-dependent
1	COL_HEADING	Headings	Grey-blue
2	COL_NORMAL	Body of list	Light grey
3	COL_TOTAL	Totals	Yellow
4	COL_KEY	Key columns	Blue-grey
5	COL_POSITIVE	Positive threshold value	Green
6	COL_NEGATIVE	Negative threshold value	Red
7	COL_GROUP	Group levels	Purple

You can use this statement to set the colours and some other attributes:

FORMAT *attribute_1 attribute_2 ... attribute_n.*

They will take effect at the next WRITE statement. An event such as the start of an event statement will reset the attributes to its default values. However, once this event is left, the original values apply once again. For example, attributes that are set in a TOP-OF-PAGE block therefore only apply to this block. You set the colour with this statement, using the US spelling shown:

FORMAT COLOR *color*.

Here, *color* is either one of the numbers listed in Table 3.34 or one of the predefined descriptors. The colour number can also be transferred dynamically, i.e. as a value from a field:

FORMAT COLOR = *field*.

In this case *field* is an I-type data field. The field contains one of the colour numbers. Apart from the colours you can also set the intensity by using the INTENSIFIED or INTENSIFIED OFF addition. The INVERSE or INVERSE OFF addition reverses the foreground and background colour. Here, too, you can dynamically define each particular option (ON or OFF). When you do so, the system will interpret field contents '0' as OFF, and all other values as ON.

You can also use the options described for the FORMAT statement in the WRITE statement. In the WRITE statement you define the attributes for the output of an individual field. The program below demonstrates some variants of the WRITE statement:

```
REPORT yz334160 NO STANDARD PAGE HEADING.
DATA n TYPE i VALUE 0.
DO 8 TIMES.
  WRITE: / 'Color: ' NO-GAP COLOR = n ,
           n COLOR = n,
           'Color: ' NO-GAP COLOR = n INTENSIFIED OFF,
           n COLOR = n INTENSIFIED OFF,
           'Color: ' NO-GAP COLOR = n INVERSE ON,
           n COLOR = n INVERSE ON.
  ADD 1 TO n.
ENDDO.
```

Exercises

1. Add some statements for formatting output to a few programs (i.e. YZ334010). For example, you can highlight intermediate headers or lines with totals in colour.

2. Insert your own headers in the reports you have just generated.

3. Write a report that generates a sufficient number of output lines with random contents. Test the statements for explicitly defining page length and page width.

4. Add column headers to report YZZ32100. Test the statements for anchoring lines or columns.

3.5   Interactive reports

The reports described in Section 3.4 allow you to call some default functions, such as character string searches or list printing, from the menu. However, true interactivity cannot be achieved by this simple form of list processing. There are some simple additions that fit seamlessly into the concept we are discussing, which expand simple reports into an interactive list-processing function that can react to special, user-triggered events. Using these additional programming language elements you can, for example, program the following functions:

- select a record in a list and return the information to a calling program (example: search help);

- jump to secondary lists with additional information;

- flexible representation of data structures or multilevel lists (example: Object Browser);

- Input and process values in the report (example: expansion level in various error lists, i.e. transport management system);

- Creation of hypertext applications (example: screen program-based online help).

  To upgrade a report by adding interactive elements, up to four steps are necessary:

1. Generate an interface with your own function codes.

2. Link this interface with the report.

3. Intercept your own function codes with event statements.

4. Program the individual functions.

  The next section explains these steps in more detail and creates examples for practical application.

3.5.1 Events in interactive reports

In addition to the events already described, three events groups are important for interactive reporting. They are needed to recognize and process user activities. Each of these events are processed using a separate event statement.

  If the user double-clicks or presses (F2), this triggers an event which is recognized through this event statement:

`AT LINE-SELECTION.`

  For this to happen, the `PICK` function code must be present, and the (F2) function key must have been assigned in the current status of the report. In the automatically set default status for reports, F2 is already assigned. To find out more information about the selected line you can use some system fields or the `HIDE` statement, which has not yet been described.

All function codes that are not automatically processed by the system are handled by this statement:

`AT USER-COMMAND.`

This event statement is a generalized form of `AT LINE-SELECTION`. At this event, all system fields are filled when the user double-clicks with the mouse or presses (F2), just like during list line selection. In addition, the system fills the `SY-UCOMM` field with the function code of the selected function. It processes the function code within the instruction block of the event statement in a similar way to a dialog application's function code in the `OK-CODE` module. The line in which the cursor was positioned will be used as the current line.

The advantage of the `AT USER-COMMAND` event over the `AT LINE-SELECTION` is that in it several different actions can be executed for the current line. Individual function codes that can be evaluated using `AT USER-COMMAND` are only available if a separate interface is generated with the Menu Painter and called in the report.

The following event statement takes on a special role:

`AT PFxx.`

If one of the function keys has been assigned to function code `PFxx.`, where xx represents the number of the function key, the system processes `AT PFxx`. instead of `AT USER-COMMAND`. As function codes should not really begin with the letter 'P', this statement is primarily suitable for test purposes. Before you can use this event statement, you must also modify the interface.

3.5.2 Details lists

One of the most important tasks of interactive reports is to react when the user selects a line in the list by double-clicking on it or by pressing function key (F2). The following short report demonstrates this principle:

```
REPORT yz334170 NO STANDARD PAGE HEADING.
DO 30 TIMES.
  WRITE: / 'Line', sy-index.
  WRITE /.
ENDDO.

AT LINE-SELECTION.
  WRITE: / 'List level :', sy-lsind COLOR 4.
  WRITE: / 'Line rel. :', sy-curow COLOR 4.
  WRITE: / 'Column rel. :', sy-cucol COLOR 4.
  WRITE: / 'Linenumber :', sy-lilli COLOR 4.
  WRITE: / 'Content :', (40)sy-lisel COLOR 4.
```

First, the report generates a list which outputs 30 lines of text, each of which is followed by an empty line. If you double-click on one of these lines, you jump to a new screen which displays some values. These values are the list number, the position of the mouse pointer with reference to the screen window, the final line number and the contents of the selected line. Any information is provided from system fields that have been filled automatically. In general terms, the first list is called a *basic list* and all others a *details list*.

Even this short program allows for some interesting experiments. One double-click in the details list results in the creation of a new list. This becomes apparent, above all, in the way that the value for SY-LSIND increases. Each double-click in the list increases the displayed value by one, and each time you press function key (F3), you return to the previous list. You can only select lines that have actually been written in the list. If you double-click after the last line, the report does not react.

During line selection, the system sets some system fields. As shown in the example, these can be queried and evaluated in the further course of the program. Table 3.35 shows the system fields that are important in interactive reporting.

Table 3.35 System fields for interactive reporting

System field	Meaning
SY-LSIND	Number of the list (basic list = 0)
SY-CUROW	Line position of the cursor in the last list displayed
SY-CUCOL	Column position of the cursor in the last list displayed
SY-LISEL	Contents of the selected line
SY-LILLI	Absolute line number of the selected line
SY-LISTI	List number of the selected line
SY-PFKEY	Name of the current status of the interface
SY-CPAGE	First page displayed
SY-STARO	First row displayed
SY-STACO	First column displayed

After the AT LINE-SELECTION statement, the code for creating a new list begins. That is why this statement can be followed by other statements that define basic settings for a new list. Consequently, you can use SET PF-STATUS to set a new status, change the dimensions of the list, etc. These settings only apply to the details list and not to the basic list. If, for example, you set a new status in a details list, the original status becomes active again after you return to the basic list. Apart from one exception, there are no special statements for details lists. This exception is the TOP OF PAGE statement. It ensures that page headers are generated within basic lists. For details lists this event is not processed. Instead, you use a similar statement:

```
TOP OF PAGE DURING LINE-SELECTION.
```

Within this event, the system processes all details lists. If you also want to set different headers for details lists at different levels, you have to analyze the system field for the list level as part of TOP OF PAGE processing.

Any numbers of branches can be generated in the example above, but in practice this is neither necessary nor practical. If you want to prevent further branches, you must use an IF statement to query the list level. Note that the value for SY-LSIND immediately after AT LINE-SELECTION already corresponds to the new list level. If there is no output, no new list level is displayed on screen either. To terminate the branch after the first details list, you need to make the following modification:

```
AT LINE-SELECTION.
   IF SY-LSIND < 2.
      WRITE: / 'List level   :', SY-LSIND COLOR 4.
      WRITE: / 'Line rel.    :', SY-CUROW COLOR 4.
      WRITE: / 'Column rel.  :', SY-CUCOL COLOR 4.
      WRITE: / 'Linenumber   :', SY-LILLI COLOR 4.
      WRITE: / 'Content      :', (40)SY-LISEL COLOR 4.
   ENDIF.
```

A selected line is made available in SY-LISEL in the same way it was written to the list. This means that, if any evaluation is taking place, only the information appearing in the list would be available. For hypertext applications (i.e. the online help) this is very helpful because you can determine the term at the cursor position with SY-CUCOL from SY-LISEL. In other applications, however, this feature is a disadvantage. If, for example, you wish to use the information in the basic list to select a record and then display additional information on it in the details list this would only be possible if the complete key appeared in the basic list and could be filtered out of the SY-LISEL value. This procedure is rather time consuming, would result in illegible lists and, above all, would fail if multiline entries were made to the list. Instead, you can use a special statement to insert additional data for each line of the list into a *hidden data area*. This data is stored and only made available again when the line is selected. The data does not appear on the screen. To use the hidden data area, you need to use a special statement and a program structure that is tailored to it. The statement is as follows:

HIDE *field.*

This statement places the current contents of the field in the hidden data area of the current line. The field can also be a simple field, a structure or the header line of a table. With HIDE you can handle any fields. If you want to enter multiple fields in a HIDE statement, you must precede them with a colon:

HIDE: *field_1, field_2, ... field_n.*

When data has been hidden with HIDE, you can use certain statements that refer to a line in the list, to load it back into the particular field. One of the statements that trigger this, for example, is the AT LINE-SELECTION event statement. The following example program demonstrates how the HIDE statement is used:

```
REPORT yz334180 NO STANDARD PAGE HEADING.
DATA: line TYPE i VALUE 1.


FORMAT COLOR 4.


DO 30 TIMES.
  WRITE: / 'Line', sy-index, AT sy-linsz ' '.
  HIDE line.
  WRITE: / 'Next line, AT sy-linsz ' '.
  HIDE line.
  WRITE: /.
  ADD 1 TO line.
ENDDO.


AT LINE-SELECTION.
  IF sy-lsind < 2.
    WRITE: / 'Selected line:', line COLOR 4.
  ENDIF.
```

You can also use this report for your own experiments. When it is executed, the list displays two lines that belong together each time. They are highlighted in colour to make them easier to recognize. For each of these lines, the report uses HIDE to place the value from the line field in the hidden data area. The line groups are separated by an empty line for which no HIDE statement has been entered.

After you select a line by double-clicking on it, the report again brings out the value for the line field from the hidden data area and displays it. No additional program statements are necessary for this: the process is controlled automatically by the system. The contents of fields that were not hidden with HIDE, remain unchanged after a line selection. Therefore, if you select a line for which no information has been hidden, its current field contents will not change. This characteristic results in an undesirable feature of the report. Although no HIDE statement has been programmed for the separators, the system creates a details list each time you double-click on one of the empty lines. Here, the value displayed for the line field corresponds to the previous current value. It does not change even after you select different empty lines.

Suppressing this feature requires a small modification of the program. The way the report branches into new lists now depends on whether data for the selected line is present in the hidden data area. As a result, in many cases there is no longer any need to evaluate SY-LSIND. For test purposes, simply copy the last program and then modify the copy:

```
REPORT yz334190 NO STANDARD PAGE HEADING.
DATA: line TYPE i VALUE 1.
FORMAT COLOR 4.
```

```
DO 30 TIMES.
  WRITE: / 'Line', sy-index, AT sy-linsz ' '.
  HIDE line.
  WRITE: / 'Next line', AT sy-linsz ' '.
  HIDE line.
  WRITE: /.
  ADD 1 TO line.
ENDDO.

CLEAR line.

AT LINE-SELECTION.
  IF NOT line IS INITIAL.
    WRITE: / 'Selected line:', line COLOR 4.
    CLEAR line.
  ENDIF.
```

In general, the report resembles the previous version. The only new thing is that, after the report generates the list, it uses the CLEAR statement to set the line field to its initial value. Now, there is no longer a query for the list level within the instruction block for line selection. Instead the report tests the line field to determine its initial value. The report will only generate the details list if the *line* field is given a value that is not equal to the initial value. This is only the case if a line has been selected, in which information in the line field was hidden with HIDE. After the details list is created by the report, line must naturally be reset to its initial value. When you are evaluating data fields derived from the hidden data area of a line, you must be sure that the field names are absolutely identical. Errors will result if the HIDE statement is used to hide several individual fields from a structure, but the whole structure is later checked for the initial value.

Because no HIDE statements are executed in the details list, the IF statement simultaneously prevents the creation of additional details lists. The various details lists, or lines from a list, can place different data fields in the hidden data area. Then, at the AT LINE-SELECTION event, the actual functionality of the application can be defined either by means of the current field assignments or by using the SY-LSIND system field.

In the examples above, the details list always fills the complete screen. You can now use the following new ABAP statement to define windows (dialog boxes) of any size, in which a details list can be displayed:

WINDOW STARTING AT x1 y1 **ENDING AT** x2 y2.

The co-ordinates define the top left (x1, y1) and bottom right (x2, y2) corners. The ENDING AT addition with the two parameters x2 and y2 is optional. If this addition is missing, the dimensions of the window are automatically set to the current dimensions of the list. Here is a short example of how this statement is used (the changes concern only the creation of the details list):

```
AT LINE-SELECTION.
  IF NOT line IS INITIAL.
    WINDOW STARTING AT 5 5 ENDING AT 50 10.
    WRITE: / 'List level :', SY-LSIND COLOR 4.
    WRITE: / 'Line rel. :', SY-CUROW COLOR 4.
    WRITE: / 'Column rel. :', SY-CUCOL COLOR 4.
    WRITE: / 'Line number :', SY-LILLI COLOR 4.
    CLEAR line.
  ENDIF.
```

It is not absolutely necessary to create a list at the AT LINE-SELECTION event. Other activities, such as calling a dialog application, are also possible. The following example demonstrates how to call a function module:

```
REPORT yz334200 NO STANDARD PAGE HEADING.
TABLES: trdir,        "Table with ABAP programs
        textpool.     "Structure for texts

* internal table for texts
DATA: BEGIN OF itext OCCURS 20.
        INCLUDE STRUCTURE textpool.
DATA: END OF itext.

FORMAT COLOR 4.

SELECT * FROM trdir
  WHERE cnam = sy-uname          "User
    AND appl <> 'S'              "no generated programs
    AND subc IN ('1', 'M', 'F') . "no includes

* write program name
  WRITE: /(60) trdir-name.
  HIDE trdir.

* read texts
  CLEAR itext.
  REFRESH itext.
  READ TEXTPOOL trdir-name INTO itext LANGUAGE sy-langu.

* find description
  CLEAR itext.
  itext-id = 'R'.
  READ TABLE itext.
```

```
* write description
  IF sy-subrc = 0.
    WRITE: /(60) itext-entry.
    HIDE trdir.
  ENDIF.
  WRITE /.
ENDSELECT.

CLEAR trdir.

AT LINE-SELECTION.
  IF NOT trdir IS INITIAL.

* call editor for program
    CALL FUNCTION 'EDITOR_PROGRAM'
      EXPORTING
        program = trdir-name
        message = ' '
        display = 'X' ' SPACE for edit, X for show only
        trdir_inf = trdir.
    CLEAR trdir.
  ENDIF.
```

In the listing, the attributes of all current user-created programs are read from the TRDIR table. The system tests some of the attributes to ensure that no include files or system-generated programs appear in the list. The TRDIR table only contains some general administration information. The short description must be read separately. All the language-specific elements of an application, such as the text elements, headings or the short description, are saved separately from this administrative data. If the language-specific data is required, it must be read using additional statements. To do so, you can use a special variant of the READ statement. It is not necessary to directly access tables with the SELECT statement. The READ statement inserts various types of text in an internal table. The system must use a code letter to find and load the short text for the program from the internal table. If there is a short description, it is also displayed in the list. For both lines, the system inserts the whole header line from the TRDIR table in the hidden data area. When a user selects a line, the system calls the program editor for the program. The DIS-PLAY flag is used to ensure that the editor works in display mode after it is called.

Interactive reporting is often used to trigger the following functions, besides calls to function modules:

● provision of information about a selected record in global fields or cross-application memory areas, and about the use of LEAVE to terminate the report;

● CALL TRANSACTION for calling a transaction;

● SUBMIT for calling another report;

- CALL FUNCTION for calling function modules;

- CALL DIALOG for calling dialog modules;

- CALL SCREEN for calling screen programs belonging to the current program.

The last statement listed is especially interesting, because even a report can have its own screen programs. In a similar way to this, you can use the LEAVE TO LIST-PROCESSING statement within a dialog application to switch on list mode. This has the effect of breaking down the borders between reports and dialog applications to some extent. However, if you mix list and dialog processing a great deal, in an application this will quickly lead to confusing programs.

If you want to create a screen program in a report, you can do so either by using the Object Browser's object list or by using the navigation functions. You enter the CALL SCREEN statement in the source code. After you double-click the number of the required screen program, the system generates that screen program. However, you do have to enter some additional data in various screen programs.

All the examples described above also work for the AT USER-COMMAND event, if this event is processed by triggering a separate function code. Also, in this event, the system selects the line defined by the current cursor position. If, however, only one action is ever to be executed for a line, such as 'always branch to another list', it is simpler for the user to select this line by double-clicking, i.e. by first placing the cursor on a line and then clicking on a pushbutton, or even selecting a menu option. In a similar way, the modification statements described below can also occur at the AT LINE-SELECTION event.

3.5.3 Making modifications to the list

Not all actions within a list require the creation of a detail list. Frequently, all you need to do is process or modify lines in the current list. An example of this is various selection lists, such as the one in search help. Depending on the list type, you can select one or more records and transfer them to the calling program. To some extent, this selection requires you to modify the entries in an existing list.

The MODIFY statement is the most important statement for modifying a list. There are several variants of this statement, each of which has some additions. To demonstrate the principle on which it works, let us use this statement as an example for now:

MODIFY CURRENT LINE.

This statement always refers to the last line selected by a user, using a line selection function. In the basic form of the statement shown above, the contents of the SY-LISEL system field are displayed in the list, where the line is positioned. You can only use the MODIFY statement to change existing lines. You cannot use it to create new ones. If the system executes the statement successfully, it fills the SY-SUBRC system field with the value 0. If MODIFY is unable to find the line that is to be changed, SY-SUBRC is filled with a value other than 0. The error code always depends on whether the system has found the line to be changed or not. The additions, which are still to be described, affect the contents of SY-SUBRC.

The processing of the examples below requires statuses that can provide two sets of function codes. These are the default function codes required for list processing, and also four additional function codes whose format is FNCx. Create a status. Then choose EXTRAS | ADJUST TEMPLATE from the menu in the Menu Painter to assign the default values for a report to that status.

The aim is for the individual function codes, which are assigned to the status, to be available to users if they press one of the function keys, starting with (F5), or by choosing certain pushbuttons. To create the different examples, you can copy the first program several times and then modify each copy accordingly. In each case, you have to explicitly mark the 'GUI status' item in the dialog box where you select the elements to be copied. The actual program is a bit more extensive because an internal table is required so that all options can be demonstrated:

```
REPORT yz334210 NO STANDARD PAGE HEADING.
DATA: BEGIN OF itab OCCURS 5,
   select,
   name(20),
END OF itab.

itab-select = ' '.
itab-name = 'Line 1'.
APPEND itab.

itab-name = 'Line 2'.
APPEND itab.

itab-name = 'Line 3'.
APPEND itab.

itab-name = 'Line 4'.
APPEND itab.

itab-name = 'Line 5'.
APPEND itab.

SET PF-STATUS 'STAT1'.

LOOP AT itab.
   WRITE: / itab-select, itab-name.
ENDLOOP.

AT USER-COMMAND.
   CASE sy-ucomm.
      WHEN 'FNC1'.
         sy-lisel+30 = 'modified'.
         MODIFY CURRENT LINE.
   ENDCASE.
```

In this program, you use the function code FNC1 to add additional text to the line where the cursor is located (you cannot double-click here to select the line!). While the original lines of the list are displayed in a highlighted colour (usually blue, depending on the system default), the added character strings are represented in normal colour (usually black).

It is easy to change the output format later. To do so you can slightly expand the AT USER-COMMAND part of the first example by evaluating a second function code:

```
AT USER-COMMAND.
. . .
  WHEN 'FNC2'.
    MODIFY CURRENT LINE LINE FORMAT INTENSIFIED OFF.
```

The function code FNC2 switches off the intensified display for the current line. After the FORMAT statement you can use all its options. In this example, they refer to the whole line. This is defined by the repetition of LINE in the statement. The multiple use of LINE in the statement may not be particularly elegant, but it is completely correct syntactically. The first LINE belongs to CURRENT and the second one defines that FORMAT should apply to the whole line. Due to the specific use of LINE, it can be assumed that the individual fields of a line can also be modified. To modify their format, use this addition:

```
... FIELD FORMAT field_1 format_1 ... field_n format_n.
```

Here you enter the names of the fields to be modified and their particular formats sequentially. It is also possible to use a third function code to demonstrate this statement. This changes the colour used to display the first two fields of the line:

```
AT USER-COMMAND.
. . .
  WHEN 'FNC3'.
    MODIFY CURRENT LINE  FIELD FORMAT itab-select COLOR 7
                         INVERSE ON itab-name COLOR 5.
```

You can only modify the colour of specific fields if data fields have been output in the list. You cannot change the characteristics of fixed values afterwards in this way. For ABAP, text elements are also a type of data field, which is why they can also be assigned new formats.

To enable you to modify individual fields, the internal control logic has to store the output fields with their output positions for each line. This information also allows you to assign new contents to the fields in a line. The statement you use to do so resembles the one used to assign new formats:

```
... FIELD VALUE field_1 FROM value_1 ... field_n FROM value_n.
```

The lines below demonstrate how this statement is used. They set the itab-select field in the current line to the value 'X' and, as a result, select the record for later evaluation, if required:

```
AT USER-COMMAND.
...
   WHEN 'FNC4'.
      MODIFY CURRENT LINE FIELD VALUE itab-select FROM 'X'.
```

You can simplify the statement slightly by entering the new values directly into the fields to be changed. In the MODIFY statement, you can then omit the FROM clause. In an individual statement like the one shown in this example, there is no advantage in using this version of the statement, but it does make the MODIFY statement a lot easier to understand, if several fields have to be changed:

```
WHEN 'FNC4'.
   ITAB-SELECT = 'X'.
   MODIFY CURRENT LINE FIELD VALUE ITAB-SELECT.
```

If the modified fields were used in a HIDE statement during the creation of the list, changes will also be made to the hidden data area. Naturally, these changes to fields only apply to the values in the list or in the hidden data area. This type of assignment has no effect on the internal table or even the database table used to create the list. This causes a new problem: the most recently used function code highlights a line. In real-life applications, this information must of course be analyzed. This is why there must be a means of reading the current field values from the list. You cannot use SY-LISEL because it is a very cumbersome way of selecting individual values. You can use a special form of the READ statement to read current values directly from the list. It is the counterpart to the MODIFY VALUE statement. As shown here, the MODIFY statement works together with the current line, due to the CURRENT LINE addition. Besides this addition, a few others are possible. These extend the scope to any line in every list that exists in the program. You can use these additions both for READ and for MODIFY. Therefore the example below shows how the READ statement can be used in this way. This example is based on one of these alternative additions that can also be used with the MODIFY statement. In practice, there is more often a need to read data from a list when required than to write data to a list. The syntax of the READ statement is:

```
READ LINE index FIELD VALUE
   listfield_1 INTO progfield_1 ...
   listfield_n INTO progfield_n.
```

The system accesses the line, identified by its line number, and reads from it the names of the fields to be entered in the list. It then inserts them in fields within a program. If the INTO PROGFIELD addition is missing, the system makes the contents of the list fields available in the original fields. All unspecified fields remain unchanged. In addition to reading the specified fields, the system also loads all the field contents hidden with HIDE into this line. If no values are present in the hidden data area, the associated fields remain unchanged. Consequently, the result of the READ statement is only really meaningful if all fields to be read by READ are initialized immediately before the READ statement is executed. This has already been shown for the evaluation of the HIDE fields. The example below, YZ334220, is broadly similar to program YZ334210, which has already been

used. However, even in the main program some changes are necessary. First of all, you
have to create an additional data field and two event statements. Due to the event statements for the title, another statement is necessary to mark the start of the 'main program'.
That is why the statements below must be inserted between the declaration for the internal table and the first assignment for the table's header line:

```
REPORT yz334220 NO STANDARD PAGE HEADING.
DATA: BEGIN OF itab OCCURS 5,
   select,
   name(20),
END OF itab.
DATA i TYPE i.

* Header main list
TOP-OF-PAGE.
   WRITE: / 'Please select'.
   SKIP.

* Header sub list
TOP-OF-PAGE DURING LINE-SELECTION.
   WRITE: / 'Selected lines:'.
   SKIP.

* create main list
START-OF-SELECTION.
   itab-select = ' '.
   itab-name = 'Line 1'.
   APPEND itab.

   itab-name = 'Line 2'.
   APPEND itab.

   itab-name = 'Line 3'.
   APPEND itab.

   itab-name = 'Line 4'.
   APPEND itab.

   itab-name = 'Line 5'.
   APPEND itab.

   SET PF-STATUS 'STAT1'.

   LOOP AT itab.
      WRITE: / itab-select input,
               itab-name.
   ENDLOOP.
   CLEAR itab.
```

```
* push buttons
AT USER-COMMAND.
  CASE sy-ucomm.

* set flag
    WHEN 'FNC1'.
      MODIFY CURRENT LINE FIELD VALUE itab-select FROM 'X'.

* reset flag
    WHEN 'FNC2'.
      MODIFY CURRENT LINE FIELD VALUE itab-select FROM ' '.

* show selected lines
    WHEN 'FNC3'.
      i = 1.
      CLEAR itab.

* read first line from screen
    READ LINE i FIELD VALUE itab-select itab-name.

* SY-SUBRC <> 0 -> line i doesn't exist
    WHILE sy-subrc = 0.

      IF itab-select <> ' '.
        WRITE: / itab-name.
      ENDIF.

* read next line
      i = i + 1.
      CLEAR itab.
      READ LINE i field VALUE itab-select itab-name.

    ENDWHILE.

  ENDCASE.

* select line with double click
AT LINE-SELECTION.
  CLEAR itab.

* read flag
  READ CURRENT LINE FIELD VALUE itab-select.
```

```
* modify flag
  IF itab-select = ' '.
    MODIFY CURRENT LINE FIELD VALUE itab-select FROM 'X'.
  ELSE.
    MODIFY CURRENT LINE field VALUE itab-select FROM ' '.
  ENDIF.
```

Up to the point where the status is specified, this program is the same as the previous example. Later, when the list is being read, the I field takes on the function of a line counter. The loop for creating the basic list also contains a modification. When the system is outputting the SELECT field, it assigns it the INPUT format. A field of this kind is ready for input in the list and the user can enter a value in it manually. This value only exists within the list: this input does not change the internal table. This functionality is similar to that of MODIFY when it is used to make changes to fields. The entries in a field of this kind are later read with the READ statement.

When the AT USER-COMMAND event occurs, the function codes FNC1 and FNC2 are used to either set or reset the flags. These statements do not contain anything new; they have already been used in the previous example. However, what is interesting is the processing of function code FNC3. Here, the system reads all the records in the basic list. It writes all the selected data records to a detail list.

The form of the READ statement mentioned above is used for reading data. To read data, a record counter is required. Before the system accesses the first line, this record counter must be set to an initial value. The structure that belongs to the fields that are to be read by the READ statement is also initialized before each READ statement. The READ statement's return code is the same as that for the MODIFY statement. For this reason, it merely tells you whether the line to be read exists or not. You cannot see from the READ statement's error code whether the field to be read is present in this line. After the READ statement, the contents of ITAB-SELECT only differ from the initial value if the field was actually found, and was filled with a value other than a blank in the list. This is the only case where the NAME field of each particular line is output in the detail list. The detail list is not displayed until all the statements in the AT USER-COMMAND block have been processed. That is why all further READ statements still read data from the basic list. In more complex programs, you must always take care that you know which of the lists is currently active, to prevent the system reading data from the wrong list.

Once a line in the list has been evaluated, the line counter is increased by one and the system reads the next line. If you want a particular line to be read after the end of the list, READ returns a return code that is not zero. This can then act as a termination criterion.

In these types of selection list, you can of course also use line selection as a way to switch a selection on or off. The AT LINE-SELECTION event shows the statements you need to do this. First of all, the system reads the current line. Depending on the flag's status, it is then either set or reset. This is one of the situations where it is a good idea to use the CURRENT LINE addition to read the current line.

You can also enter a value manually in the selection flag fields in each record. The example program regards all contents, with the exception of a blank, as a set flag. In the screen programs, where you can define checkboxes or radio buttons, the internal control logic ensures that selected fields are always represented by the letter 'X'. It may happen that other applications have been programmed so that, instead of checking for values that do not equal a blank, they check for values that are equal to the letter 'X'. If the user makes an incorrect entry, the application may not function correctly. For this reason, the WRITE statement only gives one additional option for structuring checkboxes. You can test this by simply exchanging one single line in the example:

```
WRITE: / itab-select AS CHECKBOX,
         itab-name.
```

The list now displays a checkbox instead of the input field that can contain any alphanumerical data. Simply click on this field to toggle its status. One single mouse click is all it takes! Within the application, a selected field is marked with an 'X'. An unselected field is represented by a blank. You do not need to use the statements after AT LINE-SELECTION to toggle the selection. The two MODIFY statements of this event can be temporarily commented out. However, the line selection ensures that you can still double-click anywhere in the line to select it. In contrast, the checkbox input fields only react when you click within them.

In the previous examples, you could only make modifications within a line without changing the structure or length of the list. However, some of the previously described situations, where you can use interactive reporting, presume that the list is recreated when you select a line. If you double-click on a node in the Workbench object list, the system restructures the current (basic) list and no detail list appears. The easiest way to use this functionality is to link a screen program with the embedded list-processing function. In this case, the actual screen program is inactive; it is processed in the background with the SUPPRESS dialog. In the PAI part of the screen program, the LEAVE TO LIST-PROCESSING statement is used to create a list. A user statement or a line selection in this list triggers an event statement which uses LEAVE LIST-PROCESSING to temporarily end list processing. In this case, the screen program is executed again, i.e. the list is recreated. At the end of this section, you will find a more comprehensive example that demonstrates the relationship between dialog-oriented applications and list processing.

3.6   Logical databases

The previous sections have already mentioned that selecting the data required for a report can be rather time consuming. It often happens that several tables are logically dependent on each other and form a hierarchy. When you select data, each report must take these hierarchical dependencies into account by using nested SELECT statements or similar constructs. If several reports which perform similar evaluations need to access the same files and always have to take the same dependencies into account, identical or almost identical queries will be required again and again. You can use *logical databases* to reduce the amount of time and effort that programming this requires.

Logical databases are not objects that can be used independently. It only really makes sense to use logical databases in conjunction with a report. When you generate a new report, you can enter the name of a logical database in the attributes screen. The report then automatically uses this logical database to select records.

3.6.1 Task and component parts

A logical database is a specially created program. It selects records in several tables that are linked together logically and then makes the records it reads available to the actual report. The report receives the records in the correct sequence and then only has to evaluate and display them. You use the PUT and GET pair of statements to arrange for the provision of the records by the logical database and for the reading of these records in the actual report. In this case, GET is an event statement.

A logical database consists of three basic elements:

- structure (table hierarchy);
- selections;
- database program.

Structure

The tables to be processed by the logical database must be sorted by a tree structure. Each table may only exist once in this structure. The structure's branches define how the tables interdepend on each other. You use an editor with a graphical interface to maintain this structure. Starting from a root, the system assigns the lower level tables step by step. The structure is not an object that you can use directly. It merely represents the tables that will be included in the logical database and their dependencies on each other. The system uses this data to generate two program files: the database program and the selection include. In the more recent Releases of R/3 software, the actual database program itself consists of several includes.

Selections

Selections, as their name implies, are a series of SELECT-OPTIONS statements. The system generates a separate SELECT-OPTIONS statement for each key field in all the logical database's tables. The system stores these statements in an include file which, in turn, is included in the database program. This file, together with the selections, must then be processed by the programmer according to their special requirements. You can insert selections or parameters for additional fields or delete existing selections. The following extract from a program shows a basic selection program. The name of the selection include is structured according to template **DB**<code>1db_name</code>**SEL**.

```
*_____*
*  INCLUDE DBYLB1SEL
*  It will be automatically included into the database program.
*_____*
```

```
. . .
SELECT-OPTIONS :
*                       ? FOR TADIR-PGMID,
*                       ? FOR TADIR-OBJECT,
*                       ? FOR TADIR-OBJ_NAME.
   s_author for tadir-author.

* Parameter for search pattern selection (Type SY-LDB_SP):
* PARAMETERS p_sp AS SEARCH PATTERN FOR TABLE TADIR.

* SELECT-OPTIONS :
*                       ? FOR E071-TRKORR,
*                       ? FOR E071-AS4POS.

* SELECT-OPTIONS :   ? FOR E070-TRKORR.
. . .
```

Database program

The database program is the logical database's main program. After it has been generated, the subroutines it contains are either empty or they consist only of comments and
therefore do not have any functions. At this point, the database program also contains
SELECT statements for each table in the logical database. Depending on the R/3 Release
you are using, this program may even consist of multiply-nested includes. The template
SAPDBldb_name defines the name of the database program.

The system generates a WHERE clause for the SELECT statements. This clause contains
the queries for all the key fields in each particular table. In these queries, the system
enters 'automatic comparison with key fields of the higher-level table' as a prompt value.
It does this if the table fields are based on the same data element. This ensures that the
corresponding records in the secondary table(s) are read for the higher level record. You
must modify the WHERE clause to suit your own requirements. For example, you can add
the selections from the selection include, if they have been defined. To achieve correct and
usable results, you must always take the current values of the key fields of the higher
level table(s) into consideration. In the SELECT statement, the PUT statement sends the
current record to the evaluating report.

The system takes the dependencies predefined in the structure of the logical database
into consideration in the WHERE clauses it generates. The extract from a database program
(below) shows how the key fields in the higher level table are referenced when the system
reads a secondary table. If the tables are to be linked by fields that are not key fields in the
two tables, you will have to program these queries yourself.

```
FORM PUT_TADIR.
   SELECT * FROM TADIR
*    INTO TADIR
*    INTO TABLE ? (choose one!)
*    WHERE PGMID = ?
*      AND OBJECT = ?
*      AND OBJ_NAME = ?.
   where author in p_author.
   PUT TADIR.
   ENDSELECT.
ENDFORM.                "PUT_
...
FORM PUT_E071.
* SELECT * FROM E071
*    INTO E071
*    INTO TABLE ? (choose one!)
*    WHERE TRKORR = ?
*      AND AS4POS = ?.
   PUT E071.
* ENDSELECT.
ENDFORM. 'PUT_
...
FORM PUT_E070.
* SELECT * FROM E070
*    INTO E070
*    INTO TABLE ? (choose one!)
*    WHERE TRKORR = E071-TRKORR.
   PUT E070.
* ENDSELECT.
ENDFORM.                "PUT_
```

In addition to the subroutines for the SELECT statements there are other subroutines that
the system calls automatically on particular events when the selection screen is processed.
The names of the subroutines and the corresponding events are shown in Table 3.36.

Table 3.36   Subroutines and events in a logical database's selection screen

Subroutine	Description
LDB_PROCESS_INIT	Initialize multiple processing of a logical database; called immediately after the program starts
LDB_PROCESS_CHECK_SELECTIONS	Check selections after selection values have been entered
INIT	Executed once before the selection screen is displayed for the first time
PBO	Executed prior to each display of the selection screen
PAI	Executed after each display of the selection screen
BEFORE_EVENT	Execution before different event statements
AFTER_EVENT	Executed after different event statements

3.6.2 Dynamic selection

Although logical databases make programming reports less complicated, their predefined
selection options also limit their flexibility. Dynamic selection provides a solution to this.
It allows a report's user to formulate any selection criteria for one or more tables while
the application is running. This avoids having to program a multitude of individual selections or parameters.

Practical application

If a dynamic selection has been defined for a table, the DYNAMIC SELECTIONS pushbutton
appears in the selection screen's application toolbar (*see* Figure 3.64).

After you click this pushbutton, the system splits the screen program into two. The
left-hand side displays a list of all tables for which dynamic selections have been defined
(*see* Figure 3.65). However, this overview shows the table's short description instead of its
name. Although this is very useful for the end user, programmers will need to get used to
this feature.

To display a list of the table fields, click the icon in front of the table name. Click a field
in this list to select it. If you press the button with the arrow symbol, a selection for the
selected field appears in the right-hand window (*see* Figure 3.66). The report user can
now select all the fields that they are interested in.

In this way, you can transfer all the fields you require into the list of selections. You
enter the requested selection values in the same way as you enter values in the report's
selection screen. After you have finished entering data, you choose Selections | Save from
the menu to store the values you have just entered for the dynamic selection. If you
return to the report's initial screen, a message inside the dynamic selections icon will
draw your attention to the additional selection criteria. You can now execute the report in
the usual manner and evaluate the selection values of the dynamic selection.

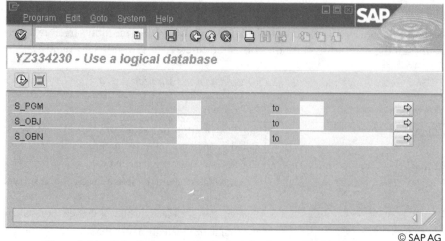

Figure 3.64   Selection screen of a logical database with dynamic selection

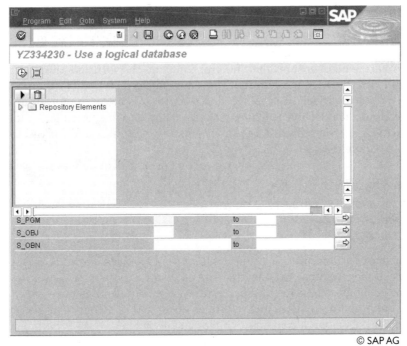

© SAP AG

Figure 3.65   Selection of tables for a dynamic selection

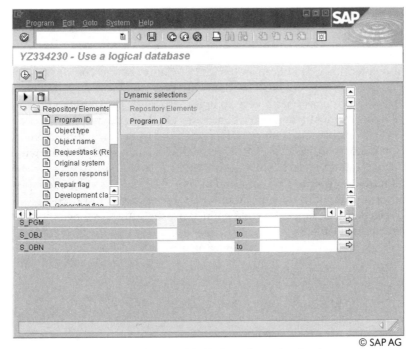

© SAP AG

Figure 3.66   Selection of fields for a dynamic selection

Programming dynamic selections

You require two things before you can implement a dynamic selection in a logical database. One is a special statement in the database program's selection include (DBxxxSEL). This special statement ensures that the user can enter the corresponding selection criterion. You enter the selection criterion for a dynamic selection in a different way from simple parameters or selection tables, and the program also evaluates it in a different way. Therefore, the selection statement must be tailored to the particular table so that the table can evaluate this selection criterion. This section will introduce you to the statements you require in more detail.

In the DBxxxSEL selection include, the following statement defines the database table for which a dynamic selection is to be implemented:

```
SELECTION-SCREEN DYNAMIC SELECTIONS
  FOR TABLE table
  [ID ident].
```

If dynamic selections are to be supported for several tables, a statement is required for each table. If the report uses a table that is intended for a DYNAMIC SELECTION, the Dynamic selections pushbutton appears in the selection screen. Any entries made when the application is running for any dynamic selections are stored in a complex data object called DYN_SEL. This data object contains an internal table called CLAUSES. Each data record in this table contains another internal table called WHERE_TAB. The selection criteria for all the database tables are stored in this internal table. You must use this special variant of the SELECT statement to evaluate these selection criteria:

```
SELECT * FROM table
  WHERE (itab).
```

This variant of the SELECT statement reads the selection criteria from an internal table. You can also enter other conditions in the WHERE clause. Before you do this, the internal table used in the WHERE clause must be filled with data from the DYN_SEL dataset.

The DYN_SEL data object has a very complex structure. The definition is stored in the RSDS type pool. Its most elementary component is the type definition for an internal RSDS_WHERE_TAB table. This internal table is derived from a structure stored in the Data Dictionary. It merely consists of a CHAR-type field with a length of 72 characters.

```
TYPES: RSDS_WHERE_TAB LIKE RSDSWHERE OCCURS 5.
```

This definition flows into the definition of the RSDS_WHERE structure. This structure has a TABLENAME field, in which you enter a table name, and a WHERE_TAB internal table. The selection criteria for the table defined in the TABLENAME field are stored in the WHERE_TAB internal table.

```
TYPES:
  BEGIN OF RSDS_WHERE,
    TABLENAME LIKE RSDSTABS-PRIM_TAB,
    WHERE_TAB WHERE_TAB TYPE RSDS_WHERE_TAB,
  END OF RSDS_WHERE.
```

You use this type of structure to define another internal table. This second internal table stores the selection criteria for several Data Dictionary tables.

```
TYPES: RSDS_TWHERE TYPE RSDS_WHERE OCCURS 5.
```

Finally, the table definition shown above is incorporated into the RSDS_TYPE type description. This type now contains the CLAUSES field, which contains an RSDS_TWHERE-type table.

```
TYPES:
  BEGIN OF RSDS_TYPE,
    CLAUSES TYPE RSDS_TWHERE,
    TEXPR TYPE RSDS_TEXPR,
    TRANGE TYPE RSDS_TRANGE,
  END OF RSDS_TYPE.
```

This data type has two additional fields that also contain very complex objects. The TEXPR field contains the selection criteria in a form that can be stored, whereas the TRANGE field saves these criteria in some of the RANGES tables. If necessary, the CHECK statement can use these RANGES tables. Finally, you use data type RSDS_TYPE to generate a real data object. You use the following statement to do this:

```
DATA DYN_SEL TYPE RSDS_TYPE.
```

You will find more details about the structure of the other components in DYN_SEL in the type pool we mentioned above.

From the data types discussed above, you can see that DYN_SEL always stores data in all tables where dynamic selections have been used to enter selection criteria. Therefore, you usually access values in DYN_SEL by using the name of the database table as a limiting criterion.

3.6.3 Using a logical database

Before you can use a logical database in a report, you must enter its name in that report's attributes screen. The name of a logical database consists of three characters. However, you enter this name in two parts in the attributes screen. SAP recommends that you use one character to emphasize that the logical database belongs to an application group. The two other characters are the user-definable part of the name. You do not need to make any more direct references to the logical database in the report.

In the actual report, you use the TABLES statement to declare all the tables from which data is to be read. After this, you can then use the following event statement to define the processing of a record in the report:

GET *table.*

The PUT and GET statements work together in a relatively complicated way. They are actually controlled by the system. First of all, the system ensures that the SELECT loop is executed for the highest table in the hierarchy. Once a data record has been read, the PUT statement transfers it to the report. When the PUT statement is called, it triggers an event that processes the GET event for the table that has just been processed in the report. For example, the record may be output there. After the GET event, the database program executes all the PUT subroutines for the subsequent tables in the hierarchy, if GET processing has been programmed for these tables in the report. When you call the subroutines, the system even takes into account dependencies that span several levels. If a report only evaluates one table, and that table is located several hierarchical levels below the root, it still reads all the tables between the root and the table.

In the form described here, the GET event for a higher level table is always called before the GET event of the lower level table. You use the addition shown below to select GET events that are only processed after all the lower level tables have been processed:

GET *table* **LATE**.

You use this addition to write evaluations concerning the lower level table (i.e. addition of field values) to the list. In a report, each table may only have one GET event and one GET LATE event.

3.6.4 A practical example

The example below is based on the practical requirements of program development. Occasionally you will need to know who has processed particular development objects and when they did so. As long as no local, private objects are involved, Table E071 tells you which tasks and statements contain a particular object. You will find information about the person responsible for processing an order or a task in Table E070. For this reason, this example will list all the tasks and statements, as well as their operator, connected with an object contained in the TADIR table. It does this by evaluating the TADIR table as well as Tables E070 and E071. To do this, you must create a logical database.

You call the processing of a logical database from the CASE menu by choosing DEVELOPMENT | PROGRAMMING ENVIRONMENT | LOGICAL DATABASES. This menu option has transaction code SE36.

In the first screen program of this transaction (*see* Figure 3.67), you enter the name of the logical database. Previous Releases of R/3 software restricted the length of this entry to only three characters. This restriction has now been removed.

After you enter the name, you click on the Create button. Like all the other elements in the development environment, you must also enter a short text for the logical database. You do this in a dialog box, as shown in Figure 3.68. You also click on the Create pushbutton to close this dialog box.

Each logical database has a table structure that has exactly one root node. You use the editor provided for that purpose to process an existing structure. However, you define the root node for a new database in a further dialog box (Figure 3.69).

In this dialog box, you enter the name of the node and a short text to describe it. Here, we recommend that you use the names of the tables involved. In addition to this, you must also specify which table to evaluate.

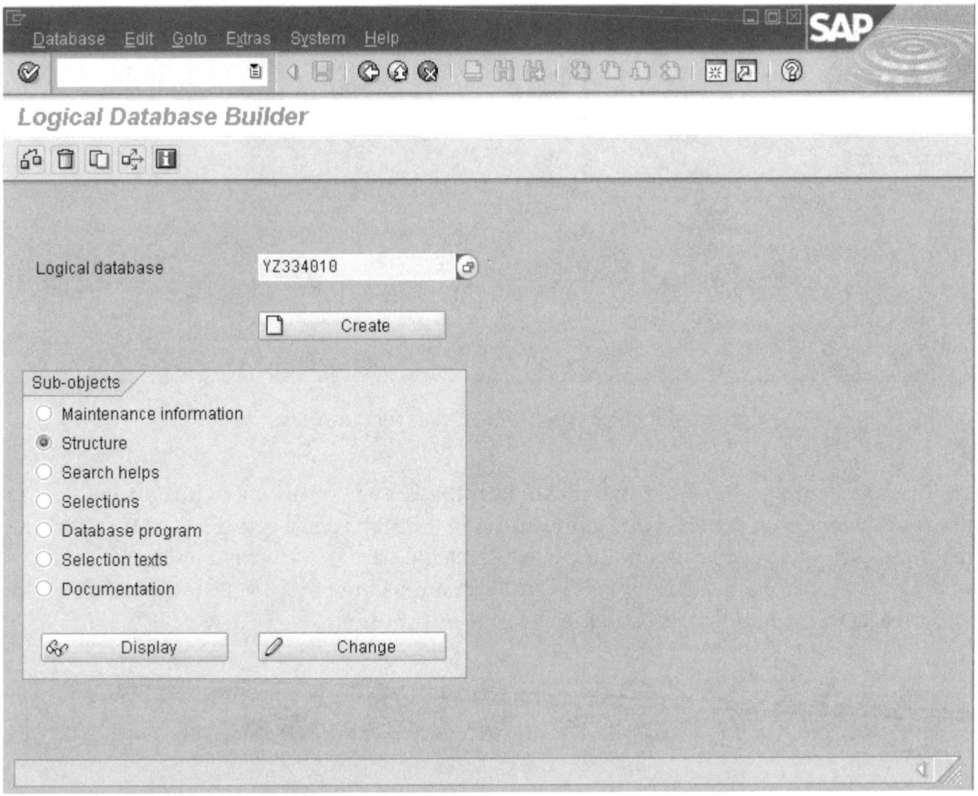

Figure 3.67   Initial screen of transaction SE36

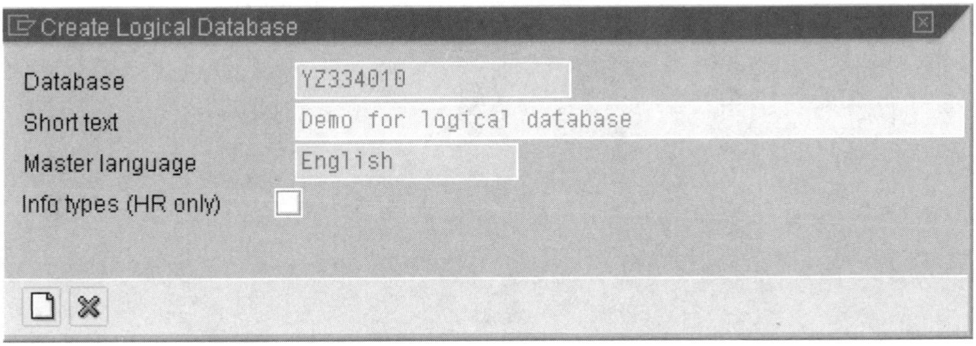

© SAP AG

Figure 3.68   Defining the short text for a logical database

© SAP AG

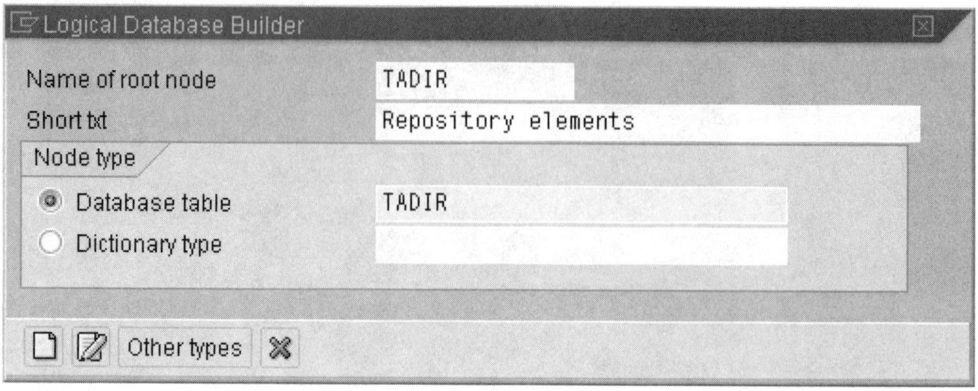

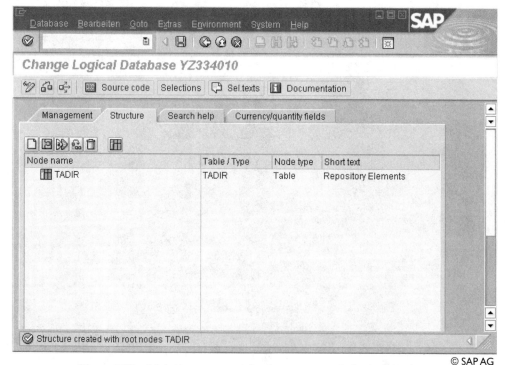

© SAP AG

Figure 3.69   Defining the root node for a table hierarchy

After confirming your entry by clicking on the Create button, you jump to the actual maintenance screen where you maintain logical databases (Figure 3.70). You can also reach this screen program in another way: enter the name of an existing logical database in the initial screen of Transaction SE36. You then select the Structure radio button in the Sub-objects frame and finally click the Change pushbutton.

© SAP AG

Figure 3.70   Maintenance screen for the structure of a logical database

In the structure maintenance screen you now create two additional nodes in the table hierarchy. To do this, position the cursor on the node under which you want to insert a new node, and click the Create icon that you see immediately above the actual work area in the tabstrip area. You enter all the data for the new node in a dialog box that looks like the one in which you create the root node (*see* Figure 3.71).

This dialog box contains a new additional input field where you can specify the node under which the new node should be inserted. This field is preselected by means of the cursor position. However, you can change its contents at any time. The system even provides input help that displays all the current existing nodes.

You create the two additional nodes according to the structure shown in Figure 3.72.

The selections are created once you have defined the table structure. You create selections by choosing GOTO | PROGRAM | SELECTIONS from the menu or by clicking on the SELECTIONS button that you see in the application toolbar.

You can use the table hierarchy you have just defined as a starting point for the program you are about to generate. In a dialog box (Figure 3.73), you must click on the Yes pushbutton to confirm that you want selections to be made on the basis of the table structure in the generated program.

The next dialog box (Figure 3.74) also allows you to provide search help in the selection fields. You do not need this for the current example, and can therefore cancel the prompt by clicking on the No button.

After the system prompts you as to whether you want to create search help, a last dialog box (Figure 3.75) is displayed. In it you select the tables for which you want to generate the dynamic selections or field selections. For the moment, we will disregard these elements. To close the dialog box without making any changes, click on the TRANSFER pushbutton.

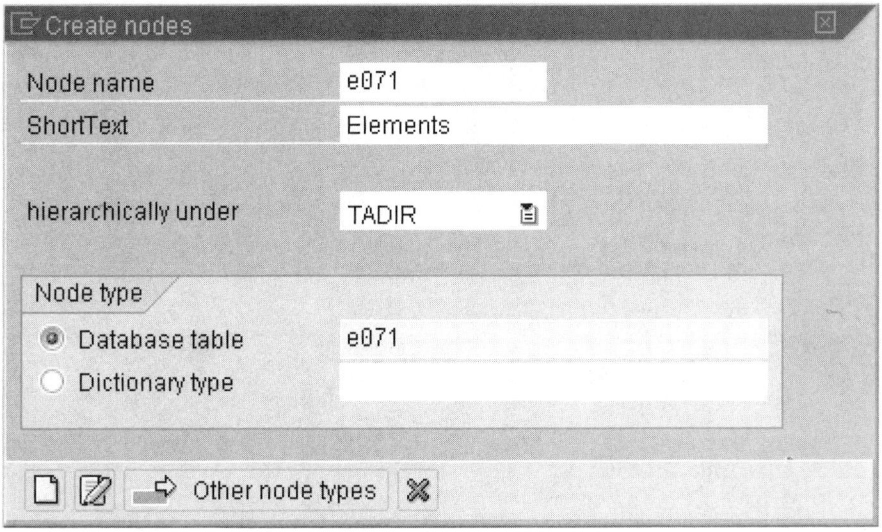

© SAP AG

Figure 3.71   Creating a new node

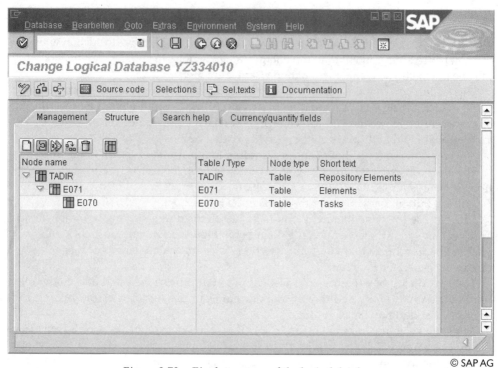

Figure 3.72   Final structure of the logical database

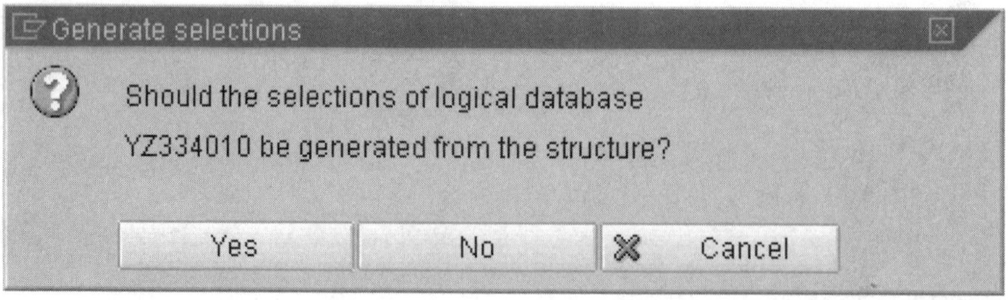

© SAP AG

Figure 3.73   Confirmation prompt when you generate selections

© SAP AG

Figure 3.74   Decision to create search help

© SAP AG

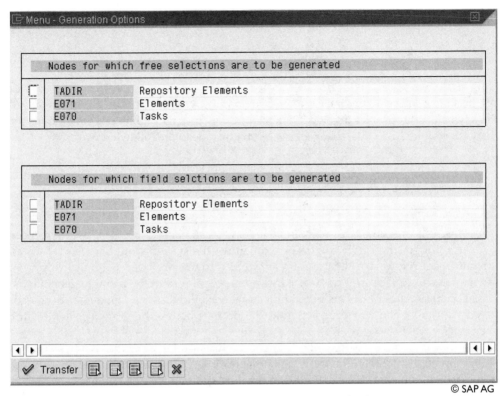

© SAP AG

Figure 3.75   Selecting tables for dynamic selections

The system now displays the editor with the generated source code. Some comment lines have been removed from the listing below:

```
*_____*

*  INCLUDE DBYZ334010SEL
*  It will be automatically included into the database program.
*_____*


*  SELECT-OPTIONS :
*                       ? FOR TADIR-PGMID,
*                       ? FOR TADIR-OBJECT,
*                       ? FOR TADIR-OBJ_NAME.

*  Parameter for search pattern selection (Type SY-LDB_SP):
*  PARAMETERS p_sp AS SEARCH PATTERN FOR TABLE TADIR.

*  SELECT-OPTIONS :
*                       ? FOR E071-TRKORR,
*                       ? FOR E071-AS4POS.
```

```
* SELECT-OPTIONS :   ? FOR E070-TRKORR.

* Enable DYNAMIC SELECTIONS for selected nodes :

* Enable FIELD SELECTION for selected nodes :
```

The source code contains a basic (commented-out) SELECT-OPTIONS statement for all the key fields of the tables involved. You should now program three selection options for the TADIR table. To do this, change the selection include in the following way:

```
SELECT-OPTIONS :
  s_pgm FOR TADIR-PGMID,
  s_obj FOR TADIR-OBJECT,
  s_obn FOR TADIR-OBJ_NAME.
```

Because this program deals with an include, you can neither execute a program check nor carry out generation. If you tried to do either, the system would always return an error message. Now save the program and return to the structure maintenance screen. There, you choose GOTO | PROGRAM | DATABASE program from the menu to generate the actual database program. This function is only available if change mode has been activated. You must confirm your action at the prompt before the system generates the program for real *(see* Figure 3.76).

You now access the source code. In the more recent releases of the R/3 System, this source code only contains INCLUDE statements. To give you a better overview, all the non-essential comments have once again been removed in the listing below:

```
include DBYZ334010TOP . " header
include DBYZ334010NXXX . " all system routines
* include DBYZ334010F001 . " user-defined include.
```

The important elements are contained in the second include, whose name ends in NXXX. If you double-click on this program name again, the following source code appears. Once again, this source code only consists of includes:

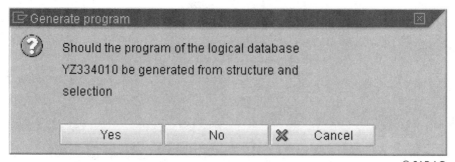

Figure 3.76   Confirming that you want to generate the database program

```
include DBYZ334010N001 . " Node TADIR
include DBYZ334010N002 . " Node E071
include DBYZ334010N003 . " Node E070
include DBYZ334010FXXX . " init, PBO, PAI
include DBYZ334010SXXX . " search help.
```

In contrast to previous Releases of SAP software, where all the SELECT statements were contained in one file, a separate include file is now generated for each table involved. You cannot tell from the file name which file is handled by each include. However, the comment at the end of each line tells you this. You should therefore switch to this file by double-clicking on program name DBYZ334010N001. Here you will find a subroutine with a commented-out SELECT statement:

```
FORM PUT_TADIR.

* SELECT * FROM TADIR
*    INTO TADIR
*    INTO TABLE ? (choose one!)
*    WHERE PGMID IN s_pgm
*    AND OBJECT IN s_obj
*       AND OBJ_NAME IN s_obn.

   PUT TADIR.

* ENDSELECT.
ENDFORM.                    „PUT_
```

This statement is syntactically and logically correct. You can activate it by removing some of the comment characters:

```
SELECT * FROM TADIR
*    INTO TADIR
*    INTO TABLE ? (choose one!)
   WHERE PGMID IN s_pgm
      AND OBJECT IN s_obj
      AND OBJ_NAME IN s_obn.

   PUT TADIR.

ENDSELECT.
```

You must also process the other two includes. Because Tables TADIR and E071 are not linked by shared key fields, you must delete the WHERE clause that was generated for Table E071 and insert the SELECT statement shown below instead:

```
FORM put_e071.
   SELECT * FROM e071
*     INTO E071
*     INTO TABLE ? (choose one!)
      WHERE pgmid = tadir-pgmid
         AND object = tadir-object
         AND obj_name = tadir-obj_name.
      PUT e071.
   ENDSELECT.
ENDFORM.                           „PUT_
```

E070 and E071 are linked by a shared key field so that the WHERE clause that the system generates can be transferred.

```
FORM put_e070.
   SELECT * FROM e070
*     INTO E070
*     INTO TABLE ? (choose one!)
      WHERE trkorr = e071-trkorr.
      PUT e070.
   ENDSELECT.
ENDFORM.                           "PUT_
```

Once you have finished processing the selection subroutines, you return to the first program file of the database program. There you activate all the programs you have processed. In this case, these are the three NXXX includes, the selection include and the SAPDBYZ334010 framework program. Once you have activated these programs successfully, you can again return to the structure maintenance screen. In this state, the logical database is generally ready for use. However, you should still maintain the selection texts to ensure that it remains easy to use. To do this, click on the Sel.texts button. You can now enter any selection text you like in the text symbol maintenance transaction that you are already familiar with (Figure 3.77). You must also activate these texts before they can take effect.

For peace of mind you can still run a final check on the logical database. To do this, choose Database | Check from the menu in the structure maintenance screen or click on the Check pushbutton. A dialog box (Figure 3.78) informs you about the status of the logical database.

Now you can create the actual evaluation report. To do this, you must generate a new program (YZ334230). In the program attributes, you enter the name of the logical database in the appropriate input field. Figure 3.79 shows the maintenance screen. Take care here that you enter the name of the logical database and not the name of the database program.

The actual evaluation report is very short. The listing below shows the source code:

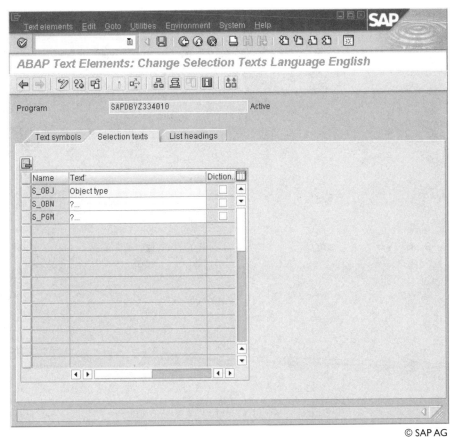

Figure 3.77   Maintaining selection texts

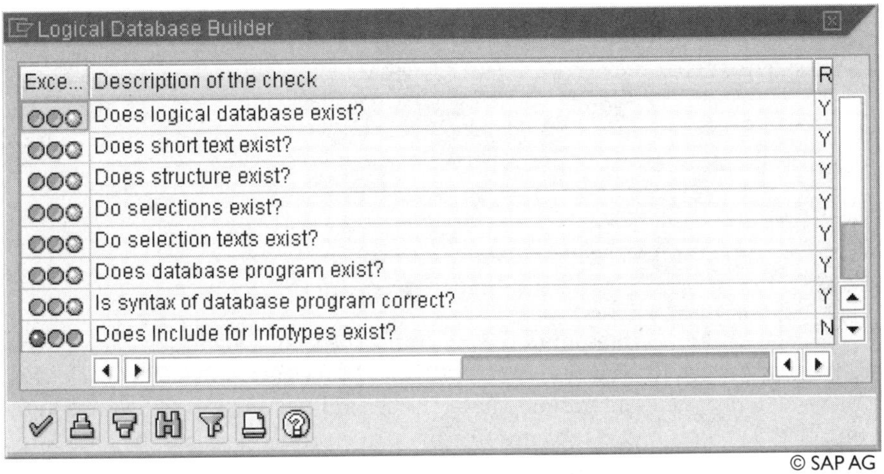

© SAP AG

Figure 3.78   Check results

© SAP AG

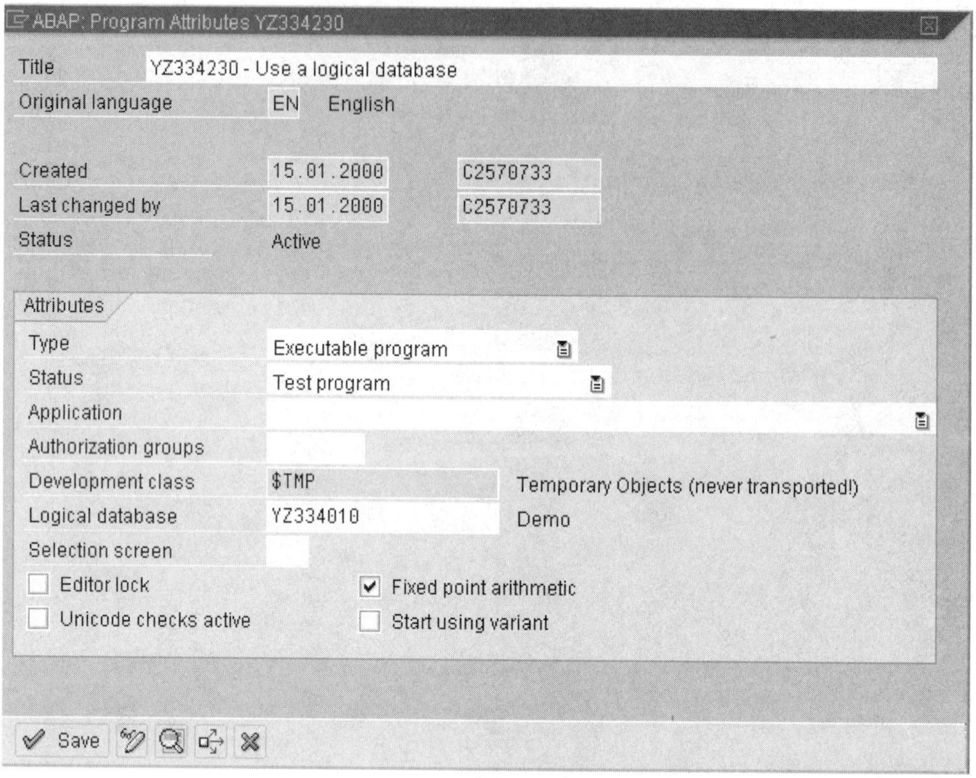

Figure 3.79   Attributes of the evaluation report

© SAP AG

```
REPORT yz334230.
TABLES:    tadir,
           e070.


START-OF-SELECTION.

  GET tadir.
    FORMAT COLOR 1.
    WRITE: / tadir-pgmid, tadir-object, tadir-obj_name.

  GET e070.
    WRITE: / e070-trkorr, e070-as4user, e070-as4date.
```

Two GET statements are present in the program. The first is always triggered when the logical database reads a record in the TADIR table. In the next statement block, this data record is used to output an interim heading. The second GET statement belongs to the last node of the table hierarchy. You can derive the name of the user who has modified this object from the corresponding table.

Despite the fact that this application is so easy to use, it still has one major restriction. The available selection criteria and the links between individual tables are predefined and unchangeable. However, there are a lot more options you can use, especially when you select objects to be analyzed from the TADIR table. Instead of programming each selection criterion separately, you can use dynamic selections. If you do this, all the table fields in one or more tables become available as potential selection fields, and with relatively little programming effort. If you have not already included dynamic selections when you created the logical database, you will have to add the necessary statements manually later on.

This part of the example defines a dynamic selection for the TADIR table. To do this, you must first edit the selection include. You then add the following statement at the end of the source text:

```
* Enable DYNAMIC SELECTIONS for selected nodes :
SELECTION-SCREEN DYNAMIC SELECTIONS
    FOR TABLE tadir.
```

With this statement you specify that the TADIR table is reserved for dynamic selections. As a result of this statement, the system automatically generates the dyn_sel_clauses internal table during runtime. You can enter selection statements in this table in a screen program that is also generated automatically. The contents of this internal table must be evaluated in the database program. You must also modify the PUT_TADIR subroutine for that purpose.

```
FORM put_tadir.
    DATA il_cl TYPE rsds_where.
    READ TABLE dyn_sel-clauses
      WITH KEY 'TADIR'
      INTO il_cl.

    SELECT * FROM tadir
*      INTO TADIR
*      INTO TABLE ? (choose one!)
      WHERE pgmid IN s_pgm
        AND object IN s_obj
        AND obj_name IN s_obn
        AND (il_cl-where_tab).
      PUT tadir.

    ENDSELECT.
ENDFORM.                    "PUT_
```

First, you use the selection statements to extract the part which contains statements for the TADIR table from the internal table. That part is then copied to a second internal table called il_cl. This table is then transferred into the WHERE clause as another part, in addition to the selection criteria that are already present. This concludes the program modifications. You can now test the program.

Tasks

1. Create and test the program.

2. Add a new selection for the date area and evaluate this selection when you access Table E070.

3. Create a dynamic selection for Table E070.

3.7   Dialog applications

A report does not have enough functionality to create complete, interactive applications. The R/3 System has provided dialog-oriented applications for this purpose. Like reports, the application's basic structure is predefined, and the ABAP statements used here are at a lower level than this basic structure. Dialog-oriented applications are primarily based on the use of screen templates called *screen programs* in the R/3 System. The main concept for dialog applications is therefore also called a *'screen program'* concept.

Some of this concept's basic features have already been mentioned in the section that described the selection screen for reports. Although selection screens use some of the functionality of screen programs, the implementation of true dialog applications, in technical programming terms, is totally different. These applications are more complicated to program, but compensate for this by having much more powerful functionality.

3.7.1 A simple introduction

Dialog applications provide the user with the input and control elements that are available in modern graphical interfaces. These elements can be divided into two main groups. The first group contains the elements that make it possible to process data, i.e. editable fields, etc. These elements are integrated in the screen program and appear in the screen program's work area. The second group consists of all the elements that a user can use to trigger a function. They include, for example, menus, pushbuttons and icons. Unfortunately, in ABAP tasks, these elements are grouped together under the rather misleading term *interface*. You should not use this term to refer to the entire user interface, i.e. the window; it merely includes the elements named above. In SAP terminology, the objects in a screen program's work area do not form part of the interface. An interface consists of one or more *statuses*. Because the term 'status' helps to avoid misunderstandings, it will generally be used from now on. The term *fullscreen* has come to be used to refer to the screen template, i.e. the actual work area of the screen program. Section 3.3.3 has already described how you process the interface or a status.

To ensure that an application runs correctly and behaves as you expect, all the dialog elements must be linked with elements of the program. When you select a menu entry, you want it to execute the function you require or transfer values from entry elements into data fields, etc. For this reason, you require program code in addition to the screen program and the interface. A report in its simplest form consists only of a single program file that can also be processed directly. In contrast, a dialog application includes the following elements:

- one or more input templates (screen programs);

- one or more statuses (interface);

- ABAP statements.

Dialog applications are executed in a very different way from reports. This makes it a little harder for users who are familiar with the usual procedural programming languages to get accustomed to the working methods required here. A report contains a program section that is vaguely comparable to the main program of commonly used programming languages. This is generally the section where data is read and displayed, i.e. the section after the START-OF-SELECTION event. The actual program activities take place in this section. All other events are similar to subroutines, even if they are not called directly, but are executed by events and event statements. They carry out help tasks. There are also certain similarities with programs written in procedural languages. The author has consciously taken advantage of these similarities in the previous section to make this introduction to the ABAP programming language easier.

A dialog application does not have this kind of program core. In the source code, you will find only a number of *modules*, i.e. a type of subroutine. For this reason, the actual program file is called a *module pool*. The module pool is indirectly similar to a library that offers a series of help routines. It is neither possible nor a good idea to process the statements in the module pool sequentially. Despite this, the name of the module pool is also the name of the application.

It is the screen programs that play the decisive role in controlling the program flow in dialog applications. When you process a dialog-oriented application, you Call screen programs instead of programs or subroutines. It is screen programs that execute individual modules from the module pool at precisely specified events. Modules are called up in the *flow logic*. The flow logic is a special piece of source code that is provided for each screen program and can be individually programmed for each screen program. The flow logic is saved together with the screen program. You cannot find it directly in the module pool.

The screen program and the module pool are inseparably linked with each other. The module pool is used by several screen programs in an application. You can therefore identify screen programs by the name of the module pool and by their number.

Dialog applications must be linked with a transaction. You use the transaction name to call the application. The module pool name and the number of the first screen program to be executed are transferred to this transaction.

The section that follows is designed to familiarize you with dialog-oriented applications. This is why the first two subsections will deal with how you process a very simple dialog application. The next subsection describes the characteristics and various contents of a screen program in more detail. After this we shall introduce some special programming techniques that are of special interest in the context of dialog applications.

Creating a simple dialog-oriented application takes considerably more time and effort than writing the 'Hello world' program. You cannot even test the application until you have created several of its component parts. Relationships only become apparent after the amount of information acquired exceeds a certain threshold. That is why the most important elements of a dialog application are generated first, while its functionality remains restricted to the absolute minimum required. When you recreate the examples in your system, you should ensure that all the elements are created as local private objects.

The first dialog application should implement a simple calculator. In the first screen program, you enter two operators and select the calculation operation to be executed. The second screen program shows you the result.

Because a dialog application consists of different objects, which in turn can themselves contain several parts, you must carry out the following steps to create and test a dialog application:

- create a module pool;

- declare the global data;

- generate the statuses;

- generate the screen programs (masks and flow logic);

- program the modules;

- generate a transaction.

Creating a module pool

New screen programs must be assigned to a module pool. You therefore start programming a dialog application by creating a module pool. To do so, you first launch the development environment.

In the Repository Browser initial screen, enter the name of the module pool in the Program input field, in the Object list frame. This first program is called SAPMY310. In addition to this, you must select the appropriate radio button. Figure 3.80 shows the initial screen of the Repository Browser at this event. We will not discuss the naming conventions in the SAP System at this stage.

You then click on the Display pushbutton. If the module pool is not yet present, the system generates a prompt similar to the one in Figure 3.81. You confirm this by clicking on the YES pushbutton.

Another dialog box (Figure 3.82) is now displayed. In addition to the name of the program you want to create, this dialog box also contains a checkbox for a top include. In contrast to the reports in module pools, this include should always be present. It is designed to be used for declaring global data. Select the checkbox, then click on CONTINUE or its icon, the green checkmark.

Now a third dialog box (Figure 3.83) is displayed. In it you enter the name of the top include. You must use the name MYZ10TOP. This has already been automatically predefined by the system.

After you confirm these actions, the initial screen of the familiar program editor appears. You can then enter the program attributes in this screen (Figure 3.84).

The Type field, for the program type, is already filled with 'M' for module pool. Just like reports, you now only have to enter a short description and the application ID. The system saves the attributes. You can now click on the Source code pushbutton to access and process the source code. After you switch to the editor, the screen shown in Figure 3.85 appears:

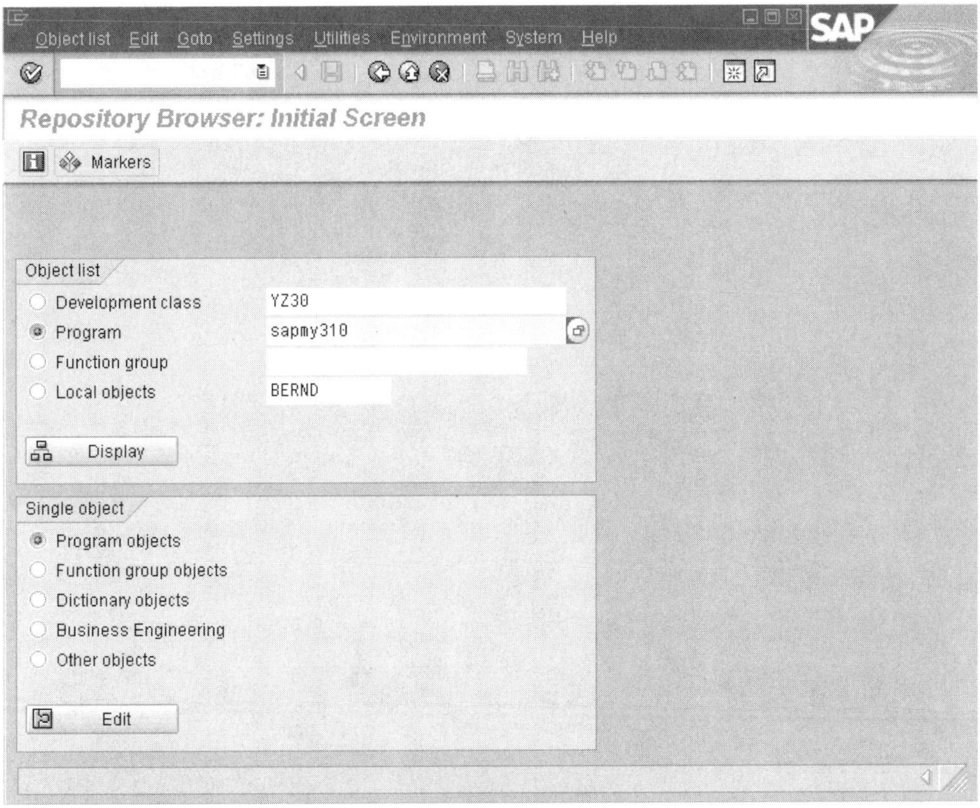

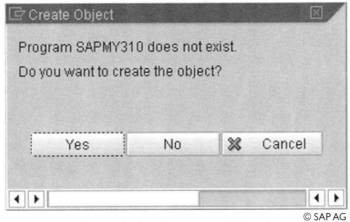

Figure 3.80   Object Browser initial screen

© SAP AG

Figure 3.81   Creating a module pool

© SAP AG

Create Program
Program
SAPMY310
With TOP INCL.

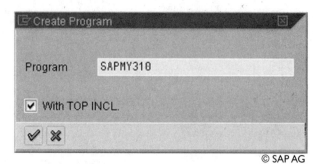

© SAP AG

Figure 3.82 Prompt for the program's name

Create Program
TOP include
MY310TOP

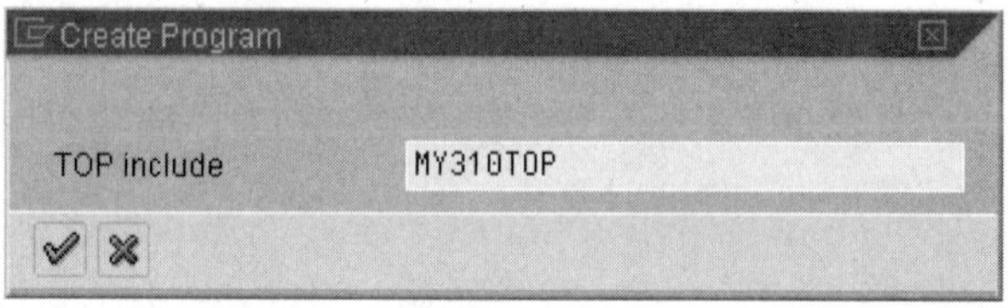

© SAP AG

Figure 3.83 Prompt for the include name

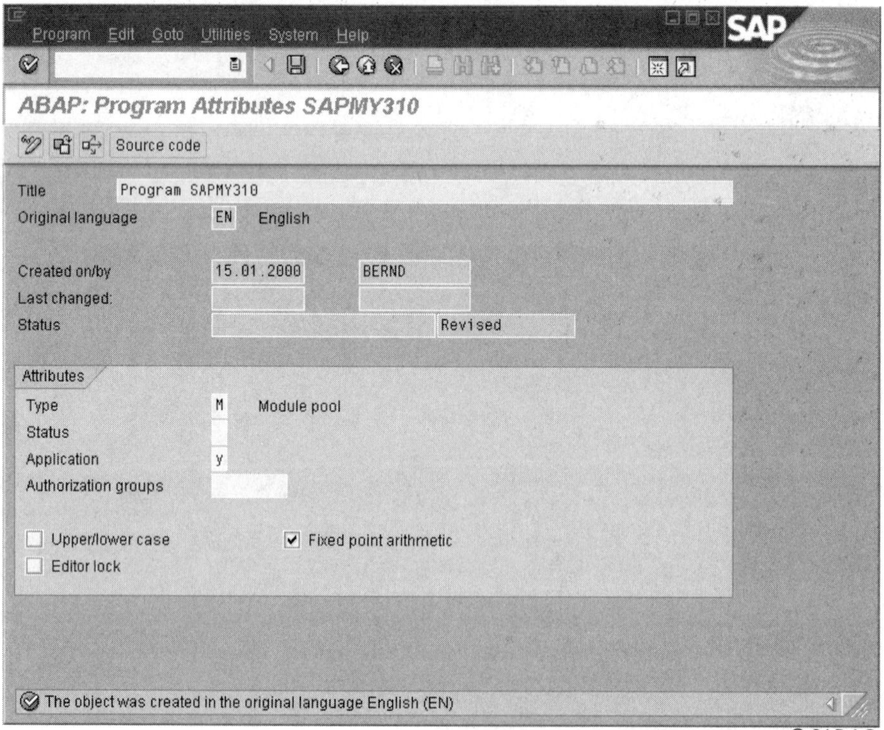

Program Edit Goto Utilities System Help
SAP
ABAP: Program Attributes SAPMY310
Source code
Title
Program SAPMY310
Original language
EN
English
Created on/by
15.01.2000
BERND
Last changed:
Status
Revised
Attributes
Type
M
Module pool
Status
Application
y
Authorization groups
Upper/lower case
Fixed point arithmetic
Editor lock
The object was created in the original language English (EN)

© SAP AG

Figure 3.84 Defining program attributes

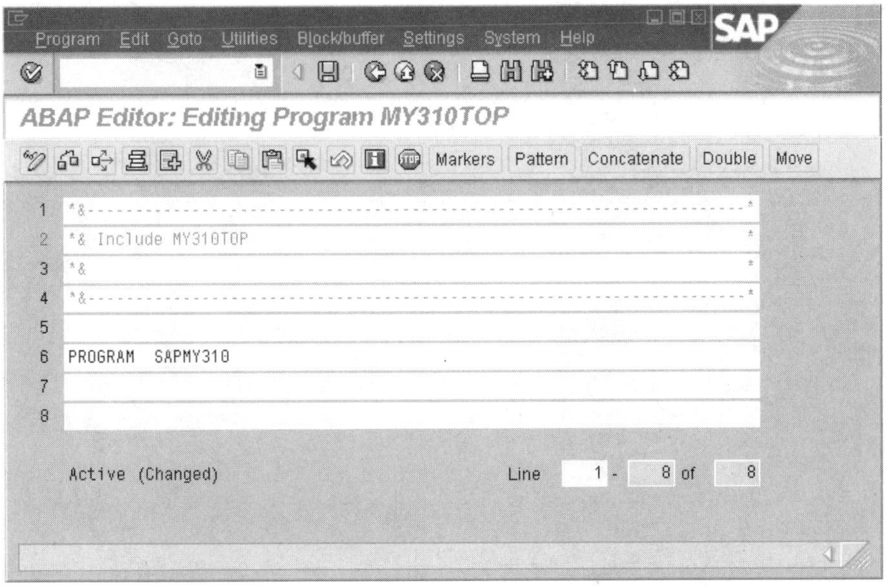

© SAP AG

Figure 3.85   Editor with top include

The editor switches immediately to the top include, not to the actual module pool. You will notice that the PROGRAM statement appears in the include and not in the main program. The actual module pool only consists of a few INCLUDE statements. Here, you can add data to the PROGRAM statement in the source code and enter the following field declarations:

```
PROGRAM sapmy310.
DATA:
  fcode LIKE sy-ucomm,
  value1 TYPE p,
  value2 TYPE p,
  result TYPE p,
  op.
```

Now save your changes. After this you can leave the editor. However, you do not return directly to the initial screen, but to the Object Browser's elements list or objects list. This list is the central element of the Object Browser and contains all the elements that belong to the application. Figure 3.86 shows the still rather modest object list that is formed after you create the module pool. The elements are divided into groups according to their type (programs, modules, subroutines, Data Dictionary objects, etc.). You can double-click on the name of a group or single-click on the icon in front of the group name to display or hide the element list for that group. Double-click on an element to start the editing tool for this element. The element is then loaded into the tool where you can process it.

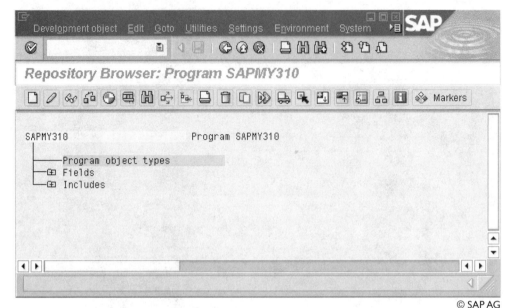

Figure 3.86   The Browser's object list

Here you position the cursor on the program name and activate the existing application (from the menu OBJECT | GENERATE/ACTIVATE). This makes it much easier for you to process the screen program that is now being created.

The first screen program

After the module pool has been created, you can generate a first version of the screen program. You use the Screen Painter to process screen programs. You access this from the initial screen of the development environment (not from the Repository Browser) by choosing DEVELOPMENT | SCREEN PAINTER from the menu or by clicking on the corresponding pushbutton. Enter transaction code SE51 to call the Screen Painter directly. In addition to calling the Screen Painter, you can also generate a screen program directly from the Browser's object list.

The Browser's object list contains all the elements of the current program. Because only one module pool and one include have been generated so far, the list is relatively short. Position the cursor on the module pool's name field and choose DEVELOPMENT OBJECT | CREATE from the menu. A dialog box is displayed (Figure 3.87). In it you can click a radio button to select its associated object type. You enter the name of each object you want to create in the input field to the right of the radio button. In this example, you should assign the number 100 to the screen program.

After you click on the Create pushbutton or select the corresponding icon, the system displays a window. In it you can enter important attributes for the screen program. Figure 3.88 shows this input template. You must also enter a short description here, just like for

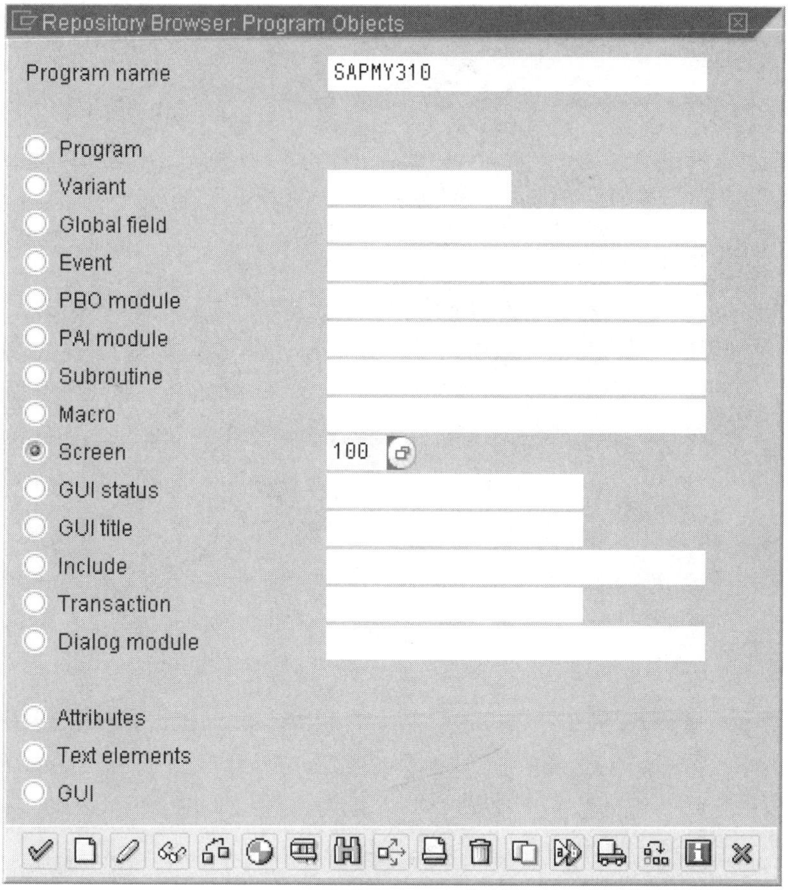

© SAP AG

Figure 3.87   Creating a new screen program

all other elements described above. You have to select the Normal checkbox for the screen program type unless the system has automatically preselected it. All the other fields remain unchanged.

The system saves the values in this screen program. You can now click on the Layout pushbutton or choose GOTO | LAYOUT EDITOR from the menu to process the screen program's graphical interface. You will first see an empty screen, which is divided into individual lines (see Figure 3.89).

All screen program elements are now placed in the work area that you see here. The screen program treats each unbroken character string in the fullscreen editor as a field no matter what characters it contains. The system automatically includes a field in the screen program's *field list*. The entries in the field list allow data fields within the program to be linked with the screen program fields. This means that data can be exchanged between the program and the screen program.

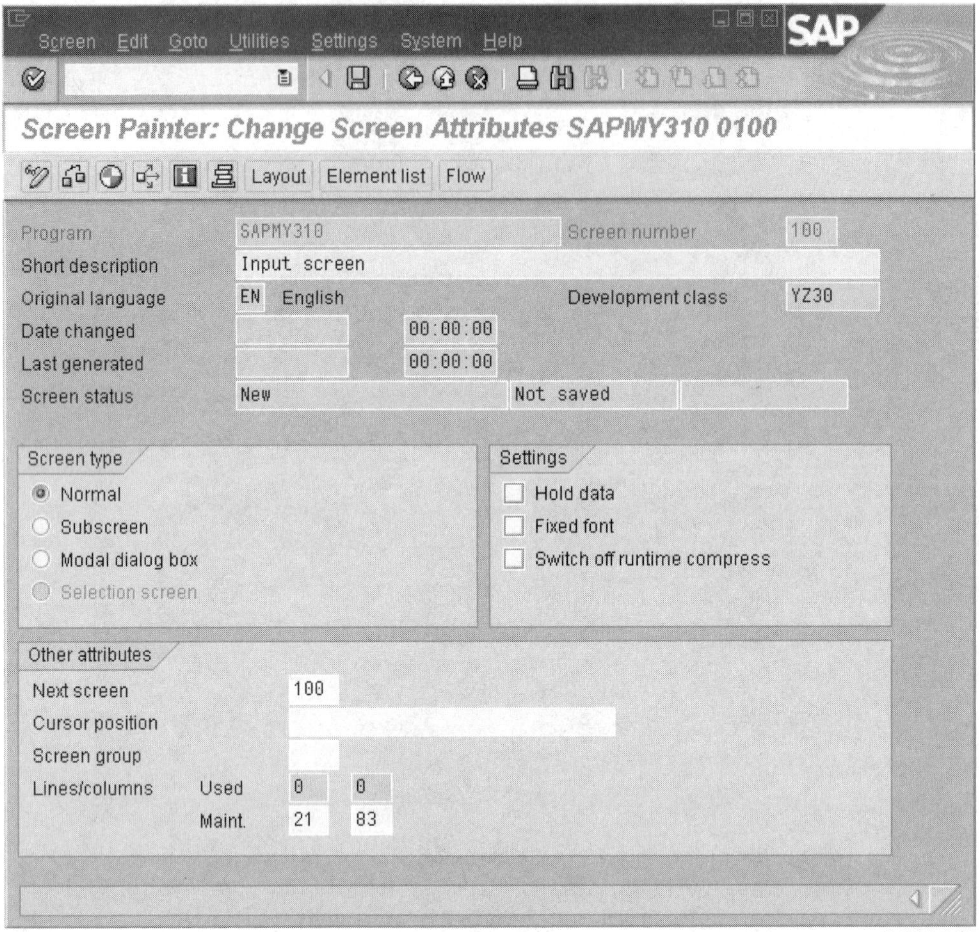

Figure 3.88   Attributes screen for screen programs

A range of different attributes define how the field later appears in the screen program. This means that a field can be represented as an editable field, as a pure display field without editing tools, as a checkbox or radio button or as simple text. Section 3.7.2 describes the different attributes or the way a field is displayed.

You can set or change a field's attributes in different ways. One way is to process the field list manually. You can achieve the same result by choosing EDIT | ELEMENT ATTRIBUTES from the menu to assign the attributes. This displays a dialog box for the field on which you have positioned the cursor. In this dialog box, you can display all the field's attributes and also make changes to them. Special editing tools, such as the one for converting a field into a graphical element, also affect some of the attributes. You must use a specific editing tool to set these special attributes. You can achieve the same effect by using a special tool that supports the creation of screen program fields. This tool then enters some of the attributes automatically.

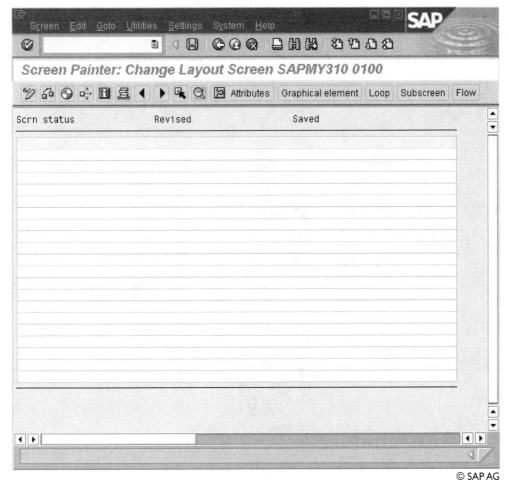

Figure 3.89   Fullscreen editor

You can use the tool mentioned above to create screen program fields and simultane-ously link them with data fields that have already been declared in the module pool or with table fields from the Data Dictionary. This tool also ensures that additional fields, with the appropriate descriptions, are generated for input fields that reference the Data Dictionary. This is why you should not usually create screen program fields by making entries manually in the fullscreen editor and then assigning individual attributes to them, unless this is absolutely necessary. In general, you should use the insertion tool described below. You should also note that this tool can only find the internal fields used in the pro-gram, in the generated version of a program.

To call this tool, choose GOTO | DICT./PROGRAM FIELDS from the menu. A dialog box (Figure 3.90) is displayed in which you must first specify which fields to insert.

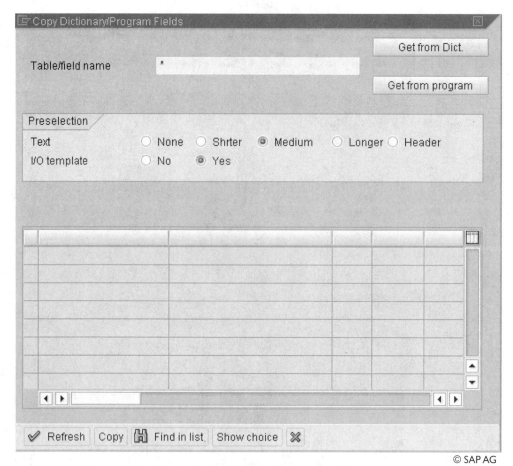

Figure 3.90   Copying fields from the program into the screen program

If you want to copy fields from within a program, enter a template in the TABLE/FIELD
NAME input field. This template must match the names of the fields you want to insert. In
this case, you can enter an asterisk to select all the fields.

After you click on the GET FROM PROGRAM pushbutton, the system lists all the available
fields. You can click on a checkbox to the left of each field name to select the fields that are
to be copied. You use the scroll bar to scroll through the selection list. In the list, you click
on the corresponding checkbox to select the value1 and value2 fields (Figure 3.91).

Click on the Copy pushbutton to copy the selected table fields into the screen program.
The dialog box disappears and the fullscreen editor's user interface is displayed again.
You double-click on the fields you have previously selected to insert them. Alternatively,
you can press (F2) to do this. Unfortunately, the layout editor only allows left-aligned
insertion no matter where you have positioned the cursor. Figure 3.92 shows the fullscreen
editor at this point in time. The input fields are represented by a sequence of underscores.

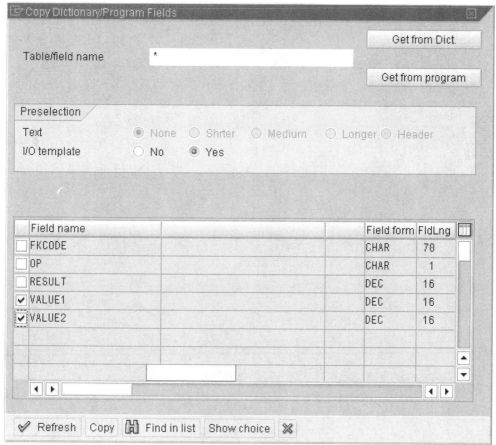

Figure 3.91   Selecting fields from within a program

© SAP AG

To create space for the field identifiers, you also have to move the input fields after you have inserted them. To do this, double-click on the field to select it, position the cursor in the place you want and click the MOVE BLOCK pushbutton in the application toolbar. Alternatively, press (Shift)(F4) or choose EDIT | MOVE BLOCK from the menu.

When you insert fields from within a program, only the actual fields are copied without their description. For this reason, these fields from within a program are not used very often. It is more practical to use Data Dictionary fields, because these contain a description that can automatically be copied into the screen program. However, as no suitable Data Dictionary structure exists for this example, we have to resort to fields from within a program to keep things as simple as possible. In this case, you must enter the identifiers manually as a character string in the screen program. Here you use an underscore to separate the individual words instead of a space. Figure 3.93 shows the corresponding processed screen program. Save this screen program before going on to the next stage of processing.

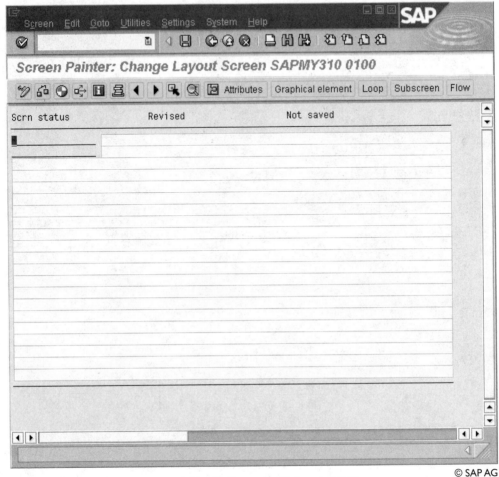

Figure 3.92   Fullscreen with inserted fields

In the element list you will find more detailed information about the fields. Older releases of the R/3 Software still use the term 'field list'. You can access this list from various points when processing the screen program, by choosing GOTO | ELEMENT list from the menu or by clicking the corresponding pushbutton. Figure 3.94 shows the element list. The list contains an entry for each of the recently inserted fields (both for the input fields and for the text). Only the last entry in the list is still empty. This entry is created automatically and is present in each screen program. It refers to a hidden field in the screen program in which the function code triggered by the user is made available. If you want to evaluate this function code in your application, you must provide a field in your program where this function code can be entered. In this case, this is the fcode field that has already been declared. Enter this field name in the last line of the element list (Figure 3.94) and save it again.

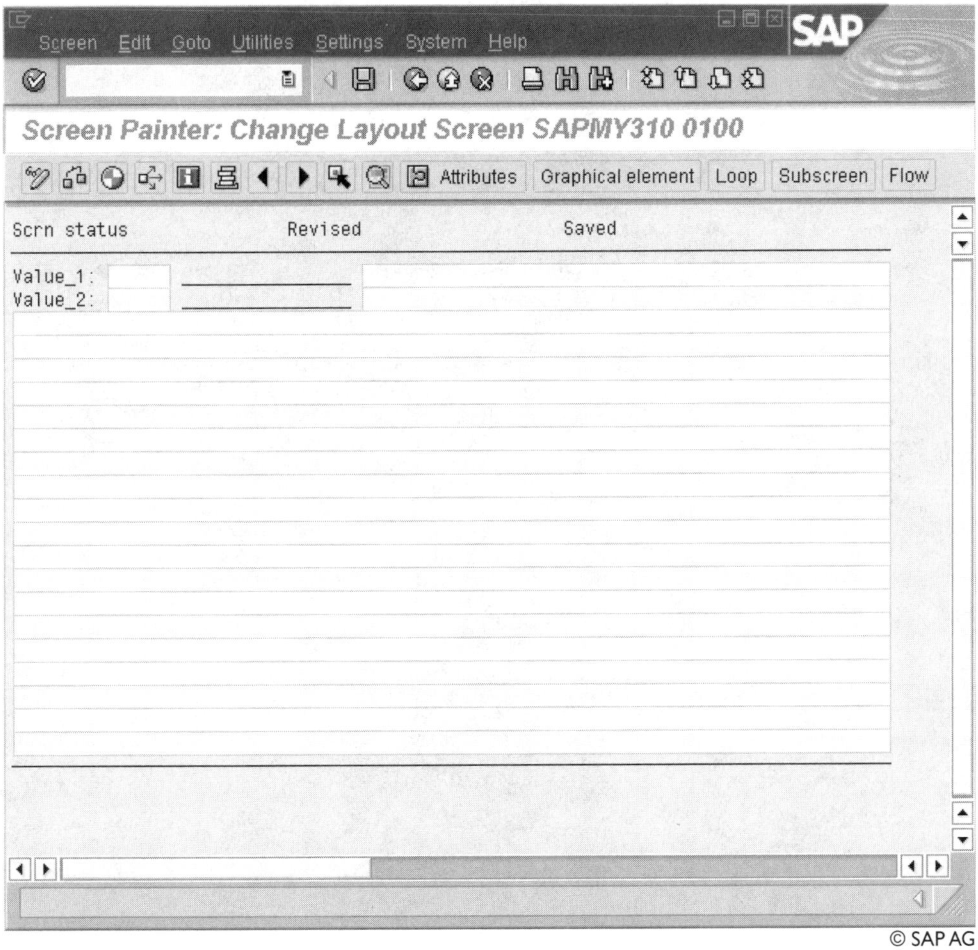

Figure 3.93 Screen program with descriptions for input fields

Now you can program the flow logic modules. This is the only way of providing the application with the functions it requires. Modules are called up in the screen program's flow logic. These modules then link the screen program with program codes. You must create these modules in the module pool and fill them with source text.

To access the flow logic, click on the Flow pushbutton or choose GOTO | FLOW logic from the menu. Initially, the flow logic for a new screen program only consists of a few lines that are automatically generated by the system. The exact contents of the flow logic depend on which R/3 Release you are using. The first two (commented-out) module calls are only automatically inserted from Release 3.0 onwards:

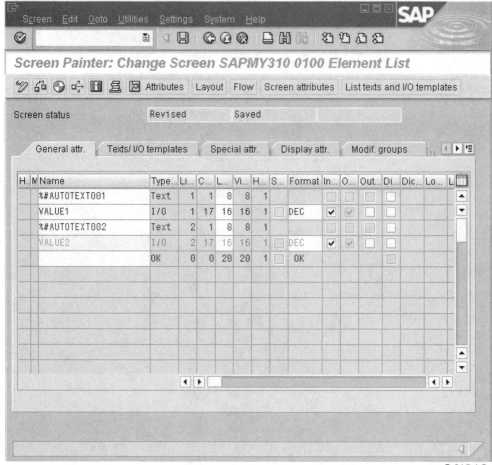

Figure 3.94   The screen program's field list

```
PROCESS BEFORE OUTPUT.
*   MODULE STATUS_0100.
*
PROCESS AFTER INPUT.
*   MODULE USER_COMMAND_0100.
```

The two statements, PROCESS BEFORE OUTPUT and PROCESS AFTER INPUT, are event statements. They are called before or after you call the screen program. At first glance, the flow logic seems to be a normal ABAP program. However, this impression is deceptive. There are only a few special statements that may be used in the flow logic and these differ considerably from the statements used in normal ABAP programs.

In the flow logic, you now remove the comment characters for the two module calls. This results in the following source code:

```
PROCESS BEFORE OUTPUT.
  MODULE STATUS_0100.
*
PROCESS AFTER INPUT.
  MODULE USER_COMMAND_0100.
```

The flow logic and also the screen program are saved and activated at this point. If they were not activated, the module calls would be present in the screen program's flow logic, but they would not be recognized when it is processed and would therefore not be executed. This error is relatively difficult to detect because the statements appear to be completely correct in the source code.

Both modules carry out basic tasks. That is why they are present in almost all screen programs and sometimes even have almost identical names. A status is loaded in the STATUS_0100 module. This is the only way of ensuring that the menu functions and function keys that are created there are available in the screen program. However, the USER_COMMAND_0100 module evaluates the data that has been entered and the function code so that it can access follow-up activities.

Module names can be up to 20 characters long. Apart from that, the same recommendations apply as for the names of subroutines or fields. However, there are a few (unwritten) rules for naming modules. It often happens that modules for several screen programs are present in one module pool. For the sake of clarity and to keep module names relatively uniform, many developers start a module's name with a word that indicates its task. They then add the number of the screen program to the end of the module name. If, for example, there are several screen programs, each with a different status, you will require several STATUS modules. These modules must all be given unique names. You can use screen program numbers to make the module names unique without losing their descriptive character. Sometimes you may want to group similar functions for several screen programs into one module. Then you could select the actual functions to be executed within this module by using the number of the current screen program that is contained in the SY-DYNNR system variable. However, using modules together may result in rather complex and confusing programs. Complex modules of this kind also make it more difficult to document specific screen programs or use selected screen programs from other programs.

Once you have created the module calls in the flow logic, you must of course create the corresponding source code in the module pool. Just like the general ABAP editor, the flow logic editor has fairly easy-to-use navigation functions. This means you do not have to leave the Screen Painter and switch to the program editor. You simply double-click on the module name to start the ABAP editor for the module pool. This tells the system that the module to be processed does not yet exist. The system then displays a prompt to see whether you want to create this module (Figure 3.95).

In another dialog box you enter the name of the program file in which the module is to be created. This dialog box displays a list of all the existing include files in the module pool. You can select a file from this list or enter a new name in an input field. This field contains a default value that you can overwrite if required. The system automatically generates the include file that you have just named and uses the INCLUDE statement to include it in the module pool.

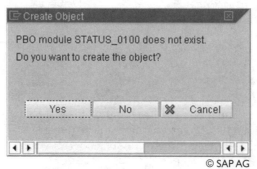

Figure 3.95   Prompt at which you confirm creation of a new include

The names of the include files for modules are created in the same way as the names of top includes. This means that you can only define the last three digits. Of these three digits, the first one should identify the event that the module belongs to. PBO modules use the letter 'O', and PAI modules use the letter 'I'. Very often, the first two digits of the screen program number are used for the last two digits, but you can also enter a sequential number if required. In this example, include MY310O01 is created for a PBO module. To do this, enter this name in the dialog box as the name of a new include. Figure 3.96 shows the dialog box.

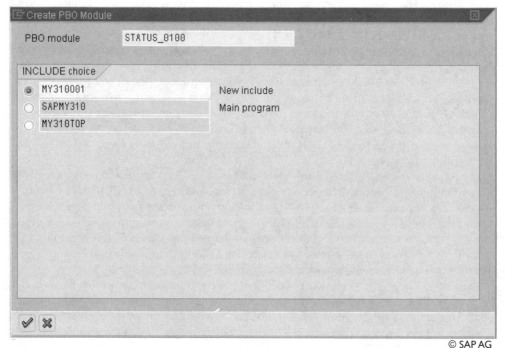

Figure 3.96   Selecting an include file for the PBO module

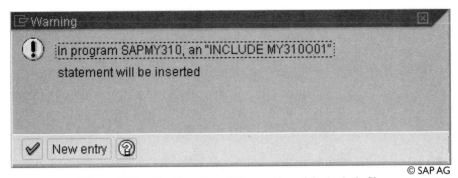

Figure 3.97 Confirmation of the creation of the include file

After you confirm the name, the system uses the Object Browser to create the include file. In a third dialog box (Figure 3.97) you then confirm that the includes have been created and inserted in the framework program.

The Browser then starts the ABAP editor for the include file and transfers the automatically generated source code to the programmer for further processing. The newly created include already contains the remaining parts of a module (the MODULE and ENDMODULE statements) and a few comments.

In the module, you add the lines shown in the following listing:

```
*---------------------------
*&--------------------------*
*& MODULE STATUS_0100 OUTPUT
*&--------------------------*
* text
*
*--------------------------*
MODULE STATUS_0100 OUTPUT.
   CLEAR: value1, value2, result, op.
   SET TITLEBAR '001'.
   SET PF-STATUS 'STAT1'.
ENDMODULE.                    "STATUS_0100 OUTPUT
```

This statement initializes the global fields and loads status STAT1. This means that the screen program can now use the menus and other elements that are defined there. The SET PF-STATUS statement expects the name of the status as a parameter. This status name must be programmed as a character string constant, i.e. enclosed in simple quotation marks. The name of the status must also be entered in upper-case letters.

The system automatically adds the term OUTPUT after the module's name. When you declare a module, you must clearly assign it to a section of the screen program processing procedure. When the system executes a module, it only searches among those in each current processing section. You mark a module as a PBO module by adding the output addition. When PAI modules are declared, they are either not labelled at all, or labelled with the `input` addition. This means that two modules that have identical names can exist in the same module pool, because one of them has the `output` addition. However, to ensure that your programming code remains as clear as possible, you should avoid using this option.

The function codes that are made available by the status must also of course be evaluated after the screen program has been processed in the PAI section of the flow logic. You evaluate these function codes in the second module. You use the method described above to create the `MY310I01` include. The listing below shows its source code:

```
MODULE user_statement_0100 INPUT.
  CASE fcode.
    WHEN 'OPCA'.
      result = value1 + value2.
      op = '+'.
      LEAVE TO SCREEN 200.
    WHEN 'OPCS'.
      result = value1 - value2.
      op = '-'.
      LEAVE TO SCREEN 200.
    WHEN 'OPCM'.
      result = value1 * value2.
      op = '*'.
      LEAVE TO SCREEN 200.
    WHEN 'OPCD'.
      result = value1 / value2.
      op = '/'.
      LEAVE TO SCREEN 200.
    WHEN 'FT03'.
      LEAVE PROGRAM.
  ENDCASE.
  CLEAR fcode.
ENDMODULE.                        "USER_COMMAND_0100 INPUT
```

The function of the module is relatively simple. A `CASE` statement evaluates the function code that is triggered by the user. Depending on the function code, the system calculates the appropriate result from the contents of the `value1` and `value2` fields. The test for division by zero, which is actually essential, has deliberately been left out in this version of the example. This test may be added later. After the calculation, you use the `LEAVE TO SCREEN 200` statement to call a second screen program that you still have to create. The result of the calculation is displayed in this second screen program. The module also evaluates function code `FT03` to end the program correctly. The module reacts to this function code by executing the `LEAVE PROGRAM` statement, which closes the currently running program. After the function code has been evaluated, the contents of the `fcode` field are deleted. The contents of this field must always be deleted. The reason for this is due to the way the system handles the (Enter) key. This key is always available in screen programs, even though it is not assigned a function code. It normally triggers processing in the PAI part of a screen program to execute the test routines contained there. You will find more information about this below. However, you cannot press (Enter) to change the existing contents of the function code field in the screen program if this key does not have a function code. This may lead to unwanted side effects because the user statement module would then receive a function code that was not triggered in the screen program.

You have now finished programming the first screen program. You can now check that the application's syntax is correct and generate the application. However, you cannot carry out a test run just yet.

The second screen program

In the flow logic of the first screen program, you call screen program 200 to display the results. You must also create this screen program. Its structure is simpler than that of the first one. You can also make it much easier to create the new screen program. To create the new screen program, you need not return to the Repository Browser's object list. In the user statement module of the first screen program, you simply double-click on the number 200 in the LEAVE TO SCREEN statement. The navigation function of the development environment recognizes that you want to trigger a jump to screen program 200. However, as this screen program does not yet exist, the system creates it for you. The procedure is the same as one already described above and therefore the explanation does not need to be repeated.

The results should now appear in the new screen program. Therefore, as shown in Figure 3.98, you first enter a descriptive text directly in the screen program. You then use the insert tool to insert the program's own result field after this text.

The default settings determine that the new field is generated as an input/output field. This is not a practical solution for the example described here. You should therefore remove the input function from the field. To do this, position the cursor on the field and click the ATTRIBUTES pushbutton. A dialog box appears (see Figure 3.99) in which you can maintain the attributes of the screen program field.

In this dialog box, you must deactivate the INPUT FIELD flag and activate the two-dimensional display (2D DISPLAY) flag instead. This setting causes the field to be displayed without its frame, which gives it a three-dimensional look. It therefore appears as normal text.

To finish processing the second screen program, enter the FCODE field in the field list to return the function code. You have now finished generating the visual part of the screen program.

The flow logic only uses one single module to evaluate the function code. The source code shown in the next listing demonstrates this:

```
PROCESS BEFORE OUTPUT.
*
PROCESS AFTER INPUT.
  MODULE user_statement_0200.
```

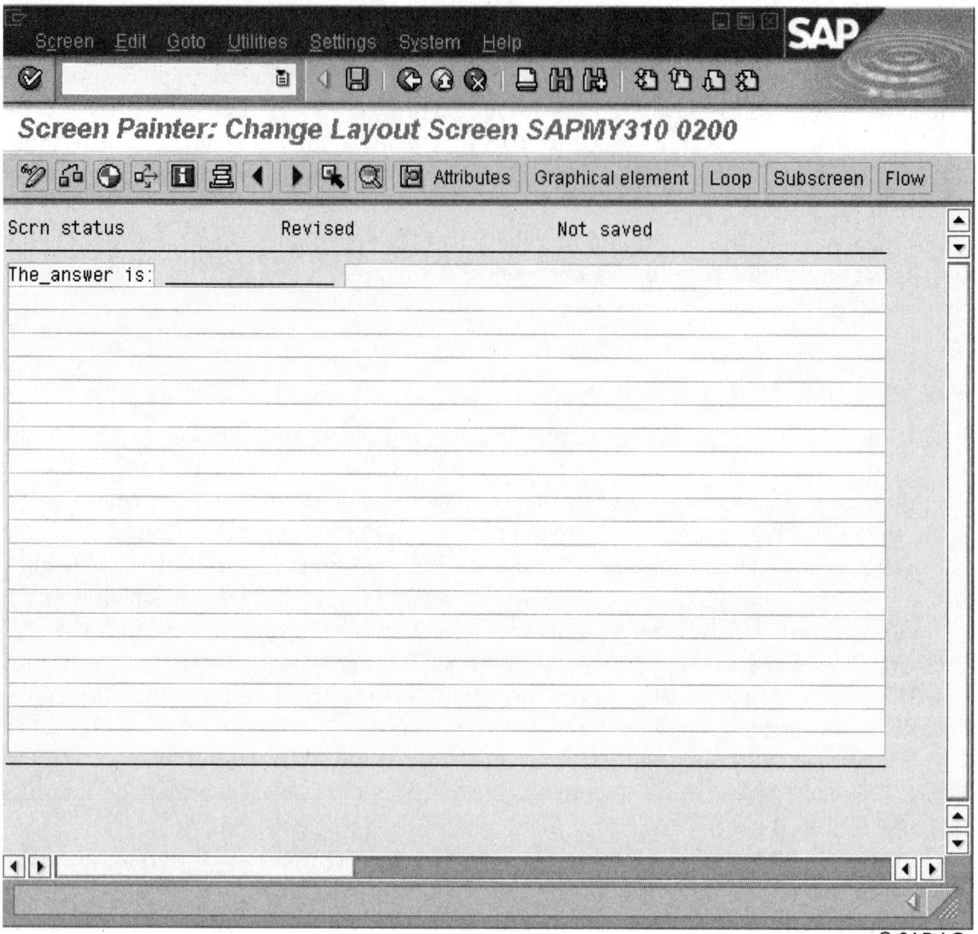

Figure 3.98   Screen program 200 of the first example

The actual user statement module of the second screen program is also shorter than that of the first screen program, because it only has to evaluate one single function code. At this point in the application, you simply program the return to screen program 100. This is shown in the next listing:

```
MODULE user_statement_0200 INPUT.
   CASE fcode.
   WHEN 'FT03'.
   LEAVE TO SCREEN 100.
   ENDCASE.
ENDMODULE.                      "USER_COMMAND_0200 INPUT
```

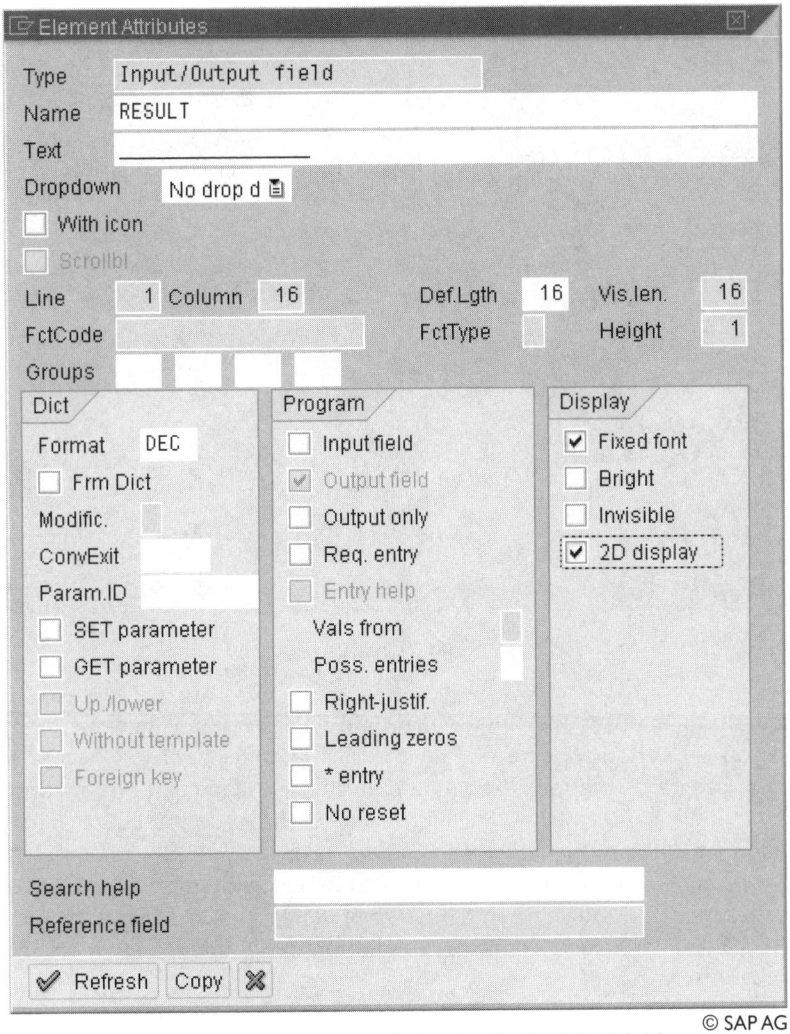

© SAP AG

Figure 3.99   Attributes dialog for the RESULT field

Menus and function keys

The next step towards a fully operational application is to create a status. It is only the elements of a status that enable the user to actively communicate with the application. Each application only contains one interface which, because it is clearly linked with the application, does not need to be described in detail. This interface includes one or more statuses, each of which has its own unique name. In different phases of processing, it is quite possible that one screen program can set several statuses. However, one status can also be used in several screen programs that follow each other sequentially. You will find

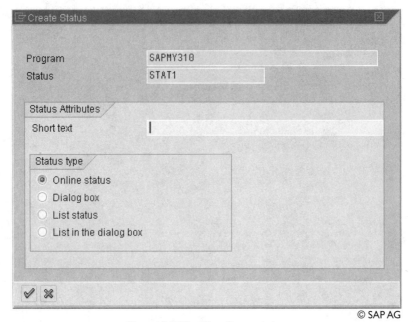

Figure 3.100   Creating a status

more details about statuses and how to maintain the individual elements in Section 3.3. For this reason, we shall now focus on how the Menu Painter works.

When you program an application, you mainly use the navigation function to create new elements. To do this, switch to the source code of the USER_COMMAND_0100 module and then double-click on the name of the status in the SET PF-STATUS statement. The system now prompts you to enter a short text and to select the status type (Figure 3.100).

In this example, you must select status type 'Dialog box'. As usual, the short text is optional. After you confirm your entry, you automatically jump to the Menu Painter initial screen (Figure 3.101).

Click on the icon with the green 'Plus' symbol to open the menu's work area. Directly underneath the Menu bar text you see another icon with the label Display standards. Click on this icon to trigger this function. The Menu Painter adds some default menu entries. If you double-click on the first menu option labelled '<object>', you can open its corresponding pull-down menu. Figure 3.102 shows you the Menu Painter in this state.

In the menu you must now store the function codes that have already been evaluated in the flow logic. In the appropriate columns in the menu, you enter the function code on the left and the descriptive text on the right. You must also replace the '<object>' placeholder with a suitable description for the menu. Figure 3.103 shows you what the Menu Painter looks like at this point.

This menu only stores the four function codes that trigger a mathematical operation. Function code FT03, which is also used here, is created in the GOTO menu for the BACK option. This menu option should return you to the previous screen program. This is part

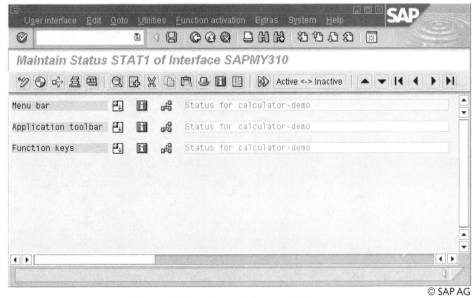

Figure 3.101   Menu Painter initial screen

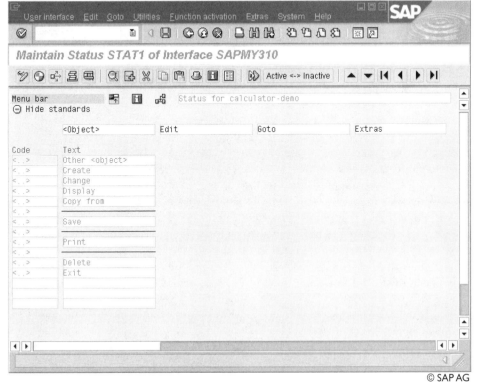

Figure 3.102   Menu Painter with pre-defined menu

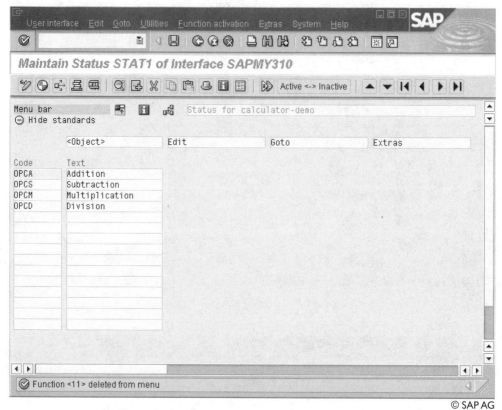

Figure 3.103   Maintaining the first pull-down menu

of the default functionality which according to the SAP Style Guide should always be triggered by (F3), the GOTO | BACK menu option and the green left arrow icon. For this reason, the GOTO menu already contains an entry for this function.

You do not require the EDIT, EXTRAS and ENVIRONMENT menus in this example. To delete them, position the cursor on the menu and choose EDIT | DELETE from the menu. Alternatively, click the corresponding button in the application toolbar.

In principle, the menu you have just generated is able to operate the application. However, the function keys and pushbuttons make the application more convenient to use. To do this, click the icon with the red minus character to close the menu work area and open the work area for the function keys (Figure 3.104) instead.

Just like in the figure, you enter the four OPCx function codes under function keys (F5) to (F8) and function code FT03 under the back icon (green arrow). You do not have to maintain any descriptions in function key entries. The system automatically copies these from the menu.

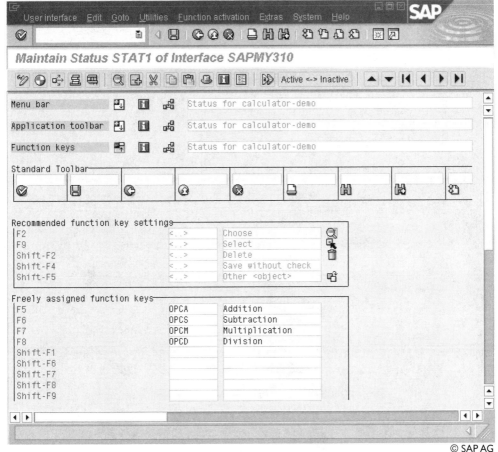

Figure 3.104   Maintaining the function keys

© SAP AG

You use a similar procedure for the pushbuttons. First, store the current status and open the work area for the pushbuttons. Just like in Figure 3.105, you enter the four OPCx function codes in the first four fields in this work area.

This completes the status maintenance procedure. You can now generate the status. To do so, choose USER INTERFACE | GENERATE from the menu or click the appropriate button in the application toolbar. Then press (F3) or select the corresponding menu options to return to the source code editor. In the source code editor, you use the navigation function to create the title. When the application is running, this title is displayed in the window's title bar. To maintain the title, simply enter the appropriate text in a dialog box (Figure 3.106).

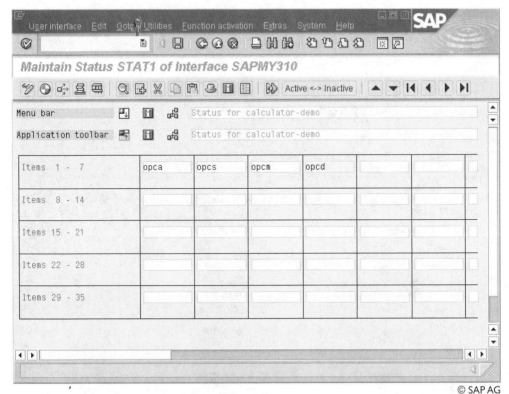

© SAP AG

Figure 3.105   Maintaining the pushbuttons

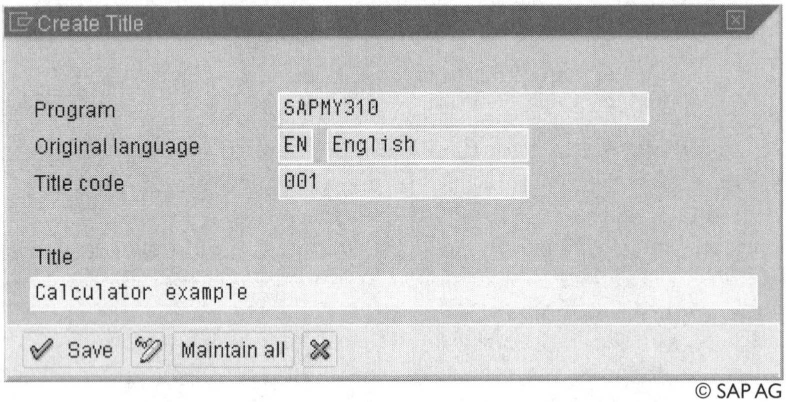

© SAP AG

Figure 3.106   Maintaining the title text

By maintaining the status, you have generated all the objects you will require for a fully operational application. Maintaining the window title is optional. You can now return to the Repository Browser's object list and re-activate the whole application to ensure that everything runs smoothly.

The application is already in a state in which it could be executed. However, you can only execute a dialog application once you have linked it with a transaction. You must now create the transaction.

From the Repository Browser's object list, choose DEVELOPMENT OBJECT | CREATE from the menu to maintain the transaction, just as you do in the Screen Painter. Once again, a dialog box is displayed. In it you select the development object and enter its name (Figure 3.107). Transaction code Y301 is used in the demo application.

After you enter the transaction code, click the Create pushbutton to start creating the transaction. In the next dialog box, you now enter the transaction type. If the default setting DIALOG TRANSACTION or PROGRAM AND SCREEN is correct, you can confirm this setting at the prompt. Figure 3.108 shows the dialog box. You also maintain the short text for the transaction in this dialog box.

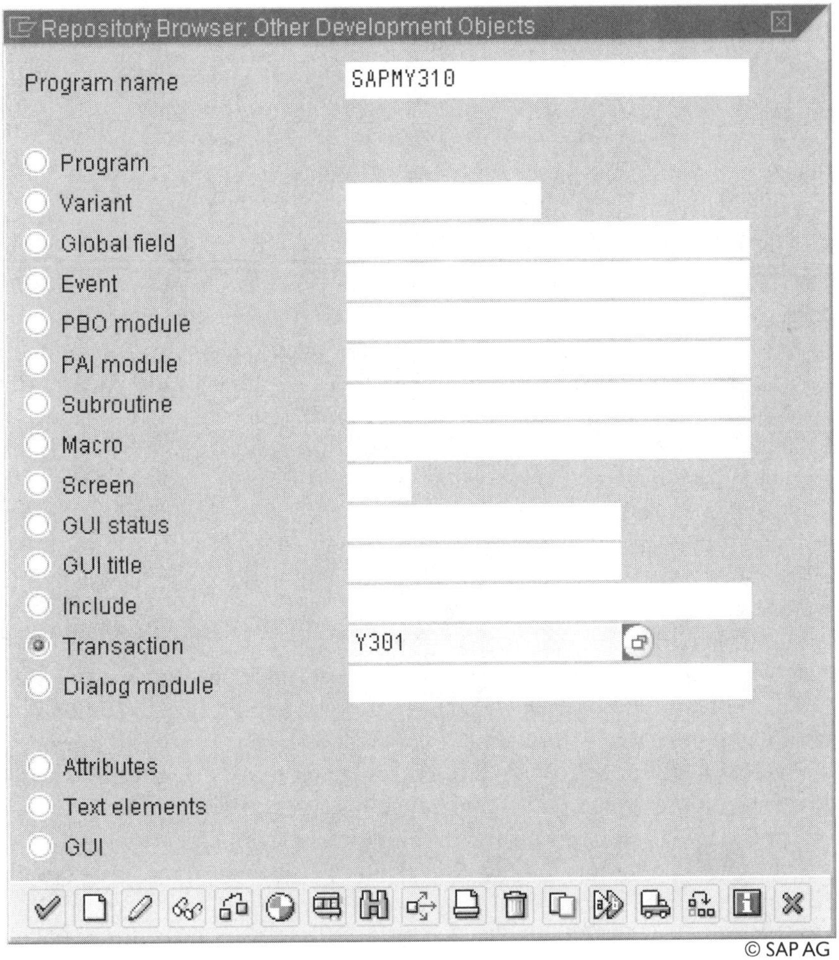

© SAP AG

Figure 3.107   Creating a transaction

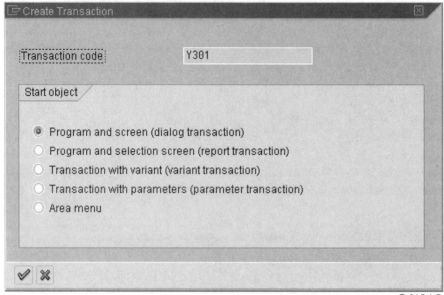

© SAP AG

Figure 3.108   Selecting the transaction type

You can also call the transaction maintenance screens from the general development interface by choosing DEVELOPMENT | OTHER TOOLS | TRANSACTIONS from the menu. The transaction code for calling the transaction maintenance screens directly is SE93.

After confirming the transaction type you require, you must enter special data for the transaction in another dialog box (Figure 3.109). This information is the module pool name (SAPMY310) and the number of the first screen program to be called (100).

After you have entered and stored the data, enter the transaction code in the statement field to execute the first dialog application. Because the initial transaction maintenance screen is still active at this point, enter /nY301 in the statement field and press (Enter). This terminates the current transaction and starts a new one.

After the transaction you have just generated starts, screen program 100 appears. You enter two operators in this screen program (Figure 3.110).

You trigger one of the four operations by clicking one of the buttons in the application toolbar. The application shows the result of this in the second screen program (Figure 3.111).

Although the application you have just generated has the basic attributes of a dialog application, it still has to be improved in many respects. For example, it does not have a check that prevents division by 0. In addition, the method of closing the application from the second screen program is somewhat clumsy, because you must still return to the first screen program. If you enter an incorrect value in one of the operator fields (i.e. '2123-456'), another special feature of the R/3 System comes to light. The system itself recognizes that the value you entered does not match the field's data type and generates an error message. This check takes place before the PAI section modules are executed.

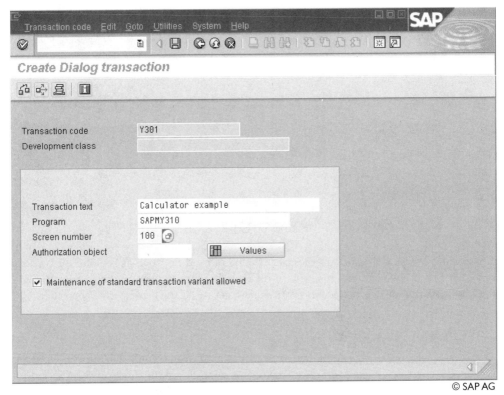

Figure 3.109   Transaction data

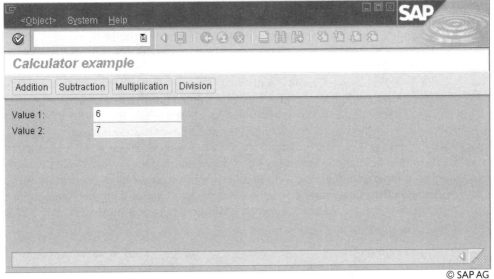

Figure 3.110   Initial screen of the first example

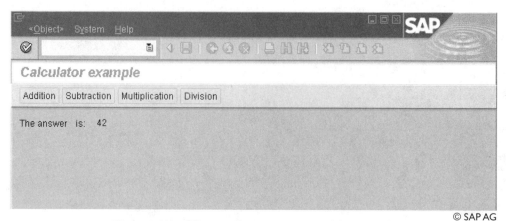

Figure 3.111   The second screen program of the example

The evaluations programmed in the user statement module, such as the one for function code FT03, will therefore not take place. As a result, you can only continue working with the application after you replace the value that has caused the error with a correct entry.

Completing the functionality

This section illustrates more details involved in dialog programming. Here, the emphasis is placed on improving user-friendliness, rather than the main functions of this kind of application. You should now make a copy of the application and only carry out these additions in the copy (program SAPMY320).

First of all, how do you check field contents? You can or sometimes must run checks that you have programmed yourself in addition to the checks that are automatically run by the system. If these checks detect an error, you must correct the incorrect entries in the screen program fields, i.e. start processing the screen program from the beginning.

You can also execute field-specific checks in a screen program. This means that you can create a separate check routine for each field or for a group of logically matching fields. You link the field(s) and check routine with each other by a special statement in the flow logic. If a check routine triggers an error message, you can only enter values in the input fields of the screen program that were linked with the check routine. The cursor is positioned in the first field to be processed. This procedure makes it easier to keep a clear view of the data and prevents new errors occurring if correct values are overwritten by mistake. You can also make field checks dependent on whether the contents of the field have been processed. This saves unnecessary checks and improves the application's performance.

The principle of check routines can quite easily be demonstrated in the demo application. To carry out a check routine, insert an additional statement in the PAI part of the flow logic:

```
PROCESS AFTER INPUT.
  FIELD value2 MODULE check_0100.
  MODULE USER_COMMAND_0100.
```

The flow logic is now saved and generated. Double-click on the CHECK_0100 character string to create the missing module in include MY310I01. The system then checks the module to see whether the current function code triggers a division. If it does, the system checks whether the value2 field contains the value 0.

```
MODULE check_0100 INPUT.
  IF fcode = 'OPCD' AND value2 = 0.
    MESSAGE ID 'YZ' TYPE 'E' NUMBER '000' with 'Division by Zero!'.
  ENDIF.
ENDMODULE.                    "CHECK_0100 INPUT
```

After you enter the source code, generate the screen program and activate the entire program, you can now test the application again. If you now enter a 0 in the value2 field, an error message should be displayed when you carry out a division. The way you maintain the message text, as well as the statements used to trigger a message, have already been described in Section 3.2.16. If, as described in that section, you have created the message class and the dummy message, you will see the error message shown in the listing.

Triggering an error with the statement MESSAGE restarts the processing of the current screen program. Now, all fields that were linked with the module causing the error through a FIELD statement in the flow logic are ready for input. In this example, this applies only to the field value2.

However, just as before, the problem still persists that a screen program in whose PAI section an error message was triggered cannot be terminated. After all, the module we have just inserted does not apply to the automatic checks. For this reason, there is a special function code type that is evaluated by specific modules, which in turn are processed before the automatic error checks. These modules are always called as the first modules in the PAI section of a screen program. The flow logic of screen program 100 must therefore be updated again:

```
PROCESS AFTER INPUT.
  MODULE exit_0100 AT EXIT-COMMAND.
  FIELD value2 MODULE check_0100.
  MODULE user_statement_0100.
```

By setting the AT EXIT-COMMAND addition for the exit_0100 module, you define that this module is only to be called if the function code is of function type E for 'Exit statement'. In the module, application termination is programmed for the two exit function codes. In the module, a CASE statement is used, although this could also be achieved with a shorter IF statement. However, it is a lot simpler to extend a CASE statement, if additional function codes have to be evaluated later.

```
MODULE EXIT_0100.
  CASE FCODE.
    WHEN 'FT12' OR 'FT15'.
      LEAVE PROGRAM.
  ENDCASE.
ENDMODULE.
```

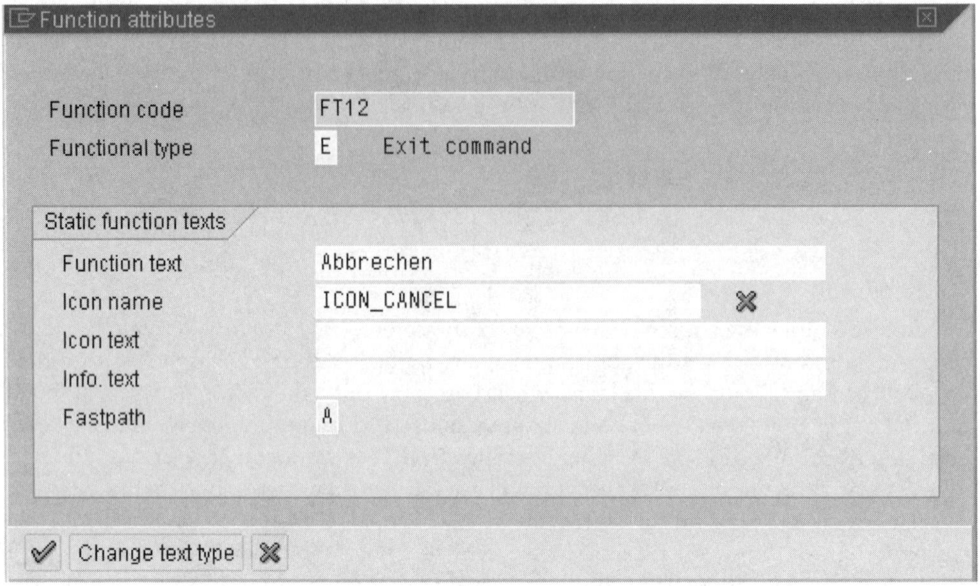

Figure 3.112   Set function type   © SAP AG

The two function codes must naturally also be created in the status to ensure they can be triggered at all. As the descriptions of the function codes show, the two function keys (F12) and (F15) are used for this. These function keys have a predefined meaning. The icon with the oblique red cross is assigned to function key (F12). The corresponding menu option is EDIT | CANCEL. The yellow up arrow or the Exit menu option in the first pull-down menu is assigned to function key (F15). The method for creating menu options and function codes has already been described. At this point, we would like to focus only on setting the function type.

First of all, insert both the function codes named here into the menu and the icon bar. Then, select GOTO | OBJECT LISTS | FUNCTION LIST from the menu to jump to the screen where you process these function codes. This list shows all the function codes that are used in the different statuses of the interface. Double-click on one of the two new function codes to display a dialog box (Figure 3.112) in which you can enter the function TYPE. In the type column, enter type E (for exit code) for function codes FT12 and FT15. The system now saves the status and generates the new interface. You can now leave the Menu Painter.

To complete the task, you should now also modify screen program 200. You can also insert an exit module here.

```
PROCESS BEFORE OUTPUT.
*
PROCESS AFTER INPUT.
  MODULE exit_0200 AT EXIT-COMMAND.
  MODULE user_statement_0200.
```

```
MODULE EXIT_0200.
  CASE FCODE.
    WHEN 'FT12'.
      LEAVE TO SCREEN 100.
    WHEN 'FT15'.
      LEAVE PROGRAM.
  ENDCASE.
ENDMODULE.
```

You can now test the application. You can close the program either by pressing (F15) or clicking on the exit icon. In screen program 100, click on the Cancel icon or press (F12) to close the program. However, in screen program 200 this function code, like FT03, will return you to screen program 100. Here, it is important that you can still press (F12) or (F15) to close screen program 100, even if an incorrect value has been entered in one of the two input fields.

This example clearly illustrates why function codes are divided into two groups and are evaluated separately. Particular activities, such as saving data or linking to other screen programs, are only permitted if the entries in the screen program are correct. However, it must be possible to carry out other functions such as closing an application, especially if incorrect entries have been made. The easiest way of meeting these requirements is to evaluate the exit function codes before executing a field check, and to evaluate the other function codes after the field check. If the system processes an exit module, and processing is not terminated because, for example, the user did not confirm this action when prompted, the system executes all the other modules. If this happens, the other modules can also evaluate an exit function code. Exit function codes are mostly used so that you can save the values you entered in the screen program before you leave the application. The detailed example in Chapter 7 demonstrates this programming technique.

3.7.2 The screen program in detail

Screen programs form the core of a dialog application. The input elements you see in the screen program's fullscreen comply with the SAA/CUA standard. A range of elements is available, in addition to the editable field you have been using until now. You can also use a series of attributes to modify the characteristics of the screen program's elements. Statements that have been specially tailored to the screen program concept are used in the flow logic and the various modules. This section will deal with this information in greater detail.

Screen program types

In its basic form, a screen program always takes up the entire work area. In special cases, i.e. when displaying additional information, it is a better idea to use dialog box screen programs whose size has been hard-coded. Report selection screens are also screen programs, but the system processes them in a different way from normal screen programs. There are five different types of screen program described below. However, you can only actually process three of these types. The system generates the other two types automatically.

Normal

All the screen programs you have generated in the demo applications are screen program type 'normal'. When you execute them, the screen programs take up the entire work area. Their flow logic can (and indeed must) be processed by the user. Normal screen programs are processed sequentially, one after the other. You define the sequence in which they are processed by setting the Next screen attribute or by setting various statements in the flow logic (such as SET SCREEN ..., LEAVE ...). For this reason, processing this type of screen program is similar to processing program statements because the processing steps are carried out sequentially.

Subscreens

Subscreens are screen programs that must be dynamically included in another screen program when the application is running. You cannot run subscreens independently. Subscreens must comply with special restrictions. For example, they cannot process any exit function codes and they must not contain any fields in which the user could enter a function code. Apart from that, subscreens do not influence the current interface (status). You use a special statement in the flow logic of the higher level screen program to call a subscreen. You will find more details about how to use this screen program type in the 'Flow logic statements' sub-section on page 307.

Modal dialog windows

You can use a range of special statements in the flow logic to process several screen programs in a different way. You would usually process them sequentially, but these statements allow you to call any screen program as a virtual subroutine. You use the CALL SCREEN statement to do this. If you use the LEAVE TO SCREEN 0 statement to close a screen program that you called with CALL SCREEN, you do not close the entire program. This statement merely returns you to the calling screen program.

     You can use a range of special additions to the CALL statement to display this type of screen program as a dialog box. If you do this, the calling screen program is not replaced by the new screen program, but appears in its own window instead. You can only enter data in this window. The application's menu and the statement field do not have any effect here. The dialog box now only reacts to the function keys and pushbuttons that were defined in the current status. The pushbuttons are displayed in a dialog box in the window's lower margin. You can only call MODAL DIALOG BOX-type screen programs as dialog boxes.

Selection screen programs

If an application uses statements that define a selection screen, the system automatically generates a selection screen program. Although you can load this type of screen program into the Screen Painter, you must not change it under any circumstances. However, the flow logic of selection screen programs contains modules that you can access directly. You cannot modify these modules because they do not exist as real ABAP program code. Any changes you make to the flow logic of selection screen programs are very likely to cause the report to function incorrectly!

Class screens

The class screen is part of the object-oriented extension of the ABAP programming language and is therefore not described in any detail here.

Field types in the screen program

When you design a screen program, you create elements in which users can enter and output data in the screen program's visible interface. These elements are called *screen program fields*. When you edit a screen program in Screen Painter, the fields are represented by groups of different alphanumerical characters. These characters act as placeholders. You can generate the fields manually by entering a specific placeholder character in the fullscreen. Alternatively, you can use a range of other tools to generate the screen program fields. You use the field type and various attributes to define a field's characteristics. Programmers can define the field type and some of the attributes when they generate the screen program. However, the Screen Painter automatically predefines some particular attributes, which therefore cannot be processed by the programmer.

The Screen Painter has several tools; one of them is the Layout Editor. This is used to structure the visual interface of the screen program.

The Screen Painter always labels fields, regardless of their type, with a block that is a different colour from the background. You must use the various functions of the Layout Editor to process this type of block, because you can no longer process it character by character in the usual way. The Layout Editor is itself a screen program. This means that any manual entries (i.e. when you create a field manually) are not recognized and evaluated until PAI processing is executed for the Fullscreen Editor's screen program. To trigger PAI processing, select the corresponding menu option, click the appropriate pushbutton or press (Enter). Only then for example does the system convert a character string into a real screen program field.

There are three main groups of field type that you can use in a screen program. These are:

1. elementary elements with processing functions;

2. static elements that are used to graphically structure the screen program;

3. complex elements (controls).

The demo example has already given an example of the first two groups of field types. Both these groups have a basic element from which all the other elements of the group are derived.

First of all, this section describes all the field types and how they are generated. It then describes the attributes you can use to make additional changes to the characteristics of these fields.

An input field is usually made up of two elements: a field identifier, i.e. the descriptor (or in SAP terminology, the keyword) and the field template, which is the actual input area. Both these elements are displayed on screen. The keyword is a text element that cannot be changed by the program user. However, the field template is the actual input field where editing takes place. The edited value must be linked with a data field to ensure that this value is available in the program. This data field then automatically defines some characteristics of the input field.

If you want to follow the explanations below in your system, you should either create a new program or a new screen program in one of the existing applications. Now enter the following data declarations in the top include:

```
TABLES:
  tadir.

DATA:
  rb1 TYPE c,
  rb2 TYPE c,
  rb3 TYPE c,
  cb1 TYPE c,
  cb2 TYPE c,
  cb3 TYPE c.
```

Key fields

Key fields are static text elements in the screen program's work area. They display general information or the names of input fields. You usually use the insertion tool (from the menu, choose GOTO | DICT./PROGRAM FIELDS) to create key fields. If you use this tool to transfer Data Dictionary fields into the screen program, the input fields and key fields automatically reference the Data Dictionary. Each corresponding text is taken from the description of a data element in the Data Dictionary. When you use the insertion tool to create a field, you can define which one of the texts available for the data element is to be selected. This selection is stored in the Modific. attribute of each particular field.

If you use the insertion tool, the field templates and key fields are usually created simultaneously. However, you can also generate each field type individually.

You can subsequently modify the contents of a key field that you inserted with the insertion tool. The fields you have modified in this way are marked with a code letter in the Modific. attribute in each particular field. You can also create key fields that do not reference the Data Dictionary. To do this, enter the text you require directly in the screen program.

You will increase the amount of work required to translate your program into other (natural) languages in the future if you modify existing key fields that reference the Data Dictionary or generate individual key fields that do not reference the Data Dictionary. For this reason, you should avoid using these variants as much as possible.

The easiest way of inserting key fields together with the field templates described below is to use the tool specifically designed for this purpose. To call this tool, choose GOTO | DICT./PROGRAM FIELDS from the menu. This tool uses a dialog box to control the dialog (Figure 3.113).

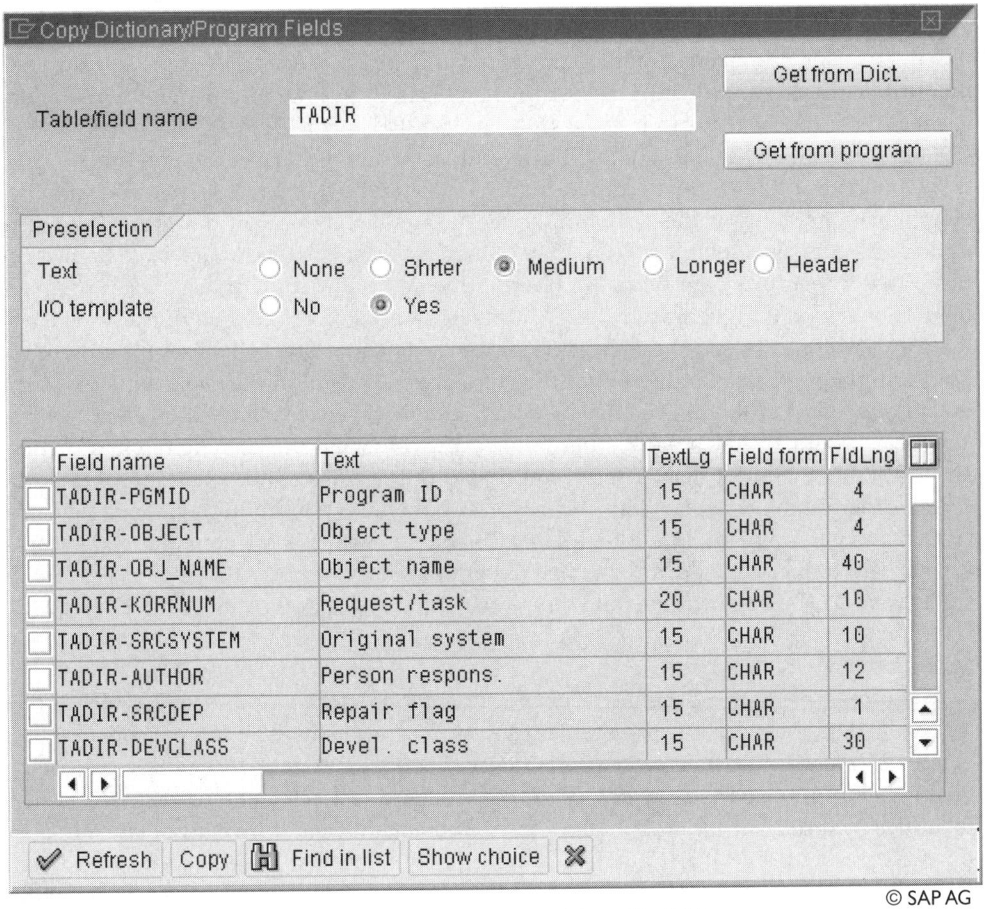

© SAP AG

Figure 3.113 Insertion tool for table fields

In the TABLE/FIELD NAME input field, you enter the name of the Data Dictionary table (or structure) from which you would like to copy the fields. Then, click the GET FROM DICT button. The table that now appears in the lower part of the dialog box displays a list of all the fields in the table. To select one or more fields, simply click on the checkbox in the first column in the table. If the screen program already contains fields from this table, these fields are still inactive, although they are present in the table. In the PRESELECTION window, you can now define the key field's type and specify whether you want to insert a field template or not. After this, click on the Copy button to copy the fields you have selected. This returns you to the Layout Editor where you insert the fields by double-clicking in the location you want them to appear. If you select several fields, they are inserted together as a block. That is why the screen program must have enough room for all the fields.

Field templates

You must create *field templates* for the actual input fields. Because you enter or output data in input fields, these fields must refer to a Data Dictionary, or at least to a field in the program, so that the system can transfer out the data. For this reason, you usually generate field templates with the input help. This has already been mentioned several times.

In the Layout Editor, field templates are represented by a range of special characters. Here, each character in the placeholder represents a character in the input field. The underscore acts as a default placeholder. Other characters symbolize special characteristics of the screen program field. In contrast, the actual function of the screen program field depends on each character itself and its position. For example, a question mark in the first position represents a mandatory input field. If they are in the first position of the field template, other characters that trigger a special function are the asterisk and the exclamation mark. All other characters, no matter what their actual position, simply act as a wildcard character. Each means that this specific character must be entered in a particular position in the input field. The system checks this automatically when it processes the screen program in an application. When you use the insert program to create a field, the system generates a default field template. This default setting only contains underscores. If you want to insert a wildcard character, you must do so in the Attributes dialog box in the TEXT field. For example, the field template might consist of the following characters:

_ _ _-_ _ _/_ _ _

In this case, the user must enter '-' after entering the first three characters, which can be any characters they choose. They must also enter '/' after the next three characters they enter, which can be any characters they choose. The system's control logic checks that the data entered in the mandatory fields and the wildcard characters are correct. The system identifies incorrect entries and displays them in the status bar. It then automatically positions the cursor in the (first) incorrect field. If existing data is displayed in a field with template characters, the screen program logic enters the data field characters sequentially into the free characters of the mask, i.e. no data is lost. If a field has the contents 123456789, the template shown above would display it as 123-456/789 and then save it with that data.

You can also generate field templates manually. To do this, enter the placeholder characters in the screen program. A field template can also start with a question mark instead of an underscore. This converts the field into a mandatory input field. You can also insert wildcard characters immediately. You can process the screen program's character string in the Layout Editor or press (Enter) until you select a function. You must do this before the Layout Editor can recognize the character string and convert it into a genuine screen program field. You must then set all the other field attributes in the Attributes dialog box or in the different variants of the field list editing procedure. This is especially important for the link with a data field.

Radio buttons

Radio buttons are input elements that can only include Yes/No information. A radio button is either selected or not. Several radio buttons are gathered in one group. You can only select one radio button at once within a group. A group is not identical with the surrounding frame. It is more like an internal summary in the screen program that cannot be identified on screen. Despite this, you can still highlight the fields that do match by putting them in an additional frame. However, this frame is not necessary for the fields to function correctly.

Each radio button has a corresponding data field in the program. If you select a radio button, the corresponding data field contains 'X'. If you do not select a button, this field contains a blank. This means that the corresponding data field is a C-type field and has 1 as its length.

You cannot create radio buttons directly. First of all, you must generate a field template for each radio button and then link it with a data field by making an entry in the screen program's field list. You then insert the three fields in the program (rb1 to rb3) in the screen program, as shown in Figure 3.114.

You can insert the fields either manually or with the insertion tool that has already been described in some detail. To create the fields manually, enter the three underscores '_' in the screen program and then assign the corresponding field names in the Attributes dialog box.

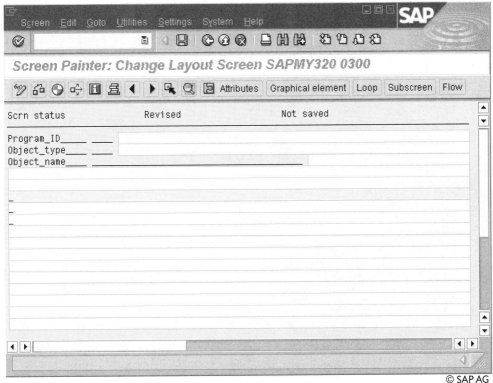

Figure 3.114   Starting point for creating radio buttons

If you use the insertion tool to copy the fields, you can only insert these fields at the left-hand margin of the screen program. This means you still have to move the fields within the screen program. Double-click in the top field again to select the field you require (Figure 3.115).

Double-click again on the bottom field to select the whole block. In this case, the block contains three fields (Figure 3.116). For obvious reasons, the horizontal position of the end of the block must not be located directly under its starting point. You can also select rectangular blocks, i.e. those that consist of field templates and key fields.

You have now selected the block you want to copy. Now place the cursor in the target position (Figure 3.117) and move the block to this position by clicking the BLOCK MOVE button or by pressing (Shift)(F4).

The Layout Editor moves the fields. After this, they are available again in the Layout Editor's initial screen (Figure 3.118) and can process additional elements.

Now you can convert these simple input fields into radio buttons. To do this, position the cursor on the upper left-hand screen program field. It does not matter if this is a key field or a field template. Then click the GRAPHICAL ELEMENT pushbutton.

The fullscreen editor then changes the view. The new screen program is used to process the graphical elements which, among other things, include the radio buttons. In this new screen, you can only process the elements by using the different functions of the Screen Painter. You can no longer make manual entries in the fullscreen.

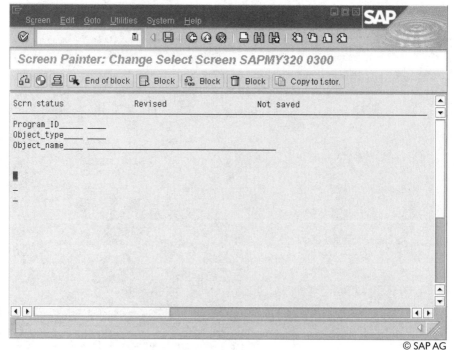

© SAP AG

Figure 3.115   Selecting the start of a block

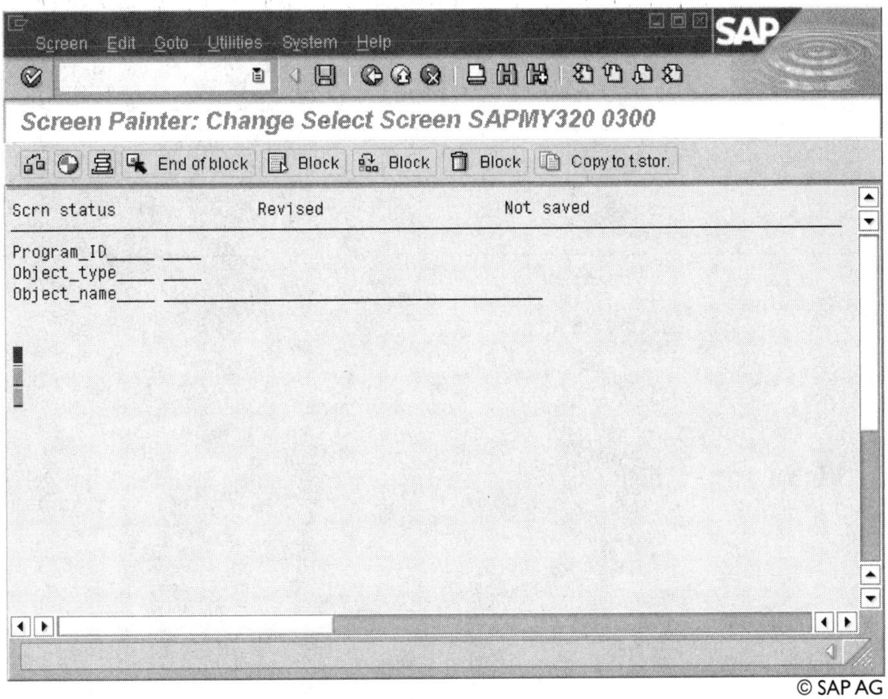

© SAP AG

Figure 3.116 Defining the end of a block

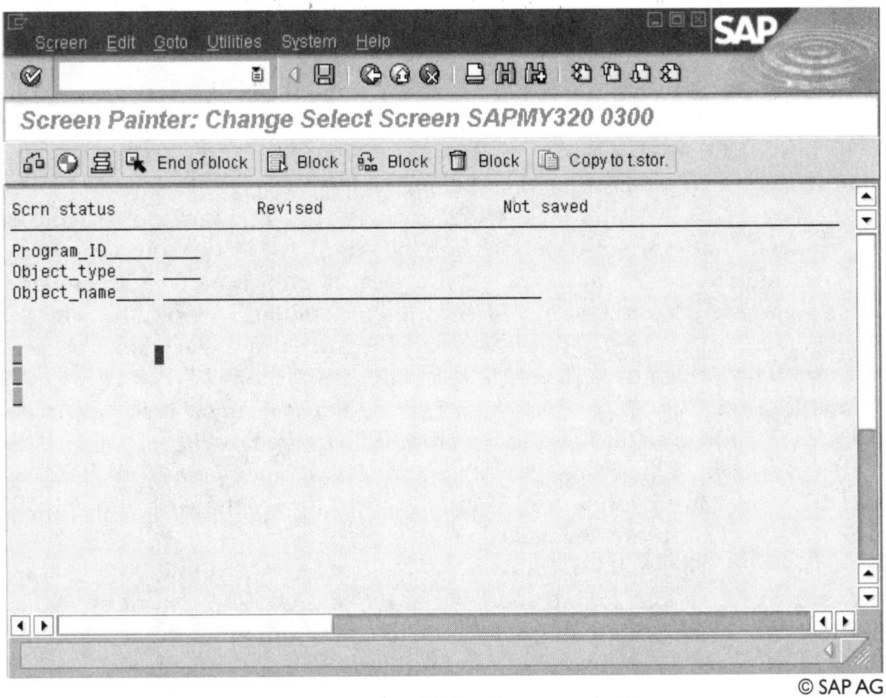

© SAP AG

Figure 3.117 Specifying the target position

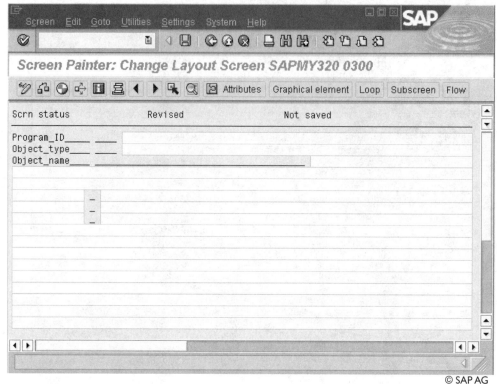

Figure 3.118   Final result of the move process

The field on which the cursor was previously positioned is highlighted in a different colour. The cursor now appears on the actual lower corner of the radio buttons group. If you now click on the END OF BLOCK pushbutton or double-click, the system combines all the elements into a block that the next function will then reference. This next function consists of clicking on the Radio buttons pushbutton. When you do this, the system converts all the field templates in the selected area into radio buttons. These radio buttons are displayed in the fullscreen editor and are identified by an appropriate icon (see Figure 3.119).

After you generate the radio buttons, the fullscreen editor view or more precisely its status and therefore the range of functions available will change again. You now combine the radio buttons into a group to ensure that only one of the fields can be selected at a time. You click the DEFINE GRAPH.GROUP pushbutton to call the function you use to do this. This function applies to all the fields in the previously selected block.

You can execute these functions immediately after each other because the fields remain selected after they have been converted into radio buttons. Otherwise you will have to select all the fields before you define the graphical group.

The radio buttons boxes do not necessarily have to be located under each other. You can also arrange them in several columns or insert empty rows between the individual fields. You do not have to transform all the fields into radio buttons at once. You can

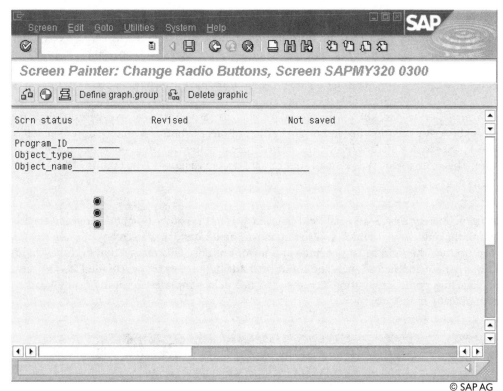

Figure 3.119 The screen program with three checkboxes

© SAP AG

transform them field by field if required. However, if you do this, the fullscreen editor requires you to quit the graphical elements tool each time, after you define each graphical element. Once you have defined all the radio buttons, you must generate the graphical radio button group. To do this, position the cursor once again on the graphical element that is located at the top left. Then click on the GRAPHICAL ELEMENT pushbutton to call the graphical elements processing tool. Because the cursor is already positioned on a graphical element, the function used to define the group is immediately available. Now position the cursor to the bottom and on the right-hand side of the screen, so the rectangle you define encloses all fields that are to be included in the group. Now click the corresponding pushbutton to generate the group.

To ungroup a group or to transform a radio button back into a simple field template, simply position the cursor on the particular element and click the GRAPHICAL ELEMENT pushbutton. The fullscreen editor screen program which you see next now only offers the functions available for the selected element. This means that the fullscreen editor works in a context-sensitive or object-oriented manner. You can reverse each particular characteristic (group or radio button) by clicking the DELETE GRAPHIC or DISSOLVE GRAPH.GROUP pushbuttons.

Checkboxes

Checkboxes are similar to radio buttons, but there are no dependencies between them. You can select any number of checkboxes in one screen program, so you do not need to group them together. However, you do need to link each checkbox with a data field. A checkbox has the same characteristics as radio buttons (type char, length 1). Enter 'X' in the data field for each checkbox you select.

You generate checkboxes in a similar way to radio buttons, except you click the Checkboxes pushbutton instead of the Radio buttons pushbutton. In the fullscreen editor, checkboxes look different from radio buttons because they are marked with a placeholder icon. This icon is shown as a small square with drawn diagonals (*see* Figure 3.120).

Frames

A frame merely acts as a visual field boundary. It has no other functions. In a screen program, the only way in which you can create a frame is by using a screen program field. If you do this, the field must not have any input options. This means that both key fields and any field templates where the Input field attribute has been deactivated, can serve as the starting point for creating a frame. You use field templates to set the frame heading dynamically in the program.

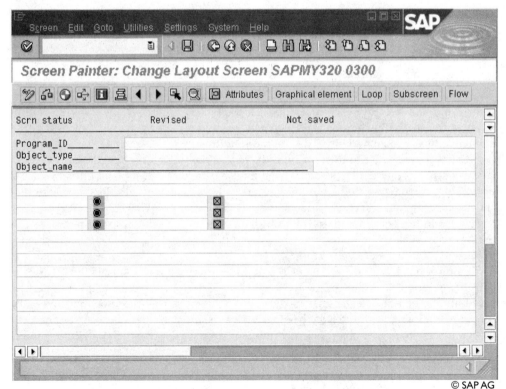

© SAP AG

Figure 3.120   Screen program with three checkboxes

To generate a frame, you first create a screen program field. This field can, of course, reference a Data Dictionary field, but does not have to. If the screen program field is to be based on a Data Dictionary field, you can simply take a (static) description from the Data Dictionary. If you cannot find a suitable text in the Data Dictionary, you can also create the frame's key field manually by entering the appropriate description in the fullscreen editor. When you position the field, you should ensure that the upper left-hand corner of the frame is generated immediately to the left of the screen program field. This ensures that the heading is always left-aligned in the frame's header line. You cannot align the header in any other way. Figure 3.121 shows the screen program in which a text acts as the starting point for a frame.

If the field for the frame description is present, the system positions the cursor on this field and activates the GRAPHICAL ELEMENT pushbutton. In the next screen program, you can then click the BOX pushbutton to launch the creation of the frame. The status changes, as you can immediately see because the application toolbar has changed. Now select the true bottom corner of the frame by positioning the cursor on it (Figure 3.122).

You then generate the frame either by clicking the END OF BOX pushbutton or by double-clicking with the mouse. The frame must not touch any other screen program field, or overlap with the screen program's page margins. The Layout Editor identifies

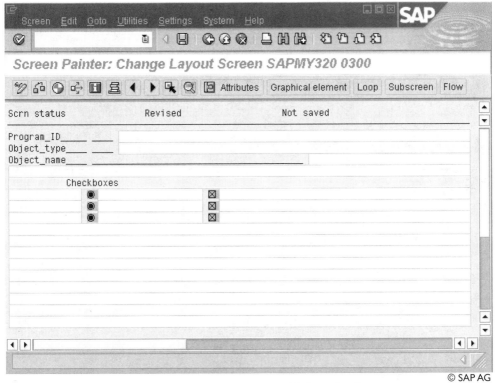

© SAP AG

Figure 3.121 Screen program with frame heading

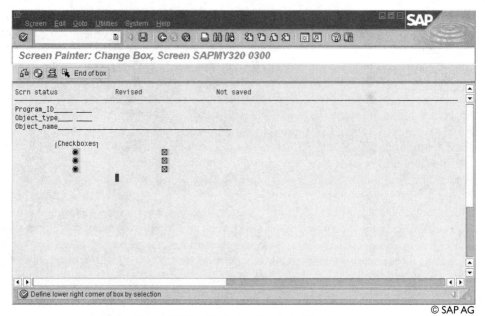

Figure 3.122   Defining the size of the frame

this type of error and rejects it. In the Layout Editor, the frame is marked with coloured
lines (Figure 3.123).

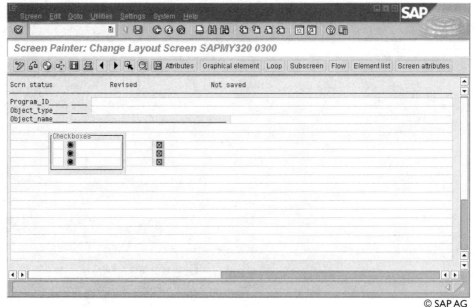

Figure 3.123   Screen program with frame

Pushbuttons

In addition to the pushbuttons in the interface's application toolbar, you can create these types of control elements within the screen program. The function codes you trigger by clicking on screen program pushbuttons have the same effect as those you trigger in the interface itself. Like a frame, screen program pushbuttons are derived from an existing screen program field. Once again, this screen program field can be a key field or a field template without input authorization. If you use the latter, you can set the text shown in the pushbutton.

You generate a pushbutton in a similar way to the elements that have already been described above. First you create the appropriate screen program field. Then position the cursor on this field and click on the GRAPHICAL ELEMENT pushbutton. In the next screen program, you now click on the PUSHBUTTONS pushbutton to transform the field into a pushbutton. In the general fullscreen editor screen, you still have to assign a function code and a function type to the pushbutton. You do so in the Attributes dialog box for the corresponding element. The structure of this dialog box and the fields in it are discussed below after the various elements have been described.

You can link pushbuttons with an icon. You can add this icon in addition to the text or instead of the text. You must take the screen program field type into consideration when you assign an icon. For key fields, you can assign an icon directly in the Attributes dialog box by selecting the ICON NAME attribute. To help you select the appropriate icon, the input help for this attribute lists all the possible icons and their descriptions. You will find more details about this in the section that discusses the attributes of screen program fields.

Subscreens

We have already referred to subscreens when we mentioned screen program attributes. When an application is running, you can dynamically integrate this type of screen program with another screen program as an include. Before this can happen, the higher level screen program must reserve a special area for the subscreen screen program. For reasons of simplicity, this area is also described as a *subscreen*. You can insert several of these subscreens into one screen program. Each subscreen is given a unique description. Subscreens provide the user with a simple method of inserting their own functions into standard SAP programs if the standard programs allow this kind of extension by embedding this type of subscreen. In addition to that, you can display specialized subscreens to maintain various objects in a general framework program.

To generate a subscreen, choose EDIT | CREATE ELEMENT | SUBSCREEN from the menu. Starting from the current cursor position, the system selects all the free space in the screen program. Figure 3.124 shows the Layout Editor at this point in time.

Double-click on any point within the selected area to define the size of the subscreen area. A dialog box is now displayed (Figure 3.125) in which you can maintain the subscreen area's attributes, especially its name.

You have now created the subscreen area. However, you still require special statements in the flow logic before you can actually display a screen program in the subscreen area. You will find more details about this in Section 3.7.2

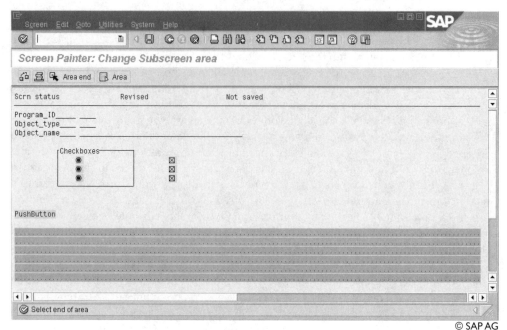

Figure 3.124   How to insert a subscreen

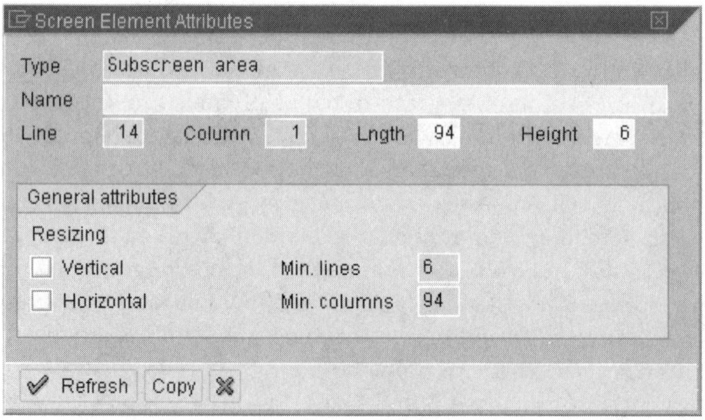

Figure 3.125   Attributes for the subscreen area

Step loops

The screen program elements described so far are designed to always process only one data record at a time. Occasionally, this has a negative effect on an application by making it run less effectively or more slowly. For this reason, you use step loops (also simply known as *loops*) to display and process several data records at once. Before you can use loops, you must generate the corresponding elements in the screen program and insert special statements in the flow logic. You will find more details on how to program loops later in this section.

To generate a loop, you must first create a block in the Layout Editor. This block consists of one or more field templates. Theoretically, it might also contain text fields, but in practice this is only rarely the case because it slows down the application. The block can include several lines and forms the template for the loop's structure. This structure consists of multiple repeats of this block. Figure 3.126 shows a line that has been prepared for a step loop.

After you have created the block, position the cursor on the top left field in the block and click the Loop pushbutton. The fullscreen editor switches to a different editing mode, in which you select the end of the template block. This is the field located at the bottom right of the block to be duplicated. To select it, double-click on the bottom right-hand corner or position the cursor and click END OF LOOP BLOCK. Figure 3.127 shows the Layout Editor at this point in time.

After you have defined the end of the block, Screen Painter automatically generates another duplicate of the selected block directly underneath it (see Figure 3.128). The template block and its copy are highlighted in different colours. The fullscreen editor remains in editing mode for loops and also provides a new status with some new functions.

A loop is first created as a *fixed loop*. The size of a fixed loop when it appears in the completed screen program is always the size originally defined for it in the Layout Editor. Because Screen Painter initially generates a loop that only consists of two blocks, you can click the END LINE OF LOOP pushbutton to extend the loop section as far as the current

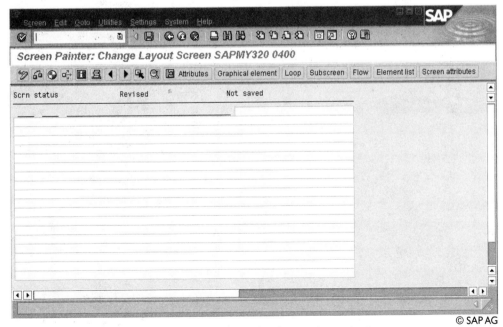

© SAP AG

Figure 3.126   Starting point for creating a step loop

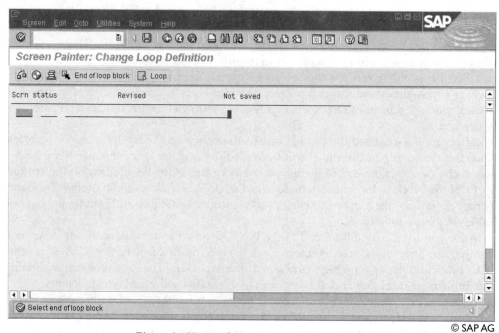

Figure 3.127   Defining the end of a loop block

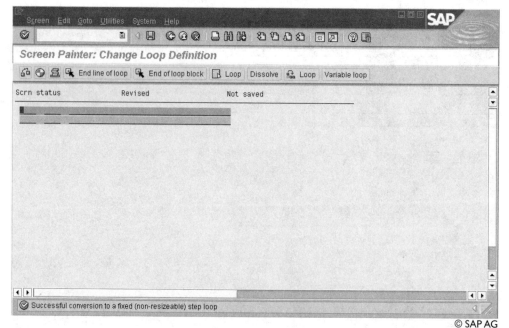

Figure 3.128   Rudimentary step loop with two blocks

cursor position. To do this, position the cursor in the end line you require and click on the END LINE OF LOOP pushbutton.

Another pushbutton or menu option allows you to transform this fixed loop into a *variable loop*. When the screen size changes, the number of visible duplicates is adjusted to fit the current size of the window. This line number change does not affect the spacing with regard to other screen program fields above and below the loop section. If you should insert another field two lines below a variable loop, these two lines underneath the loop would remain unoccupied, even though the window size has been changed. If you should put a frame around a variable loop, the frame size would change to fit the size of the loop.

You must remember one special feature when you position the key fields for a loop. That is that if the key fields are located together with the field templates inside the loop block they will be automatically duplicated in each following block. This often makes it harder to see what is actually going on in the screen program. For this reason, you can also position key fields outside the actual loop as a table heading. In this case, the key fields and field templates are located in different screen program areas. The Screen Painter does not allow this. When you generate the screen program, a corresponding error message appears. In this case, the reference table for the key fields is made available with a different table name. This table name is derived from the actual table name by prefixing it with an asterisk, '*'. You must also specify this table in the declaration part of the application. In this case it would be:

```
TABLES: TADIR, *TADIR.
```

The obvious solution to this problem is to copy the key fields and the field templates into the screen program by calling the insertion tool twice. However, you can also change the field name in the field list manually.

Table control

From Release 3.0, *controls* have been implemented to make it easier to display and process data in screen programs. *Table view* is one of these controls; it is a modern variant of the step loop. Table views provide a table work area which unlike a loop no longer consists of individual screen program fields that appear separate from each other, but appears as a complete object instead. An example of this kind of table control are the tables in the screen program element list (Figure 3.129).

Just like step loops, you must enter special statements in the flow logic before you can use table views. Again, like a loop, you click on the appropriate pushbutton or choose EDIT | CREATE ELEMENT | TABLE CONTROL from the menu option to generate a table view. The Layout Editor reserves an area for the table view in the screen program. You must confirm the actual dimensions of this area by double-clicking on the position you require in the bottom right-hand corner. You must then enter the name of the table view in a dialog box (Figure 3.130).

In the module pool, you must later use the following statement to generate a TABLE-VIEW-type data object that has the same name:

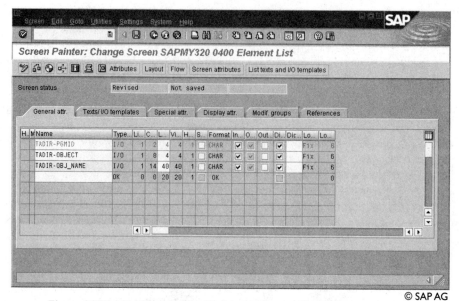

© SAP AG

Figure 3.129   Table control to display the element list in a screen program

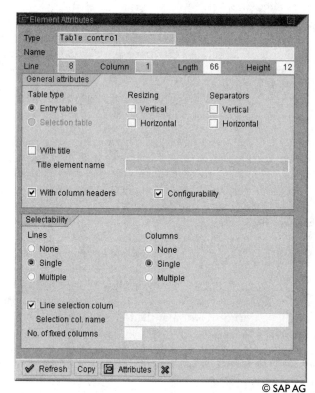

© SAP AG

Figure 3.130   Dialog box for maintaining the values for a table control

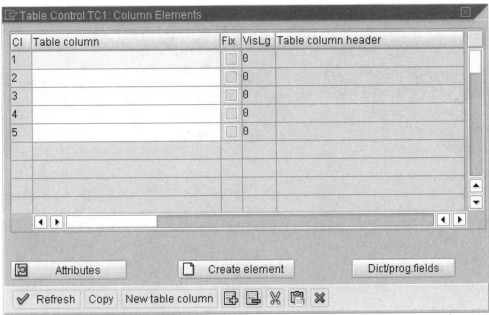

© SAP AG

Figure 3.131   Dialog box for the table view fields

CONTROLS `tableview` **TYPE TABLEVIEW USING SCREEN** `dynpronumber`.

You can only ever use one table view in one screen program, because you must specify the screen program when you declare the table view.

After you have assigned its name, you can process the table view in the Layout Editor. Click on the CTRL ELEMENTS pushbutton to insert the fields you want to display in the table view area. The dialog box shown in Figure 3.131 appears. In it you can either enter the field names manually or insert them using the input help for Data Dictionary fields. If you use the input help, you should be aware of a small difference in functionality: to copy the selected fields into the table view, you do not click the COPY pushbutton as you might expect. Instead you must click the INS.TABLE COLUMN pushbutton in the dialog box for the table view fields. The Ins.table column pushbutton only appears as an icon and is therefore easily missed.

Tabstrip

Version 4.0 of the SAP R3 System contains another screen program control. This is called the *tabstrip*. A tabstrip consists of a series of tabs and a subscreen area. When you activate one of the tabs, you switch to the contents of the subscreen area. This is how you can display and process a real subscreen in each subscreen area of a screen program. In older releases of the R/3 software you can of course mimic the tabstrip function by using a normal subscreen area and a few pushbuttons. However, a tabstrip provides a more attractive-looking interface and makes operation more intuitive. An example of a tabstrip is the element list in Screen Painter (Figure 3.132).

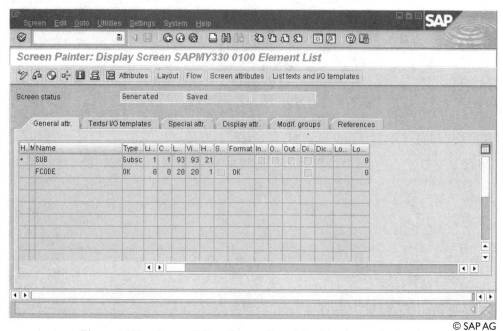

Figure 3.132   Screen Editor element list with table view and tabstrip

It takes quite a lot of time and effort to define a tabstrip control. In the screen program's maintenance transaction, you call the EDIT | CREATE ELEMENT | TABSTRIP CONTROL function. You first select the bottom right-hand corner of the tabstrip by double-clicking on it, just like you do for subscreens. The system then displays a dialog box in which you enter the tabstrip's name (Figure 3.133).

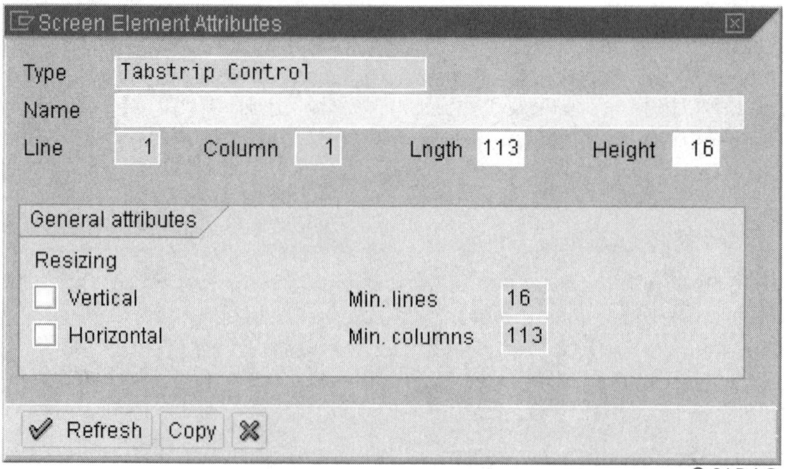

Figure 3.133   Defining the tabstrip's name

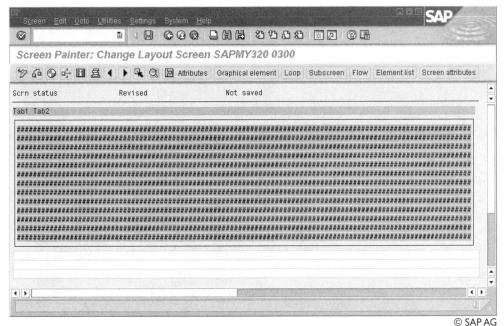

© SAP AG

Figure 3.134   View of a tabstrip in the alphanumerical Screen Painter

After you enter the tabstrip name, the program returns to the main program maintenance screen. A tabstrip looks quite similar to a subscreen (see Figure 3.134). However,
the difference is that a tabstrip has the additional line with the tabs. The system automatically creates two of these tabs with the names `Tab1` and `Tab2`.

Once you have generated the tabstrip, you must maintain the individual elements. It is
particularly important that you provide the tab with function codes. To do this, double-
click in the tabstrip area to switch to the control maintenance interface. Then choose EDIT
| CTRL ELEMENTS from the menu option. You jump to a dialog box in which you can main-
tain the tab and the remaining tabstrip elements.

In this screen (see Figure 3.135), you must assign function codes to the existing tabs
and name the subscreen area. You can also generate additional tabs here. You enter the
name of the subscreen area in the lower table view. This name is optional. It is used later
in the application's flow logic. After you have entered the name, press (Enter). In the next
dialog box, the system prompts you to confirm the subscreen name and to set its size. The
subscreen you insert later in the application can only be of the size you define here. Of
course, the subscreen area and the subscreen displayed later in the application must not
be larger than the tabstrip area.

After you enter the subscreen area, you assign the necessary information to the tabs. In
the reference subscreen column, you enter the name of the subscreen you have just
defined. You enter a freely definable function code in the `FCODE` column. Now click the
Copy pushbutton to leave the dialog box. The system highlights the subscreen area in the
screen program's maintenance interface (Figure 3.136).

© SAP AG

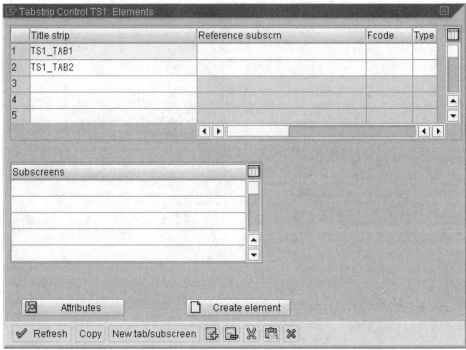

Figure 3.135 Maintaining tabstrip control elements

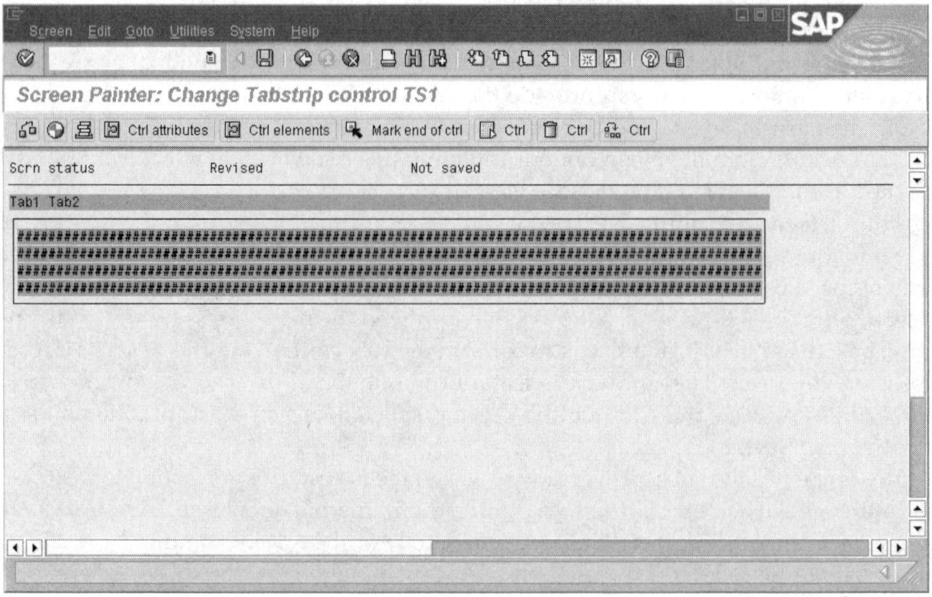

© SAP AG

Figure 3.136 Screen Painter with tabstrip and subscreen area

The way you handle a tabstrip, in technical programming terms, is relatively simple and resembles that of the subscreens. First of all, you use the CONTROLS statement to declare a tabstrip:

CONTROLS *tabstrip* **TYPE TABSTRIP**.

When a user clicks a tab, the system triggers a function code that is evaluated in the User Command module. This function code is used to set the number of the screen program that is to be inserted. In the flow logic you display this with the CALL SUBSCREEN statement in the subscreen area of the tabstrip. The object you create with the CONTROLS statement has three fields. If necessary, you can set all these fields dynamically. These are the prog, dynnr and activtab fields. In the prog field you enter the name of the program from which the inserted subscreen is to be taken. As a result, the dynnr field is filled with the number of the screen program you want to insert. In the activetab field, you enter the name of the tab that is to appear as the active tab.

Icon

From Release 3.0 onwards, you can also use icons in screen programs. When you use the term 'icon', you should be aware that the SAP System uses both 'icons' and 'symbols'. These terms name two completely different elements, even though 'symbol' means 'icon' in German! At this point, we will only deal with the icons because these are the only ones that can be used in screen programs.

Icons can only be assigned to particular fields in which you cannot enter data. These are key fields, output fields and pushbuttons. You assign key fields in the Attributes dialog box where you see a corresponding field with input help. The fields are assigned statically, which means that you cannot change their assignment when the application is running.

You can assign an icon dynamically in field templates, where you have to reset the INPUT FIELD attribute. You do this in two steps. The first step is to select the With icon attribute in the screen program for the field you want. This is not absolutely necessary, but it makes it easier for the Screen Painter to calculate the field's output length correctly. The second step is to assign the icon to the field. You cannot assign an icon's name directly. Instead the ICON_CREATE function module converts the icon's name into a special character string that must be assigned to the data element. In simple terms, a function module is a special subprogram. Function modules are discussed in greater detail in another section. You must also transfer some parameters to these modules. You can then use these parameters to influence the appearance of the display field. You can also transfer some optional parameters to the function module to influence some of the icon's display options.

Attributes of elementary screen program fields

If you position the cursor on a screen program field, you can display or maintain the field attributes by choosing EDIT | ELEMENT ATTRIBUTES from the menu or clicking the pushbutton that also has this name. This function calls a dialog box in which you can maintain the attributes of all screen program elements except those of controls.

The appearance of the dialog box depends partly on the type of field to be processed. Although the dialog box in Figure 3.137 appears for input and output fields, the push-buttons have a different dialog box (Figure 3.138).

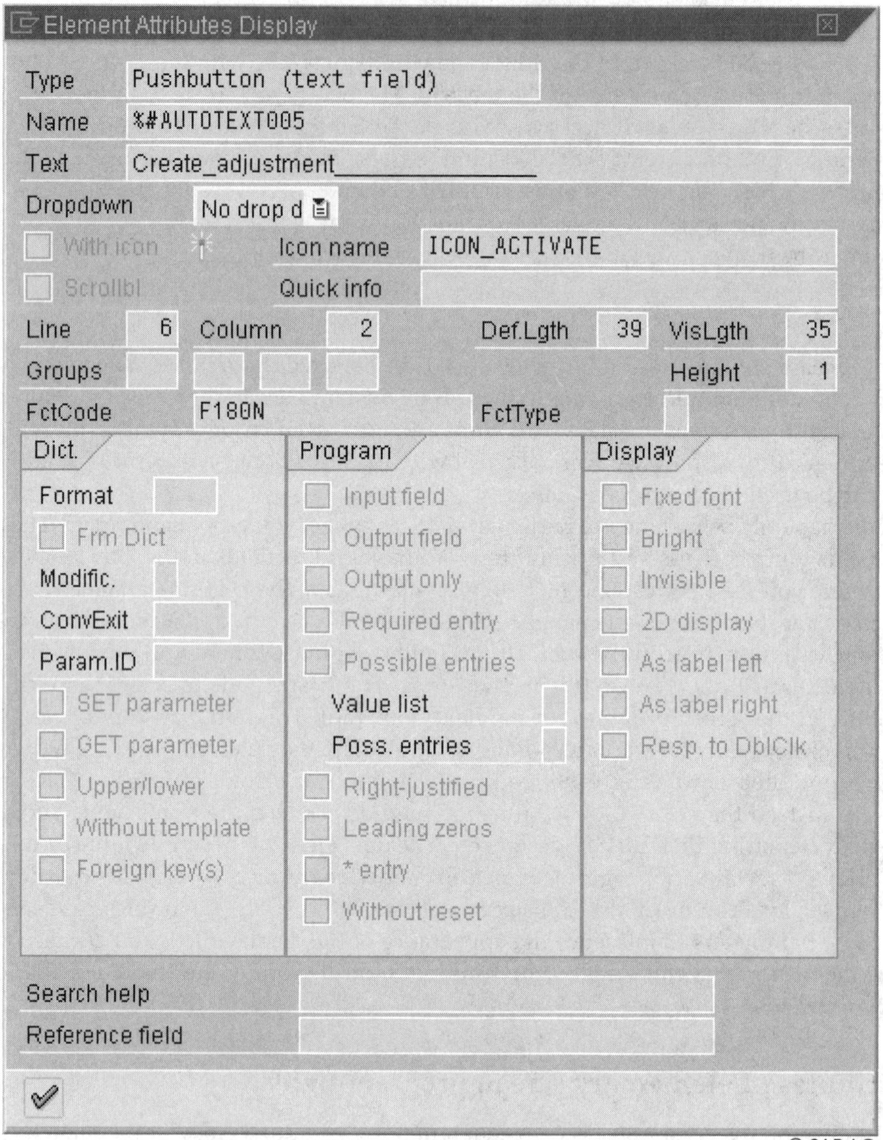

Element Attributes Display			⊠
Type	Pushbutton (text field)		
Name	%#AUTOTEXT005		
Text	Create_adjustment_____		
Dropdown	No drop d ▣		
□ With icon ☀	Icon name	ICON_ACTIVATE	
□ Scrollbl	Quick info		
Line	6 Column	2	Def.Lgth 39 VisLgth 35
Groups			Height 1
FctCode	F180N	FctType	

Dict.	Program	Display
Format	□ Input field	□ Fixed font
□ Frm Dict	□ Output field	□ Bright
Modific.	□ Output only	□ Invisible
ConvExit	□ Required entry	□ 2D display
Param.ID	□ Possible entries	□ As label left
□ SET parameter	Value list	□ As label right
□ GET parameter	Poss. entries	□ Resp. to DblClk
□ Upper/lower	□ Right-justified	
□ Without template	□ Leading zeros	
□ Foreign key(s)	□ * entry	
	□ Without reset	

Search help

Reference field

✓

© SAP AG

Figure 3.137   Dialog box for maintaining screen program field attributes

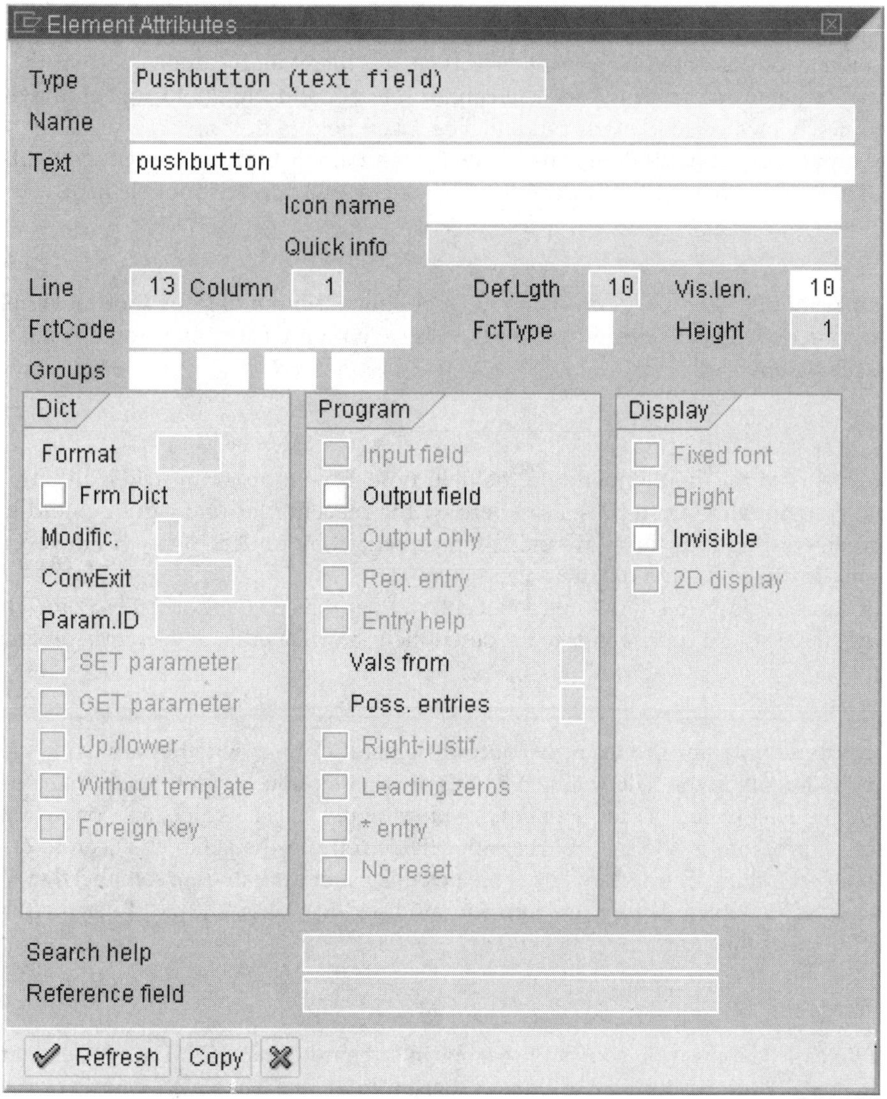

Element Attributes ☒

Type	Pushbutton (text field)
Name	
Text	pushbutton

Icon name

Quick info

| Line | 13 | Column | 1 | | Def.Lgth | 10 | Vis.len. | 10 |
| FctCode | | | | FctType | | Height | 1 |

Groups

Dict
Format
☐ Frm Dict
Modific.
ConvExit
Param.ID
☐ SET parameter
☐ GET parameter
☐ Up./lower
☐ Without template
☐ Foreign key

Program
☐ Input field
☑ Output field
☐ Output only
☐ Req. entry
☐ Entry help
Vals from
Poss. entries
☐ Right-justif.
☐ Leading zeros
☐ * entry
☐ No reset

Display
☐ Fixed font
☐ Bright
☐ Invisible
☐ 2D display

Search help

Reference field

✓ Refresh   Copy   ✖

Figure 3.138   Dialog box for maintaining field attributes

You cannot maintain every attribute for each of the field types described below. You will find more information about how to do this in Section 3.7.2.

The Attributes dialog box is divided into five areas. The upper area contains input fields or display fields for the general attributes. The middle part of the screen program consists of three columns, each with logically associated attributes. At the lower edge of the dialog box, you see two fields that are part of the Data Dictionary group, but do not fit into the corresponding column because they are too wide.

Type

The contents of the Type field set the field type and therefore the appearance of the field in the completed screen program. You cannot set or modify the field type in the dialog box. A newly created field starts out either as a key field (a descriptor) or as a field template (input/output field). You can use the Screen Painter tools to change the field type and therefore also change the appearance of the field, which is an input element.

Name

The majority of screen program fields must be linked with a data field or table field to enable data exchange. The name of this field is saved in this attribute. You can modify it in the dialog box.

Text

The contents of this field depend on the field type. Screen program fields with input or output functionality are represented here by the placeholder that can be found in the fullscreen editor. Input fields are usually represented by underscores '_'. However, the placeholder can also contain pattern characters.

In the case of fields in which you cannot enter values directly (i.e. key fields, frames, pushbuttons), the field text corresponds to the description shown later on in the screen program.

Dropdown

This attribute only applies to input/output fields. It defines whether any value can be entered manually in the field (value: SPACE) or whether you can only select a value from a predefined list (value: 'L' for list box). If you can only select a value, an icon appears in the screen program to the right of the input field. You can then click this icon to display the list of set values. The system either creates this list of set values automatically when it evaluates value tables, or you use function module VRM_SET_VALUES to create this list when the program is running (PBO event).

With icon

From Release 3.0 onwards, you can use icons in screen programs. You can either set these icons statically as attributes of a screen program field (see *Icon name*, below) or display them dynamically in output fields. To do this, generate an output field and mark the With icon field. Then, in the PBO module, a function module uses the icon name to determine an identifier for that icon. The system then assigns this identifier to the data field that works with the screen program's output field. The icon is then displayed in the screen program instead of the identifier.

Icon name

Certain types of fields (pushbutton and key fields) can have an icon added to them. Alternatively, they may only consist of an icon. The ICON NAME input field is active in these fields. You can use the value help key to display a list of the available icon names.

Quick Info

If the mouse pointer remains on an icon for a short while, the system displays a descriptive text in a coloured field directly below the icon. You can set this text in the QUICK INFO field. After you select an icon, the system prompts you with a default value. If required, you can overwrite it.

Scrollbl (scroll bar)

In input fields that are not based on Data Dictionary data types TIMS, DATS, QUAN, CURR, DEC, INT1 or INT2, you can set a visible length for the input field that is less than the total field length. However, you can only do this if the SCROLLBL field is selected. While you are processing the field contents, the contents will keep scrolling when you reach the right-hand or left-hand field margin.

Line, column

These two fields contain the co-ordinates of the screen program field. You can only modify the co-ordinates by moving a field in the fullscreen editor. In the Attributes dialog box, these fields only appear as display fields.

Defined length, visual length

The defined length of a screen program field determines the maximum number of characters this field can contain and process. In input fields, the defined length of the screen program field must equal the length of the corresponding data field. If not, the contents of the data field will be cut short. In exceptional cases, you may want this to happen, i.e. if you want to enter numbers with a maximum number of digits that is smaller than the maximum value permitted. When you use the fullscreen editor's insert help to generate screen program fields, the system copies the length defined for the original data element.

The visual length is the width of the field that you can see in the screen program. It normally corresponds to the defined length. From Release 3.0 onwards, you can scroll the fields. If the corresponding SCROLLBL attribute has been set, you can select a smaller visual length than the length that has been defined. When you edit the field, the contents will then scroll when you reach the true left-hand or right-hand margin.

Height

This output field represents the height of a particular screen program element.

Groups

The internal description of a screen program field contains four fields with the names GROUP1 to GROUP4. The system evaluates these fields and their contents when a screen program is modified dynamically. You can enter any values in the four input fields of the GROUPS attribute. These values merely represent a classification and do not directly affect how the field appears in the screen program. More detailed examples of the dynamic processing of screen programs are described below.

FctCode, FctType

You can even define pushbuttons in screen programs as well as in the statuses of an interface. However, these pushbuttons must also have a function code which in turn identifies a function type. You can set both values in the Attributes dialog box for screen program pushbuttons. You cannot use the interface's function list to change these values! There are a few dangers lurking here because the system may now generate identical function codes with different function types. Because the function type is not displayed when you debug an application, you may get seemingly inexplicable deviations when you evaluate the function codes.

Context menu

In this field you enter a name that the system uses to create the name of a subroutine, by prefixing it with the ON_CT_MENU_ character string. You call this subroutine by right-clicking in the corresponding field.

LoopType, LoopCount

To make it easier to process large amounts of data, you can process several data records of a table in one screen program. You use a special input element, called a *loop*, to do this. This loop can have two different types that give you information about the number of input lines in the loop. If the loop has the type 'Fixed', it has a fixed number of lines, regardless of the window size. This setting is displayed in the LoopCount field. You can only change the number of lines by processing the loop in the fullscreen. If the loop has the type 'Variable', the system adjusts the number of loop lines to fit the size of screen being displayed. Although the LoopCount field also shows the number of the loop lines from the fullscreen editor here, it does not affect how the loop appears in the screen program.

Format

This display field contains the data format of the data field linked with the screen program field. In fields that refer to the Data Dictionary, the data type is set automatically. If the linked data element is a field in the program and does not refer to the Data Dictionary reference, you must enter the data type here. To do this, use the input help (function key (F4)) because not all data types are permitted in screen programs.

Frm Dict (from Data Dictionary)

In this checkbox, you specify whether all the information for this screen program field is to be copied from the corresponding Data Dictionary field. This information is the length for field templates, and the field text for key fields.

Modific. (modified)

You can use the insert help to copy various key texts from the Data Dictionary. Then you can also modify these texts. The contents of this attribute identify the key text type or show that this text has been changed manually. The input help for this field displays all the available values.

ConvExit

Conversion routines can become active when you input or output fields. The system stores these routines as function modules. These function modules are called CONVER- SION_EXIT_xxxxx_INPUT or CONVERSION_EXIT_xxxxx_OUTPUT. Their predefined structure means that you only need five characters to identify them. You enter these characters in the CONVEXIT field.

Param. ID, SET parameter, GET parameter

The GET and SET parameters are data fields that can be used by more than one transaction. They are stored in a global, cross-application memory which is active throughout an entire user session. You use the GET PARAMETER or SET PARAMETER statements to fill or read these parameters. You do not need to use ABAP statements for screen program fields. You set the SET PARAMETER or GET PARAMETER flags to initiate data exchange with the parameter. This means, for example, that you can automatically copy important key fields into screen programs as default values.

Upper/lower

If you select this field, the system transfers lower-case letters and upper-case letters without changing them. If this field is not selected, the letters are all converted to upper case. Using this option is a good way of ensuring that your code remains clear in key fields.

Without template

Some characters, i.e. '?' or '!', have a special meaning in input fields. You can set a flag to prevent the system evaluating these characters, so you can enter them just like any other character.

Foreign keys

If a field has had a foreign key check defined for it in the Data Dictionary, the system also checks the field's entries against the check tables. This happens in every case, no matter when field checks may take place in the flow logic. You must set this flag to activate this check. If you do not require the automatic foreign key check, simply deactivate the flag.

Reference field

This attribute only contains an entry for currency fields or unit fields. It contains a field name which in turn contains the currency key or the unit key when the application is running. The system processes the screen program field in accordance with the characteristics of the currency or unit of measure. In the case of Data Dictionary fields, the reference field is assigned directly to the table field.

Input field

You must set this flag to ensure that the system transfers the values entered in this field from the screen program field to the data element. The system resets this flag automatically in key texts. You can deactivate it in field templates. The field now appears with a differently coloured background to show you that it is inactive. However, the field's frame remains unchanged.

Output field

If this flag is selected, the system transfers data from the data field in the program to the screen program field. If the flag is not selected, the system does not display the contents of the corresponding data field. After the screen program has been processed, the flag no longer affects how data is transferred from the screen program field to the data field.

Output only

This flag is only suitable for use in field templates. There it outputs the field contents as a key field, i.e. without the frame that normally surrounds field templates. You use this kind of field to dynamically display texts as key fields.

Req. entry

You can label those input fields that must always be given a value, such as key fields, as required entry fields. The screen program's internal control logic evaluates the exit module. Then the internal control logic checks whether the contents of all fields labelled as required entry fields contain an entry that is not their initial value. If one or more fields do not have a value, the system displays a default error message and screen program processing starts again from the beginning.

Entry help

The Screen Painter sets this attribute automatically for input/output fields. Users cannot process this attribute directly. If this field has been selected, the system provides entry help for the input field. This entry help is provided in several different ways (foreign key reference, value list in the domain, search help, value help that you program yourself).

Value list

You can only set this attribute for input fields in which the 'Dropdown Box' attribute has also been set. The permitted values (space or 'A') define how the values for the list of recommended values are acquired. If you enter a blank in this field, the system uses the existing default mechanisms to generate a list of recommended values (domain fixed values, tables containing values, search help). However, if you enter 'A', you must enter the values in the actual value list on the PBO event by calling function module VRM_SET_VALUES. You must use this module even if you are programming your own value help for the POV event. However, POV modules form part of the value help standard methods, and can therefore only be called if the Value list attribute field is blank.

Poss. entries

You use this attribute to define whether or not an existing value help should be active for this field. The value of this attribute also influences when the value help icon is displayed next to the field. Table 3.37 shows the possible entries.

Table 3.37   Value range of the value help key attribute

Value	Status value help	Icon for value help displayed
SPACE	Value help is active	If cursor is positioned in the field
0	Value help is switched off	
1	Value help is active	If cursor is positioned in the field
2	Value help is active	Always

Right-justif.

The contents of this field are displayed right justified. This only applies to output fields unless they are numerical fields.

Leading zeros

The system provides right-justified numerical values in field templates with leading zeros.

* entry

This attribute is no longer used. In input fields that have this attribute, you can enter an asterisk '*' in the first position. If you do so, a PAI module, which is identified by a special addition, is called for this field.

Without reset

If a user enters '!' in the first position of an input field, the system initializes the field as soon as all the data have been entered in the screen program. This means that no values are copied. To deactivate this mechanism, call the WITHOUT RESET attribute. This means you can now enter exclamation marks in the first position in a field.

Search helps

Search helps are a special kind of input help that enables you to search for keywords by using non-keywords. Matchcodes were used for this up to Release 3.x. Search helps are generated in independent maintenance programs and are given a unique name. If the name of a search help is entered in this attribute, you can later press (F4) to call the search help for that particular screen program field. From Release 3.0 onwards, you can also transfer the name of the matchcode or the search help dynamically when the application is running. In this case, the MATCHCODE attribute contains the name of the field. This field name must be preceded by a colon. When the application is running, the field in the PBO part of the screen program is filled with the names of each matchcode to be used.

Fixed font

The entry you make in this field defines the particular conditions under which texts are output in a fixed font, i.e. in a font where all characters have the same width.

Bright

You can tell when this field is activated because it appears in a different colour or is brighter or fainter than the others.

Invisible

This attribute is used for fields that have a password function. You cannot see the data you enter or output in fields with this attribute because the field only displays asterisks. An example of this is the password entry field that appears when you log on to the R/3 System.

2D display

The field templates and pushbuttons in the screen program are displayed in such a way as to give a three-dimensional feel. You set this flag to deactivate this function.

As label left/As label right

You should only use these flags for text fields. If one of these flags has been set, a thin line appears to symbolize that this text field belongs to the screen program element standing to its right (for 'As label left') or to its left (for 'As label right'). If necessary you can also use this flag for field templates that look like text fields in the screen program, because their entry function has been reset and the three-dimensional display has been switched off.

Resp. To DblClk

You can only set this flag set for text fields and input/output fields in which the user double-clicks to trigger a function. You set the flag labels in a particular field to draw attention to its special function.

Table View Attributes

The attributes contained in table views differ from the screen program elements described above. This is why you maintain these attributes in a different dialog box (Figure 3.139). For this reason, the table views attributes are described separately.

Name

The Name attribute field contains the table view's name. You must ensure you have used the CONTROLS statement to declare the table view in the declaration part of the program.

Entry table / Selection table

Both these checkboxes determine whether you can edit the data displayed in the table view or simply display it. Users can use selection tables to select records. The program's structure then defines how these records are processed later on.

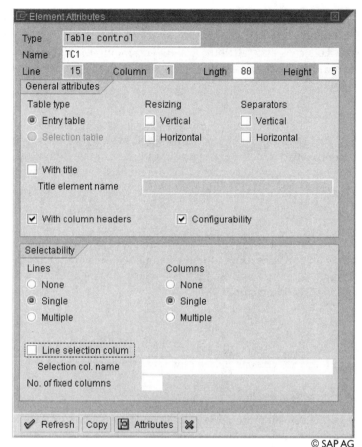

© SAP AG

Figure 3.139   Attributes dialog box for table views

Resizing Vertical, Horizontal

These two attributes control how the table view reacts when the SAPGUI window is resized. If these attributes are set, the distance between the table view and the lower or right-hand edge of the window remains constant for as long as possible. This means that the table view may become smaller if necessary. These attributes ensure that any fields displayed underneath or to the right of the table view remain visible.

If these attributes are not set, the size of the table view remains constant. If the SAPGUI window becomes smaller and therefore does not have enough room to display the screen program in full, the system automatically provides the window with a scroll bar.

Separators Vertical, Horizontal

You use these two attributes to display separators between the individual table rows or columns.

With title, Title element name

You can give the table view a title. This title is stored in a data field whose name you enter in the TITLE ELEMENT NAME attribute. When you maintain this attribute, the system prompts you to decide whether a key field (hard-coded text) or a field template (dynamic text) should be used.

With column headers

If this attribute is set, a column header is displayed above each column in the table view. The column header is also either a key field or a field template, just like the table title. You enter the corresponding field names in the dialog box where you maintain the table view fields.

Configurability

You can only set this attribute if the With column headers attribute is also active. If there are no restrictions on configurability, the user can save their own changes in the table view layout (column sequence and width). The next time the screen program is called, the table view is displayed in its modified form.

Selectability

You use the checkboxes that belong to this attribute to define whether rows or columns can be selected. If they can, you can define how many rows or columns can be selected.

Line selection column, Selection column name

If this attribute is set, a pushbutton appears in front of each table row. You use this pushbutton to select the row you require. If the attribute is activated, you must assign a field name. The rows you select are marked with an 'X' in the corresponding data field. This field applies only within the LOOP at the PAI event.

No. of fixed columns

In the table view, you can fix columns at the left-hand margin of the table. These columns remain in this position. The horizontal scroll bar only starts after this column. You enter the number of fixed columns in the NO. OF FIXED COLUMNS attribute.

Flow logic statements

The module pool's program module is called in a screen program's flow logic. The statements contained there define the screen program functions. The flow logic consists of several sections that are processed at certain events. These events are defined by four different event statements:

1. PROCESS BEFORE OUTPUT.

2. PROCESS AFTER INPUT.

3. PROCESS ON HELP REQUEST.

4. PROCESS ON VALUE REQUEST.

Not all of these four events can be found in every piece of flow logic. The last two are relatively rare because the system itself already provides powerful mechanisms for input help and general help. However, you will find the first two statements in every screen program. That is why they are automatically written into the flow logic when a new screen program is generated. Despite this, it is quite possible that no actions are performed at one of the named events, although the event statement is present.

The modules called in the various sections perform special actions, which only apply to each particular section. Some of these actions are discussed below. The flow logic contains some special statements that are similar to ABAP statements, but not identical to them. The only task of some of these statements is to call modules from the module pool. This is why the flow logic contains so few different statements. Just like ABAP statements, you use a range of parameters to modify the effects of the flow logic statements. Although some of the statements described below resemble ABAP statements, they have very few features in common apart from their names. In this section, the term 'statement' refers to the flow logic statements. These are sometimes also described as SCREEN PROGRAM STATEMENTS.

The FIELD statement

You use the FIELD statement in the PAI part of a screen program to trigger field-specific activities. The statements that are programmed in conjunction with the FIELD statement then refer only to the field entered after FIELD. The basic format of this statement is as follows:

FIELD *field*.

In this case, the statement merely addresses a field. You should only use this statement in a CHAIN-ENDCHAIN chain. If there are no additions to follow, you can also use colon notation to address several fields:

FIELD: *field_1, field_2, ... field_n*.

The statement becomes much more useful if you link the FIELD statement with the MODULE statement, as shown below:

FIELD *field* **MODULE** *module*.

This statement calls the module. If a message (error message) is generated in the module, you can only enter data in the field defined in the FIELD statement. You can define more additions (that belong to the MODULE statement and are described there) to make module processing dependent on particular conditions.

Using a second variant of the FIELD statement you can test a field directly against a table, without having to write a separate module for that purpose. This is:

FIELD *field* **SELECT** ....

You can also use the SELECT statement as an independent statement. This is why it is described separately. When you link the SELECT statement with the FIELD statement, only the field you specify will be ready for input if the SELECT statement triggers an error message.

You can only use the variant of the FIELD statement described below for fields whose type is CHAR or NUMC. This variant checks the field against a list of values that are coded directly in the source code:

FIELD *field* **VALUES** (*value_list*).

The value list that you enclose in round brackets consists of one or more individual values. You must enclose these values in single quotation marks and separate them from each other with commas. You use the NOT operator to identify a value that is not permitted. You can similarly use the BETWEEN AND or NOT BETWEEN AND operators to identify ranges that are permitted or not permitted.

You can use several of the additions described above in one FIELD statement. You must use the following syntax to enter the additions:

```
FIELD field : VALUES ... ,
              MODULE ... ,
              ... .
```

The MODULE statement

You use the following statement to call modules from the module pool:

MODULE *module*.

You can use this statement for all four events. It also has a few additions that can influence how it operates. The addition shown below has already been demonstrated in an example. It results in the module only being called if a function code of type E has been triggered:

... AT EXIT-COMMAND.

For this reason, you should only really use this addition in the PAI part of the flow logic. An exit function code typically closes a screen program. This is why you should only use one statement with this addition in each screen program. This statement should also be the first statement at the PAI event.

You can only use all the other additions if the FIELD statement if used to call the module in a field assignment. Table 3.38 lists the possible additions and their effects.

The CHAIN...ENDCHAIN statements

These two statements form a framework. They usually include a FIELD statement for several fields and one or more associated MODULE calls. The CHAIN statement links these statements to form a processing block or a processing chain. If an error message is triggered in the CHAIN, all fields in the chain that are addressed with FIELD will once again become ready for input. This is a useful function if for example a user has to enter several

Table 3.38   Additions for the MODULE screen program statement

Addition	Effect
ON INPUT	Processing only takes place if the corresponding field has a value that is not its initial value
ON CHAIN-INPUT	Processing only takes place if at least one field in the chain has a value that is not its initial value (only useful in CHAIN brackets)
ON REQUEST	Processing only takes place if an entry has been made in the corresponding field
ON CHAIN-REQUEST	Processing only takes place if an entry has been made in at least one field in the chain (only useful in CHAIN brackets)
ON *-INPUT	Processing only takes place if an asterisk, '*', has been entered in the corresponding field and the field has the asterisk entry attribute
AT CURSOR-SELECTION	Processing only takes place if a user has made a selection by double-clicking or by pressing (F2)

keywords, or other values that depend on each other, in one screen program. In this case, an error can no longer be clearly assigned to a particular field. A (theoretical) example of a CHAIN could look like this:

```
CHAIN.
   FIELD:   CREDCARD-TYPE,
            CREDCARD-NUMBER.
   MODULE   CHECK_CREDIT_CARD ON CHAIN-REQUEST.
ENDCHAIN.
```

The CHECK_CREDIT_CARD module is designed to check whether a payment made with the credit card details entered here is authorized. The permitted credit card number ranges depend on who issues the particular credit card. An error can occur if either the wrong credit card type or an incorrect number has been entered by mistake. For this reason, both fields must become ready for input if an error occurs. The only way you can do this is to use CHAIN. Despite the fact that you can enter several fields after the FIELD statement if a module is called directly in the FIELD statement, the system only makes the last field of the field list ready for input if an error happens.

The SELECT statement

The system provides a special form of the SELECT statement in the flow logic. You use this statement in the PBO part to read a record from a table and make this record available in the screen program. In the PAI part, the statement is used to check values from the screen program against a table. This screen program statement is now only rarely used in new developments. It can easily be replaced with a module in which easy-to-use variants of the SELECT statement are available.

The basic form of the flow logic SELECT statement looks like this:

```
SELECT * FROM table
  WHERE tablefield = inputfield ....
```

You can define several selection conditions in the WHERE clause. However the system only tests for data that matches the conditions. Therefore, the only operator permitted here is the equals sign. You can use any fields from the current program in the WHERE clause. There is no limit to the fields you can use in the current screen program. This means you can process the selection depending on the values entered in other screen programs. For example, you could request key fields in a screen program and then use these key fields to read a record in the PBO part of the next screen program. To do this, place the contents of the record that has been read in the table's header line. You do this with the following addition:

```
... INTO table.
```

The record can only be transferred into the header line of a Data Dictionary table. For this reason, the screen program fields must be linked directly with the table fields. Although the SELECT statement would still find the record, even if it didn't have the INTO addition, it would not be able to make the record available for further processing. This would be useful in the PAI part when check routines are used.

The result of the SELECT statement can affect how the program works later on. The only way you can influence the program flow within the flow logic is by sending messages. To do this, you use two further additions that you can make dependent on the results of the search process. The addition shown below outputs an error message if the data selection was successful:

```
WHENEVER [NOT] FOUND
  SEND [ERRORMESSAGE | WARNING] number WITH messageparameters.
```

You can also use the NOT FOUND statement instead of FOUND to trigger the error message if no record with the corresponding key is present. You can trigger a hard-coded error message (restarts screen program processing) with the ERRORMESAGE addition. You use the WARNING addition to generate a simple warning that does not trigger a restart of screen program processing. After you press (Enter) or click the corresponding icon to acknowledge the warning, the system continues processing the screen program.

You do not have to display an individual error message. The system generates a standard error message if the WHENEVER addition is not present and the data selection has been unsuccessful. However, you usually do not want this to happen in the PBO part. This is why the SELECT statements in the PBO part almost always issue a warning if they cannot find the record.

As already mentioned in the FIELD statement, you can use the SELECT statement as an addition for this statement. In this case, the field linked with FIELD once again becomes ready for input if the SELECT statement generates an error message. If you want several fields to accept input, you should use SELECT together with a FIELD statement for several fields in a CHAIN. Three typical examples of how you can use the SELECT statement are shown below.

Searching for a record in the PBO section:

```
PROCESS BEFORE OUTPUT.
...
SELECT * FROM KNA1
  WHERE CUSTNO = KNA1-CUSTNO
  WHENEVER NOT FOUND
    SEND WARNING 123 WITH KNA1-CUSTNO.
```

Checking an individual field in the PAI section with a standard message:

```
FIELD KNA1-CUSTNO SELECT * FROM KNA1
  WHERE CUSTNO = KNA1-CUSTNO.


SELECT in a CHAIN:


CHAIN.
  FIELD:  INVOICE-PAYTYPE
          INVOICE-CURRENCY.
  SELECT * FROM PERMTYPE
    WHERE PAYTYPE = INVOICE-PAYTYPE
      AND CURRENCY = INVOICE-CURRENCY
    WHENEVER NOT FOUND
      SEND ERRORMESSAGE 345.
ENDCHAIN.
```

The LOOP and ENDLOOP statements

We already mentioned loops and table views in the section that discussed the visual elements of screen programs. You can use these statements to process several records in one screen program. Because the individual blocks in a loop represent copies of a template block and therefore contain identical field names, you cannot address the fields in these blocks directly. For this reason, you must use a special statement to process the individual blocks in the loop sections of a screen program.

In the flow logic, the LOOP and ENDLOOP statements form a loop in which all the blocks in the screen program's loop section are run once. At this point in time, you can address the fields in the current blocks by their field names. The field contents must, of course, be processed in a module that is called in the LOOP. If a screen program contains several loop sections, you must therefore also use several LOOP statements. In the flow logic, the loop section and the statement are assigned in the same sequence as the areas were declared in the screen program.

You need a LOOP both at the PAI event so you can enter data in the screen program fields, and at the PBO event, to check data and reload it to the database table if required. A missing LOOP-ENDLOOP loop triggers an error message when the system generates a screen program with a step loop section. A simple piece of flow logic for a screen program with a loop section could look like this:

```
PROCESS BEFORE OUTPUT.
...
  LOOP.
    MODULE READ_LINE.
  ENDLOOP.

*
PROCESS AFTER INPUT.
...
  LOOP.
    MODULE PROCESS_LINE.
  ENDLOOP.
```

In this case, the LOOP for each step loop line that appears in the screen program is run just once. The loop contains the SY-STEPL field. The system automatically increases the value in this field by 1 each time it runs the loop. Once you leave the loop, the value in the SY-STEPL field is not defined. If you require the number of step loop lines for other evaluations, you must save the value in the SY-STEPL field in the LOOP to a global data field in the application. This example of the LOOP statement addresses all the step loop lines in the screen program one after another. If necessary, you can use your own module to acquire the data to be entered into these fields. If you cannot display the entire dataset on screen, you may have to program your own functions to scroll through the dataset.

You will require a LOOP in the PAI part of the flow logic, even if you do not intend to read modified values from the screen program. This is why you always need a LOOP-ENDLOOP pair. However, if you want to read data from the screen program and then continue to use the modified data in the program, you must once again use a special module where you use the SY-STEPL loop index to determine the correct table row.

A second variant of the LOOP statement automatically creates a link between an internal table and the step loop. The version of the statement for the PBO event looks like this:

LOOP AT *itab* **CURSOR** *cursor*.
ENDLOOP.

This statement always reads the entire internal table and transfers it to the step loop fields. You do not need a special module in the LOOP to do this if the screen program uses internal table fields. If the table has more rows than can be displayed on screen, the system automatically provides the screen program with a scroll bar. You use this scroll bar to scroll through the internal table within the loop section. The communication between the scroll bar and the LOOP statement occurs automatically. You do not have to generate or evaluate any function codes.

The cursor acts as a pointer to the records and should be derived from the SY-INDEX field. In the LOOP statements this field contains the index of the most recently edited record. Outside the LOOP statement this field contains the index of the first data record shown in the loop. You can set the value of this field dynamically in the program. When you do this, the system scrolls through the list as when you use the scroll bar.

You do not require the CURSOR addition at the PAI event. However, the system still automatically updates the value for the cursor in the LOOP. You require a specially designed module to reload the values from the step loop back into the internal table. In this module, you can use the value of the cursor field to identify the particular record.

```
LOOP AT itab.
  [ MODULE modify_itab. ]
ENDLOOP.
```

You can enter additional options for both variants of the LOOP statement. The following addition merits particular mention:

```
... INTO record.
```

This addition writes a record from an internal table to a separate work area. You need this addition to process tables that do not have their own header lines.

Besides the CURSOR addition, the LOOP statement for an internal table can also process the following additions:

```
FROM first.
```

and

```
TO last.
```

The first and last fields must also be derived from the SY-INDEX field. They must be provided dynamically in the program because you cannot use direct values. The entries limit the scrolling area to the records between the two range limits. If one of the values is missing, the first or last record is taken as the range limit.

You need another variant of the LOOP statement to process table views. A global data object with a unique name is present for each table view. Just like step loops, the LOOP statement runs through the individual rows of a table view in the flow logic. The basic form of this statement, which you must call both in the PBO part and in the PAI part, looks like this:

```
LOOP WITH CONTROL tableview.
  MODULE ... .
ENDLOOP.
```

Here tableview represents the element declared with this statement:
```
CONTROLS tableview TYPE TABLEVIEW USING SCREEN dynpronumber.
```
You call a module for each line in the table view. You then process the individual fields in the table line in this module (fill the fields in the PBO section, evaluate the fields in the PAI section). You can access the fields by their names just like in the loops. If you need the index of the current line in table view, use this field to display it:

```
tableview-current_line.
```

In this simple form, you must enter the values manually in the table view fields. You can make this task much easier by entering a cursor (just like for simple step loops). You can then use this statement to link an internal table with a table view. The statement corresponds to the variant already described for internal tables. The only difference is that you also specify the name of the table view. At the PBO event, you also need the following statement:

```
LOOP AT itab WITH CONTROL tableview CURSOR cursor.
ENDLOOP.
```

This statement ensures that the system runs through the internal table and places each line of the table in a line in the table view. You do not need to call a module if the field names in the table view correspond with those in the internal table. Once again, the cursor is a data field in the program that can be derived from the SY-INDEX field.

At the PAI event, you must read the records in the table view, check them and write them back to the internal table. The LOOP statement and module you need to call for this are the same as the statements already described for a loop using internal tables.

```
LOOP AT itab.
  MODULE ... .
ENDLOOP.
```

The CALL SUBSCREEN statement

The term subscreen has already been described. It is a special screen program type. If you want to insert a subscreen into another screen program when the application is running, this screen program must contain a subscreen area that is identified by a clear and unique name. When the application is running, you use the following statement to insert a subscreen screen program into another screen program:

```
CALL SUBSCREEN name INCLUDING program screen.
```

This statement must of course be located in the PBO part of the flow logic. The name parameter is the name of the subscreen area as it was entered in the Screen Painter. This parameter is placed directly, i.e. without quotation marks, in the statement. The two other parameters, program and screen, identify the subscreen screen program. These two values appear as a character string, i.e. enclosed in single quotation marks in the statement. Alternatively, you can use data fields that contain the values you require. It is much easier to call subscreens dynamically if you use fields.

In the PAI part of the higher level screen program, you now need another somewhat simpler statement:

```
CALL SUBSCREEN name.
```

When you use the CALL statement to call a subscreen screen program, the system executes a part of its flow logic. If the CALL statement is present in the PBO part, this means that the system only processes the PBO module. The CALL statement in the PAI part of the higher level screen program then processes the PAI modules of the embedded screen program.

Embedded screen programs cannot change the interface of the calling screen program or process the function code. For this reason, you cannot assign a data field to the field used to transfer the function code in the field list of the subscreen screen program. Therefore it is a good idea to run field checks or initialize the screen program fields in the flow logic of a subscreen screen program. If the subscreen area was not directly defined in a screen program but was supplied by a tabstrip, you use the name of the tabstrip in the CALL SUBSCREEN statement instead of the program name.

Context-sensitive and value help

The term 'value help' has already been mentioned when we described the attributes of a screen program field. You can use various methods to display the range of values available for each input field in the screen program. Two of the help options, implicit value help and search help, are based on Data Dictionary elements and are described in the Data Dictionary. These elements primarily use dependencies between the tables defined in the Data Dictionary. These dependencies are called *foreign keys*. Although their functionality is very wide ranging, it is still sometimes not extensive enough. If this is the case, you can write customized value help for each screen program field. To do this, call a corresponding module at the PROCESS ON VALUE REQUEST event. This call is like the one for a field check:

```
PROCESS ON VALUE REQUEST.
  FIELD value1 MODULE help_values.
```

This statement ensures that the system displays the value help icon in the screen program next to the value1 input field. If a user clicks this symbol, this has the same effect as if they press (F4). If a user presses that key, the application only processes the statements after the PROCESS ON VALUE REQUEST event. If the FIELD statement has been used to link the field where the screen cursor was located at this moment to a module, the system also processes this module. There are no restrictions on what this module can contain. Using an appropriate method, a value is determined and placed in the screen program field at the end of the module. As a simple test to illustrate this principle, you can implement the additions mentioned above in the flow logic and then add the following module in the SAPMY310 example application.

```
MODULE help_values.
  value1 = '12345679'.
ENDMODULE.
```

If this kind of value help exists for a field, the system ignores any other value helps that may be present for this field (foreign key or search help).

The context-sensitive help you call by pressing (F1) works in a similar way to the value help. In addition to the four keywords with different lengths and the short description, you can enter more detailed documentation for data elements in the Data Dictionary. If this documentation is present, you can press (F1) to display it. If not, at least the short description will appear.

You must use the help function that you program yourself if the documentation is not sufficiently descriptive or if you want the system to display an additional help text for fields that do not refer to the Data Dictionary. This help function differs from the value help because it has a different timing instruction (PROCESS ON HELP REQUEST) and requires different functionality from the module. However this option is not actually used very often.

After the system executes the individual input help or value help modules, it starts the processing of the screen program again at the PBO event. The PAI event is not processed.

LOOP for database tables

Besides using the LOOP statement to maintain internal tables, you can use another variant of it to work directly together with database tables. The syntax for this LOOP statement looks like this:

```
LOOP AT databasetable.
ENDLOOP.
```

This statement executes a series of actions in the background. Its function is therefore much more extensive than you would assume, despite its similarity to the basic form of the LOOP statement. This variant of the LOOP statement requires a specially structured screen program. In addition to the actual loop section whose input fields are linked with the header line of the database table, the screen program must also contain a second input area for the table's key fields. These input fields are also linked with the database table, but in them the asterisk variant of the name will be used. The tables do not have to be declared with the TABLES statement. The typical flow logic consists of just a few lines:

```
PROCESS BEFORE OUTPUT.
  LOOP AT databasetable.
  ENDLOOP.


*

PROCESS AFTER INPUT.
  LOOP AT databasetable.
    MODIFY databasetable.
  ENDLOOP.
```

The PBO LOOP statement enters the first of the table's data records into the loop blocks. In the PAI LOOP the contents of the loop block are loaded back into the table. No module is necessary for this. A screen program variant of the MODIFY statement is available in loops over Data Dictionary tables and only there.

The hidden functions of this LOOP statement apply to browsing in the table. When the user presses the (Enter) key, the system reads the contents of the input fields based on the * table. It searches for these values in the database table. If it finds a matching record, it uses it as the first record in the loop section. If it finds no matching record, it places the next largest record similar to the search pattern in the first loop block. If the fields for the search pattern are empty, the flow logic will scroll down one screen.

You will rarely use a LOOP through a database table in your own programs, as you can achieve much more user-friendly applications with other programming methods. Up to Release 2.2, this form of the LOOP statement was primarily used in automatically gener-ated maintenance programs. For certain tables, so-called *extended table maintenance* may be permitted in the Data Dictionary. If you select a special menu option (Generate table screen), the Data Dictionary generates a program and a screen program that fulfil the conditions mentioned above. You can use transaction SM31 or choose SYSTEM | SERVICES | TABLE MAINTENANCE | EXTENDED TABLE maintenance from the menu to call these programs. Transaction SM31 prompts the user to enter the name of a table and then calls the corresponding maintenance screen program. This simple option for data maintenance is used primarily when different system tables are being processed and during customizing. It is common practice to edit the modules for extended table maintenance manually after their creation. However when a new table screen program is created, these changes will be lost. In contrast to all the other naming conventions, the generated module pools start with the three letters MST, followed by the name of the table. Because the maximum length of a module pool's name is eight digits, a maintenance program of this kind can only be generated for tables whose names consist of a maximum of five digits.

From Release 3.0, other tools are available for table maintenance. These generate more complex maintenance programs in which the LOOP statement is no longer used in the way described above.

3.7.3 Complex elements in the screen program – an example

This section contains a small example which demonstrates the subscreens and other more complex elements. It has no practical meaning whatsoever, but combines some of the illustrated statements and elements into an application that is ready to be run. In the initial screen of this program, you can display one of two input templates in a subscreen. You can toggle between the input templates by clicking on a pushbutton in the application toolbar or by selecting menu options. The input templates supply search terms for a query in the TADIR table. Optionally, you can display the search result to be in a step loop or in a table view. These elements are included in normal screen programs. In a second phase of development, the application will then combine the two input templates into one tabstrip.

First of all, create a new module pool called SAPMY330. Then enter the following declaration in the top include:

```
PROGRAM sapmy330 MESSAGE-ID y1.
TABLES:
  tadir.

DATA:
  g_subscreen    LIKE sy-dynno VALUE '1000',
  itadir         LIKE tadir OCCURS 10 WITH HEADER LINE,
  fcode          LIKE sy-tcode,
  excode         LIKE sy-tcode OCCURS 10 WITH HEADER LINE,
  target_screen  LIKE sy-dynno VALUE '2000',
  start_screen   LIKE sy-dynno VALUE '100',
  i TYPE i.

CONTROLS tc1 TYPE TABLEVIEW USING SCREEN 3000.
CONTROLS ts1 TYPE TABSTRIP.
```

After defining the global data, you must generate the program. Although this step is not required to ensure its operation, it is necessary so the insertion tool can find the program's internal data fields during subsequent processing of the screen program. Now generate a status called STAT1 that supplies the functions shown in Table 3.39.

Table 3.39   Functions of the status STAT1

Function code	Function type	Menu	Function key
FT03	E	Jump I Back	F3 (activate predefined icon in icon bar)
FT15	E	Edit I Cancel	F12 (activate predefined icon in icon bar)
SUB1		Settings I User data	F5 (generate pushbutton)
SUB2		Settings I Object data	F6 (generate pushbutton)
STEP		Settings I Step loop	F7 (generate pushbutton)
TABV		Settings I Table view	F8 (generate pushbutton)

Subscreen containers for subscreens

Subscreens are screen programs that can be dynamically displayed in specially designated areas of a *subscreen container*. Both screen programs must fulfil special requirements. This means that there is much more work to do in the subscreen container than in the subscreen. First of all, we generate the subscreen container.

Working in the Layout Editor

Generate a new screen program, number 100 and then switch to the Layout Editor. A subscreen area will now have to be created in the subscreen container. To do so, you position the cursor on the top left-hand corner of the area to be inserted. Then you activate the SUBSCREEN pushbutton or choose EDIT I CREATE ELEMENT I SUBSCREEN from the menu. After you confirm the entry at the prompt, the Screen Painter fills the maximum space available in the screen program with a block consisting of dots and highlighted in colour. Place the cursor where you want the subscreen to end (bottom right-hand corner). To confirm the final size of the subscreen, click on the Mark end of the subscreen pushbutton, double-click or choose EDIT I MARK END OF SUBSCREEN from the menu.

In a dialog box (Figure 3.140) the Screen Painter prompts you to enter the name of the subscreen area. You can enter any name. For reasons of simplicity, the name 'SUB' has been used here.

No input fields are required in the subscreen container. However, you must link the screen program's statement field with the program's internal fcode field to ensure that the function code is transferred correctly.

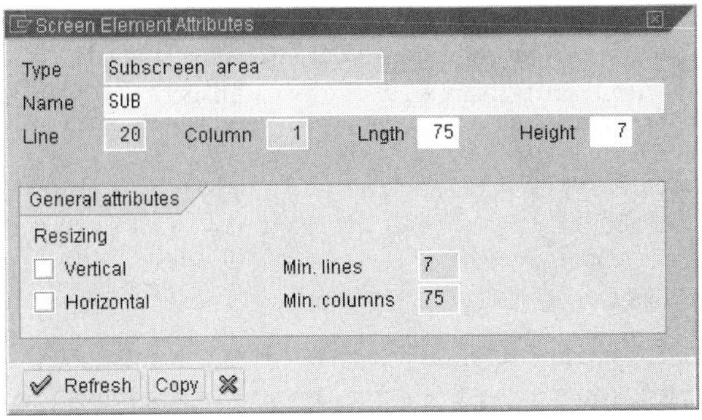

Figure 3.140 Dialog box in which you enter the name of the subscreen area © SAP AG

Flow logic

In the subscreen container's flow logic, you can call the subscreen(s) to be inserted in addition to the modules you know about already (for setting the status and evaluating the function codes). To do so, you use the CALL SUBSCREEN statement. This statement must be called for both the PAI and PBO events. It ensures that the correct subscreen is displayed in the subscreen container. Apart from that, it calls the subscreen's modules. The syntax of this statement is different for each of the two events. At PBO, the system has to pass on the name of the subscreen area in the subscreen container as well as the name of the module pool and the number of the screen program that is to be inserted:

CALL SUBSCREEN *subscreen_area* **INCLUDING** *program screen_number*.

Here you can enter the values for program and screen_number either as literals (character strings enclosed in simple quotation marks) or as field contents. In the latter case, the fields will not be enclosed in oval brackets, as is usual during dynamic data transfer in normal ABAP statements. Instead they will be inserted without any further additions.

In the PAI part of the flow logic, the INCLUDING addition is no longer necessary:

CALL SUBSCREEN *subscreen_area*.

No check modules referring to fields in subscreens should be called in the subscreen container. Because subscreens can be exchanged dynamically, checking for fields in an inactive subscreen might trigger redundant error messages. Apart from that, it would adversely affect the modularization that the subscreens are designed to achieve.

This is the flow logic of screen program 100:

```
PROCESS BEFORE OUTPUT.
  MODULE status_0100.
  CALL SUBSCREEN sub INCLUDING 'SAPMY330' g_subscreen .
*
PROCESS AFTER INPUT.
  MODULE exit_0100 AT EXIT-COMMAND.
  CALL SUBSCREEN sub.
  MODULE user_statement_0100.
```

In the `status_0100` module you merely set the status. Apart from that, the number of the start screen program is stored in a global variable. This field is later used for navigation because a second initial screen program will be created for the tabstrip. The module's source code is fairly simple:

```
MODULE status_0100 OUTPUT.
  SET PF-STATUS 'STAT1'.
  start_screen = sy-dynno.
ENDMODULE.                  "STATUS_0100 OUTPUT
```

The flow logic `CALL` statement (shown below) embeds a subscreen screen program into the sub subscreen area. You will see this subscreen screen program's number in the g_sub-screen field. You use the statement to change the subscreen dynamically. This is clearly illustrated by the user statement module's source code (function codes `SUB1` and `SUB2`):

```
MODULE USER_COMMAND_0100 INPUT.
CASE fcode.
    when 'SUB1'.
      g_subscreen = '1000'.
    when 'SUB2'.
      g_subscreen = '1010'.
    when 'STEP'.
      target_screen = '2000'.
    when 'TABV'.
      target_screen = '3000'.
    WHEN 'SEL1'.
      SELECT * FROM tadir
        INTO TABLE itadir
        WHERE devclass = tadir-devclass
          AND author = tadir-author.
      IF sy-dbcnt > 0.
        leave to screen target_screen.
      ENDIF.
    WHEN 'SEL2'.
      translate TADIR-OBJ_NAME using '*%'.
      SELECT * FROM tadir
        INTO TABLE itadir
        WHERE pgmid = tadir-pgmid
          AND object = tadir-object
          and obj_name like tadir-obj_name.
      IF sy-dbcnt > 0.
        leave to screen target_screen.
      ENDIF.
  ENDCASE.
ENDMODULE.                  "USER_COMMAND_0100 INPUT
```

The full functionality only becomes apparent after you have familiarized yourself with the function and the structure of the two subscreen screen programs. In screen program 1000, there are two input fields for the development class (`tadir-devclass`) and the program author (`tadir-author`) as well as a pushbutton that triggers function code `SEL1`. If the user clicks this pushbutton, the contents of these two fields are used to select entries from the `TADIR` table. The entries the system reads are stored in an `itadir` internal table. Screen program 1010 that contains the three fields `tadir-pgmid`, `tadir-object` and `tadir-obj_name` as well as a function key for function code `SEL2`, works in a similar fashion.

After the system selects the records you require, it displays another screen that shows the records it has found. The number of the screen program that calls this display is set dynamically because you should be able to display it both in a step loop and in a table view. To select this number, enter the `STEP` and `TABV` function codes or click the corresponding pushbutton in the application toolbar in the initial screen.

In the initial screen program, you only require a very simple module to evaluate the two exit function keys:

```
MODULE exit_0100 INPUT.
   LEAVE TO SCREEN 0.
ENDMODULE.                    "EXIT_0100 INPUT
```

Creating subscreen screen programs

You can create a subscreen screen program in the same way as any other screen program. However, you should be aware of the following points:

- You must not make an entry in the statement field in the subscreen screen program's field list.

- The subscreen screen program cannot set a status.

- The area occupied in the subscreen screen program must be adjusted to fit the space available in the subscreen container.

- You must set the subscreen screen program attribute.

You first create subscreen 1000. This subscreen must contain two input fields, so that you can enter search words, as well as a pushbutton. To do this, create screen program 1000 in the module pool that you have already generated. Set the Subscreen attribute in Figure 3.141.

In the fullscreen editor, you enter the two input fields (`tadir-author` and `tadir-devclass`) for the program author and development class. Figure 3.142 shows how the screen program appears when it is being processed.

To generate the pushbutton, enter the text for the key in the location you require in the screen program (*see* Figure 3.143).

Now position the cursor on the text and click on the Graphical element pushbutton. The Layout Editor highlights the selected text in colour and provides other editing options (Figure 3.144).

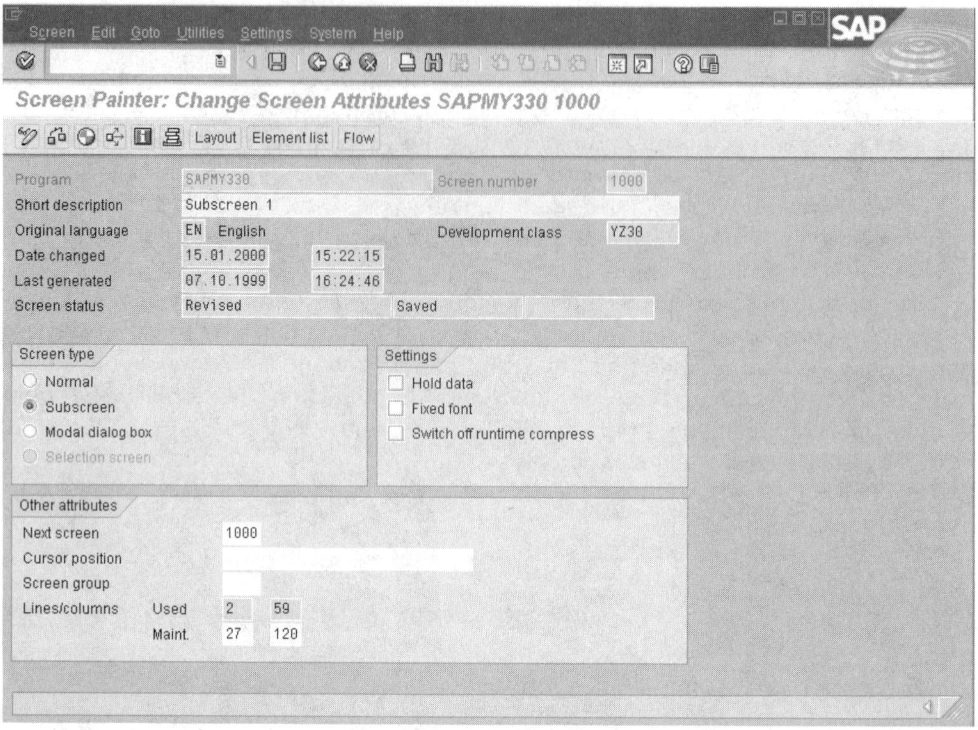

Figure 3.141   Attributes of a subscreen screen program

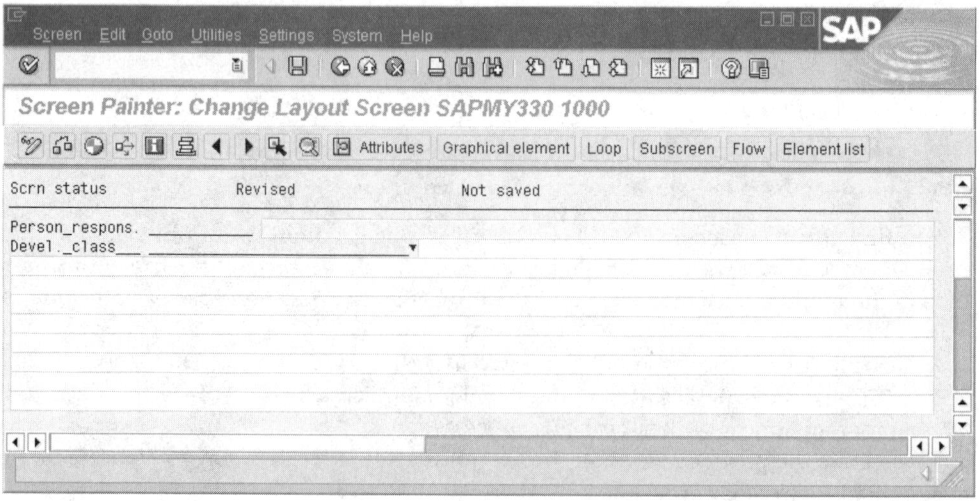

Figure 3.142   Subscreen screen program during processing

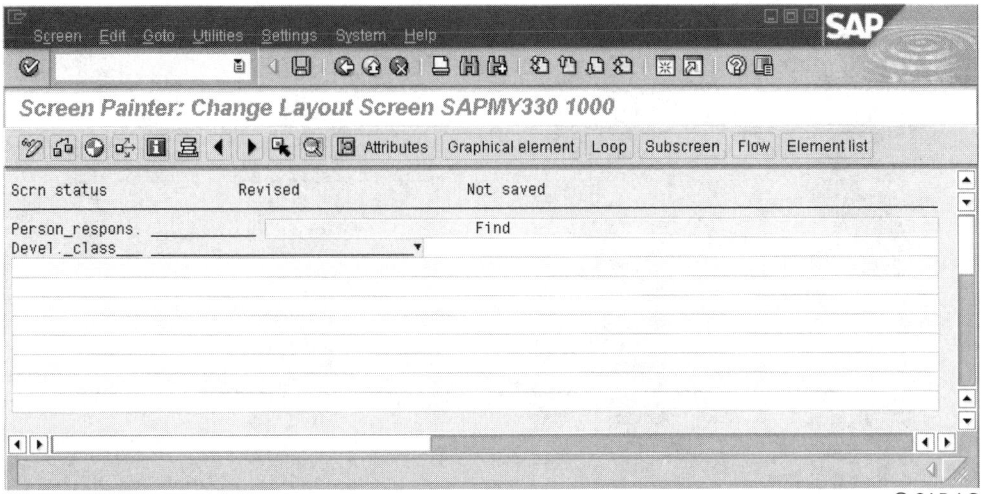

Figure 3.143   Generating a pushbutton

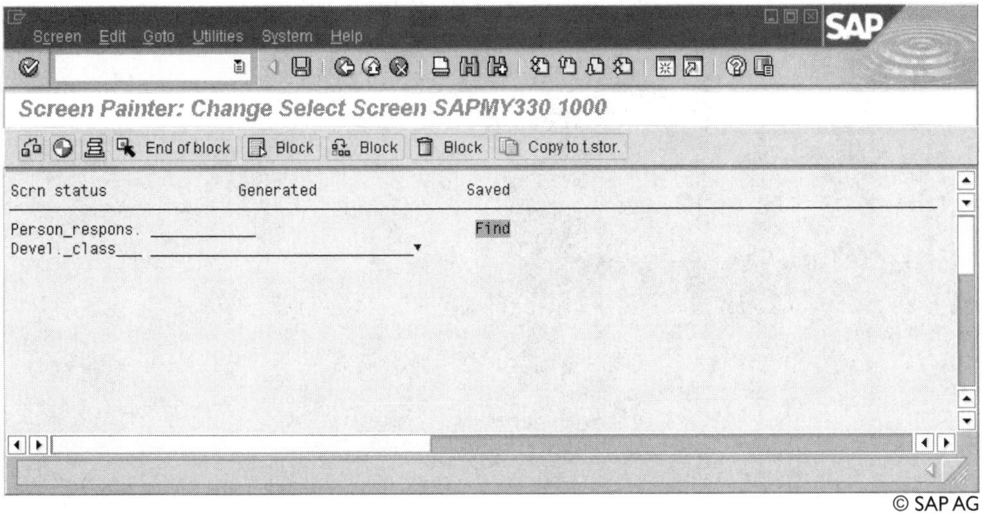

Figure 3.144   Processing a graphic element

The cursor is still positioned on the text field. You can now click on the Pushbuttons button to convert this highlighted field into a pushbutton. After it has been converted, a message appears in the status bar to tell you that the conversion was successful. Now press (F3) or select the corresponding menu option to return to the main screen of Layout Editor. In this screen, the pushbutton you have just generated is now highlighted in colour (Figure 3.145).

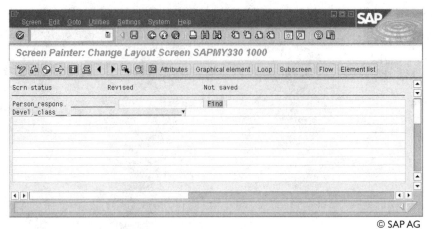

© SAP AG

Figure 3.145   Screen program with pushbutton

Finally, you still have to assign a function code to this pushbutton. To do this, position the cursor on the button and click on the ATTRIBUTES button. A dialog box is displayed (Figure 3.146) in which you enter a name for the pushbutton in the NAME field. You must also enter function code SEL1 in the FCTCODE field in this dialog box.

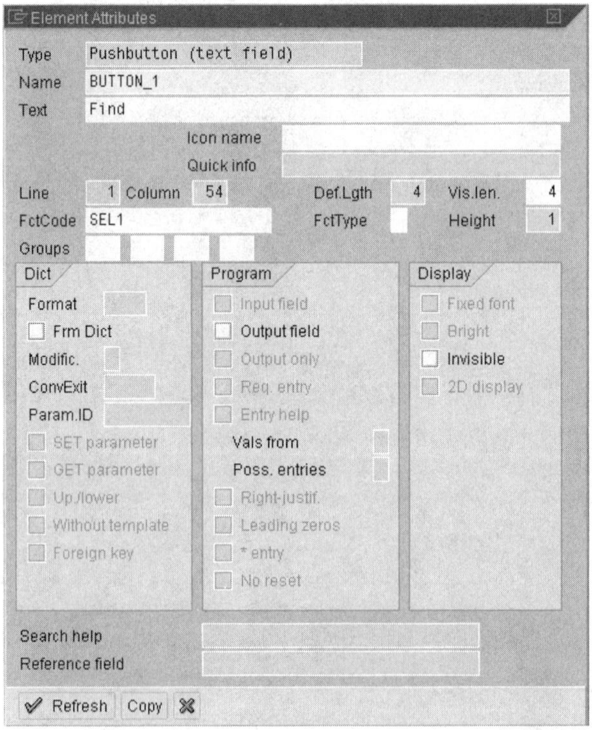

© SAP AG

Figure 3.146   Assigning a function code to the pushbutton

You can create another subscreen screen program, number 1010, in the same way. In this screen program, you enter the `tadir-pgmid, tadir-object` and `tadir-obj_name` fields as well as a pushbutton for function code `SEL2`.

Flow logic of the subscreen screen program

Both screen programs have their own flow logic. However, this flow logic is pretty basic because the user statement module is always missing. As no status is set either, the PAI part is totally empty. The system only initializes the input fields in the PBO section of the flow logic. The flow logic of screen program 1000 is shown here to represent both flow logics:

```
PROCESS BEFORE OUTPUT.
  MODULE init_1000.
*
PROCESS AFTER INPUT.
```

The source code of the initialization module is very simple:

```
MODULE init_1000 OUTPUT.
  tadir-devclass = '$TMP'.
  tadir-author = sy-uname.
ENDMODULE.                 "INIT_1000 OUTPUT
```

The initialization in screen program 1010 is equally simple:

```
MODULE init_1010 OUTPUT.
  tadir-pgmid = 'R3TR'.
  CLEAR tadir-object.
  CLEAR tadir-obj_name.
ENDMODULE.                 "INIT_1010 OUTPUT
```

After you have programmed the flow logic and the two modules, you can now generate the two screen programs.

Step loops

Step loops consist of a repeated series of tables in a block. The block can be made up of one or more fields and can extend over several lines. You use the `LOOP` statement in the flow logic to process the contents of a step loop. In this example, the step loop should contain the `pgmid, object, obj_name, devclass` and `author` fields from the `itadir` internal table.

Working in Layout Editor

You will need another screen program, numbered 2000, to demonstrate the step loop. This is a completely normal screen program, not a subscreen. In the Layout Editor, you first create the template block for a table row. To do this, copy the fields of the `itadir` internal table that are listed above into the screen program. Some of these fields are very long. That is why you first have to set a sensible output length for the fields, especially for `itadir-obj_name` and `itadir-devclass`. You can modify the output length in the Attributes dialog box. You must select the Scrollbl flag so that you can enter a suitable value in its Vis.len field. Then you line up all the fields in the third line of the screen program. The top line is reserved for the column headings.

Before you can actually generate the step loop, you should insert the title. To do this, use the insertion tool to copy the appropriate key fields from the `TADIR` table. Make sure you do not copy any of the field templates. Then move the key fields to their correct position above the field templates. If necessary, you might have to align the position of the field templates with the position of the descriptor in the title or use the Attributes dialog box to change the text of individual title elements. Now position the cursor on the first field in the line that contains the field templates. Figure 3.147 shows what the Layout Editor looks like at this point in time.

Now click the LOOP pushbutton. This switches the Layout Editor to a different editing mode. Double-click on the last field of the line at the end of the loop block to select this field. The Layout Editor once again switches mode (see Figure 3.148).

In the Layout Editor, you will now see a table that has two rows. The interface also provides other editing tools that are specially designed for step loops. After you have generated a step loop, its size, i.e. the number of lines in the table, is initially predefined. This type of step loop is called a fixed loop. To change the number of lines in the table, position the cursor in the required location and click on the END LINE OF LOOP pushbutton or choose EDIT | MARK FINAL LINE OF LOOP from the menu. However, you can also position the cursor at any location in the loop area and click on the VARIABLE LOOP pushbutton or choose EDIT | CONVERT | VARIABLE LOOP from the menu to convert the loop into a variable loop. The second method is used in this example. The two lines in the screen program will provide enough space because the system automatically adjusts the number of lines in the loop to fit the area available.

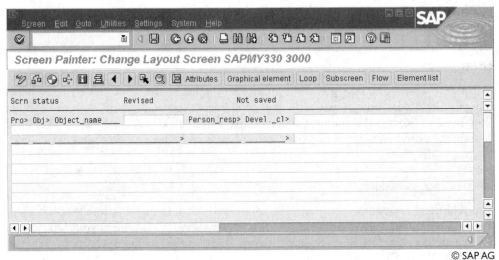

Figure 3.147   Layout Editor with table header and template line

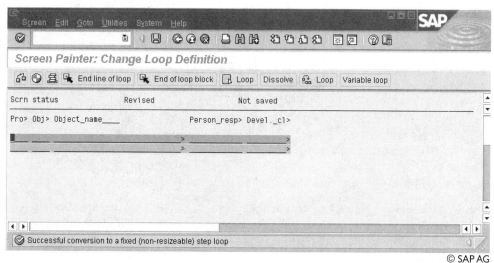

Figure 3.148   Step loop with two blocks

Flow logic

We shall not discuss any scroll functions that you might program yourself because they are so seldom used in practice. Here, the `itadir` internal table is to be linked completely with the step loop. To allow this, we will extend the flow logic of screen program 2000 as shown below:

```
PROCESS BEFORE OUTPUT.
  LOOP AT itadir CURSOR i.
  ENDLOOP.
*
PROCESS AFTER INPUT.
  MODULE exit_2000 AT EXIT-COMMAND.
  LOOP AT itadir.
    MODULE modify_itab.
  ENDLOOP.
```

The system automatically transfers the rows in the internal table into the step loop without using any other statements. However, you will require a few additional statements if you want to transfer modified values from the screen program back into the internal table. To demonstrate this, a module call that carries out this task is inserted into the LOOP block in the PAI section. Once again, the actual module is fairly simple:

```
MODULE modify_itab INPUT.
  MODIFY itadir INDEX i.
ENDMODULE.  *                    "MODIFY_ITAB INPUT
```

You must structure the exit module correctly to ensure that you can exit the application or return to the initial screen in the proper way. Obviously, you must also remember to link the statement field in the field list with the `fcode` field in the program.

```
MODULE exit_2000 INPUT.
  CASE fcode.
    WHEN 'FT03'.
      LEAVE TO SCREEN start_screen.
    WHEN 'FT15'.
      LEAVE TO SCREEN 0.
  ENDCASE.
ENDMODULE.                                   "EXIT_2000 INPUT
```

After you have generated and activated all the parts of the application and generated a dialog transaction (330), you are ready to test the application. Figure 3.149 shows the completed application.

Click on the appropriate pushbutton to select one of the two input templates. There, enter the selection criteria you want and click on the Search button in the screen program. If the system finds records that match your selection criteria, the application lists them in screen program 2000. There you use the scroll bar to browse through the table. You can also change data there. Although these changes do not affect the contents of the database table, they are saved in the internal table. However, you cannot yet switch to the table view because you have not yet programmed this screen program. If you try to do this, it will cause a runtime error. Press (F3) to return to the initial screen. Press (F12) to exit the application.

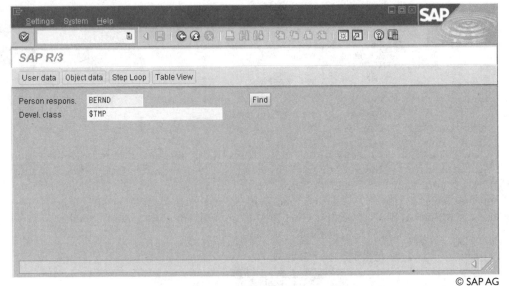

© SAP AG

Figure 3.149   Initial screen of the application

Table views

From Release 3 of the R/3 System onwards, there is another element that can display data in table format in addition to the step loop. This element is the table view. This looks like the tables available in many Windows applications. However, there are changes that do not only apply to the appearance but also to the functions and the programming model.

Working in Layout Editor

First create a new screen program, numbered 3000. Once again, this is a normal screen program and not a subscreen. Position the cursor on the top left-hand corner of the work area and choose EDIT | CREATE ELEMENT | TABLE CONTROL from the menu. The Layout Editor will now reserve all the free space in the screen program for the new control (see Figure 3.150). You now double-click in the selected area to define the size of the control. You can always change the dimensions of the control later on. For this reason, you should select dimensions that are as large as possible at this point.

After you double-click to define the size, the system automatically displays a dialog box in which you set the control's attributes (Figure 3.151).

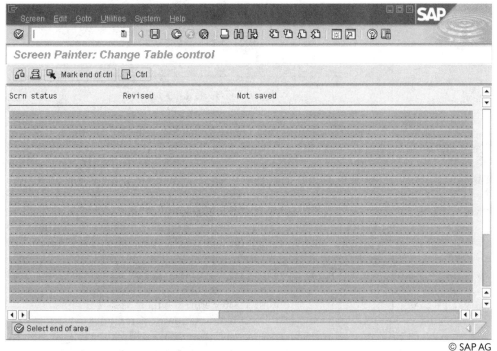

© SAP AG

Figure 3.150   Reserved area for a table view

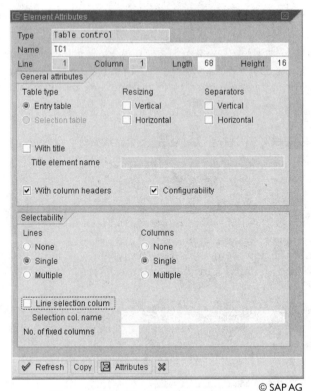

© SAP AG

Figure 3.151   Attributes for the table view

You must make two changes in this dialog box. Enter the value TC1 in the NAME field. The corresponding control has already been declared in the top include at the start of the example. The second change concerns the line selection column. The SELECTABILITY frame contains a check box labelled LINE SELECTION COLUMN. This field is activated by default. For this example, however, it must be deactivated. Click on the COPY button to confirm the attributes. An empty control now appears in the Layout Editor (Figure 3.152).

You now assign the fields that you want to display to the table view. To do this, position the cursor in the selected area and click on the GRAPHICAL ELEMENT pushbutton. This switches to a different Layout Editor mode in which you can edit options for the table view. Alternatively, you can access this mode by double-clicking in the selected area.

From the available functions, click on the CTRLELEMENTS pushbutton. This function activates a dialog box (Figure 3.153) in which you define the table view columns.

In this dialog box, you enter the fields you want manually. Alternatively, you can also use the insertion tool, which you are already familiar with, by clicking on the DICT/PROG.FIELDS pushbutton. As already described for step loops, you now select the five fields in the itadir internal table. After you have made the selection in the insertion tool, position the cursor in the first row of the TABLE COLUMN column in the table view dialog box. Now click on the Ins. Table column pushbutton. This key is only present as an icon. As an alternative to the pushbutton, you can also use the key combination (Ctrl)(Shift)(F1).

© SAP AG

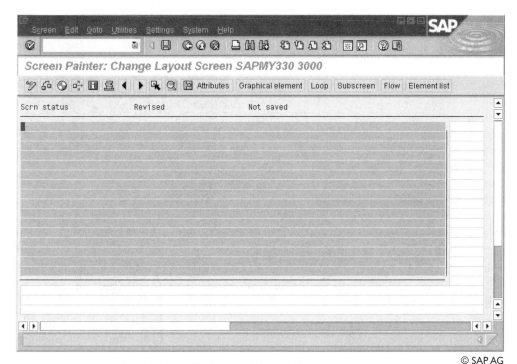

Figure 3.152 The Layout Editor with an empty table view

© SAP AG

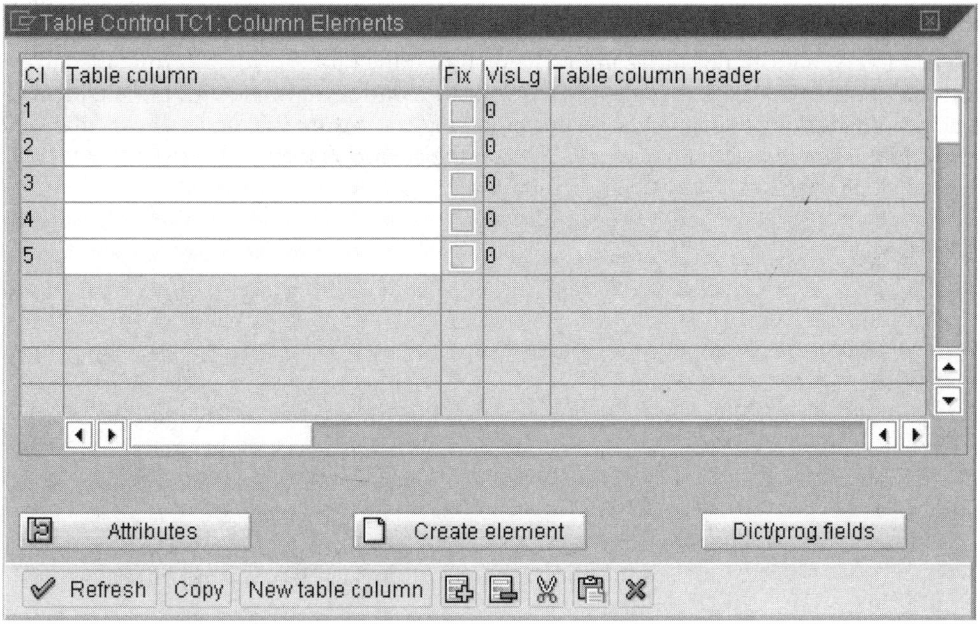

Figure 3.153 Defining the table view columns

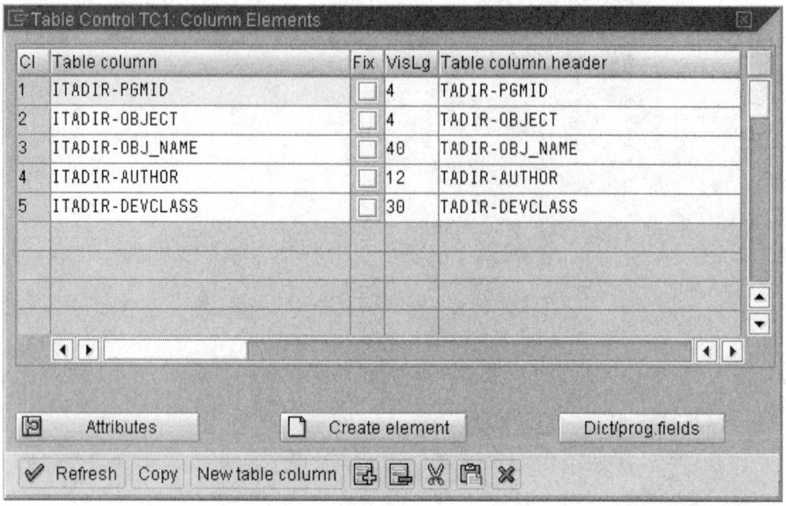

© SAP AG

Figure 3.154   Finished dialog box with entries for a table view structure

You also use the insertion tool to copy the descriptors from the TADIR table into the Table column header column. You must do this separately for each individual field. You can also enter the field name manually. However, if you do so, the system prompts you to enter the field's characteristics in several successive dialog boxes.

After you have copied the fields, you should once again change the output length for the `itadir-obj_name` and `itadir-devclass` tables. To do this, overwrite the values in the VisLg column. Figure 3.154 shows you the finished dialog box with its entries.

After you confirm the entries in the dialog box at the prompt, you return to the Layout Editor. The area that was previously empty for the controls now contains placeholders for the headings and the table fields. At this point you can reduce the dimensions of the table view to the size you actually require. Position the cursor on the bottom right-hand corner and click on the MARK END OF CTRL pushbutton.

Flow logic

The flow logic is similar to that in the step loop example. It basically contains the same statements:

```
PROCESS BEFORE OUTPUT.
  LOOP AT itadir CURSOR i WITH CONTROL tc1.
  ENDLOOP.
*
PROCESS AFTER INPUT.
  MODULE exit_3000 AT EXIT-COMMAND.
  LOOP AT itadir.
    MODULE modify_itab_tc.
  ENDLOOP.
```

You now add the WITH CONTROL tc1 addition to the LOOP statement. This is the only way to link the internal table with the table view. The exit module is the same as that used in the step loop screen program, and is therefore not listed again here. However, the statement used to write the modified values back into the internal table is not the same as that used in the step loop screen program. Although you must use the CURSOR addition in the LOOP statement just like in the table view screen program, you will no longer see the number of the current record in the cursor field at the PAI event. You must use a special field in the table view to do this. This is why you require a new module:

```
MODULE modify_itab_tc INPUT.
  MODIFY itadir INDEX tc1-current_line.
ENDMODULE.                              "MODIFY_ITAB_TC INPUT
```

Once you have generated the screen program, you can now test the application once again. You should also be able to get a correct result by selecting the table view in the initial screen as shown in Figure 3.155.

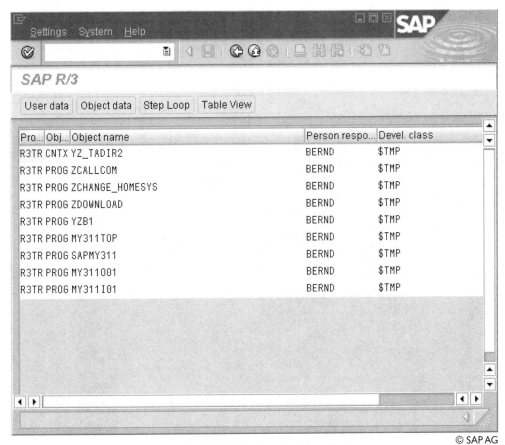

© SAP AG

Figure 3.155   Table view in the application

Tabstrips

Tabstrips combine several subscreens together and represent them as index cards in a screen. In this example, it makes sense to link the two input templates into one tabstrip. You create the tabstrip in a new screen program that functions as an alternative initial screen program.

Working in Layout Editor

Create a normal screen program, numbered 200. Once again position the cursor in the top left-hand corner and choose EDIT | CREATE ELEMENT | TABSTRIP from the menu. The Layout Editor once again reserves the entire free space for the control you want to create. As in the table view, you now select the bottom right-hand corner by double-clicking. After this double-click, the system then automatically prompts you to enter some important attributes of the tabstrip in a dialog box (Figure 3.156).

One of these attributes is the name. In this case you use TS1 as the name because this type of element has already been declared. You do not need to enter any data in the other fields. Click on the COPY pushbutton to close the dialog box. In the Layout Editor, a tab-strip appears that contains two tabs, but is otherwise empty (Figure 3.157).

Now you enter elements in the tabstrip. You enter these elements in a similar way as in the table view. Double-click in the selected area or click the GRAPHICAL ELEMENT pushbutton to switch to the editing mode for the control. There, click on the CTRL ELEMENTS pushbutton to activate a dialog box (Figure 3.158) in which you define the appearance of the tabstrip.

Two tabs are already preset in this dialog box. Your task is to assign a function code, a text and the name of a subscreen area to these tabs. You can enter the function code and the subscreen area name directly in the displayed dialog box and maintain the text in the Attributes dialog box. To call this dialog box, position the cursor on the element you want to maintain and click on the ATTRIBUTES pushbutton in the tabstrip dialog box. You could for example use the texts 'user' and 'object'.

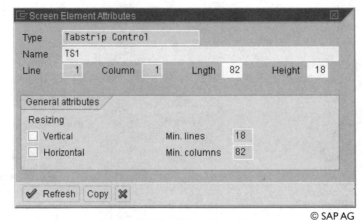

Figure 3.156   Tabstrip attributes

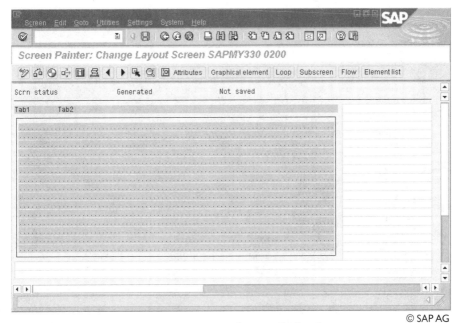

© SAP AG

Figure 3.157   Newly created tabstrip

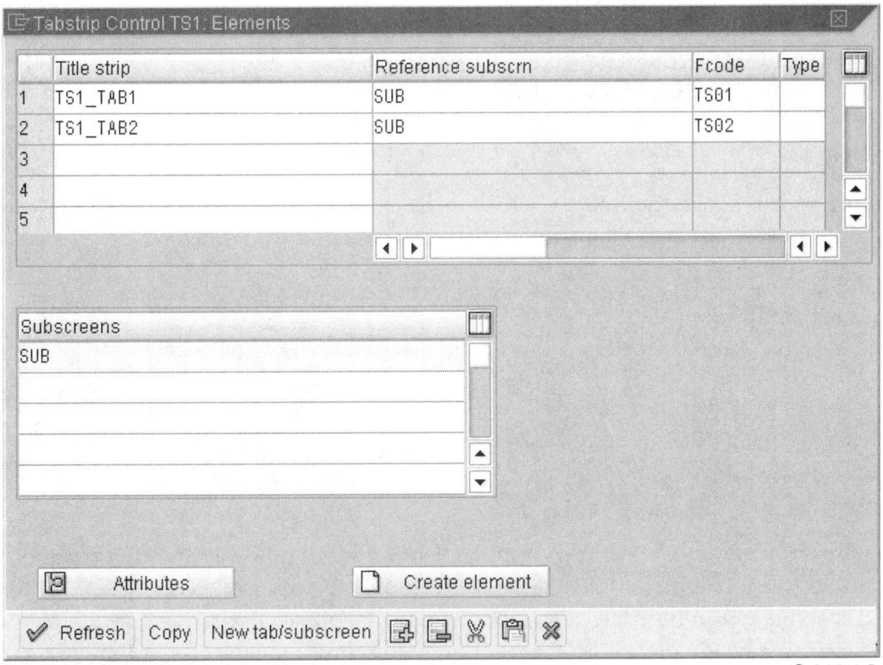

© SAP AG

Figure 3.158   Defining tabstrip elements

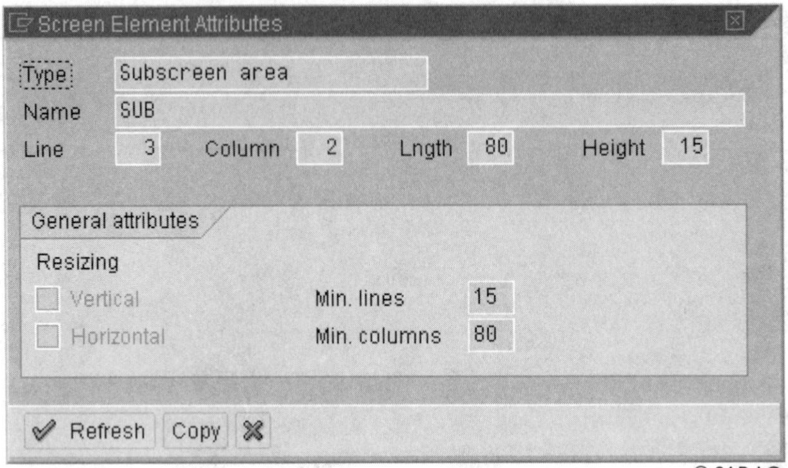

Figure 3.159   Defining the size of the subscreen area

In the SUBSCREENS subarea, enter the name of the subscreen area that is available in the tabstrip area so you can display subscreen screen programs. You can only use subscreens that have been defined in this table as reference subscreens for the individual tabs. When you copy the data by clicking on the COPY pushbutton, the Layout Editor prompts you to define the size of the subscreen area (Figure 3.159). You should select values that make full use of all the free space in the tabstrip. You do not have to explicitly create this subscreen to do this. All you need to do is enter the listing in the dialog box and define the size. This completes your work in the Layout Editor.

Flow logic

The flow logic is somewhat more complex because you must enter data both in the actual flow logic and in the user statement module. First of all, the flow logic:

```
PROCESS BEFORE OUTPUT.
  MODULE status_0200.
  CALL SUBSCREEN sub INCLUDING 'SAPMY330' g_subscreen.
*
PROCESS AFTER INPUT.
  MODULE exit_200 AT EXIT-COMMAND.
  CALL SUBSCREEN sub.
  MODULE user_statement_0200.
```

A tabstrip contains a subscreen area that, from a technical programming point of view, is handled like a completely normal subscreen. For this reason, you need a CALL SUB-SCREEN statement in both the PBO section and the PAI section. This CALL SUBSCREEN statement must be identical with that used in screen program 100. The differences become visible in the user statement module:

```
CASE fcode.
    WHEN 'TS01'.
        g_subscreen = '1000'.
        ts1-activetab = 'TS01'.
    WHEN 'TS02'.
        g_subscreen = '1010'.
        ts1-activetab = 'TS02'.
    WHEN 'STEP'.
        target_screen = '2000'.
    WHEN 'TABV'.
        target_screen = '3000'.
    WHEN 'SEL1'.
        SELECT * FROM tadir
            INTO TABLE itadir
            WHERE devclass = tadir-devclass
                AND author = tadir-author.
        IF sy-dbcnt > 0.
            LEAVE TO SCREEN target_screen.
        ENDIF.
    WHEN 'SEL2'.
        TRANSLATE tadir-obj_name USING '*%'.
        SELECT * FROM tadir
            INTO TABLE itadir
            WHERE pgmid = tadir-pgmid
                AND object = tadir-object
                AND obj_name LIKE tadir-obj_name.
        IF sy-dbcnt > 0.
            LEAVE TO SCREEN target_screen.
        ENDIF.
    ENDCASE.
ENDMODULE.                          "USER_COMMAND_0200 INPUT
```

You will find the relevant sections, i.e. where function codes TS01 and TS02 are evaluated, at the start of the module. You can now no longer use the two pushbuttons in the application toolbar to toggle between the two input templates. Instead you use the tabs in the tabstrip. The system evaluates the function codes that are initiated by these tabs in the same way as those initiated by the pushbuttons. However, you must also define which of the tabs is to be highlighted by assigning it to the activetab field in the tabstrip control.

Because you no longer require the application toolbar's two pushbuttons, you can deactivate them in the status_0200 module:

```
MODULE status_0200 OUTPUT.
    REFRESH excode.
    excode = 'SUB1'. APPEND excode.
    excode = 'SUB2'. APPEND excode.
    SET PF-STATUS 'STAT1' EXCLUDING excode.
    start_screen = sy-dynnr.
ENDMODULE.                          "STATUS_0200 OUTPUT
```

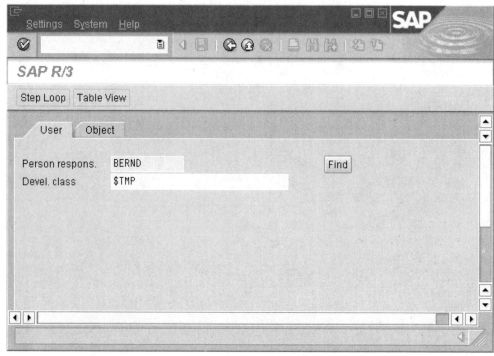

Figure 3.160   Initial screen with tabstrip

The exit module is the same as that used in screen program 100.

After you have programmed the flow logic and activated the new screen program, you must create a second transaction. Although this second transaction also starts program SAPMYZ330, it uses the newly created screen program 200 as its initial screen program. Figure 3.160 shows the new initial screen.

Exercise

1. The two pushbuttons used to define the display format of the internal table in the initial screen have no function in screen programs 2000 and 3000. Change these two screen programs so that you can switch directly to the other display format.

3.7.4 Special programming techniques in dialog applications

A module pool provides the program modules for one or more screen programs. Global data is also declared in the module pool. Theoretically, you could fit the entire source code into only one file. However, it is a lot easier to work with shorter files in the editor. It is therefore common practice, but by no means absolutely necessary, to split module pools up into several include files. This involves six important sections that also consist of six include files or groups of include files. There are recommended names for the different file groups:

- data declaration;

- PBO modules for processing before the screen program display;

- PAI modules for processing after the screen program display;

- include files for subroutines (forms);

- modules for help (F1);

- modules for permitted entries (F4).

The actual module pool only contains the various INCLUDE statements, it does not usually contain any other source code. For reasons of simplicity, the program header required for each program is moved into the top include. That is why it always has to be placed first in the source code. This special role is also reflected in the include name, which ends with TOP.

A module pool name always starts with SAPM. After that, the next letter should identify the application group that the module pool is designed for, i.e. F for finance. Just like reports, the two letters Y and Z in this position are reserved for customers' own developments. All other letters are reserved for use by SAP. The other characters are used to identify the actual module pool.

Similar conventions apply to the names of the include files. They start with the name of the module pool, abbreviated to the first three characters, i.e. MY310. This is followed by a letter that indicates the type of elements contained in the include. The letter O represents files that contain PBO modules. The letter I represents includes that contain PAI modules. Files with subroutines, i.e. form routines, are given the letter F. The last two characters are used to identify the individual files in a group.

This section now describes important actions that you should carry out in dialog applications and the ABAP statements you require for them. Even though these statements are described in the context of dialog applications, this does not mean that they can only be used there. You can also use some of these statements in reports.

Modifying screen program fields dynamically

In the Screen Painter you predefine attributes for the screen program fields. You can change some of these attributes dynamically when the application is running. For example, you can withdraw input authorization from some fields and transform them into pure display fields. You could also delete the fields from the screen program. In this way, you can modify a screen program with relatively little programming effort to match specific user authorizations or to meet the special requirements of the record you want to process.

The SCREEN table

You carry out dynamic modifications at the PBO event. You use a special variant of the ABAP LOOP statement (not the flow logic statement that has the same name) to process all screen program fields. When a screen program is executed, the most important data for each field template but not for key fields is placed in the SCREEN internal table. The structure of this table is shown in Table 3.40.

Table 3.40   Table for screen program fields

Field name	Type	Length	Contents / Effect	Should I edit this field?
SCREEN-NAME	C	30	Field name	
SCREEN-GROUP1	C	3	Evaluation of modification group 1	
SCREEN-GROUP2	C	3	Evaluation of modification group 2	
SCREEN-GROUP3	C	3	Evaluation of modification group 3	
SCREEN-GROUP4	C	3	Evaluation of modification group 4	
SCREEN-REQUIRED	C	1	Mandatory entry	X
SCREEN-INPUT	C	1	Ready for input	X
SCREEN-OUTPUT	C	1	Field is displayed	X
SCREEN-INTENSIFIED	C	1	Highlighted	X
SCREEN-INVISIBLE	C	1	Password input	X
SCREEN-LENGTH	X	1	Length (hexadecimal)	X
SCREEN-ACTIVE	C	1	1 = field appears in the screen program 0 = field does not appear in the screen program; overwrites all other attributes	X
SCREEN-DISPLAY_3D	C	1	3D display	X
SCREEN-VALUE_HELP	C	1	Value help exists	
SCREEN-REQUEST	C	1	Input takes place	

In the LOOP, you can use the MODIFY statement to change some attributes and save them to the SCREEN table. You should not do this for all the attributes because some of them only tell you about a field's special characteristics. A first example is shown below:

```
LOOP AT SCREEN.
  SCREEN-INPUT = '0'.
  MODIFY SCREEN.
ENDLOOP.
```

You can use these statements to remove input authorization from all the screen program's fields. The character '0' (zero) denotes a deactivated attribute. Enter '1' to activate an attribute.

If you only want to modify selected screen program fields, you can request them by field name in the LOOP. This field name is the same as the field that appears in the fullscreen editor or the screen program's field list:

```
LOOP AT SCREEN.
  IF SCREEN-NAME = 'KNA1-KUNNR'.
    SCREEN-INVISIBLE = '1'.
    MODIFY SCREEN.
  ENDIF.
ENDLOOP.
```

You can use modification groups if you need to modify a larger number of screen program fields. In the fullscreen editor, you can maintain four attributes for each screen program field. These attributes are labelled as modification groups 1 to 4. You can enter any three-digit character string in each of these four fields. You can enter any values here because there are no restrictions or checks. These modification groups are simply four additional descriptors for the field. Later on, you use the four fields SCREEN-GROUP1 to SCREEN-GROUP4 to determine the contents of these attributes. For example, let us assume that a screen program contains some fields that should always be hidden together. In the fullscreen editor, you set modification group 1 to the value '001' for these fields. You then hide them with the following statements:

```
LOOP AT SCREEN.
  IF SCREEN-GROUP1 = '001'.
    SCREEN-ACTIVE = '0'.
    MODIFY SCREEN.
  ENDIF.
ENDLOOP.
```

You can of course choose any modification group and value for this attribute. The transaction code is often used as the criterion for this type of modification. In addition to a transaction that you use to maintain data, there is often one that is used exclusively to display data. For example, all the tools you have used so far have this mode. In this case, the initial screen displays separate menu options or pushbuttons for displaying and modifying data. You will see the transaction code in the SY-TCODE system field.

Although step loops consist of several lines, the LOOP AT SCREEN statement only supplies one single record for the step loop. Any changes you make in this record apply to the entire step loop, i.e. to all the lines you can see in the screen program. One exception to this is when you call LOOP AT SCREEN in the flow logic's LOOP. In this case, the step loop is also only provided with one record, which references the current line in the step loop. In this special case, any potential changes will only affect this line.

Processing table views

The structure of table views is considerably more complex than normal screen program fields or step loops. Therefore you cannot use the LOOP AT SCREEN statement to process them, even though there is a line in the SCREEN table for each table view column.

You must declare table views in the module pool, unlike other screen program elements. This is why there is a data object in the program that has a relatively complex structure in addition to the screen program element. This data object has the same name as the table view in the screen program. The data object is used to store any information about the table view (apart from the actual data). If you want to modify the way the table view reacts, you must modify some of the fields in this data object. The system uses other fields to store status information. These fields then operate like system fields.

The data object consists of a structure. Some simple fields in this structure control the global characteristics of the table view. The structure also contains an internal table that supplies information about individual columns in the table view. Unlike the structure in the SCREEN table, the structure for both elements is not derived from standard system objects. It is described by two type declarations in the CXTAB type pool. When you declare a table view, the system evaluates this information automatically. Table 3.41 shows the structure of data type CXTAB_CONTROL. This data type describes the entire data object of a table view:

Table 3.41   Structure of data type CXTAB_CONTROL for table views

Field name	Type	Contents / effect	Should I edit this field?
FIXED_COLS	I	Number of fixed columns at the left margin	X
LINES	I	Number of lines	
TOP_LINE	I	Start line for display	X
CURRENT_LINE	I	Contains the current line in LOOP over the table view	
LEFT_COL	I	First movable column displayed	
LINE_SEL_MODE	I	0 - no line selection	
		1 - single line selection	
		2 – multiple line selection	X
COL_SEL_MODE	I	0 - no column selection	
		1 – single column selection	
		2 – multiple column selection	X
LINE_SELECTOR	C(1)	Display button for line selection	X
V_SCROLL	C(1)	X – display vertical scrollbar	(No function)
H_GRID	C(1)	X – separation line between lines	X
V_GRID	C(1)	X – separation line between columns	X
COLS	CXTAB_COLUMN	Internal table for column description	

There is also a data type that you use to describe the structure of the COLS internal table. This structure is called CXTAB_COLUMN and is described in Table 3.42. In this data type, the SCREEN field is described by the structure of the internal table also called 'screen'. The result of this is that names are generated on several levels.

Table 3.42   Structure of data type CXTAB_COLUMN for column descriptions in table views

Field name	Type	Contents/effect	Should I edit this field?
SCREEN	SCREEN	Column attributes	X
INDEX	I	Number of lines	X
SELECTED	ICON-OLENG	X - column is selected	X
VISLENGTH	ICON-OLENG		X
INVISIBLE	C(1)	X - column invisible	X

The excerpts from a program below demonstrate how to modify a table view dynamically. They refer to the example about the complex elements in the screen program. You can upgrade screen program 3000 in this example by adding another module to test the programming method. You should be aware that the internal COLS table does not have a header. This means you must declare a work area before you can access the table. To do this, refer back to data type CXTAB_COLUMN that is contained in the CXTAB type pool. First, declare the data objects you require. As usual, you do this in the top include:

```
TYPE-POOLS CXTAB.
DATA CL TYPE CXTAB_COLUMN.
```

Later in a PBO module you define the first three columns of the table view as fixed columns that cannot be modified. You then hide the itadir-devclass field:

```
MODULE init_3000 OUTPUT.
  LOOP AT tc1-cols INTO cl.
    IF cl-index < 4.
      cl-screen-input = ' '.
    ELSE.
      IF ( cl-screen-name = 'ITADIR-DEVCLASS' ).
        cl-invisible = 'X'.
      ENDIF.
    ENDIF.

    MODIFY tc1-cols FROM cl.
  ENDLOOP.
  tc1-fixed_cols = 3.
ENDMODULE.
```

Using icons

Another way of changing the appearance of screen program fields before you display the screen program is by using icons. To do this, you enter a special identifier in the data field that is linked with the screen program. The system recognizes this as a reference to an icon and displays the icon in its place when it outputs the field. In this case, you can only use output-type screen program fields. This also works for dynamic texts for function codes. To determine the icon's identifier, you first call a special function module. This expects you to enter the icon's name as a parameter. The return code consists of a special character string that the screen program recognizes as a reference to an icon. If necessary, you can display the icon together with text. You can also define a quick info text for the icon.

It is very easy to test the dynamic generation of icons and the function modules they require. To do this, declare a global data field (P1) that is long enough (35 characters) and embed it in the fullscreen of the screen program. Assign the OUTPUT ONLY and WITH ICON attributes to this field. This deactivates the INPUT FIELD attribute that is set automatically. The length of the field and the output length to be reserved in the screen program depend partly on the type of icon and text to be output. In addition to the icon's identifier, the data field must be large enough to contain the actual text and the quick info text for the icon.

You usually assign icons to the screen program field in a PBO module. Quite often screen programs have a module in which you can make all the modifications to the interface. The listing below shows how you use this function module. For example, you will see the icon names in the input help for the corresponding field in the Screen Painter Attributes dialog box.

```
. . .
CALL FUNCTION 'ICON_CREATE'
     EXPORTING
        NAME                       = 'ICON_GREEN_LIGHT'
        TEXT                       = 'text for the icon
        INFO                       = 'quick info'
        ADD_STDINF                 = 'X'
     IMPORTING
        RESULT                     = P1
     EXCEPTIONS
        ICON_NOT_FOUND             = 01
        OUTPUTFIELD_TOO_SHORT      = 02.
. . .
```

Recognizing changes to data

Almost every screen program provides at least one function code that allows you to leave the screen program immediately. If data has already been entered, it is a good idea to tell users that they may lose this data before they leave the screen program. The system fills the SY-DATAR system field (Data Received) with 'X', if values have been processed in the screen program. The screen program initializes this field before each run. If necessary, the field's contents must also be stored in a flag in the program. This system field is the only way you can recognize changes to data in EXIT modules. The system does not transport data from screen program fields to fields in the program until the EXIT module has been executed. This is why you cannot save data in the EXIT module. If you need to save data, you must not close screen program processing with an EXIT module. The application example shown in Chapter 7 gives a detailed demonstration of what to do in such cases.

Another way of recognizing data changes is to use a global flag that is set in a special module. You use the ON REQUEST addition in a `module` statement to ensure that this module is only called if data has been changed. In the flow logic, you use the FIELD statement to link the fields whose contents you want to monitor, with a module where you set a global flag:

```
* flow logic
PROCESS AFTER INPUT.
...
  FIELD fieldname "a statement for each field
    MODULE DATA_CHANGED ON REQUEST.
...

* module pool
MODULE DATA_CHANGED.
  FLG_DATA_CHANGED = 'X'.
ENDMODULE.
```

The system must reset the flag if new data is entered in the screen program. However, unlike SY-DATAR, this flag has no effect if the screen program terminates immediately the first time it is processed. This means you must use both methods to make absolutely sure that you can identify any changes.

Evaluating the data field at the cursor position

Only data transfer takes place in LOOP statements. If you want to edit internal tables, you can sometimes also use additional function codes to edit a selected record in the screen program. For example, this would allow you to add a new record or delete an existing one. From the user's point of view, the easiest way of doing this is if the cursor's position in the screen program identifies the record they want to modify and they do not need to work through any additional selection fields, etc. To program these functions, you must determine the loop block in which the cursor has been positioned in the PAI module, but outside the LOOP. You then use this value to determine the record's index. You can determine the loop block's number quite simply by using this next statement:

GET CURSOR LINE *line*.

This statement places the number of the current loop block in the field you entered as the parameter. You should note here that one loop block can consist of several lines in the screen program. The GET statement determines the same value for all the lines in a block.

To find out the actual number of the record on which the cursor is positioned, the system adds the loop block number determined in the way described above, to the number of the first record shown in the loop (ITAB_OFFSET in example 1 or value of loop cursor I in example 2) and deducts 1 from the result.

The GET CURSOR statement has several options that you can use to get meaningful results even if the screen cursor is not positioned in a step loop area, but in a simple screen program field. In addition to the return parameter, the statement therefore also tells you whether the screen cursor is located in a loop area (SY-SUBRC = 0) or not (SY-SUBRC = 4). It gives this information in the SY-SUBRC system variable.

This statement is quite easy to use. The previous example acts as our starting point. In the status, function code FT02 is assigned to function key (F2). This function code must insert a new record in front of the record where the screen cursor is located and enter a value in the new record (line number + 100). You only need to write one FCODE module to analyze the function code and include this module in the flow logic:

```
MODULE FCODE INPUT.
  CASE FCODE.
    WHEN 'FT02'.
      GET CURSOR LINE CL.
      IF SY-SUBRC = 0.
        CL = CL + I - 1.
        ITAB-Z = CL + 100.
        INSERT ITAB INDEX CL.
      ENDIF.
  ENDCASE.
ENDMODULE.
```

Filling list boxes

From Release 4.x onwards, screen program input fields also have list boxes. These contain values that users can select. The range of values can be set automatically by the system. You can also set it manually in the program. You use function module VRM_SET_VALUE to control the definition of the value range. This module expects you to enter a VRM_VALUE-type internal table as an input parameter. You will find the definition of this data type in type pool VRM. Therefore your first task is to include the type pool and to declare the internal table:

```
TYPE-POOLS vrm.
DATA possible_values TYPE vrm_value OCCURS 0 WITH HEADER LINE.
```

At the PBO event, this table is filled with values and then transferred to the function module:

```
possible_values-key = 'KEY1'. possible_values-text = '1st item'.
APPEND possible_values.
possible_values-key = 'KEY2'. possible_values-text = '2nd item'.
```

```
APPEND possible_values.
possible_values-key = 'KEY3'. possible_values-text = '3rd item'.
APPEND possible_values.

CALL FUNCTION 'VRM_SET_VALUES'
  EXPORTING id      = 'TADIR-AUTHOR'
            values = possible_values[].
```

The function module expects you to enter the name of the field for which the list box has to be filled and the table with the values to be set as input parameters. The table in this example has a header line, so when you transfer the parameter you must clearly show that the system is to transfer the table and not the header line. You do this by enclosing the table name in square brackets.

Program links from screen programs

You can jump to various other elements from a screen program. In most cases, this branching takes place in the PAI section. However, you can also call other programs or parts of programs in the PROCESS ON VALUE REQUEST section. You have the following link options:

- continue with different screen program;

- execute a report;

- start another transaction;

- close the application.

You use three basic statements with a few variants to call elements. These statements are LEAVE, SUBMIT and CALL. They control the program flow in different ways. If you use LEAVE, the application is continued sequentially. CALL is more like a subroutine call. However, you can use various additions with the SUBMIT statement to implement both linking methods.

Many of the statements discussed in this section can also be used in reports. However, in practice this is done much less frequently than in the dialog applications discussed here.

Link with LEAVE

You use the LEAVE statement to call elements that logically follow each other in sequence. Screen programs are an example of this type of element. The called element is given complete control over how the program is then executed. If you finish processing this type of element without calling a follow-on element, the same thing happens as when you close the application.

You can use the different variants of the LEAVE statement to call different elements. You usually require two statements to call a screen program. First, you use this statement to set the number of the calling screen program:

SET SCREEN *screen*.

You do not have to use this statement if the number of the new screen program has already been set as the next screen in the current screen program. You then use this next statement to jump to the new screen program:

LEAVE SCREEN.

From Release 3.0 onwards, you can combine both statements into one. This will read:

LEAVE TO SCREEN *screen*.

This type of link is final. It must not be confused with a subroutine call. This means that you do not automatically return to the calling screen program after you close the screen program you called. The jump to screen program 0 is a special function and closes the application. You can achieve the same function with the following statement:

LEAVE PROGRAM.

You jump to another transaction with the next statement:

LEAVE TO TRANSACTION *transactioncode*.

Here, you must enter the transaction code in upper-case letters and enclose it in single quotation marks. You can give this statement the optional addition:

... AND SKIP FIRST SCREEN.

This addition suppresses the display of the initial screen program in the transaction you call. However, the system still processes the flow logic of the first screen program correctly. This is why you must fill the fields of this screen program automatically. You do this either by using the GET/SET parameters, together with corresponding attributes in the screen program or by using statements in the PBO modules. If all mandatory input fields have been entered correctly, the user has no way of entering data. Processing continues immediately with the PAI modules. The current function code is the one for (Enter), default: blank. It is a good idea to use this type of statement and skip data entry in the first screen program if the called transaction has a special structure. This will be dealt with in more detail at the end of this section.

Branching with SUBMIT

You can also call reports, as well as other screen programs and transactions. Instead of using the LEAVE statement, you use the statement shown below:

SUBMIT *report*.

Around 20 different additions are available for this statement. You can use them to transfer various things to the report, ranging from the format of the output list to printing or archiving. Most of these additions are only of interest in special cases. At this point, only 5 additions are of real importance. They are described below.

You use this first addition to return to the calling program after the report has been executed:

`...` **AND RETURN.**

After the `SUBMIT` statement, the calling program then continues. The report is started immediately without any existing selection screen being processed. This means that the user cannot restrict the volume of data that the report searches through. However, the programmer can still ensure that the report has parameters and selections. The simplest way of doing this is to name a variant with:

`...` **USING SELECTION-SET** *variant.*

You can also use the following two statements to transfer preassigned parameters and selections to the report:

`...` **WITH** *parameter* `...`

or

`...` **WITH SELECTION-TABLE** *selection.*

If the user still has to process the selection screen, you can use the next addition:

`...` **VIA SELECTION-SCREEN.**

This triggers the processing of the selection screen. If the `WITH` statement has been used to set default values for parameters and selections in the calling application, the user can change the default values that were transferred before they execute the report. They change these values in the selection screen.

The CALL statement

This statement processes the called application or the called element as a subprocess. After the called application terminates, the calling application continues from where it was interrupted. This statement is most frequently used to call dialog boxes in screen programs. You have already encountered lots of dialog boxes, in particular those in which you input individual values or those in which you confirm specific activities. You use a variant of the `CALL` statement to call all these dialog boxes.

You use the next statement to call screen programs:

CALL SCREEN *screen.*

In the called screen program the `LEAVE TO SCREEN 0` statement no longer closes the entire application. It merely returns you to the point at which the screen program was called. If you use the basic form of the statement, the new screen program fills the whole work area, i.e. it completely replaces the previous screen program. The called screen program should be a normal screen program.

A dialog box is a screen program in whose attributes the screen program type *Modal dialog* box is selected instead of *Normal*. When you call the dialog box, you must be specific where you want it to be displayed. You specify this position in relation to the current screen program:

CALL SCREEN *screen* **STARTING AT** *line column.*

In this type of call, the system ensures that the size of the dialog box corresponds to the area actually occupied in this screen program. Very long dialog boxes whose length would exceed the space available on the screen are automatically restricted to the height and width of the screen and are given a scroll bar. However, this can only ever be a solution for emergencies. Therefore if necessary you can specify the exact final position. However this only makes sense if you have also defined a start position.

CALL SCREEN *screen* **STARTING AT** *line column*
  ENDING AT *line column*.

The system handles dialog boxes somewhat differently from simple screen programs. It moves the application toolbar to the bottom edge of the dialog box. The menu, icon bar and statement field are not available. You can only display the function key assignment by clicking on the right mouse button. This is why in screen programs that are to be processed as dialog boxes all the important functions must be assigned to function keys.

You can only use CALL SCREEN to call screen programs in their own application. If there were screen programs whose functionality was required in several applications, using this statement would require too much programming time and effort. This is why these general screen programs are programmed as dialog modules that can be called from any application. You will find more details about dialog modules in another section. Here, we will only demonstrate how to call these modules:

CALL dialog *dialog*.

As these dialog modules do not belong to the current application, they cannot access data fields in the application that is running. If you want to transfer data to the dialog modules or have them return data, you must specify the fields involved when you call the dialog modules. To do so, you use export and import parameters respectively. Export parameters are the elements that are transferred to the module:

... **EXPORTING** *field_1* **FROM** *param_1* ... *field_n* **FROM** *param_n*.

The dialog modules have a defined interface. This interface lists all the parameters that have values assigned to them or that can read values. You use the FROM addition to assign a value from the current program (param...) to one of these interface parameters (field...). If the names of the fields in the calling program and in the dialog module are identical, you do not need the FROM addition. You then simply define the name of the field to be exported. You use a similar procedure to return values. The next addition uses the dialog module's parameters to return data to elements in the calling program:

... **IMPORTING** *field_1* **TO** *param_1* ... *field_n* TO *param_n*.

If the names are identical, you can use the same simplified procedure as for the EXPORTING statement described above.

A dialog module does not necessarily have to consist of one single screen program. Within a dialog module, you can link to other screen programs. For this reason, you can also use the AND SKIP FIRST SCREEN addition for the CALL DIALOG statement.

You can also use the CALL statement to jump to other applications. You use this next statement to call the selected transaction as a subprocess, i.e. as a subroutine:

`CALL TRANSACTION` *transactioncode*.

Like in `LEAVE TO TRANSACTION`, you can use this next addition to skip the first screen program if all the mandatory input fields contain correct values:

`... AND SKIP FIRST SCREEN.`

In the called transaction, all the statements that close this transaction in the normal way (i.e. `LEAVE TRANSACTION`, `LEAVE TO SCREEN 0`) return you to the calling application.

Processing embedded lists

Up to now we have not yet pointed out that you can combine dialog processing with list processing. You can embed list-processing elements in dialog applications or call screen programs in reports. This option is used quite frequently in practice. For example, you use the following statement to temporarily activate list processing in a dialog application:

`LEAVE TO LIST-PROCESSING.`

As this issue can get pretty complicated, we have dedicated Section 3.8 to it.

3.7.5 Discussion

The statements introduced in this section and the relationships between them explain how a screen program functions. However, you will need to know more before you can create usable applications. When you design an application, the screen program concept and some of the statements mentioned above require you to take into consideration a program schema and some of SAP's (unwritten, in-house) recommendations. A large number of applications in the SAP system have a relatively simple basic structure. Occasionally, although radical changes are made to this basic structure, it is never completely ignored. Despite the fact that you can deviate from these basic principles, you will later pay the price for the freedom you had when you designed the application by having to handle a more complicated program structure that requires time-consuming maintenance. Anyone who is working with ABAP for the first time should be guided by the rules below. These are the fundamental issues you should consider when you develop an application:

- A dialog application (and therefore a transaction) is used to process an object or to fulfil a task that cannot be subdivided any further. Of course this does not mean that it only processes one table. However, if an application (for example `SE38`) is used to process the source code of a report, no other elements such as text elements or messages are processed directly in this application. You will require separate transactions for this. You can call them from the current transaction.

- A transaction is completely autonomous. You must not have to meet any technical programming conditions before you can call a transaction.

- Although they are independent, you should regard transactions as modules of the overall system. In particular, the transactions should be structured in such a way that they can also be called from other applications. One example is maintaining text elements in your transaction or in transaction SE38. Because you cannot include any parameters when you call a transaction from a program (with CALL TRANSACTION), many dialog applications contain several transaction codes. You use these transaction codes, for example, to decide whether an object is created, processed, deleted or displayed in a program. The transaction code is evaluated within the application. In addition, you evaluate the SY-CALLD system field to determine whether an application has been called directly or with the CALL TRANSACTION statement.

- A dialog application frequently consists of two parts, each of which consists of at least one screen program. In the first part (therefore in the first screen program, i.e. the initial screen program), you specify which exact object is to be processed by entering the values for the key fields. The subsequent screen programs then process the selected object. The fields in the first screen program are usually linked with GET/SET parameters. When you call the application from another transaction, the system fills the global parameters and the AND SKIP FIRST SCREEN... statement is used to prevent the first screen program of the called transaction from being displayed. This ensures that the user can process a predefined element without having to enter the key values.

- When you plan an application, your primary concerns are the 'What' and 'When', but not the 'How'. It is fairly easy to extend the pure functionality of an application by adding to the screen program flow logic. However, it is harder to change the program structure and such changes can lead to undesirable side effects.

- When you implement the functions, you should take into consideration the characteristics of the two parts of the flow logic. The system carries out initializations that affect data and screen programs in the PBO part. In contrast, the data is actually checked and evaluated in the PAI part.

3.8   Relationship between list and dialog processing

Until now we have assumed that reports and dialog-oriented applications are strictly separated. However, in certain cases this strict distinction can be overcome. You can embed lists in dialog applications and also use screen programs in reports.

3.8.1 Lists in screen programs

The extent to which you can dynamically structure screen programs is very limited. This is why screen programs are not flexible enough to display and process values in the way required by some applications. In these cases, programmers often resort to processing lists interactively. To do this, they use the statements described below that can also be directly embedded in screen program processing. An example of how lists are embedded are the search help dialog boxes where lists are displayed. Users can then select an entry from these lists. The Object Browser (that you are already familiar with) or, more precisely, its object list, is based on list processing. Within dialog processing, you can use the next statement to temporarily activate list-oriented processing:

LEAVE TO LIST-PROCESSING.

You can now execute all the statements that are only permitted in list processing (i.e. WRITE). The list is displayed on screen if the PAI part of the current screen program's flow logic has been processed completely or explicitly ended with the LEAVE SCREEN statement. If you did not have embedded list processing, you would normally jump to the next screen at this point. However, if an inserted list is present, the system displays this list first and the next screen is only called after list processing has been completed. The next screen is the screen program that was either defined with the NEXT SCREEN attribute or with the SET SCREEN statement. When embedded lists are used in a production system the screen program in whose PAI part the list was generated is usually called again and again.

The system executes an embedded list in the same way as a list that was created with a separate report. This also means that the system automatically evaluates some of the function codes, such as the one used to close list processing. This is why all the necessary function codes must be available within list processing. You also require a function code that closes list processing. However, when the system calls embedded list processing, it does not automatically call the default status for the lists that would provide these function codes. The status of the calling screen program remains activated. Therefore without additional programming there is always the danger that an embedded list cannot be closed.

There are several ways of providing the list with the function codes it requires. The easiest way is to define the function codes in the status of the screen program. If for example you assign the BACK function code to function key (F3) or the corresponding icon, you will be able to close the list. However, this only works because BACK is one of the function codes that are automatically evaluated by the system.

The safest option is to set the predefined list processing status. You can achieve this very easily with the next statement:

SET PF-STATUS ' '.

Because the specified status is not yet present, the system uses the default status that is used for list processing. The system intercepts the default function codes (i.e. Quit, Print, Find) and processes them. This ensures that the list functionality you are already familiar with in reports is available. Therefore you simply press (F3), (F12) or (F15) or choose the corresponding menu option to return to dialog processing.

However, in many cases this status cannot be used because the functionality you want to implement in the embedded list is totally different from the functionality found in normal reporting. You may often have to analyze the actual function codes and to use this next statement to return to dialog processing:

LEAVE LIST-PROCESSING.

When you close list processing, you return to the PBO part of the screen program from which you called list processing. You can deviate from this default setting, even when you call list processing, by using the following statement:

LEAVE TO LIST-PROCESSING AND RETURN TO SCREEN *screen.*

After you close list processing, the program now jumps to the screen program you have specified in this statement.

After the LEAVE TO LIST-PROCESSING statement, the system no longer evaluates function codes individually in the usual way that you will recognize from screen programs, i.e. in the screen program's flow logic. Instead the function codes are evaluated by the event statements for reports or within the system itself. Event statements that refer to list processing must be programmed directly in the module pool.

The example below (SAPMY340) shows how list processing is embedded in a screen program. Further on in the code, you will only see the relevant extract from the module pool. You must generate the surrounding application yourself with the help of the previous examples. The screen program's status should provide three pushbuttons that you use to trigger function codes FNC1, FNC2 and FNC3. These function codes should also be assigned to function keys (F6) to (F8). Function key (F15) must also be available as an exit function key (as described above) so that you can close the application correctly. You must assign function code FT15 to this function key. It is important to note here that this function code must be an exit code and that the screen program must have an exit module. You can then use your own screen program number as the next screen.

The screen program should have one module in the PBO part and two modules in the PAI part of the flow logic. You set the status described above in the PBO part. The PAI part has two modules: the familiar exit module and the following PAI module that is used to evaluate function codes. The flow logic listing looks like this:

```
PROCESS BEFORE OUTPUT.
  MODULE status_0100.
*
PROCESS AFTER INPUT.
  MODULE exit_100 AT EXIT-COMMAND.
  MODULE user_statement_0100.
```

The user statement module contains the most important parts of the program logic:

```
MODULE user_statement_0100 INPUT.
  CASE fcode.
    WHEN 'FNC1'.
      LEAVE TO LIST-PROCESSING.
      NEW-PAGE NO-TITLE NO-HEADING.
      SET PF-STATUS ' '.
      WRITE / 'Embedded list processing'.
      WRITE 'with standard status for reports.'.
      WRITE / 'End with F3 or similar.'.
```

```
   WHEN 'FNC2'.
     LEAVE TO LIST-PROCESSING.
     NEW-PAGE NO-TITLE NO-HEADING.
     WRITE / 'Embedded list processing,'.
     WRITE 'screen program's status still applies..
     WRITE /
        'Quit with function key F12 or 3rd pushbutton.
   ENDCASE.
 ENDMODULE.                              "USER_COMMAND_0100 INPUT
```

In the PAI modules include, you enter the following event statement manually as well as the statement block that belongs to it:

```
AT USER-COMMAND.
  IF sy-ucomm = 'FNC3' OR sy-ucomm = 'FT12'.
    LEAVE LIST-PROCESSING.
  ENDIF.
```

Enter function code FNC1 to display the first list. After you have activated list processing, the default title and the list heading are deactivated using the NEW-PAGE statement. In this case, this statement does not generate a page break because no data was output in the list before the statement was called. Here this statement is only used to deactivate the title and the heading. An empty character string acts as a descriptor for the status to be set. Because no such status is present, the system uses the default status for list processing. The system itself evaluates the functions provided by this status, so you do not need to carry out any additional programming tasks. For example, you can print the list without any trouble because printing is one of a report's default functions.

In the second version of list generation, which you trigger with function code FNC2, the system does not set a new status. This is why the screen program's status continues to be available. However you can now no longer press (F3) to close list processing because the status does not provide the function code that is automatically evaluated by the system. You must use the various list-processing event statements that you program yourself to close list processing. For this reason, one of these event statements is shown as an example of this programming method immediately below the module. If you trigger any function code that is not processed by the system, the system in turn triggers the AT USER-COMMAND event. If you click the third pushbutton and press (F12), a corresponding query closes list processing.

This example displays a screen program in which you use pushbuttons to select one of the two different lists. This screen program also has its own functions. In practice, you usually do not need to make this kind of selection. In this case, the screen program simply forms the frame that actually makes it possible for you to insert list processing functions into a dialog application. To retain the modular character of the screen program within the application, you should separate dialog processing from list processing. This is why no dialog processing normally takes place in a screen program that carries out list processing. This is not an essential requirement, but experience has shown it to be a useful way of working. It is easier to program and maintain applications that are structured in this way than applications that combine several functions in one screen program. In such cases, you should not display the dialog screen, because it would only cause confusion. This is why the ABAP statement set includes a statement that allows you to skip the dialog in a screen program and to execute PAI processing immediately. This statement looks like this:

`SUPPRESS DIALOG.`

This statement can be demonstrated in an application (`SAPMY350`) that you generate by making slight changes to the previous example. In the PBO part of the screen program, you only need one module to execute the new `SUPPRESS DIALOG` statement. You do not need to set a status. You also cannot trigger a function code because you skip the actual dialog. This is why you also only need one module in the PAI section of the screen program. This module is where the list is generated:

```
MODULE user_statement_0100 INPUT.
  LEAVE TO LIST-PROCESSING AND RETURN TO SCREEN 0.
  NEW-PAGE NO-TITLE NO-HEADING.
  SET PF-STATUS ' '.
  WRITE / 'Embedded list processing'.
  WRITE 'with standard status for reports.'.
  WRITE / 'End with F3 or similar.'.
ENDMODULE.
```

The system does not evaluate any function codes, because they cannot be generated without a dialog. If you do not use the AND RETURN TO SCREEN 0 addition to the LEAVE statement, the screen program would be executed again after you leave list processing. This would happen because the PBO part of the calling screen program would always be executed again after list processing was closed. This is why you can only end the screen program by using the event statement shown above. Depending on how the screen program was called up, the event statement combined with the AND RETURN addition either closes the entire application (screen program called with LEAVE TO SCREEN) or simply returns you to another screen program (called with CALL SCREEN). In most cases, we recommend that you insert a list into the dialog application in the second variant.

3.8.2 Input help

In practice, embedded list processing is often used to implement input help. At the end of this subsection, we will therefore demonstrate how you use an interactive report as input help for a screen program field. Because not all program development steps are described in detail, you will have a good opportunity to practice using the development environment and the various tools to create the program.

First, generate a screen program that includes a simple list-processing function. This list initially displays the numbers of all available colour attributes. Double-click on a number to display or hide additional lines in the list, together with examples of the colour concerned and other attributes.

In a second section, generate another screen program that only has one input field. For this input field, you program an input help text that uses the screen program you created in the first part.

To create the complete example, simply work through the following steps:

1. Create a module pool. You can select any name that conforms to the existing conventions. The module pool should have a top include where you enter the following declarations:

```
DATA: BEGIN OF itab OCCURS 20,
  index TYPE i,
  col TYPE i,
  detail,
  text(20),
END OF itab.
```

```
DATA: g_init VALUE 'X',    " Flag: Screen program run for first time
      g_line TYPE i,        " Top-most displayed line
                            " in the list
      g_page TYPE i,        " Top-most displayed page
                            " in the list
      g_int TYPE i,         " Help field
      g_col(20).            " Global field for returning the
                            " selected line, for part 2
```

2. Create a screen program (numbered 100) in this module pool. The fullscreen of this screen program remains empty. You do not need to make an assignment to the statement field. The next listing shows the flow logic:

```
PROCESS BEFORE OUTPUT.
  MODULE status_0100.
*
PROCESS AFTER INPUT.
  MODULE user_statement_0100.
```

3. Generate the two modules in accordance with the following listing:

```
MODULE status_0100 OUTPUT.
* Set status for list
  SET PF-STATUS 'STAT1'.

* Creation of the help table on first call
  IF g_init = 'X'.

* Initialize internal table
    CLEAR itab.
    REFRESH itab.
```

```
* Initialize global fields
    CLEAR: g_init, g_int, g_line, g_page.

* A record for each colour
    WHILE g_int < 8.
      itab-index = g_int + 1.
      itab-col = g_int.
      itab-detail = ' '.
      itab-text = 'Color'.
      itab-text+7(5) = g_int.
      APPEND itab.
      ADD 1 TO g_int.
    ENDWHILE.
  ENDIF.

* Suppress input in screen program
  SUPPRESS dialog.

ENDMODULE.                          "STATUS_0100 OUTPUT


MODULE user_statement_0100 INPUT.
  LEAVE TO LIST-PROCESSING.
  NEW-PAGE NO-TITLE NO-HEADING.

* Output each line of the Itab
  LOOP AT itab.
    WRITE: / itab-text INTENSIFIED OFF.
    HIDE itab.

* If flag is set, then examples of colour and attributes
    IF itab-detail = 'X'.
      WRITE: /5 'Normal            '    COLOR = itab-col
                                        INTENSIFIED OFF
                                        INVERSE OFF.
      HIDE itab.

      WRITE: /5 'Intensified       '    COLOR = itab-col
                                        INTENSIFIED ON
                                        INVERSE OFF.
      HIDE itab.
      WRITE: /5'Inverse            '    COLOR = itab-col
                                        INTENSIFIED OFF
                                        INVERSE ON.
      HIDE itab.
```

```
      WRITE: /5 'Intensified Invers'  COLOR = itab-col
                                      INTENSIFIED ON
                                      INVERSE ON.
      HIDE itab.
      WRITE /.

   ENDIF.
  ENDLOOP.


* due to LINE-SELECTION
  CLEAR itab.

* In case of re-generation of the list after line selection,
* jump back to the old position
  SCROLL LIST TO PAGE g_page LINE g_line.
ENDMODULE.                        " USER_COMMAND_0100 INPUT
```

4. You have to generate the STAT1 status that is called in the INIT module. In the interface editor, choose Extras | Adjust template from the menu to derive this status from a list status. In this status, you create a new function SELE that must also be accessible from a function key and a pushbutton. You can use 'Copy' as its text. You must also modify the function code for Cancel (function key F12) to FT12. This function code must be an exit function code.

5. In the module pool, you must now program the following two event statements. The first one is AT LINE-SELECTION:

```
AT LINE-SELECTION.
  IF NOT itab IS INITIAL.

* Remember current position of the first line displayed
    g_page = sy-cpage.
    g_line = sy-staro.

* Toggle flag for detail display
    IF itab-detail <> ' '.
      itab-detail = ' '.
    ELSE.
      itab-detail = 'X'.
    ENDIF.

* Change record in table
    MODIFY itab INDEX itab-index.
```

```
* Jump back to the PBO part of the screen program -> Regenerate
     the list
     LEAVE LIST-PROCESSING.
   ENDIF.
```

The second event statement is AT USER-COMMAND:

```
AT USER-COMMAND.
   CASE sy-ucomm.
     WHEN 'FT12'.
        LEAVE TO SCREEN 0.
   ENDCASE.
```

Now generate a transaction that uses screen program 100 as its initial screen program. Test the application. It should generate a short list with the numbers of the colours available in lists. Double-click on one of these lines to display four additional lines with examples of how the colours appear.

6. Generate a second screen program (200). In the fullscreen of this screen program, the system generates an input field for the g_col global data field. The flow logic of the second screen program contains three module calls:

```
PROCESS BEFORE OUTPUT.
   MODULE status_0200.
*
PROCESS AFTER INPUT.
   MODULE exit_0200 AT EXIT-COMMAND.
PROCESS ON VALUE REQUEST.
   FIELD g_col MODULE get_color.
```

7. Create the modules called by screen program 200:

```
MODULE status_0200 OUTPUT.
   SET PF-STATUS 'STAT1'.
ENDMODULE.                        "STATUS_0200 OUTPUT

MODULE exit_0200 INPUT.
   LEAVE TO SCREEN 0.
ENDMODULE.                        "EXIT_0200 INPUT

MODULE get_color INPUT.
   g_init = 'X'.
   CALL SCREEN 100 STARTING AT 5 5 ENDING AT 30 10.
ENDMODULE.                        "GET_COLOR INPUT
```

8. In the AT USER-COMMAND event statement, you must add a function for evaluating the function codes you have just created. To do this, you simply require a second WHEN branch.

```
WHEN 'SELE'.
  IF NOT itab IS INITIAL.
    g_col = itab-text.
    LEAVE TO SCREEN 0.
  ELSE.
    MESSAGE ID 'Y!' TYPE 'I' NUMBER '000'.
  ENDIF.
```

9. Generate a second transaction that uses screen program 200 as its initial screen program and then test the application. A small button appears next to the input field. You
can click on this button to call screen program 100 as a dialog box. In this dialog box,
you can select an entry and click on the Copy button to add it to the input field.

Discussion

In step 1, you first declare the data that is required in the program. The internal table or
more precisely the detail flag later controls how the additional lines containing the
examples of the output formats are displayed. The index and col fields, just like the
text, are only included to make the program slightly simpler. In principle, the information
in these fields can also be derived from the index (record number) of the internal table
when the application is running.

You need a screen program before you call a list in a dialog application. You create this
screen program in steps 2 and 3. The system fills the internal table in the INIT module
with eight records. In the first part of the example, you do not need to empty the table
before the system fills it with data. The reasons for this will be described later. Apart from
creating the list, the system also initializes a few global fields to achieve a predefined
basic state. You save the list's current line later.

At the end of the INIT module, the SUPPRESS DIALOG statement is used to suppress
dialog processing. This means that the application immediately continues processing, but
only processes the single PAI module. In this module, list processing is activated and the
list is created. At least one line appears in the list for each line in the internal table. If the
detail flag is activated in the internal table, the system displays four additional lines
with the different attribute combinations. When the system creates the internal table, it
resets this flag, i.e. the list only contains eight single lines. For each output line, the HIDE
statement places the entire record in the hidden data area.

After the system has displayed the list, the user can carry out two activities. They can
press (F12) or click the corresponding icon to trigger function code FT12. This is
processed by the AT USER-COMMAND event statement and closes the application, because
it returns to screen program 0. At this point you must not use the default function code
recommended in the Menu Painter. The system would evaluate the default function code
and would only close list processing and not the entire application. However, the calling
screen program is activated again after list processing. This would cause the list to be
regenerated immediately. You can only close the application correctly by programming
your own evaluation of a function code.

The most interesting part of the application is the AT LINE-SELECTION event that is programmed in step 5. After a line is selected, the record placed in the hidden data area with the HIDE statement is automatically brought back to the itab header line, if you selected one of the data lines in the list. You can see this from the introductory IF statement.

The main task of the detail flag in the records in the internal table is to display the list on screen. You toggle this flag in the internal table's header line. You can then use the record index contained in the header line to update the contents of the internal table. Using the index simplifies the application. If the record's index cannot be directly derived from the returned data, you should first search for the record in the internal table. For this reason, it is essential that you save a unique key for each record in the hidden data area. After you have modified the internal table, use the appropriate statement to close list processing. The PBO part of screen program 100 is processed again. This obviously means that the list is displayed again. This list is now completely regenerated in accordance with the flags that have just been set or reset.

When the system regenerates a list, the list is displayed from its first line. Because even this small demo list can extend far beyond one screen page, you may after a double-click be taken to a completely different page in the list from the one you were in before you selected the line. To avoid this, if you use the AT LINE-SELECTION statement, the system saves the current line number and page number in global fields. After the list has been regenerated, you then use the SCROLL statement to jump to a particular line in the list.

Embedded list processing is frequently used to provide users with input help, in which they can make a selection from a particular range of values. The main procedure can be demonstrated very easily by using the program you have just generated. First, generate screen program 200 with an input field, as in step 6 of the instructions above. The only task of this screen program is to demonstrate the provision of input help for a data field. It does not have any real functions other than this. The data field that works together with the input field must be accessible from both screen programs (100 and 200) because it is used to transfer data between the two screen programs. Screen program 200 is executed in dialog mode. For this reason it needs a status, which must contain a function code that you can use to close the application. For the sake of simplicity, you can use STAT1 here, even if it contains some function codes that are not required.

You create the actual input help by using another event in the flow logic of screen program 200. This input help is processed if you press (F4) in the input field. The statements used to call the input help are extremely simple. First, set the flag to trigger the initialization of screen program 100. If the input help is called several times, screen program 100 is always called each time, but because the itab internal table is located in the application's global data area, it remains intact until the user leaves the transaction. To display the base form of the list each time you start the input help, use the g_init flag to regenerate the help table.

Now, use the CALL statement to call screen program 100. You can use the STARTING AT and ENDING AT additions to display the execution of the screen program and therefore that of the list in a dialog box. Screen program 100 is now fully ready for operation. The dialog box now displays the list. Double-click in this list to display a record's details. Press (F12) in this list to return to screen program 200. Because you called screen program 100 with the CALL statement, you cannot use the LEAVE TO SCREEN 0 statement to close the entire application. If you use this statement you will merely return to the calling screen program.

In screen program 100 or more precisely at the AT USER-COMMAND event you still need to transfer the data to the calling screen program. To do this you could simply enter the text from the header line of the itab table into the g_col global data field immediately before you use the LEAVE statement. This header line is also filled with data from the hidden data area at the AT USER-COMMAND event. To give users the option of cancelling without transferring data, the status of screen program 100 contains an additional function code SELE which is used to copy data. This function code is also evaluated at the AT USER-COMMAND event. When you trigger that function code, the system enters a value from the selected line in the g_col global field before it is returned. However, you can only use this function code to close the screen program if you have selected a correct line. As already mentioned in the listing, the system should display an error message if it is unable to find a line. Because it is highly likely that neither the message class nor the message are currently present, the system simply displays an empty dialog box without an error message. Even if a message class and message do exist, there is no relationship between the message text and the cause of the error.

3.8.3 Screen programs in reports

Calling a screen program does not entirely depend on whether the program is a module pool or not. It is primarily the program type that influences how the application starts. However, the program type does not affect the elements the application contains. This is why reports can also contain and execute screen programs and modules. In this way, you can solve special problems faster than you could if you only used dialog applications. Calling a screen program has the following advantages:

- In a report, it is relatively easy to create and modify a selection screen in which you preselect data. You do not need to process a screen program to do this. You simply need a few PARAMETERS statements or SELECTION statements.

- You can use any existing logical databases to make selecting the data easier.

- You can display the selected records for selection in an interactive report (i.e. select them by double-clicking). The records are processed in a genuine screen program. It is easier and quicker to program this type of a report than a screen program with a step loop or table view that has the same function.

Mixing list processing with dialog processing makes using this kind of application a little more complicated. This is why these applications are often used for low-level tasks and only by small groups of users.

To call a screen program in a report, use this next statement:

CALL SCREEN *screen.*

The modules that belong to the screen program must be available in the current program.

In a report, there are two ways of creating a screen program. The easiest method is to use the navigation function. After you double-click the screen program number in the **CALL SCREEN** *screen* statement, the R/3 System generates the screen program, along with all its elements. You can of course also create the screen program from the Object Browser's object list.

This procedure can be demonstrated quite simply in program YZZ34200. You replace the call to the function module that displays the source text with a small dialog in which the user can change the program's description.

First, you must add some more declarations to the actual report. It is also a good idea to give it a simpler structure so the important points can be identified more easily. The listing for the modified report is shown below; you create it by simply copying program YZZ34200 and then modifying a few lines. You must add two more data fields in the declaration part. These are the L_TEXT field that temporarily contains the program title and the FCODE field that stores the function code during the dialog.

```
REPORT yz336010 NO DEFAULT PAGE HEADING.

TABLES: trdir,        "Table with ABAP program
        textpool.     "Structure for texts

* Internal table for texts
DATA: BEGIN OF itext OCCURS 20.
  INCLUDE STRUCTURE textpool.
DATA: END OF itext.

DATA:
  fcode    LIKE sy-ucomm,
  l_text   LIKE itext-entry.

PARAMETERS p_name LIKE trdir-cnam.
TRANSLATE p_name USING '*%+_'.

FORMAT COLOR 4.

SELECT * FROM trdir
  WHERE cnam LIKE p_name          "User
    AND appl <> 'S'               "no generated programs
    AND subc IN ('1', 'M', 'F')   "no includes
  ORDER BY name.

*    Text for program in itab
  CLEAR itext.
  REFRESH itext.
  READ TEXTPOOL trdir-name INTO itext LANGUAGE sy-langu.
```

```
* Find the description
    itext-id = 'R'.
    READ TABLE itext.

* Write program name
    WRITE: / trdir-name, (60) itext-entry.
    HIDE: trdir, itext-entry.

* Separator
    WRITE /.
ENDSELECT.

CLEAR trdir.

AT LINE-SELECTION.
    IF NOT trdir IS INITIAL.
        l_text = itext-entry.
        CALL SCREEN 100.
        MODIFY CURRENT LINE FIELD VALUE itext-entry.
        CLEAR trdir.
    ENDIF.
```

Now generate the program so the insertion tool can find the fields in the program in the screen program.

Double-click on the screen program number to ensure that the system generates a new screen program. In this screen program, you generate an input field for the L_TEXT data field, and also a display field for TRDIR-name. Because the L_TEXT field is very long, you should restrict its visible length in the screen program. You should also allow entries in upper-case or lower-case letters in this field. The flow logic and the two modules tell you about the screen program's functions and also indirectly tell you about the generation of the status. Of course, you must also generate this structure. The flow logic is the same as that in the automatically generated default value.

```
PROCESS BEFORE OUTPUT.
    MODULE status_0100.
*
PROCESS AFTER INPUT.
    MODULE user_statement_0100.
```

In the status module, you simply set the status.

```
MODULE STATUS_0100 OUTPUT.
    SET PF-STATUS 'STAT_1'.
ENDMODULE.                              " STATUS_0100 OUTPUT
```

The three function codes evaluated in the user statement module allow the user to close the screen program with or without saving the edited value. These function codes also let users restore the old contents without having to leave the screen program. Please create status STAT_1 on your own so that the three function codes can be generated. For once, you do not need to set an exit attribute for the function codes. This is because all the function codes are evaluated in the user statement module and there is no exit module.

```
MODULE user_statement_0100 INPUT.
  CASE fcode.

*.....Save and exit
    WHEN 'FT11'.
      CLEAR itext.
      REFRESH itext.
      READ TEXTPOOL trdir-name INTO itext LANGUAGE sy-langu.
      CLEAR itext.
      itext-id = 'R'.
      itext-key = space.
      READ TABLE itext.
      itext-entry = l_text.
      IF sy-tabix = 0.
        APPEND itext.
      ELSE.
        MODIFY itext INDEX sy-tabix.
      ENDIF.
      INSERT TEXTPOOL trdir-name FROM itext LANGUAGE sy-langu.
      LEAVE TO SCREEN 0.

*.....Exit without saving
    WHEN 'FT03'.
      LEAVE TO SCREEN 0.

*.....Restore text
    WHEN 'UNDO'.
      l_text = itext-entry .
  ENDCASE.
ENDMODULE.                        "USER_COMMAND_0100 INPUT
```

Saving the modified value to the database is somewhat more complicated. This is because the text pool must first be read again to an internal table in which the system must find and overwrite the corresponding entry. Then the entire internal table must be written back to the text pool. If the system only wrote one modified entry for the program title to the textpool, all the other entries (text elements, etc.) would be lost.

3.9   Function modules and dialog modules

Function and dialog modules have already been mentioned in the context of the statements discussed so far. These modules have sometimes also been used without further explanation. Function modules are primarily very powerful resources that are used to modularize applications.

Function modules are stored in a function pool. A function pool includes one or several function modules that logically belong together. The function pool contains global data declarations and subroutines that can be used in any application (form routines) for all the function modules contained in it. In this respect, it is like a module pool. The contents of the data fields declared in the global data area (in the framework program) remain in force as long as the calling program is active. For this reason it is also called a *local memory*.

Function modules are like subroutines (forms). They encapsulate program code and data. You can only access data from the function module's interface. However, there are also considerable differences between function modules and normal subroutines:

- Function modules must be contained in a special type of program. These special programs are called *function pools*. Function modules may have access to a function pool's global data. A function pool that has function modules is also called a *function group*.

- You can use a function module's name to call it from other programs. The function pool does not have to be specified in these programs. This means that function modules must have unique names throughout the system.

- You use a specially designed maintenance transaction (transaction SE37) to maintain function modules independently of the function pool.

- Function modules have a precisely defined interface that you can also provide with documentation. You can extend this interface under certain special circumstances without having to modify the existing programs used to call the function module.

- It is easier to check and maintain function modules in a test environment. For each module, you can store test data that is then used to check how a function module behaves after it has been modified.

3.9.1 Generating function modules

As in the previous sections, this section first describes how you generate a function group and a simple function module. It also demonstrates the test environment. You will find more detailed information in the section that follows.

When you generate a new function module, you must first specify which function group it belongs to. If no suitable function group exists, you must create one. Just like other development objects, you can generate function groups and function modules in different ways. In the end, all these methods will bring you to the same tool: the function module editor. You access this tool directly with transaction code SE37 or from SAP Workbench's main menu, by clicking on the corresponding pushbutton or by choosing DEVELOPMENT | FUNCTION BUILDER from the menu.

Once again, the simplest way to generate a function module is to use the Object Browser. The Object Browser's initial screen provides a separate input field for function groups. You enter the name of the function group in this field. You can use any name you want, although the first letter should comply with the conventions that have already been described (A-X for SAP, Y and Z for customer developments or reserved naming range). The system creates the function pool's name from the SAPL character string followed by the name of the function group. In this example, we use YZZ1 as the name of the function group. The Y is predefined and the 1 represents the first function group. The second and third characters, in this case ZZ, should be used to identify a particular user if this example is used by several programmers. Figure 3.161 shows the Repository Browser's initial screen at this point in time.

After you click on the DISPLAY pushbutton, the Object Browser creates the object list for existing function groups. If the function group you want does not exist, the Object Browser creates it. To do this, it displays a number of dialog boxes, i.e. the dialog boxes for the transport management system. In one of these dialog boxes, you enter a short description of the function group (see Figure 3.162).

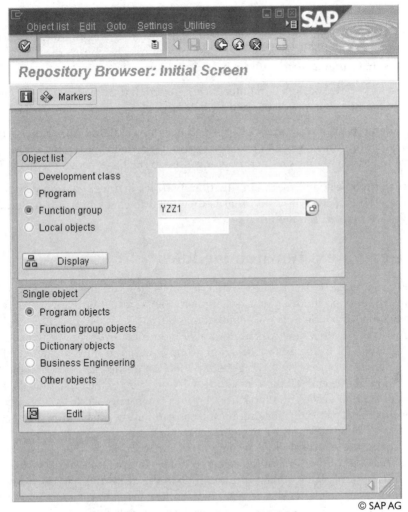

© SAP AG

Figure 3.161   Repository Browser's initial screen

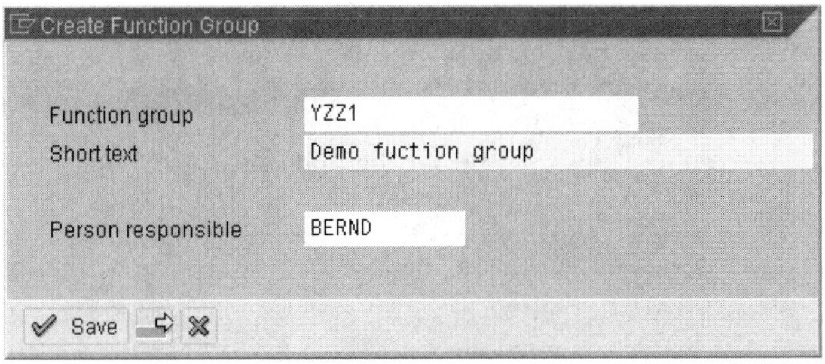

© SAP AG

Figure 3.162   Entering the short description of a new function group

The Object Browser now automatically creates the function group. Right from the start, this function group contains two include files. Figure 3.163 shows the function group's object list. You name the include files in a similar way to the include files in module pools. The name starts with an L, followed by the name of the function group. The end of the name consists of three characters that are almost always predefined by the system. However, unlike other program types, when you process function groups it is much less likely that you will have to create your own include files. This is because many are automatically generated by the system. In a newly created function group, you will always find a TOP include (here LYZZ1TOP) in which you enter declarations, and an include that

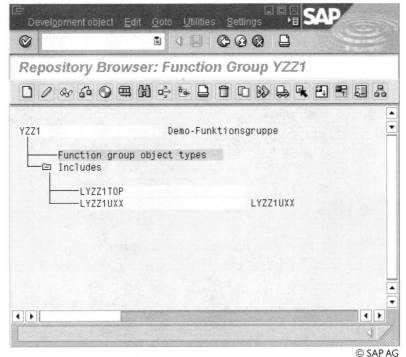

© SAP AG

Figure 3.163   Object list of a newly created function group

contains administration information. This always has the ending UXX. You cannot process this include manually. Each function module is stored in its own include, whose name is given the ending Unn, where nn represents a two-digit number. When you create a function module, the system generates these includes automatically.

The top include contains the program header and will later contain the data declarations. The data fields in the top include apply globally within the function group. You can either enter the declarations manually or create them from the function modules using the navigation function. When you access a function group for the first time from within an application, the system only initializes all the global fields of the function group the first time you call a function module. You can only make other changes to these fields by using the various function modules in the function group. The values of the global elements remain in effect until the calling application is closed.

It is very easy to create the individual function modules from the Repository Browser's object list. To do this, place the cursor on the function group's name. You then choose DEVELOPMENT OBJECT | CREATE from the menu, or press (F5) or click the corresponding icon to generate a new development object. Once again, you do this by entering the name of the function module you want to create in a dialog box (see Figure 3.164). This dialog box looks like the one used for dialog applications, but you enter different data in it.

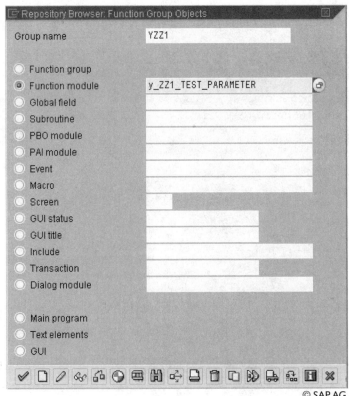

© SAP AG

Figure 3.164   Dialog box for generating a function module

In this dialog box, click on the Function module radio button and enter the module's name in the input field. Enter Y_ZZ1_TEST_PARAMETER as the name of the first module you want to create. The function module names must be unique throughout the entire R/3 System. That is why the function module names often start with the name of the function group. This makes it easier to identify them by avoiding confusion if you are dealing with similar-sounding names, but is not absolutely necessary. In addition to that, the actual descriptors of the function modules can show their functions clearly without you having to use special tricks or unusual abbreviations to assign clear unique names. Function modules that are generated in client systems must begin with the letters 'Y' or 'Z' and have an underscore '_' in the second position in their name.

The first function module is used to demonstrate the parameter interface and its characteristics. After you confirm your entry by clicking on the Create icon in the dialog box, the system prompts you to enter more data for the function module. You use two important tools to maintain a function module. One is the editor in which the source code is actually processed. The second tool provides a number of screen programs in a tabstrip in which you maintain administration information and the interface description. First of all, the system requests the administration information (see Figure 3.165).

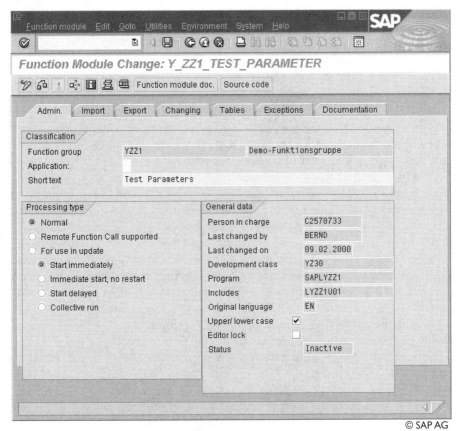

Figure 3.165   Function module administration information

This data refers to the short description, the application and the processing type. You must enter a short description. The APPLICATION field is only of secondary importance. For this reason, it is not a mandatory input field and can remain empty. The Normal entry is the default setting in the PROCESSING TYPE group. You must either set a new value for this entry or leave it unchanged. The next section will tell you about the background. The information you enter in this screen program has approximately the same meaning as the attributes in reports or screen programs. However, this information is described as *administration information* for function modules.

The system saves the data in the administration screen program. It then adds data to some of the status fields in the screen program. For example, it adds the name of the include file, in which the source code for the new function modules will be stored later on. Each function module is given its own include file. You should never process these files directly, for example with the standard editor (SE38). In particular, you must not delete them manually. You can only ensure that function groups remain consistent by processing them with the Object Browser or by processing function modules with transaction SE37. To maintain the parameter interface in the current screen program, select the corresponding tabs or the source code by clicking the appropriate pushbutton.

In simple subroutines (form routines), you code a number of statements when you declare the subroutine to determine the interface used to transfer data. In contrast, you define a function module's parameters in a few specially designed input templates. The parameter interface is divided into five subareas, each of which has a separate tab. These are three input templates for simple parameters (fields or structures), one for tables and one for exceptions. Initially we are only going to use simple parameters as part of this example. These parameters are divided into import, export and changing parameters. Figure 3.166 shows the input template for import parameters.

Each parameter is identified by a unique name within the function module. You enter this name in the IMPORT PARAMETER field. You can specify the parameter's data type in greater detail in the REF.FIELD/STRUCTURE OR REFERENCE TYPE fields. These entries are optional. The system handles any parameters that are not declared in more detail as a CHAR field. You can assign a default value (fixed value or system field) to any parameter. If you do not assign a value to the parameter when you call a function module, this default value will apply. The interface of a function module can be expanded later on. To ensure that you do not have to change module calls that you have already programmed later on, you can or must use a flag to mark the additional parameters as optional parameters. Parameters with default values automatically become optional parameters. When you call a function module, you can transfer a value for this kind of parameter, but this is not absolutely necessary. If you set the REFERENCE flag in the last column, the system is forced to save the transferred value temporarily. You must select this flag if you want to change an import parameter temporarily within the function module.

In the three tabs, you should generate the parameters shown in Table 3.43 for the first test.

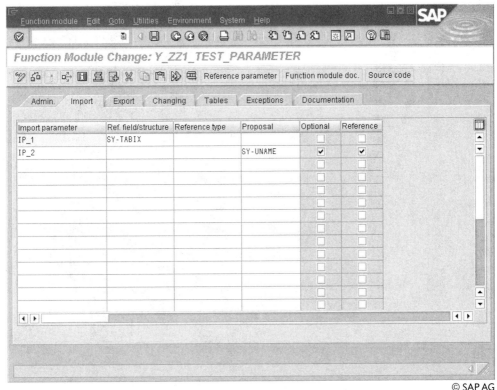

© SAP AG

Figure 3.166   Maintaining import parameters for a function module

Table 3.43   Parameters of the new function module

Parameter type	Parameter	Structure/field	Type	default	Optional	reference
Import	IP_1	SY-TABIX				
Import	IP_2			SY-UNAME	X	X
Changing	CP					
Export	EP_1	SY-TABIX				
Export	EP_2					

After you enter the parameters, the system saves the settings. You choose Goto |
F.module source code from the menu to call the editor in which you process the source
text. This editor operates in more or less the same way as the editor you are already
familiar with from transaction SE38. However, some of its pull-down menus are different
because they contain functions that are specific to each particular development object. For
function modules, the system first generates a framework that consists of the FUNCTION

and ENDFUNCTION statements. You enter the interface's description as comments in this framework. You can derive all the characteristics of the parameters that are set in the parameter screen from these comments in the interface. Of course, any changes you make to this comment do not influence the interface's structure.

You can now program a few statements in the function module. In this example, you only need to manipulate some of the data and assign values to the parameters. The complete source code of the function module, including the automatically generated comments, is shown below:

```
FUNCTION Y_ZZ1_TEST_PARAMETER.
*"----------------------------------------------
*"*"Local interface:
*"          IMPORTING
*"                VALUE(IP_1) LIKE SY-TABIX
*"                VALUE(IP_2) DEFAULT SY-UNAME
*"          EXPORTING
*"                VALUE(EP_1) LIKE SY-TABIX
*"                VALUE(EP_2)
*"          CHANGING
*"                VALUE(CP)
*"----------------------------------------------

  ep_1 = ip_1 * 5.
  ep_2 = ip_2.
  cp = cp + ep_1.

  ip_1 = 9999.          "No effect on calling program

ENDFUNCTION.
```

In this example, new values are assigned to the output parameters. These new values result directly or indirectly from the import parameters so that you can see how they are evaluated. You can test the function module directly from the development environment, just like you test a report. However, just like a report, you must activate a function module before you execute it. You can usually do this directly from the editor for an individual function module. As the function group was also newly created in this example and has therefore not been activated yet, you must return to the function group's object list in the Repository Browser and activate both the function group and the function module there. To do this, place the cursor on the name of the function group and then choose DEVELOPMENT OBJECT | GENERATE/ACTIVATE from the menu. Alternatively, click the appropriate icon or press (Ctrl)(Shift)(F8).

The activation of function modules is dependent on the general procedure for administering active and inactive program sources. This means that each time you modify a function module, you must activate it so that these changes can take effect. This is the major difference between this Release and previous Releases, in which you could not manage inactive source texts. In these systems, you also had to activate function modules, but this procedure was more like releasing the function modules. You only had to carry out this activation once. Any changes to the source code did not require repeated activation.

After you have activated the function module successfully, you can now test it. To do this, place the cursor on the function module's name in the Repository Browser's object list and choose DEVELOPMENT OBJECT | TEST/EXECUTE from the menu. You jump to the test environment for function modules. Alternatively, press (F8) or click the TEST/EXECUTE icon in the application toolbar. From the module's source code you can jump to the test environment by choosing UTILITIES | TEST ENVIRONMENT from the menu. The test environment's initial screen program (Figure 3.167) contains input fields for all the import and changing parameters of the module to be tested. The fields are filled with the default values that you declared in the interface. The width of each input field depends on the data type. The system provides quite a wide input field for parameters whose type is not defined (in this case for the CP changing parameter). In this way, the system deviates from the default length of 1 for data fields without type definition in the case of function module parameters.

All parameters that have default values are filled with those default values in the input screen. You can, of course, overwrite the defaults. The screen programs in the test environment use embedded list processing with interactive elements. This makes it easy to adapt the user interface to the interfaces of a wide variety of function modules. After you have entered the test values, press (F8) or click the corresponding icon to start the test. After processing is complete, the system displays the return parameters in a second screen program in the test environment (see Figure 3.168). You can easily use the function module to process parameters. In this case, you should be aware that you have to move the visible part of the image to the right edge with the scroll bars if you want to see the result of the changing parameter.

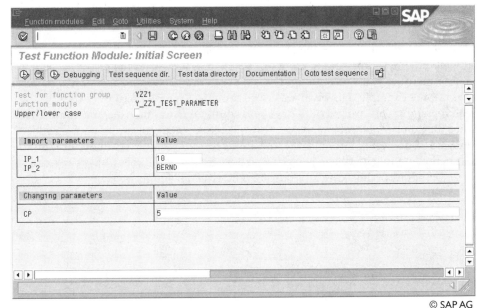

Figure 3.167   Test environment for function modules: input screen

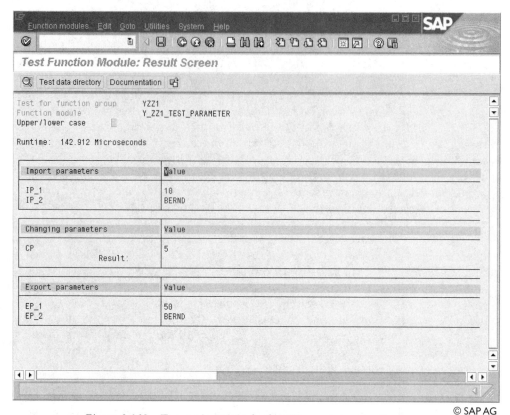

© SAP AG

Figure 3.168   Test environment for function modules: results screen

The results screen displays the current parameter values. The two export parameters that were previously missing in the input screen also appear in the results screen. In the function module, you can reassign the import parameters in certain cases, as demonstrated in the example. However this does not affect the fields in the calling program. These reassignments are only effective within the function module and can be used to reduce the number of local data fields. However, this is not good programming style.

Instead of the test environment, you can of course also use a small application to call the function module you have just generated. A good way of doing this is to use a separate report or one of the demo programs for embedded list processing:

```
REPORT yz337010.
DATA:  x TYPE i VALUE 2,
       y TYPE i VALUE 3,
       n TYPE i,
       s(20).
```

```
CALL FUNCTION 'Y_ZZ1_TEST_PARAMETER'
      EXPORTING
            ip_1 = x
            ip_2 = 'MEIER'
      IMPORTING
            ep_1 = n
            ep_2 = s
      CHANGING
            cp = y.

WRITE: / n,
       / s,
       / y.
```

At this point, you should pay special attention to how the terms *import* and *export* are used. Data that is received by a function module, i.e. imported, must be sent by the calling program, i.e. exported. During a call, the function module's import parameters therefore appear under the EXPORTING statement. In contrast, the parameters declared as export parameters in the function module are marked as IMPORTING.

All formal parameters that return values to the calling program must have data fields assigned to them as current parameters. You can also assign direct values to all the parameters that are merely used to transfer values to the module.

3.9.2 Function modules in detail

In ABAP applications, function modules are used for a wide variety of different tasks. Consequently, the characteristics you can set for function modules are just as numerous. The way you program a module must also be adapted to suit the intended purpose. Before some of our examples illustrate how you program and use function modules, the next section will provide you with the basic knowledge you will require.

Processing types

When you create a new module, you must choose one of the available processing types (see Figure 3.165). These function types have an enormous influence on how a function module is processed. A Normal-type module is the original form of function modules. You call it from applications and it is executed immediately. You can only continue the calling program after the function module has been completely processed. In this type of call, the called function module must be present within the current R/3 System. Using the RFC (Remote Function Call) *mechanism,* you can call and execute function modules in other systems. This makes it possible for different SAP systems to communicate with each other and exchange data. In this case, the systems involved may have different R/3 Releases and maintenance levels. In certain situations, you can even communicate with non-SAP systems. Function modules that you want to call from other systems must be of the REMOTE FUNCTION CALL supported type.

All other function types are designed for *update tasks*. Update tasks are special function modules that require you to enter specific data both when you declare them and when you call them again. Making changes to the database, i.e. writing data to the database, requires a certain amount of time. If many tables are affected by the changes and these changes in turn trigger further actions (i.e. updating indexes or search help), the time required may become so long that dialog processing becomes almost impossible, because the application has to wait until the writing process has finished. For this reason, more complex database changes are not executed at the same time as the rest of the program, but are instead moved to update modules that run asynchronously. These modules are only executed if the calling program triggers a COMMIT WORK statement. During the call, they are identified with this next addition:

```
...  IN UPDATE TASK.
```

When you call a module that is marked like this, the system automatically saves the transferred parameters without executing the function module. You can also call the module repeatedly with different values for the parameters each time. The system only executes the updates and transfers the correct parameters to them if you use a COMMIT WORK statement. This type of execution is very useful because it transfers the parameters just like in other function modules. You can even design and test update modules as normal function modules to start with and only transform them into genuine updates later on.

Because updates do not run at the same time as the calling application, they cannot return values. They must therefore not contain any export parameters. However, if processing errors occur, the updates can trigger error messages which still appear in various error logs, although they cannot be output in the calling application.

The main difference between the various update function types is the time at which they are processed. The system immediately executes updates of the type START IMMEDIATELY and IMMEDIATE START, NO RESTART. Here the calling program does not wait for these update tasks to be complete, but continues to run. Both processes therefore run in parallel with each other. This type of update task is also called a V1 update. Because the system stores the data to be updated internally, you can usually repeat a failed update process. You will require the second function type if you want to prohibit (prevent) a repeated update.

The last two function types START DELAYED and COLLECTIVE RUN define updates that run with a time delay. Here you can move the starting point to times when the system is not busy. This type of update is also called a V2 update.

In the case of all asynchronous updates, you must be aware that you cannot predefine the exact time at which the update occurs. It may happen that, although a record has been written by a transaction, an application that started later is unable to find this record because the update has not yet been processed. You must take these effects into account when you program your own applications, where you often have to make compromises about the current status of the data and application performance.

Parameters

Parameters are used to exchange data between the function module and the calling application. Here the parameters are identified by their names. When you call a function

module, the transfer values (current parameters) are assigned directly to the formal parameters named in the interface. This means that the sequence of the parameters is of no
importance when you call a function module.

There are three types of function module parameters. These are simple data fields or
structures, tables and exceptions. A simple data field contains the subgroups import,
export and changing parameters. These parameters can have different characteristics and
attributes. The attributes are described first below. However, not all attributes are available for all parameter types. You set the attributes in the parameters screen.

You can assign a type description to the formal parameters in a function module's
interface. If you do this, the system carries out a check when the application is running to
see whether the type or the characteristics of the current parameter match the formal
parameter. If they do not, the control logic will generate a runtime error.

Function module parameters are usually only local, i.e. they only apply within the
function module. However, you can choose EDIT | GLOBALIZE PARAMETERS from the menu
to globally broadcast a function module's interface to the entire function group. If you do
this, no other global data with the same name may be present in the function group. In
contrast to other global data, the contents of a function module's global interface are only
known in the period between when the module is called and it is left. To prevent an inter-
face from being globally applicable, choose EDIT | LOCALIZE PARAMETERS from the menu.

In some cases, global interfaces make it easier to access data, especially if the function
group contains screen programs that are used to access the parameters of a function
module. However, global interfaces contravene the usual rules concerning the validity of
data and can quickly lead to programs becoming confusing and give rise to undesirable
side effects. Therefore it is safer to ignore global interfaces and to copy the contents of the
parameters into the global data fields in the function group instead.

Parameter name

A *parameter name* is used to identify a parameter. You create this name in accordance with
the naming conventions for data fields. To improve your overview of the data it is sometimes but not absolutely necessary to show the parameter's type (import, export,
changing, table) by defining a prefix. Because changing parameters have only been in
existence since Release 3.0, but recursive calls still require data fields that act both as
import and export parameters, you can create import and export parameters with identical names. If you do this, the parameters must have the same data type. In addition, you
must also set the REFERENCE flag.

Reference structure

When you declare data fields, you can use the LIKE statement to cause them to take on
the data type and some other characteristics of existing fields or structures. You can also
describe function module parameters in more detail in this way. To do this, enter the template field or the structure in the REF.FIELD/STRUCTURE attribute or the REFERENCE TYPE
attribute. The name of the attribute depends on the actual tab involved. Table parameters
can only be described by a structure.

In the function module's source code, you use the LIKE or STRUCTURE statements to
refer to the kind of type assignment in the additional comments that describe the interface.

Reference type

From Release 3.0 onwards, you can declare types in ABAP. You can enter these types directly in programs. You can also move them into type pools. You use this next statement to include these type pools in an application:

TYPE-POOL `type-pool`.

If you do this within the framework program of a function group, you can also declare parameters that reference data types from this type pool.

Proposal

You can give simple parameters a default value. The system uses this value if no specific value has been assigned to a parameter when the function module is called in a program. The default value can either be a constant of the particular data type or one of the (SY-...) system fields. Although you can enter a field in the program, i.e. from the global data area of the function group, it has no effect at all when the function module is executed.

Optional

Where this flag has been set, you do not necessarily have to assign all the parameters a value when the function module is called. These parameters are therefore optional. If you change the interface of a module that has already been used in programs and the new parameters are marked as optional, you do not have to change the existing calls. The system automatically handles all the parameters that have a default value as optional parameters. If a mandatory parameter assignment is missing when you call a module, the system issues a runtime error.

Reference

When they transfer parameters to a subroutine, some commonly used programming languages such as C or Pascal distinguish between value and reference parameters. For value parameters, the value of the current parameter is copied into a local data area to which the formal parameter then points. If the value of the formal parameter is changed in the function module, this does not affect the value of the current parameter. When parameters are transferred by a reference, the formal parameter refers directly to the contents of the current parameter. This also means that any changes to the formal parameter have a direct effect on the current parameter. You use the REFERENCE FLAG to define the type of parameter transfer for simple parameters in function modules. Tables are always transferred as reference parameters.

In ABAP, reference parameters are not functionally necessary for function modules. The concept of import and export parameters ensures that values are transferred to the calling program anyway. Despite this, transfers with a reference save memory and make the application run slightly faster because the system does not need to copy data. For this reason, tables have always been transferred as a reference.

If an exception is triggered in the function module, you must be aware that reference parameters have one special feature. This feature is approximately similar to the trigger-

ing of a message in screen programs. The processing of the function module stops immediately and the calling program continues from the point at which the function module
was called. All the values assigned to reference parameters become effective immediately
they are assigned. This means they remain effective, even if the function module is closed
with an exception after they are assigned. On the other hand, value parameters are only
transferred if the function module has been closed correctly.

The description of the attributes below is followed by an explanation of the different
parameter types.

Import parameters

Import parameters are used to transfer data to the function module. If these parameters are
value parameters, you can give them new values in the function module because the current parameter's value does not change when it is assigned to a value parameter. However,
if you assign new values to import reference parameters, the system triggers a runtime
error. This is because this assignment would change the value of the current parameter.

When you call the function module, you can assign both direct values and data fields
to the import parameters. It makes no difference if the import parameter is a value or reference parameter. This procedure is rather unusual in comparison with the procedures
used in other compilable programming languages. In these languages, the compiler
writes direct values directly into the generated machine code. No memory is reserved for
them in the data area and therefore you cannot transfer the values with a reference. For
import parameters, you can set all the attributes mentioned above.

Export parameters

The function module uses the export parameters to return results to the calling program.
Values are assigned to the export parameters in the function module. After the function
module has been processed, the system transfers the contents of the export parameter to
the current parameters and therefore changes their values. You can also read the export
parameters in a function module and then use them on the right-hand side of assignments. However, this is only a good idea once the export parameter has been given a
correct value. Prior to this, its contents are not defined because no data has been transferred from the current parameter to the export parameter.

Automatically, export parameters are optional parameters that do not have to be evaluated.
When you call a function module, you can comments out or delete all unnecessary export
parameters. You cannot set default values for export parameters in the interface definition.

Changing parameters

Changing parameters identify the characteristics of import and export parameters. They
take on the value of the current parameter and make it available to the function module.
If you make an assignment to a changing parameter, the value is transferred to the current parameter after the function module has been processed. You can also use all the
previously described attributes for changing parameters as well as for input parameters.

Table parameters

You use the TABLES parameter type to transfer internal tables to the function module. A transfer is always performed as a reference parameter. Any changes to the function module also take immediate effect in the table. From Release 3.0 onwards, you can label tables as optional. This was not possible prior to Release 2.2. In any case, you must create table parameters with reference to a structure or a data type.

Exceptions

Unexpected events can occur when you process a function module. The calling program must be informed about these events. For example, the system may attempt to read data from or write data to records that have already been locked by other programs or that do not exist at all. Because different applications can each call a function module in a different context, it is often impossible to react correctly to such events in function modules. You can therefore use exceptions to send error statuses to the calling program. The possible exceptions are defined in the function module's interface. These are names that describe the exception. You do not need any other entries or attributes. You should use clear and unique descriptors such as NOT_FOUND or RECORD_LOCKED for exceptions to make it easier for the function module's user to evaluate the exceptions. The way these exceptions are handled technically from a programming viewpoint is described in the next section.

Handling exceptions

For a number of reasons, function modules are often not supposed to react to unexpected events themselves, but should leave this to the calling program. This is why function modules must inform the calling program about errors or unexpected events in a suitable manner. This information should be as transparent as possible and a flexible transfer mechanism should be used. In addition, you must ensure that exceptional situations really are processed and do not remain undiscovered. The exception handling procedure carries out all these tasks. Its functions are much more extensive than a simple return value.

The system executes the exceptions in the function module's interface. In the function module itself, they appear as predefined descriptors. The ABAP statements that trigger exceptions use these descriptors. When a programmer calls a function module, they can decide which of the possible exceptions they would like to handle themselves. To do this, the programmer assigns a numerical value to the exceptions they want to process.

If a function module triggers an exception that should be handled in the calling program, the system closes the function module and places the number of the exception in the SY-SUBRC field. This system field can then be evaluated in the calling program. Assigning a number to the exception is enough to signal to the function module that this exception will be handled in the calling program. However, the function module cannot check whether the calling program actually reacts to the exception.

The triggering method in the function module defines how a function module reacts to exceptions that are not evaluated by the calling program. Exceptions must be triggered explicitly; they do not emerge automatically when a problem occurs. You use the next two statements to do this. You use this statement to trigger an exception:

RAISE *exception*.

If the calling program deals with this exception, it will be handled in the way described above. However, if the exception is not dealt with, the system generates a run-time error. The next method of generating exceptions is slightly less strict. To do this, you add the following addition to the MESSAGE statement:

MESSAGE ... RAISING *exception*.

Now the function module no longer reacts to an exception that has not been handled with a runtime error. Instead, it sends the message defined in the MESSAGE statement. An exception that is handled by the calling program is processed in the manner described above. However, the system also fills a few additional system fields, besides SY-SUBRC. The message class that applies to the MESSAGE statement is transferred into the SY-MSGID field. In the same way, the system enters the message type in the SY-MSGTY field and enters the actual message number in SY-MSGNO. You use the WITH addition to transfer up to four parameters to a MESSAGE-RAISING statement. These parameters then appear in the error message text instead of a series of placeholders. If these parameters are present, they are transferred into the SY-MSGV1 to SY-MSGV4 system fields. This is how the calling program is provided with all the information it requires to enable it to call the error message on its own, if necessary.

You do not need to assign a unique value to the exceptions when you call a function module. You can assign the same value to several exceptions. However, after one of these exceptions has been triggered, the calling program can no longer tell which exception has been triggered in the function module. If you do not require this distinction, simply program in the exceptions to be handled after EXCEPTIONS and do not assign a value. The system later returns a value for these exceptions which is undefined, but does not equal 0. No value is assigned to any of the exceptions that do not have to be handled. You must either comment out these values or delete them from the call. The OTHERS addition works in a similar way. When you call the function module, this exception (which is predefined by the system) is used to name all the function module's exceptions that have not been listed individually. You can also use this exception with or without an assigned value.

Sometimes you may not want function modules to use MESSAGE to trigger messages themselves. You can prevent this even if a message is sent in the function module, by programming a simple MESSAGE statement without the RAISING addition. To do this, use the predefined ERROR_MESSAGE exception when you call the module. If this exception has been set, all the E and A messages in the function module will automatically trigger the ERROR_MESSAGE exception. All other messages will be suppressed.

The program below demonstrates how you use the different exceptions in greater detail. First you generate a new Normal function-type function module in the function group you have already used. This is relatively easy to create. You can work out the interface structure from the comment in the source code. The input parameter is a parameter called A that is derived from the SY-TABIX field.

Exceptions are maintained in a separate tab in the interface definition. This mask only contains one input column. All the exceptions are listed in this column (Figure 3.169).

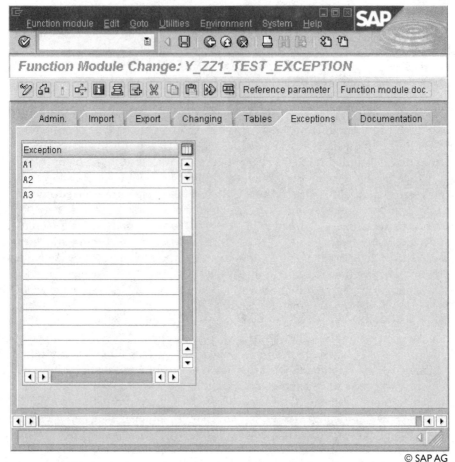

© SAP AG

Figure 3.169   Maintaining the exceptions of a function module

The source code of the second module is also relatively simple. Depending on the value of the input parameter, different exceptions are triggered with different variants of the MESSAGE statement:

```
FUNCTION Y_ZZ1_TEST_EXCEPTION.
*"----------------------------------------------
*"*"Local interface:
*"        IMPORTING
*"            VALUE(A) LIKE SY-TABIX DEFAULT 1
*"        EXCEPTIONS
*"            A1
*"            A2
*"            A3
*"----------------------------------------------
```

```
CASE A.
  WHEN 1.
    RAISE A1.
  WHEN 2.
    MESSAGE ID 'YY' TYPE 'I' NUMBER '002' RAISING A2.
  WHEN 3.
    MESSAGE ID 'YY' TYPE 'E' NUMBER '003' RAISING A3.
  WHEN 4.
    MESSAGE ID 'YY' TYPE 'I' NUMBER '000'.
  WHEN 5.
    MESSAGE ID 'YY' TYPE 'E' NUMBER '000'.
  ENDCASE.
ENDFUNCTION.
```

In the following report, the module is called with several types of exception handling. The number of the exception to be triggered is compared with the SY-SUBRC return code.

```
REPORT yz337020 NO STANDARD PAGE HEADING.

* Combined interception of several exceptions
WRITE: / 'Combined exception interception' COLOR 5.
DO 3 TIMES.
  CALL FUNCTION 'Y_ZZ1_TEST_EXCEPTION'
    EXPORTING
      a = sy-index
    EXCEPTIONS
      a1
      a2
      a3.

  WRITE: / 'Exception:', (4)sy-index, 'SY-SUBRC', (4)sy-subrc.
ENDDO.

* Selective interception of one exception + Message in the FB
WRITE: /, / 'Selective interception' COLOR 5.
DO 4 TIMES.
  CALL FUNCTION 'Y_ZZ1_TEST_EXCEPTION'
    EXPORTING
      a = sy-index
    EXCEPTIONS
      a1 = 11
      a2 = 12
      a3 = 13.

  WRITE: / 'Exception:', (4)sy-index, 'SY-SUBRC', (4)sy-subrc.
ENDDO.
```

```
* Use of OTHERS and ERROR-MESSAGE
WRITE: /, / 'OTHERS and ERROR_MESSAGE' COLOR 5.
DO 5 TIMES.
   CALL FUNCTION 'Y_ZZ1_TEST_EXCEPTION'
      EXPORTING
         a                  = sy-index
      EXCEPTIONS
         a2                 = 1
         error_message      = 33
         OTHERS             = 99.

   WRITE: / 'Exception:', (4)sy-index, 'SY-SUBRC', (4)sy-subrc.
ENDDO.
```

The three genuine exceptions and the type I message are triggered sequentially in the first DO loop. Although the three exceptions are handled by the calling program, no individual number is given to the exceptions. The output in the report shows that a value of 1 is returned for all three exceptions in SY-SUBRC. In this way, you can determine that an exception was generated in the function module. However, you cannot tell which this exception is. You can only identify the specific exception if you assign values to them, as you can see in the second loop. You can assign any value to the exceptions. However, you usually use sequential numbers instead of the arbitrary values used in the example. In the loop, the function module displays yet another message. As this message has type I , it is displayed as a dialog box that has to be confirmed. This message type does not cause the program to terminate. That is why the 0 appears as a return value in the report.

The statements in the third loop demonstrate the OTHERS and ERROR_MESSAGE additions. The second exception is dealt with separately. For this exception, return code 1 appears in the report. The OTHERS statement assigns the value 99 to all exceptions that are not executed explicitly, in this case A1 and A3. You use the ERROR_MESSAGE statement you prevent any type of error message from being sent. Neither the info dialog box nor the genuine error message that was triggered with parameter 5 will be displayed. However, this latter parameter places the value of the ERROR_MESSAGE exception into the SY-SUBRC field.

It is impossible to illustrate the additional attributes of exception handling, because they would close the program. For example, this happens if exceptions are triggered that are not intercepted by the calling program. Therefore, you should use the following method to call the function module in another report that you create yourself. You must save it each time, before you start the report!

```
CALL FUNCTION 'YZ31_TEST_EXCEPTION'
   EXPORTING
      a = 1. " after each other 1 until / up to 3
```

Calling function modules

You use the following statement to call function modules:

`CALL` *function* ... .

You must enclose the function module's name in single quotation marks. You must enter the name in upper-case letters, or else the system will not be able to find the function module. In the statement, you must list all the parameters you want to transfer. You must also use the `EXPORTING`, `IMPORTING`, `CHANGING`, `TABLES` and `EXCEPTIONS` statements to name the individual parameter groups. The ABAP program editor provides a utility that lets you insert an entire statement; this is because the interfaces of function modules can be extremely large. You can choose EDIT | INSERT STATEMENT from the menu to call a help function that can insert several complex statements into the source code. In a dialog box (Figure 3.170), the system first prompts you to enter data about the object you want to insert.

In this dialog box, select the `CALL FUNCTION` check box. In the associated input field, enter the name of the module you want to insert. If you do not know the correct way to spell the name, press (F4) to call the input help.

You then press (Enter) or click the corresponding icon to confirm the data you have entered. The system then inserts a complete statement for calling the module into the source code. This call contains all the function module's parameters. Each of these parameters stands in its own line. The system also transfers all the optional parameters into the source code, but then disables them (they are commented out). If necessary, you can

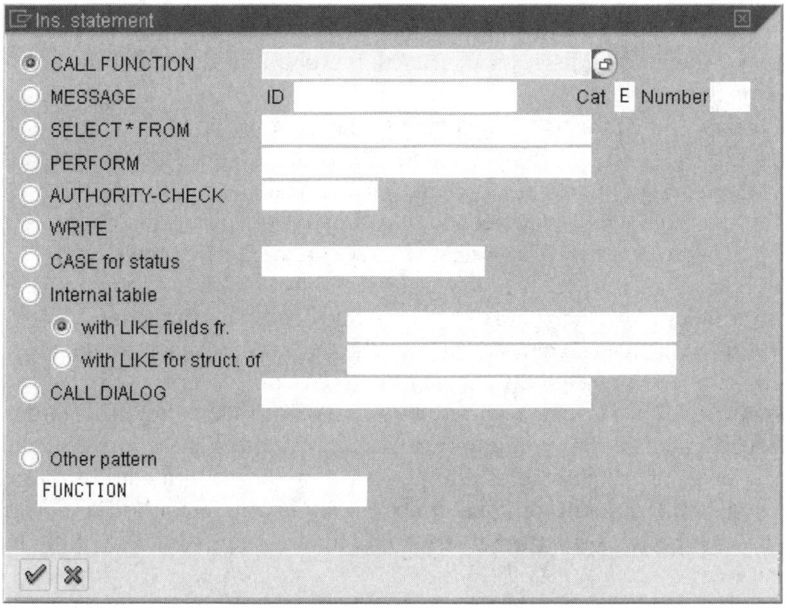

Figure 3.170   Dialog box for inserting a function module call into a program

activate these optional parameters by removing the comment characters and assigning a current parameter. If parameters have default values, the system enters these values in the assignment. Because this type of parameter is optional by default, it will of course also be disabled. You only include them in the call if you want to transfer a value that is not the default value. Disabled lines may remain in the source code. This makes it easy to carry out modifications later because you simply remove the comment character and then assign a value.

Mandatory parameters are located in genuine statement lines that are not marked as comments. However, because no value has been assigned, the system would display an error when you started the program or when it carried out a separate syntax check.

All the exceptions declared in the function module are also located in the call that the system generates automatically. The system assigns a sequential number to these exceptions. If you do not want an exception to be handled you can disable it. The programmer can change these assigned numbers quite easily.

Sometimes, this automatic disabling function causes minor errors. If all parameters are optional in one of the parameter groups, you must manually disable the particular group identifier (i.e. EXPORTING or TABLES). This is because this kind of statement without any subsequent parameters would cause a syntax error.

In addition to the simple call, as shown in the current examples, the CALL FUNCTION statement has more additions that either call special function types or ensure that the function module you call is executed in a particular way. At this point, we only want to mention the IN UPDATE TASK addition. You will need this addition to calldate function modules.

Documentation

Because function modules are often designed for use in more than one application, the documentation for the module itself for the function group as a whole and for the individual parameters is of considerable importance. A potential user should be able to get enough information about how to use the function module from the documentation for the associated components, instead of having to analyze the source code. This is why all the function modules that are designed to be used on more than one platform must be thoroughly documented. You can call the tools you need for creating this documentation at several points in the development environment. This section focuses on the Object Browser.

You can document a function group from the object list in the function group. To do this, place the cursor on the function group's name and then choose EDIT | DOCUMENTATION | CHANGE. from the menu. The Object Browser now displays a special editor (SAPscript Editor, see Figure 3.171) in which you can enter detailed documentation. This editor also works on a line-by-line basis, but this is the only feature it shares with the program editor that you otherwise use. These editors are fundamentally different, both in terms of the principles that govern how they operate and in terms of how you actually use them (menu options, function key layout, etc.). You use the SAPscript Editor to assign special formatting instructions to documents (visible at the left margin of the input area).

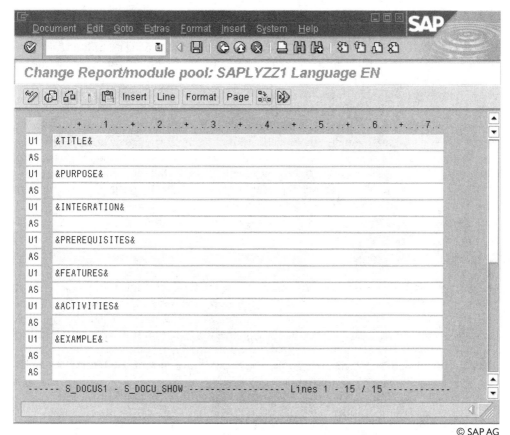

© SAP AG

Figure 3.171   Editor for maintaining a function group's documentation

You can also create documentation for the individual function modules. To do this, select a tab in the tabstrip in the administration screen program. In this input template you can assign a short, descriptive text to each parameter and each exception. You can also maintain the short text for a function module here. Double-click on one of the input fields to return to the SAPscript Editor in which you can enter a longer text.

3.9.3 Dialog modules

Dialog modules are like normal dialog transactions that have been encapsulated and can now only be accessed by using a precisely defined interface to exchange data. In this respect they are similar to function modules. However, one or more dialog modules are assigned to a module pool instead of to the function pool. This module pool contains the same elements as a normal dialog application, i.e. an interface, screen programs and modules. However it has nothing in common with *function groups*.

Apart from defining the dialog module's interface, you program it in the same way as a normal dialog application. Therefore you should first generate a module pool. You can also program the functionality, i.e. create screen programs and their associated modules. You then call the administration tool for dialog modules from the initial screen of the Workbench. To do this, choose DEVELOPMENT | PROGRAMMING ENVIRONMENT | DIALOG MODULE from the menu or enter transaction code SE35. In the administration tool for Dialog modules, you enter the name of the module, and click on the Create pushbutton to generate it. In the next screen program, you must enter the short description (as usual), the name of the module pool and the number of the initial screen program. You define the interface in other screen programs. This procedure is like the one you use to generate the function module interface, but the dialog module interface is far simpler.

Strictly speaking, dialog modules represent only one precisely defined call option for screen programs that you could otherwise also execute with the CALL SCREEN statement. This is why they are not used as often as function modules.

3.9.4 BAPIs

The way external programs access the resources of the R/3 System is rather complicated, although the RFC call of function modules does provide a simple technical solution to this. The reason for this lies in the complexity of the R/3 System and the fact that many of the applications are not integrated with others. The screen program concept also requires the internal functions to be integrated with the application's user interface. There are very few clearly defined interfaces that an external application might use to access specific resources from another application. However, this type of interface is absolutely essential for some programming techniques, such as some Internet connections or for linking programs from different vendors. From Release 3.1 onwards, SAP has provided what are known as BAPIs (Business Application Component Interfaces). Technically speaking, BAPIs are simply function modules that have RFC capability. They are designed to provide dialog-free application functions that refer to *business objects*. One of the aims of using BAPIs is to develop the visual interface separately from the application functions. BAPIs can be used both within the R/3 System, in ABAP tasks and also by external applications. For various reasons, BAPIs must be defined in the Business Object Repository as the methods of a business object.

As the development of BAPIs is currently in full swing at SAP, at this point we must refer you to SAP itself. There you can find out their current development status and obtain documentation. You will find all the most up-to-date information on SAP's world wide web server at www.sap.com.

Before you can use BAPIs in the way mentioned above, they must first meet certain requirements. These requirements also affect the applications that you program using BAPIs. They are described in brief below.

No-status requirement

BAPIs are supposed to execute an autonomous task in accordance with the 'all or nothing' principle. They should neither depend on the previous execution of other BAPIs nor leave behind a temporary system state that is a prerequisite for processing other BAPIs. Therefore they must not change any of the data fields in the global data area of their function group.

In practice, this functionality causes problems. For example, normal applications read a data record and simultaneously lock it to prevent it being processed by a third party. The user modifies the data record that is then written back to the table, which again unlocks the record. Under normal conditions, this form of processing does not cause any problems. However, because BAPIs do not have a dialog, the task cannot be carried out by one BAPI. You will require two BAPI calls, one for reading and the other for writing. As the no-status requirement means that the database must not be locked, there is no way of ensuring that the write access to the database can actually be executed. It is quite possible that the same record may be processed by another application at the same time. It is also possible that that record has been locked by a normal application. This means you must either make compromises that involve giving up some of the functionality, use a completely different programming method or alternatively make more compromises that affect the extent to which you comply with the no-status requirement.

Permanency

In contrast to the usual R/3 transactions that may sometimes change radically from one Release to the next, BAPIs must offer an interface that remains constant throughout several release cycles. This applies both to the actual technical interface and to the functionality. Otherwise, applications that use BAPIs would have to be checked and modified after each upgrade.

3.10 Function modules for general use

Many of the function modules in the R/3 System carry out tasks in more than one application. In this respect, they are like the default library provided by many other programming languages. Some important functions in the R/3 System are executed by function modules instead of by special ABAP statements. This section describes some of the most important programming techniques that are based on the use of function modules.

The examples described above have merely been used to demonstrate some characteristics of function modules. This section will present a few real-life application examples of how you use function modules.

3.10.1 Standardized dialogs

A number of default prompts are frequently required in one program. The SAP System's function library already contains a large number of this type of dialog. These dialogs meet the requirements of the SAP Style Guide. You can and indeed must use the function modules in separate applications to provide SAP System users with a uniform interface. Although the prompts are ultimately generated by a screen program, increased flexibility can be achieved by creating them as a function module. The function modules are divided into different task areas. They also belong to different function groups (SPO1 to SPO6 and STAB). There are the following different task areas:

- confirmation prompts;

- selection of alternatives;

- data entry;

- dialogs for printing;

- displaying text;

- displaying tables.

The simplest of the modules is POPUP_TO_CONFIRM_LOSS_OF_DATA. You use this module for example if you want to terminate processing in a screen program in an exit module without saving data. You will already have met this type of prompt several times during your work to date. This function module is very easy to use. This next listing shows an extract from a real program:

```
. . .
IF ( ( flg_action = c_yes ) OR ( sy-datar = 'X' ) ).
  CALL FUNCTION 'POPUP_TO_CONFIRM_LOSS_OF_DATA'
    EXPORTING
      textline1      = text-015          " Do you really want to
                                          " cancel?
"     textline2      = ' '
      title          = text-021          " Warning!
"     start_column   = 25
"     start_row      = 6
    IMPORTING
      answer         = l_answer.

  IF l_answer = 'J'.
    LEAVE TO SCREEN 0.
  ENDIF.
ELSE.
  LEAVE TO SCREEN 0.
ENDIF.
. . .
```

This example clearly shows how you use the module. Three of the parameters are mandatory. These are a text (TEXTLINE1), the title that appears in the dialog box title (TITLE) and the return parameter (ANSWER). The module uses the ANSWER parameter to return which of the two pushbuttons was activated in the dialog box. This value is either 'Y' or 'N'. The answer No is predefined as the default response in the module to ensure that the program is not terminated if the user presses (Enter) by mistake to confirm their entry in the dialog box. By analyzing this very simple module, both the source text and its other components such as the interface definition or documentation, you can gain some interesting insights into how it was programmed and also consolidate the knowledge you have already acquired.

Other function modules provide much more complex resources, but also require somewhat more involved programming. The following program, which is obviously more complicated, uses two function modules to input values and select records from a table. These function modules make it possible to generate the dialog box dynamically when a program is running, i.e. without using the Screen Painter. For a simple demonstration, the statements are first of all included in a report as a subroutine. You can use this subroutine without any modifications as input help at the PROCESS ON VALUE REQUEST event. To do this, simply call the subroutine from a POV module. The output of the selected value is then replaced by an assignment to a screen program field.

The input help should offer one dialog box in which you can enter a sample user name and another dialog box in which you enter a sample development object. Development objects are for example programs, tables or module pools. After you enter these two values, the application reads all the objects in the TADIR table that match the selection criteria you entered. It then lists these objects in a table in a second dialog box. In this dialog box, you can double-click on an entry to select it. This entry is then displayed in the actual report where you can check it.

Because the next listing is quite large, we have divided it into several sections to make its information clearer and easier to understand. Each section of the source code is separated from the next by explanations about that particular section. First of all, here is the actual main program: this simply consists of a few declarations, the subroutine call and the output of the selected entry.

```
REPORT yz337030 NO STANDARD PAGE HEADING.
TABLES tadir.

DATA: name LIKE tadir-obj_name,
      subrc LIKE sy-subrc.

PERFORM select_entry
  USING name subrc.

IF subrc = 0.
  WRITE: / 'Selection:', name.
ELSE.
  WRITE: / 'ERROR'.
ENDIF.
```

The selection process takes place in a subroutine:

```
FORM select_entry USING  p_name LIKE tadir-obj_name
                         p_subrc LIKE sy-subrc.

*...Fields for inputting the search terms
  DATA: l_name LIKE tadir-obj_name,    " Name of development object
        l_author LIKE tadir-author,    " Owner of the object
        l_returncode LIKE sy-tcode,    " Return code FB
        l_field_len TYPE i,            " Help field length
        l_lines TYPE i.                " Help field line counter
```

You must declare a few data fields at the start of the subroutine. The `TADIR` table which you want to evaluate has already been introduced in the main program. The names of the help fields all start with the prefix `L_`. This prefix identifies local fields. However, ABAP programs and in particular dialog-oriented applications make extensive use of global fields. The system often reads or writes to these global fields in subroutines, bypassing interfaces. You can make the data much clearer in an application by distinguishing between local and global fields.

```
*..Macro for declaring internal tables
  DEFINE defitab.
     data: begin of &1 occurs &3.
             include structure &2.
     data: end of &1.
  END-OF-DEFINITION.

*...Table containing input fields
  defitab i_inf helpval 10.

*...Table containing field descriptors for the list dialog box
  defitab i_tabf help_value 10.

*...Table containing data lines for the list dialog box
  DATA: BEGIN OF i_values OCCURS 100,
     lines(256) TYPE c,
  END OF i_values.
```

In addition to the simple data fields, you require three different internal tables which are used to supply the function modules with data. Two of these tables are derived from Data Dictionary structures (`HELPVAL` and `HELP_VALUE`). These structures must not be declared using `TABLES` if they are only used in the `INCLUDE STRUCTURE` statement. To ensure their descriptor is unique, the names of the internal tables are assigned the prefix `I_`. In the `I_INF` table, you enter the descriptors of the input fields in the first dialog box. The appropriate function module then returns the read values to this table. The two other tables define the structure of the list dialog box (`I_TABF`) and fill the fields of the table with values (`I_VALUES`). To save typing, a macro is used in the declaration.

```
*...Creation of the input template definition
  CLEAR i_inf.
  i_inf-tabname = 'TADIR'.
  i_inf-fieldname = 'OBJ_NAME'.
  i_inf-keyword = 'Development object'.
  DESCRIBE FIELD tadir-obj_name LENGTH l_field_len.
  i_inf-length = l_field_len.
  i_inf-value = '*'.                      " Default value
  i_inf-lowercase = ' '.
  APPEND i_inf.
```

```
CLEAR i_inf.
i_inf-tabname = 'TADIR'.
i_inf-fieldname = 'AUTHOR'.
i_inf-keyword = 'Person in charge'.
DESCRIBE FIELD tadir-author LENGTH l_field_len.
i_inf-length = l_field_len.
i_inf-value = sy-uname.            " Default value
i_inf-lowercase = ' '.
APPEND i_inf.
```

You use several parameters to ensure that the fields in the input dialog box have unique names. This naming replaces the definition of the fields in a screen program. As a result, the amount of required entries is correspondingly large. For each field in the mask, you must create a data record in the I_INF table. The TABNAME and FIELDNAME fields name a field from the Data Dictionary. The function module requires this Data Dictionary field to determine the correct structure statements. The system requires these entries to convert the type of the value you enter.

In the mask, each input field is described by a prefixed name that you enter in the KEYWORD field. The LENGTH field must contain the length you require for the input field. This value should be derived from the Data Dictionary. If you make your own modifications, you must ensure that they are not longer than the length specified in the Data Dictionary. If you make an entry in the LOWERCASE field, the system will process entries in both upper-case and lower-case letters. If you do not make an entry in the LOWERCASE field, the system automatically converts the values into upper-case letters. If the INTENS field is set, the field names appear in colour on the screen.

The VALUE field is the actual value field. The values it contains when you call a function module are displayed and edited. The function module returns the values you entered in the dialog box in this field.

```
CALL FUNCTION 'HELP_GET_VALUES'
        EXPORTING
"            cucol = 5
"            curow = 5
            popup_title = 'Search terms for development objects
        IMPORTING
            returncode = l_returncode
        TABLES
            fields = i_inf
        EXCEPTIONS
            no_entries = 01.

*...After correct input of values in program fields
  IF ( sy-subrc = 0 ) AND ( l_returncode = space ).
    LOOP AT i_inf.
```

```
     CASE i_inf-fieldname.
       WHEN 'OBJ_NAME'.
         l_name = i_inf-value.
         TRANSLATE l_name USING '*%+_'.

       WHEN 'AUTHOR'.
         l_author = i_inf-value.
         TRANSLATE l_author USING '*%+_'.
     ENDCASE.

   ENDLOOP.
 ELSE.
   WRITE: / 'Not correct input'.
 EXIT.
 ENDIF.
```

Calling the function module is relatively simple. To do this, choose EDIT | INSERT statement from the menu to insert the call into the source code. Then you complete the statement by entering a few parameters, i.e. the title and the previously created table with the field descriptions.

After the function module terminates, both SY-SUBRC and RETURNCODE will return information about how the function module was executed. If genuine errors occur, an exception is triggered that sets the SY-SUBRC field to a value other than 0. If the user terminates input, the RETURNCODE field will show a value other than SPACE.

After the function module has been called and closed correctly, the system places the values entered in the dialog box in the VALUE field in the internal table. You have to transfer these values from the table fields into local data fields of the program so that you can use them later in the program. You do this in a LOOP by using table I_INF. In this loop, the system evaluates the FIELDNAME field to assign the value in the VALUE field to the correct data field in the program. After this data has been transferred, the system converts any sample characters present. The user is generally used to working with the characters '*' and '+'. The SELECT statement's LIKE operator now expects the characters '%' and '_' instead.

```
*...Fill the table with the individual fields,
*...a record for each field
*...Sequence: 1. line, 1. field; 1. line, 2. field;
*...2. line, 1. field ...
  SELECT * FROM tadir
  WHERE obj_name LIKE l_name
    AND author LIKE l_author.

    i_values = tadir-obj_name. APPEND i_values.
    i_values = tadir-pgmid. APPEND i_values.
    i_values = tadir-object. APPEND i_values.
```

```
ENDSELECT.

IF sy-dbcnt = 0.
  WRITE: / 'No development objects found.
  EXIT.
ENDIF.
```

After the system has loaded the search terms, you can now launch the search in the database. The system must transfer each field value for the records it finds individually into the I_VALUES table. These values must be transferred in a way that conforms to the structure of the table in the list dialog box defined below. If the SELECT statement cannot find any records, it closes the program.

```
*...Creation of selection list

*...Fill the table for column names
*...First column 1 for the object name
  i_tabf-tabname = 'TADIR'.
  i_tabf-fieldname = 'OBJ_NAME'.
  i_tabf-selectflag = 'X'. " Selection field, will be returned
  APPEND i_tabf.

*...Following that, column 2 for object group
  i_tabf-tabname = 'TADIR'.
  i_tabf-fieldname = 'PGMID'.
  i_tabf-selectflag = ' '.
  APPEND i_tabf.

*...Finally column 3 for object type
  i_tabf-tabname = 'TADIR'.
  i_tabf-fieldname = 'OBJECT'.
  i_tabf-selectflag = ' '.
  APPEND i_tabf.
```

The second function module generates a dialog box which contains a list. To achieve this, you must provide the function module with the list's structure. This structure must correspond with the contents of the I_VALUES table. In particular, the number of columns in the table must match the number of values written from a record into I_VALUES. This is because the fields in the table will later be filled line by line by values from the I_VALUES table and without further checks. Declaring the table is simple; you simply transfer the table name and the field name so that the function module can gather type definitions from the Data Dictionary. One column in the table can have a special meaning. You mark that column by setting the SELECTFLAG field. When you select a line in the table, the system returns the contents of this highlighted column to the calling program.

```
*...Call function module that generates the selection list
  CALL FUNCTION 'HELP_VALUES_GET_WITH_TABLE'
"        EXPORTING
"            cucol                                = 0
"            curow                                = 0
"            display                              = ' '
"            fieldname                            = ' '
"            tabname                              = ' '
"            no_marking_of_checkvalue             = ' '
"            title_in_values_list                 = ' '
"            title                                = ' '
"            show_all_values_at_first_time        = ' '
         IMPORTING
             select_value                         = l_name
         TABLES
             fields                               = i_tabf
             valuetab                             = i_values
         EXCEPTIONS
             field_not_in_ddic                    = 01
             more_then_one_selectfield            = 02
             no_selectfield                       = 03.

  p_subrc = sy-subrc.
  p_name = l_name.

ENDFORM.
```

You complete the application by calling the second function module. You can use more parameters to modify the application. However, under normal circumstances all you need to do is transfer the two internal tables and assign a data field for the return code. The entry provided by this function module and a copy of the SY-SUBRC field are assigned to the parameters of the subprogram and returned to the calling program in this way.

3.10.2 Reading screen program fields

The example shown above introduces a different problem. Input helps that operate in accordance with the principle described above require the user to input values. The user may already have entered a value in the screen program that could now be used as a search term. However, at the PROCESS ON VALUE REQUEST event, the values contained in the screen program have not yet been transferred to the program's internal fields. Nevertheless, even this problem can be solved by using a special function module. Using this function module, values can be read directly from a screen program by bypassing the standard transfer mechanism. The DYNP_VALUES_READ function module takes over the actual work. It only expects a few parameters:

```
CALL FUNCTION 'DYNP_VALUES_READ'
        EXPORTING
                DYNAME                      =
                DYNUMB                      =
"               TRANSLATE_TO_UPPER          = ' '
        TABLES
                DYNPFIELDS                  =
        EXCEPTIONS
                INVALID_ABAPWORKAREA  = 01
                INVALID_DYNPROFIELD   = 02
                INVALID_DYNPRONAME    = 03
                INVALID_DYNPRONUMMER  = 04
                INVALID_REQUEST       = 05
                NO_FIELDDESCRIPTION   = 06
                UNDEFIND_ERROR        = 07.
```

The DYNUMB and DYNAME parameters transfer the number of the screen program and the name of the program that contains this screen program. The TRANSLATE_TO_UPPER flag ensures that the value(s) the system reads are converted into upper case. The table to be transferred with DYNPFIELDS initially contains the names of the field(s) to be read in the FIELDNAME fields. After successfully executing the function module, the system lists the values it has loaded into the FIELDVALUE fields in this table. The exact structure of the table to be transferred to DYNPFIELDS is defined in the DYNPREAD structure in the Data Dictionary.

3.10.3 Uploading and downloading data

The R/3 System was developed as a client/server application with preference given to Microsoft Windows or Microsoft Windows NT as a front end operating system. As a result, it is relatively easy to integrate external programs. This also gives rise to the need to have external data read by the front end computer. This data is downloaded to and stored in the database on the front end hard disks where it is processed by the R/3 System. For example, the program editor has the UTILITIES | UPLOAD/DOWNLOAD menu options. You can select them to upload or download the source code of a program. There is a similar menu option in list processing (SYSTEM | LIST | SAVE | LOCAL FILE). Uploading or downloading has nothing to do with the batch input process. In the batch input process, existing SAP transactions evaluate the external datasets. In contrast, you yourself must process the data the system reads during the upload.

The system provides four relatively easy-to-use function modules that you can use to upload or download data. You use them to read data from the front end hard disk or to store data there. Two of these modules, UPLOAD and DOWNLOAD, present a dialog to the user and the other two WS_UPLOAD and WS_DOWNLOAD, work without a user dialog. Apart from this difference, the function modules are fairly similar. That is why we will only focus on the modules that work with a user dialog in this section.

These modules have a comprehensive interface. In practice, however, only a few para-meters are really necessary. You must enter the name of an internal table that will be used for data exchange. The structure of this table depends on the format of the characters to be transferred. In contrast, the data on the front end can be present in different formats and fonts. The unstructured files (binary files) and those files that contain pure ASCII text are of particular importance. For binary files you must provide an internal data type-X table that consists of a single column. The system reads right through the external file and fills each table row completely. There is no specific 'end-of-file indicator'. This may result in the last line of the internal table containing partially invalid characters, so it is absolutely essential that you enter the current file size when you download binary files. When you read binary files, the upload module returns the number of bytes read.

When you process ASCII files, each line of the external file is stored in a line in the internal table. This line should provide enough space for this purpose. You do not have to specify a size for ASCII files.

In a dialog box, the module prompts you to enter two essential bits of information, the file name, with path, and the file type. The parameters are primarily used to transfer vari-ous information. Table 3.44 describes the most important parameters in more detail.

Table 3.44   Important parameters for upload and download modules

Parameter	Task
CODEPAGE	Codepage for ASCII files
FILENAME	Default value for the file name
FILETYPE	Default value for the file type (ASC, BIN...)
ITEM	Header for file dialog
FILETYPE_NO_CHANGE	User not permitted to change file type if 'X'
FILETYPE_NO_SHOW	File not displayed if file type is 'X'
FILESIZE, BIN_FILESIZE	File size of binary files (import and export parameters)
MODE	Write mode (overwrite, attach)
SILENT	If 'X', suppress message that up/download was successful

The simple report shown below illustrates how you work with the two modules. This report is also an example of how to use data clusters. The report allows you to read any files from the front end's file system, store them in the R/3 System database and write them back again later on.

```
REPORT yz337040 NO STANDARD PAGE HEADING.
TABLES:
    indx,
    rlgrap,
    sscrfields.
```

```
DATA:
  BEGIN OF datatab OCCURS 100,
    line(255) TYPE x,
  END OF datatab,

  filesize TYPE i,
  filename LIKE rlgrap-filename,
  g_ucomm LIKE sscrfields-ucomm.

PARAMETERS: name LIKE indx-srtfd.
SELECTION-SCREEN FUNCTION KEY 1.
SELECTION-SCREEN FUNCTION KEY 2.

INITIALIZATION.
  sscrfields-functxt_01 = 'Upload'.
  sscrfields-functxt_02 = 'Download'.

AT SELECTION-SCREEN.
  g_ucomm = sscrfields-ucomm.
  sscrfields-ucomm = 'ONLI'.

START-OF-SELECTION.
  CASE g_ucomm.
    WHEN 'FC01'.
      CALL FUNCTION 'UPLOAD'
          EXPORTING
              filetype = 'BIN'
              filetype_no_change = 'X'
          IMPORTING
              filesize = filesize
              act_filename = filename
          TABLES
              data_tab = datatab
          EXCEPTIONS
              OTHERS = 1.

    IF sy-subrc = 0.
      EXPORT datatab filesize filename
        TO DATABASE indx(zz) ID name.
      UPDATE indx SET usera = sy-uname
        WHERE relid = 'ZZ'
          AND srtfd = name
          AND srtf2 = 0.
```

```
ELSE.
   WRITE: / 'Error on reading', filename, '!'.
ENDIF.

WHEN 'FC02'.
   IMPORT datatab filesize filename
      FROM DATABASE indx(zz) ID name.

   IF sy-subrc = 0.
      CALL FUNCTION 'DOWNLOAD'
         EXPORTING
            bin_filesize          = filesize
            filename              = filename
            filetype              = 'BIN'
            filetype_no_change    = 'X'
         TABLES
            data_tab = datatab
         EXCEPTIONS
            OTHERS = 1.

      SELECT SINGLE * FROM indx
         WHERE relid = 'ZZ'
            AND srtfd = name
            AND srtf2 = 0.
      WRITE: / name, 'created by', indx-usera.

   ELSE.
      WRITE: / 'Object', name, 'doesn''t exist!'.
   ENDIF.

ENDCASE.
```

In the selection screen, you enter a descriptor which will be used to identify the contents of the file when stored in a data cluster in the R/3 System. To start uploading or downloading, click the appropriate pushbutton in the application toolbar. BIN is predefined as the file type. For this reason, you must save the current file size as well as the data. Apart from that, the system stores the file name so that it can prompt you with it as a default value during the download. All three data objects (the actual data, the file size and the file name) are stored in a data cluster in the INDX table. The abbreviation ZZ is used as the area descriptor.

After a successful upload and export into the database, the USERA field in the INDX table is set to the name of the current user. After a download, the system reads this information and outputs it in the report. Here this is mainly to show that the tables for data clusters can also be processed with the normal Open-SQL statements.

3.11 How to process forms

Although the output and formatting options of commonly used reports enable the user to generate printed lists, they are not suitable for printing forms. However, this is one of the most frequently required tasks. Outputting forms is a lot more complicated than creating printed lists. For this reason, there is a special procedure described in this chapter that you use to print forms. The basis for printing forms are form definitions that are created with a specialized tool in the development environment. To actually print a form, you must call special function modules in your program, in which the form definitions will be used.

In this context, the expression 'printing forms' does not mean filling actual forms. Instead, it refers to any printed output that has to be formatted or precisely positioned on the output medium. In addition to filling actual forms, such as printed cheques, forms printing is, for example, also responsible for outputting mailshots or processing long texts in the SAP help system.

In form definitions, you can include text elements that you maintain with the *SAPscript Editor*. In this case, the term *text element* does not refer to the text icons used in a program, but other objects that exist only within the form-printing procedures. Form definitions are a subset of the general text processing procedures used in the R/3 System. For this reason, the name *SAPscript* has generally come to be used as a generic term for all tools connected with maintaining text and printing forms. Forms are processed on a client-specific and language-specific basis. In the case of customer developments, the developer and the system administrator arrange the distribution of the forms and their translation, if required.

This section first describes the principle of form printing. This is followed by an example that gives you the chance to actually use the tools and the programming methods. You will find some important details in the subsections that follow the programming example.

3.11.1   Principle of form printing

You use the form editor (transaction SE71) to maintain form definitions. A form consists of a combination of different elements. The most important elements are *pages, windows, text elements* and *paragraphs*. For now, the explanation of the functional principle will only deal with these elements.

The basic element is a *window*. A window, also called a *window definition*, contains one or more *text elements*. Each of these text elements represents a text block of any size which is assigned a clear descriptor in the window. Apart from normal text, the text elements can also contain special SAPscript statements. For example, these include the placeholders for values that will be inserted dynamically. Only text elements that you have explicitly addressed will be output later on. This is why you do not have to print all of a window's text elements. A window definition can therefore contain far more text than will be printed out later.

In a window definition, you only specify the contents of a particular window and some text formats. The window definition does not contain any information about the text sequence or the location of the window on the form.

The actual finished form must consist of at least one *page*. In addition to other data, you define several *page windows* on a page. A page window defines the location at which a window is printed on a page. In contrast to pages and windows, a page window is not an independent element but exists only as a logical object within the page description. When you define pages and page windows, you specify where something has to be printed. You define a new page window for each page. You can also display a window definition in different positions on several pages, i.e. in different page windows.

Another element is *paragraph definitions*, often (incorrectly) abbreviated to *paragraphs*. You use paragraph definitions to specify how the printed text should be formatted. For reasons of simplicity, you can set a default that applies to the entire form. You can also assign attributes for individual sections of text when you maintain the text elements.

There are no special ABAP statements for printing forms. The whole forms printing process is based on calling different function modules which you have to provide with suitable parameters. The following listing contains pseudo-code to demonstrate the simplest method.

First, you call a function module that gives you your printing parameters. For example, this function module can display a dialog box where the user specifies the printer they want to use. The SAP System also displays this dialog box automatically if you are printing a printed list.

```
CALL FUNCTION 'GET_PRINT_PARAMETERS'
   EXPORTING
     OUT_PARAMETERS = print_parameters
 . . .
```

The printing parameters are temporarily stored in the application. They have to be transferred to various other function modules as parameters. You may even be able to skip calling this module because you can also call a similar printing dialog from the next function module.

After initializing the printing parameters, you generate a spool request. All the forms generated in the further course of the application are contained in this spool request. This means that all forms will later be printed in the same print run. When you generate the spool request, you can select a form at the same time. However, this is not absolutely necessary because you can always define the form later on.

```
CALL FUNCTION 'OPEN_FORM' . . .
```

This call only triggers the generation of the spool request. It does not create a specific form. To do this, you must call the next function module. During this call you can specify the language and the specific form you require. You can call this module as often as necessary. This therefore allows you to switch forms within the same spool request.

```
CALL FUNCTION 'START_FORM' . . .
```

After you select the form, you must address the elements you want to print (window and text elements), so that they are actually printed in the form. If the text to be printed contains placeholders for dynamic values, the system replaces them automatically.

```
CALL FUNCTION 'WRITE_FORM' ...
```

After you have entered all the output in the form, you close the form with this statement:

```
CALL FUNCTION 'END_FORM' ... .
```

To print another form, call the START_FORM function module again. In practice, you will arrange the three function modules, START_FORM, WRITE_FORM and END_FORM, in a loop.

After the output of all forms is completed, you must exit the spool request.

```
CALL FUNCTION 'CLOSE_FORM' ...
```

All the forms created between OPEN_FORM and CLOSE_FORM now appear in a spool request. You must always use the OPEN_FORM and CLOSE_FORM function modules, as well as the START_FORM and END_FORM function modules in pairs.

3.11.2   Example mailshot

The example below uses the TADIR table and data from the user master record to generate a mailshot. Once again, this application does not serve any purpose as a piece of real commercial software; it is only used to demonstrate the various tools and the programming model you need to print forms.

The program determines all the existing users in the current client. The system then searches the TADIR table for the objects generated or modified by each user. All the objects the system finds are output as a mailshot. The mailshot consists of an unchanging sender, an address that contains the user's name and a table that lists all the previously determined objects. If a user has not created any objects, they will still receive the letter, but it will only contain a standard text.

Generating a form

First you generate the form. You should already have selected the actual structure of the form before you call the forms editor because this is not a graphical tool, but a dialog application that is based on screen programs. We strongly recommend that you create a dimensionally accurate template.

In this example, we want our mailshot to consist of two sets of pages with different layouts: the first page and all pages that follow it. The first page will contain the name and address of the sender, as well as some body text. The subsequent pages consist only of body text.

To start the forms editor, Form Painter, choose Tools | SAPscript | Form from the menu or enter transaction code SE71. The Form Painter initial screen appears (*see* Figure 3.172).

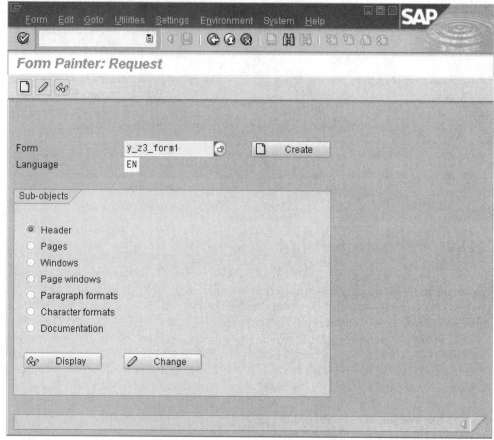

Figure 3.172   Form Painter initial screen

In the FORM input field you enter the name of the form you want to create. This name is subject to the usual naming conventions and must therefore start with the letters 'Y' or 'Z' in customer systems. In the Language field, select the language you require. This field may be preset to the logon language. Because you have not yet created a form, the selection you make in the SUB-OBJECTS area has no effect on the further process.

Now click on the CREATE button to display a screen program in which you maintain general administration data (Figure 3.173). In this screen program, you merely enter a short description of the form's task in the Description field. In the input area for the language attributes, you can define whether the form is to be translated and if so into which languages. This setting is only of importance when using the translation tools in the R/3 System. This will be mainly the case at SAP. If you are working with a system that uses the SAP translation tool, you should select the DO NOT TRANSLATE flag unless you also want to get to know the translation tool after you have learnt how to create forms. All other settings remain unchanged.

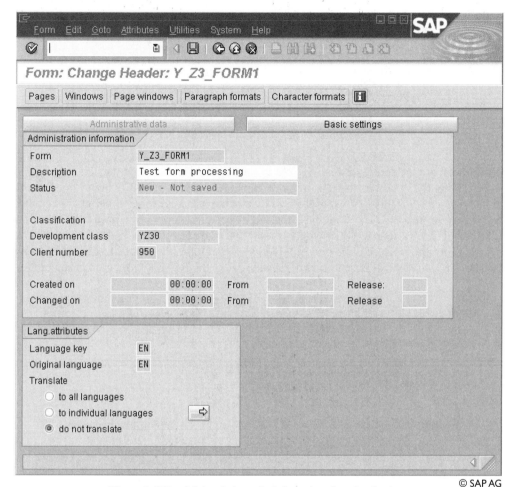

© SAP AG

Figure 3.173   Maintaining administration data for the form

After you have maintained the administration data, save the settings. The next step is to define a paragraph format. This format is used later as the default format for the form. Click on the PARAGRAPH FORMAT button to display the maintenance screen program for the paragraph formats.

The screen programs in which you maintain the various elements of a form are quite similar to each other. A work area lists all the existing elements. Double-click on one of these elements to turn it into an active element. It is then displayed in colour. You maintain the characteristics of the current element in the input fields in the lower part of the screen program. To create a new format, choose EDIT | CREATE ELEMENT from the menu. In a dialog box, you then enter the two-digit descriptor and a short text (*see* Figure 3.174).

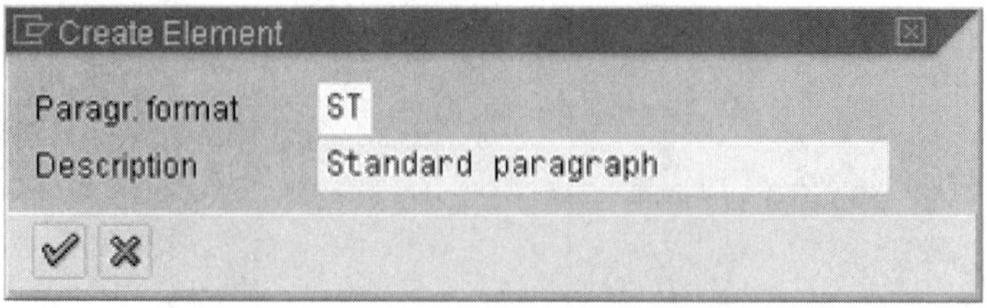

© SAP AG

Figure 3.174   Creating a new format

The format you define in this way is included in the work area of the screen program (*see* Figure 3.175). Because there is only one element, it is automatically highlighted as the active element. For this first example, you do not have to assign any other characteristics to the format. You can now store the form and go on to processing the forms pages.

To display the screen in which you maintain form pages, click on the PAGES button. The screen program looks like the one in which you maintain attributes. To generate a new page definition, choose EDIT | CREATE ELEMENT from the menu. Once again, a dialog box

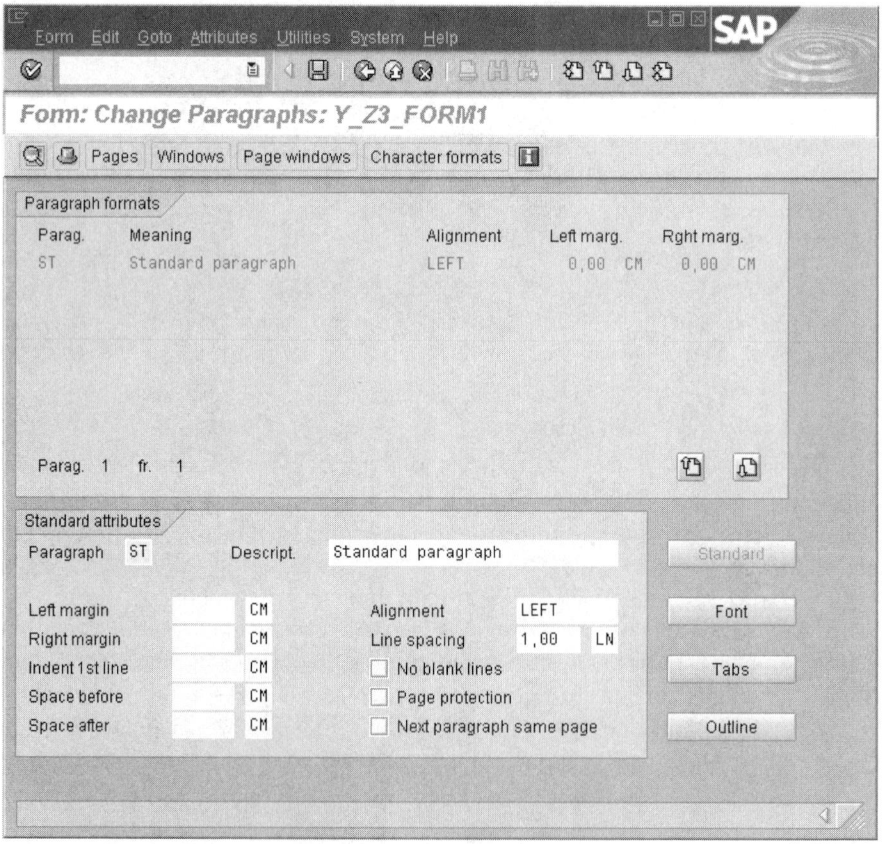

© SAP AG

Figure 3.175   Maintenance screen program for form paragraphs

© SAP AG

Figure 3.176   Creating a page description

with two input fields (see Figure 3.176) is displayed in which you enter the name of the page and a short description. First, create the FIRST page and then the NEXT page, but do not maintain attributes for these pages.

Now select the FIRST page by double-clicking on it. Maintain the NEXT PAGE attribute. Then enter NEXT as the next page (*see* Figure 3.177). The NEXT PAGE attribute ensures that the NEXT page is called after the FIRST page. This allows you to format the first page differently from the subsequent pages. You must also enter this attribute in the NEXT page

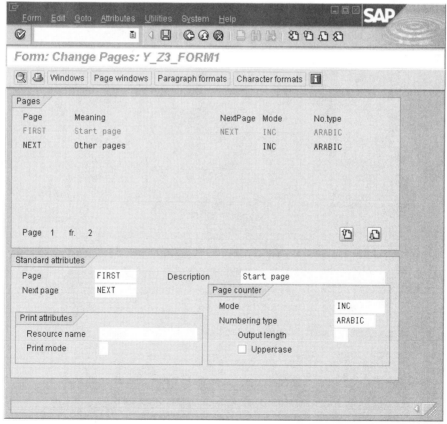

© SAP AG

Figure 3.177   Maintaining the attributes of a page description

where you also use NEXT. This is the only way you can ensure that another page format-ted with NEXT is called after the first page formatted with NEXT (i.e. the second page in the whole document) is output. Without this setting, a random next page would be called after the creation of the second page. This would terminate the program.

After the pages, you define the window as the third important element. To do this, click on the Windows button to call the appropriate maintenance screen program. Figure 3.178 shows you the initial state of this screen program.

In contrast to the two other screen programs, an element is predefined by default here. Because the MAIN window must be present in all the forms, the system has already cre-ated it for you. Now choose EDIT | CREATE ELEMENT from the menu to generate the ABS window for the sender and the ADDR window for the recipient. In a dialog box, you are now prompted to enter the name and short description of these windows, in the appro-priate fields (*see* Figure 3.179).

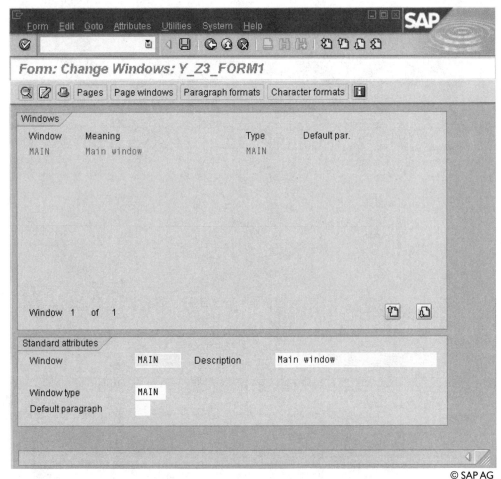

Figure 3.178   Maintenance screen program for window definitions

Figure 3.179   Creating a new window

The default values entered by the system remain unchanged. After saving these settings, you can use the window you have just generated to create the page window. To do this, position one or more windows on each of the two already defined pages, to define the dimensions of the windows. Click on the PAGE WINDOWS pushbutton to display the screen program in which you maintain the page windows (*see* Figure 3.180).

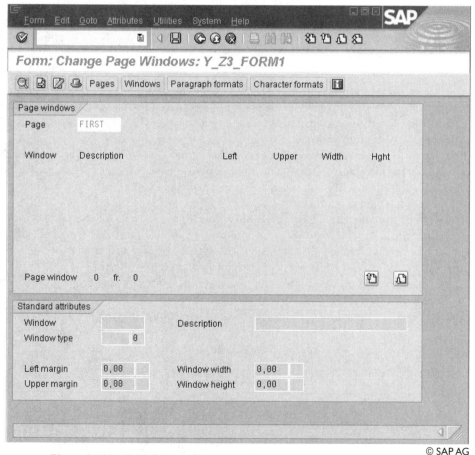

Figure 3.180   Initial state of the page window maintenance screen program

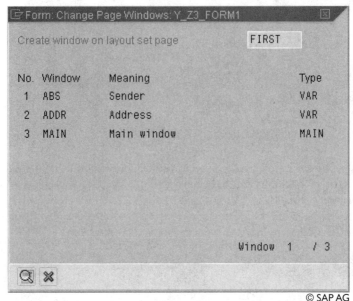

Figure 3.181   Selecting a window definition for a new page window

This screen program differs from the others in one detail. In the upper half of the work area of an input window, you first use the input help (i.e. FIRST or NEXT) to select the page you want to process. After you do so, the remainder of the screen program will display information about this form page.

Just like in the other screen programs, you choose the EDIT | CREATE element from the menu to insert a new page window. This menu option displays a dialog box, in which all the available window definitions are listed (Figure 3.181). Double-click on a definition to select the window you require.

The system transfers the selected window into the work area of the page window screen program. If several page windows are present on one page (Figure 3.182), one of them will in turn be selected for further processing. In the lower area of the screen program, you can maintain the attributes for that particular page window.

In this example, the processing is restricted to defining the size and the position of the page window.

You can see the page window to be selected and its position (in cm) in Table 3.45.

Table 3.45   Dimensions of the form's page window in cm

Page	Window	Left margin	Top margin	Width	Height
FIRST	MAIN	1	7	15	20
	ABS	1	1	5	3
	ADR	7	1	8	4
NEXT	MAIN	1	1	15	26

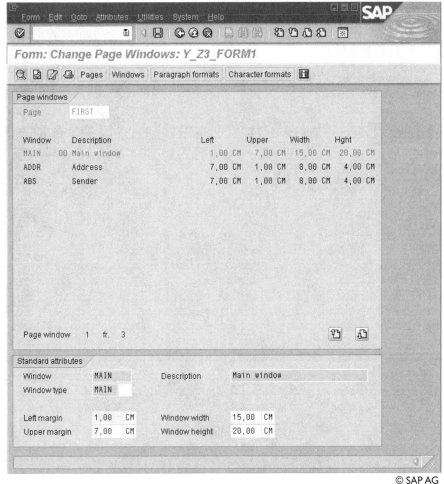

Figure 3.182   Maintaining a page window

To complete the definition of the forms structure, you must enter a default paragraph and the start page in the administration data. For this purpose, switch to the form's header data. To do this you can click on the Header pushbutton, choose GOTO | HEADER from the menu or press (F5). In the form's header data, click on the BASIC SETTINGS pushbutton to display the screen program shown in Figure 3.183. Then, in the DEFAULT PARAGR. field, enter paragraph definition ST which you created at the start. In this screen you also enter the name of the first page, FIRST, in the FIRST PAGE field.

You can now store the entire form. We recommend that you first check the accuracy of the form by choosing FORM | CHECK | DEFINITION from the menu. The result of the check is displayed in the status bar.

By following the steps described above, you have created an empty form. Although you can use it in its present state, in your application you would have to transfer the entire text you want to output into the form by calling special function modules. It is a lot more convenient to define text elements within the window. How you do this is described below.

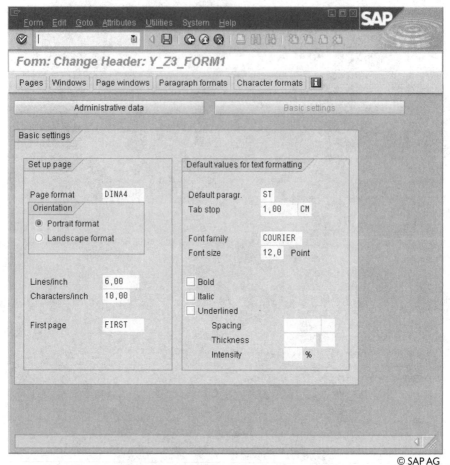

© SAP AG

Figure 3.183   Maintaining the default format and the start page for the form

Creating text elements

You create text elements as subordinate objects when you define a window. To do this, you must first call the tool you use to process the window definition by clicking on the WINDOWS pushbutton. Select the entry for the main window by double-clicking on it. Then click on the text elements icon or call the editor. To do this, choose EDIT | TEXT ELEMENTS from the menu or press (F9). The system displays the editor that provides you with an almost completely empty work area (*see* Figure 3.184).

By default, the system displays a paragraph format for the text you want to create. There are no other default settings. You will find the format options in a two-digit field to the left of the actual line. You can enter format options to the left of each line, even if some different releases do not display an input field at first; if you place the cursor to the left of the actual line, the input field and the icon for input help will appear.

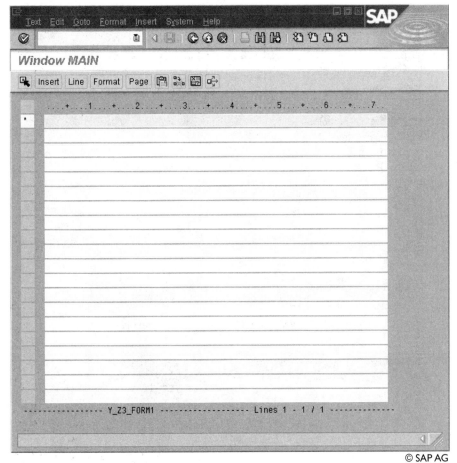

© SAP AG

Figure 3.184   Text elements editor

The format options not only define how the following text is formatted, but also switch on special functions. One of these special functions is to assign names for text elements. This name is later used by the function modules (mentioned above) to address the text element. Call the input help for the format options and select format /E from the list (Figure 3.185).

In the input line to the right of the format characters, you now enter the name of the text element. In this example, we have used INTRO. This line must not contain any other characters. The actual text must start in the next line. This is why you must press (Enter) after you have entered the name of the text element. The system adds a new paragraph. The character '*' in the format field of the next line clearly shows this. Now, you can enter the text. Generate the additional text elements in accordance with Figure 3.186. Lines for which no format is defined are follow-on lines. Because the editor does not automatically execute a line feed, it is easiest to first insert carriage returns with the (Enter) key and then delete the formats in the format column later.

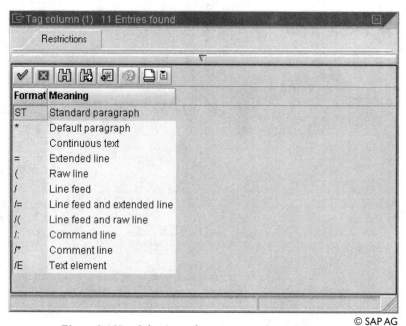

Figure 3.185   Selecting a format option for text elements

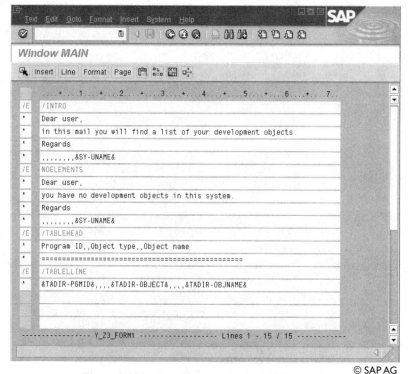

Figure 3.186   Text elements in the MAIN window

After you enter the text, the system returns you to the screen program in which you maintain the form windows. Now you assign text to the two other windows. Because these windows should only ever contain a standard text, you do not have to create specifically named text elements for these windows. All you need to do is enter the actual text.

The sender window consists of only one single line:

```
Sender: &SY-UNAME&
```

The address window contains a little more data:

```
Recipient: &USR03-BNAME&
           &USR03-NAME1&
           &USR03-NAME2&
           &USR03-ABTLG&
```

Now save the form and return to the screen program, in which you maintain header data. We recommend that you check the form once again. To do this, choose FORM | CHECK | DEFINITIONS from the menu.

You must activate a form before you can use it. To do this, choose FORM | ACTIVATE from the menu. Only by activating the forms can you ensure that the data also becomes effective for other applications. You must therefore always reactivate the forms each time you have modified them. When you process a form, the contents of the currently active version do not change.

Program for selection

The structure of the program below is similar to the one already discussed in the pseudo-code. It is merely designed to demonstrate how the various function modules can be used in real situations and is therefore kept accordingly simple. To keep its structure as clear as possible, all the function parameters that are not required have been removed from the listings, with one exception. The exceptions generated by the function module if an error occurs are dealt with individually to simplify troubleshooting. If an error does occur, the program will terminate and output the name of the function module and the error number. Because there are several WRITE_FORM calls, the output window will also be shown if messages concerning this module are displayed. This means you can determine the location in the program code that triggered the error.

The program starts with the declaration of the required tables and a few data fields. Table USR03 supplies the parts of the user master record that are relevant here. The system reads the development environment objects in the TADIR table. You will find explanations of the two f_count and f_headline data fields later on in the text. The system provides an s_user selection that you use to choose the users you want to edit, restricting the number of forms to be output.

```
REPORT yz337050.
TABLES:
  tadir,
  usr03.
DATA:
  f_count LIKE sy-tabix,
  f_headline VALUE space.
SELECT-OPTIONS:
  s_user FOR usr03-bname.
```

The first action within the application is to call the function module OPEN_FORM to generate a new output statement. To achieve this, four parameters need to be transferred. You use the SCREEN value in the DEVICE parameter to specify the screen as the output device. In this case, no print parameters need to be supplied. That is why the DIALOG parameter has been commented out. It is only required if output is to be made to a printer (DEVICE = 'PRINTER'). Within the application, the form is not changed. Therefore you can pass the name of the form to the forms administration function at this point by assigning the form name to the FORM parameter. Finally, you must also specify the language that the system is to use to search for the form. You can only use the logon language if you also have created the form in this language.

```
CALL FUNCTION 'OPEN_FORM'
    EXPORTING
      device                       = 'SCREEN'
*     dialog                       = 'X'
      form                         = 'Y_Z3_FORM1'
      language                     = sy-langu
    EXCEPTIONS
      cancelled                    = 1
      device                       = 2
      form                         = 3
      options                      = 4
      unclosed                     = 5
      mail_options                 = 6
      archive_error                = 7
      invalid_fax_number           = 8
      more_params_needed_in_batch  = 9
      OTHERS                       = 10.
IF sy-subrc <> 0.
  WRITE: / 'OPEN_FORM:', sy-subrc.
  EXIT.
ENDIF.
```

In the application, you only have to generate one single output statement. However, within this statement several forms need to be created. The additional statements are therefore located in a SELECT loop in which the system will process all user master records matching the selection criterion sequentially.

```
SELECT * FROM usr03
  WHERE bname IN s_user.
```

It is possible that no objects exist in the development environment for the current user. If this is the case, the created form should contain a text to notify you of that. It is then not necessary to output the table header. After the user master record is read, there is a statement that determines the number of entries in the TADIR table for the current user and stores them in the f_count field.

```
SELECT COUNT(*) FROM tadir
  INTO f_count
  WHERE author = usr03-bname.
```

Now, you can launch the output of a new form with the START_FORM function module. All necessary entries concerning the form have already been made in OPEN_FORM so you do not have to pass any parameters here.

```
CALL FUNCTION 'START_FORM'
   EXCEPTIONS
      form       = 1
      format     = 2
      unended    = 3
      unopened   = 4
      unused     = 5
      OTHERS     = 6.
 IF sy-subrc <> 0.
   WRITE: / 'OPEN_FORM:', sy-subrc.
   EXIT.
 ENDIF.
```

For both kinds of output, the contents of the windows for the address and sender are identical. You can output these two windows immediately after running the form. When calling WRITE_FORM, you only have to transfer the names of the two windows (ADDR and ABS) as parameters. These two windows only contain a single unnamed text, so this kind of call is absolutely clear.

```
CALL FUNCTION 'WRITE_FORM'
    EXPORTING
       window                        = 'ADDR'
    EXCEPTIONS
       element                       = 1
       function                      = 2
       type                          = 3
       unopened                      = 4
       unstarted                     = 5
       window                        = 6
       bad_pageformat_for_print      = 7
       OTHERS                        = 8.
  IF sy-subrc <> 0.
    WRITE: / 'WRITE_FORM (ADDR):', sy-subrc.
    EXIT.
  ENDIF.
```

```
CALL FUNCTION 'WRITE_FORM'
   EXPORTING
      window                          = 'ABS'
   EXCEPTIONS
      element                         = 1
      function                        = 2
      type                            = 3
      unopened                        = 4
      unstarted                       = 5
      window                          = 6
      bad_pageformat_for_print = 7
      OTHERS                          = 8.
IF sy-subrc <> 0.
   WRITE: / 'WRITE_FORM (ABS):', sy-subrc.
   EXIT.
ENDIF.
```

The field f_count contains the number of TADIR objects for the current user. If this number is greater than zero, the entire document must be output with an introductory text, the table that contains the objects and an appropriate table header. Because the document is output in the MAIN window, you will not only have to specify the window but also the window area (TYPE parameter) and the name of the required text element (element parameter). First of all, a descriptive text will be output.

```
IF f_count > 0.
   CALL FUNCTION 'WRITE_FORM'
      EXPORTING
         element                       = 'INTRO'
         function                      = 'SET'
         type                          = 'BODY'
         window                        = 'MAIN'
      EXCEPTIONS
         element                       = 1
         function                      = 2
         type                          = 3
         unopened                      = 4
         unstarted                     = 5
         window                        = 6
         bad_pageformat_for_print = 7
         OTHERS                        = 8.
   IF sy-subrc <> 0.
      WRITE: / 'WRITE_FORM (INTRO):', sy-subrc.
      EXIT.
   ENDIF.
ENDIF.
```

The text is followed by the table, which must be provided with a table header. This header is located on the follow-on pages in the TOP area of the window. However on the first page it will have to be output just after the INTRO text element. The contents of the F_HEADLINE flag control this functionality. If this flag has not been set, the system will output the table header in the BODY area of the MAIN window.

```
IF f_headline                      = space.
   CALL FUNCTION 'WRITE_FORM'
      EXPORTING
         element                   = 'TABLEHEAD'
         function                  = 'SET'
         type                      = 'BODY'
         window                    = 'MAIN'
      EXCEPTIONS
         element                   = 1
         function                  = 2
         type                      = 3
         unopened                  = 4
         unstarted                 = 5
         window                    = 6
         bad_pageformat_for_print  = 7
         OTHERS                    = 8.
   IF sy-subrc <> 0.
      WRITE: / 'WRITE_FORM (TABLEHEAD/BODY):', sy-subrc.
      EXIT.
   ENDIF.

   f_headline = 'X'.
ENDIF.
```

On all other pages, the header is written in the TOP area. Here it is not essential to test the F_HEADLINE flag again. On the first page, the statement shown below will not result in any output in the document, because outputs in the TOP area have no effect if an output has already occurred in the BODY area. The output is however scheduled for the subsequent pages and will automatically appear after a page break.

```
CALL FUNCTION 'WRITE_FORM'
   EXPORTING
      element                   = 'TABLEHEAD'
      function                  = 'SET'
      type                      = 'TOP'
      window                    = 'MAIN'
   EXCEPTIONS
      element                   = 1
      function                  = 2
      type                      = 3
      unopened                  = 4
      unstarted                 = 5
      window                    = 6
      bad_pageformat_for_print  = 7
      OTHERS                    = 8.
IF sy-subrc <> 0.
   WRITE: / 'WRITE_FORM (TABLEHEAD/TOP):', sy-subrc.
   EXIT.
ENDIF.
```

The code for outputting the table header is followed by a SELECT loop through table
TADIR. In this loop, there is another call to the WRITE_FORM function which lists the individual objects. The call type and the parameters are essentially the same as for the
previous statements.

```
SELECT * FROM tadir
   WHERE author                      = usr03-bname
   ORDER BY PRIMARY KEY.

   CALL FUNCTION 'WRITE_FORM'
      EXPORTING
         element                     = 'TABLELINE'
         type                        = 'BODY'
         window                      = 'MAIN'
      EXCEPTIONS
         element                     = 1
         function                    = 2
         type                        = 3
         unopened                    = 4
         unstarted                   = 5
         window                      = 6
         bad_pageformat_for_print    = 7
         OTHERS                      = 8.
   IF sy-subrc <> 0.
      WRITE: / 'WRITE_FORM (TABLELINE):', sy-subrc.
      EXIT.
   ENDIF.


ENDSELECT.
```

The ELSE statement below is used for evaluating the number of TADIR objects for the
current user. If this number equals zero, the system outputs a text to inform you about
this fact. No other information will be displayed.

```
ELSE. 'IF f_count > 0.
   CALL FUNCTION 'WRITE_FORM'
      EXPORTING
         element                     = 'NOELEMENTS'
         function                    = 'SET'
         type                        = 'BODY'
         window                      = 'MAIN'
      EXCEPTIONS
         element                     = 1
         function                    = 2
         type                        = 3
         unopened                    = 4
```

```
              unstarted                    = 5
              window                       = 6
              bad_pageformat_for_print  = 7
              OTHERS                       = 8.
          IF sy-subrc <> 0.
            WRITE: / 'WRITE_FORM (NOELEMENTS):', sy-subrc.
            EXIT.
          ENDIF.

      ENDIF.
```

After evaluating a user, the current form terminates. You terminate it by calling the END_FORM function module. No parameters are necessary:

```
CALL FUNCTION 'END_FORM'
    EXCEPTIONS
        unopened                     = 1
        bad_pageformat_for_print  = 2
        OTHERS                       = 3.
IF sy-subrc <> 0.
    WRITE: / 'END_FORM:', sy-subrc.
    EXIT.
ENDIF.
```

```
ENDSELECT.
```

The previous ENDSELECT statement is part of the loop through table USR03 with the user master records. After all users have been evaluated, close the output statement by calling CLOSE_FORM. This function module can also be called without any parameters.

```
CALL FUNCTION 'CLOSE_FORM'
    EXCEPTIONS
        unopened                     = 1
        bad_pageformat_for_print  = 2
        OTHERS                       = 3.
IF sy-subrc <> 0.
    WRITE: / 'CLOSE_FORM:', sy-subrc.
    EXIT.
ENDIF.
```

```
WRITE: / 'END'.
```

This completes the program. You can now execute it. In this context, please consider the exercises that follow.

At this point, we should like to draw your attention to yet another special feature. Up to and including Release 3.1x, the system only replaces placeholders automatically in the case of fields based on the Data Dictionary, i.e. for fields in tables and structures. It is only from Release 4.0 onward that it is possible to also copy the contents of internal fields from programs automatically. Despite this, it is not necessary to generate forms within a SELECT loop in previous Releases. As an alternative, you can use the EXTRACT datasets which have already been mentioned, as long as these work together with Data Dictionary fields. One of the main uses of the EXTRACT statement is therefore the printing of reports for outputting bulk data.

Exercises

1. Execute the program. If necessary, limit the number of users to be evaluated by setting a suitable selection criterion.

2. Print out a form from the screen view.

3. Change the default for the output device in PRINTER and activate the DIALOG parameter. Print the form(s). Deactivate the IMMEDIATELY OUTPUT option in the print dialog if it was previously activated. Then change to the output control function. Display the contents of the spool job and print it out.

3.11.3   Important attributes and statements

When you defined the form above, you mainly copied default settings. You can use some important attributes to modify the behaviour of the form. Below, we will describe some of these attributes in more detail.

Window types

Windows are assigned a type that defines the way they are processed and displayed. Not all types can be set for each window.

CONST

Windows of this type are of an identical size on all pages where they are displayed. Their contents are only processed once, when the system starts processing the form. You can use this window type to represent the window in an identical way on all pages.

If you enter data in the window, all information that cannot be displayed inside the window will be lost.

VAR

Every time a page is created, VAR-type windows are reprocessed by the forms processor. They can therefore have a different size on each different page. However all entries exceeding the current size of the window will also be lost in this case.

MAIN

The MAIN window type is the only one that triggers a page break during processing if the current window on a page has been completely filled. When a page break is created, the page definition may also be changed. If the new page contains no MAIN window and the same page definition is being used again as a follow-on page, this will create an endless loop. For this reason, each page should contain a MAIN window.

Within the MAIN window, there are three subareas, TOP, BODY and BOTTOM. The contents of the TOP and BOTTOM areas automatically appear on all pages once they have been defined. They are used for table headers and footer lines, for example. You select the areas by setting parameters in the WRITE_FORM function module.

Symbols

The SAPscript code can contain symbols. Symbols are descriptors enclosed in ampersands (the '&' character). Each symbol is replaced at runtime by its value. If the symbol corresponds to the name of a Data Dictionary field or an internal field within the printing program, it will be replaced by the contents of this field. Apart from that, predefined symbols exist for various headings, page numbers and dates, as well as time entries. You can choose INSERT | SYMBOLS from the menu to choose these symbols and insert them into the text elements maintenance editor.

Paragraph formats

When you are defining a form, the R/3 System provides you with some preprogrammed paragraph formats. To use one of these formats, enter it in the first column to the left of the actual text. Table 3.46 shows you the icons and the names of these formats. After the table there is a short description of each format.

Table 3.46   Predefined paragraph formats

Icon	Name
*	Default paragraph
/	New line
/:	SAPscript control statement
/*	Comment
=	Long line
/=	Long line with line feed
(	Raw line
/(	Raw line with line feed
>x	Fixed line
/E	Text element

Default paragraph

In a form's header data you have to set a default paragraph format. You must define this format first. In the form, you can use the asterisk '*', as a symbol to reference this format. Each line marked in this way will create a new paragraph, i.e. the system will execute a line feed before outputting the line.

New line

The text lines within a paragraph will be continuously formatted. If you want to force a line feed, you can achieve this with this character, '/'. Here the current formatting characteristics will remain intact.

SAPscript control statement

Within the text for a form's window you can store some control statements alongside pure text. You mark these statements with the character '/:' in the format column. There is a section all about these control statements below.

Comment

Use the character '/*' to insert a comment. The character only applies to the current line. If the comment extends over several lines, you have to enter the comment symbol for each line.

Long line

The SAPscript Editor will not apply any formatting for this line. This means that no line feed will be executed either. Consequently, the contents of this line are attached directly to the end of the previous line. No separating space will be inserted either, unless the long line begins with a space.

Long line with line feed

This text is treated exactly like a long line text, except that before the system outputs the text it will insert a line feed.

Raw line

Although this line is formatted, it will not be processed by the *SAPscript Composer*. This tool has a number of tasks, such as processing character formats within a line, icons, tab and formatting characters and hypertext links. Instead, the characters in the raw line will be output without any changes. As in the case of a long line, the raw line text is attached directly to the end of the previous line, i.e. without a separating space as a delimiter. If you require a delimiter, you must start the raw line with a space.

Raw line with line feed

This text is treated exactly like a raw line text, except that before the system outputs the text it will insert a line feed.

Fixed line

You cannot enter data in a fixed line or change or separate it. The system evaluates the first two characters of the actual text as paragraph format characters and outputs the ones that follow as normal text. The letter 'X' in the format symbol is replaced by a number or any letter to enable the user to identify and distinguish between various fixed lines.

Text element

A line marked as a text element contains the name of a text element. A text element includes the whole text up to the name of the next text element or until the end of the text. The contents of a text element will only appear in the form if the text element has been explicitly addressed using the WRITE_FORM function module.

Control statements

You can use the attribute '/:' to insert control statements into the text of a form. You can also use the CONTROL_FORM function module to trigger the same statements at runtime. Each control statement is located in its own line. This section describes the available control statements in more detail.

NEW-PAGE

This statement triggers a new page. As a result, the system closes the page that has just been edited. The follow-on page statically specified within the form's definition is normally used as the next page. However, you can also overwrite this default by passing the page you want as a parameter to NEW-PAGE.
   Examples:

```
/ :   NEW-PAGE
/ :   NEW-PAGE NEXT2
```

PROTECT

If you want to protect paragraphs from an automatic line feed, you can enclose these paragraphs in the two statements PROTECT and ENDPROTECT. If the space available on the current page is not sufficient to output the included text, the system will insert a page break. After the page break, the text is always output, even if it is too long to fit on an empty page.
   Syntax:

```
/ :   PROTECT
text
/ :   ENDPROTECT .
```

NEW-WINDOW

A form page can contain up to 99 MAIN-type windows. This is necessary for example if you want to print out text with multiple columns or labels. The windows are clearly identified by a unique number between 0 and 98. You can use the NEW-WINDOW statement to switch to the next MAIN-type window.

Syntax:

```
/: NEW-WINDOW.
```

DEFINE

You can use the DEFINE statement to assign text icons a value within the source code. There are two assignment operators. The simple equals sign '=' triggers a one-level icon replacement. If the value to be assigned contains additional text icons, they will only be replaced at runtime. The assignment operator ':=' first replaces all icons within the values (right-hand side of the assignment) and only then executes the assignment in the text.

Syntax:

```
/: DEFINE &symbolname& = 'value'.
```

SET DATE MASK

You can use the SAPscript SET DATE MASK statement to create date fields and define how they are output. After this statement is executed, all date fields will be output using the format you have defined.

Syntax:

```
/: SET DATE MASK = 'datemask'
```

In the date mask, you can use the templates listed in Table 3.47.

Table 3.47   Formatting characters for the date mask

Format characters	Description
DD	Day (two-digit)
DDD	Name of day, abbreviated
DDDD	Name of day, written in full
MM	Month (two-digit)
MMM	Name of month, abbreviated
MMMM	Name of month, written in full
YY	Year (two-digit)
YYYY	Year (four-digit)
LD	Day (processed like in additional option L)
LM	Month (processed like in additional option L)
LY	Year (processed like in additional option L)

All other characters in the mask will be interpreted as text and transferred accordingly. You activate the default by assigning an empty string. The language-independent text for the names of days and months is stored in the TTDTG table. Under normal circumstances, you should never have to change these entries.

SET TIME MASK

You can also process time entries in a similar way to formatting dates. To do so, you use the SET TIME MASK statement. The syntax of this statement is as follows:

`/: ` **`SET TIME MASK`** ` = ` `'time mask'`

In the time mask, the placeholders listed in Table 3.48 are used. All other characters will be interpreted as text and output without change.

Table 3.48   Formatting characters for time entries

Characters	Meaning
HH	Hours (two-digit)
MM	Minutes (two-digit)
SS	Seconds (two-digit)

SET COUNTRY

With this statement, you trigger the country-specific processing of special fields and values. This applies for example to the date display format, to the decimal character or to the thousands separator. When reports, etc., are being generated, the settings in the user master record will be evaluated for this purpose. Forms printing can easily generate documents in different languages (i.e. in the language of the recipient) in one single step, so you can also set language-specific processing at runtime if necessary. To do so, you can select the required country keys either by entering a value enclosed in single quotation marks or a SAPscript icon. The SAPscript icon is the most frequently used method. The syntax of the statement is as follows:

`/: ` **`SET COUNTRY`** ` country key.`

SET SIGN

You use this statement to specify whether a prefix operator will appear to the right or to the left of the number concerned. In the statement you define the position with the words LEFT or RIGHT, resulting in the two following syntax variants:

`/: ` **`SET SIGN LEFT`**

or

`/: ` **`SET SIGN RIGHT.`**

RESET

This statement resets the current paragraph number to its initial value. Here you have to pass the name of the particular paragraph format as a parameter:

```
/:  RESET  paragraph.
```

INCLUDE

The text elements of a window definition apply only within one form. Therefore, it is not possible to reuse text modules. If you would like to use reusable modules that can be inserted into several forms, you have to create them as normal SAPscript texts. You then use the INCLUDE statement to insert these texts in forms. The syntax of this statement is rather more complicated because several options are possible:

```
/:   INCLUDE  name
    [ OBJECT  object]
    [ ID  ident]
    [ LANGUAGE  language]
    [ PARAGRAPH  paragraph]  [NEW-PARAGRAPH  npar].
```

You must always specify the name of the text to be inserted. It only has to be enclosed in single quotation marks if it contains spaces. You can also use a field name placeholder to pass the name of the text. The remaining parameters of the INCLUDE statement are optional.

The forms processor searches for the language-specific contents of a form either in the logon language, or in the language specified when the SAPscript function modules were called. The same applies to includes. However you can overwrite this default setting by using the LANGUAGE option. This also applies to the format set using the PARAGRAPH parameter. In all text parts formatted with the standard format '*' this statement replaces this standard format with the one transferred as a parameter. NEW-PARAGRAPH works in a similar fashion. However, this statement only reformats the first line of a text. If no FORMAT option is set, the system will reapply standard format to all paragraphs.

The OBJECT option is irrelevant to forms creation. You can use the ID parameter to define another part of the text name.

STYLE

Use this statement to change the output style. Its syntax is very simple:

```
/:  STYLE  style.
```

If you enter an asterisk for style, the forms processor will reapply the original style.

ADDRESS

Address data located inside the statement bracket ADDRESS – ENDADDRESS is processed in accordance with the standards of the recipient's country. This country must be defined in the COUNTRY parameter.

```
/: ADDRESS [COUNTRY country] ...
   ...
/: ENDADDRESS.
```

TOP

Use the TOP statement to define a text that automatically appears at the start of each main window, immediately after it has been defined. This text can run over several lines.

```
/: TOP text
/: ENDTOP.
```

BOTTOM

Use this statement to generate a text that automatically appears as a footer line.

```
/: BOTTOM
```

text

```
/: ENDBOTTOM.
```

IF

Logical expressions can be evaluated within the text definitions. Like in ABAP, you use these statements to do so: IF, ELSE, ELSEIF and ENDIF. You can find the available operators in Table 3.49. The syntax resembles the familiar ABAP statement:

```
/: IF condition
       ...
/: ELSEIF condition
...
/: ELSE
...
/: ENDIF
```

Table 3.49 IF statement operators

Operator character	Text symbol for operator	Description
=	EQ	Equal
<	LT	Smaller
>	GT	Greater
<=	LE	Smaller or equal
>=	GE	Greater or equal
<>	NE	Not equal
	NOT	Negation link operator
	AND	Link operator AND
	OR	Link operator OR

CASE

You can also use the `CASE` statement to distinguish between cases. As above, the syntax is generally the same as for the ABAP statement:

```
/: CASE icon
 /: WHEN value_1
  ...
 /: WHEN value_2
  ...
 /: WHEN value_n
  ...
 /: WHEN OTHERS
  ...
/: ENDCASE.
```

PERFORM

The forms processor can call ABAP subroutines to perform additional evaluations or calculations with text contents. Data is exchanged using icons, i.e. placeholders for field names or predefined icons. The syntax of this statement also resembles the syntax of the corresponding ABAP statement:

```
/: PERFORM subroutine IN PROGRAM program
/: USING &invar1&
/: USING &invar2&
  ...
/: CHANGING &outvar1&
/: CHANGING &outvar2&
  ...
/: ENDPERFORM.
```

PRINT-CONTROL

In the `SPAD` transaction, you can define special print controls for each printer. Print controls are control character strings used to trigger special actions in the printer. In the form, you use the `PRINT-CONTROL` statement to trigger the sending of one of these control character strings. Because the forms processor does not evaluate these control characters, they may destroy the entire formatting of the text if used incorrectly.

The syntax of the statement is again very simple:

```
/: PRINT-CONTROL name.
```

BOX

Using the `BOX` statement, you can draw a frame and then apply shading to the enclosed area. However not all printer drivers support this statement. The syntax of the statement is as follows:

```
/: BOX
  [XPOS xpos] [YPOS ypos]
  [WIDTH width] [HEIGTH height]
  [FRAME frame]
  [INTENSITY intensity].
```

The two parameters xpos and ypos define the position of the top left-hand corner of the frame. Here you have to also consider the effect of the POSITION statement, which defines the zero point within the window. The zero point does not have to correspond with the top left-hand corner of the window. To define the exact position, you must therefore add the values of xpos and xoffset or ypos and yoffset.

You use width and height to define the width and height of the frame. You use frame to define the thickness of the frame. If you set a value of 0 for frame, no frame will be drawn.

If the data for xpos, ypos, width or height are missing, the system will pass default values or the values set with POSITION and SIZE.

In contrast to other statements, the parameters with the exception of intensity consist of a value and a measurement. Table 3.50 contains the possible units of measurement. Enter decimal numbers as character strings, i.e. enclosed in single quotation marks.

The intensity parameter defines the opacity: the amount of black applied to the

Table 3.50   Units of measurement and conversion factors

Unit	Description	Conversion
CH	Character	
CM	Centimetres	
IN	Inches	2.54 CM
LN	Line	
MM	Millimetres	
PT	Point	1/72 IN
TW	Twip	1/20 PT

area inside the box in percentage terms. The value range lies between 0 and 100.

Examples:

```
/: BOX 5 CM 5 CM 10 CM 10 CM FRAME 10 TW INTENSITY 10
/: BOX WIDTH '5.5' CM HEIGHT 1 CM FRAME 10 TW
/: BOX WIDTH 5 CM HEIGHT 5 CM INTENSITY 10
/: BOX FRAME 20 TW.
```

POSITION

Initially, the source of the co-ordinates for the BOX statement is the top left-hand corner of a window. You can use the POSITION statement to move this starting point. Here you can either assign an absolute position by entering values without a prefix or assign a position relative to the last value by entering values with a prefix.

The WINDOW and PAGE parameters are used as switches and have consequently no additions. They set the position for the source of the co-ordinates for the BOX statement to the top left-hand corner of the window or the page.

Syntax:

```
/: POSITION [XORIGIN xoffset] [YORIGIN yoffset] [WINDOW] [PAGE].
```

SIZE

You can use this statement to enter default values for the height and width of the window. As in the POSITION statement, the values you assign here can be absolute or relative. Again, the WINDOW and PAGE switches set initial values.

Syntax:

```
/: SIZE [WIDTH width] [HEIGHT height] [WINDOW] [PAGE].
```

HEX, ENDHEX

The characters between HEX and ENDHEX will be interpreted as hexadecimal values and sent to the printer without modification.

SUMMING

This statement works in a similar way to the ABAP statement that has the same name. You only enter it once. Following that, it is executed each time the specified source field is processed. The syntax of the statement is as follows:

```
/: SUMMING program symbol INTO summing symbol.
```

3.11.4 Function modules in detail

Some function modules have an important role to play in forms output. These modules are described in detail below.

OPEN_FORM

The OPEN_FORM function module launches the printing of forms. It has to be called before all other modules for the printing of forms. The module's main task is to generate a suitable spool or to find an existing spool request. To do so, it either prompts the user to provide the required information in a dialog or the required information must be transferred when the module is called. In addition, it is possible but not absolutely necessary to specify the form you want to use when OPEN_FORM is called.

The two most frequently used parameters of the OPEN_FORM function module are DIALOG and OPTIONS. With the value in DIALOG you control the call of the dialog box, in which the user enters the print parameters. In the OPTIONS parameter, which has the structure ITCPO, you transfer default values for the print parameters. The final print parameters result from the values in the OPTIONS parameter, the defaults in the user master record, and if the dialog has been released from the entries made by the user. In the RESULT export parameter, the module returns the selected print parameters.

With the contents of the DEVICE parameter, you specify the output medium. The default value for printed output is PRINTER. You can suppress the generation of a spool request, and display the document on screen instead, by setting the value SCREEN in the DEVICE parameter. In that, you can use the APPLICATION parameter to modify the interface of the screen program in which the document is displayed. Other permitted values for DEVICE are TELEX, TELEFAX and ABAP. If the form you want to use already needs to be predefined in OPEN_FORM, you can do this with the two parameters FORM and LANGUAGE.

If the required form does not exist in the specified language, the system will probably use the form in another language. The LANGUAGE export parameter will therefore return the current language of the form.

As an alternative to outputting print jobs on a printer, they can also be stored in an optical archive. The parameters ARCHIVE_INDEX and ARCHIVE_PARAMS are applicable in this case. However this section does not contain any details about them because archiving is a different area of activity to the one we are discussing here.

In the dialog where the user enters print parameters, they have the option to terminate the dialog. In addition, incorrect entries can trigger an error. It is therefore essential to analyze the exceptions initiated by the function modules. It is not sensible to continue with the printing of forms if the module terminates with the generation of an exception. During program development, the value in the exception often supplies helpful information on how to limit errors.

START_FORM

The task of the START_FORM function module is to launch the processing of a new form. Before you can call this function module, you must first of all have used OPEN_FORM to start forms printing. To do so, you have to pass the name of the form to the module in the FORM and LANGUAGE parameters, unless you have already done this when calling OPEN_FORM. Within an OPEN_FORM-CLOSE_FORM block, you can repeatedly call the START_FORM module and specify a different form each time. If you have already entered the name of the form in OPEN_FORM, this will no longer be required in START_FORM. In this case, the START_FORM call will launch the processing of a new copy of the selected form. This module will also return the language currently selected for the form in the LANGUAGE export parameter.

In a form, one page is usually defined as the start page. If you would like to change this default, you can do so by passing the appropriate page name to the STARTPAGE parameter.

The text elements in a form can contain placeholders for table fields. At runtime, these placeholders will be replaced by the contents of the particular table fields. In this case, the system will look for the fields in the current program unless you select a different program in the PROGRAM parameter.

WRITE_FORM

The WRITE_FORM function module is responsible for outputting the text elements present in the form. It can only be called if forms printing has been opened with OPEN_FORM and a form has been created with START_FORM.

When calling WRITE_FORM, you must always enter the window in which the system should output the data in the WINDOW parameter. If you split up the form into several pages, this does not affect WRITE_FORM. The system inserts a page break either when accessing a window that does not exist on the current page or if the MAIN window of the current page is full.

A window can contain several text elements. Each element's name must be passed in the ELEMENT parameter.

By selecting an output option in the FUNCTION parameter, you specify how an existing text will be handled. The effect of the parameter depends on the window. For the MAIN window, the SET and APPEND functions cause the text to be appended to the existing output. The DELETE function has no effect. In all other windows, you can use the SET function to reset the entire window contents. Any data present in the window will be deleted. To append output, you have to use the SET function. The DELETE function is effective and deletes the text in the specified window.

The TYPE parameter only applies to output in the MAIN window. This window is divided into the three areas, TOP, BODY and BOTTOM, that have to be selected with the TYPE parameter.

The PENDING_LINES export parameter affects output in the BOTTOM area of the MAIN window. If the BOTTOM area does not provide sufficient space for a text you want to output, the missing characters will appear in the BOTTOM area of the next page. You may have to specify the output of this follow-on page with NEW_PAGE. This is necessary for example if the normal text output has ended. If you see an 'X' in the PENDING_LINES export parameter, this means that the output of parts of the text in the BOTTOM area is still pending.

END_FORM

After you have entered text in a form by calling the WRITE_FORM function module, you have to end this form by calling END_FORM. You can only open a new form with START_FORM after the END_FORM call. After you have called END_FORM, it is no longer possible to output in the form that has ended. The function module will return the current print parameters in the RESULT export parameter.

CLOSE_FORM

By calling CLOSE_FORM you end the whole form printing process. The system will only output the form to the printer spool after the CLOSE_FORM call. If you only want to output a single document on screen at a time, you have to process a separate OPEN_FORM-CLOSE_FORM string for each document.

In the RESULT or RDI_RESULT parameters the module returns the current output parameters.

If an 'X' has been entered in the TDGETOTF parameter when OPEN_FORM was called in the printer parameters, no spool or screen output will occur. In this case, the OTFDATA table will return the processed output in OTF format.

PRINT_TEXT

This function module processes a text module for output and then sends it to the output device.

CONTROL_FORM

With this function module, you can dynamically transfer control statements to the form at run-time. For this, you transfer the statement in the COMMAND parameter. The triggering character for control statements ('/:') must not be transferred. There are no other parameters for this module. The form previously opened with START_FORM will be used as the current form.

3.11.5 Print parameters

The creation of forms is always connected with the generation of a spool request. The OPEN_FORM function module must be supplied with corresponding parameters for this purpose, because this module generates a spool request. Even within reports without forms processing, access may be required to the print parameters. The print parameters can be acquired in different ways. The OPEN_FORM function module controlled by a special parameter can call the standard SAP System print dialog. In it the user can define the print parameters at application runtime. However this is not recommended in all cases. If the report creating the document runs in batch mode, the corresponding dialog cannot be

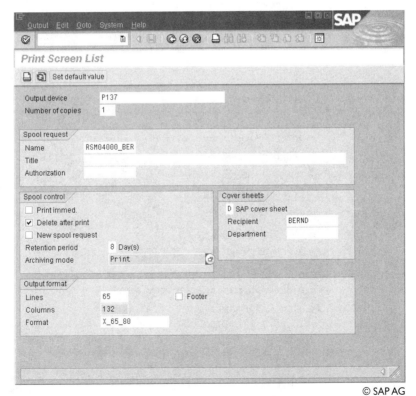

© SAP AG

Figure 3.187   Dialog in which users input print parameters

executed. Besides, it may well happen that the OPEN_FORM module is called up several times within an application. In this case, multiple copies of the dialog for the print parameters would be displayed. You can therefore transfer a data structure containing print parameters to the function module and deactivate dialog mode. You then can preset the required parameters in the program, determine them using your own dialogs (or report parameters) or alternatively call the default print dialog yourself (*see* Figure 3.187).

Data structures

Two data structures play an important role in the context of print parameters. The GET_PRINT_PARAMETERS function module, which you can use to call the default print dialog, uses the PRI_PARAMS structure to return the print parameters. However, the OPEN_FORM function module expects an input parameter based on the ITCPO structure. Both structures have fields with identical contents, but unfortunately they have different names. That is why it is necessary to transfer the parameters determined by calling GET_PRINT_PARAMETERS as fields into the structure that serves as an input parameter for OPEN_FORM.

Table 3.51 shows the design of the PRI_PARAMS structure.

Table 3.51   Design of the PRI_PARAMS structure

Field name	Description
PDEST	Output device
PRCOP	Number of expressions
PLIST	Name of the spool request (list name)
PRTXT	Text for cover page
PRIMM	'X': output immediately
PRREL	'X': delete after output
PRNEW	'X': new spool request
PEXPI	Spool residence time in days
LINCT	Length of list in lines
LINSZ	Width of list in characters
PAART	Production of the list
PRBIG	Output selections
PRSAP	Output cover page
PRREC	Recipient
PRABT	Department
PRBER	Authorization for access to spool request
PRDSN	Name of spool dataset
PTYPE	Type of spool request
ARMOD	Archive mode
FOOTL	Output footer line
PRCHK	Checksum

Each output statement must be sent to an output device (usually a printer). The output device might also define the values stored for some other attributes, for example the maximum page width and length. In the user master record, you can maintain a default for this value. This default is automatically transferred to the system. You will find the names of the output devices in the PDEST field. In the PRCOP field you can specify how many copies you would like to print.

Spool requests do not have to be printed immediately. Very often only one spool request is generated. This is especially true in the case of very large print jobs. This single spool request is later printed manually or in batch mode. You can set the PRIMM flag to define whether the output is to be automatically executed immediately after the creation of the output statement or not. After the output of a spool request, it is naturally at an end and no further output can be appended to it. This feature is connected with the PRNEW flag. If this flag is set, a new spool request is created for each output statement. If this flag has not been set, the system will first search for a suitable spool request made by the current user to which more output can be appended. In this case, the system only creates a new spool request if no suitable one exists.

After output, spool requests will remain in the spool list for a certain time. The period of time (in days) is defined in the PEXPI field. After the time entered there has passed, the spool request is automatically deleted. If it is not desirable to leave the spool request in the spool list after successful output, you can force its immediate deletion after output by selecting the PRREL flag. This is primarily of use in the case of documents or lists whose contents should not be accessible to all users. Normally, every user can view all spool requests. Not only can they see their own administration information and attributes, but also their actual contents. If increased security is required, you can store the name of an authorization, against which the spool request will be checked during access in the PRBER field.

Within spool administration, text information must be available about the individual spool requests to enable an administrator to find a particular spool request. The PRTXT field is available for this kind of information.

When outputting print jobs to printers that are available to several users, it is often sensible to insert a cover page. A cover page will always be created for the spool request if the PRSAP flag has been selected. Besides some data that the system creates automatically, the contents of the PRTXT, PRREC and PRABT fields are output to this cover page. The two latter fields show the name of the recipient and their department.

The field ARMOD is not unimportant, although seldom used. Instead of sending output requests to a printer, you can also store them in an optical archive. Optical archives are not provided with the R/3 System and must be purchased separately. You can use them to store the output documents and later display them in the form in which they were printed on paper. Many R/3 transactions link a data record in the R/3 System with its associated documents and allow transparent access to them. Use the TDARMOD flag to control the storage of a document in the optical archive. In the ARMOD field, enter the value 1 to initiate printing. If you set the value 2, the document will only be stored in the optical archive. The document will be output on both devices if you enter the value 3.

The GET_PRINT_PARAMETERS function module carries out some logical checks. You should therefore only modify the contents of PRI_PARAMS by using GET_PRINT_

PARAMETERS. So you can recognize changes outside the module, it determines a checksum that is stored in the PRCHK field.

The ITCPO Data Dictionary structure is used to transfer print parameters to the OPEN_FORM function module. In this structure (see Table 3.52), you will find some fields that have no counterpart in the PRI_PARAMS structure. In the TDPAGESLCT field, you can select the pages you want printed. Here, you identify the pages by their page number. You can separate a series of values with commas (example: 1,5,7). You can use a hyphen to set a range of pages (example: 5-7). If the first or the last value is missing in a range statement, printing will begin at the start or finish at the end of the document respectively (examples: -5,7-). The title of the spool request is contained in the TDCOVTITLE field. In addition there are three other fields: TDDATASET, TDSUFFIX1 and TDSUFFIX2.

The GET_PRINT_PARAMETERS function module

You use this function module to edit and read the current print parameters. It returns the results in a parameter called OUT_PARAMETERS, with the structure PRI_PARAMS. There are two ways to pass data to this parameter. First, the function module can call the SAP System default print dialog, in which the user can input the print parameters. Alternatively, you can transfer individual default values and the current version of the print parameter data record to the function module in a series of import parameters. It then creates a new print parameter from these values. If necessary, you can combine the two methods. If you do so, the user will find the default values you have set in the print parameters dialog. When the system is determining the print parameters, it takes any default values present in the user master record into consideration.

The function module stores a checksum in a field in the print parameter data record and uses it to check the validity of the values. Therefore you should never make changes to the print parameters by directly accessing the data record, but always exclusively by using the function module.

You use two parameters to control the actual functioning of the module. In the NO_DIALOG parameter you can set a value to specify whether the module should work in dialog mode or not. In the MODE parameter you can within certain limits influence the structure of the dialog being called up by the function module. This is described below.

When using the Export parameter, you should be aware of a special feature. If you operate the module in dialog mode, it will return a value in the VALID parameter showing whether the dialog ended correctly or was terminated by the user. It is essential to read this parameter and analyze it, to ensure your application functions correctly. If you do not use the VALID parameter value, but call a function module in one of the modes PARAMS, PARAMSEL, BATCH or CURRENT, it will react by triggering a runtime error. The same applies to the evaluation of the OUT_PARAMETERS parameter, for all modes other than DISPLAY. In previous releases of the SAP System, the system also checked the evaluation of the parameters. However, if an error occurs, the module only generates an exception and not a runtime error.

In addition to the fields mentioned in the description of the PRI_PARAMS structure, the module also processes a series of parameters that are necessary for the operation of an optical archive. These are not described here.

Table 3.52   Fields in the ITCPO structure

Field name	Short description
TDPAGESLCT	Selection of pages to be printed
TDCOPIES	Number of copies
TDDEST	Name of the output device
TDPRINTER	Name of the device type
TDPREVIEW	'X': print preview form on screen
TDNOPREV	'X': no print preview
TDNOPRINT	'X': no printout possible from print preview
TDNEWID	'X': generate new spool request
TDDATASET	Name of the spool request
TDSUFFIX1	Suffix 1 for the name of the spool request
TDSUFFIX2	Suffix 2 for the name of the spool request
TDIMMED	'X': immediately output spool request
TDDELETE	'X': delete spool request immediately after output
TDLIFETIME	Spool residence time
TDSCHEDULE	Request send time
TDSENDDATE	Required send date
TDSENDTIME	Required send time
TDTELELAND	Country key
TDTELENUM	Telecommunications partner
TDTITLE	Text description
TDTEST	Test form
TDPROGRAM	Program name
TDSCRNPOS	Screen display position for OTF
TDCOVER	'X': create cover page
TDCOVTITLE	Cover page: title
TDRECEIVER	Cover page: recipient
TDDIVISION	Cover page: department
TDAUTORITY	Authorization to access spool request
TDARMOD	Archive mode
TDIEXIT	Immediate exit after printing / faxing from print preview
TDGETOTF	Only create OTF table
TDFAXUSER	SAPoffice user
TDRDIDEV	Output device

PARAMS mode

This mode is used to call the default print dialog. This is the standard mode that is also called if the MODE parameter has not been filled. If necessary, the missing values can be derived from the user master record or filled with default values.

PARAMSEL mode

This mode is generally similar to PARAMS mode. However its dialog displays an additional field which you can use to create a printout of the selections from the report. The associated input field corresponds with the PRBIG field in the PRI_PARAMS structure.

BATCH mode

Frequently, the GET_PRINT_PARAMETERS function module is used to determine the print parameters for a program that is to run in the background. In this case, the name of the program to be started has to be entered in the REPORT import parameter. Any settings defining for page length and width are transferred from this program to the print parameters dialog. Apart from that, the print pushbutton is replaced with the Save pushbutton. The input field for the activation of the printing of selection values is also activated.

CURRENT mode

This mode should not be executed in dialog mode. It determines the current print parameters. With this mode you can find out the print parameters specified when an application was started.

DISPLAY mode

This mode is only recommended in dialog mode. It displays the current print parameters in a display box that cannot accept input.

Tasks

1. Analyze the ITCPO structure. Insert a suitable structure in program YZ337050 and enter all the default data required for printing into the structure. Then transfer this data to OPEN_FORM. Then switch off dialog mode for OPEN_FORM.

2. Set the trial print mode in ITCPO and then execute the program again.

3. Insert the GET_PRINT_PARAMETERS function module into the program, and provide the OPEN_FORM function module with the data supplied by GET_PRINT_PARAMETERS.

4 ABAP Objects

The first object-oriented extensions of ABAP, the R/3 programming language, were introduced in Release 4.0. In the current Release 4.6, ABAP has become a full-blooded object-oriented language. It is with this in mind that SAP has introduced the new name *ABAP Objects* for ABAP.

This section of the book is different from other sections. Other sections begin with examples that allow the user to make a practical start, before going into detail later. Here the process is reversed. Examples are linked in with some of the explanations of terms.

4.1 Terms from the world of ABAP Objects

The basic philosophy of object-oriented programming is to package data and the program code used to process it into compact elements, called *objects*. This method makes it easier to model the actual content of a program.

Object-oriented programming introduces a large number of new terms that are not specific to a particular programming language. This section describes the most important new terms, without intending to be a complete introduction to object-oriented programming. It contains comparisons with conventional ABAP, which are intended to make the initial introduction easier.

4.1.1 Classes

A class is the description of an object or, to put it more simply, the data type for an object. In the class you define the data, and also the program code that is allowed to access this data. Unlike conventional data types, a class definition is not only used to define simple data fields but also to contain source code. Objects are derived from the class later.

4.1.2 Objects

An object is the instance of a class, just as a data field is the instance of a data type. You work with objects in your program. You generate them, assign data to them and call functions with which you process the data for these objects. A program can contain any number of objects belonging to the same class.

4.1.3 References

A reference refers to an object, and has some similarities to a field symbol. You can only access an object through a reference. In a program, the reference appears as a special type of data field. It is possible for several references to point to the same object.

As well as reference to real objects, there are other reference types that can refer to classes or interfaces.

4.1.4 Attributes

Attributes are the data fields belonging to an object. They are declared within the class definition, with the same statements as in a normal program. The objects exist independently of each other so their attributes are also independent of those belonging to other objects. This applies even if both objects belong to the same class.

Attributes are only available when an object has been created, i.e. an instance of a class exists. The only exception is the special case of *class attributes*.

4.1.5 Methods

The source text sections that are used to access the attributes of an object are called methods. Methods are comparable with the subroutines or function modules in conventional programming languages. You always use a real object to access methods, except class methods. Therefore the methods are only available if objects, i.e. instances of a class, exist.

4.1.6 Events

Objects can trigger an event. Other objects can recognize this event and react to it. Objects can use the event function to communicate with each other. Events are linked to real objects. They therefore always relate to specific objects and not simply to every instance of a class.

Before an object can react to an event, it must first register itself for handling that event. In doing so, it must define both the triggering object data and the name of the event.

4.1.7 Class attributes

Class attributes do not apply to individual objects, but to all the objects in a class. At an application's runtime, only one instance of the class attributes exists per class. The memory for the class attributes is available before instances have been derived from its class. Class attributes can also include information that is intended to apply to all the objects in the class.

4.1.8 Class methods

A class method differs from a conventional method in its range of validity. Conventional methods apply to one specific object. In contrast, class methods apply to a class. Therefore, they exist before the objects have been generated, just like class attributes. You can use class methods to access class attributes. In practice, you use class attributes for the object-oriented processing of program functionality. It means you do not have to create an instance of a real object when you use the application later.

4.1.9 Class events

Class events apply to an entire class, just like class attributes and class methods. If objects register themselves for handling events, you do not need to specify the triggering object for class events. An event is then handled regardless of which real object triggers it.

4.1.10 Exceptions

The term *exceptions* is not specific to object-oriented programming. All the same, methods, like function modules, can trigger exceptions to signal error states to the calling program. Events are intended for normal communication between objects. Exceptions guarantee that error states are reported.

4.1.11 Interfaces

In an interface you define both attributes and methods. However, you do not implement the methods. Instead, you simply define their call parameters. The classes that integrate the interface into their declaration carry out the implementation. Using an interface guarantees that you can address all the various classes through an identical interface. So the interfaces offer a second means of defining the interfaces for several classes, alongside the inheritance function.

4.1.12 Constructors

A class can contain a constructor, although it does not have to. This is a method that is automatically called when you generate an instance of a class. You normally use constructors to initialize a generated object. They can be provided with parameters to do this. There are two constructors. The class constructor (predefined name CLASS_CONSTRUC-TOR) is called once when a class is accessed for the first time. The instance constructor (pre-defined name CONSTRUCTOR), however, is executed for each newly created object.

4.1.13 Visibility

You can provide both attributes and methods with parameters that restrict their visibility. There are three levels of visibility. Public attributes and methods are visible from the surrounding program without restriction. These attributes have both read access and write access. Protected attributes and methods are only visible within the class and possible inheritors, i.e. they cannot be accessed from outside. Private elements are subject to even more stringent constraints: they are only visible within the class.

4.1.14 Inheritance

The term *inheritance* is used to describe new classes derived from classes that already exist. Each new class receives all the characteristics (attributes and methods) from the class it inherits from. All these characteristics are available in the new class as if they had been defined there. The class that the elements are inherited from is called the *superclass*.

More attributes can be added to an inheriting class and methods can even be redefined (provided with new functions).

The subordinate classes can accept assignments from references that have the data type of the superclass.

4.1.15 Encapsulation

You can hide the internal functions of an object from the outside world by restricting the visibility of its attributes and methods. An object's users only access its resources through the public interface, without knowing how it functions internally.

4.1.16 Polymorphy

Different classes can implement methods that have the same name. These methods may then behave in completely different ways.

4.1.17 Classes pool

A classes pool is a special type of program in the R/3 System. In a classes pool you define classes that can be used throughout the whole system. You process the classes in a classes pool using the *Class Builder*.

4.2   Commands

This section describes the most important new language elements that have been created as part of the object-oriented extensions to ABAP. You can use these commands to generate and use object-oriented elements in your own programs.

4.2.1 Defining a class

A class definition always consists of two blocks. Each of these is introduced by the CLASS command and concluded by ENDCLASS. The first block contains the actual definition.

The second is used to implement the methods. Additional keywords are used within the CLASS statement to distinguish between the two blocks.

You must first define a new class. To do this, you define the attributes and the interfaces of the methods. You cannot define classes in subroutines or function modules. You cannot nest class definitions either. The syntax of the command for defining a class is:

```
CLASS class DEFINITION
    [ INHERITING FROM superclass |
      ABSTRACT  |
      FINAL     |
      PUBLIC    |
      CREATE ( PUBLIC | PROTECTED | PRIVATE )
    ]
    [ PUBLIC SECTION. ]
      Component definitions...
    [ PROTECTED SECTION. ]
      Component definitions...
    [ PRIVATE SECTION. ]
      Component definitions...
ENDCLASS.
```

The CLASS keyword introduces the definition. It is followed by the names of the classes that are to be created and the DEFINITION keyword. You use this syntax to generate a class that is only known within the current program. Although the class is part of the global definitions within the program, the term local class is used because the class is not visible from outside the program.

You can use additional keywords to modify the characteristics of a class. With one of them, INHERITING FROM, you can use the inheriting mechanism. You use INHERITING FROM to determine that the new class inherits all the non-private elements from a given superclass. You can reimplement all the inherited methods in the new class unless this is expressly forbidden. Each class can only inherit from one other class. In this way a class tree emerges with the OBJECT class located at the top, as it is implicitly available.

The ABSTRACT addition marks a class as abstract. This means instances (objects) cannot be created from this class. Classes like this are normally used as the starting points for branches in the class tree. If several similar objects share a number of attributes and methods, these objects are often implemented in an abstract class. This saves having to implement identical functions many times.

The FINAL addition has the opposite effect. It defines that no further subclasses can be derived from a particular class.

The CREATE addition defines who may create instances for the class. The default setting is CREATE PUBLIC and you do not need to define this. It allows you to generate an instance at any point in the program code. If you use CREATE PROTECTED, you can only generate an instance within the class itself or within a subclass. Finally, the CREATE PRIVATE addition only allows you to generate instances within the class itself. This requires the provision of a class method in which the instances for the class are generated. This method must return a reference to the generated instance.

The PUBLIC addition creates a class known throughout an SAP System. You can only create classes of this type in the Class Builder. This automatically appends the PUBLIC addition. You cannot use this addition if you define the class manually.

Once you have entered the data concerning the class itself, you define the components of the class. Three different sections are available for this (PUBLIC SECTION, PROTECTED SECTION and PRIVATE SECTION). Not all the sections have to be present in a class, but if present, they must be defined in the sequence shown above. The sections define the validity range of the attributes and methods that are defined within them. Public elements (PUBLIC SECTION) can be accessed from anywhere. Protected elements (PROTECTED SECTION) are only available within the class itself and the subordinate classes. Private elements (PRIVATE SECTION) can only be used within the class itself.

Three groups of components exist in a class. You cannot create every component in the sections named above. The first group of components is the interface components. You use the INTERFACE and ALIASES statements to generate them.

The second group of components is the class components. They are also called *static components*. This group includes type and constant definitions (TYPES and CONSTANTS), class data (CLASS-DATA), class methods (CLASS-METHODS) and class events (CLASS-EVENTS).

The third group contains instance-specific data, methods and events. You use the DATA, METHOD and EVENT statements to define them. The syntax for component definitions is as follows:

```
[ INTERFACES interface ]
[ ALIASES name FOR interface~component ]
[ TYPES type declaration ]
[ CONSTANTS constant declaration ]
[ CLASS-DATA field definitions ]
[ CLASS-METHODS method declaration ]
[ CLASS-EVENTS event declaration ]
[ DATA field definitions ]
[ METHODS method declaration ]
[ EVENTS event declaration ]
```

The syntax for the individual statements is described in more detail directly after this section. This example focuses on the definition of the class as a whole.

The syntax for the implementation section is much simpler as it can only contain methods:

```
CLASS class IMPLEMENTATION.
{
  METHOD header.
    method implementation
  ENDMETHOD.
} . . .
ENDCLASS.
```

All the methods that were declared in the definition section, or imported through interfaces, must be implemented in the implementation section.

There are two other forms of the `CLASS` statement. They only consist of one line:

CLASS *class* **DEFINITION DEFERRED.**

   or

CLASS *class* **DEFINITION LOAD.**

The `DEFERRED` addition only announces the name of the class. It is defined later. However, you can then start using the class name in other definitions before you actually define the class.

The `LOAD` addition is only necessary in the context of a common (`PUBLIC`) class. It ensures that the definition of the class is loaded.

4.2.2 Defining an interface

You define an interface in a similar way to a class. However, in an interface, all the visibility groups are missing. All elements are automatically public. You can define the same components as in classes. Consequently, you can encapsulate interfaces within each other.

INTERFACES *interface* [**DEFERRED**] **.**
  [**INTERFACES** *interfaces*]
  [**ALIASES** *name* **FOR** *interface~component*]
  [**TYPES** *type declarations*]
  [**CONSTANTS** *constant declarations*]
  [**CLASS-DATA** *field definitions*]
  [**CLASS-METHODS** *method declarations*]
  [**CLASS-EVENTS** *event declarations*]
  [**DATA** *field definitions*]
  [**METHODS** *method declarations*]
  [**EVENTS** *event declarations*]
ENDINTERFACE **.**

To access the elements of an interface within a class that is using this interface, use this command:

interface~component

4.2.3 Defining components

You can define various components within classes and interfaces. Some of the statements used to do this (e.g. `DATA` and `TYPES`) are already familiar, and others are new. This section describes the various components and the necessary statements in detail. It primarily concentrates on the new statements.

Declaring events

You can declare events within class and interface definitions. To do so, you use the
EVENT keyword. Its complete syntax is as follows:

```
EVENTS event EXPORTING {
  VALUE(parameter) [
    TYPE type | LIKE field [OPTIONAL | DEFAULT default]]}.
```

This kind of event can provide the recipient with further information, in addition to
the fact that it exists. When you are defining the event, you must define and set the type
of further information, in much the same way as you set a method's export parameters.

A class-related event cannot pass on additional parameters. The command syntax for
defining this kind of event is therefore simply:

```
CLASS-EVENTS event.
```

Defining methods

Methods resemble function modules in terms of their characteristics and the way they
work. Therefore, similar statements are also used for defining them. However, in contrast
to the function modules, you do not maintain the interface definition by using a special
tool in several consecutive screen programs. You enter it directly in the source code, just
like our old friend the subroutine.

You define methods and their interfaces in a class's definition section:

```
METHODS method
  [ IMPORTING ( [[VALUE | REFERENCE](parameter)] | parameter
      [TYPE type | LIKE field]
      [OPTIONAL | DEFAULT default] ) . . . ]
  [ EXPORTING ( [[VALUE | REFERENCE](parameter)] | parameter
      [TYPE type | LIKE field]
      [OPTIONAL | DEFAULT default] ) . . . ]
  [ CHANGING   ( [[VALUE | REFERENCE](parameter)] | parameter
      [TYPE type | LIKE field]
      [OPTIONAL | DEFAULT default] ) . . . ]
  [ RETURNING VALUE(parameter) [ TYPE type | LIKE field ] ]
  [ EXCEPTIONS { exception } ]
  [ ABSTRACT ]
  [ FINAL ]
  [ REDEFINITION ].
```

The way you use the IMPORT, EXPORT and CHANGING keywords to define import and
export parameters is similar to the procedure for function modules. Just as for subroutines, you can use the TYPE or LIKE additions to define parameters' types. However, this
type definition is mandatory. Finally, you can use OPTIONAL to define that parameters
are optional. If you do so, the parameter is filled with the initial value that is appropriate
for the parameter's type, if that value is not transferred. The DEFAULT addition also
defines an optional parameter and assigns it a default value.

Data types from the program and Data Dictionary are not the only things whose type you can set with TYPE. Table 4.1 shows all the typing variants.

Table 4.1   Different typing variants

Statement	Description
Type	Parameter corresponds to the data type.
ANY	Parameter is compatible with all data types.
REF TO class	Parameter is a reference to a class or interface.
LINE OF itab	Parameter corresponds to the line structure of an internal table.
TYPE [ANY │ INDEX │ STANDARD │ SORTED │ HASHED] TABLE	Parameter is an internal table with the defined characteristic (ANY, etc.)

You can also use one major extension in functionality, which is not available for function modules. After the RETURNING addition you can enter a parameter that then applies as the sole return code for the method. When you use this addition you exclude the use of the EXPORTING and CHANGING parameter types. If you use the RETURNING addition, this means that the return code method can later be used directly in expressions. At the moment this type of value transfer is only possible in special cases. In this context, also note the section on implementing methods and the examples.

If a method's parameter names are the same as the names of its attributes, the parameters in the method hide the attributes. To access the attributes, you can still use the ME-> prefix. Note also program YZ342040.

Use the EXCEPTIONS addition to define the exceptions that the method can trigger. This is exactly the same as the procedure for function modules.

You can use three statements, ABSTRACT, FINAL and REDEFINITION, in the context of the inheritance of classes. If you want to take a method from a superclass and reimplement (overwrite) it in a derived class, you must mark the method with the REDEFINITION keyword in the definition section of the derived class. You are not allowed to assign further options, apart from the FINAL addition, to methods that are to be overwritten. This means that you must not change the interface when overwriting methods. For example, you cannot add parameters. The only two possible statements that can be used with REDEFINITION are:

```
METHOD method REDEFINITION.
METHOD method FINAL REDEFINITION.
```

A method marked as ABSTRACT is not implemented in the current class. It will be implemented in the derived classes. In contrast to this, a method marked with the FINAL addition can no longer be overwritten.

In the context of event processing, there are special methods that are used for handling events. You must define these methods in an appropriate way, and later register them as handling methods for the event. You define a method for event handling as follows:

```
METHODS method FOR EVENT event OF class
   [ IMPORTING { parameter } ]
   [ ABSTRACT ]
   [ FINAL ]
   [ REDEFINITION ].
```

The imported parameters must correspond to the export parameters of the event.

You define class methods in much the same way as simple methods. However, class methods have no interface. Hence the definition is simply as follows:

```
CLASS METHODS method [ FOR EVENT event OF class ].
```

Method implementation

The methods you define in a class's definition section must be implemented later. In a class's implementation section, you use this statement to begin implementation of the methods:

```
METHOD method.
```

To close implementation of the methods, you use this statement:

```
ENDMETHOD.
```

You do not have to repeat the interface definition. Enter the source code for the method between the two statements.

Calling methods

You use the CALL METHOD command to call a method, in much the same way as you call a function module. The parameters are transferred as for conventional function modules. The RECEIVING keyword is new here: it is used to receive the RETURNING parameters for the method. The PARAMETER-TABLE and EXCEPTION-TABLE additions have been added to the call syntax. These options allow you to transfer parameters or exceptions to an internal table.

```
CALLING A METHOD objectreference->method
   [ EXPORTING    { parameter = value } ]
   [ IMPORTING    { parameter = field } ]
   [ CHANGING     { parameter = field } ]
   [ RECEIVING      parameter = field ]
   [ EXCEPTIONS [{ exception = value } ]
   [ PARAMETER-TABLE itab ]
   [ EXCEPTION-TABLE itab ].
```

As simple methods are always linked with existing objects, you have to use the object reference to call the method.

If the complete interface for a method consists of a single import parameter, you can simplify the call to the method by enclosing the import parameter in round brackets:

CALL METHOD *objectreference->method(single_parameter)* .

You can use a similar form of call if the interface for the method consists solely of import parameters. In this case, you can transfer the parameters for a call as name/value pairs:

```
CALL METHOD objectreference->method( param_name_1 = param_value_1 ...
                              param_name_n = param_value_n) .
```

For both these two forms of parameter transfer, there are special cases where the call can be further simplified if the method returns a value, i.e. if a RETURNING parameter has been defined in the interface. In these cases, you can omit the CALL METHOD keyword. The method call can then stand directly as the operand in statements. This is possible, for example, in assignments (a method call as the source in a MOVE statement, or as an arithmetical operand in conventional assignments) and in logical expressions. Note here that the round brackets are part of the syntax, i.e. you must always enter them, even if the method has no import parameters. If so, you must leave a space between the opening and closing brackets!

Generating object references

You require an object reference to access objects. A reference is rather like a field symbol that points to a specific memory space. You can find the object in precisely this location. Several references can point to one object. Assignments to object references do not change the object; they merely modify a pointer that points to it. In the same way, deleting an object reference does not automatically delete an object. The memory space occupied by the object is only released automatically if no more object references point to that object. You generate object references using this command:

DATA *reference* [**TYPE REF TO** *class* | **TYPE** *referencetype* | **LIKE** *reference*] .

Naturally, you can also use the TYPES statement to declare your own data types for object references:

TYPES *referencetype* [**TYPE REF TO** *class* | **LIKE** *reference*] .

When you generate an object reference, you have not yet created an object. You merely create a field that can point to an object. Please note that in the statements above, the placeholder class stands for both full-blown classes and for interfaces.

Two object references are implicitly available within each object. These are the so-called *self-reference*, ME and the *pseudo-reference*, SUPER. The ME reference points to its own object. As a result you can access each component of an object by explicitly entering

ME->component .

This is sometimes necessary because the components of the object can be hidden by parameters, etc., that have the same name.

The SUPER pseudo-reference does not point to a real object, but to a higher level class. You use it to access the corresponding methods for the superclass in overwritten methods.

Generating objects

Objects must be generated explicitly. The simplest way to do this is to use the following statement:

CREATE OBJECT *reference.*

The type of reference field in this statement defines the type of object you generate. Sometimes you deviate from this approach. To do this, you explicitly transfer the type of class that is to be generated:

CREATE OBJECT *reference* **TYPE** *class* | *(class_field).*

To do this, there must be assignment compatibility between the type of class to be generated and the type of reference field. You can enter the class name of the object you generate as a direct value, or it can be determined dynamically from the contents of a field.

After this command is executed, it creates an object, along with the object reference defined by you that points to this object. You can access the elements within an object using the statements in Table 4.2, providing the visibility classes permit it.

Table 4.2   Accessing elements in objects

Element	Access
Attribute	Reference ->attributes
Method	CALL reference ->method
Attributes from an interface	Reference -> interface attribute
Method from an interface	CALL reference -> interface method

When you generate an object, a constructor can be called automatically. This constructor is a method with the predefined name CONSTRUCTOR. You can transfer parameters to this method. To do this, you assign this addition to the CREATE statement:

EXPORTING *param_name_1 = param_value_1 ...*
          param_name_n = param_value_n.

A constructor can trigger exceptions that you can also define using CREATE. Use the following addition:

EXCEPTIONS *exception_name_1 = exception_value_1 ...*
          exception_name_n = exception_value_n.

If a constructor has no optional parameters, you must provide them using CREATE OBJECT.

Triggering exceptions and events

Use the following command to trigger an exception in an object's method, just as you do for function modules:

RAISE *exception.*

The same command, with some additional keywords, is responsible for events.

RAISE EVENT *event* [**EXPORTING** { *parameter s = value* }].

Fundamentally, you can transfer additional parameters to simple events (and not to class events). The method that is defined later can transfer and evaluate these parameters for event handling.

Apart from the optional parameter list, there is no difference between calling simple and class events. However, in class methods you can only trigger class events, while both types of event are available in methods relating to instances.

Event handling

To deal with events, you must first define a method as an event handler within a class definition. To do so, use the FOR EVENT addition in the method definition. You must still register this method within the application. When you do this, you assign a real event-triggering object to the event-handling object if this is necessary.

To set the handler for class events, use this statement:

SET HANDLER *handlerlist* [**ACTIVATION** *field*].

handlerlist is a list of the event-handling methods. You must specify these methods fully using the following syntax:

*object->*method.

When you enter the individual methods, only separate their names from each other with a space. The SET HANDLER command does not accept the use of the colon after the statement.

Registration of instance-related events is slightly more time consuming as you still have to specify the event-triggering event. To do so, use the FOR addition followed by the object reference:

SET HANDLER *handlerlist* **FOR**
  [*objectreference* | **ALL INSTANCES**]
  [**ACTIVATION** *field*].

If you want to carry out event handling for all instances (objects) in a class, you can use the ALL INSTANCES addition after the FOR keyword, to determine that this is the case.

In both forms of the command, you can use the ACTIVATION keyword to deactivate or reactivate event handling. To do this, you transfer a field with length 1 and type C. If this field is empty, event handling is deactivated. If the field has the value 'X', or the ACTIVATION addition is missing, event handling is activated.

4.2.4   Examples

The examples in this section demonstrate object-oriented programming with ABAP Objects. Several programs at the start primarily demonstrate the new statements. The problems solved by these programs are not typical or practical uses of object-oriented concepts, but they do provide a simple introduction to the issues involved.

Defining a class

The first program presents a class that performs arithmetical calculations. So you can also use the classes defined here in the next example, their definitions and implementation are grouped in an include statement. Look first at the contents of this include. Line numbers have been added to simplify the explanation that follows:

```
 1  *------------------------------------------------------------*
 2  *    INCLUDE YZ34_CALC1
 3  *------------------------------------------------------------*
 4 CLASS calc1 DEFINITION.
 5   PUBLIC SECTION.
 6     METHODS:
 7       constructor
 8       IMPORTING   value1 TYPE f
 9                   value2 TYPE f,
10     do_operation
11       IMPORTING operation TYPE c
12       EXPORTING result TYPE f.
13   PROTECTED SECTION.
14     DATA: op1 TYPE f,
15           op2 TYPE f.
16 ENDCLASS.
17
18 CLASS calc1 IMPLEMENTATION.
19   METHOD constructor.
20     op1 = value1.
21     op2 = value2.
22   ENDMETHOD.
23
24   METHOD do_operation.
25     CASE operation.
26       WHEN '+'.
27         result = op1 + op2.
28         CLEAR: op1, op2.
29       WHEN '-'.
30         result = op1 - op2.
31         CLEAR: op1, op2.
32       WHEN '*'.
33         result = op1 * op2.
34         CLEAR: op1, op2.
35       WHEN '/'.
36         result = op1 / op2.
37         CLEAR: op1, op2.
38     ENDCASE.
39   ENDMETHOD.
40 ENDCLASS.
```

Between lines 4 and 16 you find the definition of the class. The statement in line 4 opens the definition of the class, which is assigned the name `calc1`. In lines 5 and 13, you find the statements defining the area of visibility for the subsequent definitions. As both fields `OP1` and `OP2` are located in the `PRIVATE` area, they will not be visible from outside later. These fields are filled when you generate the real object. To do this, the program defines a special method, `constructor`, that is automatically called when you generate a new object. A class need not have a constructor, but in many cases it is very helpful. For example, when you are defining a real instance you can immediately set useful values for its attributes. Without the constructor, you would need another method that you would have to call separately.

The constructor is assigned two values that it stores in both the object's private fields. In the `PUBLIC` section, you find the `do_operation` method. It receives an `operation` code in the operation input parameter and returns the result in the `result` parameter. We do not intend to deal with the potential problem of a division by zero in this example. Calculated results are returned using export parameters, just like function modules.

Because the `METHODS` statement supports colon notation, you can define both the named methods in one go, without having to enter the `METHODS` statement before each method. However, this means you must close the definition of the constructor with a comma and not with a full stop.

Initially, the definitions only define the interface for the methods. After definition, you must store these methods with the program code in the implementation section (lines 18 to 40). You do this by entering the source code between the `METHOD` and `ENDMETHOD` statements. The functionality of both methods is very simple. In `constructor`, `OP1` and `OP2` are filled with the values of the import parameters. The `do_operation` method links both fields on the basis of the transferred operational characters.

You can now use the `calc1` class in programs to create instances of objects. Here is the source code of a simple program:

```
 1 REPORT   yz342010.
 2 INCLUDE yz34_calc1.
 3 PARAMETERS:    a(20),
 4                b(20),
 5                op.
 6 DATA:  r   TYPE REF TO calc1,
 7        f1 TYPE f,
 8        f2 TYPE f.
 9
10 START-OF-SELECTION.
11    TRANSLATE a USING ',.'.
12    TRANSLATE b USING ',.'.
13    f1 = a.
14    f2 = b.
15
16    CREATE OBJECT r EXPORTING    value1 = f1
17                                 value2 = f2.
18
```

```
19    CALL METHOD r->do_operation
20      EXPORTING
21        operation = op
22      IMPORTING
23        result = f1.
24
25    WRITE: / f1 EXPONENT 0.
```

In the main program, the include is first linked with the class definition. You then define three parameters that can receive both the numerical input values and the operational characters.

To be able to use the class, you must generate an object reference and later link it to an object. The statement in line 6 deals with generating the reference. This statement generates a reference, r, that can point to an object of the calc1 class.

Individual statement blocks, similar to subroutine declarations, are used to define and implement a class. The ABAP interpreter can only find statements after such a block if the beginning of a new statement block is programmed explicitly. In line 10, the START-OF-SELECTION statement is used to do this. Immediately after this statement, the input parameter available as a character string is changed into decimal numbers. To do so, implicit type conversion is defined in lines 13 and 14. The correct decimal separator (comma or point) is set beforehand to prevent problems arising.

An object is generated immediately afterwards in line 16, using the object reference. Because you have to program an object reference relating to a particular class, you do not need to reference the class again if you use CREATE OBJECT to generate the object. The class being used here has a constructor whose import parameters are required parameters, so you must provide the CREATE OBJECT statement with an EXPORTING part. Both the numerical values will be transferred into this.

The actual calculation is performed by calling the do_operation method in line 19. The call itself resembles the call for a function module. All the same you must enter the names of the object and the method. You must separate them with the characters '->'. The results are displayed as soon as processing is complete.

Inheritance

The next example demonstrates the principle of inheritance. Division by 0 is not intercepted within the do_operation method for the calc1 class and causes a runtime error. You should remove this problem by programming a new class called calc2. You reimplement the method in this class. All other characteristics are to be inherited from the existing calc1 class. You define and implement the new class directly in the main program. Its listing is as follows:

```
1 REPORT  yz342020.
2 INCLUDE yz34_calc1.
3
4 CLASS calc2 DEFINITION INHERITING FROM calc1.
5   PUBLIC SECTION.
```

```
 6      METHODS do_operation REDEFINITION.
 7 ENDCLASS.
 8
 9 CLASS calc2 IMPLEMENTATION.
10   METHOD do_operation.
11     IF operation <> '/' OR op2 <> 0.
12       CALL METHOD super->do_operation
13         EXPORTING
14            operation = operation
15         IMPORTING
16            result = result.
17     ELSE.
18       CLEAR result.
19     ENDIF.
20   ENDMETHOD.
21 ENDCLASS.
22
23 PARAMETERS: a(20),
24             b(20),
25             op.
26 DATA: r  TYPE REF TO calc2,
27       f1 TYPE f,
28       f2 TYPE f.
29
30 START-OF-SELECTION.
31   TRANSLATE a USING ',.'.
32   TRANSLATE b USING ',.'.
33   f1 = a.
34   f2 = b.
35
36   CREATE OBJECT r EXPORTING    value1 = f1
37                               value2 = f2.
38
39   CALL METHOD r->do_operation
40     EXPORTING
41       operation = op
42     IMPORTING
43       result = f1.
44
45   WRITE: / f1 EXPONENT 0.
```

First you integrate the include with the calc1 class in line 2. This makes the class available in the current program. You define the calc2 class in line 4. The INHERITING FROM addition defines that the new class inherits all its characteristics from the calc1 class. The calc2 class will behave just like the calc1 class if the definition of the calc2 class contains no additional statements, and the CLASS statement immediately follows the ENDCLASS statement. Although you can create and use references from the new class, calls to either method are immediately passed to the calc1 class. In line 6, you determine that the do_operation method is to be redefined. Because the interface cannot be changed by the redefinition, you do not have to program it again, i.e. the corresponding method from the calc1 class continues to be valid. However, you still have to program the source code for the new method in the implementation section. In this special case there are two possibilities. You could transfer the complete source code for the method from the calc1 class, and only build in an additional check, in the CASE branch for division. Alternatively, you could check the operators and operational characters first and call the do_operation method for the class calc1 if all the values are correct. The latter approach is more elegant, as it saves you reimplementing available functionality.

In line 11 of the source code, you can see the corresponding check. Line 12 contains the call to the higher level class for the method. As both methods must have the same name, you must use the super pseudo-reference to define that you want to access the method in the base class. If you do not enter this reference, the ABAP interpreter will call the do_operation method from calc2 class and so generate an endless loop.

The rest of the program is identical to the first example, with the exception of the r reference. The best way to understand the program functions is to debug the complete program step-by-step.

Compatibility of assignments

In practice you derive several different subclasses from a base class through the application of inheritance, as demonstrated above. In this case, each class essentially represents a separate data type. The type checks that take place during the assignment of objects are not directly comparable with the checks that take place during assignments between elementary fields. Under certain conditions, you can assign object references of another type to objects of different classes. Generally, a reference field can point to all objects belonging to the class of that reference field, as well as to all objects derived from this base class. This is independent of the degree of inheritance.

The program that follows presents the different kinds of assignment and the effects associated with them. The starting point is the c1 class that stores a simple character string. You can use the set_value method to set the value of this attribute, and use get_value to load it. You derive both classes c11 and c12 from this class. Both redefine the set_value method. Within the new methods, the character string is converted into either capital or lower-case letters. In addition, class c12 defines a further method called clear_value.

In the data declaration section for each of the three classes, you create an object reference and declare two character string fields. At the beginning of the program you create instances of three objects and test them. They are assigned three character strings, each of which is either in its original form, completely in capital letters, or completely in lower-case letters. The program teaches you nothing new, up to this point. Here is the source code:

```
 1 REPORT yz342030.
 2 TYPES mychar(60).
 3
 4 CLASS c1 DEFINITION.
 5   PUBLIC SECTION.
 6     METHODS:  set_value IMPORTING imp TYPE mychar,
 7               get_value EXPORTING exp TYPE mychar.
 8   PROTECTED SECTION.
 9     DATA value TYPE mychar.
10 ENDCLASS.
11
12 CLASS c1 IMPLEMENTATION.
13   METHOD set_value.
14     value = imp.
15   ENDMETHOD.
16
17   METHOD get_value.
18     exp = value.
19   ENDMETHOD.
20
21 ENDCLASS.
22
23 CLASS c11 DEFINITION INHERITING FROM c1.
24   PUBLIC SECTION.
25     METHODS: set_value REDEFINITION.
26 ENDCLASS.
27
28 CLASS c11 IMPLEMENTATION.
29   METHOD set_value.
30     CALL METHOD super->set_value EXPORTING imp = imp.
31     TRANSLATE value TO LOWER CASE.
32   ENDMETHOD.
33 ENDCLASS.
34
35 CLASS c12 DEFINITION INHERITING FROM c1.
36   PUBLIC SECTION.
37     METHODS: set_value REDEFINITION,
38       clear_value.
39 ENDCLASS.
40
41 CLASS c12 IMPLEMENTATION.
42   METHOD set_value.
43     CALL METHOD super->set_value EXPORTING imp = imp.
44     TRANSLATE value TO UPPER CASE.
```

```
45    ENDMETHOD.
46
47    METHOD clear_value.
48       CLEAR value.
49    ENDMETHOD.
50 ENDCLASS.
51
52 DATA: r1  TYPE REF TO c1,
53       r11 TYPE REF TO c11,
54       r12 TYPE REF TO c12,
55       cimp TYPE mychar VALUE 'abcDEF',
56       cres TYPE mychar.
57
58 START-OF-SELECTION.
59    CREATE OBJECT r1.
60    CALL METHOD r1->set_value EXPORTING imp = cimp.
61 CALL METHOD r1->get_value IMPORTING exp = cres.
62    WRITE: / cres.
63
64    CREATE OBJECT r11.
65 CALL METHOD r11->set_value EXPORTING imp = cimp.
66 CALL METHOD r11->get_value IMPORTING exp = cres.
67    WRITE: / cres.
68
69    CREATE OBJECT r12.
70 CALL METHOD r12->set_value EXPORTING imp = cimp.
71 CALL METHOD r12->get_value IMPORTING exp = cres.
72    WRITE: / cres.
73
74    r1 = r11.
75 CALL METHOD r1->set_value EXPORTING imp = cimp.
76 CALL METHOD r1->get_value IMPORTING exp = cres.
77    WRITE: / cres.
78
79    r1 = r12.
80 CALL METHOD r1->set_value EXPORTING imp = cimp.
81 CALL METHOD r1->get_value IMPORTING exp = cres.
82    WRITE: / cres.
83
84 * r1 and r12 point to the same object!!!
85    CALL METHOD r12->set_value
86       EXPORTING imp = 'An other string'.
87 CALL METHOD r1->get_value IMPORTING exp = cres.
88    WRITE: / cres.
```

```
89 CALL METHOD r12->clear_value.
90
91 * not possible:
92 * CALL method r1->clear_value.
93 *    r11 = r1.
94 *    r12 = r1.
95 *    r11 = r12.
```

The first important statement is in line 74. This statement assigns the contents of the r11 object reference to the r1 object reference. This does not mean that the contents of the class-c11 object are copied to the object in the class. The object reference merely points to the existing class-c11 object. The r1 and r11 references now point to exactly the same object! The object that was previously generated in class r1 is lost as there is no longer a reference pointing to it. Without a reference you cannot access the object.

As r1 now points to an object in class c11, the next time you call the method (lines 75 and 76), the methods of this object will be executed too. That is, the character string will be converted into lower-case characters. In the same way, r1 can naturally also point to an object in the c12 class, as the statements in lines 79 to 82 make clear. As r1 and r12 now point to the same object again, it does not matter which object reference you use for calling the method. There is an example of this in the listing (lines 85 to 87).

You can assign r11 or r12 to r1 because classes c11 and c12 inherit from class c1. When they inherit they can extend, but not restrict, the definition from c1. As a result, the subclasses always contain the elements in the definition of class c1, and you can also address them through object references that only know the elements in the base class. This also means that you cannot use object reference r1 to address elements that you have only defined in the derived classes. In the example, the clear_value method in the class c12 is such an object. The object reference r1 after the assignment of r12 points to an object in c12 class, but you cannot use it to address the clear_value method. The attempt leads to a syntax error.

The system does not carry out type checks by simply comparing names. It also includes the inheritance hierarchy. For this reason, this statement also leads to an error:

```
r11 = r12.
```

This is in spite of the fact that r12 contains all the elements that are contained in the definition of class c11 which defines type r11.

These assignments are not correct either:

```
r11 = r1.
```

and

```
r12 = r1.
```

Because inheriting classes can extend the definition of the base class, both these statements would allow access to elements that are not available to the assigned object. Attempts of this kind must naturally be prevented.

Simplifying the transfer of parameters

When calling the methods, we followed conventions similar to those for calling function modules. However, there are several ways in which it is simpler to call methods. These are described in the practical example below. In it we shall again use a class that performs an arithmetical operation. No inheritance will be involved. The `calc3` class will be completely reimplemented and has different interfaces from the `calc1` and `calc2` classes.

```
 1 REPORT  yz342040.
 2 CLASS calc3 DEFINITION.
 3   PUBLIC SECTION.
 4     METHODS:
 5       constructor
 6         IMPORTING value1 TYPE f
 7                   value2 TYPE f,
 8       set_op
 9         IMPORTING op TYPE c,
10       result
11         RETURNING value(result) TYPE f.
12   PROTECTED SECTION.
13     DATA: op1 TYPE f,
14           op2 TYPE f,
15           op  TYPE c.
16 ENDCLASS.
17
18 CLASS calc3 IMPLEMENTATION.
19   METHOD constructor.
20     op1 = value1.
21     op2 = value2.
22   ENDMETHOD.
23
24   METHOD result.
25     CASE op.
26       WHEN '+'.
27         result = op1 + op2.
28         CLEAR: op1, op2.
29       WHEN '-'.
30         result = op1 - op2.
31         CLEAR: op1, op2.
32       WHEN '*'.
33         result = op1 * op2.
34         CLEAR: op1, op2.
35       WHEN '/'.
36         IF op2 <> 0.
37           result = op1 / op2.
38           CLEAR: op1, op2.
```

```
39              ENDIF.
40        ENDCASE.
41     ENDMETHOD.
42
43     METHOD set_op.
44        me->op = op.
45     ENDMETHOD.
46
47 ENDCLASS.
48
49 PARAMETERS: a(20),
50               b(20),
51                 op.
52 DATA:  r   TYPE REF TO calc3,
53         f1 TYPE f,
54         f2 TYPE f.
55
56 START-OF-SELECTION.
57    TRANSLATE a USING ',.'.
58    TRANSLATE b USING ',.'.
59    f1 = a.
60    f2 = b.
61
62    CREATE OBJECT r EXPORTING  value1 = f1
63                                value2 = f2.
64    CALL METHOD r->set_op( op ).
65
66    f1 = r->result( ).
67
68 WRITE: / f1 EXPONENT 0.
```

The way the new class functions is different from previous classes. Both the operands are still transferred to the constructor, but the non-standard method set_op is available for setting the operational characters. It stores the operational characters in an attribute for the class. The additional attribute for the operational characters is also an extension of previous variants. The result method returns the result of the operation. This method has no input parameter. It returns only one parameter and uses the RETURNING statement, not the EXPORTING statement.

The source code for the constructor and the result method teach us nothing new because they are similar to methods we have already encountered. It is only within the set_op method (line 44) that a new syntax variant appears. The input parameter for the method, and the attributes of the object, both possess the same name, op. Thus the input parameter conceals the attribute. Consequently, it is not so readily available. Access to the attribute is only possible through the me reference. This reference always points to the current object, and so allows you to access concealed elements in a targeted manner.

The next special syntax feature is in line 64. There, the set_op method has only one parameter available to it, so the value for this parameter can be transferred without the EXPORTING clause and a name reference. It can be assigned clearly and without any problems. Please note that, when you call the method in this way, you must enter a space between the brackets and the formal parameter.

An even simpler method for the ABAP programmer, although it takes some getting used to, is the call to the result method in line 66. This method has no input parameter and returns its result as a RETURNING parameter. Because the input parameters are missing, the parameter list for the call can remain empty. You only have to enter the two round brackets, but these must be separated from each other by a space! Results are returned through a RETURNING parameter. In some exceptional cases, this allows you to leave out the CALL METHOD statement. Assignment of the results to another field is one of these exceptions. Thus, in line 66 the RETURNING parameter is written to the f1 field.

Interfaces

In the examples you have seen so far, you have defined the interfaces for the classes directly in the classes, using the inheritance function from a higher level class. As a result, a class tree emerges whose elements' assignments are only upwardly compatible within a branch. Sometimes it is desirable, or necessary, to have completely different classes with methods that have the same names. The way these methods function internally may be different, but outwardly they may have identical interfaces and fulfil similar tasks. This behaviour is known as *polymorphism*. In practice, this kind of method could write the attributes for an object to a database or call a dialog that allows you to edit the attribute. This type of programming makes it easier to write generic applications that can work with objects in different classes. The problem is that each object you process requires an object reference whose type corresponds to the particular class. If the affected classes lie in different branches of the class tree, and have no common predecessor that offers the desired method in its own interface, you need a reference variable for each class. This can become very difficult if a large number of classes is affected, or if you are dealing with classes that do not yet exist. You cannot write generic applications in this way.

The example below demonstrates the use of an interface. This interface defines a single method called show. You use this method used later with real objects to display a development object's name and type. The interface is implemented by two classes (cprog and ctable) that are not assignment-compatible with each other. One class records the names of programs, and the other the names of tables. Each of these classes has an additional method with which the attributes can be set, in addition to the method defined through the interface.

The task of the program below is to determine the program name and table name from the TADIR table and to create an instance of an object of the appropriate class for each of the data sets. These objects must be saved in an internal table. Then each object must be addressed in a loop through the internal table. Each object must display the name and the type of the development object assigned to it. Here is the source code for the program:

```
 1 REPORT yz342050.
 2 INTERFACE ishow.
 3   METHODS show.
 4 ENDINTERFACE.
 5
 6 CLASS cprog DEFINITION.
 7   PUBLIC SECTION.
 8     METHODS:
 9       set_progname
10         IMPORTING prog TYPE sobj_name.
11     INTERFACES ishow.
12   PROTECTED SECTION.
13     DATA: progname TYPE program.
14 ENDCLASS.
15
16 CLASS ctable DEFINITION.
17   PUBLIC SECTION.
18     METHODS:
19       set_tabname
20         IMPORTING table TYPE sobj_name.
21     INTERFACES ishow.
22   PROTECTED SECTION.
23     DATA: tablename TYPE tabname.
24 ENDCLASS.
25
26 CLASS cprog IMPLEMENTATION.
27   METHOD set_progname.
28     progname = prog.
29   ENDMETHOD.
30
31   METHOD ishow~show.
32     WRITE: / 'Program: ', progname.
33   ENDMETHOD.
34 ENDCLASS.
35
36 CLASS ctable IMPLEMENTATION.
37   METHOD set_tabname.
38     tablename = table.
39   ENDMETHOD.
40
41   METHOD ishow~show.
42     WRITE: / 'Table  : ', tablename.
43   ENDMETHOD.
44 ENDCLASS.
45
```

```
46 TYPES:
47   t_objref TYPE REF TO ishow,
48   ti_objects
49     TYPE STANDARD TABLE OF t_objref
50     INITIAL SIZE 0.
51
52 DATA:
53   ref_prog TYPE REF TO cprog,
54   ref_tabl TYPE REF TO ctable,
55   ref_obj  TYPE REF TO ishow,
56   iobjects TYPE ti_objects WITH HEADER LINE.
57
58 TABLES:
59   tadir.
60
61 START-OF-SELECTION.
62   SELECT * FROM tadir
63     WHERE devclass = 'SBF_WEB'
64       AND ( object = 'PROG' OR object = 'TABL' )
65     ORDER BY obj_name.
66
67   IF tadir-object = 'PROG'.
68     CREATE OBJECT ref_prog.
69     CALL METHOD ref_prog->set_progname
70       EXPORTING prog = tadir-obj_name.
71     ref_obj = ref_prog.
72   ELSE.
73     CREATE OBJECT ref_tabl.
74     CALL METHOD ref_tabl->set_tabname
75       EXPORTING table = tadir-obj_name.
76
77     ref_obj = ref_tabl.
78   ENDIF.
79   APPEND ref_obj TO iobjects.
80
81   ENDSELECT.
82
83 LOOP AT iobjects.
84   ref_obj = iobjects.
85   CALL METHOD iobjects->show( ).
86 ENDLOOP.
```

Three object references are declared in the declaration part of the application, one each for both the classes, and one for the interface. Although the declarations appear the same, they can subsequently only use the reference fields that point to classes to create instances of objects. The assignments of these two reference fields are not compatible with each other. However, you can assign the contents of both fields to the interface reference ref_obj, as both classes implement this interface. You can only access the parts of the objects that are defined through the interface. In this case, this is only the show method. This is sufficient to complete the task, however. You can call the show method in the LOOP through the internal table without knowing the object's type. As the complete object lies behind this reference, the method called can give the correct data output.

Events

So far you have addressed objects directly to use their functions. However, this demands that a reference always points to an object. If you want to trigger a special function, you have to know which object to address. As object-oriented models can be very complex, this can lead to an equally complex data structure for administering the objects. Yet it is these complex data structures that object-oriented programming is supposed to simplify. This is why events are used to enable objects to communicate with each other without causing errors. The fundamental idea is that an object sends a message without knowing the precise recipient. For each possible message, a receiving object is created that reacts in the desired manner.

The event mechanism is for example used very frequently in graphic interfaces. There a menu option can trigger an event that is processed through an event handler.

The following example demonstrates the statements necessary for sending and dealing with an event:

```
 1 REPORT yz342060.
 2 TYPES mychar TYPE tadir-obj_name.
 3 CLASS cevent DEFINITION.
 4   PUBLIC SECTION.
 5     EVENTS: modify_content EXPORTING value(upp) TYPE c,
 6             show_content.
 7     METHODS:  create_event_modify IMPORTING value(upp) TYPE c,
 8               create_event_show.
 9 ENDCLASS.
10
11 CLASS cevent IMPLEMENTATION.
12   METHOD create_event_modify.
13     RAISE EVENT modify_content EXPORTING upp = upp.
14   ENDMETHOD.
15
16   METHOD create_event_show.
17     RAISE EVENT show_content.
18   ENDMETHOD.
19 ENDCLASS.
20
21 CLASS cstring DEFINITION.
```

```
22    PUBLIC SECTION.
23      METHODS:  set_value IMPORTING imp TYPE mychar,
24                modify   FOR EVENT modify_content OF cevent
25                  IMPORTING upp,
26                show     FOR EVENT show_content   OF cevent.
27    PRIVATE SECTION.
28      DATA value TYPE mychar.
29 ENDCLASS.
30
31 CLASS cstring IMPLEMENTATION.
32    METHOD set_value.
33      value = imp.
34    ENDMETHOD.
35
36    METHOD modify.
37      IF upp = 'X'.
38        TRANSLATE value TO UPPER CASE.
39      ELSE.
40        TRANSLATE value TO LOWER CASE.
41      ENDIF.
42    ENDMETHOD.
43
44    METHOD show.
45      WRITE: / value.
46    ENDMETHOD.
47 ENDCLASS.
48
49 DATA: re TYPE REF TO cevent,
50       rs TYPE REF TO cstring.
51
52 TABLES tadir.
53
54 START-OF-SELECTION.
55    CREATE OBJECT re.
56    SELECT * FROM tadir
57      WHERE devclass = 'SBF_WEB'
58        AND object   = 'DTEL'.
59
60      CREATE OBJECT rs.
61      CALL METHOD rs->set_value
62        EXPORTING imp = tadir-obj_name.
63      SET HANDLER rs->modify FOR re.
64      SET HANDLER rs->show FOR re.
65    ENDSELECT.
66
```

```
67    CALL METHOD re->create_event_modify EXPORTING upp = ' '.
68    CALL METHOD re->create_event_show.
69    CALL METHOD re->create_event_modify EXPORTING upp = 'X'.
70    CALL METHOD re->create_event_show.
```

Events can only be triggered within a class. For this reason you first define a class called `cevent`. The `EVENTS` statement for this class declares the `modify_content` and `show_content` events. The `modify_content` event has one parameter available to it. The events are triggered within the class in which they are defined. In this example, this is done using two methods specially intended for that purpose, `create_event_modify` and `create_event_show`. It is not always necessary to trigger events in specially written methods. It is much more usual for events to be triggered within methods that also contain other functions.

Two methods in the `cstring` class serve as the recipients of the events. The objects of this class take on a character string, whose format (capitals or upper case) can be modified through one of these events. Apart from that, the objects should be able to display their contents on the screen on demand.

If you want to use a method as an editing tool, you must first declare it as an event handler. You do so using the `FOR EVENT` addition in the methods declaration. In it you must enter the names of each event, and the class to which the event belongs. If an event has a parameter, the parameter must also be declared in the method that deals with it. You do so with an `IMPORTING` statement. This statement is an option for the `FOR EVENT` statement and does not correspond to the normal `IMPORTING` statement in the methods declaration. The parameter list of this `IMPORTING` statement must correspond to the parameter list of the event. In the example, the `upp` parameter belonging to the event triggers the conversion of the character string into capitals.

The entries described only make it possible to handle the event. They prescribe that a method belonging to a class can be used as a handling routine, although it does not have to be. At runtime, you still have to define which method reacts to a particular message. Both sender and recipient must be specified, i.e. as an object. This means that different recipients can react to an event according to the transmitting object. You can make this requirement less strict by not distinguishing between the various transmitters of an event (using the `FOR ALL INSTANCES` addition).

In the example, an instance of an object of the `cevent` class is created in line 55. This object is used later to trigger the events. Following this, the system reads some data elements from a selected development class (lines 56 to 58). It generates a `cstring`-class object for each of these elements, and fills it with the name of the data element. Lines 63 and 64 contain the actual assignment of the event-handling methods to the triggering event. Note that the generated objects are not grouped in an internal table. Instead, the object reference is always described again.

A call to a `cevent`-class method in line 67 finally triggers the first event. Because all instances of the `cstring` class are intended to deal with this event, all the character strings are converted into lower-case characters. The next event, initiated in line 68, commands all `cstring` objects to display their values on screen. The two subsequent commands demonstrate the procedure again, although it now commands conversion into capitals.

Exercises

1. Change the `calc1` class so that the input parameter of the constructor is optional. Generate additional methods so you can set both the operands independently of the constructor, and test the new methods in a program of your own.

2. Create a new class in which a division by zero triggers an exception.

3. Change program `yz342060` so that two objects are ready to trigger exceptions, and alternately assign one of the two objects to the `cstring` objects as a valid transmitter for the `modify` event. Now test the way the events are handled.

5 Maintaining Data Dictionary Elements

When you create an ABAP task, in addition to the programming work involved in writing source code you often have to create elements in the Data Dictionary. The only way you can carry out special subtasks, such as implementing input help texts or maintenance modules, without programming, is by maintaining Data Dictionary elements. This chapter describes the Data Dictionary elements with their special attributes and the tools you need to maintain the objects. The examples presented in this chapter, along with the objects generated, form the basis of other examples in this book, in particular the comprehensive demo application in Chapter 7. That is why we recommend that you work through all the examples and exercises. The sections in this chapter are designed in a similar way to those in Chapter 4. The practical demonstration comes first and is followed by more extensive sections with theoretical explanations.

You can access all the tools described in this chapter in the main menu of ABAP Workbench, by clicking on the DICTIONARY button, by choosing DEVELOPMENT | DICTIONARY from the menu, or by entering transaction code SE11. The initial Data Dictionary maintenance screen (Figure 5.1) appears first.

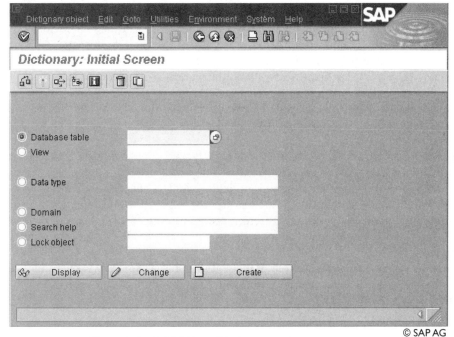

Figure 5.1   Initial Data Dictionary maintenance screen

This is the initial screen. You enter the name of the object that you want to process in the only input field. You use the check boxes to predefine the object type. Three pushbuttons in the screen program take you to the typical processing types, create, change or display. Different types of objects can have identical names. However, this does not apply to all types. Views, structures, tables and data elements have a common name range. Objects in these four groups must have unique, multitype names. The names must be unique because you use these elements as type identifiers in the data declaration.

All the elements you will generate in this chapter have the character Z in their names. You can replace this character if necessary to allow several programmers to work on one system at the same time.

5.1   Domains, data elements, tables and structures

The principal relationships between domains, data elements and tables have been described in Chapter 2, so they are not repeated here. You use the Data Dictionary elements described in this section to construct two very simple tables. These tables will store the code letters for different business sectors and the language-dependent long texts for these code letters.

5.1.1 Domains

Domains provide the basis on which you define table fields. They are the direct link to the database. They contain technical attributes, such as the data type and the length. You can also enter additional data to further restrict the predefined stored values according to data type and field length. Domains have to some extent lost their character as purely technical elements for description. This is because of the use of automatic value checks in conjunction with fixed values or value tables and the associated foreign key dependencies. Many domains also indirectly contain application-specific information. So, when you create domains it is usual, and sometimes essential, to consider how you are going to use them later on in applications. Looking at them from a technical point of view is not enough. The reasons for this will become clear after you have created the tables mentioned above.

The first domain you generate is YZ3DESCR. The table field based on this domain will later include a name, i.e. an explanatory text. You create a domain in the following way: enter the name of the domain in the input field of the Data Dictionary maintenance tool, select the DOMAIN radio button and click on the CREATE button. The screen program illustrated in Figure 5.2 appears. This screen program contains a single input field for the short descriptions on three tabs in a tabstrip. You can enter all the important data for a domain in this field.

First you enter a short description of the domains in the same way as for almost every other object in the development environment. This is only used for information, so the content is not critical.

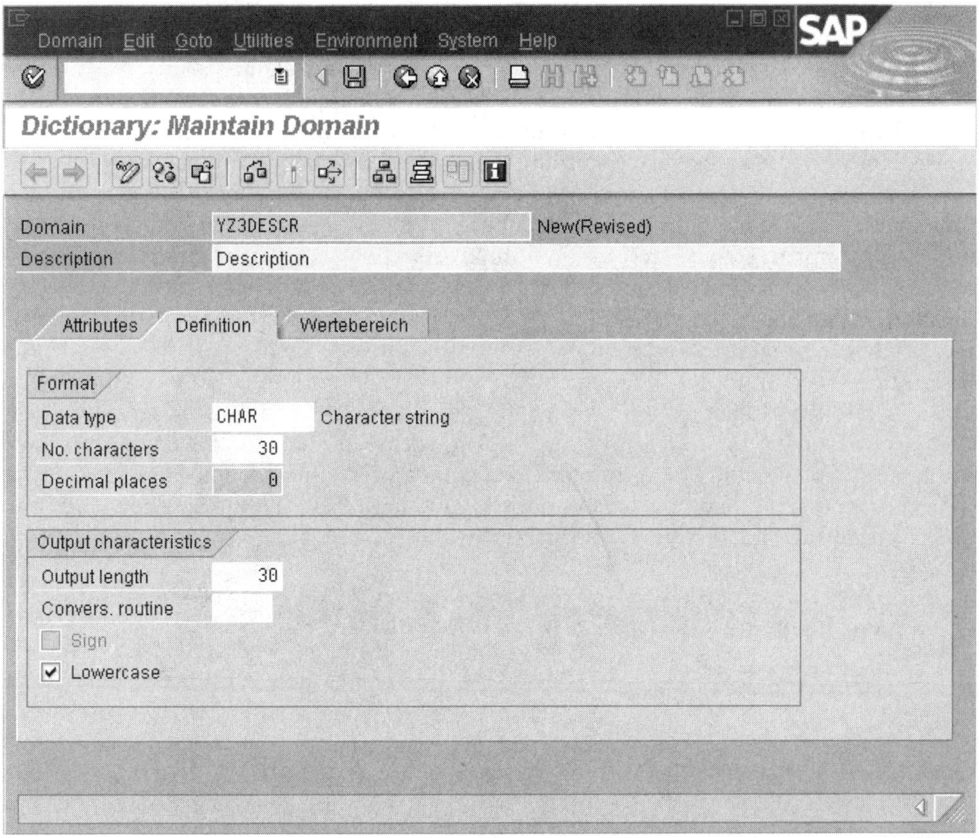

© SAP AG

Figure 5.2   Maintenance screen for a domain

Once you start maintaining a domain, the DEFINITION tab becomes active. You enter information about the data and the output format in this card. The DATA TYPE and NO. CHARACTERS (number of characters) fields are especially important. The new domain you are creating is given the data type CHAR (character string), and a length of 30, as you can see in Figure 5.2. The other fields can remain empty.

You select the LOWERCASE check box to prevent the field contents being converted into upper-case letters. The data you enter is saved. The OUTPUT LENGTH field is filled automatically when you do this. Additional fields will sometimes be filled automatically for other data types. You do not require any more data for domain YZ3DESCR. The ATTRIBUTES tab merely contains output fields that tell you, for example, when the last changes were made. The values range tab lets you restrict the permitted values range for table fields that are based on this domain. You will see this demonstrated in the next domain you create. However, you must first complete domain YZ3DESCR.

A new domain, or changes to an old domain, only take effect after the domain is activated. You select the appropriate menu option or click on the pushbutton to activate the

domain. If a domain is already being used in data fields and tables, you will have to activate it again after you have made changes. When this happens, you also have to activate
all the objects that are dependent on the domain (tables, data elements, etc.), because the
new attributes also have to take effect there. It may take you some time to activate the
dependent objects if there are a large number of them. This is why you should decide the
entire data structure at the very beginning when you develop a new application. This will
minimize the number of alterations that you have to make later and therefore minimize
time-consuming regenerations. However, there are situations in which you cannot avoid
processing domains step by step, with multiple activation.

Domain YZ3BRA, which you are about to create, will now be used to describe how you
define the domain's fixed values. The system checks these fixed values when you enter
them in screen programs. You cannot enter invalid values. To make entering these values
easier, the system automatically generates input help for domains with a values check.
This displays the available values, which are stored in a selection list. You create the new
domain with data type CHAR and length 1. In this case, the LOWERCASE check box is not
activated so you can only enter capitals. You enter and save the data in the same way as
for the first domain, then you switch to the VALUES RANGE tab. Figure 5.3 shows this part
of the screen program. It basically consists of two tables.

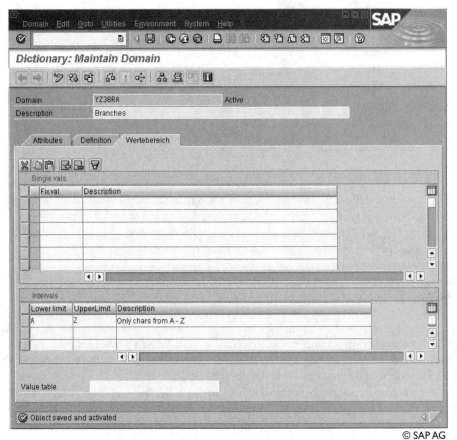

Figure 5.3   Maintaining the fixed values for a domain

In both tables, you enter either fixed values or ranges. In the last field in both tables, you can enter a short name or description for each value or range. These descriptions appear later in the input help that is generated automatically. This means you should make the descriptions as clear as possible. The domain settings in Figure 5.3 ensure that you can only enter the letters A to Z in a data field that is based on this domain. The domain is activated after you enter the fixed values. You have now created the domains for the first two example tables. The rest of this section describes some of the important attributes of the domains.

Format

When you maintain a domain, it is assigned a format or a data type. The data types available for domains are not the same as those for ABAP data types or those used in database systems. Instead they are an intermediate layer from which conversions in both directions are possible. From the Data Dictionary, they can easily be converted into actual data types, for a database system or into an ABAP data type. Domain data types have functionality that is similar to that of a database system. This is because the domains are responsible for links to the database system, or, to be more precise, the link to individual fields in a database table.

The domain's data type also defines the basic attributes of the Data Dictionary field. You use the domain to generate the Data Dictionary field later on. Some data types have an output mask for displaying the values on screen. The data types available for domains are listed in Table 5.1. For this reason, the term *external format* is also used instead of *domain data types*. When you select an external format, you must take the length or value range for the value to be stored there into account, because the various external formats (types) have different lengths and value ranges available to them. For example, external formats INT1, INT2 and INT4 can have integer values with a length of 1, 2 or 4 bytes. In an ABAP program, all these formats are converted to ABAP data type I.

Some data types have a predefined length. You can specify the field length for other data types within certain limits. In each case, you must make an entry in the NO. CHARACTERS (number of characters) field because the screen program carries out an input check. You still have to do this, even if the system automatically sets, or corrects, the field length to a standard value later when you save the value or press (Enter). If you use the input help to select the data type, the correct number of digits is set automatically if this is possible.

All data types that are used in domains are later mapped to the ABAP data types by the Data Dictionary. This means that different external formats can be transformed into the same ABAP data type. If you want a data field within the program to include the contents of a table field, it must have the type and the length of the external data type into which it is to be converted. The easiest way to do this is to use the LIKE statement to declare the data field. Table 5.2 shows some information about how external data types are converted into ABAP types if you do not want to use the LIKE statement.

Table 5.1   Data types for domains, data used in tables (a: thousands and decimal separators are set by the system, b: the number of decimal places depends on the currency)

Data type	Description	Mask	Number of digits	Decimal places/ default	Output Length/ default
ACCP	Posting period YYYYMM	____.__	6		Any/ 6
CHAR	Character strings		<=255		Any/ number of digits
CLNT	Client		3		3
CUKY	Currency key, referenced from CURR fields		5		5
CURR	Currency field, stored as DEC	a, b	<=17	<= number of digits / 2	Any / number of digits + separator + prefix operator
DATS	Date field (YYYYMMDD), stored as CHAR(8)	__.__.____	8		10
DEC	Calculation or amount field with decimal point and prefix operator	a	<=17		Any / number of digits + separator + prefix operator
FLTP	Floating-point number with 8-byte accuracy		16	16	Any / 22 + prefix operator
INT1	1-byte integer, decimal number <= 254		3	3	Any /
INT2	2-byte integer, only for length field in front of LCHR or LRAW		5		Any / 5 + prefix operator
INT4	4-byte integer, decimal number with prefix operator		10		Any / 10 + prefix operator

Table 5.1   Continued

Data type	Description	Mask	Number of digits	Decimal places/ default	Output Length/ default
LANG	Language code		1		1
LCHR	Long character string, requires preceding INT2 field		>255		Any / number of digits
LRAW	Long character string, requires preceding INT2 field		>255		Any / number of digits
NUMC	Character string containing only numbers		Any		Any / number of digits
PREC	Accuracy of a QUAN field				
QUAN	Quantity field, refers to a unit field with format UNIT	a	<=17	<= number of digits	Any / number of digits + separator + prefix operator
RAW	Uninterpreted sequence of bytes		Any		Any / doubled number of digits
RAW STRING	Variable long sequence of bytes		Any		Any / 15
STRING	Variable long sequence of bytes		Any		Any / 15
TIMS	Time field (HHMMSS) stored as CHAR (6)	__:__:__	6		Any / 8
VARC	Long character string, not supported from Rel. 3.0		Any		Any
UNIT	Unit code for QUAN fields		2 or 3		Number of digits

Table 5.2   Representation of external formats in ABAP (n = places, m = digits after the point, s = 1 for prefix operator, otherwise 0)

External data type	Mapping in ABAP
ACCP	N(6)
CHAR n	C(n)
CLNT	C(3)
CUKY	C(5)
CURR n,m,s	P((n+2) / 2) DECIMALS m (NO-SIGN)
DATS	D(8)
DEC n, m, s	P((n+2) / 2) DECIMALS m (NO-SIGN)
FLTP	F(8)
INT1	I
INT2	I
INT4	I
LANG	C(1)
LCHR	C(n)
LRAW	X(n)
NUMC n	N(n)
PREC	
QUAN n, m, s	P((n+2) / 2) DECIMALS m (NO-SIGN)
RAW n	X(n)
RAWSTRING n	XSTRING n
STRING x	STRING n
TIMS	T(6)
VARC n	C(n)
UNIT	C(n)

Values range

This section refers to the values range tab shown in Figure 5.3. When you enter values in screen programs, the system can check whether these values are permitted in the fields. This check involves using the appropriate statements in the flow logic, especially if the check is more extensive. The system can also check the values automatically against a predefined value set. A side effect of this is that the system also provides input help that displays all the permitted value sets for all the fields in which these types of checks occur.

The checking mechanism for special maintenance modules provided by the system (e.g. transactions SM30 and SM31) is particularly important. You can use these tools to maintain table contents without having to write your own programs for them. This maintenance tool is especially useful when you are customizing existing programs.

You make it possible for the system to carry out automatic checks by defining the value set in a domain. You can do this either by defining the fixed values or by specifying a value table. This value table must have a key field that is based on the particular domain. The only values that users are allowed to enter later are those contained in the corresponding field in the value table. However, you need to do more than specify a value table before you can carry out a check. You must also define *foreign keys*. This is a very complicated subject and is therefore described in greater detail in Section 5.1.6.

The fixed values of a domain, as well as the value table's name, are processed in their own area in the screen program. A table can only act as the value table for one domain. If the table you specified in the VALUE TABLE field is already the value table for another domain, the system displays an error message when you activate this table.

Output characteristics

You enter attributes in the OUTPUT CHARACTERISTICS field group on the DEFINITION tab. These attributes influence how the fields in a list or screen program are displayed. Some data types include fractions. You can enter the number of decimal places you want to permit in the DECIMAL PLACES field. This value is predefined for some external formats, such as FLTP, for floating point numbers. You can choose any value for other formats. If you want to reserve a place for the prefix operator, you must select the SIGN flag. The number of digits needed to output a value may be different from that of the field length. However, this depends on the internal representation of a value, as well as the number of places required for decimal places and prefix operators. The system automatically calculates the output length when you change the other values and displays it as a default in the corresponding input field. You can overwrite this value manually. A warning usually appears if the value in the OUTPUT LENGTH field is different from the calculated length. If necessary, you can select an output length that is different from the real length. If the CHAR field is very long, it is a good idea to select an output length that is shorter than the length of the database field. Some standard tools, such as those in the data browser (transaction SE16) or the two tools for table maintenance (SM30 and SM31) access the data in the Data Dictionary to generate output lists or maintenance screen programs. These tools would then try to display these very long fields at their original length on the screen. This would make the display very complicated and confusing. You can reduce these undesirable side effects by setting shorter lengths for these output fields in the domains.

Conversion exits (in particular the variants of the WRITE statement) have already been mentioned in Section 3.4. Conversion exits are function modules that convert the value of a field before output or after input. You can specify a conversion exit of this type for each domain. The variable part of the name of a conversion exit is five characters long. You can enter it in the CONVERS. ROUTINE field. However, you do not use this type of conversion routine very often. The last flag, LOWER CASE, is much more important. This flag is not normally active. When not active, it automatically converts all the letters you enter in screen programs into upper-case letters. This feature is especially important for key fields, because it ensures that they are written in a consistent, uniform style. The letters are not converted if the flag is activated, and therefore the characters are saved in the format in which you enter them.

The program does not convert your entry into upper-case letters when you enter the value in the database. It converts the letters when it processes the screen program. This means that you can write values containing lower-case letters to a database when the LOWER CASE flag is deactivated, but you cannot do this in a screen program. You could enter values that contain lower-case letters by hard-coding them in the program. For this reason, this flag does not protect against programming errors.

5.1.2 Data elements

After you have declared the domains, you can generate the data elements. Data elements access the technical data of a domain and add commercial or program-specific information to it. Data elements and domains have separate name ranges so they can have identical names. Domains and data elements are often assigned directly to each other, so it actually makes things clearer if they have identical names.

In the initial screen of the Data Dictionary maintenance tool, you create data elements in a similar way to domains. After you enter the name YZ3DESCR in the input field, and select the DATA ELEMENT field, you can click on the CREATE button. The maintenance screen for data elements is displayed (Figure 5.4). Its structure is similar to that of the domain's maintenance screen.

First you must, as usual, enter the required short description. When you generate a data element, you are actually assigning a technical data type. Since object-oriented programming was implemented in ABAP, data elements can belong to one of two different data type groups. The first group consists of simple fields. These fields have a single unstructured value of a particular type. You can define this data type in two ways: either through a domain or directly, by using a standard data type. These have been described elsewhere, in the description of domains. However, this second method does not have the advantage of the values range check. You then select one of these options by activating the ELEMENTARY TYPE radio button and one of the two radio buttons, DOMAIN or BUILT-IN-TYPE.

The second selection you can make is part of object-oriented programming. When you select the REFERENCE TYPE field, the data element defined in this way will include a reference to a class or an interface. In this case, you must enter the name of a class or an interface in the REFERENCE TO input field.

As data elements define the semantic meaning of the field, you must still maintain the field texts that are used as key texts in screen programs. These descriptors appear as key fields in screen programs, or as column headings in automatically generated lists. Therefore it is important that they are correct and as clear as possible. Finally, the short description and the field descriptor determine how the field is interpreted in the applications. These descriptions tell you what information will be saved in the corresponding table field. Select the FIELD LABEL tab to maintain the descriptor (*see* Figure 5.5).

© SAP AG

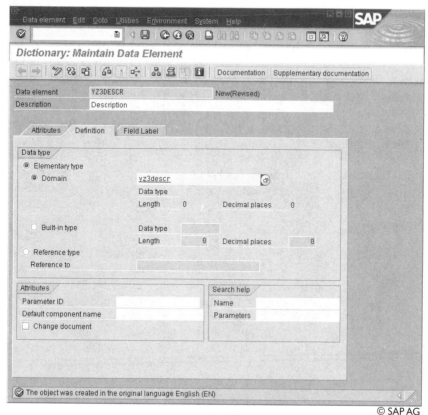

Figure 5.4 Maintaining a data element

© SAP AG

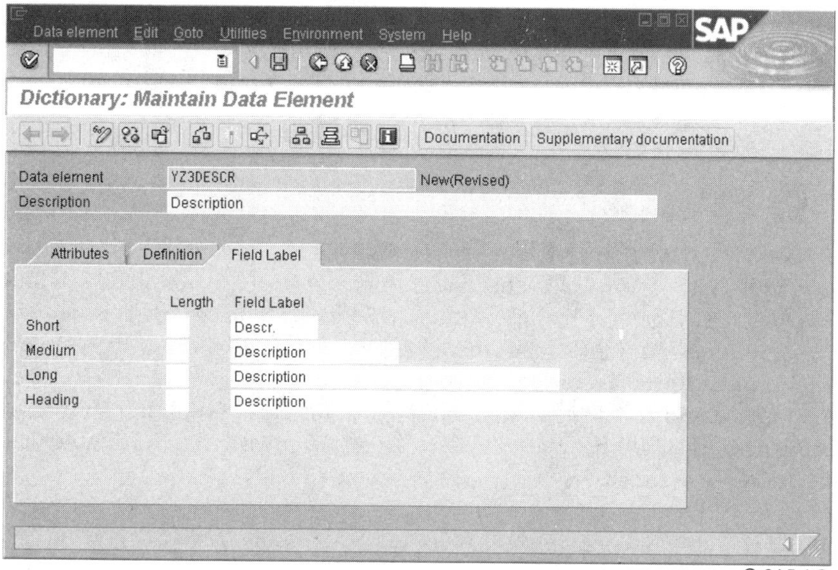

Figure 5.5 Maintaining the descriptor

In this screen, you enter the text you require and set its maximum length. Older Releases used standard default values here.

The data element is not activated until you have entered all the attributes. Just as for domains, any changes to data elements only become effective after they have been activated. If the data element is already being used, all the dependent Data Dictionary objects are also activated automatically.

When you have successfully created the data element YZ3DESC, repeat the procedure for the data element YZ3BRA. Link it with domain YZ3BRA and give it the name *Sector*.

A few more input fields are displayed in the lower part of the DEFINITION tab. These fields can be very useful in professional applications. The R/3 System provides several processes for exchanging data between applications, using global memory ranges. One of these processes involves Get/Set parameters. This kind of parameter is given a unique descriptor. You use special ABAP statements (SET PARAMETER, GET PARAMETER) to write values to this kind of parameter, or read values from it. The parameter keeps its contents for an entire user session, i.e. from logon to logoff. You can assign screen program fields as attributes to this kind of parameter. When the screen program is processed, the field is then automatically filled with the parameter's contents or the value of the field in the parameter. In some situations this can save you making time-consuming entries in various transactions. For example, the system stores the name of the program you are processing in this kind of parameter. The input field for program names is automatically filled when you call the various maintenance tools, e.g. in the Screen Painter or the Menu Painter.

If you have assigned a parameter of this type to a data element, the parameter is automatically assigned to a screen program field based on the corresponding data element.

The SAP System has a function that allows you to selectively log data changes. To do so, you use a special transaction to generate *change document objects* and add a few more functions to programs. These functions automatically recognize changes to a record and then generate a change document. This document only takes account of changes made in data fields where the CHANGE DOCUMENT flag is set.

You can use a search help to link data elements. When you use this data element in a screen program, the search help is always active, no matter what table field you are using. You always enter the data for the search help in the SEARCH HELP NAME and PARAMETERS input fields.

5.1.3 Tables

Once all the necessary data elements and domains have been made available, you can generate a table. Unlike data elements and domains, tables are not merely definitions in the Data Dictionary. They are real objects that exist in the database. This is why you must work through some additional steps when you generate a table. These steps are described in the section that follows. You will generate two tables to include a code letter for an industrial sector and a language-dependent text for this code letter. In the example described below, you will use these tables to validate entries in a third table where you enter the master data for shares.

Table structure

First you define the table's general attributes and structure. To do this, enter the table name (YZ3B) in the Data Dictionary maintenance initial screen, select the DATABASE TABLE radio button, and click on the CREATE button. A screen program is displayed, structured as a tabstrip. You will recognize its similarity to the maintenance screen programs you have already seen. In this screen program, you maintain the table's data fields, as well as some of the other attributes.

Now, as usual, you enter a short description. You can select any text you wish. However, this text should refer to the table's actual task, i.e. only including permitted industry sectors. In the current ATTRIBUTES tab, there are only two fields in which you can make entries (*see* Figure 5.6).

You must make an entry in the DELIVERY CLASS field. In the context of this example, the contents of the field are relatively meaningless. In production SAP applications, the delivery class influences whether this table is allowed to import entries from other systems, and the extent to which it can do so. You can use delivery class C (customizing table) for Table YZ3B, and for Table YZ3BT which you create after it.

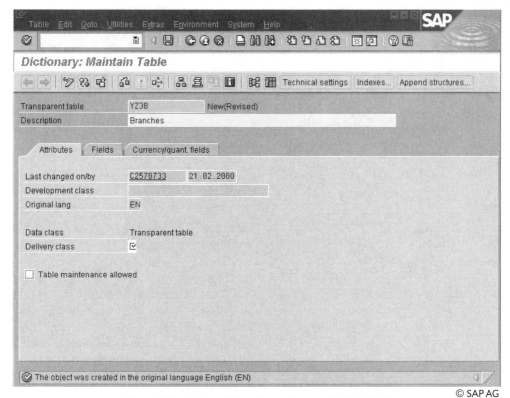

© SAP AG

Figure 5.6   Maintaining the attributes of Table YZ3B

We have already mentioned several times that you can generate special maintenance programs for tables. However, you can only do this if the TABLE MAINTENANCE ALLOWED flag is set. You should set the flag for both the YZ3B and YZ3BT tables, because you will maintain them later on using these kinds of tools. This flag does not affect how these tables are processed in the dialog applications you have programmed.

Once you have completed this preliminary work, you can define the data structure. To do this, switch to the FIELDS tab. Here you find a table that allows you to define several fields in one step. Enter the name of the field you want to create in the FIELDS column. You should follow the same conventions you use for the names of internal program data fields, apart from the length of the field. The field names must, of course, be unique within a table. If you want the field to be a key field, select the KEY flag. The key fields must be positioned at the beginning of the table. To describe the attributes of the data field, enter a data element in the third column that is ready for input.

A little extra information is needed here. From Release 3.0C onwards, you can enter a data type directly instead of referring to a data element. This is a good idea for help fields that will never appear in screen programs, or reports, as you will then never have to

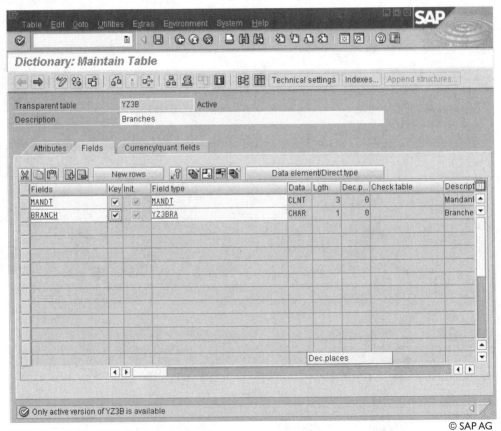

Figure 5.7   Maintaining the data fields in a database table

maintain headings, descriptions or foreign key dependencies for these kinds of fields. You can only input data types directly after you choose EDIT | DIRECT TYPE from the menu, or press the DATA ELEMENT/DIRECT TYPE pushbutton, to switch to maintenance mode for the table fields. However, this option will not be used in this example.

The first table, YZ3B, will only include two fields. The SAP System has multiple clients. The development objects you generate are valid throughout the entire system, no matter whether they are programs, tables or other elements. For this to work, the tables that contain client-specific data must have a field in which you can specify the client. The Data Dictionary processes this field automatically when it accesses the table. You do not have to analyze this field in any way in applications. However, in client-dependent tables, you must always create this field as the first field in the table. This field is always called MANDT (client). It is a key field and is based on the MANDT data element. This data element is already present in the standard R/3 System. You cannot, and indeed must not, create it or process it yourself.

The second field in the table is the SECTOR field. It is also a key field and uses the YZ3BRA data element. After you enter the values and press (Enter) or save the entries, the system uses the data elements to determine some of the important entries. It then inserts this data in the remaining columns in the table definition. The maintenance screen program should now look like Figure 5.7.

Currency and quantity fields

You handle table fields that contain currency amounts or quantity definitions (CURR and QUAN types) in a special way. Data about the currencies and units of measurement is stored in central tables (e.g. TCURC and T006). In these tables, a key is assigned to each currency or unit of measurement. This key is unique throughout the entire system. You use this data to describe a field with currency amounts or units of measurement more precisely. That is why you must assign an additional field to every field of the type CURR or QUAN. This additional field is called the *reference field*. When an application is running, this field contains a key for the currency or unit of measurement. This field may be in its own table or in a different table. When this kind of field is displayed in a screen program, the system determines the currency or unit key and formats the field accordingly. Reference fields are assigned in the third tab. You can only enter the types of fields mentioned above in reference table input fields and reference fields.

Technical settings

Relational database systems do not create tables haphazardly in the hard disk storage area. They try to optimize capacity requirements and access speed. To do this, some database systems expect programmers to enter specific data. This data, and some other entries, form a table's *technical settings*. You enter these settings in a second screen program (Figure 5.8). You can access this either by clicking on the TECHNICAL SETTINGS button or choosing GOTO | TECHNICAL SETTINGS from the menu. Sometimes the system also jumps to this screen program automatically, e.g. when you attempt to activate a table without technical settings.

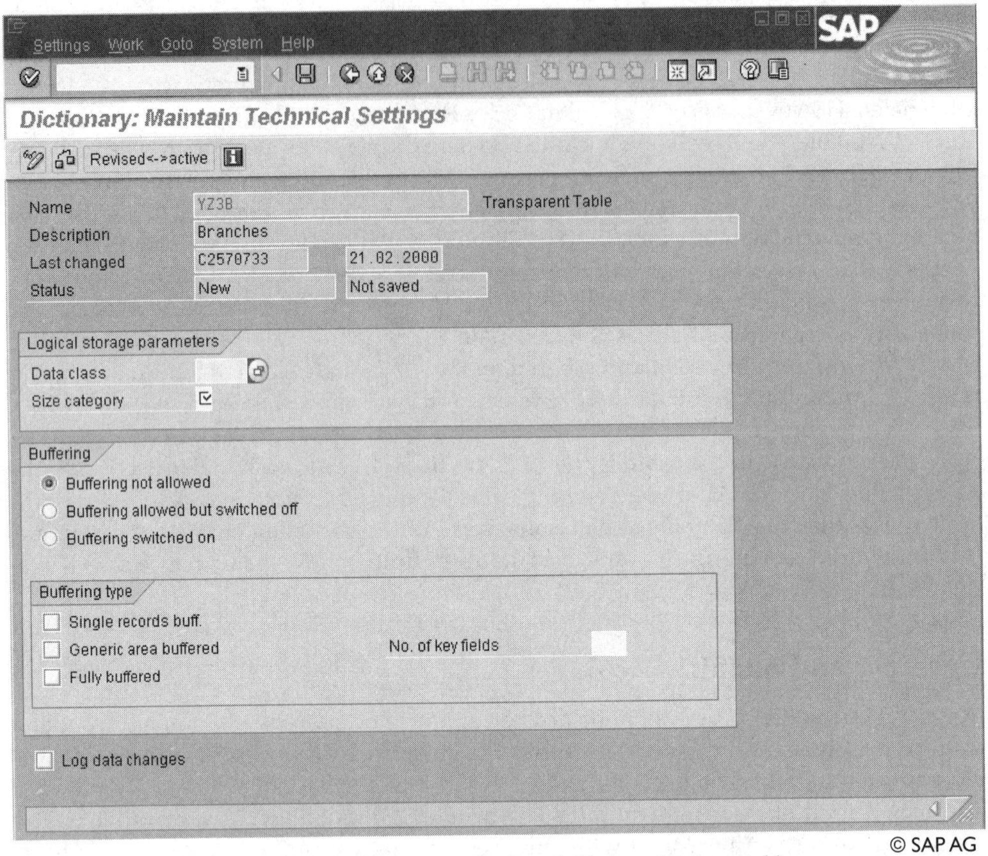

Figure 5.8   Maintaining the data fields in a database table

For this reason, you only need to enter data in this screen program to allow the database system to optimize access to the table. The technical settings do not affect the table's main functions. They only affect the speed at which the system accesses the table. They are therefore not critical for an application's functionality, but do affect performance.

The possible values for technical settings may differ from one database system to the next. For this reason, you should use the input help and find a suitable entry from the values listed there.

Three values are particularly important. The first is called DATA CLASS, for the data type. It provides information about the frequency of access. In the example, APPL2 is selected for customizing data that is rarely accessed. The second field is called SIZE CATEGORY. It tells the database about the expected number of records. The database can then reserve contiguous memory capacity for the table. In our example, we are only working with a small number of records, so the lowest value is perfectly adequate. The third vital piece of data concerns the buffer type. The system selects BUFFERING NOT ALLOWED as the default setting. You can keep this default if required.

Several additional pieces of information are required for buffering data. The SAP System can store tables, or selected parts of tables, in an internal buffer. This speeds up access to the data. Buffering is only a good idea if records are going to be read several times within a transaction. The effectiveness of the buffer deteriorates when you write data to the table. Depending on the type of buffer that is set, when you read one entry in a database table, other entries are accessed and stored in a buffer. If you were to select full buffering, the table would either be completely loaded into the buffer, or not at all, if there was not enough memory capacity available. This type of buffer is only recommended for very small tables, up to approximately 30 KB.

If you select generic buffering, all records are buffered with an identical key. This is why you must name the number of key fields that the buffer has to evaluate if you use this type of buffer. This number has to be smaller than the total number of key fields by at least a value of 1, or the buffering would be the same as described above. It is a good idea to use this type of buffering for language-dependent tables. If you want to buffer a table generically, you must optimize the sequence of key fields accordingly. The start of the key text should be as consistent as possible for the records that are to be read later, so that the buffer does not have to be continually refilled. In practice, this means that the field with the language key should immediately follow the client field in language-dependent tables.

If you use individual buffering, records are stored in a buffer once they have been read for the first time. This type of buffer is only really useful if you frequently access a relatively small number of records, and read them with completely different keys.

You can save the technical settings once you have processed them. Press (F3) or select the appropriate icon to return to the main maintenance screen program for table maintenance. You activate the table there. When it is activated, the table is both marked as active in the Data Dictionary and created in the database as a physical table.

After you have successfully processed Table YZ3B, you can create the second Table, YZ3BT. This table is to have an explanatory text for each sector. This text can be maintained separately for each logon language. Table 5.3 shows the fields and data elements to be included in the table:

Just like MANDT, the SPRAS data element (for 'language') is a predefined standard SAP element. You must use this data element and a language field that is based on it for tables with language-dependent texts. Of course, the language field must belong to the key, but it does not have to be positioned directly after the client field. You maintain the technical settings in the same way as for Table YZ3B, and you can use the same values. Then you activate the table. You can now process another two tables.

Table 5.3   Structure of Table YZ3BT

Field name	Key	Data element
MANDT	X	MANDT
LANGU	X	SPRAS
SECTOR	X	YZ3BRA
DESCR		YZ3DESCR

It is relatively simple to process table definitions in the Data Dictionary. You can work out most of the available menu options from their names or simply by trying them out. Here are a few details about the table characteristics to supplement the information you have read so far.

If you want to add new fields to existing tables, you can usually insert the new fields into the field list. If possible, you should always insert fields at the end of the table. In this case it is simpler for the database system to adapt the structure of the database table. In the tables maintenance screen, you click on the NEW FIELDS pushbutton to add new table fields. This function adds new fields to the end of the table. You click on the INSERT LINE pushbutton to create a new field directly in front of the field where the cursor is positioned.

Defining a foreign key

Although the two tables are not linked technically, they are closely linked logically. In a later application, the user must enter a value in Table YZ3B and also enter the corresponding language-dependent description in Table YZ3BT. Instead of your own dialog transaction, you should use the table maintenance functions the system provides to allow the user to do this. To use the system's maintenance function, you must generate a maintenance module for Table YZ3B later on. You must create a *foreign key* so this module can link the two tables correctly with each other. A foreign key defines the table dependencies. The system uses a range of tools to automatically evaluate the foreign key. The basic theory of foreign keys is described in a separate section. This section simply demonstrates how you use a foreign key to link Tables YZ3B and YZ3BT with each other.

You use the SECTOR table field to link the two tables. The texts in YZ3BT should be assigned to a sector and therefore to a record from YZ3B. You use the database field's domain to create the actual link.

The text table is the subordinate table. It should only contain texts for sectors that are already present in YZ3B. This is why you enter a value table in the YZ3BRA domain alongside the fixed values. This value table is YZ3B. You can call the domain from the Data Dictionary maintenance function initial screen so that you can make entries in the value table. However, just like when you maintain a program, you can also use a specially designed navigation function in the Data Dictionary maintenance screen. You simply double-click on the name of a data element in the table structure's field list to jump straight to a screen program in which you can maintain that data element. There, you can double-click again on the name of the domain. You can now maintain that domain. The maintenance transaction you call initially works only in display mode. This is intended to prevent incorrect entries. If you really want to process an object, you must click on the appropriate pushbutton or choose the relevant menu option to switch to change mode.

No matter how you maintain the domain, you enter 'Table YZ3B' in the VALUE TABLE field. You then activate the domain. Specifying the value table does not directly influence the checks for the domain. It only defines the table against which the check is to be made. The system only executes the check if you later define a foreign key relationship for that table field.

Adding a value table can be one of the reasons for processing an active domain again. A cyclical dependency arises because the domain itself is used in the value table. You can only enter the value table in the domain if Table YZ3B is present. But you can only create Table YZ3B if the `YZ3BRA` domain is present.

In older Releases of the R/3 System, the system shows that a check table is available in the table maintenance tool by inserting and displaying an asterisk in the CHECK TABLE column. This asterisk tells you that a value table is present for the underlying domain, but that no foreign key has been defined. You always create the foreign key in the dependent table, in this case `YZ3BT`. To do this, you place the cursor on the line for the `SECTOR` field in the table maintenance transaction and choose GOTO | FOREIGN KEY(S) from the menu. Alternatively you can press (F8) or click on the appropriate pushbutton. Because no foreign key is present yet, a dialog box appears. In it the system can display a proposed value for the foreign key. Click on the YES pushbutton to confirm this dialog box.

The system displays a second dialog box in which you can process the foreign key (Figure 5.9). The system uses the key fields and the domain of the field for which the foreign key is being created to determine the proposed value. You must select the CHECK REQUIRED flag in the SCREEN CHECK frame, if it has not already been set automatically. Select the KEY FIELDS OF A TEXT TABLE radio button in the SEMANTIC ATTRIBUTES group. This selection defines that the maintenance modules you create will later automatically evaluate the language field in Table YZ3BT. You can now click on the ENTER pushbutton to

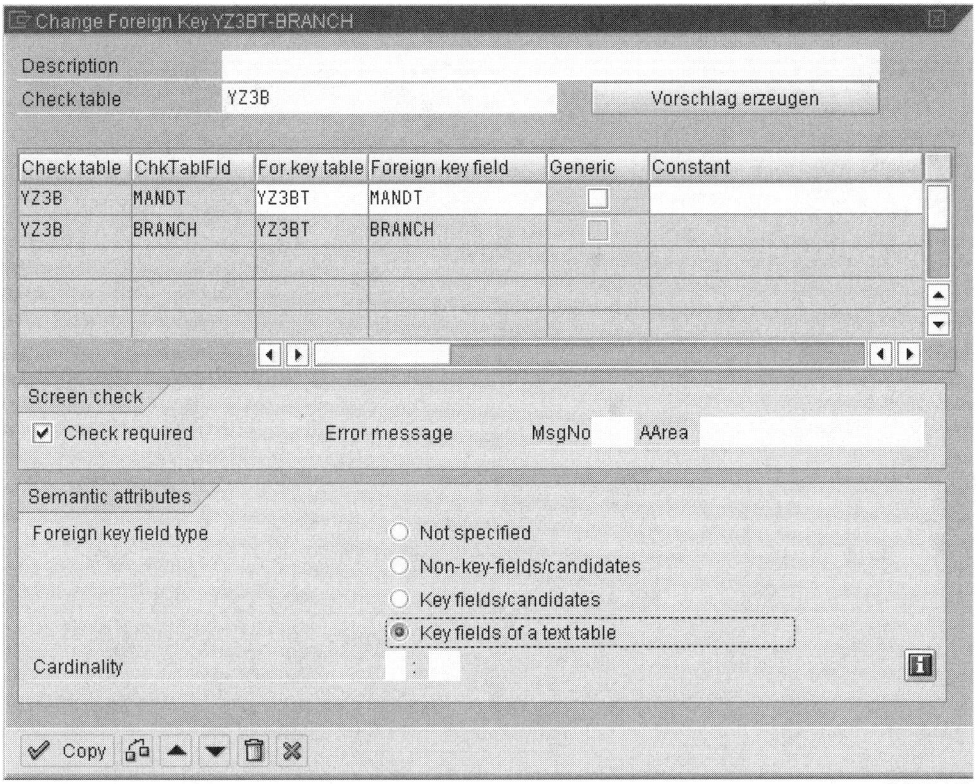

Figure 5.9   Proposed value for a new foreign key

insert the foreign key definition in the table definition. The name of the table against which the field is checked now appears in the CHECK TABLE column, replacing the asterisk. You can then activate the table.

Generated table maintenance

Now that you have defined the foreign key, you have completed the preparations for creating a maintenance module for Table YZ3B. This maintenance module forms the basis for transactions SM30 and SM31. You use these transactions to maintain the table contents. You generate the maintenance modules in the table maintenance base screen. You choose UTILITIES | TABLE MAINTENANCE GENERATOR from the menu to do this. This menu option is only active, i.e. you can only use it, if you are processing the table in change mode. From R/3 Release 3.0, the table maintenance generator is a relatively complex tool. Unlike in earlier Releases, it does not generate a module pool with one single screen program. Instead it generates a complete function group. You can process this group manually later on and modify it to meet your particular requirements. You can regenerate selected parts of the function group after you have made changes to the table, although under certain circumstances, manual additions can remain unchanged.

You only need to make a few entries in the table maintenance generator's screen program (Figure 5.10) to generate a simple maintenance module for Table YZ3B and its associated texts.

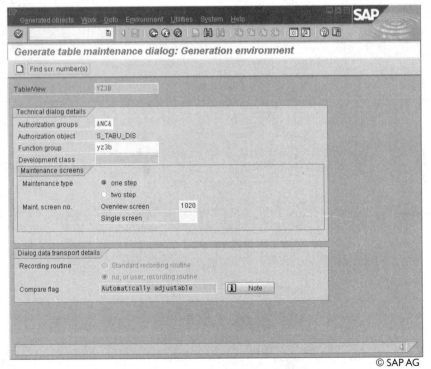

© SAP AG

Figure 5.10   Maintenance screen program for the table maintenance generator

Enter the name of the function group in the FUNCTION GROUP field. All the objects generated for maintaining the table are stored in this function group. The name YZ3B has been selected for the example. Select the ONE STEP radio button in the MAINTENANCE GROUP group. The number 1020 is used as the screen program number of the maintenance screen (maintenance screen program). It is not possible to make a universally applicable statement about the contents of the AUTHORIZATION GROUPS field at this point. This is the only field restricted in this way. Before you can maintain a table, you must assign an authorization group to a maintenance module. Only a special group of users is permitted to use this tool. In the input help for the authorization group, the system will probably prompt you to use the entry '&NC&'. This means for 'no authorization group'. If this entry is not available or causes problems later, you must ask your system administrator to inform you of a suitable authorization group or create one for you.

After you have entered all the values, you can generate the maintenance modules by clicking on the CREATE pushbutton or selecting GENERATE OBJECTS | CREATE from the menu. A message in the window's status bar tells you whether the task has been executed correctly. You can then call the table maintenance module you have just generated directly from the table maintenance generator screen program. To do this, you simply enter transaction code /nSM31 in the command field. This ends the application that is currently running and calls the initial screen for table maintenance (Figure 5.11).

In this screen program you simply enter the name of the table you want to maintain and click on the MAINTAIN pushbutton to select the right processing type. The transaction then calls the maintenance functions needed for processing. If you have not changed

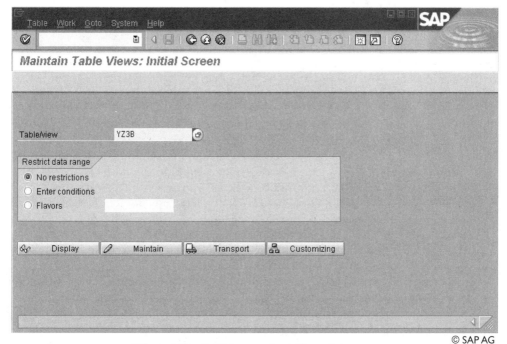

© SAP AG

Figure 5.11   Initial screen for table maintenance

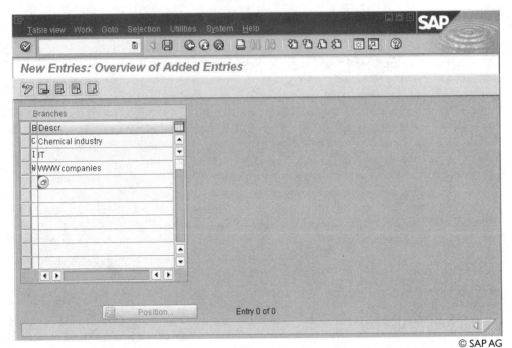

© SAP AG

Figure 5.12   Entering new records using table maintenance functions

these functions manually, they display the table contents in a list. Choose EDIT | NEW ENTRIES from the menu or click on the NEW ENTRIES pushbutton to access a list where you can enter new records. Figure 5.12 shows what the screen program looks like after you have entered two records. You must save the changes to the data after you have entered them.

The maintenance screen program has an input help text for the SECTORS input field. A dialog box is displayed after you call the input help (by pressing (F4) or selecting the icon on the right, next to the input field). This window displays the range of permitted values. To do this, it evaluates the fixed values defined in the YZ3BRA domain.

You must enter the name of the table you want to process in the initial screen of transaction SM30 and transaction SM31. Because you mainly use both these tools within customizing, you can use a parameter transaction to jump directly to the table's processing screen. You can add this transaction to a menu. As a result, you can maintain a specific table in a targeted manner without having to enter any additional data. The next example describes how you use this function together with transaction SM30.

You must first create a new transaction that contains the name YZ3B for the sake of clarity. Select the TRANSACTION WITH PARAMETERS transaction type in the following dialog box (Figure 5.13).

The structure of the next dialog box (Figure 5.14) is more complex than that used for processing simple dialog transactions.

A parameter transaction can either call a transaction or call a screen program directly from a module pool. The second call type is useful if no transaction is present yet for the module pool or program or if you want to execute the call from an alternative screen program. In this example, you want to call an existing transaction. You therefore select the

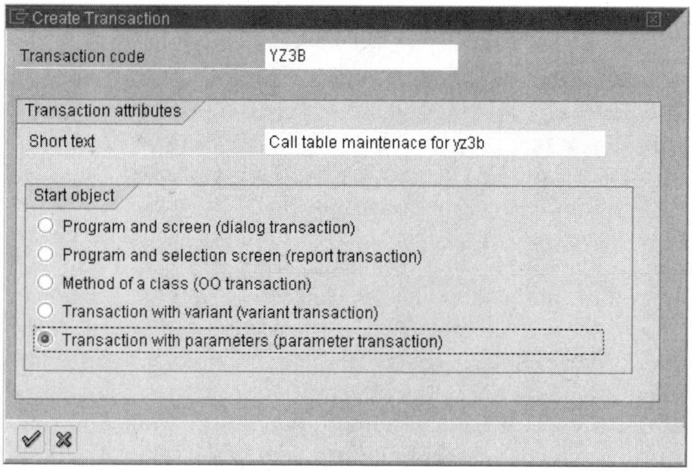

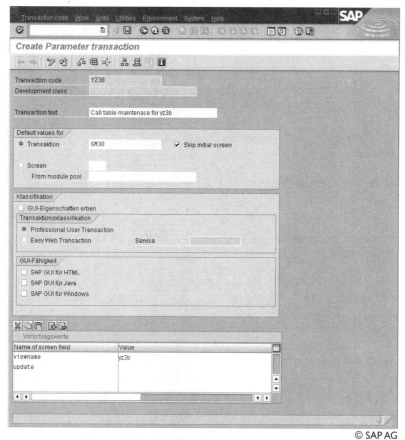

© SAP AG

Figure 5.13   Creating a parameter transaction

© SAP AG

Figure 5.14   Details of a parameter transaction

TRANSACTION radio button and enter the code of the transaction you want to run in the input field next to it. Because you want to access table maintenance directly, you must skip the initial screen of transaction SM30. To specify this, select the SKIP INITIAL SCREEN flag under the field where you enter the transaction code. To ensure that the transaction you call works correctly, you must transfer the values that you would otherwise enter in the initial screen in another way. This is precisely the reason for using parameter transactions. You can enter the parameters you want to transfer in the input fields that appear in the lower third of the dialog box. In the left-hand column, you also enter the name of a screen program field in the initial screen of the transaction you are calling. In the right-hand column, you enter the value you are transferring. After you have entered the parameters as shown in Figure 5.14, you can save the new transaction and execute it immediately.

A programmer who develops a parameter transaction must be familiar with the transaction to be called or at least know the structure of the start screen program. You cannot create a correct parameter transaction without this information. You can find this information either in the relevant documentation or by evaluating the source code of the application you want to call. You can click on function key (F1) to display first-level help. When you click on this button and place the cursor over the screen program the system displays a help text (Figure 5.15) for most screen program fields.

A TECHNICAL INFO pushbutton appears in this dialog box. You click on this pushbutton to display another dialog box (Figure 5.16) in which you see technical data about the screen program field, e.g. its name or the underlying table field.

Figure 5.15   Help text for screen program fields

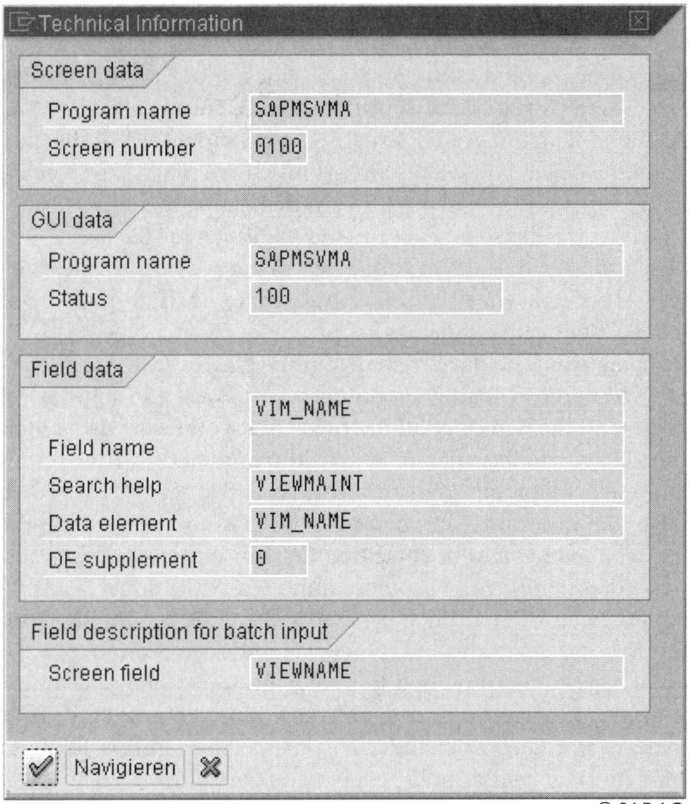

© SAP AG

Figure 5.16   Technical information about a screen program field

However, in transaction SM30 in particular, you need to do more than simply analyze the start screen program. If you use parameter transactions you can only fill the fields in the start screen program. You cannot use any buttons. This is why the start screen program for transaction SM30 contains hidden input fields, e.g. the UPDATE field. Compare this with screen program 100 in program SAPMSVMA. At the PAI timepoint, the flow logic not only evaluates the triggered function code, but also the status of these input fields. The flow logic handles an 'X' in the UPDATE field in the same way as when you click the MAINTAIN pushbutton. The developer of a parameter transaction must be familiar with these kinds of internal issues.

Include and append structures

You cannot and should not add new fields directly to the original table every time. The include and append structures provide you with two other options. You use include structures to add existing structure definitions to other tables or Data Dictionary structures. This allows you to use more extensive definitions several times. This can save you a lot of programming work. An include structure makes it easier to make changes if you want to use a substructure in several places. Then you only have to maintain these changes in one location. Includes are available in all releases.

When you are processing a table, you can choose EDIT | INCLUDE | INSERT from the menu to add an existing structure to the current table. The term . INCLUDE appears in the table as a field name. The integrated structure appears instead of the data element. You enter the name of the object you want to insert in a small dialog box (see Figure 5.17). You can also enter a group name and name suffix in this dialog box.

Both these fields have the same effect as the additions for the INCLUDE statement (see Section 3.2.). The group name allows you to access the added substructure as an independent subobject. The name suffix prevents problems that may occur if different substructures have identical field names.

Usually, the name suffix field can remain empty. However, you can use a suffix to prevent repeated field names causing problems when you add includes. These character strings are attached to the names of all the fields that you insert using includes. This prevents ambiguity. However, this changes the field names and you must therefore take this into consideration when you program applications that access this kind of table.

Includes also have a more important role to play in customer modifications. Sometimes applications have to be modified to meet particular customer requirements. This means that you often have to provide tables with additional fields. When new SAP software is implemented in a modified system, and a table containing customer modifications is resupplied by SAP, the customer's changes are often overwritten. Special maintenance tools have been provided to allow you to maintain customer modifications and avoid losing data during upgrades. This task can be made easier if the fields added by the customer are stored in an include. This means that, during the upgrade, you only need to integrate the new include and not every single field.

From Release 3.0 onwards, you can solve this problem even more elegantly by using append structures. An append structure is a table structure that contains a reference to a higher level table in its administration data. The higher level table does not have to contain a reference to the append structures. When you activate a higher level table, all the append structures are automatically assigned to that higher level table. You do not have to make manual adjustments because the subordinate structures are automatically dependent on the higher level table even if you have changed its structure through an SAP upgrade. You generate append structures in the same way as includes by choosing GOTO | APPEND STRUCTURE from the menu when you maintain a table.

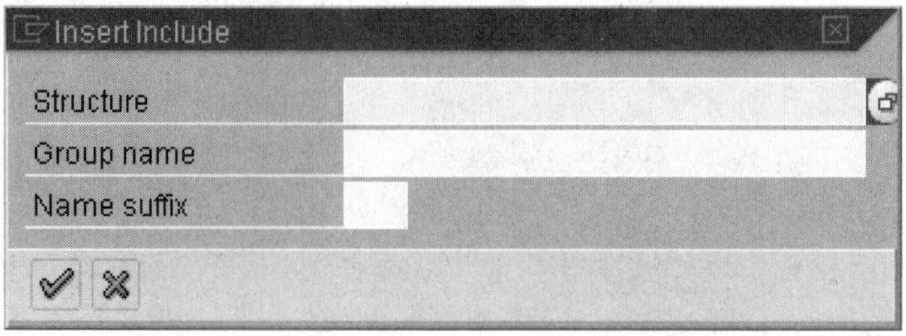

© SAP AG

Figure 5.17   Adding an include structure to a table definition

5.1.4 Data cluster tables

As already mentioned, tables in which data clusters are stored require a special structure. However, you create them as normal transparent tables and process them using the appropriate statements (e.g. SELECT). Their true functionality only becomes apparent when you use them with the EXPORT and IMPORT statements. These tables, and how they interact with these two statements, are a good example of how closely you can interlink different objects within the SAP R/3 development environment.

Table 5.4 shows the structure of this type of table. If you want the table to be client-dependent, the first field must be the MANDT client field. The second field is a mandatory field. It must have the name RELID, data type CHAR and have length 2. This field stores the code for the area. It is a key field. You can link any number of key fields to this field, but their type must always be CHAR. These fields form the actual key for the data cluster. However, the IMPORT or EXPORT statements only expect a single field as their key. The contents of this field are then transferred into the key fields character by character. Once again, the last key field is predefined. It has the name SRTF2 and must be an integer field with the length 4.

The EXPORT statement automatically fills the key fields with data. All the key fields, apart from the client field and the SRTF2 field, are formed from the values entered when you use the EXPORT or IMPORT statements. The system always fills the SRTF2 field with data automatically.

You can join any number of other fields to these key fields. These fields can contain additional information about the data saved in the data cluster. You use the standard statements for working with tables (SELECT, UPDATE, etc.) to process these fields.

The two fields CLUSTR and CLUSTD form the end of the table. They have data type INT2 or LRAW. The CLUSTD field includes the actual data. The length of this field is, of course, limited so the data can be saved in several consecutive records or read from several records. The SRTF2 field acts as a counter.

Table 5.4   Structure of a data cluster table

Table field	Key	Type	Data supplied by EXPORT/IMPORT
MANDT	X	MANDT	Client handled automatically or specified with CLIENT
RELID	X	CHAR2	Area
any key fields	X	CHAR	Key (as individual CHAR field without internal structure)
SRTF2	X	INT4	Filled automatically
any table fields			Not handled by IMPORT/EXPORT
CLUSTR		INT2	Internal administration information. Filled automatically
CLUSTD		LRAW	Data field for cluster data. Filled automatically

If you want to store additional information in optional fields in a data clusters table you usually only have to do this once for each data cluster. This is not affected by the actual number of records you really want to store. In this case, you must enter a valid value in key field SRTF2. In practice, this is always 0 because you always write at least one record for each data cluster. You will find an example of the structure of a data cluster table and how to process this table in Chapter 3, Section 3.10.3.

Indexes

You can speed up searches in tables by using appropriate indexes. An index contains selected fields from a table in a database system. The records are always sorted. You can now use an appropriate procedure, such as a binary search, to find a record very quickly. An indicator in the index refers to the location in the database table at which you can find the record that belongs to the index term. The database system uses indexes automatically. When you access a table, e.g. using SELECT...WHERE, the database system searches for an index that matches the WHERE clause. The system uses this index if it is present. If not, the system carries out a sequential search in the database table. The database system automatically updates the indexes when you add or delete records.

The system creates a *primary index* for each database table. This index contains all the key fields. In the SAP System, both programmers and users can also generate additional *secondary indexes*. You do this in the main table maintenance screen by clicking on the INDEXES pushbutton or by choosing GOTO | INDEXES from the menu. From R/3 Release 3.0 onwards, indexes are identified by the table name and a three-digit code. When you maintain an index from the table maintenance functions screen the table name is, of course, predefined. You simply enter the three-digit index code in a small dialog box (Figure 5.18).

An index's code is only used to distinguish between the various indexes in the maintenance tool. As the database system uses index automatically, you cannot reference a particular index in programs.

Before you can process the index, you must enter a code and confirm the code by pressing (Enter). Figure 5.19 shows the corresponding screen program.

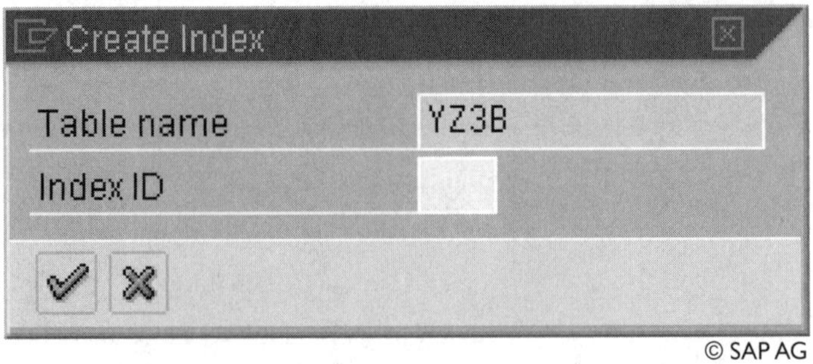

Figure 5.18   Selecting an index for processing

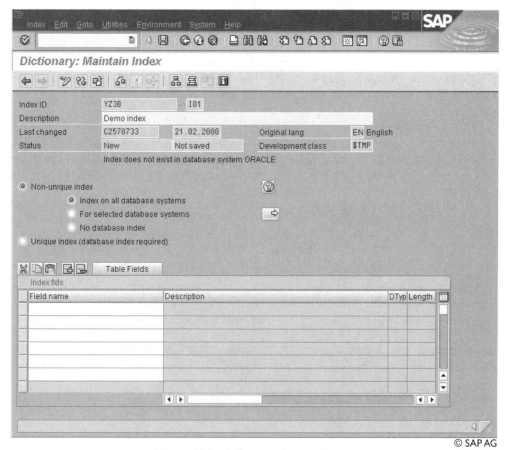

Figure 5.19   Index maintenance screen

First of all, you must enter a short description. A UNIQUE INDEX flag defines whether the entries in the index table are meant to be unique. If this flag is set, the database checks not only that the key fields for the table are unique, but also whether the index file is unique. This means that a record may not be included in a table, although this should be possible according to the values in its key fields. You should only use this setting for secondary indexes in exceptional circumstances. In fact, this setting is often inadvisable because this type of additional data check can damage the functionality of existing applications.

In the table view area of the screen, you now enter all the table fields that you are going to use to create the index. The input help button in each field name input field calls an input help text. This help contains all the fields that are to be transferred. You can transfer these fields to the index definition by clicking on them. The sequence in which you add the fields to the index can have a considerable effect on the efficiency of the index.

After you enter the fields, you must activate the index. While the index is being activated, it is also being generated in the database. Once the index is active, its processing is complete.

You should carefully consider the design of secondary indexes that are used for run-time-critical search processes. This means that you must modify the sequence of the fields in a WHERE clause and the index fields so that they match each other. The first index field should already enable you to make an extensive selection. The contents of these fields should therefore change frequently. In the WHERE clause, you should list the fields in the same sequence as they occur in the index definition. You can only evaluate an index to the same extent as the valid fields (from the index's point of view) in the WHERE clause.

Here is an example of how the index and the WHERE clause work together. A table is predefined with the CUSTNO (key field), NAME1, NAME2, STREET, ZIP and CITY fields. If you frequently use the name and location as search criteria, you should create a secondary index for NAME and CITY. The WHERE clause then contains these fields in this sequence:

```
. . .
WHERE NAME = . . .
   AND CITY = . . .
. . .
```

A WHERE clause created in this way uses the index very efficiently to find records with the required names. If it finds several entries, it will also use the index to determine the record's location. If the sequence of the fields in the WHERE clause was mixed up, you would probably not be able to use the index. However, suppose you create the index using the three NAME, NAME2 and CITY fields. Here you can only use the index up to the NAME field for the search. You would then have to carry out a sequential search through the records you identified in this way to find the location you require. This is because the WHERE clause does not contain a value for the NAME2 index field.

Database utilities

Several maintenance tools have a *database utility*. You can always access this utility by choosing UTILITIES | DATABASE UTILITY from the menu or by entering transaction code SE14. The Data Dictionary's tools only process the logical definitions for the different objects. You frequently still have to generate these physically in the database. For example, after you define the structure of a table, you must also still generate it as a physical table in the database system before you can save any data. The Data Dictionary merely provides the table description from the SAP System viewpoint. You use the database utility to generate or delete objects in the database. However, you rarely need to call this tool manually because the system usually starts it automatically when you activate a table and it runs in the background. You may need to call this tool manually if problems arise after an import or an upgrade.

When you call the utility from the Data Dictionary tools, some parameters will already have been set, e.g. the name of the object. You can then select various activities in the database utility (create, delete, convert) and various modes of operation (e.g. online or background processing). Some of the maintenance functions, especially those used to create new objects, call the database utility automatically. The activation logs of the various elements tell you if you have to use the database utility manually. The ADJUST TABLE function is especially important. You must call this function when you need to change a table's structure. All the old data is also transferred into the new table structure during the conversion procedure.

You can only delete a Data Dictionary object that is present in the database after you have deleted the object from the database. In previous releases, you had to call the database utility manually. This is no longer necessary in the current Release 4.6.

Delivery classes

The *delivery class* of a table determines whether SAP or the customer is responsible for maintaining the data in the table. It also determines how the table behaves in a client copy or upgrade. The delivery class of a maintenance view is taken into consideration when you enter view data using extended table maintenance. The tables in the SAP System contain completely different kinds of information. Some tables contain *transaction data*. This is the data a user creates during their everyday tasks. Other tables are used to customize the R/3 System to meet user requirements, and others contain data that the R/3 System requires in order to function correctly, e.g. authorizations, exchange rate factors for currencies, etc. Some applications are also in part controlled directly by the entries in some tables. The reasons and methods for modifying the contents are just as varied as the tasks the tables carry out. Many of the tables are filled with default values when you install the SAP software. Later deliveries of corrections, new Release upgrades or client copies may have to overwrite these contents. It is crucial that user-specific settings are not changed or deleted. In the same way, users must not be able to change system tables as this may affect the functional ability of the whole system. For this reason, individual tables are assigned a special attribute called the *delivery class*. This attribute defines who may update the contents of the table and in what form it is supplied by SAP. Table 5.5 shows the various delivery classes.

Application tables contain the data generated by the various business administration applications. Tables of this type are always empty when they are delivered by SAP. The contents are only entered by the customer. The customizing tables are used to tailor the

Table 5.5   Delivery classes

Delivery class	Description
A	Application table
C	Customizing table
G	Protected table
L	Temporary data
E	General system table
S	SAP System table
W	Table used for system operations

system to customers' needs. Tables of this kind are supplied with default settings when an R/3 System is installed. These tables are later maintained by the customer. As a rule, R/3 upgrades do not change the contents of these tables. Protected tables are similar to customizing tables. However, an R/3 upgrade can add values to protected tables, but cannot change existing values. The temporary data tables behave in a similar way to the application tables. These tables are empty when they are delivered by SAP and are never filled with values by SAP. These tables differ from the application tables because when you copy client data you can also copy the contents of the application tables. You cannot do this with temporary tables. The general system tables have a name range for customers. SAP upgrades do not affect this name range, although entries in the SAP name range can be changed. However, the R/3 System tables can only be maintained by SAP. These tables are already filled with data when the system is delivered. System tables whose class is S or E include information that is more static in character. In contrast, the system operation tables (class W) contain data that is changed indirectly by a range of transactions. These tables contain data that the R/3 System needs to support its functions, e.g. descriptions of Data Dictionary elements or program source code. The contents of these tables are not subject to special protection.

5.1.5 Structures

Like a table, a Data Dictionary structure has a name and a field list. However, no database table is generated for a structure. The structure maintenance tool is therefore very similar to the one you use to process tables, although some functions relating to the database are missing.

   In more recent R/3 Releases, Data Dictionary elements and global data type declarations are becoming more and more similar to each other. As a result, structures are tending to be managed as components of data types. That is why there is no longer a STRUCTURE check box in the initial screen of the transaction you use to maintain the Data Dictionary (SE11). It has been replaced by the DATA TYPE field. Before you create a new data type, you define what kind of data type you want to create in detail in a small dialog box (see Figure 5.20).

   You can use Data Dictionary structures in two different ways. You can use them in a program as a structure. You can also assign data to them. To do this, you use the TABLES keyword to declare them in the program, just as you do for tables. Data Dictionary struc-

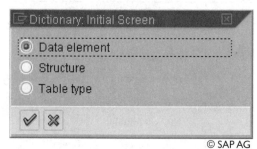

© SAP AG

Figure 5.20   Selecting the required data type

tures combine the joint handling of several data fields that are logically connected, with the advantages of a Data Dictionary element (typing, foreign key checks, field descriptors, simple transfer to screen programs).

The second option is to use structures as a data type. You can use a structure to describe the attributes of your own data objects in the DATA statement. If you only use a structure as a data type, you do not have to declare it with TABLES.

If you want to maintain fields from several tables in one screen program, a structure that contains all these fields makes programming much easier than using the tables directly. When you process the screen program, you can insert all the necessary fields into the screen program's fullscreen in one step. In an application, this kind of structure makes it easier to handle the data. The program is also clearer because you only work with one structure to access the screen program data. It is also easier to see how data is transferred to check routines or update tasks because it requires one parameter.

5.1.6 Foreign key dependencies

The various tables in a database all interrelate with each other. The aim of the relational database concept is to store information in SAP tables with the minimum possible data redundancy. It then links these tables with each other by using common keys. When a database is created, these assignments are carried out at the purely logical level. The Data Dictionary in the SAP System also implements physical dependencies via foreign keys. Depending on their actual definition, these *foreign keys* can fulfil several tasks, such as:

- documenting table relationships and therefore the data model;

- preparing information about table links for other tools;

- executing value checks in screen programs.

You define foreign keys in a table for each table field. You define how the contents of this field depend on the contents of another field in an upper level table (also called a *check table*). The table that contains the foreign key is also known as the *foreign key table*. The field for which the foreign key was created, i.e. the table it checks, is called the *check field*. A foreign key can contain more fields, in addition to the check field. These are called *foreign key fields*. Foreign key fields are the key fields in the check table.

Tables YZ3B and YZ3BT, which you have already defined, provide a simple example of foreign keys. Both tables contain a SECTOR field. Table YZ3BT should only contain supplementary texts that handle the records in YZ3B. For this reason, you may only enter values in the YZ3BT-SECTOR field that are contained in the YZ3B-SECTOR field. This is why a foreign key has been defined in table YZ3BT. The YZ3BT table is therefore the foreign key table and the YZ3BT-SECTOR field is the check field. Table YZ3B is the check table for the foreign key.

To fulfil its tasks, a foreign key requires some important information:

- Which table is the check table?

- Against which field in the check table should it check?

- Should additional fields be taken into consideration to restrict the value set from the check table?

- What should be the dependency on the check table?

The system determines some of the necessary information when you create a foreign key. You must specify some additional data manually. You process foreign keys in the dialog box that you have already seen in Figure 5.9. Below there is more detailed information on the characteristics of foreign key definitions.

Check tables and check table fields

If you want the system to check a field, you must clearly define against which field and in which table it is to carry out the check. You cannot select just anything as these two foreign key attributes. These attributes are defined by the domain on which the field you want to check is based. You can enter a value table in the attributes of a domain. The system prompts this value table as a check table when you define a foreign key. The system searches in the check table for a field from this table, that is based on the same domain. It then checks against this field.

You can overwrite the check table that the system proposes. However, if you do this, you may only select a table that is directly or indirectly linked with the actual value table for the domain by foreign key dependencies. You enter the new table name in the foreign key dialog box, in the appropriate input field. The foreign key field and the proposed assignments are updated when you press (Enter). In this case, the values table and the check table are different.

Key fields

When you define a foreign key, the system tries to find corresponding fields in the foreign key table (the subordinate table) for all the key fields in the check table. To do this, the system evaluates the domains for the check table's key fields one after the other. Fields in the foreign key table, which are based on the same domains, are included in the foreign key. If no suitable fields are present in the foreign key table, the system tells you that the foreign key cannot be entered completely.

If you later check the contents of a field in a foreign key table, the system takes the current values from the foreign key fields in the foreign key table and uses them to create a key for the check table. Only records identified using the key are used to check the check table.

You can reduce this wide-ranging restriction on the range of values by removing the field assignments to key fields in the check table. You do this by selecting the GENERIC flag in the foreign key dialog box. The contents of this field are then no longer involved in selecting records in the check table during the foreign key check.

Dependency

You can maintain *semantic attributes* for foreign keys. These provide information about how foreign key fields depend on the check table. They are not important for the data check in screen programs. However, they are used when you create *aggregates* (views, input help, etc.).

The cardinality defines the number of dependent records that may exist for each record in the check table. You enter this number in the format n:m. If n has the value 1, there should be one record in the check table for each record in the foreign key table. However, the value C permits the foreign key table to contain records for which there is no record in the check table. The value m predefines how many records may exist in the dependent table for each check table record. 1 stands for exactly one, C for a maximum of one, N for at least one and CN for any number.

The degree of dependency defines whether the foreign key fields uniquely identify the records in the check table or not. These foreign key fields do not necessarily have to be key fields in the foreign key table. It is particularly important that you select the KEY FIELDS OF A TEXT TABLE radio button in this case. This specifies that the foreign key fields for the foreign key table, except for an additional language field, correspond exactly to the key fields of the check table and are key fields themselves.

5.2 Views

Views provide a view of one or more tables. You very often use views to link information from several tables without using complicated queries or programs. Views can also be used to allow specific users to only view selected fields in a table. Views are often used for customizing or for special tasks and are often generated automatically. They do not play such a significant role in general programming as tables or screen programs. For this reason, this section only demonstrates how to generate simple views. You will find an introduction to views in Chapter 2.

The Data Dictionary maintenance functions contain an option that you choose to use to process views, just like for tables and structures. You can use views in a similar way to tables, especially when you use the TABLES statement to implement them in applications. For this reason, you must use a name that has not already been assigned to a table or structure. When naming a view, it is a good idea to use a name that indicates that it is a view. However, this is merely a recommendation, not a requirement. For example, many of the view names supplied by SAP begin with the letter V. You can often also derive the name from the primary table used in the view. In this example, it would make sense to use the name YVZ3B. In the basic Data Dictionary maintenance screen, you enter this name, select the VIEW option and click on the CREATE button. A dialog box is then displayed in which you select the view type. In this example, you should use the DATABASE VIEW type. The initial screen in which you maintain the view is then displayed (Figure 5.21).

Just as for all the other objects, you first have to enter a short description. You actually define the view in some of the tabs in the maintenance interface. THE TABLE/JOIN CONDITIONS tab is active as soon as you start. It contains two tables. In TABLES, the left-hand table, you enter all the tables that contain fields that you want to include in the view. In this example these are tables YZ3B and YZ3BT.

The conditions that link the records from the Tables you are using are contained in the JOIN CONDITIONS range. The system provides input help to make it easy for you to main-

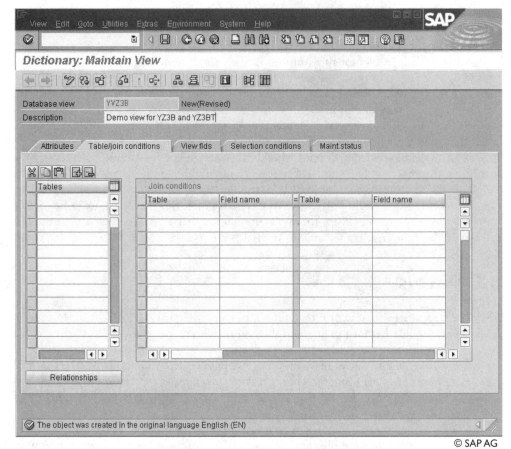

Figure 5.21   *View maintenance*

tain the join conditions. This input help bases its information on existing foreign key dependencies and jointly used data elements or domains. Place the cursor on Table YZ3B in the left-hand table and click on the RELATIONSHIPS button under this table. The system now displays a dialog box. This dialog box lists all the tables that have a relationship to the previously marked table. You can also double-click on a line to display the possible relationships (joins) of the fields for both tables. Figure 5.22 shows the dialog box.

You click on the COPY button in the dialog box to transfer the selected relationship with the corresponding field links to the right-hand view in the maintenance dialog screen. If necessary, you can now process the JOIN CONDITIONS manually. You can also enter all the relationships between the tables involved manually, without using the input help.

At this point you can save the view definition. You then have to select the fields that you want to include in the view. To do this, switch to the VIEW FLDS (view fields) tab (Figure 5.23).

On the tab there is a button called TABLE FIELDS. A dialog box is displayed when you click on this button. In it you select the tables you want to include by double-clicking on them.

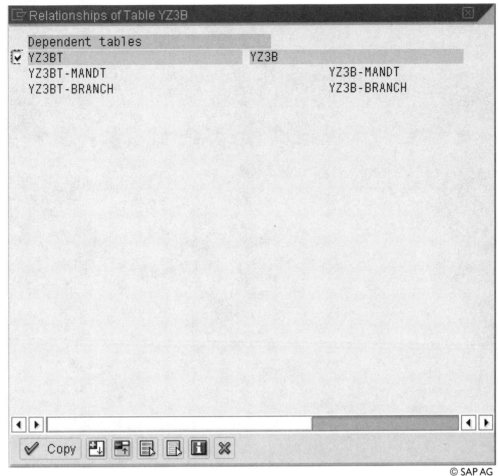

Figure 5.22   Selecting join conditions

The dialog box that follows lists all the fields in this table. Select the fields you want and click on the COPY button to transfer them to the table view. In this example, you can transfer all the fields in Table YZ3BT. This is because all the tables you are using build on each other. You then save the data you have entered and activate the view. Now you can use the view in applications.

You can only use a database view to make changes to table data if the view only contains one table. In this example, this is not the case so you can only use the view to read the data. You can tell this by the maintenance status that the system suggests automatically. You will find this status in the MAINT. STATUS (maintenance status) tab.

If you want to use a view that you have defined yourself, containing several tables to maintain data, you must use view type C (customizing view).

Database views (type D) are implemented as views of the database system. Therefore you must create them in the database in the same way as tables after you use the database utility to define them. From Release 3.0 onwards, this is carried out automatically during activation. In older R/3 Releases, you must call the database tool manually.

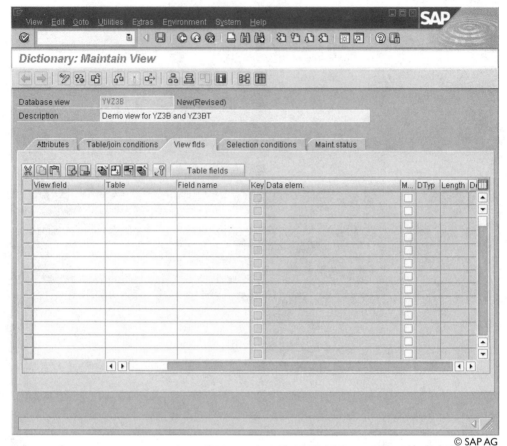

Figure 5.23   Defining view fields

5.3   Search help

In Release 4.0, the matchcodes used in previous Releases were replaced by a general search help function. Search help enables you to search for a table field's value by using other fields in the same table or a text table linked with that table. For example, in Table YZ3B you can use search help to find a single-digit descriptor of an industry sector using the short text. You use transaction SE11 to maintain the search help.

Each search help exists as an independent element and can be used separately. In this case, it is called an elementary search help. Sometimes you can use various procedures to search for a value and can therefore use a different elementary search help. Here you can combine several elementary search helps to create a collective search help. When you create a new search help, you have to decide whether to create an elementary or collective search help. Select the type you want in the dialog box with two selection fields.

When you assign a search help to a field, you can use either an elementary or a collective search help. You can assign these at different points:

- Connection with a screen program field. The SEARCH HELP attribute is part of the attribute maintenance functions for a screen program field.

- You can also assign a search help to table fields or structure fields in transaction SE11. For structures, you do this in the ENTRY HELP/CHECK tab. Place the cursor on the field you want to select in table maintenance and choose GOTO | SEARCH HELP | FOR FIELD from the menu.

- You can link search helps with data elements. The search help is passed on to all the fields that are based on this data element. You maintain the assignment of the search help on the DEFINITION tab in data element maintenance.

Search helps can do more than fill screen program fields. You can also transfer the contents of several screen program fields as the default for the search criteria. In addition, search help can call freely programmable function modules. These options let you extend the functions of the search help as you require. Figure 5.24 shows the maintenance dialog for an elementary search help.

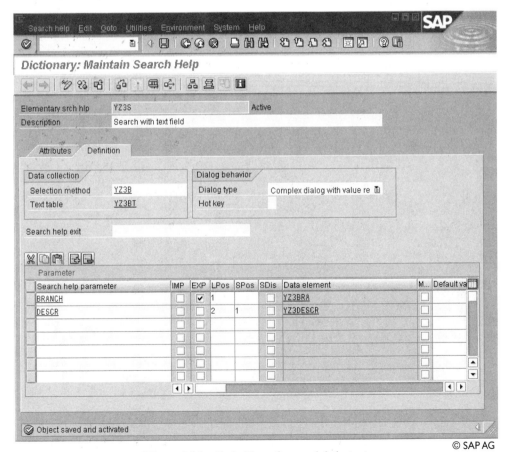

© SAP AG

Figure 5.24   Definition of a search help text

The SELECTION METHOD field is extremely important. In this field, you enter the name of the table or the view in which you are looking for values. If a text table is present for this table, the system automatically enters its name in the TEXT TABLE field. You cannot fill this field manually.

The entry you make in the DIALOG TYPE field defines the behaviour and appearance of the search help. There are three selection options available here. The 'immediate value display' dialog type immediately lists all the determined values in a list of hits, no matter how many records are found. You cannot therefore carry out a search in the more narrow sense of the term. This is more like an input help.

The 'dialog with value restriction' setting first requests your search criteria in a dialog box. The entry you make in this dialog is then used for the selection in the table. The system then displays the result of the query as a list of hits. In the Search dialog box, you can maintain the selections you already know from reports. You can use individual values, templates, ranges or value groups to restrict the number of hits.

The third possible setting is 'dialog dependent on number of hits'. This combines the two variants we have just dealt with. If the list of hits contains fewer than 100 entries, it displays them immediately. If there are more, it asks you to enter a limiting search criteria.

The SEARCH HELP PARAMETER column contains the table fields or view fields that the system should use within the search help. In that column, enter all fields that are to be used within the search help. You can only use fields from the table that is named in the SELECTION METHOD or from the text table that belongs to it. Every search help parameter has additional attributes which describe how the parameter functions in more detail. If the IMP (import) flag is set for this parameter, you can fill the search help parameters with values from the calling application. The search help only supplies values that have been determined with the search process for parameters with an activate EXP (export) flag. If the search help finds several possible values, it presents you with a list of hits from which you can select the entry you want. You can also modify the structure of the list of hits. You do this in the LPOS column by defining the sequence of the fields in the list of hits. If there is no entry in the LPOS column, the field will not appear in the list of hits. This column must be filled with values for an elementary search help. There is no point in creating search help without a list of hits. In the same way, you can also use the value in the SPOS column to define the position of the field in the dialog box where you enter the search terms. If a field has no entries in this column, it does not appear in the find-dialog box either. Sometimes it is a good idea not to offer the field you are actually searching for in the Search dialog.

If you select the SDIS flag for a field, this field is merely displayed in the dialog box mentioned above. You cannot make an entry in this field. This is useful for fields that are prefilled by the calling application.

Here is a demonstration of search help. The task here is to create a search help that searches Table YZ3B for the code letter for an industry sector using the descriptive text. The definition is relatively simple. All you have to do is enter the values you see in Figure 5.24 and activate the search help.

You can test a search help directly from the maintenance transaction by choosing SEARCH HELP | TEST from the menu. The system first generates a test screen program into which the field you are searching for is transferred as an input field (Figure 5.25).

Figure 5.25   Test environment for search help

The actual search help starts when you call the input help in this screen for the SECTOR field. In accordance with the definition, a dialog box then appears that contains the search terms (Figure 5.26).

The values found in the search are then presented in a list of hits (Figure 5.27). The column with the values you want to transfer is marked by a small icon under the column header.

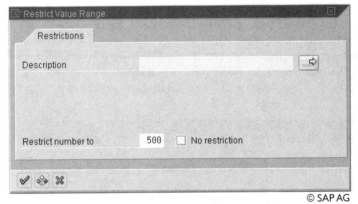

Figure 5.26   Input template for search values

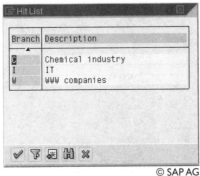

Figure 5.27   List of hits

5.4 Matchcodes

Matchcodes were the predecessors of the search help that we have just described. They were available until Release 3.1x, and were replaced by search help in Release 4.0. This section describes matchcodes once again for users of older systems.

You use a matchcode to search for the key field of a record via other fields. These fields do not have to be key fields themselves. The system generates matchcodes according to the defaults set by the programmer. You can use a matchcode as an input help in a screen program field. To do this, you simply enter it in the attributes of the screen program field concerned.

Matchcodes consist of two parts. The actual search process is controlled by a *Matchcode ID*. This defines which database fields will be used in the search. When you use a matchcode, a matchcode ID appears on the screen as a dialog box with several input fields. The user can enter search terms in these fields. One or more matchcode IDs form a matchcode object. When you execute a matchcode, the matchcode object presents the user with all the available matchcode IDs in a selection list. The matchcode object defines which table field is to be searched for. This field is valid for all matchcode IDs.

In this section you will generate a simple matchcode. It will use the description to search for a value for the SECTOR field in Table YZZB. Matchcode names can have a maximum length of four digits. Matchcodes have their own name range so they can also be given the name YZZB. In the basic Data Dictionary maintenance screen, you can enter this name in the input field and select the MATCHCODE OBJECTS check box. You then click on the CREATE button. You maintain the basic attributes of an object's matchcode in the following screen program (Figure 5.28). This includes the name of the primary table as well as the short description.

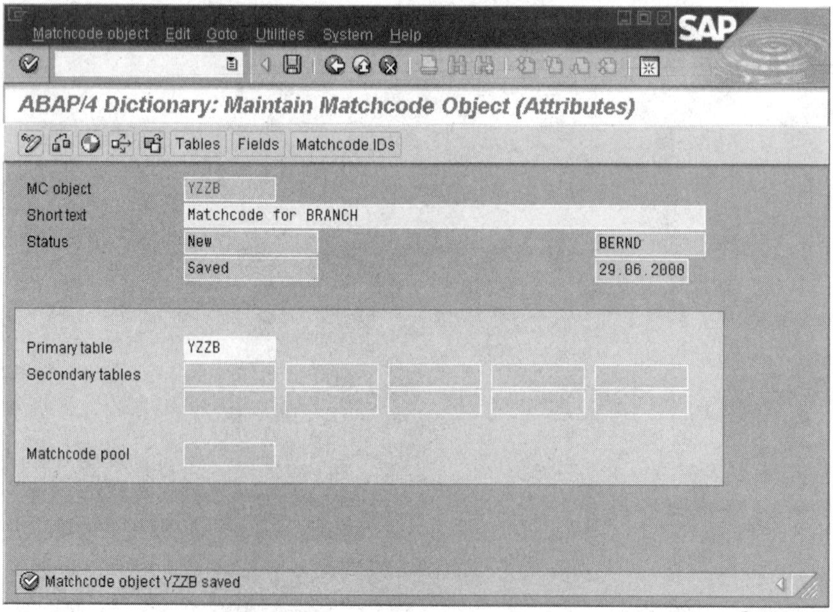

© SAP AG

Figure 5.28   Maintaining matchcode attributes

The primary table contains the data field that you want to find using the matchcode. If the primary table is linked with other tables by a foreign key, you can also search their contents. You must include these tables as secondary tables in the matchcode object. To do this, click on the TABLES button or choose GOTO | TABLES from the menu. In this screen program, you then call a dialog box (Figure 5.29) by clicking on the CHOOSE SEC.TAB button or choosing EDIT | CHOOSE SEC.TAB from the menu. You select the secondary tables in this dialog box.

You must specify all the table fields that you want to use later in the search, no matter which matchcode ID they are used in. You must include them in the field list of the object's matchcode. Click on the FIELDS button to access the field list. The key fields for the participating tables are automatically transferred into the field list. To complete the example, all you need to do is transfer the DESCR field from Table YZZBT. To do this, go to the matchcode maintenance field list, place the cursor on the field that has table name YZZBT and click on the CHOOSE FIELDS button. A dialog box now appears (Figure 5.30). Double-click on the DESCR field to select it and click on the COPY button to transfer it into the matchcode's field list.

One matchcode returns the contents of exactly one table field to the screen program field with which it has been linked. You select the TAR.FLD column to define this field. The corresponding fields are check boxes and not radio buttons. This means you can select several lines in the field list and therefore several table fields. In this case, of course, if you

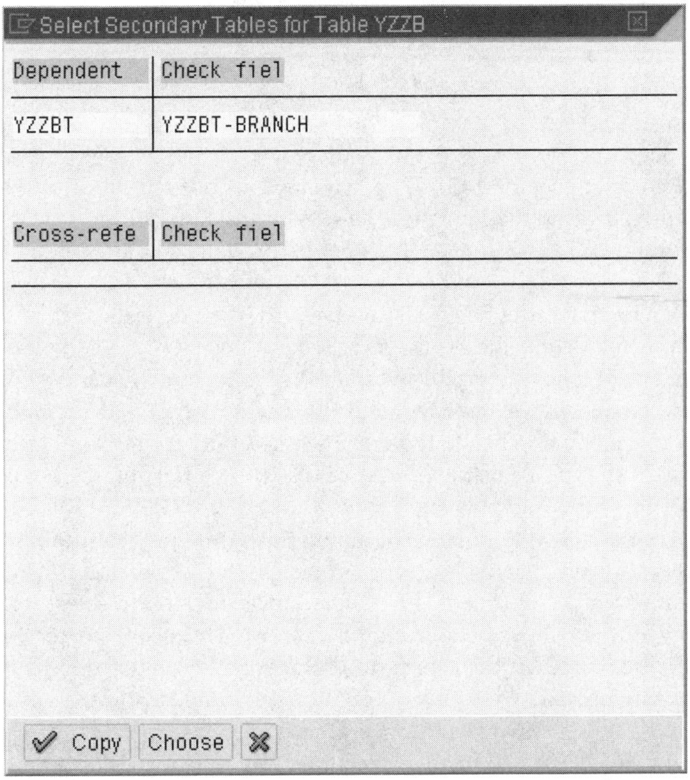

Figure 5.29   Inserting secondary tables

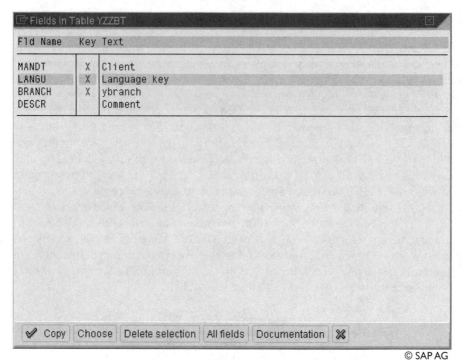

Figure 5.30   Field selection for matchcodes

check or save data an error message will be displayed. It is the programmer's responsibility to select the correct search field. The system does not check later to see whether a
matchcode returns a value that matches the screen program field it was assigned to. The
search field in this example is the SECTOR field. You will see the field list for the matchcode in Figure 5.31.

When you have created the field list, you have finished defining the matchcode object.
This definition merely forms the framework or basis for the matchcode IDs. You are now
going to create one of these. To do this, you must save the field list and return to the basic
matchcode maintenance screen (see Figure 5.28). There you activate the matchcode object.
Then you can call the maintenance tool for a single matchcode ID either by clicking the
MATCHCODE IDs button or choosing GOTO | MATCHCODE IDs from the menu. Immediately
after you select this function, you must enter a unique code letter (SAP matchcode) or a
number (customer matchcode) in a small dialog box. This character uniquely identifies a
matchcode ID within a matchcode object. It appears later in a dialog box when you work
with the complete matchcode. Here you can use this character to select which one of the
matchcode IDs you want to search for. In this example you use '1'. After you confirm the
entry in the dialog box, the screen program appears where you process the matchcode
IDs. Here, once again, you first have to enter a short description. This appears in the
selection list of an object's matchcode when the application is running. This description
should therefore be as clear and factually accurate as possible.

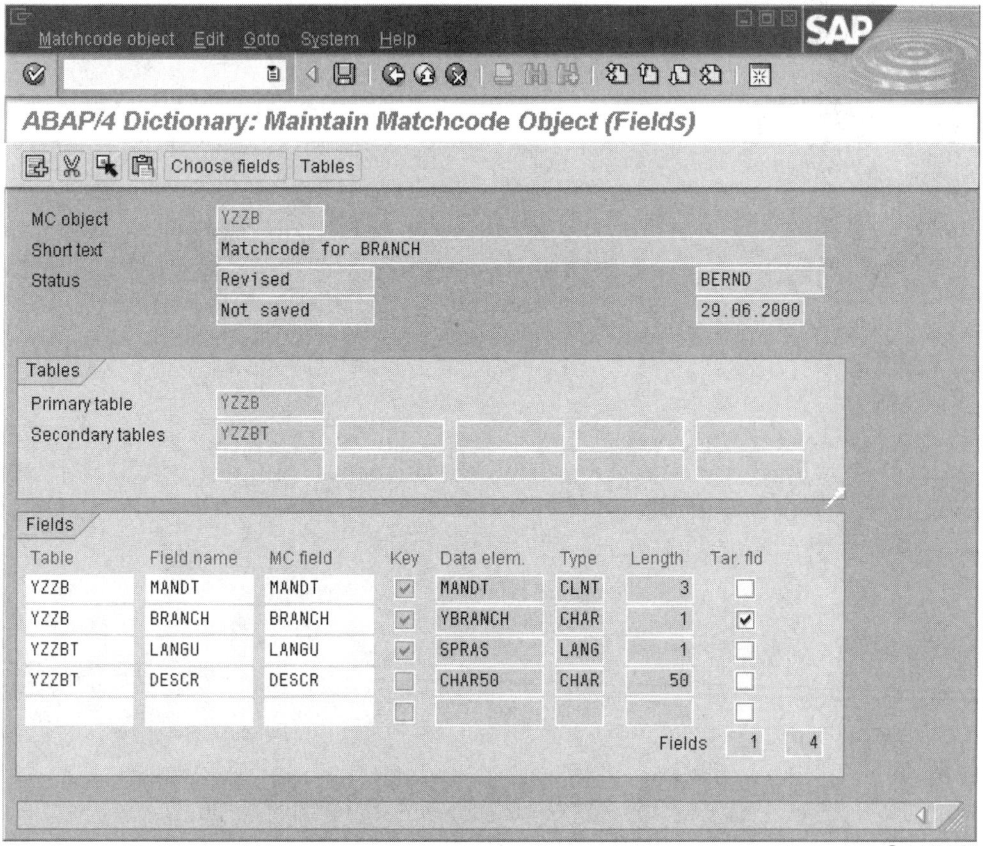

Figure 5.31   Field list of the demo matchcode

Then you select the tables that you want to make available in the IDs input fields from the tables that are declared in the matchcode object. You click on the CHOOSE SEC.TABLES pushbutton, or choose EDIT | CHOOSE SEC.TABLES from the menu to do this. In the second step, you transfer the actual table fields into the IDs field list (FIELDS button, then CHOOSE FIELDS). The sequence of the fields in the field list defines the sequence of the input fields in the matchcode dialog box and in the selection list at runtime. The records found are displayed in this selection list where you can select them. For this reason, some menu options allow you to delete or move entries in the field list.

The matchcode ID field list's structure differs from that of the matchcode object. To a certain extent, you can use additional attributes to influence the attributes of the input fields in a later dialog box. In particular, you can switch on the Get/Set parameters function and define the position of the input fields. For the example, you insert all fields into the matchcode ID. If a client field is available, it appears automatically in the field list, but is not displayed later in the input dialog box for the matchcode (see Figure 5.32).

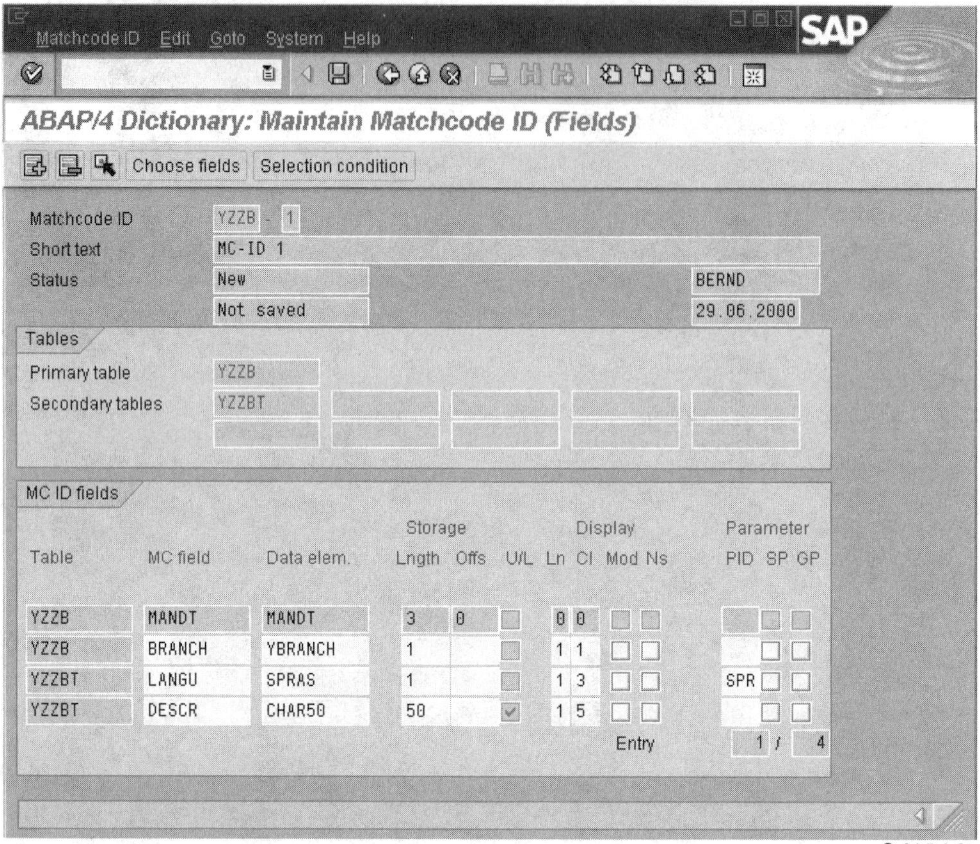

© SAP AG

Figure 5.32   Maintaining a matchcode ID

Save the field list. Then you have to activate the matchcode ID. When you have done this, the matchcode is ready for use. You can carry out the first test from the matchcode object's attributes screen program by choosing UTILITIES | MATCHCODE DATA | DISPLAY from the menu.

When you defined the matchcode ID you had to enter an activation type. The activation type has considerable influence on the technical implementation of the matchcode in the system. Some of the matchcode types originate from SAP's R/2 System. This did not work with relational databases from the outset. That is why matchcodes are not just simple search programs. Sometimes there are extensive datasets hidden behind a matchcode. These must be maintained in parallel to the actual application data.

The activation type 'I', used up until now generates a matchcode that is a database view. It also generates a program that reads the information you want through this view. This matchcode always uses this program to access the current data in the database table. This matchcode type is currently the standard recommended procedure.

A so-called *classification* is carried out within some modules in the SAP System. In it you can enter additional sort criteria for any tables and fill them with values. The customer can also create this classification. You can use matchcode type 'K' to apply this kind of classification data and search for records. However, to use the classification, you need to understand this tool very well. Apart from that you have to do extensive programming work. For these reasons, we are not going to look further into classification and the matchcodes here.

The other three matchcode types, A, S and P, build their own dataset that must always be updated in parallel to the real data. This data area contains only the fields in which you want to search using the matchcode. Apart from that there can be indexes that speed up searches. You can and must update this dataset on an ongoing basis. Sometimes people also talk about the structure of the matchcode data. There are three possible strategies. For matchcode type 'A' you update the data through a utility that operates asynchronously to the rest of the application. This type of matchcode is especially suitable for searching in datasets that are rarely updated. For matchcode type 'S' the update occurs at the same time as the changes in the actual database tables. Updating is controlled by the Data Dictionary, or more precisely the database interface. Finally, you can use an application program that also updates the matchcodes of type 'P' itself, by calling an automatically generated function module.

5.5 Lock objects

A program can use lock objects to block access to selected records or tables. You set or release the actual lock by calling a function module that is generated by the system. The locking function does not use the services provided by the database system. Instead it is implemented in the Data Dictionary with SAP's own tools. The necessary function modules are created in a lock object definition in the Data Dictionary. When you call them as parameters, these function modules are transferred as the key values for the records to be locked. There are two particularly important steps when you define a lock object. First you must define the tables that you want to block jointly. In addition to these tables, you can select the tables that are needed as the lock argument. This process is similar to the one for defining views and matchcodes.

The example below describes the definition of a shared lock object for Tables YZ3B and YZ3BT.

First you enter the name of the lock object into the Data Dictionary initial maintenance screen, click on the LOCK OBJECT radio button and click on the CREATE button. SAP recommends that the names of lock objects begin with E. You are free to choose the rest of the name, but it is usual to use the name of the primary table. The name of the lock object in this example is EYZ3B.

The screen program for maintenance of the lock object resembles the tools described earlier (see Figure 5.33).

After you start the transaction, the TABLES tab is active. You define the table you want to lock and the lock mode within the PRIMARY TABLE area. The lock mode determines whether users can access the locked records and how they can do so (read-only, etc.). SHARED LOCK mode (code letter S) allows several users to read the table at the same time. A user cannot access the data to make modifications. EXCLUSIV CUMULATIVE mode (default setting, code letter E) locks the defined records immediately and completely for all other users. But the

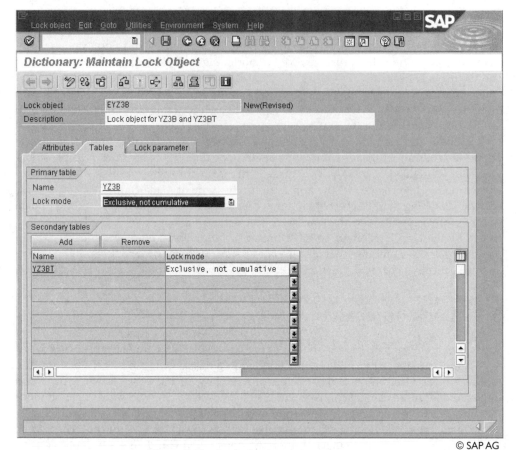

Figure 5.33   Lock object maintenance screen

user who is locking the records can lock them again. Cumulative locking is excluded through EXCLUSIVE, NOT CUMULATIVE mode (code letter X). The user can then only lock the record once, i.e. in one mode. You set the lock mode separately for the primary tables and the secondary tables. There is one input field with a list box available for each of these.

If you want to lock several tables simultaneously, you can enter additional tables in the SECONDARY TABLES area. You cannot make manual entries here. The additional tables can only be determined through an input help that you call by clicking on the ADD button. This input help determines the tables that are linked with the primary table using the foreign key dependencies, and displays them in a dialog box where you can select them.

The tool transfers all the key fields in the tables you are using as potential lock parameters. After you insert the tables, you can change to the LOCK PARAMETER tab. In this tab, you must select all the fields that you want to use later to identify the record that you want to lock. This will normally be all the key fields.

The lock object is activated after you enter all the attributes. This procedure generates two function modules. Their names consist of the prefix ENQUEUE_(lock) or DEQUEUE_ (release lock, unlock) and the name of the lock object. The two function modules in this example are therefore called ENQUEUE_EYZ3B and DEQUEUE_EYZ3B. These function modules have some general parameters and some parameters that are dependent on the lock object's lock arguments. The listing below shows the call to this module and the way it can be inserted in the program editor by choosing EDIT | PATTERN from the menu.

```
CALL FUNCTION 'ENQUEUE_EYZ3B'
*     EXPORTING
*          MODE_YZ3B        = 'E'
*          MODE_YZ3BT       = 'E'
*          MANDT            = SY-MANDT
*          SECTOR           =
*          LANGU            =
*          X_SECTOR         = ' '
*          X_LANGU          = ' '
*          _SCOPE           = '2'
*          _WAIT            = ' '
*          _COLLECT         = ' '
*     EXCEPTIONS
*          FOREIGN_LOCK     = 1
*          SYSTEM_FAILURE   = 2
*          OTHERS           = 3
```

All the parameters of the function module, apart from the actual lock parameters, have default values. The system fills the inserted statement structure with the default values, but they are initially automatically reported by the SYSTEM_FAILURE exception. Function modules that belong to lock objects with lock mode 'X' also have a third exception, OWN_LOCK. This exception is triggered if the same process has already requested a lock that overlaps with the current lock request. The whole table is locked when you use the standard defaults for the parameters of the lock module.

If the lock module generates an exception, it does so with a statement similar to this:

```
message e602(mc) with sy-uname raising foreign_lock.
```

This means that all system fields containing messages are filled. That is why you can either display a specific error message that you have programmed, or use the filled system fields to output standard messages:

```
if sy-subrc <> 0.
  message id sy-msgid type sy-msgty number sy-msgno
          with sy-msgv1 sy-msgv2 sy-msgv3 sy-msgv4.
endif.
```

No exceptions are triggered when you unlock the function modules. Their interface is therefore kept simpler, as this listing shows:

```
CALL  FUNCTION 'DEQUEUE_EYZ3B'
*       EXPORTING
*               MODE_YZ3B   = 'E'
*               MODE_YZ3BT  = 'E'
*               MANDT       = SY-MANDT
*               SECTOR      =
*               LANGU       =
*               X_SECTOR    = ' '
*               X_LANGU     = ' '
*               _SCOPE      = '3'
*               _SYNCHRON   = ' '
*               _COLLECT    = ' '
```

In addition to the parameters that have already been described, there is another parameter here called _SYNCHRON. If it is filled with 'X', the module waits until the lock is actually lifted. Without this entry the module works asynchronously.

5.6 Type groups

From Release 3.0 you find *type groups*. You store globally applicable type definitions in type groups. Type groups do not fit into the pattern of Data Dictionary objects discussed so far, because there are no database-specific objects hidden behind type groups. There are merely files containing special ABAP statements. However, as you can use Data Dictionary objects like global type definitions, it makes sense to include them here.

You declare data types or constants in a type group, also known as a *type pool*. In it you use the TYPES or CONSTANTS statements. In an application, you can use this statement to insert a type group:

TYPE-POOLS typgroup.

After that, all declarations made in the type group are available in the program. You should assign type groups to a development class. That is why SAP recommends that the name of a type group should consist of the name of the development class and one or two more letters if required. The names of the elements declared in a type group must begin with the name of the type group and an underscore.

There is no specific input field for type groups in the Data Dictionary initial screen. To maintain type groups, choose UTILITIES | OTHER DICTIONARY objects from the menu.

5.7 Exercises

1. If you can log on to your system with different logon languages, test the general table maintenance functions for both tables using different languages.

2. Generate the YZ3STOCK and YZ3PRICE tables, and also the necessary data elements and domains (domain name = data element name). Take the structure of the tables

from the overview that follows (Tables 5.7 and 5.8). There should be a foreign key relationship between the WKZ field in the YZ3PRICE table and the WKZ field in the
YZ3STOCK table. The YZ3STOCK table is therefore a value table for the YZ3WKZ
domain. Enter the YZ3STOCK-CURRENCY field as the reference field for the field
PRICE in the YZ3PRICE table. Double-click on the field names to make the necessary
input fields available. In addition create a foreign key relationship between the CUR-
RENCY field in the YZ3STOCK table and the TCURC table. Assign delivery class A to
both tables. You do not have to generate the modules for general table maintenance.

Table 5.7   Structure of the YZ3STOCK table

Field name	Key	Data element	Type	Length	Check table	Short text
MANDT	X	MANDT	CLNT	3	*	Client
WKZ	X	YZ3WKZ	NUM C	6		WKZ
NAME	X	YZ3DESCR	CHA R	30		Share name
BRANCH		YZ3BRA	CHA R	1	*	Description of branch
CURRENCY		WAERS or WAERS_CURC	CUK Y	5	TCURC	Currency key

Table 5.8   Structure of the YZ3PRICE table

Field name	Key	Data element	Type	Length	Check table	Short text
MANDT	X	MANDT	CLNT	3	*	Client
WKZ	X	YZ3WKZ	NUM C	6	YZ3STOCK	Share name
AKTDATE	X	YZ3DAT	DAT S	8		Date
PRICE		YZ3PRC	CUR R	8		Share price

6 Resources in the Development Environment

Creating an ABAP task is complex. You require a multitude of tools. Some resources exist to make the work easier. This chapter presents the most important resources in detail.

6.1 Transport Management System

The R/3 System is a very comprehensive and complex application. At SAP there are sometimes several hundred developers working on it simultaneously. The newly developed objects must be delivered to customers in a co-ordinated fashion, ensuring also that the software functions correctly. There are several tools that help you to fulfil this task. In this book, they are called *transport management tools*. They are sometimes also called Change and Transport System tools. Some of these tools work in the R/3 System, and others at operating system level.

Every software developer who is creating their own software must know about transport management and the software delivery logistics typical of the R/3 System. You must consider all the requirements of the R/3 System to guarantee that software is transferred without error and in full working order after an R/3 upgrade.

Setting up transport management tools and certain low-level activities relating to these tools is not something the programmer has to do. This chapter begins with a description of the transport management components that a developer uses on a daily basis. This is followed by examples of typical development activities. The chapter concludes with information about the organization of an R/3 software project.

From Release 3.0, the *Workbench Organizer* is the interface for all transport management tools. You call it using transaction code SE09. The tool familiar from earlier Releases (transaction SE01) is still available, although the interface has been extensively revised. It is mostly used to solve special problems for which the Workbench Organizer is not flexible enough.

6.1.1 Tasks

An application can lock a table against external access. In just the same way, a developer must be able to protect the elements that he or she is currently processing from being processed by someone else. There are two different types of locks. If a programmer wants to process a development object, the tools read this object's description from the database. This sets a normal database lock that prevents the object being processed by another developer. The lock is only effective until the developer saves the changed object and exits the development tool.

There is an alternative to this short-term lock, which differs from the lock for tables because it can function over a longer period, sometimes even weeks. This alternative lock can protect the object for the whole development period. Only the developer who created the lock can process the object during this period. The first task of the transport management system is to assign objects to a developer and to prevent access by other developers.

Another task is to create logs that record the processing of objects. All processed objects and their developers are recorded in special system tables. This allows you to find out when an object was processed and by whom. This information is important if you want to transfer a development to another system, such as a customer system.

All newly developed programs must be tested and later transported to the customer system or to your own production system. It is practically impossible to carry out development and testing in the same system, at least in the case of the large projects with which SAP is involved. For a test, you need applications to have a defined and, most importantly, unchanging status over a period of time. This would mean that no development could take place for the duration of the test. This would only be possible for a very small team of developers. This is why there is an SAP system group available for development. Completed objects are transported (physically copied) from the development system to a *consolidation system*. There they are tested. The transport management system lists the different developers and projects with all the processed objects. These lists are used to ascertain the processed objects when a development project is completed. In this way, you can select the required processed objects and transport them. Customers also usually have at least two systems, a test system and a production system. For example, preliminary corrections or reworked customizing settings are first tested in the consolidation system, and only then copied to the production system.

Newly developed objects are transported to customer systems in a similar way. Unlike a completely new installation, the only objects that are transported to the customer system are those that have been changed since the last delivery. You can also evaluate these functions using the transport management logs.

6.1.2 Principle

If a user wants to create a new object or process an existing one, he or she includes this object in a *request*. The user either creates a new request or selects it from a list of current requests. When the object is included in a request, it is locked and other developers cannot process it. A request is basically a list of items that is assigned some additional attributes. These additional attributes include a description and details of the owner. A development object that is contained in a request of this kind cannot be included in another request. This means that only the owner of the request can process that particular object. To allow several programmers within a development team to process the same object, the transport management system provides a way of combining several developers and their requests.

Each developer can create any number of this kind of request. This allows you to distinguish between different development projects. The request is released when a development project is complete. This means that the objects contained in it are no longer locked. The list of objects that were processed within this request remains intact, but it is no longer evaluated when the system determines what locks are present. Depending on the type of system, the processed objects and the system configuration, you also export the processed elements if necessary. This means that the system stores a description of all the development objects contained in the request in a file at operating system level. The structure of this file is not affected by the operating system. You can transport it to another system and load it. This is how development objects are transported to other systems. It also means you cannot transport development objects that were not entered in a request.

6.1.3 Terminology

This section describes several of the terms that are used in the context of transport management. It only applies to R/3 Releases higher than 3.0. Some of the terms already existed in earlier Releases. However, if they did, they sometimes have a slightly different meaning from Release 3.0.

Development class

A complex R/3 application consists of many different development objects. The term *development class* is used to group all the elements in an application (programs, Data Dictionary objects, transactions, etc.). The development class defines the transport properties of the objects it contains, especially the target system in the case of data export. When you generate new objects, you must enter the development class in a transport management system dialog box. In the Workbench initial screen there is a command field in which you specify the development class (transaction SE80 or SEU). The Object Browser then displays all the development objects in the selected development class.

You should create a development class before you begin a development project. You can do so as part of customizing in transaction SEU or using the general table maintenance transaction SM31. The table you want to maintain is TDEVC. Whatever method you use to call, you process the data for a development class in a dialog box as in Figure 6.1.

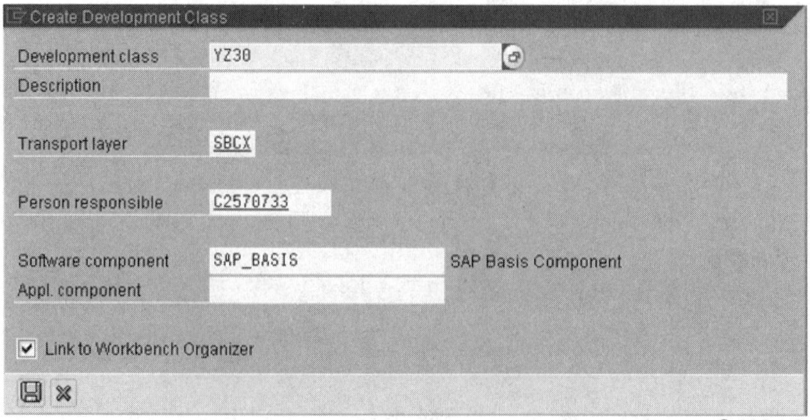

Figure 6.1   Creating a development class

© SAP AG

Besides the name and the short description, you must specify a TRANSPORT LAYER. This piece of information defines the transport route, and most importantly the target system, for all the objects that you create in the development class. The transport layers are maintained by an administrator and differ from system to system.

By entering the name of the person responsible, you can make it easier to solve problems if you are working in a big team. You can enter values in the two fields SOFTWARE COMPONENT and APPL. COMPONENT (application component) to combine development classes to form larger units. This is only important in very big development systems such as those at SAP.

Name ranges have also been defined for development classes. Names for the customer's development class must begin with Y or Z or with the name prefix that has been assigned to that customer. Classes whose names begin with T play a special role. These are local development classes. The objects in these classes cannot be transported. These classes enable you to use the transport management functions for local applications (writing logs, protection against processing by third parties).

Local objects

You can assign the status *local object* to newly created objects. You process this kind of object outside the correction system. You cannot use the correction system to protect them against processing by third parties and they cannot be transported. The only way to protect these objects is by locking them while you are directly processing them with a particular development tool. This lock is not set by the correction system. It is a normal database lock. Local private objects are assigned the development class $TMP.

Original and copy

You develop applications in a development system. The development objects are transported to other systems from here. This happens periodically to remove errors or install new functions. You can only permanently change a development object in the system from which the object was created. That is why the system records where each development object was generated. This system is also called the original system of the object and the object in this system is the original. There are only copies of the object in all other systems that are supplied through SAP upgrades, even the customer systems. When you transport objects between different R/3 Systems, the transport management system prevents the original object from being overwritten or changed. You can overwrite and change copies at any time.

Task

A task is the smallest physical organizational unit in the correction system. It is used to register the objects that are being processed and to create the processing lock. Each task has a unique number to identify it. You assign one or more tasks to a request. The programmer must enter the number of the request whenever the correction system wants to register a new object for processing. However, the information is actually stored in a task within this request. Tasks correspond in principle to the lists already mentioned. A task can only ever have one owner.

The correction system differentiates between different types of task. There are development objects with different statuses (original or copy) within a system. This distinction is necessary because these development objects require individual treatment. A task can only ever contain objects with the same status. The different types of tasks (also called *task attributes*) are listed in Table 6.1. Tasks are generally created automatically by the correction system, which also assigns the type. This type is usually unimportant for the user of the correction system.

Table 6.1   Attributes of tasks

Task type	Description
Not assigned	Newly created tasks without contents
Development / correction	Only contains objects that were newly created in the current R/3 System (originals)
Repair	Only contains objects that were created in other R/3 Systems and transported to the current R/3 System (copies)

The term 'task' did not exist in earlier Releases. That is why tasks of the type development/correction are also known as *corrections* and tasks of the type repair are described as *repairs*.

Request

A request is a logical administrative unit that groups all the tasks necessary for a self-contained development task. It can contain one or more tasks of different types and with different owners. The request defines what type of transport to other systems is used for all the objects in the tasks contained in the request. Requests are normally created automatically. This always generates a subordinate task that is linked to the new request.

If the programmer wants to register an object using the correction system, they enter the request to which they want to assign the object. The correction system automatically ascertains the actual task in which the object will be registered, on the basis of the user and the object's status. The system creates a task of a suitable type if none exists.

Requests also have a type that is defined through the transport properties of the objects contained in it, or more precisely through the first object that is to be included (see Table 6.2). All the objects that are registered in later stages of development must have the same transport properties. If this is not the case for a particular object, that object cannot be registered in this request. The correction system then creates a new request.

The owner of a request can create more tasks in their requests for other developers, using special functions in the Workbench Organizer. All the developers included in a request can process all the objects entered in the tasks within this request.

Each development class has various system tables. They determine whether or not elements in this class can be transported out of the current system. If you process a non-transportable object, the system automatically generates a local request. Otherwise it generates a transportable request.

Table 6.2   Attributes of a request

Type of request	Description
Not assigned	Empty request
Transportable	Request with objects that can be exported to another R/3 System
Local	Request with objects that cannot be exported from the current R/3 System

Release

When development is complete, you must release the tasks and requests. You do this using the special menu functions of the particular transport tool. Only the owner of the task or the request may use these functions.

When you release a task, the first effect is that the list of items for the task is copied to the list for the higher level request. The lock on the objects remains, but is now set by the request. You can release the request when all its tasks are released. This removes the lock for the objects. The objects are exported if the request is transportable. You can no longer process released tasks or requests.

6.1.4 Example of a new development in a customer system

This section describes the processes involved when you create a new object in a customer system. The names of the objects therefore follow the conventions for customer objects. For reasons of availability, this example was created for a customer system running Release 4.5. If you are working on a customer system and have the necessary authorizations, you can complete this example in your own system. The transport management system depends a lot on system-specific settings. This means that the workflow in your system may differ from the one described here. You must only create transportable objects in your system and actually transport them when you understand their effects on your system.

Figure 6.2   Assigning a development class

In this example, you want to process report YZ361010. You create a report with this name using transaction SE38 or the Workbench. You enter a short description and program type in the program editor attributes screen. These steps are exactly the same as the ones when you created the 'Hello World' program in Chapter 3. The first dialog box for the correction system is displayed when you want to save the data in the attributes screen (see Figure 6.2). In all the other examples in this book, you generally close this dialog box by activating the LOCAL OBJECT button. This creates objects that are not subject to control by the transport management system.

If you want to create the object with the correction system, you must enter a development class (in this example YZ30) in this dialog box. This copies the transport properties of this class (target system) to the new object. Then you close the dialog box by clicking on the SAVE button. The correction system recognizes that the new object must be included in a request, so it prompts you to specify the request number in a second dialog box (Figure 6.3).

You can click on the OWN REQUESTS button to display any of your own requests that are present as an input help. Their attributes must allow the inclusion of the current object. Sometimes the last number processed is automatically inserted into the command field as

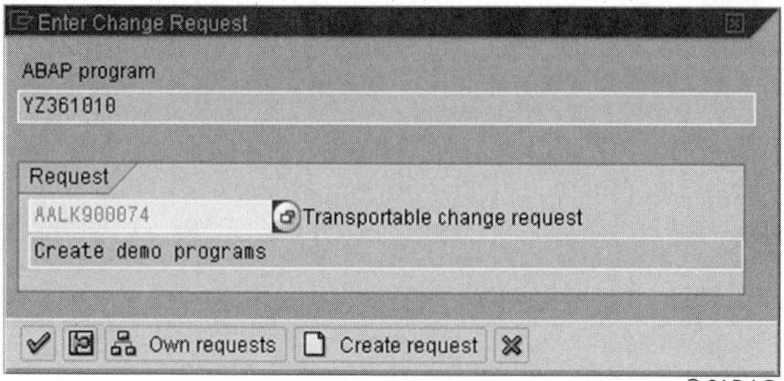

Figure 6.3   Defining the request

a suggested request number. Click on the CREATE REQUEST pushbutton to generate a new request. If you do so, you must enter a short description in a third dialog box. After you save the third dialog box, you return to the second dialog box. In it you create the request by clicking (Enter) or the appropriate pushbutton (green tick). You can include more objects in this request if you need them.

When you finish the development you must release the request. You use the *Workbench Organizer* to do this. This must not be confused with the actual Workbench. You can access the Workbench Organizer through transaction code SE09 or from the main menu for program development. Choose OVERVIEW | WORKBENCH ORGANIZER from the menu. Figure 6.4 shows the interface for this tool.

You can maintain all the requests and tasks from the initial screen of the Workbench Organizer. The right-hand side of the screen (GLOBAL INFORMATION) displays an overview of all the transports carried out by the current user. If the system is included in a *transport group*, this overview includes transports from other systems.

On the left-hand side of the screen, you can use the attributes of the tasks and requests that you want to process to select them. All the tasks and requests that have the marked attributes appear in a second screen after you click on the DISPLAY pushbutton (Figure 6.4).

You can click on the MODIFIABLE or RELEASED radio button to differentiate between released, i.e. completed, requests and those that you can still process.

To release the request you have just generated, you must click on the MODIFIABLE and TRANSPORTABLE radio button. After you click on the DISPLAY pushbutton, the transaction generates a new screen that contains the interactive report (see Figure 6.5).

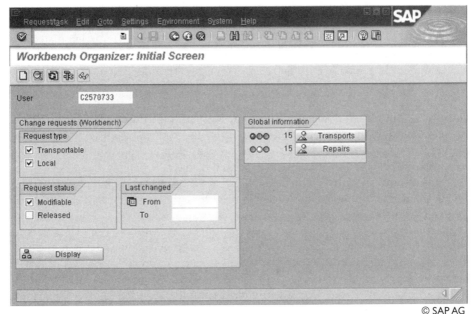

© SAP AG

Figure 6.4   The Workbench Organizer

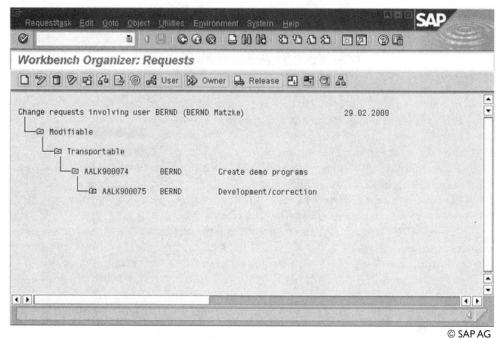

Figure 6.5   Tasks and requests overview

To display all the tasks belonging to a request, single-click on the folder icon to the left of the request's number. Click on the request's folder icons to show the contents of the associated tasks. When you want to release a request, you must first release all its tasks. To do this, place the cursor on the number of the task you want to release and click on the RELEASE button. In the course of the release, you can enter documentation for each task; this is not mandatory. You can simply save the sample suggested by the system and leave the documentation editor by clicking (F3). Released tasks are highlighted in a different colour in the Workbench Organizer. Then you can repeat the process for the request. After you release a task, the system copies the list of the processed objects to a list that is assigned to the request. As a result, the lock is retained until the request is released. After you release the request, other users can process the object.

Various errors can occur when you export out of the system and import into a different system. That is why the system creates a log. To view this log, choose GOTO | TRANSPORT LOGS from the menu.

The detail screen for the tasks and requests offers several more important processing functions. You can assign a different owner to a marked object by clicking on the CHANGE OWNER pushbutton. The owner is the only person who can process a request or a task, i.e. insert new objects or release the request. If the owner of a request or a task is absent and the request has to be changed, another employee can then continue processing the object. You can also perform this function with other peoples' objects, i.e. you can fetch objects from other employees.

If you do not want to change the owner, you can also assign a request to additional employees. To do this, mark the request with the cursor and then click on the ADD USER pushbutton. You can enter the name of an additional employee in a dialog box. A task is then created specifically for this employee. Only the owner of the request can perform this function.

6.2   Authorization concept

Authorizations are extremely important to protect programs and data from unauthorized access. You should therefore also use them in your own development projects. However, authorizations are based on a very complicated system. Apart from that, maintaining authorizations for different users is very time consuming. Each additional authorization increases the maintenance workload and the probability that problems will occur. For these reasons, you should use existing authorizations in your own applications wherever possible. You can usually do this, as most customer developments are limited to extensions to existing SAP applications. Even if you have to create your own authorizations, you can very often fall back on preprogrammed elements called *authorization objects*. When you build authorization checks into your own applications, you must choose one of three approaches that involve different amounts of work:

1. use existing authorizations;

2. create and use new authorizations based on existing authorization objects;

3. generate new authorization objects and derive your own authorizations from them.

You need special authorizations to maintain the various elements of the authorizations system. These should not be available to every user for reasons of system security. The work described in this section is not performed by every developer, but by a system administrator. Apart from that, the checks within authorization maintenance are organized so that the two jobs of creating and releasing authorizations can be assigned to two different administrators. This guarantees that there is dual control when there are changes affecting security. Depending on your actual authorizations within your system, you may not be able to perform the example below. If you are not able to do so, the descriptions combined with the screenshots at least provide you with an overview of the elements in the authorization system.

The example describes the entire process. It begins with the creation of an authorization field, and ends with the insertion of an authorization into a user master record. This is achieved using an authorization for the demo program in Chapter 7. This description contains the three points mentioned above, but in reverse order. For the demonstration, you need an R/3 System set up as a customer system. That is why we are using a Release 4.5A System in this case. In newer Releases, there are more transactions available for authorization maintenance (such as Profile Generator PFCG). Otherwise there are no significant differences.

6.2.1 Authorization classes, fields and objects

An authorization object is a template for an authorization. The authorization object contains fields that you later fill with values in the authorization. An authorization object is therefore slightly similar to a type declaration. Several authorization objects for an application group (e.g. accounting or materials management) form an authorization class. This authorization class is only used to create logical groups for the authorization objects and to make things clearer.

All the fields that you want to include in authorization objects must be contained in three Data Dictionary structures. Normally you always use the authorization maintenance transactions. However, you can process these structures directly with the table maintenance tools (transaction SE11).

You use different structures for the authorization fields used in the SAP Basis system tools, SAP applications and customer developments. By using these different structures, you can see what is happening and keep the development areas separate from each other more easily. These structures have the following names: AUTHA for fields in application development, AUTHB for fields in the SAP Basis system tools and ZAUTHCUST for the fields in the authorizations created by the customer. AUTHA and AUTHB are always present, but you may have to generate ZAUTHCUST by copying the AUTHC structure. If the ZAUTHCUST structure does not exist in your system yet, generate it by copying the AUTHC structure. You can do this in the Data Dictionary maintenance screen (transaction SE11). You will find it hard to understand the example at the end of this section without this structure.

The ZAUTHCUST structure can cause particular problems in customer systems that are supplied from different sources (in-house developments, other suppliers). There is a danger that changes can be overwritten by both sides if this table is maintained in different source systems and transported to the customer system. That could mean that the authorization fields are missing, and that the authorizations based on them become invalid. In such cases, you should create append structures for ZAUTHCUST with the transaction SE11. Then each source system no longer supplies the complete ZAUTHCUST structure. They only supply an append structure, whose name is clearly defined beforehand. You can only use the transactions for authorization maintenance to display fields generated in this way. You cannot process them.

6.2.2 Authorization groups

If you use explicit authorization maintenance incorrectly, you can create security loopholes. The R/3 System performs some checks automatically. These do not have to be programmed within an application program. It monitors the calling of transactions for table maintenance or the modification of applications.

These checks are based on authorization groups. You define an authorization group through an entry in the TPGP table. The TPGPT table contains the short texts for the authorization groups. You generate an eight-character descriptor in the TPGP table. You do this separately for each application area. This descriptor is the name of an authorization group. You can enter this name as an additional attribute when you maintain objects. The system checks against the S_DEVELOP authorization object before a program is started or edited. Maintenance of the program attributes or access to other tools in the development environment is protected by S_PROGRAM.

A user has the right to access the object if they have an authorization derived from the S_DEVELOP or S_PROGRAM authorization object in the BC_C (basis development environment) authorization class. The authorization must also contain the name of the authorization group in the P_GROUP field.

6.2.3 Protecting transactions

From Release 3.0E, you must explicitly release all the transactions that a user is to be allowed to access. You do this by entering the transaction codes (or a suitable wildcard pattern) in the TCD field of the S_TCODE authorization object.

6.2.4 An example

Up to three steps are required to generate your own authorization objects:

1. define the authorization fields;

2. create an authorization class;

3. create an authorization object.

For these steps you need the tools described below. You can access them from the development environment main menu by choosing DEVELOPMENT | OTHER TOOLS | AUTHORIZATION OBJECTS | FIELDS (transaction code SU20) or DEVELOPMENT | OTHER TOOLS | AUTHORIZATION OBJECTS | OBJECTS (transaction code SU21) from the menu.

First, you must create an authorization field. Use transaction SU20 to do this or one of the menu options listed above. In the start screen of this transaction (Figure 6.6), select the category you want for the new authorization fields by clicking on one of the pushbuttons there.

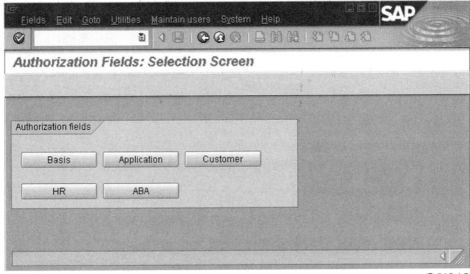

© SAP AG

Figure 6.6   Creating authorization fields

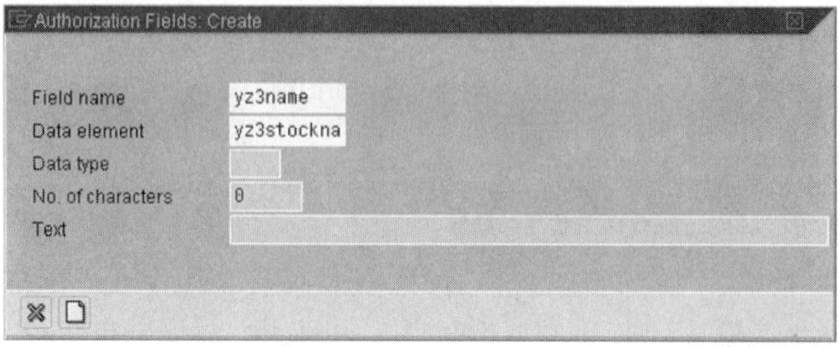

Figure 6.7   Defining a new authorization field

Then, the system checks that the selection matches the current system type. If the selection is correct, it displays the authorization fields available in the particular group in a list. You can now click on pushbuttons or choose menu options to create new fields or process present fields. When you create new fields, the system prompts you for just two pieces of information in a dialog box (Figure 6.7).

It is the name of the authorization field and the name of the data element that define the attributes of the authorization field. In accordance with the naming conventions, they are both freely definable. In this example, the name of the authorization field is YZ3NAME and the name of the data element is YZ3STOCKNA. The three display fields in the dialog box are only updated when you save the data, and the values in them vary according to the attributes of the data element. These entries also appear in the list. You can create more fields using the same procedure. For this example, one field is enough.

In the second step, you create a new authorization class. The procedure is basically the same as the procedure for creating a new field. First you start transaction SU21 either by entering the transaction code or by choosing its menu option. Although the menu option is called OBJECTS, not CLASSES, the system displays a list of all the authorization classes. To generate the new class, click on the appropriate pushbutton or choose the associated menu option. You enter the data for the new class (description and description) in a dialog box (Figure 6.8).

The class you have just created now appears in the list of available classes. In it you can process the objects in a class by double-clicking on the class names or by clicking on the LIST OBJECTS pushbutton. These objects are also displayed in a list. You can add new objects to this list by clicking on the appropriate pushbutton or choosing the associated menu option. In the dialog box for defining an authorization object, you are prompted to enter the object name and a short description. You can also change the authorization class if you need to. As well as this data, you can enter up to ten authorization fields in the lower area of the dialog box (Figure 6.9). The fields must already exist at this point.

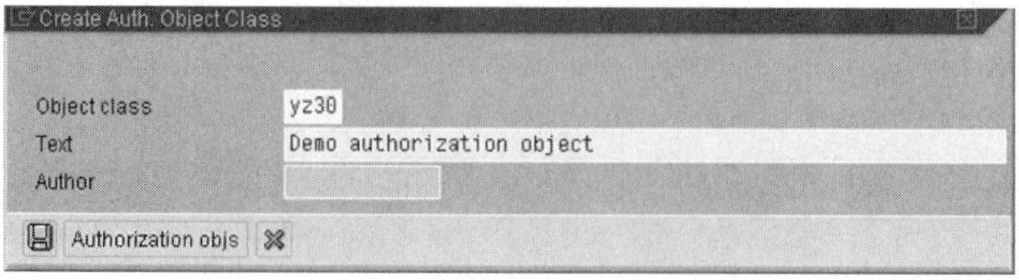

Figure 6.8   Creating an authorization class

© SAP AG

Figure 6.9   Creating authorization objects

When you have defined the authorization object, the first phase of the authorization maintenance work is complete.

You can now use the authorization object to define an authorization. An authorization is an instance of an authorization object. You assign it a unique name. It contains all the fields present in the authorization object and you can assign values to the fields. Later, the system carries out the authorization check against these values.

There are several ways in which you can call the authorization maintenance function. In the screens for transactions SU20 and SU21, you can choose the MAINTAIN USERS menu's three options: AUTHORIZATION, PROFILE and USER. The same menu is also present in the system administration area menu. You can choose it from the R/3 System base menu (area menu S000) by choosing TOOLS | ADMINISTRATION. The transaction codes for the three menu options are SU01 (user), SU02 (profiles) and SU03 (authorizations).

To create an authorization, you call transaction SU03. First, the system displays a list of all the available authorization classes. This only displays a short description, not a technical definition. As the list is sorted alphabetically by these short descriptions, the order of entries is different from that in the list you see in transaction SU21. Double-click on an entry in the list to branch to a list of all the authorization objects in this class. This list also only contains the short description. However, you can also display the actual description by clicking on the TEC.NAMES pushbutton. All authorizations derived from an authorization object are displayed in a third list. This appears after you double-click on the name of the authorization object. In our example this list is still empty. Click on the CREATE pushbutton

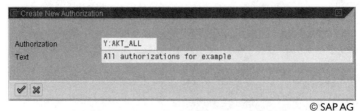

© SAP AG

Figure 6.10   Maintaining an authorization

or choose AUTHORIZATION | CREATE from the menu to generate an authorization. A dialog box is displayed. In it you must enter the name of the authorization and a short description. As an authorization contains specific values and permits or forbids precisely defined actions, you must give it a unique name. In our example, the first authorization (*see* Figure 6.10) should receive the name Y:AKT_ALL. Note that according to the SAP naming conventions, you are not allowed to enter an underscore in the second position in the names of customer authorizations. You can enter any short description you want.

The authorization you have just generated is then displayed in the list of authorizations, but is still empty. You assign values to it by clicking on the MAINTAIN VALUES pushbutton, by choosing GOTO | MAINTAIN VALUES from the menu, or by double-clicking on the name of the authorization. You can enter one or more individual values or value pairs in the dialog box that is now active (Figure 6.11).

After you define the field values, you must save and activate the authorization. The values you have entered only become effective after activation. The authorization status

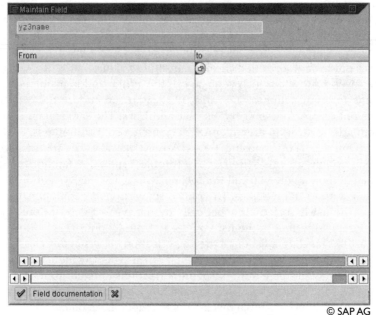

© SAP AG

Figure 6.11   Assigning values to an authorization

(revised, active) is displayed in the list of authorizations. Sometimes the authorizations for maintenance and activation are split between two different administrators. This means that changes made by one person have to be confirmed by someone else before they become effective. That is why you save two versions when you are revising an existing authorization: the current version that is valid for the user, and a maintenance version. Only activation converts the maintenance version to the current version. During activation, the system places the current and the maintenance version opposite each other. This makes it easier for the activating administrator to check them. Final activation only occurs after you perform the ACTIVATE function again.

You can create any number of authorizations with different field values for an authorization object. Each authorization must be stored in a user's master record to define the user's actual rights. You cannot do this directly. You have to insert *profiles*. A profile groups one or more authorizations that belong together logically, and thus makes it easier to maintain a user's data. You cannot directly assign an authorization to the user master record.

To create a profile, you call transaction SU02 or choose MAINTAIN USERS | PROFILES from the menu. The initial screen for this transaction contains a command field. In it you can make a preliminary selection of the profiles for processing from the list that is then displayed. You can skip this initial screen without entering a value by pressing (Enter). The result of this is that all the available profiles appear in the list. You can generate a new profile in this list by pressing the CREATE pushbutton, in much the same way as you create authorization objects or authorization classes. You must enter the description of the profile (Y:AKT_PROALL) and a short description in a dialog box (see Figure 6.12).

In this dialog box, you must also choose between a single profile and a composite profile. A single profile contains authorizations. A composite profile groups other profiles. In this example we will create a single profile.

A screen with a relatively large table view is displayed (see Figure 6.13). In it you create the new profile. The profile's authorizations are automatically listed in this table view. You can either create authorizations manually, by entering the name of the authorization object and authorization or by using a special function for each. You can call these functions by clicking on the INSERT AUTHORIZATION or INSERT OBJECT pushbuttons or by choosing EDIT | INSERT AUTHORIZATION or EDIT | INSERT OBJECT from the menu. These functions display input help which you can use to select an object or an authorization. They first display a list containing all the authorization classes. You can select one of

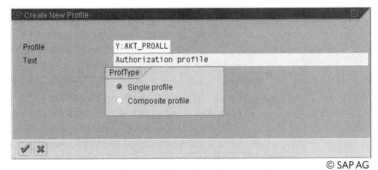

© SAP AG

Figure 6.12   Creating a profile

© SAP AG

Figure 6.13   Creating a profile

these classes by double-clicking on it. The system then displays a list of all the authorizations for all the authorization objects in that class. You can now select one of these
authorizations and when you do so, the system inserts it in the profile.

Changes to a profile only become effective after activation, in just the same way as
changes to an authorization. Here too, the active and the maintenance versions are first displayed together. A profile is only activated after you confirm that you want to activate it.

After you generate the profile, you can store it in the user's master record. You can test
the authorizations by creating a new user (or having a new user created for you) or by
inserting the new authorization into your own user master record. You can maintain your
user master record with transaction SU01 or by choosing MAINTAIN USERS MAINTENANCE |
USERS from the menu. You enter the name of the new user or the one you want to change
in the only command field in this transaction, and click on the CREATE or CHANGE pushbuttons. You can enter the Y_AKT_PROALL profile in the step loop area of the screen that
now follows. Then save the data. These changes will take effect the next time the user
logs in to the system.

7 An Example

This section uses a small example to explain the basic programming techniques you use to create a dialog application. The emphasis here is on the program's structure and on describing the programs of the individual program parts, not on how you use individual tools or how you create the application. Many of the applications in the SAP System use a relatively standardized program structure. This structure has become well established over the years. It enables clear programming, lets you use the programs in a fairly uniform manner and link transactions quickly and easily.

This example makes it possible for you to create share price indexes. To do this, in the YZ3STOCK table you first maintain the shares whose index values (prices) you want to enter. The indexes have their own YZ3PRICE table. You should already have created both these tables as part of the exercises in Chapter 5. The YZ3B and YZ3BT tables that you have already used are used again here. Figure 7.1 shows the relationship between the tables. This figure uses the normal entity relationship representation used at SAP.

You should find that the existing table maintenance functions that have been generated will also allow you to process the YZ3B and YZ3BT tables. Separate programs are only generated for YZ3STOCK and YZ3PRICE in the programming examples below. The program for YZ3STOCK should allow you to create, change, display and delete records. In this case, the delete function is created as a subfunction of the program's change function. The second program enables you to enter or edit index data for all the records managed in YZ3PRICE. No simple display or delete functions are planned here. You must start with the program for YZ3STOCK because you can only manage indexes for shares that have a record in YZ3STOCK.

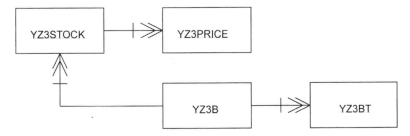

Figure 7.1   Relationships between the tables in the demo application

7.1   Program structure

A program consists of one or more screen programs that are called one after another. Together with the flow logic statements, each screen program executes a precisely defined subtask. When the system jumps from one screen program to another in a program, this means that one subtask has been completed and that it can now carry out another subtask. This means that each screen program represents a status within the program. For this reason, the first thing you do when you create a program is to split up the actions to be carried out into subtasks. You then assign these subtasks to the various screen programs. Next, you define when these screen programs are to be processed, i.e. the conditions that must be fulfilled and the actions that launch the screen programs. It is relatively easy to define the subtasks you require to maintain YZ3STOCK. There are only two subtasks involved here:

1. select the record;

2. process the record.

Each of these programs is transferred to a screen program. More complex programs may require you to subdivide the programs described above even further and therefore increase the number of screen programs.

However, two screen programs are quite sufficient here because the example has deliberately been kept very simple.

After you have defined the number of screen programs and their programs, you must define the possible screen programs that can be accessed from each screen program. You should only use these kinds of transitions in the PAI part of a screen program. However, this part is only processed when the user triggers a function in the screen program. You also need to decide which functions and function codes are to be available in a screen program and what effect they should have. Both the basic requirements of the SAP Style Guide and application-specific demands play a role here. For example, the SAP Style Guide requires system-wide uniform reactions to the BACK command, function key (F3), CANCEL command, function key (F12) and EXIT command, function key (F15). Not all these commands are needed in every screen program, but when they are the user should be able to predict how the program will react.

Figure 7.2 shows the navigation structure of the demo application. This graphic needs a little explanation. You do not usually have to write an individual program for each of the subtasks, such as create, change, display and delete. Instead you use the transaction codes to branch to the various parts of an individual program. For this reason, a program's initial screen often provides a range of menu items that allow you to switch from one of the program's basic functions to another one. Each time you use these function codes, the program is called again by the corresponding transaction code. In addition, each initial screen in a program must provide at least one way of closing the program.

After you have entered your selection criteria in the initial screen, press (Enter) to access the processing screen. This feature is used throughout the system, so that the AND SUBMIT FIRST SCREEN addition functions correctly when you use CALL TRANSACTION to call a transaction.

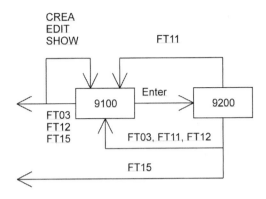

Figure 7.2 Navigating between screen programs

If you press (Enter) in the processing screen, it usually allows you to check the data you have entered and if necessary calls another screen program in which you enter additional data. If you press (Enter) in the processing screen in the example, you return to the processing screen because the example does not have another screen program. The processing procedure is completed when you save the data. You do not need to stay in the processing screen after you have saved the data; you can also return to the program's initial screen.

You must also be able to leave the processing screen without checking and saving the data. To do this, you use the BACK, CANCEL and EXIT functions that are described above. Although in the initial screen these three functions close the program, according to the SAP Style Guide they must have a different effect in the processing screen. If possible, the CANCEL function should return to the previous screen program. If the user has entered data in the current screen program, they must be warned that this data may be lost. The user should then be prevented from using the CANCEL function. The BACK function should also return to the previous screen program, to allow the user to save any changes they have made. The user should also be able to use the EXIT function to save their data. However, the EXIT function closes the entire program as well as the current screen program.

If you want to delete a record, it is not practical to check the current screen program's data. For this reason, you can delete the data in the exit module. However, you will have to confirm your action at the system prompt. Of course, you must return to the initial screen once you have deleted a record.

7.2 Program 1: SAPMYZ3S

The program structure description is a prerequisite for analyzing the source code. Because an application consists not only of the actual source code, but also of other elements, these elements are described below.

To call the application, use one of these three dialog transactions: YZ3I (create), YZ3U (change) and YZ3S (display). All of them execute screen program 9100 from module pool SAPMYZ3S.

Screen program 9100 contains the YZ3STOCK-WKZ mandatory field. Because this type of field does not accept a value that consists only of blanks, it ensures that no nameless data records can be generated.

Table TPARA contains the all Get/Set parameters. A parameter called YZS has been defined in this table. You use transaction SM31 to maintain table TPARA. When you maintain screen program 9100, you must activate the Get/Set mechanism for the single input field. You must also enter parameter YZS in data element YZ3WKZ as the data element's PARAMETER ID attribute.

Screen program 9200 is shown in Figure 7.3. This figure also shows the field names of the screen program fields. In this screen program, only YZ3STOCK-NAME, YZ3STOCK-SECTOR and YZ3STOCK-CURRENCY are input fields. All the others are display fields. The attribute TWODIMENSIONAL has also been set in some of these fields.

Both screen programs store the function code in the FCODE field.

There are two statuses: STAT_G for the initial screen (9100) and STAT_A for the work screen program (9200). In Figure 7.2, you can already see the basic function codes and the type of the codes required in these statuses. All the function codes whose lines lead out to the left or below a screen program (FT03, FT12, FT15, CREA, EDIT, SHOW) are exit function codes. All the others are simple function codes. The function code programs define how the function codes are assigned to the icons in the icon bar. However, you must make these assignments manually. The only key defined here is for function code F14 (delete).

Both the YZ3STOCK and YZ3PRICE tables have a lock module.

A few global data fields and constants (e.g. C_TRUE, C_ FALSE) have been declared in the declaration part of the module pool. You will find the source code of the declaration part at the end of this section.

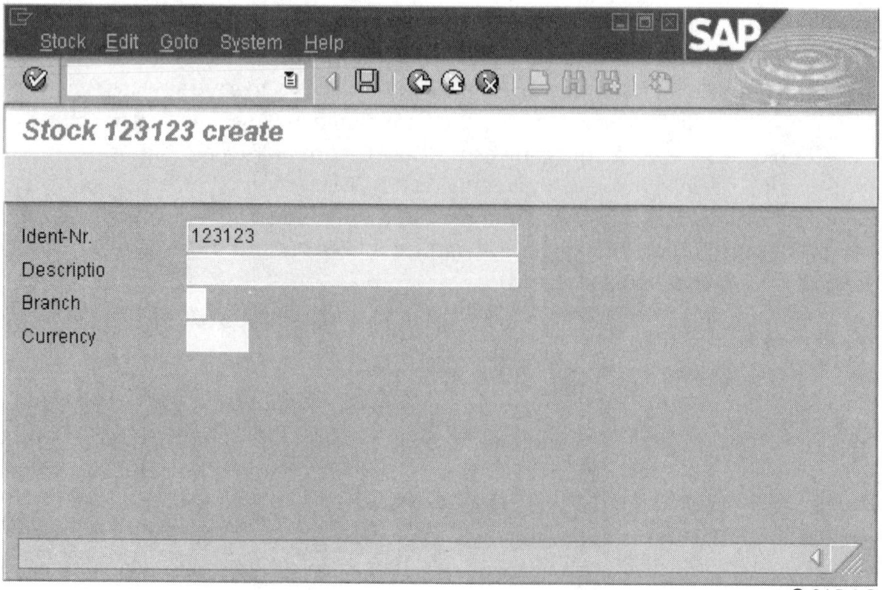

Figure 7.3   Demo application screen program 9200

The screen programs and their flow logic are the starting points for analyzing an application. The listing below begins with the flow logic of screen program 9100.

```
PROCESS BEFORE OUTPUT
*…initialize screen program
MODULE status_9100


PROCESS AFTER INPUT
*… evaluate exit codes

    MODULE exit_ 9100 AT EXIT COMMAND
    *…check whether the entry value is correct for the transaction
    FIELD yz3stock-wkz
    MODULE read_record_9100.

    *…go to the next screen
    MODULE user_command_9100.
```

All initializations should take place in the `status_9100` module. You will find this type of module in almost all screen programs.

You do not have to carry out any other actions in the PBO section. The PAI part also does not have any special features. You need one module to evaluate the exit function code. You require a second module to evaluate all the other function codes. In screen program 9100, because you want to read the record that is to be processed, you require a third module.

The `status_9100` module has a very simple structure. First of all a header is generated, depending on the transaction code. The header consists of a fixed text 'Share &&' into which you can insert one or two variable parameters. Only one parameter is used in screen program 9100. In contrast, screen program 9200 uses both parameters. The wording of the variable part, which has been programmed here as a numbered text element, is inserted after the statement as a comment.

```
MODULE status _9100 OUTPUT

*… Set the window header line
CASE sy-code
  WHEN 'YZ31'
      SET  TITLEBAR '001' WITH text-001."create
  WHEN 'YZ3U'
       SET TITLEBAR '001' WITH text-002.   " change
    WHEN 'YZ3S'.
     SET TITLEBAR '001' WITH text-003.   " display
  ENDCASE

*... Set status for initial screen
  SET PF-STATUS 'STAT_G'.

*...Delete the table's header line
  CLEAR yz3stock.
ENDMODULE.                    " STATUS_9100  OUTPUT
```

After you have specified the title, you set the status to ensure that the function codes are available. For security reasons, the YZ3STOCK header line is also initialized. This ensures that a blank record is always available when you create new records in screen program 9200.

If you decide against initialization, in some cases the contents of the most recently processed screen program might appear when you create a new record in screen program 9100. However, the Get/Set parameter always sets the YZ3STOCK-WZ field to the current value.

The PAI module EXIT_9100 is also very simple. Its only unique feature is the way in which it handles the screen program's function codes. The field provided for function codes, the FCODE field, is a global data field. If no function code has been assigned to the (Enter) key, you cannot overwrite the contents of the FCODE field by pressing (Enter). Note that it is only possible to assign no function code to the (Enter) key from Release 3.0 onwards, but even then it is very rarely done. If you did press (Enter) here, this field would still contain the function code that has so far applied. In many programs which were not developed specifically for Release 3.0 or completely redeveloped for it, the function code was stored in a second field and the actual function code field was deleted. Although this example was developed for Release 4.6, these old programming techniques should be used here. This means you will still be able to execute the program correctly, even if you are using older releases.

```
MODULE exit_9100 INPUT.
*...Save and delete function code field, see text
  g_fcode = fcode.
  CLEAR fcode.
*.....three function codes branch to other transactions
  CASE g_fcode.
    WHEN 'CREA'.
      LEAVE TO TRANSACTION 'YZ3I'.
    WHEN 'EDIT'.
      LEAVE TO TRANSACTION 'YZ3U'.
    WHEN 'SHOW'.
      LEAVE TO TRANSACTION 'YZ3S'.
  ENDCASE.

*...If you do not want to branch, close the program
  LEAVE TO SCREEN 0.
ENDMODULE.                         " EXIT_9100   INPUT
```

In the exit module, you must first evaluate the three function codes CREA, EDIT and SHOW, because they must be handled differently. All the other exit function codes are designed to close the program. For this reason, you can only switch to screen program 0 after the CASE statement.

The module used to evaluate the normal function codes is even simpler than the exit module. Screen program 9100 only uses the (Enter) key. You press (Enter) to process a specific record.

Because the record you select is processed in screen program 9200, you only need to program the switch to screen program 9200 in the corresponding module:

```
MODULE user_command_9100 INPUT.
  g_fcode = fcode.
  CLEAR fcode.

*...If ENTER pressed, process record
  IF g_fcode = ' '.
    LEAVE TO SCREEN 9200.
  ENDIF.
ENDMODULE.                            " USER_COMMAND_9100  INPUT
```

The READ_RECORD_9100 module contains the screen program's actual functionality. The record you want to process is made available in it. In this case, you have to decide whether you want to create a new record or process an existing one. This is necessary because you cannot combine the functions of the create and change transactions. For this reason, the program first attempts to use the key term you entered in the screen program to read the record in the module. It then evaluates the return code of the SELECT statement, in accordance with the transaction code. If the record has been read successfully you must call the lock module to protect it from unauthorized access.

Messages are triggered in the module if the SELECT statement's result does not match the current transaction code. If this happens, the screen program is processed again and the USER_COMMAND_9100 module is therefore not executed.

```
MODULE read_record_9100 INPUT.
*....Try to read the required record
  SELECT SINGLE * FROM yz3stock
    WHERE wkz = yz3stock-wkz.

*...SY-SUBRC shows whether the record has been found
  IF sy-subrc = 0.

*.... No record must be present if you use the create transaction
  IF sy-tcode = 'YZ3I'.
*.......Text: Share &/& already present!
    MESSAGE e001 WITH yz3stock-wkz yz3stock-name.

ENDIF.

*.....Lock record
  CALL FUNCTION 'ENQUEUE_EYZ3STOCK'
    EXPORTING
      mode_yz3stock  = 'E'
      mandt          = sy-mandt
      wkz            = yz3stock-wkz
```

```
*          X_WKZ              = ' '
*          _SCOPE             = '2'
*          _WAIT              = ' '
*          _COLLECT           = ' '
        EXCEPTIONS
           foreign_lock    = 1
           system_failure = 2
           OTHERS          = 3.

    IF sy-subrc <> 0.
*....... Text: record cannot be locked!
       MESSAGE e005.
    ENDIF.

*...Record does not exist
   ELSE.

*.....Record must be present if you use the change and display
transactions.
IF sy-tcode = 'YZ3U' OR sy-tcode = 'YZ3S'.

*....... Text: Share &/&  not yet present!
       MESSAGE e002 WITH yz3stock-wkz yz3stock-name.
    ENDIF.

    ENDIF.
ENDMODULE.                            " READ_RECORD_9100   INPUT
```

You could also program the functionality of this module in the user command module. However, separating the functions clearly shows how the program can be modularized.

Screen program 9200 carries out all the maintenance tasks for the record selected in screen program 9100. One of these tasks is to check the values entered in the screen program and save the data. Because the tasks are more extensive and the exit function codes have to be handled differently, the source code for this module is a little more comprehensive. You can already see this from the flow logic.

```
PROCESS BEFORE OUTPUT.
*...Initialize screen program
   MODULE status_9200.

*...Read additional information
   MODULE read_info_9200.

PROCESS AFTER INPUT.
   MODULE exit_9200 AT EXIT-COMMAND.
*...Identify data changes
```

```
CHAIN.
    FIELD: yz3stock-sector,
           yz3stock-name,
           yz3stock-currency.
    MODULE data_changed_9200 ON CHAIN-REQUEST.
ENDCHAIN.

*... Check sectors
    FIELD yz3stock-sector MODULE sector_check_9200.

*...Evaluate function code
    MODULE user_command_9200.
```

Once again, you first require a STATUS module so that you can set the status and modify it if required. In table YZ3STOCK, the CURRENCY and SECTOR fields only contain abbreviations. Users often find it helpful to see the long texts for these abbreviations. The fields you require for these long texts are already present in the screen program. You must, of course, fill these fields with values before you display the screen program. This program has been moved into a second PBO module called read_info_9200.

In the PAI part, you must first evaluate the exit function codes. In the CHAIN shown below, all the input fields in the screen program are checked for possible entries. If the data has been changed, the system must set the corresponding flag. This flag influences the data security prompts you see when you close the program. You need the CHAIN statement if you want to connect several fields with one module. It is therefore a good idea to program three separate module calls, as shown below:

```
FIELD yz3stock-sector
    MODULE data_changed_9200 ON CHAIN-REQUEST.

FIELD yz3stock- name
    MODULE data_changed_9200 ON CHAIN-REQUEST.

FIELD yz3stock- currency
    MODULE data_changed_9200 ON CHAIN-REQUEST.
```

An additional range of permitted values has been defined in the domain on which the YZ3STOCK-SECTOR data field is based. The automated field checks only check the contents of a screen program's field against this value range. If you also want to restrict the permitted values to those entries that are maintained in Table YZ3B, you will require another check module SECTOR_CHECK_9200. Finally, you have to process the normal function codes. This screen program contains a lot of normal function codes.

Because the program reacts differently to function keys (F3), (F12) and (F15), you must co-ordinate the two modules so that you can process the function codes. However, we shall first describe the other four modules.

In the STATUS module, you require two new activities in addition to the tasks demonstrated in screen program 9100. You must first modify the screen program dynamically.

For example, in the display transaction, all the fields must be converted into output fields. In the other transactions, the only field you have to lock against entries is the YZ3STOCK-WKZ field. In screen program 9200, this field is only displayed to provide information. Of course, it should no longer be possible to change the key after you have selected and locked the record.

```
MODULE status_9200 OUTPUT.
*...set screen program fields to inactive
*...display everything, otherwise name only
  LOOP AT SCREEN.
    IF screen-name = 'YZ3STOCK-WKZ'
      OR sy-tcode = 'YZ3S'.
      screen-input = c_off.
      MODIFY SCREEN.
    ENDIF.
  ENDLOOP.

*...Set save function to inactive for the display transaction
    CLEAR i_fcode
  REFRESH i_fcode.
  IF sy-tcode = 'YZ3S'.
    i_fcode-fcode = 'FT11'.
    APPEND i_fcode.
  ENDIF.

*...For all transactions, except change,
*...deactivate the delete code
  IF sy-tcode <> 'YZ3U'.
    i_fcode-fcode = 'FT14'.
    APPEND i_fcode.
  ENDIF.

*...Set status for change screen program
  SET PF-STATUS 'STAT_A' EXCLUDING i_fcode.

*...Initialize global flags
  g_exit    = c_false.
  g_delete = c_false.
  g_exit_module = c_false.

*...Add WKZ to title
  CASE sy-tcode.
    WHEN 'YZ3I'.
      SET TITLEBAR '001' WITH yz3stock-wkz text-001.   " create
```

```
    WHEN 'YZ3U'.
      SET TITLEBAR '001' WITH yz3stock-wkz text-002.   " change
    WHEN 'YZ3S'.
      SET TITLEBAR '001' WITH yz3stock-wkz text-003.   " display
  ENDCASE.
ENDMODULE.                                   " STATUS_9200   output
```

The second new task is to deactivate function codes that are not required. To do this, enter these function codes in an internal table. The EXCLUDING addition transfers this table to the system when you set the status. In screen program 9200, some flags control how the program operates. Some of these flags are reset every time the PBO part runs. You will see how you need this process later on when you look at both function code modules.

The module you use to read both the descriptions for sector and currency are so simple that it does not require further explanation:

```
MODULE read_info_9200 output.
*... Provide sector designation
  SELECT SINGLE * FROM yz3bt
  WHERE sector = yz3stock-sector AND
        long  = sy-long.

*... Delete old contents, if search unsuccessful
  IF sy-subrc <> 0.
    CLEAR yz3bt.
  ENDIF.

*... Provide currency code
  SELECT SINGLE * FROM tcurt
  WHERE waers = yz3stock-currency AND
        spras = sy-lungu.

*...Delete old contents if search unsuccessful
  IF sy-subrc <> 0.
  CLEAR tcurt.
  ENDIF.
ENDMODULE.                                   " READ_INFO_9200   output
```

The same applies to both PAI modules.

```
MODULE data_changed_9200 input.
*...SY-DATAR is always newly initialized,
*...must therefore be saved
  IF sy-datar = c_true.
    g_changed = c_true.
  ENDIF.
ENDMODULE.                                   " DATA_CHANGED_9200   input
```

The DATA_CHANGED module merely sets a global flag. This flag must of course remain accessible when the screen program is processed again because data has changed due to, for example, an error occurring or because the (Enter) key has been pressed. For this reason, you must not initialize this flag in the PBO part! In contrast, the SECTOR_CHECK_9200 module is so simple that no further description is required.

```
MODULE sector_check_9200 input.
  SELECT SINGLE * FROM yz3b
  WHERE sector = yz3stock-sector.

  IF sy-subrc <> 0.
*.....text: Sector & not maintained!
    MESSAGE e006 WITH yz3stock-sector.
  ENDIF.
ENDMODULE.                          " SECTOR_CHECK_9200
```

However, both the screen program's function code modules are really complicated. The exit module's source text comes first. This module makes extensive use of a few subroutines because some functions are required in both the exit command module and in the user command module. It is therefore a good idea to store these functions in subroutines.

```
MODULE exit_9200 input.
  g_fcode = fcode.
  CLEAR fcode.
  g_exit_module = c_true.

*...Handle deletion separately, as it is not affected by data
changes
  IF g_fcode = 'FT14'.
    PERFORM delete_question_9200.
  ELSE.

*.....if data is changed, then confirmation prompt
    IF g_changed = c_true OR
       sy-file  = c_true.

*......Set.G_CHANGED, so that contents make
*....... correct evaluation possible in the first run
      g_changed = c_true.

*.......confirmation prompt if required
*....... and set EXIT flag
      PERFORM check_save_9200.
```

```
*.......to close without saving data,
*.......then return directly to the EXIT module
      IF g_exit = c_true AND
         g_save = c_false.
         g_changed = c_false.

*......... Unlock record then return
         PERFORM dequeue_9200.
         PERFORM navigate_9200.
      ENDIF.

   ELSE.

*.......if no data changed
*....... Set G_EXIT against evaluation in NAVIGATE_9200
      g_exit = c_true.

*....... Unlock record, then return
      PERFORM dequeue_9200.
      PERFORM navigate_9200.
    ENDIF.
  ENDIF.
ENDMODULE.                                " EXIT_9200   input
```

The function code is first saved to a second field, and the field that is linked to the screen is initialized. A flag is set to record the fact that the exit module was called. Not all the exit function codes cause the application to be terminated. If processing of the screen continues, it must be as easy as possible to recognize that the exit module is being executed in the user command module.

After you set the flag, the program checks whether the record is to be deleted. If it is to be deleted, the user must confirm this action in a dialog box. If any other exit codes occur, the program checks whether data has changed. You still cannot set the G_CHANGED flag if an exit function code was triggered in the first screen program processing run. This is why you must test both SY-DATAR and G_CHANGED in the exit module. You can set this flag when necessary so that all further checks can access G_CHANGED in the same way.

Depending on the exit code, users should be given the option of cancelling the process or at least saving the data they have entered before closing the screen program, if they made changes to the data. You control these options by using the two G_EXIT and G_SAVE flags. The CHECK_SAVE_9200 subroutine executes the confirmation prompt and evaluates the results. You can call this subroutine without parameters and set both the G_EXIT and the G_SAVE flags. If you want users to be able to leave the screen program without saving data, the record that has been processed is unlocked directly in the exit module and the users leave the screen program. These two functions are also executed by subroutines. The system executes them without prompting the user for confirmation if an exit code has been triggered (apart from FT14) but no change was made in the screen program.

The two function codes (F3) and (F15) should allow users to save the data they changed. However, the current screen program contents are not yet available in the exit module. In addition, no field checks have been carried out. For this reason, you should not close the screen program function codes that are linked to these two function keys directly in the exit module in case data has to be saved. Instead, you should only set the different flags and continue the program. For this reason, the system may execute both check modules and the user command module after executing the exit module. This user command module does not contain very many functions, as they are stored in the sub-routines. Then the function code is once again saved in a second field. This is only necessary if the exit module run was not completed. In this case, you do not have to call subroutine CHECK_SAVE_9200 again.

```
MODULE user_command_9200 INPUT.
*...if FCODE is already reset in EXIT module
IF g_exit_module = c_false.
    g_fcode = fcode.
    CLEAR fcode.


*.....establish whether data has to be saved
*.....and  whether screen program may be left, prompt only
*.....necessary, if EXIT module not effective

    PERFORM check_save_9200.
  ENDIF.

*... save data
  PERFORM save_9200.

*...return, target depends on the function code
  PERFORM navigate_9200.
ENDMODULE.                        " USER_COMMAND_9200  input
```

Both the SAVE_9200 and NAVIGATE_9200 subroutines are run until complete in any case, even if you press (Enter). However, both the G_EXIT and G_SAVE flags are set in accordance with the CHECK_SAVE_9200 function code and they are evaluated in these routines, so the execution of these routines is not the same thing as ending the program. The listing below shows the NAVIGATE_9200 routine:

```
FORM check_save_9200.
  CASE g_fcode.
```

```
*.....ENTER key
*.....-> only data check
    WHEN ' '.
       g_save = c_false.
       g_exit = c_false.

*.....F3 = BACK
*.....-> option of saving data if data has changed
    WHEN 'FT03'.
       PERFORM save_question_9200.

*.....F11 = SAVE
*.....-> save data and close the screen program
    WHEN 'FT11'.
       g_save = c_true.
       g_exit = c_true.

*.....F12 = Cancel
*.....-> only information about possible data loss

    WHEN 'FT12'.
       PERFORM cancel_question_9200.

*.....F15 = EXIT
*.....-> option to save if data has changed
    WHEN 'FT15'.
       PERFORM save_question_9200.

  ENDCASE.
ENDFORM.                          " CHECK_SAVE_9200
```

Depending on the function code, the system sets global flags or executes confirmation prompts. The function codes for these are stored in separate subroutines to make them easy to access. To execute the actual confirmation prompt, call one of the function modules supplied by SAP. The result determines whether the global fields are set.

```
FORM save_question_9200.
DATA: l_answer.

*...prompt only necessary if data has been changed
IF g_changed = c_true.
```

```
      CALL FUNCTION 'POPUP_TO_CONFIRM_STEP'
        EXPORTING
*          DEFAULTOPTION = 'Y'
           textline1     = text-012   "Data will be lost!
           textline2     = text-013   "Save first?
           title             = text-010   "Warning
*          START_COLUMN  = 25
*          START_ROW     = 6
        IMPORTING
           answer        = l_answer
        EXCEPTIONS
           OTHERS        = 1.

      CASE l_answer.

*.......Save and close
        WHEN c_yes.
           g_save = c_true.
           g_exit = c_true.

*.......Close without saving
        WHEN c_no.
           g_save = c_false.
           g_exit = c_true.

*.......Cancel the function -> screen program is not closed
        WHEN c_cancel.
           g_save = c_false.
           g_exit = c_false.

      ENDCASE.

*...close, if no data changed
*...always possible
      ELSE.
         g_save = c_false.
         g_exit = c_true.
      ENDIF.
ENDFORM.                              " SAVE_QUESTION_9200
```

The POPUP_TO_CONFIRM_STEP module has three pushbuttons for three possible options: Yes, No and Cancel. In the confirmation prompt, these choices mean 'Exit and save', 'Exit without saving' or 'Do not exit the screen program'. In contrast, the module POPUP_TO_CONFIRM_LOSS_OF_DATA only provides the options Yes and No, which mean 'Exit without saving' or 'Do not exit the screen program' in the application.

```
FORM cancel_question_9200.
DATA: l_answer.

   CALL FUNCTION 'POPUP_TO_CONFIRM_LOSS_OF_DATA'
      EXPORTING
         textline1    = text-011    "Really Cancel?
*        TEXTLINE2    = ' '

         title        = text-010    "Warning
*        START_COLUMN = 25
*        START_ROW    = 6
      IMPORTING
         answer       = l_answer
      EXCEPTIONS
         OTHERS       = 1.

*...If really Cancel, then set EXIT flag
   IF l_answer = c_yes.
      g_exit = c_true.
      g_save = c_false.

*...otherwise reset EXIT flag
   ELSE.
      g_exit = c_false.
   ENDIF.
ENDFORM.                          " CANCEL_QUESTION_9200
```

The confirmation prompt that appears when you delete a record is similar to those above, apart from the texts. However, the G_DELETE flag is set here to inform the SAVE_9200 routine, so that instead of saving the record from YZ3STOCK, it is to delete it, together with all the index data from YZ3PRICE.

```
FORM delete_question_9200.
DATA: l_answer.

   CALL FUNCTION 'POPUP_TO_CONFIRM_STEP'
      EXPORTING
         defaultoption = 'N'
         textline1    = text-021    " Really delete record with all
         textline2    = text-022    " following records?
         title        = text-023    " DELETE
*        START_COLUMN  = 25
*        START_ROW     = 6
      IMPORTING
         answer       = l_answer
      EXCEPTIONS
```

```
      OTHERS          = 1.

  IF l_answer = c_yes.
    g_delete = c_true.
    g_exit   = c_true.

  ELSE.
*.....not absolutely necessary, only for safety reasons
    g_delete = c_false.
    g_exit   = c_false.
  ENDIF.
ENDFORM.                           " DELETE_QUESTION_9200
```

Once again, these two fundamentally different tasks (save and delete) make SAVE_9200 somewhat more complex:

```
FORM save_9200.
  IF g_save = c_true.

    MODIFY yz3stock.

*.....test database operation status
    IF sy-subrc <> 0.

*.......text: error when saving the record!
      MESSAGE e003.
    ELSE.

*.......text: data saved for &.
      MESSAGE s004 WITH yz3stock-wkz.
    ENDIF.

*.... remove record lock
    PERFORM dequeue_9200.

*..... save changes permanently
    COMMIT WORK.

*.....reset data change flag
g_changed = c_false.

  ENDIF.

*...if data is to be deleted
  IF g_delete = c_true.
    DELETE FROM yz3price
```

```
        WHERE wkz = yz3stock-wkz.

    DELETE FROM yz3stock
        WHERE wkz = yz3stock-wkz.

    COMMIT WORK.
    g_exit = c_true.
  ENDIF.
ENDFORM.                          " SAVE_9200
```

In contrast, it is very easy to see how NAVIGATE_9200 functions and therefore this is not described here.

```
FORM navigate_9200.
  IF g_exit = c_true.
    CASE g_fcode.

*.......F3 = BACK
*.......-> Return to previous screen program
      WHEN 'FT03'.
        LEAVE TO SCREEN 9100.

*.......F11 = SAVE
*.......-> Return to previous screen program
      WHEN 'FT11'.
        LEAVE TO SCREEN 9100.

*.......F12 = CANCEL
*.......-> Return to previous screen program
WHEN 'FT12'.

        LEAVE TO SCREEN 9100.

*.......F14 = DELETE
*.......-> Return to previous screen program
      WHEN 'FT14'.
        LEAVE TO SCREEN 9100.

*.......F15 = EXIT
*.......-> Close entire program
      WHEN 'FT15'.
        LEAVE PROGRAM.
    ENDCASE.
  ENDIF.
ENDFORM.                          " NAVIGATE_9200
```

To ensure you have all the information you need, the global data declarations and the subroutine used to release the database lock are listed here:

```
PROGRAM   sapmyz3s MESSAGE-ID y3.
TABLES:
  yz3stock,
  yz3price,
  yz3b,
  yz3bt,
  tcurt
. " TABLES

CONSTANTS:
  c_true              VALUE 'X',
  c_false             VALUE ' ',
  c_yes               VALUE 'J',
  c_no                VALUE 'N',
  c_cancel            VALUE 'A',
  c_on        type i VALUE 1,
   c_off      type i VALUE 0
. " CONSTANTS

DATA:
  fcode             LIKE sy-ucomm,

  g_fcode           LIKE fcode,
  g_changed         LIKE c_false VALUE c_false,
  g_save            LIKE c_false VALUE c_false,
  g_exit            LIKE c_false VALUE c_false,
  g_delete          LIKE c_false VALUE c_false,
  g_exit_module  LIKE c_false VALUE c_false,

  BEGIN OF i_fcode OCCURS 5,
    fcode LIKE sy-ucomm,
  EXIT OF i_fcode
. " DATA
FORM dequeue_9200.
  CALL FUNCTION 'DEQUEUE_EYZ3STOCK'
    EXPORTING
      mode_yz3stock = 'E'
      mandt         = sy-mandt
      wkz           = yz3stock-wkz
*     X_WKZ         = ' '
*     _SCOPE        = '3'
*     _SYNCHRON     = ' '
*     _COLLECT      = ' '
  .
ENDFORM.                      " DEQUEUE_9200
```

7.3   Program 2: SAPMYZ3P

After this extensive description of the first program, you should have no problem in creating the second one yourself. Its structure is like that of the program described above. This also means that the source code is very similar.

You enter a date in the first screen program. In the second screen program, you then enter the index value (share value) for this day, for each of the shares that are maintained in the YZ3STOCK table. If a date is already present, you can change it if required. There are no functions for deleting or just displaying the records. Therefore there is only one dialog transaction, YZ3P.

The system generates an internal table that you use to process the index data. This table has a similar structure to table YZ3PRICE. The system inserts a record for each share from YZ3STOCK into this table and adds an index value if one is present. In the processing screen program, you use a table view to process this table. Figure 7.4 shows the structure of this screen program.

You can then copy the existing SAPMYZ3S module pool with all its components. You could call the target SAPMYZ3P. When copying this data, you must ensure that all the components (status, includes, etc.) are actually copied. During the copying process, a dialog box appears in which you must select all the elements you want to copy. In the copy, you can then remove all the application-specific source text elements and reprogram them after you have processed the screen program. You should first try to program this second application yourself. To help you do this, you can refer back to the source code of the first program and to some of the examples in previous chapters. If you have any problems, you will find the complete source code at the end of Chapter 10.

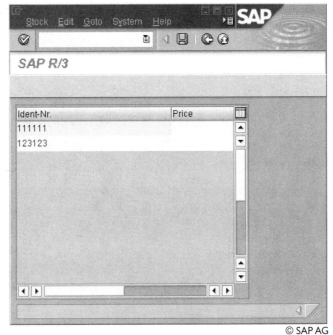

© SAP AG

Figure 7.4   Screen program for maintaining index data

8 Tips and Traps

8.1 TIPS

8.1.1 How to generate screen program fields

You should always generate screen program fields with a reference to the Data Dictionary. This guarantees the fields are translated correctly. The *Field attributes* dialog box contains some data about the current Data Dictionary reference. However, the key field and the corresponding input screen may belong to different tables or it may happen that only the key field refers to the Data Dictionary in order to produce a translatable text and the input screen itself refers to another field within the program. You can also generate Data Dictionary structures for screen programs that contain all the fields required in the screen program.

8.1.2 Side effects of function codes

The function code in a screen program is often stored in a global field in the module pool. Various screen programs use the module pool for this purpose. Problems may arise if you use the CALL command to call another screen program, for example as a dialog box, in the PAI part of a screen program. After you return from the object you found with CALL, the contents of the global field for the function code will probably have changed. This can lead to problems if you have to evaluate this field again in the PAI part after you have used the CALL command. You can avoid such problems by storing all the function code's evaluations for one screen program in a subroutine. You do this by copying it into the local field there. After this, only the local field is involved in evaluations.

8.1.3 Field checks

You only need field checks when you want to save data or to evaluate it further in the next screen program. Therefore it is a good idea to test the transaction code in the modules responsible for field checks and only carry out the checks if these transaction codes really result in the storing of the data. This for example prevents the system from carrying out unnecessary error checks when you call a supplementary dialog box that automatically returns to the main screen.

If one module pool is used for several transactions, you should test the transaction code as well as the function code. If you do this, you can also suppress field checks for transactions that merely display the data.

8.1.4 Field entries for select options

The correct syntax for the SELECT-OPTIONS command is:

SELECT-OPTIONS selection **FOR** field.

This means that the system creates a selection for the field you enter. The name of this field is important for the following reasons:

- The field you enter defines the format of the field on the selection screen, especially the length of the field.

- If you use the selection in a CHECK command with the following format, the command automatically checks the selection that is filled at the beginning of the report against the field set in the SELECT-OPTIONS command:

CHECK selection.

This field may be for example a field in a table that runs in a loop.

However, if you use the IN operator to use a selection in a SELECT statement or an IF statement, the field name is not affected if you explicitly specify the comparison field. In contrast, however, if you use the abbreviated form as shown below, the system uses the field you have specified in the SELECT-OPTIONS statement:

IF selection.

8.1.5 Structures

Although structures do not store data in a database table, they do have or are automatically assigned a header that they can use to store data temporarily. This header works in a similar way to a structure. It can also link one structure to screen program fields without you having to derive a structure from the structure.

8.1.6 Unlock

Once in a while, because of a network problem or a client crash, it may happen that you can no longer process some elements. The SAP System appears to think that they are still being processed, because the system has not been informed that their processing has been completed correctly. The elements remain locked for as long as this message is missing and you cannot access them again to change them. The system then displays a message like 'User xyz is already processing abc'.

You must remove the block before you can continue processing. To do this, choose TOOLS | ADMINISTRATION | MONITOR | LOCK ENTRIES from the menu. In the next screen program, you enter the limiting search terms. The system then displays a list that contains the current lock entries. You click DELETE to select and then delete these entries.

8.1.7 Formal parameters and offset data

You can access individual characters or character groups in a field by entering their offset and length. However, you cannot do this for the formal parameters in a subroutine. Despite this, if you want to use the offset to process these formal parameters, you can copy the contents into a local variable and process it there, then transfer it back into the formal parameters. Alternatively, you can use a field symbol that refers to the parameter. You can access the field symbol by entering the offset and the length.

8.1.8 Field validity ranges

Modules do not form a separate validity range for fields. This means that in modules you cannot define fields that are already present in the framework program. However, the fields you create in modules still continue to be valid outside these modules.

If you use the DATA statement to define a field within a FORM routine, you can only access this field until the ENDFORM statement of the particular routine is reached. If another routine is called from the first routine, you cannot use the field there.

If you use the LOCAL statement to define a field in a FORM routine, the current field contents which must already exist must be saved internally and not retrieved until you leave the routine. This means that you always work directly with the globally defined field. From time to time, this field also contains other data independently of the program block that contains the LOCAL statement. This data is also valid if you call another routine!

8.1.9 Function keys

In subscreens, such as dialog boxes that display list options, you will see pushbuttons displayed on the lower edge of the screen. These pushbuttons are defined in the interface for these subscreens just like the usual pushbuttons in normal screen programs.

The size of a dialog box is often defined dynamically and therefore depends on the length of the data lines that are displayed. Sometimes the dialog box is not wide enough to display all the pushbuttons. Although these buttons are active, they are not visible. Therefore it is useful to click the right-hand mouse button to display the function key assignment if you cannot see important functions that should be available in the dialog box. To do this, position the mouse cursor within the dialog box. When you create the interface, you should define the most important pushbuttons first so that they appear as far as possible to the left.

8.1.10 Pushbuttons

You maintain the pushbutton function codes in the working area of screen programs and maintain the Menu Painter function codes separately, even if they have the same function code. This means that both a pushbutton and a function key can trigger the same function, but with a different function type. In some situations, the flow logic handles these function codes differently, although it looks like the same function code! This error can be caused if there are two pushbuttons in a screen program, which means several keys with the same function code and different function types! You can only see the function types in the interface or screen program maintenance functions. You do not notice them when you are debugging a program!

8.1.11 Syntax check

The system checks the entire syntax of the function pool in a function group. Even if you call a function whose code is not being processed, syntax errors in another program part or include may block all the function group's functions. You can only prevent this by ensuring that each active program code does not contain any syntax errors when you save it. That does not mean that it has to work without errors. This is why you should not activate any program parts that contain syntax errors.

8.1.12 Returning to a transaction's start screen

Many programs have an initial screen in which you enter key terms and from which you branch to the actual processing functions. This initial screen is always displayed again after you leave the actual processing screen program. In the PAI part of the processing screen program, this happens in two different ways. First, you can specify the next screen program, for example:

```
LEAVE TO SCREEN 100.
```

In this case, you do not leave the transaction, so the global data is retained. Alternatively, you can restart the transaction:

```
LEAVE TO TRANSACTION SY-TCODE.
```

This reinitializes everything and database locks are released, etc. This often avoids problems with update elements, etc.

8.1.13 Modifying screen programs

You use a loop through the automatically generated SCREEN table to modify a screen program's appearance (input, hide...). You use the ACTIVE attribute in a field to remove it completely from the screen program. All the fields that are displayed below this field move up and the system automatically updates the frames.

8.1.14 Pushbuttons in selection screens

In selection screens, you can create as many pushbuttons as you require in the screen area and create one or two pushbuttons in the icon bar. Even if you declare them, pushbuttons only appear on the screen if at least one selection or one parameter is present.

You must evaluate the function codes provided by the pushbuttons. For example, this may happen at the AT-SELECTION-SCREEN event. The problem is that only the function codes you select branch to the list creation screen (START-OF-SELECTION). All the other function codes merely return you to the selection screen. Therefore if you want a push-button to start the report, usually after you have set a special flag, the function code is first evaluated in AT-SELECTION-SCREEN by SSCRFIELDS-UCOMM. The function code is then placed in SSCRFIELDS-UCOMM, which triggers the jump to the list processing screen, usually ONLI.

```
CASE SSCRFIELDS-UCOMM.
   WHEN 'TEST".
      G_CHANGE = ' '.
      SSCRFIELDS-UCOMM = 'ONLI'.
   WHEN 'COPY'.
      G_CHANGE = 'X'.
      SSCRFIELDS-UCOMM = 'ONLI'.
ENDCASE.
```

8.1.15   Making entries in initial screens

Many screen programs are created in such a way that you must enter the key values in the request screen. The data for these values is then entered in the next screen. If the key values you enter do not fit any of the records, all the input fields have to be reactivated for the key. To achieve this, the read routines or check routines and a FIELD statement for all the key fields must be placed in a CHAIN. If you want to read directly in the module where the function codes are also evaluated, you must execute this module in the CHAIN.

```
PROCESS AFTER INPUT.
CHAIN.
   FIELD: TAB-A, TAB-B, TAB-C.
   MODULE OKCODE.
ENDCHAIN.
```

8.1.16   Missing authorizations

You can call Transaction SU53 if you receive an error message when you execute an application because of insufficient authorizations. This transaction shows you the most recently checked authorization with the checked values, as well as the values contained in your authorizations.

8.2   TRICKS

8.2.1 Function parameter (Release < 3.0)

Up to Release 2.2, function modules only had import and export parameters. The system read input parameters in the module and did not return any data when you closed the procedure. In contrast, export parameters were only used to return data. They were not used to transfer data to the function module. If you wanted a function module to read the contents of a parameter, change them and then return them, you had to create an import and export parameter for that purpose. Each time you called the module, this parameter was always assigned to the same field, similar to the following example:

```
CALL FUNCTION 'UPPER_CASE'
  IMPORTING
    IP_WORD = L_WORD
  EXPORTING
    OP_WORD = L_WORD.
```

From Release 3.0, you can use the CHANGING parameter to do this.

8.2.2 Screen program

If you want to enter more values in a screen program and the screen program does not have enough space, you can enter these values in a 'follow-on' screen program. To make it easier to work with this kind of screen program, the next screen is often displayed as multiply-nested dialog boxes. So that users do not have to run through all the screen programs step by step when they finish entering data, the closing function code is available in all the dialog boxes.

For example:

```
Screen program 400:
...
CALL SCREEN 500 STARTING AT 10 10.
* Subscreen 500 is called and processed.
* The function is closed e.g. by function code DATU
* (transfer data) and EABB (cancel)
* The function code is stored in global field FCODE ,
* The function code in screen program 500 is not deleted

IF FCODE = 'DATU".
  CLEAR FCODE.   "Only in the first dialog box
  SET SCREEN 0.
  LEAVE SCREEN.
ENDIF.
...

DYNPRO 500:
...
IF FCODE = 'DATU'.
  SET SCREEN 0.
  LEAVE SCREEN.
ENDIF.
...
```

The statements shown above result in the following procedure:

Screen program 400 is to be called. This screen program is to be the first dialog box to be called from an initial screen. The lines shown above derive from the flow logic of screen program 400. Screen program 500 is called and processed, also as a dialog box. This screen program should contain the function keys COPY DATA (function code DATU) and CANCEL (EABB). The COPY DATA key should allow you to return to the initial screen and therefore close all the dialog boxes at the same time. For this reason, the FCODE in the screen program 500 is not deleted, but is passed on to screen program 400. There the FCODE is evaluated immediately after the CALL SCREEN statement and the screen program is closed. To prevent undesirable side effects in the calling initial screen, the FCODE is initialized beforehand.

If an abnormal end occurs over several levels, the statements are transferred from screen program 400 as appropriate into all the other screen programs. You can then of course only initialize FCODE in the screen program that you have called from the initial screen.

8.2.3 A simple way to output char fields

Many test reports contain lists of important table fields, which are usually C-type and N-type key fields. To achieve this in the output statement, you must program all the fields that are to be output. If only C-type and N-type fields are to be output, you can use the procedure shown below to save yourself a lot of work. First you create a structure that contains all the table fields you want to output. You insert a blank field between each of these fields as follows:

```
DATA: BEGIN OF F_TEST,
  LNAME LIKE TAB-LASTNAME,
  SPACE1,
  FNAME LIKE TAB-FIRSTNAME,
  SPACE2,
  BDATE LIKE TAB-BDATE,
END OF F_TEST.
```

In the program, you then use the MOVE-CORRESPONDING statement to assign the contents to this structure in the SELECT loop. The structure is then output with this statement:

```
WRITE / F_TEST.
```

The structure is displayed correctly because the system handles it entirely as a C-field. However, this does mean that transformations, particularly those based on data types such as converting functions controlled by the data element, will not be effective.

8.3   Traps

8.3.1 String comparison with CA (contains any) and NA (not any)

The length of strings is predefined. If a character string's compare pattern is entered as a field and not as a string constant, the pattern must have exactly the same length as the field. It must therefore fill the field completely. Otherwise, the following problem occurs:

the system fills empty spaces with blanks and that may also include any unfilled spaces in the string you are testing. The comparison will then return the result TRUE, because both strings contain blanks. Not only is this response undesirable, but the error is also very hard to detect.

8.3.2 Searching for strings with SEARCH

You can use the SEARCH command to search for a particular pattern within a string. When you do this, the system automatically ignores the final blanks when you enter the pattern. If you are searching for a blank, the following statement is never successful:

```
SEARCH string FOR ' '.
```

If you want to suppress the automatic interpretation of special characters or blanks, you must add two full stops at the end of the character. The correct command is therefore:

```
SEARCH string FOR '. .'.
```

8.3.3 Numerical values in character fields

You can use automatic type conversion to enter numerical values, even in C-type fields. You can then use these values without any problem in expressions. However, things become complicated if the character field is not long enough for the numerical value.

8.3.4 Transferring data from screen programs

After you leave a screen program, the data you have just entered does not become valid until after an AT EXIT-COMMAND statement. Until this happens, you will still find the old values in the screen program fields. This means that you cannot save data in the AT EXIT-COMMAND modules!

For this reason, you should only use the AT EXIT-COMMAND modules to finish processing without saving data. Another way to pass on the information that data has been changed is also available in the AT EXIT-COMMAND module. This is the SY-DATAR system variable, which contains an 'X' if data has been changed. The system can display a prompt to at least warn the user that they risk losing data. However, this field is reinitialized during each PBO run and is only set if data has been changed in that particular run.

However, there are problems with using screen programs in HELP REQUEST modules. In exceptional cases, you can use R/3 Basis function modules to read these fields directly from the screen program (see Chapter 3, Function modules).

8.3.5 Initializing screen program fields

You can initialize screen program fields in the PBO modules. In the case of transactions that create new records, it is a good idea to clear the fields for the new entries each time you call the screen program; otherwise, the screen program fields may still contain values from previous transactions if the second screen program (where the actual processing takes place) is interrupted after you enter the data. However, in this special case you can initialize the screen program by branching from the first screen program. Usually initial-ization takes place in the PBO modules of the second screen program; otherwise, the fields would be reinitialized each time an error message occurs in the second screen pro-gram, as the screen program completely processes new error messages.

Alternatively, you can use a flag. You set this flag the first time you execute a call after you initialize the screen program fields. The flag is then reset every time you use the LEAVE statement. This means you can now initialize the screen program fields in the PBO modules. However, this does not really solve the problem because you must ensure that this flag is correct every time you jump in or out of this function and you also have to process it.

8.3.6 SELECT INTO

Records that you have found by using a SELECT command are usually displayed in the work area (header row) of the table which you have scanned. You can then evaluate these records in that work area. After a SELECT-ENDSELECT loop, the most recently found record is displayed in the table's header row. This record is not the last record in the table. This is useful for checking whether any records without a complete key are present. No activities whatsoever take place in the SELECT-ENDSELECT loop. The header record is not processed until you leave the SELECT-ENDSELECT loop.

If you use the following additions, the system reacts differently:

INTO TABLE itab

   or

INTO workarea.

In this case the header of the table that you have scanned is always blank! The results are displayed either in the structure or in the table that you specify after the INTO com-mand. Therefore, the header row in the internal table is also blank. Only the work area is immediately usable. It contains the record that was read most recently after the ENDSELECT command.

If you are working with an internal table, you must use the following statement to fill the table's header record:

READ itab INDEX 1.

If you do not do this, the table is processed in a loop.

8.3.7 Several assignments in the UPDATE statement

If you want to use a WHERE clause to link several assignments in one UPDATE statement, you must enter the assignments one after the other without commas. For example:

```
UPDATE YZ3STOCK
   SET SECTOR = 'S' CURRENCY = 'USD'
   WHERE WKZ = '123456'.
```

In this case, neither of the two assignments are executed until the condition is met. In the UPDATE statement, the absence of a colon after SET is also syntactically correct. However, this has a significant effect on how the UPDATE statement behaves. In the following statement, the WHERE clause only applies to the last assignment:

```
UPDATE YZ3STOCK
  SET: SECTOR = 'S', CURRENCY = 'USD'
  WHERE WKZ = '123456'.
```

The first assignment is executed for all the table's records.

```
UPDATE YZ3STOCK
  SET: SECTOR = 'S' WHERE WKZ = '123456',
       CURRENCY = 'USD' WHERE WKZ = '888888'.
```

8.3.8 Using READ in internal tables

In internal tables, you can use the READ statement to read a record, no matter what type of key it has. However, before you can do this, you must enter blanks in the fields that are not involved in the search. You use the following command to do this:

MOVE SPACE TO record.

You may not achieve the result you want if you use the following command for initialization instead:

CLEAR record.

This is because some fields (depending on their type) are not filled with blanks, but with other characters. The system then automatically searches for these characters. This usually means that no records can be found!

8.3.9 Incorrect structure for form routines

In form routines, you can use the keyword STRUCTURE (or a few other constructs) to assign a structure to a parameter that has been transferred as a structure. This means you can access individual fields in the structure by using their names. This structure assignment does not check the types. The system only checks the parameter length when you call a form routine. When you enter the real parameter, you must ensure that its length is not less than the length of the structure that has been selected, otherwise you may select a completely incorrect structure. This will simply overlay the real data. If the structure and the ABAP Dictionary structure do not match, the system may misinterpret data, as the following example shows:

```
REPORT BMPRIV20.
DATA: BEGIN OF S1,
  A(5) TYPE C,
  B(10) TYPE C,
END OF S1.
```

```
DATA: BEGIN OF S2,
  A(10) TYPE C,
  B(3) TYPE C,
END OF S2.

S1-A = 'aaaaa'.
S1-B = '1234567890'.

PERFORM F1 USING S1.
WRITE /.
WRITE /.
PERFORM F2 USING S1.

FORM F1 USING P STRUCTURE S1.
  WRITE / P-A.
  WRITE / P-B.
ENDFORM.

FORM F2 USING P STRUCTURE S2.
  WRITE / P-A.
  WRITE / P-B.
ENDFORM.
```

This report outputs the following data:

```
aaaaa
1234567890
aaaaa12345
678.
```

8.3.10   Global data

Global data is only globally applicable within the program in which it has been declared. For example, if you call a function module from a module pool, its function pool may contain a data field that has the same name as an item of data in the calling module pool. However, these data fields may have different contents.

8.3.11   Global fields as subroutine parameters

Subroutine parameters are often reference parameters. This means that they merely point to the actual data field. The subroutine's parameters are affected if you change the contents of the original fields in nested subroutines. The following program shows how this happens. Problems may often occur when you transfer system fields (e.g. SY-SUBRC) to reference parameters. This is because these fields are frequently changed, often implicitly, by various statements.

```
REPORT   zxxxxx001.
data: global value '1'.

perform sub1 using global.

form sub1 using parameter like global.
  write: / 'before:', parameter.
  perform sub2.
  write: / 'after :', parameter.
endform.

form sub2.
  global = '2'.
endform.
```

8.3.12 LOCAL

You use the LOCAL statement in form routines. It ensures that the contents of a global field are stored in an internal temporary buffer and that these contents are saved when the routine ends. This means you can use the field in any way you require within the routine. However problems occur if the LOCAL variable is also transferred as a parameter. This may be caused by poor programming style or be unintentional:

```
REPORT BMPRIV04.
DATA V1(10) TYPE C.
V1 = 'A'.
WRITE: / 'before:  ', V1.
PERFORM TEST USING V1.
WRITE: / 'after   ', V1.

FORM TEST USING V2.
LOCAL V1.
  V1 = 'B'.
  WRITE: / 'TEST 1  ', V1.
  V2 = V1.
ENDFORM.
```

The contents of global field V1 are changed within the form routine, because V1 is transferred to the routine as a reference parameter with the name V2. This is what you want to happen. However, when you leave the routine, the LOCAL statement returns the original contents to V1. You can prevent this kind of side effect if you use the DATA statement instead of the LOCAL statement. This is also better programming style (true local variable).

8.3.13   Deleting views (Release 2.2)

You must make an entry in the TVDIR file if you want to create views that are to be used later on in Transaction SM30. This entry ensures that the system generates some screen programs in which you can maintain the view. If you delete the view later on, you must also delete the entry in the TVDIR file.

8.3.14   Validity range of function groups

Function groups or their internal data area only apply within the limits of the calling program. If you call a function group from different levels in one program, you may create different instances of this function group and therefore different data areas for it. The following example shows how this may happen:

Function group 1 contains functions A and B. Function group 2 contains function C. If you call C from within A and then call B again, three data areas are created. This is because the system creates a new instance of function group 1, when you call B from C. Therefore, if B data is stored in the global fields in the function group, you cannot access this data in A. In this case, you must use the memory to transfer the data (e.g. with the EXPORT and IMPORT statements).

8.3.15   External performs

When you call external subroutines, the command interpreter processes the declaration part of the external program. If the external routine accesses global variables, the variables in the program containing the subroutine are always used, not the variables in the calling program.

8.3.16   SY-DATAR

When you enter data in a screen program, the SY-DATAR system variable is automatically set to 'X'. This variable is reset each time the screen program is run even if, for example, an abnormal end is suppressed by a user prompt in the EXIT module and the screen program is processed from the beginning. If this happens, SY-DATAR is reset although changes have been made and not yet saved.

8.3.17   Parameters and selections for calling reports

If you use the SUBMIT statement to call a report from a screen program, the system does not check whether all the report's parameters or selections are really filled. It also does not check whether all the parameters or selections coded in the call are actually present in the report. Typing errors mean that values are not transferred to the report.

8.3.18   Data declarations in modules

Modules do not represent self-contained units in terms of the validity scopes of data fields. Any fields that you declare in a module in a module pool take effect globally as soon as you declare them. For this reason, if you call the module several times, the declaration and therefore the assignment of the initial value is only carried out the first time you call the module. This also happens when the screen program to which the module belongs is left and then called again. If you unintentionally declare a field in a module and you want that field to act as a numerical variable for loops or something similar, you must use an assignment to set this field to its initial value. You may not get the result you require if you only assign the initial value when you declare the field.

8.3.19   SELECT ... INTO TABLE

You use the `SELECT INTO TABLE` statement to save the result of a `SELECT` statement directly to an internal table. To achieve this, the structure of the internal table must correspond to the structure of the data returned by the `SELECT` statement. This is because the records found by the `SELECT` statement are written to the internal table, no matter what their structure.

8.3.20   Specifying an area for data clusters

In the `IMPORT FROM DATABASE` or `EXPORT TO DATABASE` commands, you must enter an area as an additional key. You must also program this value as a constant; you cannot transfer it dynamically from a field's contents. If you enter a field name by mistake in this case, the system does not query this as a syntax error. The command simply interprets the first two characters of the field name as an area entry. It does not evaluate the field contents.

8.3.21   Incorrect parameters for function modules

When you call function modules, the parameters are transferred by name reference. If you make a typing error when you enter the parameter names manually, the function modules do not accept the parameters. If the parameter you want to transfer in the function module is an optional parameter, the error will not be detected either when the system checks the syntax or by checks the system carries out at runtime. The error causes the module to function incorrectly because the parameter that appears to have been transferred does not actually arrive.

8.3.22   Function values are not returned

When you call function modules, they ignore any parameters that are transferred along with the parameters that you declared when you defined the interface. If the `IMPORTING` statement is not activated by deleting the comment character after you insert a reference example for a function module, the calling program handles the IMPORTING parameter as an EXPORTING parameter. Therefore it does not return values to the parameters. In the following example, parameter L_ID remains empty, because an incorrect comment causes it to appear as an EXPORTING parameter:

```
CALL FUNCTION 'NUMBER_GET_NEXT'
    EXPORTING
        NR_RANGE_NR                 = '01'
        OBJECT                      = 'Z123'
        . . .
*    IGNORE_BUFFER                  = ' '
*  IMPORTING
        NUMBER                      = L_ID
        . . .
    EXCEPTIONS
        INTERVAL_NOT_FOUND          = 1
        . . .
```

8.3.23   Update

In dialog applications, every time you switch screen a COMMIT WORK is triggered. This is how the system permanently saves changes to database tables. However, this implicit COMMIT WORK does not execute update routines such as function modules with the ON UPDATE TASK addition. You can only execute these function modules by specifically using this statement:

COMMIT WORK.

8.3.24   Secondary indexes

For Data Dictionary tables, you can create secondary indexes in addition to the ubiquitous primary indexes. These secondary indexes can evaluate any of the fields in the tables. You use the UNIQUE flag to declare these additional indexes as unique indexes. As a result, the new records you want to add must be unique, not only with regard to their own table key, but also with regard to the contents of the fields in the secondary index. This is usually not the effect you require. This problem is usually caused by a design fault or handling error. You can tell that an unwanted unique secondary index may be present if both the MODIFY command and the INSERT command issue return code 4 when you add a record.

8.3.25   Release-specific differences in SELECT

The SELECT command has one variant. In this variant you can enter the list of fields to be read in the database dynamically. This variant needs an INTO clause. Before Release 3.1x, the data types of the fields in the INTO clause did not have to be identical to the data types of the fields read by the database. However, this requirement applies from version 4.0 onwards.

8.3.26 Data Dictionary problems when upgrading to Release 4.x

When you define your own Data Dictionary structures, you may often access the data elements in the standard R/3 System. This is not only a good idea, but also the correct way to work, because it ensures that your own applications always work with the correct data formats. However this may lead to problems when you are upgrading from a Release 3.x System to a Release 4.x System. This is because various data elements have been renamed. These elements have been renamed because from Release 4.0 onwards, data elements and Data Dictionary structures are located in the same name range. Obviously, a data element can now no longer have the same name as a Data Dictionary table.

You must fix the errors manually, because there is no automatic way of solving the problem. However in most cases all you have to do is to use the old data element names as part of a search pattern because the new names were often created by simply adding a suffix.

9 Summary Reference

The contents of this book provide a more or less complete reference guide to all ABAP commands. The availability and functional scope of many commands depend on the system release and you can use the system online help at any time to call valid documentation, so this section simply contains a list of the ABAP commands and a short description of each. This will be enough to show you the power of the language and to give you an overview of the commands and their variants.

9.1 Metasymbols description

In this chapter, a meta-language is used to describe the command syntax. The syntax is sometimes very complicated and in some cases even this meta-language is inadequate to describe it clearly. One of the topics most likely to cause ambiguity is which combinations of the various additions and parameters are permitted and how many of them there are. That is why if you are uncertain you should read the description in this chapter or the R/3 System online help.

The syntax descriptions use the following icons and font styles:

- **Bold**: command components which must be entered in this format.

- *Italics*: placeholder for other elements such as field names.

- Normal text: metasymbols, described in Table 9.1.

Table 9.1   Meta symbols used in this chapter

Symbol	Meaning
[ ]	Optional parameters and additions are enclosed in square brackets. Elements of this kind can occur only once
{ }	An element enclosed in curly brackets can occur one or more times
|	Alternative: you can only use one of the elements before or after the bar (pipe) character
( )	Elements group
...	Any repetition of the element in front of the dots

9.2 References and parameter repetition

The ABAP programming language uses two special syntactical components which can be used in many different commands: references and parameter repetition.

A reference consists of a field name enclosed in round brackets. At runtime, the system replaces the reference with the contents of a particular field. In this way, you can also modify commands dynamically at application runtime. There must be no delimiter between the brackets and the field name.

Through parameter repetition, you can use several parameters in some commands. To do so, the command ends with a colon and the parameters are separated from each other with commas. For example:

```
MOVE: A TO B,
      C TO D.
```

This is not to say that a colon may only stand after the first keyword. In some cases, for which SAP has unfortunately not provided specific descriptions, parameter repetition can only be applied to parts of a command. For example, this command is also correct:

```
MOVE A TO: B, C.
```

It fills the fields B and C with the contents of field A.

Regrettably, there is no general rule that states the commands in which these two language elements are permitted, and those in which they are not. As a result, you should refer to the description of each command.

9.3 ABAP commands overview

ADD *value* **TO** *field*.

The contents of value (field or constant) is added to field and the result is saved in `field`.

ADD *field_1* **THEN** *field_2* **UNTIL** *field_Z* **GIVING** *field*.

The contents of fields `field_1` to `field_Z` are summed and the results saved in `field`. `field_1` is the first of a series of fields with identical offset, and `field_Z` is the last. All fields must be of the same type and have the same length. The offset between the fields is defined through the offset between `field_1` and `field_2`.

ADD *field_1* **THEN** *field_2* **UNTIL** *field_Z* **TO** *field*.

Summation (calculation of a total) as in the previous example. The result is added to the current contents of `field`.

ADD *field_1* **THEN** *field_2* **UNTIL** *field_Z*
  ACCORDING TO *sel* **GIVING** *field*.

Summation and assignment as in command example two above. Only the fields whose index has been set using the `sel` selection table are included in the summation. The first field has the index 1. SELECT OPTIONS or RANGES must be used to create the selection table.

ADD *field_1* **FROM** *first* **TO** *last* **GIVING** *field*.

Field `field_1` is the first of an uninterrupted series of fields of the same type and length. The `first` and `last` values set the index of the first and last fields that are to be summed. The result is stored in `field`.

ADD-CORRESPONDING *record_1* **TO** *record_2*.

Only the fields whose names occur both in `record_1` and in `record_2` are included. The contents of the fields in `record_1` are summed with the contents of the fields with the same names in `record_2`.

ALIASES *alias* **FOR** *interface~component*.

You use this command to generate an alias name for an interface component in the declaration part of an object. This reduces the amount of typing you have to do and is also a way for an interface component to replace a normal element transparently.

APPEND [*record* **TO**] *itab*
  [**SORTED BY** [*field* | (*field_name*)]].

This command adds a new record to the `itab` internal table. The data is taken either from the field list or the header rows of the internal table to which the record is to be added. There is no limit to the number of records that the table can hold.

The SORTED BY `field` addition is used to sort the new record in the table in descending order, depending on the contents of `field`. The SORTED BY addition restricts the number of records in the table. If the number of records exceeds the value set for the OCCURS parameter in the internal table declaration, the last record is lost if the new record is inserted before it. You can define the sorting field dynamically. To do so, enter the name of the sorting field in the SORTED BY parameter. The dynamic parameter must be enclosed in round brackets. You can enter an offset and length to restrict the sorting criterion.

APPEND INITIAL LINE TO *itab*.

Adds a record to the internal table and fills it with initial values as defined in the table's structure.

APPEND LINES OF *itab_1*
  [**FROM** *index_1*] [**TO** *index_2*] **TO** *itab_2*.

Adds the contents of internal table *itab_1* to internal table *itab_2*. You can use the optional additions FROM and TO to define the numbers of the records that are to be added from `itab_1`.

```
ASSIGN [LOCAL COPY OF]
  [field[+offset][(length)]] |
  (field_name)] |
  dataref->*
  TO <field_symbol>
    [CASTING type]
    [CASTING TYPE type]
    [CASTING LIKE field]
    [TYPE type]
    [DECIMALS decimal_places].
```

The `field_symbol` refers to the contents of a data field. If no additions are used, the `field`'s characteristics (type, length, conversion exit) are transferred. You can use the `TYPE`, `CASTING` and `DECIMALS` additions to overwrite these characteristics. Depending on which addition you use, either the system interprets the source field on the basis of the type entered or it interprets it on the basis of the field symbol type or else the field symbol type is set at runtime.

You can set the source field directly by entering its name. Alternatively, the system can determine it dynamically by transferring the name into an additional field or through a data reference. If you enter the source field name directly, you can also specify its offset and length. If you specify the length by entering `*`, the system monitors the field length when data is assigned to the field. The offset and length cannot be defined if the field name is assigned dynamically. In this case, the system searches for the field at several levels (local data, global data, `TABLES` naming range, external naming ranges).

You can use the optional `LOCAL COPY OF` addition to create a copy of `field` before assigning it. In this way, assignments to the field symbol do not change the contents of the original field. This addition can only be used in subroutines. The field symbol used must be defined locally in the subroutine.

```
ASSIGN component index | name OF STRUCTURE record
  TO <field_symbol>.
    [CASTING type]
    [CASTING TYPE type]
    [CASTING LIKE field]
    [TYPE type]
    [DECIMALS decimal_places].
```

This variant of the `ASSIGN` statement is similar to the previous example. However, in this case the field symbol does not refer to an individual field, but to the subfield of a structure. You can either specify the subfield through its index (initial value 1) or by entering a name.

```
ASSIGN TABLE field (field_name) TO <field_symbol>.
```

Like `ASSIGN field_name`, but the system only looks for the field in the `TABLES` naming range.

```
AT LINE-SELECTION.
```

This is an event statement which is used in list generation. The statement block concerned is always processed if a user selects a valid line in a list. They can do so by double-clicking with the mouse, running executing function code PICK, or by pressing (F2), which is the usual method. They can also click on a hotspot.

AT USER-COMMAND.

This event statement's statement block is processed if a user starts a function or enters data in the command field. It only applies to function codes that are not intercepted by the system.

AT PFxx**.**

The system processes this event statement if a user presses a function key that has function code PFn assigned to it. Here, n is a numerical value between 00 and 99.

AT NEW *field.*
  ABAP statements
ENDAT.

You should only use this statement within a LOOP running over an internal table or an EXTRACT dataset. Here, field is a subfield in the internal table or dataset. The system executes the statements between AT NEW and ENDAT if there is a change to the contents of field or of a field that is placed before field in the structure definition. The system compares the current record with the record that has just been processed in the last loop. In this way, the start of a new group can be recognized.

AT END OF *field.*
  ABAP statements
ENDAT.

Similar to AT NEW. However, in this case the system compares the current record with the one that follows it. In this way, the end of a new group can be recognized.

AT FIRST.
  ABAP statements
ENDAT.

You should only use this statement within a LOOP. The system executes the statements in this block before running through the loop for the first time.

AT LAST.
  ABAP statements
ENDAT.

You should only use this statement within a *LOOP*. The system executes the statements in this block after running through the loop for the last time.

AT *fieldgroup* [**WITH** *fieldgroup_1*]**.**
  ABAP statements
ENDAT.

You should only use this statement within a `LOOP` through an `EXTRACT` dataset. The system only executes the statement block if the current record has been created with `EXTRACT fieldgroup` and therefore belongs to `fieldgroup`. Furthermore, the `WITH` addition ensures that the statement block is only executed if the current record is followed by a record that was created with `EXTRACT fieldgroup_1`.

`AT SELECTION-SCREEN ON` `[parameter | selection]`.

You should only use this event statement in reports that have selection screens. The system processes it after a user enters data in the selection screen. If an error message is triggered in the statement block, only the parameters entered or the selection will be ready for input.

`AT SELECTION-SCREEN ON BLOCK` `block`.

You should only use this event statement in reports that have selection screens. The system processes it after a user enters data in the selection screen. If an error message is triggered in the statement block, only a field in the selected block will be ready for input.

`AT SELECTION-SCREEN ON END OF` `selection`.

You should only use this event statement with selection screens. Every time the user makes a selection, the system can display a second selection screen in which the user can enter several records or ranges that belong to the selection table. The system processes the event statement after the user has finished input in the second screen program. On this event, all values entered are available in the selection table so the user can check them there. However if there is an error message, the second screen program is not ready for input!

`AT SELECTION-SCREEN ON HELP REQUEST`
   `FOR` `[parameter | selection-LOW | selection-HIGH]`.

This event statement, which calls online help, expects either the name of a parameter or a selection as an addition. If you specify a selection, you must enter the actual input field name with the `-LOW` or `-HIGH` addition after the name. The system then processes the event statement if the mouse pointer is placed in the named field and the user presses function key (F1) to activate online help in a selection screen.

`AT SELECTION-SCREEN OUTPUT`.

The system processes this event statement immediately before outputting the selection screen on the screen.

`AT SELECTION-SCREEN ON RADIOBUTTON GROUP` `radio_button_group`.

You should only use this event statement in reports that have selection screens. The system processes it after a user enters data in the selection screen. If an error message is triggered in the statement block, only the radio buttons belonging to `radio_button_group` will be ready for input.

`AT SELECTION-SCREEN ON VALUE REQUEST`
   `FOR` `[parameter | selection-LOW | selection-HIGH]`.

This event statement expects either the name of a parameter or of a selection as an addition. If you specify a selection, you must enter the actual input field name with the addition -LOW or -HIGH after the name. The system then processes the event statement if the mouse pointer is placed in the named field and the user presses function key (F4), input values. At the selection screen runtime, the system displays the icon for input help to the right of the input field.

AT SELECTION-SCREEN ON EXIT-COMMAND.

The system processes this event statement if the user activates an exit command function code in the selection screen.

AUTHORITY-CHECK OBJECT *authority_object*
  { **ID** *authority_field* **FIELD** *value* }
  [**ID** *authority_field* **PLACEHOLDER**] .

This statement checks the authorizations present. In this statement, authority_object is the name of the authorization object. The authority_field value sets the authorization object's authorization fields. After this command is executed, the SY-SUBRC system field provides information on whether the current contents of the authorization fields entered match value. If so, the user has the necessary authorization. Up to ten authorization fields can be passed as parameters to the command. If no check is required for a field, you can use the entry ID authority_field DUMMY to cancel it.

BACK.

In list processing, places the mouse pointer on the first line of the current page after TOP-OF-PAGE processing. It you use the BACK command together with the RESERVE statement, this places the mouse pointer on the first output line after the RESERVE statement.

BREAK *user_name.*

Interrupts the execution of a program and runs the debugger if the current user has the name that has been set. In this way, user-specific breaks can be added in the development phase which do not affect the work of other users. In batch mode or posting update mode, the program is not actually interrupted; instead the system generates a system log message.

BREAK-POINT [*field*].

Unqualified break-point. Interrupts the execution of the program and runs the debugger. In batch background or posting update mode, the program is not actually interrupted. Instead the system generates a system log message. If you specify a field, the contents of that field can be transferred into the message.

CALL DIALOG *dialog*
  [**AND SKIP FIRST SCREEN**]
  [**EXPORTING** { *dialogfield_x* [**FROM** *program_field_x*] }]
  [**IMPORTING** { *dialogfield_x* [**TO** *program_field_x*]   }]
  [**USING** *itab* **MODE** *mode*] .

Calls the `dialog` dialog module. If this module consists of several successive screen programs, you can use `AND SKIP FIRST SCREEN` to specify that the system processes the first screen program without displaying it. You use the `EXPORTING FROM` statement to transfer data to the dialog module. As a result, the value of a program field is assigned to a field defined in the dialog module. You use the `IMPORTING TO` statement in a similar way to return values from the dialog module to the calling program. If the field names in the dialog module and the calling program are identical, the `FROM` or `TO` additions are not required.

You can use the `USING` addition to transfer an internal table that contains data in batch Batch input Input format. The dialog module then carries out mass processing. You can set a value for `mode` (see Table 9.2) to define the display type for processing Batch Input data.

Table 9.2   Processing modes for batch background operation

Mode	Description
A	Screen programs are displayed (default)
E	Screen programs are only displayed if an error has occurred
N	No display

```
CALL FUNCTION function
    [ EXPORTING        { parameter = value } ]
    [ IMPORTING        { parameter = field } ]
    [ TABLES           { parameter = itab  } ]
    [ CHANGING         { parameter = field } ]
    [ EXCEPTIONS [  { exception = value } ]
                    [ OTHERS = value ]
                    [ ERROR_MESSAGE = value ]].
```

Calls the `function` function module. The names can either be a string variable in inverted commas or a field that contains the name.

After `EXPORTING`, you should list the values that are to be transferred to the function module. After `IMPORTING`, you should list the fields that are used to hold the return values. List internal tables after `TABLES`. You can use the `CHANGING` addition to declare combined import and export parameters. List the exceptions that are to be handled by the calling function module after `EXCEPTIONS`.

```
CALL FUNCTION function STARTING NEW TASK task_name
   [DESTINATION [dest | IN GROUP [group_name | DEFAULT ]]]
   [PERFORMING subroutine ON END OF TASK ]
   [EXPORTING  { parameter = value } ]
   [TABLES     { parameter = itab  } ]
   [EXCEPTIONS   exception = value [MESSAGE field ]].
```

Runs the `function` function module asynchronously, in a new mode (or if defined with `DESTINATION` in another system identified by `dest`). The calling program starts without waiting for the called function module to end. As a result, it is not possible for the called function module to use its parameters to return values and exceptions. However if required, you can use `PERFORMING` to name a subroutine. The only exception is errors that may occur when a connection is being set up to a remote system. You must use `EXCEPTIONS` to intercept them. You can use the `MESSAGE` addition to name a field in which the system places an explanatory text if a system error occurs. For this kind of call, all systems involved must have at least R/3 Release 3.0.

When you create a call with `DESTINATION`, you can also use `IN GROUP` to name a group of application servers on which the function module can undergo parallel processing.

```
CALL FUNCTION function IN UPDATE TASK
    [EXPORTING { parameter = value } ]
    [TABLES    { parameter = itab  } ].
```

The system does not execute the function module immediately. Instead it marks it for processing. The transferred values are automatically held in a temporary buffer. It only executes the function module using the values held in the temporary buffer after a `COMMIT WORK` statement.

```
CALL FUNCTION function DESTINATION dest
    [EXPORTING       { parameter = value } ]
    [IMPORTING       { parameter = field } ]
    [TABLES          { parameter = itab  } ]
    [CHANGING        { parameter = field } ]
    [EXCEPTIONS      [{ exception = value } ]
                     [OTHERS = value]
                     [ERROR_MESSAGE = value]
                     [MESSAGE field]].
```

Calls and executes the named function module in the `dest` system. This type of execution is called a *Remote Function Call* (RFC). `dest` can be a string constant or a field that contains the name of the system that is to be called. The calling program waits until processing is complete so it can also receive return values. It handles exceptions in the same way as normal function modules, but `MESSAGE` can also be used for the special handling of some connection-related exceptions.

```
CALL FUNCTION function IN BACKGROUND TASK
    [AS SEPARATE UNIT],
    [DESTINATION dest],
    [EXPORTING { parameter = value } ]
    [TABLES    { parameter = itab  } ].
```

Marks the function module for asynchronous updating. The transferred values are held in a temporary buffer. If required, you can use the `DESTINATION` addition to force the execution of the function module on another system. You can use the `AS SEPARATE UNIT` addition to force the execution of the function module in a separate transaction.

```
CALL CUSTOMER-FUNCTION identifier
   [EXPORTING     { parameter = value } ]
   [IMPORTING     { parameter = field } ]
   [TABLES        { parameter = itab  } ]
   [CHANGING      { parameter = field } ]
   [EXCEPTIONS [{ exception = value } ]
                [ OTHERS = value ]
                [ ERROR_MESSAGE = value ]].
```

SAP provides *Customer Exits* as a simple way for customers to extend existing applications. These are function modules supplied with no content. Customers can upgrade them to meet their requirements. SAP defines the interface, the event at which they are called and the actual name. The `identifier` is a three-digit, numerical string constant, or a field with corresponding contents. The additions for parameter transfer are the same as described for the `CALL FUNCTION` statement above. To define customer exits, SAP uses the `SMOD` transactions. To activate customer exits, customers use the `CMOD` transactions.

```
CALL METHOD method [
   [EXPORTING     { parameter = value } ]
   [IMPORTING     { parameter = field } ]
   [CHANGING      { parameter = field } ]
   [RECEIVING      parameter = field   ]
   [EXCEPTIONS [ { exception = value } ]
                 [ OTHERS = value ]
                 [ ERROR_MESSAGE = value ] ]
] |
[
   [PARAMETER-TABLE param_tab ]
   [EXCEPTION-TABLE excep_tab ]
].
```

You use this statement to call a method present in an object in ABAP Objects. The way it transfers parameters is very similar to the call to a function module. There are two procedures to transfer parameters. You can only use one at a time. Either the first five additions transfer each parameter individually, or the parameters in internal tables are transferred instead. After `EXPORTING`, the system executes the parameters that are sent to the method. After `IMPORTING`, the system executes the parameters that are returned by the method. You can use `CHANGING` to define a combination of import and export parameters for transfer. If the method only returns a single parameter, `RECEIVING` can receive it. In special situations, parameters of this kind can also be used directly as a value for the method call in expressions. As in the case of function modules, the `EXCEPTIONS` addition is used to handle exceptions.

Besides transferring individual parameters, you can also insert the parameters and exceptions in their own internal table, close it and transfer it to the method.

```
CALL METHOD method ( parameter ).
```

You can use this form of the CALL command to transfer a single import parameter easily to an ABAP Objects method.

CALL METHOD *method* ({ *parameter* = *value* }) .

Use this command to call a method in ABAP Objects. If you use this form of the call, the method must only have import parameters. The command's syntax requires these parameters to be entered in round brackets after the method name. Their name will be used as a reference to transfer them.

CALL METHOD OF *object method*
   [= *field*]
   [**EXPORTING** { *parameter* = *field* }]
   [**NO FLUSH**] .

You can enter the name of a method present in an OLE object called object . If required, you can use the first addition to store the method's return code in a data field. If you want to transfer parameters to the method, do so in the same way as you call function modules with EXPORTING. If you make several successive OLE calls, the system buffers them and transfers them together if a non-OLE statement follows. You can use the NO FLUSH addition to set up more extensive buffering. If you do so, the system only executes the OLE calls after the FREE command.

CALL SCREEN *screen*
   [**STARTING AT** *x1 y1* [**ENDING AT** *x2 y2*]] .

Use this to call the screen screen program of the current main program. This command also executes the screen program's flow logic. After the system has finished processing the screen program, it continues with the statement that follows the CALL statement. If required, you can use STARTING AT to position the screen program that you have called on the screen. The system then displays it as a dialog box. You can set the size through the actual area of the screen program used (screen program attribute Used). Alternatively, you can define it explicitly by setting parameters for ENDING AT.

CALL SELECTION-SCREEN *screen*
   [**STARTING AT** *x1 y1* [**ENDING AT** *x2 y2*]] .

You can use this statement to call a selection screen. You use the SELECTION SCREEN BEGIN OF SCREEN and SELECTION SCREEN END OF SCREEN statements to define a selection screen.

CALL TRANSACTION *transaction*
   [**AND SKIP FIRST SCREEN**]
   [**USING** *itab*
      [**MODE** *mode*]
      [**OPTION FROM** *params*]
      [**UPDATE** *update*]
      [**MESSAGES INTO** *message_table*]] .

You can use this statement to call the named transaction. After the system has finished processing the called transaction, it continues processing the current program, beginning at the statement after the CALL statement. You can set the name of the transaction that is to be called, either by entering a string constant or by entering a field that contains the name. You can use the AND SKIP FIRST SCREEN addition to miss out the first screen program of the called transaction if all input fields in it have been filled with meaningful values by suitable means such as GET/SET parameters.

You can use the USING addition to transfer a table with screen programs in Batch Input format to the called transaction. If you do so, you can use some other parameters listed in Table 9.3 to modify the behaviour of the transaction.

Table 9.3   Additions for background processing

Addition	Parameter	Effect
MODE	A	Display screen programs
	E	Only display screen programs if an error occurs
	N	Do not display screen programs
UPDATE	A	Asynchronous update
	S	Synchronous update

Besides using the MODE and UPDATE command additions, you can also use values in the *params* structure to control the called transaction. This structure is used with the OPTIONS FROM addition.

During batchbackground processing, error messages cannot be output on the screen. Instead you can use the MESSAGES INTO command addition to collect them in an existing internal table. This table must have the structure BDCMSGCOLL. This structure is defined in the Data Dictionary.

CASE *field.*

You use the CASE statement to introduce a complex statement block which the system uses for case distinction to distinguish between upper case and lower case. This block ends with ENDCASE. Within the block you can use the WHEN value statement to compare the contents of field with the contents of value. If they are identical, the system executes the statements up to the next WHEN branch. You can use the WHEN OTHERS statement, which you must enter as the last WHEN branch, to introduce a statement block for all other values.

CATCH SYSTEM-EXCEPTIONS   { *systemexception* = *returncode* }

You can use this statement to intercept runtime errors. The parameter list contains the runtime error to be checked and any numerical return code. If the runtime error occurs within the next CATCH – ENDCATCH block, the system continues processing at the statement after the ENDCATCH statement. It also fills the SY-SUBRC system variable with the return code assigned to the runtime error.

CHECK [*condition* | *selection*].

This statement checks the logical expression or the selection. In the case of the selection, you should ensure that the table header rows or structure for which the check is to be carried out have already been stated when the selection table is declared. If the check is positive, the system continues processing with the next statement. If not, the way it now reacts depends on the current statement block's type. In loops, the system jumps to the start of the loop, and begins the next run through the loop from there. If the statement block is a modularization unit (subroutine, module, function module or event statement), the system quits it.

CHECK SELECT-OPTIONS.

You should only use this event statement after a GET event when processing logical databases. The system checks the contents of the current record for the database table defined after GET, for all selections concerning this table. The dynamic selection feature makes this kind of check superfluous.

CLASS *classname* **DEFINITION**
   [**PUBLIC**]
   [**INHERITING FROM** *superclass*]
   [**ABSTRACT**]
   [**FINAL**]
   [**CREATE** [**PUBLIC** | **PROTECTED** | **PRIVATE**]].

You use the CLASS ... DEFINITION statement to define a class in ABAP Objects. In the definition you declare all fields and define the methods with their interface.

Only the Class Builder sets the PUBLIC addition. It marks classes that are used throughout the whole system. You can use INHERITING FROM to activate the inheritance function. The new class inherits all the attributes of the superclass entered. You can use the ABSTRACT addition to prevent instances from being generated from this class. Classes to which you assign the FINAL addition cannot be used as a superclass in an inheritance chain. Consequently they end inheritance. You can use the CREATE addition to define whether instances of the class can be generated everywhere.

CLASS *classname* **DEFINITION DEFERED**.

You simply use this variant of the CLASS commands to announce the name of a new class. You actually define it later.

CLASS *classname* **DEFINITION LOAD**.

You use the LOAD addition to load a class if the system accesses static components or the class is required to define an event-handling routine.

CLASS *classname* **IMPLEMENTATION**.

You use this statement to introduce the implementation section of a class in ABAP Objects. In this section, you program the individual methods.

CLASS-DATA *data definitions*.

Within a class, this statement defines static class attributes. The data definitions have the same syntax as the ones for the DATA statement.

CLASS-EVENTS *event*.

You use this statement to define static (class) events within ABAP Objects.

CLASS-METHODS *method parameters*
[**FOR EVENT** *event* **OF** *class*].

You use this statement to define a static method within a class definition. The syntax is identical to that of the METHODS statement. If you add FOR EVENT, class methods can also act as handling routines for events.

CLASS-POOL [**MESSAGE-ID** *id*].

This statement introduces a classes pool. Class Builder generates this type of program and therefore this statement. You do not enter it manually.

CLEAR *field* [**WITH** (*value* | **NULL**)].

The system sets the field to its type-dependent initial value. In contrast, if you add WITH NULL, the system fills the field with blanks. If this field contains a value, instead of NULL, (field or direct value), the system fills it with the first byte of the value.

CLOSE CURSOR *cursor*.

You use this to close the database cursor. You only need to use this command if you want to use the cursor more than once to read database records.

CLOSE DATASET *filename*.

The system closes this file. You only need to use this command if you want to open the file in an application several times one after the other. In the command, the filename can be either a string constant or a field with corresponding contents.

CNT(*field*).

The CNT statement is not a true ABAP statement. It is a field that the system generates and fills automatically. If you want to evaluate the field contents, it is a good idea to use a sorted extract data set in a LOOP. In addition, field must form part of the sorting code. After a group end, CNT returns the number of different values in field.

COLLECT [*record* **INTO**] *itab*.

This statement adds a new record, either to the internal itab table or to an existing entry with the same key. The system uses the data from the itab header row in the internal table, or from a structure `record` which you have entered. The key usually consists of all the fields that are not numerical, i.e. whose type is not I, F or P. If the `COLLECT` statement finds a record in the internal table whose key is the same as that of the record you want to add, the system adds all the numerical field values of the new record to those which are already present. In this case, no new record is added to the internal table. There is no limit to the maximum number of records the table can hold.

COMMIT WORK [**AND WAIT**] .

This statement will commit all database changes. The system executes all the update routines (`PERFORM ON COMMIT`, `CALL FUNCTION IN UPDATE TASK`) and pre-flagged background processes (`CALL FUNCTION IN BACKGROUND TASK`). The database locks are released. The system defines the area between two `COMMIT WORK` statements as a logical processing unit (*logical unit of work, LUW*).

An exception to this process occurs when you call `COMMIT WORK` in dialog applications that were called using `CALL DIALOG`. Only database locks are released here. The actual commit, i.e. the confirmation of database changes and the start of update routines, is not carried out until after the `COMMIT WORK` statement is executed in the calling program.

If you add `AND WAIT`, this makes the application wait until all update routines have been completed.

COMMUNICATION ... .

Using the different variants of the `COMMUNICATION` statement, shown below, several programs can communicate with each other, using the CPI-C protocol. CPI-C stands for Common Programming Interface-Communication.

... **INIT DESTINATION** *dest* **ID** *ident* [**RETURNCODE** *ret*] .

You can use this command to create the link to the `dest` system. In `ident` the system returns an ID number for the link. If necessary, the system can return the return code with an addition of the same name to a specifically-named `ret` field. You will usually find the return code in `SY-SUBRC`.

... **ASSIGN ID** *ident* [**RETURNCODE** *ret*] .

When you use this command, the system sets up the initialized link.

... `ACCEPT ID ident` [`RETURNCODE ret`] .

You use this variant to create and initialize a link you have requested.

... **SEND ID** *ident* **BUFFER** *buffer*
    [**RETURNCODE** *ret*]
    [**LENGTH** *length*] .

When you use this command, the system sends the `buffer` contents to the recipient location. If you add the `LENGTH` addition, the system displays the number of characters to be transferred.

```
... RECEIVE ID ident
       BUFFER buffer
       DATAINFO info
       STATUSINFO status
          [ RETURNCODE ret ]
          [ LENGTH length ]
          [ RECEIVED number ]
          [ HOLD ] .
```

When you use this command, the system receives the data sent from the recipient location and stores it in the `buffer`. The `info` and `status` fields display information about the transfer. You can use the `LENGTH` addition to limit the number of characters to be read. `RECEIVED` stores the number of characters that were actually read. The `HOLD` variant switches off the asynchronous receive mode. The receiving process then waits until the end of the data transfer.

```
... DEASSIGN ID ident [ RETURNCODE ret ] .
```

This statement closes and dismantles the link. If required, you can use a return code to evaluate how successful this action was.

```
COMPUTE field = expression .
```

The system calculates the (arithmetical) result of the `expression` expression and stores it in the `field` field. You do not have to use the `COMPUTE` statement; instead you can use this short form:

```
field = expression .
```

```
COMPUTE ref1 ?= ref2 .
```

The system carries out a reference between reference variables. To do this, it carries out a type conversion.

```
CONCATENATE { value } INTO field
    [ SEPARATED BY separator ] .
```

In this statement, the system interprets all the values (field contents or constants) as character strings and links them into one character string. When it does this, the system ignores final blanks. It stores the result in `field`. You can use `SEPARATED BY` to define a character string, which the system inserts between the individual elements as a delimiter.

```
CONDENSE field [ NO-GAPS ] .
```

The system interprets the contents of `field` as a character string, regardless of the actual type of data. You can combine several blanks which follow each other, to form one blank or suppress them completely (`NO-GAPS`). The system displays the result again in `field`.

```
CONSTANTS field[(length)]
    [TYPE typ | LIKE like_field] VALUE ( value | IS INITIAL ) .
```

This statement is used to declare a data field, `field`, with fixes contents. The value is assigned with the `VALUE` option. In addition to assigning an actual value, you can use `IS INITIAL` to assign the initial value which belongs to a particular data type. You can set the constant's type by using the assigned value by entering a type or by deriving it from an existing field.

```
CONSTANTS:
  BEGIN OF record,
    declaration ...
  END OF record.
```

This statement declares a structure with fixed contents. You must use `VALUE` to assign a value to each field in the structure when you declare the subfield.

```
CONTEXTS context.
```

You use this statement to identify a data context in a program.

```
CONTINUE.
```

You should only use this statement in loops. It causes the system to jump to the beginning of the loop and start the next run.

```
CONTROLS name TYPE control_type.
CONTROLS name TYPE TABLEVIEW USING SCREEN screen_number.
CONTROLS name TYPE TABSTRIP.
```

Use the `CONTROLS` statement to define an object which is used to display data visually. The `control_type` defines the object's type. This type is not a standard data type. Instead, it is the name of one of the elements programmed by SAP.

At present, the system supports two controls. You could describe the view table as a further development of the loops step. Before you can declare a views table, you must add additional parameters to the `CONTROL` statement. You can use a tabstrip to program a multipage dialog, and use a few tabs to select its pages.

```
CONVERT DATE date INTO INVERTED-DATE field.
```

The system inverts the date in `date`, which can consist of field contents or constants, (nine's complement of the internal representation) and stores the result in `field`. This conversion means that the most recent date has the lowest numerical value. This can be very useful when you are searching by date.

```
CONVERT INVERTED-DATE date INTO DATE field.
```

This statement converts an inverted date back to its original value.

```
CONVERT TEXT value INTO SORTABLE CODE hexfield.
```

This command converts `value`, regardless of the currently set language. This conversion makes it possible for you to sort data correctly, because it includes language-specific special characters such as accents.

CONVERT TIME STAMP *tstamp* **TIME ZONE** *zone*
  INTO DATE *date* **TIME** *time*.

This statement converts a time stamp into a date and a time.

CONVERT DATE *date* **TIME** *time*
  INTO TIME STAMP *tstamp* **TIME ZONE** *zone*.

This statement is used to convert a date and time entry into a time stamp.

CREATE DATA *ref* (**TYPE** *type* | **TYPE** (*namefield*) | **LIKE** *field*).

This statement generates a data object to which the ref reference refers. The system determines the data object type either from a data type that has been entered statically or dynamically or by referring to an existing field. Before this happens, you must first use DATA ref TYPE REF TO DATA to define the reference. You can only access these data objects using field icons.

CREATE OBJECT *classref* [**TYPE** *class* | **TYPE** (*namefield*)].{}

You use this command to generate an instance of a class. When this happens, the system uses the class reference you entered to define the class name. However, if you are using references that you did not enter, the system uses the TYPE addition together with static or dynamic transfer to define the class name.

CREATE OBJECT *object class* [NO FLUSH | QUEUE-ONLY].

This statement generates an OLE2 object that you can process with other commands.

DATA *field*[(*length*)]
  [**TYPE** *type* | **LIKE** *template*]
  [**VALUE** *value*]
  [**DECIMALS** *decimal_places*]
  [**TYPE** *ref* **TO DATA**]
  [**TYPE** *ref* **TO** *class*]
  [**READ-ONLY**].

In this statement, the system declares an elementary field data field. If you do not want to use the default values, you can use various additions to define the type and other characteristics. The length entry defines the size of the data field. You must enter this value in round brackets without a delimiter immediately after the field name. Use TYPE to give the object the predefined or user-defined type. You use LIKE to transfer the characteristics of an existing data object. With VALUE, you can assign a value at the same time as you declare it. In the case of elementary P-type fields, you use DECIMALS to fix the number of decimal points.

The last three options mentioned above are part of the object-oriented extension of ABAP. The TYPE ref TO DATA addition generates a reference to a data object. You can use TYPE ref TO class to create a field that refers to references the instance of a class. You can only use the READ-ONLY addition within the declaration part of a class. Although you can read this kind of field from outside the class, you can only change it by using the class's own methods.

```
DATA: BEGIN OF record,
  declaration ...
END OF record.
```

```
DATA record[(length)]
  [ TYPE typ | LIKE template ]
  [ TYPE LINE OF itab_typ | LIKE LINE OF itab ].
```

You can use both these variants of the DATA statement to create a structure. In the first variant you must declare the subfields of the structure between BEGIN OF record and END OF record. You can also use the additions described in other variants of the DATA statement. This therefore means that you can also include complex elements, even tables, in a structure. You must separate the individual declarations from each other by a comma.

The second variant of this statement defines the structure's structure. To do this it either references a structure type or another existing structure. It can also use the line structure of an internal table.

```
DATA: BEGIN OF itab OCCURS roll_area,
  declarations ...
END OF itab [ VALID BETWEEN field_1 AND field_2 ].
```

```
DATA itab
  [ ( TYPE linetype | LIKE record ) OCCURS n
      [ WITH HEADER LINE ] ] |
  [ ( TYPE | LIKE ) RANGE OF ( type | field )
      [ INITIAL SIZE size][ WITH HEADER LINE ] ] |
  [   TYPE itabtype [ WITH HEADER LINE ] ] |
  [ ( TYPE | LIKE ) TABLE OF ( linetype | record ) ] |
  [ ( TYPE | LIKE ) tabkind OF ( linetype | lineobj )

      WITH [ UNIQUE | NON-UNIQUE ] key
      [ INITIAL SIZE size ][ WITH HEADER LINE ] ].
```

The system uses both these DATA statements to declare internal tables. The first variant requires the system to list all the elements in the internal table. The roll_area parameter contains the number of records to be stored in RAM. This data is only stored on the swap area of the hard disk if this number is exceeded. The system automatically generates a header row for tables created with this command variant. The VALID BETWEEN addition defines two fields in the table. The PROVIDE command then uses these fields to create a validity range.

The other variants of the statement use existing data types for structures or internal tables or use existing structures and tables to describe how the new internal table is created. In some cases, you must enter OCCURS. By default, tables that are created in this way are not given their own header row. If you need a header row in this kind of table, you must define it with the WITH HEADER LINE addition.

```
DATA: BEGIN OF COMMON PART name,
  declaration ...
END OF COMMON PART.
```

You use this statement to define a data block in the global memory area. This data block can be used by several programs at the same time, if it is declared with the same name and identical structure in each program. In practice, a common part is usually declared in its own file. You use an INCLUDE statement to include this common part in all the programs which are to use it. If you only want to use one common part, you do not have to use its name. Despite this, you declare the data block's structure in the same way as for structures.

```
DEFINE name.
  ABAP statements   ...
END-OF-DEFINITION.
```

You use the DEFINE statement to define a macro. This macro is made up of ABAP statements. The END-OF-DEFINITION statement concludes the macro's definition. The macro can contain positioning parameters &1 to &9. The system replaces these parameters with the macros definition statements when the program is translated (before it is run for the first time).

```
DELETE FROM table | (namefield) WHERE condition [CLIENT SPECIFIED].
```

You use this statement to delete records from a database table. The system deletes all the records that are identified through the WHERE condition. You can either enter the table name as a direct value in the statement or transfer it from a data field. By default, the system only deletes records in the current client. You can use the CLIENT SPECIFIED addition to switch off automatic client-handling. If you do this, you must also enter the client in the selection condition, just like any other table field.

```
DELETE table | *table | (field_with_tablename)
  [CLIENT SPECIFIED]
  [FROM workarea].
```

You use this statement to delete individual records from the table you specify here. Alternatively, you can transfer the table name statically in the statement or dynamically in a data field. You must transfer the entire key of the record you want to delete into the table's header record, or into a work area which you have specified (FROM ...). If you transfer the table name dynamically, you must also enter the work area. The system transfers the contents of the work area character by character into the table's key fields. For this reason, the work area must be able to include all the key fields. You must therefore ensure that the key values are included in the work area in the same sequence and length as agreed for each particular table in the Data Dictionary. However, the work area's internal structure does not have to be the same as the table's structure. This means that the work area does not have to be a structure. Instead, for example, it could be a C-type or N-type data field, which is long enough. You use the CLIENT SPECIFIED addition to switch off automatic client handling.

```
DELETE table | (field_with_tablename)
  FROM TABLE itab
  [CLIENT SPECIFIED].
```

You use this statement to delete all the records whose key matches one of the records in the internal `itab` table from the database table you have specified. The records in the internal table are subject to the same requirements as defined for the work area in the version of the DELETE statement described above. Once again, you can use the CLIENT SPECIFIED addition to switch off automatic client-handling. You can transfer the database table's name either statically or dynamically.

DELETE *table* | **table* **VERSION** *field_with_tablename*.

You use this variant to transfer dynamically the table name in the `field_with_tablename` field. However, table names are subject to some restrictions. Because you can now use other versions of the DELETE statement to transfer names dynamically, this command variant is only supported for reasons of compatibility, and should no longer be used for new development.

DELETE *itab*
  [[**INDEX** *index*] |
    [**WHERE** *condition*][**FROM** *start*][**TO** *last*]].

You use this statement to delete records from an internal table. If you do not use an addition, you should really only use this statement in a LOOP through the table. If you do this, the system deletes the current record each time. If you use the INDEX addition, you can delete a specific record without using loops if you know the record number. This can for example be determined by some of the READ command's variants. The system starts counting from 1. You can use the WHERE, FROM and TO additions as alternatives to INDEX to create an area which is to be deleted. The FROM or TO entries, together with WHERE, ensure that the system only examines the area of the internal table that you have specified.

DELETE TABLE *itab* [**WITH TABLE KEY** { *key* = *value* }].

You use this statement to delete the first record that matches the key you enter from the internal table.

DELETE TABLE *itab* [**FROM** *record*].

You use this statement to delete the record whose key matches the record's key in the header row or the specific work area you specify from the internal table.

DELETE ADJACENT DUPLICATES FROM *itab*
  [**COMPARING** [*field_1 ... field_n*] |
           (field_with_fieldname) |
           COMPARING ALL FIELDS]].

You use this statement to delete repeated entries from the internal table. Identical entries are those that match one of these criteria:

- they have field contents that all match and that have an elementary data type that is not I, P or F (default function without COMPARING addition);

- they have field contents that all match and that are listed in the COMPARING command addition;

- they have field contents that all match (COMPARING ALL of a field).

This command can only function correctly if the identical records follow immediately after each other. You must presort the internal table in accordance with the compare criterion you want to use.

DELETE FROM DATABASE *table(area)* *ID key*
    [**CLIENT** *field*].

You use this statement to delete what is known as a *data cluster* from the `table` table and the `area` area. Both entries are direct values. The round brackets around `area` are part of the statement's syntax. A `key` is used to identify the cluster. You can enter this key either as a direct value or as field content.

DELETE FROM SHARED BUFFER *table(area)* *ID key*
    [**CLIENT** *field*].

You use this command to delete a data cluster from the inter-transactional buffer. The `table` and `area` entries are direct values. The round brackets around `area` are part of the statement's syntax. A `key` is used to identify the cluster. You can enter this key either as a direct value or a field content.

DELETE DATASET *filename*.

You use this statement to delete the file you specify in the `filename` parameter at operating system level. This file is not a table. It is usually a file in a different format such as a text file or binary file from another system.

DEMAND { *context_field* = *program_field* } **FROM CONTEXT** *context*
    [**MESSAGES INTO** *itab*].

You use this command to read values from a data context.

DESCRIBE FIELD *field*
    [**LENGTH** *result_field*]
    [**TYPE** *result_field*]
    [**TYPE** *typ* **COMPONENTS** *number*]
    [**OUTPUT-LENGTH** *result_field*]
    [**DECIMALS** *result_field*]
    [**EDIT MASK** *result_field*]
    [**HELP-ID** *Id*].

You use this statement to determine one or more characteristics of a field and then enter them in the `result_field` field. You must use at least one addition. If you enter several additions at the same time, you will of course need different result fields.

DESCRIBE TABLE *itab*
    [**LINES** *lines*]
    [**OCCURS** *roll_area*]
    [**KIND** *tablekind*].

You use this command to fill the `lines` field with the number of records in the `itab` internal table and to fill the `roll_area` field with the value of the `OCCURS` parameter which you entered when you declared the internal table. You use the `KIND` option to determine the table type (standard-type table, sorted table or hash table). You must enter at least one of the additions.

DESCRIBE DISTANCE BETWEEN *field_1* **AND** *field_2* **INTO** *distance*.

The system enters the distance in bytes between the fields `field_1` and `field_2` in the `distance` field.

DESCRIBE LIST [**INDEX** *index*] **NUMBER OF LINES** *lines*.

You use this command to enter the number of list lines in the `lines` field. If required, you can use `INDEX` to enter the list level so that you can access lists other than the one currently displayed.

DESCRIBE LIST [**INDEX** *index*] **NUMBER OF PAGES** *pages*.

You use this command to enter the number of list pages in the `pages` field. If required, you can use `INDEX` to enter the list level so that you can access lists other than the one currently displayed.

DESCRIBE list [**INDEX** *index*] **LINE** *A* **PAGE** *pages*.

You use this command to return the number of the page on which the line you specify is present. You can also use `INDEX` to enter the list level here, so that you can access lists other than the one currently displayed.

DESCRIBE LIST [**INDEX** *index*] **PAGE** *pages*
  [**LINE-SIZE** *result_field*]
  [**LINE-COUNT** *result_field*]
  [**LINES** *result_field*]
  [**FIRST-LINE** *result_field*]
  [**TOP-LINES** *result_field*]
  [**TITLE-LINES** *result_field*]
  [**HEAD-LINES** *result_field*]
  [**END-LINES** *result_field*].

The various additions for this command return information about the structure of a specific page in a list. If you use several additions at the same time, you will of course require different fields in which to enter the results. Table 9.4 shows the return values of the individual additions.

DIVIDE *field* **BY** *divisor*.

You use this statement to divide the value in `field` by a `divisor`. The system displays the result in `field`. You can enter the divisor either as a direct value or as a field.

DIVIDE-CORRESPONDING *record_1* **BY** *record_2*.

You use this statement to search for fields with matching names in both structures. If the system finds these fields, it divides the contents of one field in `record_1` by the contents of the field with the same name from `record_2`. It then displays the result in the `record_1` field.

Table 9.4   Additions of the DESCRIBE LIST PAGE command

Addition	Returns
LINE-SIZE	Line length
LINE-COUNT	Permitted number of lines
LINES	Number of output lines
FIRST-LINE	Absolute line number of the first line on the page
TOP-LINES	Number of lines output in the page header (title + column headings)
TITLE-LINES	Number of lines output as a title
HEAD-LINES	Number of lines output as column headings
END-LINES	Number of footers reserved for the page end

```
DO.
  ABAP statements ...
ENDDO.
```

This statement is an endless loop. The system repeats the statements between DO and ENDDO until you leave the loop with EXIT, STOP or REJECT.

```
DO VARYING field FROM start NEXT distance.
  ABAP statements ...
ENDDO.
```

The system processes this endless loop until you leave it with EXIT, STOP or REJECT. In this statement, start and distance are field names. Each time the loop runs through, the system assigns a new value to field (which is also a data field). The first value is taken from the contents of the start field. The system determines the next field by adding the distance between start and distance to the memory address of each current field. If the system has assigned a value to field, this change will also be effective in the place in the RAM from which the system read the current contents of field. You can combine several VARYING additions in one DO statement.

```
DO n TIMES.
  ABAP statements ...
ENDDO.
```

The system runs through the loop n times.

```
DO n TIMES VARYING field FROM start NEXT distance.
  ABAP statements ...
ENDDO.
```

You use this statement to combine a DO VARYING statement with a predefined number of loop runs. The system assigns values to field in the same way as for DO VARYING.

EDITOR-CALL FOR *itab*
  [**TITLE** *title*]
  [**DISPLAY-MODE**]
  [**BACKUP INTO** *backup_tab*].

You use this statement to load the itab internal table into the program editor where you can process it. The table can only be made up of C-type fields and be a maximum length of 72 characters. The system only saves changes in the internal table if you use the SAVE command, function key (F11), in the editor. You use TITLE to specify a title. The DISPLAY-MODE addition prevents anyone processing the table and only allows it to be displayed. Use the BACKUP INTO addition to generate a backup copy of the table in a second internal table.

EDITOR-CALL FOR REPORT *program* [**DISPLAY-MODE**].

You use this statement to load a specific program into the program editor where you can process it. Use the DISPLAY-MODE addition to set the editor to display mode. The program can now no longer be processed.

ELSE.

You use the ELSE statement within an IF statement to introduce a statement block. The system ignores this block if the condition entered after IF is not fulfilled.

ELSEIF condition.

You use this statement to link the ELSE statement with a new IF statement. This means you can create nested comparisons. You can replace this statement at any time with separate ELSE and IF statements.

END-OF-DEFINITION.

You use this statement to end a macro definition.

END-OF-PAGE.

You use this statement to execute a statement block which belongs to this event statement. This happens when the system reaches the END-OF-PAGE area of a page when it is outputting a list or if the RESERVE statement does not contain the required number of free lines. This event statement has no effect if LINE-COUNT was set to the default value 0 or a specific page feed takes place with NEW-PAGE.

END-OF-SELECTION.

You use this statement to execute the statement block of this event statement, after all the statements of the current selection part of a report have been executed. This happens when for example the system has read all the records in a logical database.

ENDAT.

You use this statement to end the statement block of an AT statement.

ENDCASE.

You use this statement to end a CASE branch.

ENDCATCH.

You use this statement to end a CATCH block.

ENDCLASS.

You use this statement to end the definition block or implementation block of a class which started with CLASS.

ENDDO.

You use this statement to end a loop which was introduced with DO.

ENDEXEC.

You use this statement to end a native SQL statement.

ENDFORM.

You use this statement to close a subroutine.

ENDFUNCTION.

You use this statement to end a function module.

ENDIF.

You use this statement to end an IF statement.

ENDINTERFACE.

You use this statement to end the definition part of an interface in ABAP Objects.

ENDLOOP.

You use this statement to end a LOOP.

ENDMETHOD.

You use this statement to end a method declaration.

ENDMODULE.

You use this statement to end a module declaration.

ENDON.

You use this statement to end the statement block of an ON statement.

ENDPROVIDE.

You use this statement to close a PROVIDE loop.

ENDSELECT.

You use this statement to end a SELECT loop.

ENDWHILE.

You use this statement to end a WHILE section.

EVENTS *event* **EXPORTING** {
  VALUE (*parameter*) [
    TYPE type | LIKE field [OPTIONAL | DEFAULT default]]}.

You use this statement to declare instance events within an ABAP Objects class. The system can assign parameters to events. These parameters must always be value parameters. For this reason, you must mark them with the VALUE keyword and enclose them in round brackets. You must not leave any blanks between the brackets and the parameter name. You can use the TYPE or LIKE option to assign a type to a parameter. You can also use OPTIONAL to declare a parameter as an optional parameter. You use the DEFAULT addition to predefine an initial value.

EXEC SQL [**PERFORMING** *subroutine*].
  SQL statement
ENDEXEC.

This statement means that there is a native SQL statement between EXEC and ENDEXEC. As the system passes this statement directly to the database, it must take into consideration any special features of the specific database system. The system uses ABAP data fields to exchange data between ABAP and native SQL. These fields are marked with a colon in the SQL statement. You use PERFORMING to define an ABAP subroutine which is executed once for each record that the SQL statement returns. It may happen that you cannot port native SQL statements. For this reason, you should only use them if you do not have an alternative.

EXIT.

You use this statement to leave a processing section. The exact system reaction depends on the statement's position within the program. If this statement is in a loop, the system only closes the loop. If the statement is in a modularization unit (subroutines, statement block of an event statement) but outside a loop, the EXIT statement closes the processing unit. In a report, the EXIT statement ends further processing and the system displays the list it has generated so far.

EXIT FROM STEP-LOOP.

This statement relates to the LOOP statement in the flow logic of a screen program. The system closes the corresponding loop, as a result of which no further records are created or read in the step loop area of the screen program.

EXIT FROM SQL.

You use this statement to close native SQL processing which was introduced by EXEC SQL PERFORMING.

EXPORT (*itab*) | { (*field* | *itab* [**FROM** *source*]) }
  TO DATABASE table(area) [**FROM** *record*] [**CLIENT** *client*] **ID** *key*.

You use this statement to write fields or internal tables to a table database table. There they are stored in what is known as *a range* area. You can store several objects using the same key. You use the CLIENT addition to specify a target client, if you do not want to use the current client. You can use the FROM addition which you must enter for each element you want to store in order to store an element in the table with another name. The database table you use must have a predefined structure. The second FROM addition after TO DATABASE uses a separate structure instead of the table work area.

Instead of entering all the fields you want to transfer separately, you can transfer all the values in an internal table. This table must have a suitable structure. It must be made up of one or two Char-type columns. The first column must contain the names of the objects to be transferred. The second column optionally contains an alternative name for each object. This is automatically used as a parameter by the FROM or TO clause. If the second column in the internal table is missing or empty, the FROM or TO clause has no effect.

```
EXPORT (itab) | { (field | itab  [FROM source]) }
  TO MEMORY [ID key].
```

You use this statement to write fields or internal tables to a global memory area from where they can be read by other applications. This means you can transfer data between applications within one user session. You can use the FROM addition to store an object under another name. The ID addition gives the stored object an identifier which you can use to load them again. The EXPORT command works across applications. If you carry out several exports, the system deletes all existing objects that have the same identifier. Instead of using the value list, you could also transfer all the values from an internal table.

```
EXPORT (itab) | { (field | itab  [FROM source]) }
  TO SHARED BUFFER table(area)
  [FROM record] [CLIENT client] ID key.
```

You use this statement to write fields or internal tables to a buffer which is used for more than one transaction. This buffer is managed on the application server. This means that the data is only available for processes which run on this server. The parameters are the same as for the EXPORT TO DATABASE command.

```
EXTRACT fieldgroup.
```

You use this statement to write the current contents of the fields defined in fieldgroup to a program's extract dataset. If you declared a field group HEADER, its contents are inserted as a prefix to act as a key.

```
FETCH NEXT CURSOR cursor INTO record.
```

You use this statement to read the next record from a dataset that was specified with OPEN CURSOR. The system stores the result in record.

```
FIELDS field.
```

You use this statement to inform the extended program check that the fields you enter are to be used. This prevents the check program from returning error messages if the fields in the program cannot be accessed or only accessed dynamically. This statement does not have functionality relevant to real programs.

FIELD-GROUPS *fieldgroup*.

You use this statement to declare a *field group*, which is used together with extract datasets. A field group logically groups several existing fields to form one object. It is created dynamically at runtime. Field groups therefore differ considerably from structures.

FIELD-SYMBOLS *<fieldsymbol>*
    [**STRUCTURE** *table* **DEFAULT** *record*] |
    [**TYPE** *type*] |
    [**TYPE LINE OF** *type*] |
    [**LIKE** *field*] |
    [**LIKE LINE OF** *record*] |
    [**TYPE** *tablekind*] |
    [**TYPE REF TO** *class*].

You use this command to declare a field symbol. The pointed brackets that enclose the field symbol's name are part of the command's syntax. You must enter these brackets. A field symbol is a pointer which you assign later to a data field with the ASSIGN command. If you do not use one of the additions, the system does not define the field symbol type until it is assigned (see ASSIGN). You use the STRUCTURE addition to create a field symbol that can point to a structure that is completely defined in the Data Dictionary. You can then use <fieldsymbol>-fieldname to access the individual fields in the structure later on. You must make a record work area available for these types of field symbol. This work area must be the same size as the Data Dictionary structure. You can use other additions to define field symbol types. The system checks the type during an ASSIGN.

FORM *subroutine*
    [**TABLES**   { *itab* [*typing*] }]
    [**USING**   { [*parameter* | **VALUE**(*parameter*)] [*typing*] }]
    [**CHANGING** { [*parameter* | **VALUE**(*parameter*)] [*typing*] }].

You use this statement to define a subroutine. It ends with the ENDFORM statement. You can transfer internal tables as parameters to the subroutine, as well as transferring fields and structures. The system assigns the current parameters to the formal parameters in the same sequence as the parameter when the subroutine was called. You must use one of the TABLES additions to identify internal tables and the USING and CHANGING additions to identify field parameters. The system mainly handles the parameters as reference parameters. It only handles them as value parameters if you use the VALUE addition. You can assign additional type definitions to any parameter. At runtime, the system checks whether the current parameter has the correct type. The statements you can use to assign types are listed in Table 9.5.

Table 9.5   Possible additions for assigning types to parameters

Statement	Effect	For single parameters	For internal tables
... STRUCTURE record	The parameter corresponds to the structure of record	Yes	Yes
... TYPE type	The parameter has a type that you have specified	Yes	Yes
... TYPE LINE OF itab	The parameter has the structure of a record in the itab table that does not have a header row	Yes	No
...TYPE REF TO class	The parameter is a reference to an object in the class you have specified	Yes	No
...TYPE REF TO DATA	The parameter is a data reference	Yes	No
... LIKE field	The parameter has the characteristics and type of field	Yes	No
... LIKE LINE OF itab	The parameter has the structure of the itab internal table	Yes	No
...TYPE [C | N | X | P] ...	The parameter has the type you have specified. The length and decimal points are not taken into account	Yes	No
... TYPE TABLE	The current parameter must be a table without header rows	Yes	Yes
... TYPE ANY	Any type is permitted		
... TYPE [ANY | INDEX | STANDARD| SORTED | HASHED] TABLE	The parameter is a table of the table type you have specified	No	Yes

FORMAT
```
  [COLOR [color | OFF]]
  [INTENSIFIED  [ON] | [OFF]]
  [INVERSE      [ON] | [OFF]]
  [INPUT        [ON] | [OFF]]
  [HOTSPOT      [ON] | [OFF]]
  [RESET].
```

You use this statement to set or reset the output parameter when you are processing lists. The ON switch is the default value. Unlike OFF, you do not have to enter it in the program code. New settings come into effect from the next WRITE statement onwards. When you enter a new processing event, some of the settings are reset to their default value.

FREE *dataobject*.

You use this statement to release the memory required to process the specified dataobject. In this case, dataobject can be a field, structure, internal table or complex data object.

FREE MEMORY [**ID** *key*].

You use this statement to delete the global memory area. The basic form of this statement without an addition deletes all the data, even data which has been assigned a key. You must specify the key before you can delete specific, individual data groups.

FREE OBJECT *object* [**NO FLUSH**].

You use this statement to release the object ole object.

FUNCTION *function*.

You use this statement to introduce the definition of a function module.

FUNCTION-POOL.

You use this statement to introduce a function group's framework program. The system automatically generates this statement when you create a new function group. It is equivalent to a report statement.

GET *node*
  [**LATE**]
  [**FIELDS** { *field* }].

You can only use this event statement in reports which work with a logical database. The node parameter can either refer to a database table or to a logical node. The system inserts the next record from node into the header row with the same name. At the same time, the system calls the contents of all the tables that are higher level to the table. You use the LATE addition to continue processing after the system has read all the tables that are lower level to the table. You can use FIELDS to restrict access to the fields you have entered. This can improve system performance because the logical database then only has to fill the selected fields with data.

```
GET CURSOR FIELD field
  [OFFSET offset]
  [LINE line]
  [VALUE value]
  [LENGTH length].
  [AREA area].
```

You use this command to return the name of the field on which the cursor currently stands. The additions also give information about the cursor's offset within the field, the number of any step loop line or absolute list line present, the current value, the field's output length, or the name of a control if present. You can use this command both in dialog processing and in interactive reporting.

```
GET CURSOR LINE line
  [OFFSET offset]
  [VALUE value]
  [LENGTH length].
```

You use this command to return the number of the list line or the step loop line that the cursor is in. The additions are only effective within list processing. They return the cursor's offset in the line, the contents or the length of the entire line.

```
GET PARAMETER ID parameter_name FIELD field.
```

The system reads the parameter with the name you specify from the global memory and displays it in the specified field. You can enter the parameter name as field contents or a direct value.

```
GET TIME [FIELD field].
```

You use this statement to fill the SY-UZEIT field with the current time. The system also resets SY-DATUM, the system date field. If you use the field addition, the system does not update the system fields. Instead it merely fills field with the current time.

```
GET RUN TIME FIELD field.
```

The first time you call GET RUN TIME, the system initializes the field field. Each time it is called after that, the system fills field with the time that the application has been running since the first time you called GET RUN TIME. The time elapsed is shown in microseconds.

```
GET TIME STAMP FIELD field.
```

You use this statement to return a time stamp.

```
GET LOCALE LANGUAGE lang COUNTRY country MODIFIER mod.
```

You use this statement to determine the current test environment. The system stores the values it reads in the lang, country and mod fields.

```
GET PROPERTY OF object attributes = field [NO FLUSH] [QUEUE-ONLY].
```

You use this statement to read the characteristics of an OLE object and display them in the field you enter. You use the NO FLUSH addition to collect several OLE requests in order to execute them together. You can use QUEUE-ONLY to define conditions that suppress the updating of the return values in the OLE object.

GET BIT *n* **OF** *field* **INTO** *result*.

The *field* must be a hexadecimal field (type X or XSTRING). The bits in this field are numbered from the left, starting with 1. The command writes bit n from *field* into the *result* field.

GET PF-STATUS *status* [**PROGRAM** *prog*] [**EXCLUDING** *itab*].

You use this statement to read the name of the current status and store it in the *status* field. If the current status belongs to another program, you can use the PROGRAM addition to find out this program's name. You can use the EXCLUDING addition to write currently deactivated function codes to an internal table.

GET REFERENCE OF *field* **INTO** *ref*.

You use this statement to fill the *ref* reference with a reference to the *field* field.

HIDE *data*.

You use this statement to place the content of the *data* field in a hidden memory area and link it with the number of the current line. The hidden content becomes active again when you select a line in interactive reporting. The *data* field may be a single field, a list of fields or a structure.

```
IF condition.
  ABAP statements ...
[ELSE. | ELSEIF condition.]
  ABAP statements ...
ENDIF.
```

You use this statement to evaluate a logical expression. If it is fulfilled, the system executes the statements which immediately follow it up to the next ELSE, ELSEIF or ENDIF statement. If it is not fulfilled, the system evaluates the next ELSEIF expression or continues processing after an ELSE statement.

```
IMPORT (itab) | [field | itab] [TO target]
  FROM DATABASE table(area) TO record
    ID key [CLIENT client] |
    MAJOR-ID maid MINOR-ID miid.
```

You use this statement to import data clusters, i.e. groups of data fields or internal tables, from one area of a special table. You must have used EXPORT TO DATABASE to export these values. The data the system reads must either all be stored together in an internal table or stored individually. You can use the TO addition which you must enter separately for each individual parameter in order to store read values in other fields. You can either enter the entire key, using the ID or in two parts with MAJOR-ID and MINOR-

ID. If the table is client-dependent, you can also use CLIENT to transfer the client number. In the statement, table and area are direct values. The round brackets around area are part of the command's syntax. Unusually, in this case, they do not refer to a field content. You can use the TO record statement after you have entered the table and area to store the control data in a separate work area.

```
IMPORT DIRECTORY INTO itab
    FROM DATABASE table(area) [CLIENT client] ID key.
```

You use this statement to return a directory of the objects which were stored using a particular key in a specific table in a particular area. The itab table must a predefined structure.

```
IMPORT (itab) | [field | itab] [TO target] FROM MEMORY [ID key].
```

You use this statement to read objects from the global memory which were stored there with EXPORT. You can use the TO addition to store values in other fields.

```
IMPORT (itab) | [field | itab] [TO target]
    FROM SHARED BUFFER table(area) TO record
        ID key [CLIENT client].
```

You use this command to import data from a buffer which is used by several transactions. The parameters are the same as those used for the IMPORT DATABASE command.

```
INCLUDE file.
```

The file file contains ABAP source code. The system includes this statement in the current ABAP program. The ABAP program behaves as if the statements were coded directly in its own program. One include file may be included in several programs.

```
INCLUDE STRUCTURE record
    [AS name [RENAMING WITH SUFFIX suffix]].
```

You should only use this statement within a BEGIN OF REC ... END OF REC statement. It adds the structure of the structure that you have specified to the declaration. This thereby expands the structure. However, the system does not add the entire structure, it only adds the fields contained in the structure. However, if you enter an alias name for the added structure, you can continue to access it as an independent element. You can also include one structure several times. If you do this, the suffix which is added to all the field names in the substructure acts as a unique field descriptor.

```
INCLUDE TYPE record_typ
    [AS name [RENAMING WITH SUFFIX suffix]].
```

You should only use this statement within a BEGIN OF REC ... END OF REC statement. It adds the structure of the structure type you specify to the declaration. This expands the structure of the individual fields. Although the structure has been expanded, you can assign an alias name to the substructure so that you can continue to access it as an independent element. A suffix which is added to the substructure's field name prevents conflicts between substructures which have identical field names.

```
INFOTYPES nnnn
  [NAME name]
  [OCCURS roll_area]
  [MODE Mode]
  [VALID FROM first TO last].
```

You use this statement to define an *Infotype*. An infotype can be simply described as an internal table that corresponds to a database table. Infotypes are only used occasionally in special applications.

INITIALIZATION.

This is an event statement used in reporting. The system processes the event you enter once at the beginning of a report immediately after it creates the parameters.

```
INSERT table | *table | (field_with_tablename)
  [CLIENT SPECIFIED]
  [FROM workarea].
```

You use this statement to add a record to a database table. You can transfer the table's name as a direct value from a field with appropriate contents. The system takes the data either from the header row of the table or from workarea, which can be unstructured. If you use this variant of the command, the record must also have a unique key with reference to the table and all UNIQUE indexes. You can use the CLIENT SPECIFIED addition to switch off automatic client processing.

```
INSERT table | (field_with_tablename) [CLIENT SPECIFIED]
  FROM TABLE itab [ACCEPTING DUPLICATE KEYS].
```

You use this Open SQL statement to add several records to a database table. You can transfer the table's name as a direct value from a field with appropriate contents. The system takes the records you want to add from the itab internal table. The way this table is created must fulfil the same requirements as the workarea in both previous variants of the statement. You use the ACCEPTING addition to prevent the system generating a run-time error if you attempt to add records that have identical keys. Once again, you can use CLIENT SPECIFIED to switch off automatic client processing.

```
INSERT [[workarea | INITIAL LINE] INTO] itab [INDEX index].
```

You use this command to add a record to a standard-type internal table. The system either takes the data from a specific work area that you have specified or from the table's header row. If required, you can use INITIAL LINE to add a record that is filled with initial values. You use the INDEX addition to set the position in which it is to be added. The first record has index number 1. You can use the table in a LOOP if you do not want to specify the index. If you do this, the new record is added in front of the current record.

```
INSERT [[workarea | INITIAL LINE] INTO] TABLE itab.
```

You also use this command to add a record to an internal table. However, this command works generically and can therefore be used for all types of internal table. The table type of the table you want to process defines how the new record is added.

```
INSERT LINES OF itab_1
  [FROM first] [TO last]
  INTO itab2 [INDEX position].
```

You use this command to add records from the `itab1` internal table to the `itab2` internal table. You can enter additional parameters to specify exactly which records are to be transferred, as well as the position at which they are to be added. The `itab2` table must be a standard-type table.

```
INSERT LINES OF itab_1
  [FROM first] [TO last]
  INTO TABLE itab2.
```

You use this statement to add records generically from `itab1` to `itab2`. In this case, `itab2` can be any type of table.

```
INSERT { field_x } INTO fieldgroup.
```

You use this statement to add data fields from a field group which you have previously declared using `FIELD-GROUPS`. This procedure does not involve any data transfers, it merely defines which data fields should belong to the field group. Although according to SAP documentation this statement is an operational statement and not a declarative statement, the task it performs is a comparable task to a declaration.

```
INSERT INTO table | (field_with_tablename)
  [CLIENT SPECIFIED]
  VALUES workarea.
```

This is an Open SQL statement. You use this statement to add a record to a database table. The system takes the data from `workarea`, in accordance with the table's structure. Although the work area itself can be unstructured, it must contain all the data in the correct sequence and it must have the correct length. You can transfer the table's name as a direct value from a field with the appropriate content. The system will only add the record if neither the table nor any of the `UNIQUE` indexes contain a record that has the same key. You can use `CLIENT SPECIFIED` to switch off automatic client processing. If you do this, you must fill the `MANDT` field with data, just like any other key field in the program.

```
INSERT REPORT program FROM itab.
```

You use this statement to add a program to the global programs set. The system reads the source code from the `itab` internal table.

```
INSERT TEXTPOOL program FROM itab LANGUAGE language.
```

You use this statement to add text elements for the program in the language you set in the global programs set. The system takes the texts from an internal table.

```
INTERFACE interface
  [SUPPORTING REMOTE INVOCATION] |
  [DEFERRED] |
  [LOAD].
```

You use this statement to define an interface within ABAP Objects. The statement describes the interface without defining actual methods in it. You use the ENDINTERFACE statement to close the define.

You use the SUPPORTING REMOTE INVOCATION addition to call the interface methods remotely.

Both the other additions merely return controlling information to the runtime system. If you use these additions, you will not create a true definition. The statement stands alone and does not introduce a block that is concluded with ENDINTERFACE.

The DEFERRED addition only introduces the interface's name. The definition takes place later. You use LOAD to load the definition of an interface which already exists globally.

INTERFACE-POOL.

This statement is used to introduce an interface pool. The class builder stores global interfaces in it. You never need to code this statement manually because it is generated by the class builder.

INTERFACES *interface*.

You use this statement to add an interface to a class or to another interface.

LEAVE.

You use this statement to close an application (transaction, dialog, report) that you called with CALL and then continue the calling application with the statement after the CALL call.

LEAVE LIST-PROCESSING.

You use this statement to close a list-processing session that is embedded in a dialog and was started with LEAVE TO LIST-PROCESSING.

LEAVE program.

You use this statement to leave the current program.

LEAVE SCREEN.

You use this statement to finish processing the current screen program and to execute the screen program that was set in the screen program attributes, or that you entered previously with SET SCREEN.

LEAVE TO LIST-PROCESSING [AND RETURN TO SCREEN *screen_number*].

You use this statement to temporarily activate list-processing within a dialog application. After you close list-processing, the system executes the PBO part of the current screen program or the PBO part of the screen program that you set with RETURN TO SCREEN.

LEAVE TO SCREEN *screen_number*.

You use this statement to finish processing the current screen program and to execute the screen program whose number you have specified.

LEAVE TO TRANSACTION *transaction_code*
  [**AND SKIP FIRST SCREEN**].

You use this statement to leave the current transaction and start a new transaction. The SKIP addition ensures that the system does not process the first screen program of the transaction you have called on screen if all the input fields of this screen program have been filled with the appropriate values by the appropriate functions.

LOAD-OF-PROGRAM.

This is an event statement. The system always processes this event when a program of type 1 (online report), type M (module pool), type F (function group) or S (subroutine pool) is loaded into an internal mode.

LOCAL *field*.

You can only use this statement within subroutines, i.e. after a FORM statement. It saves the current contents of field and recreates them after you leave the subroutine. For this reason, you can handle the global field like a local data field in a subroutine. You can make assignments to this field, but they have no effect outside the subroutine.

LOOP.
  ABAP statements ...
ENDLOOP.

In this loop, you can use all the records in an application's EXTRACT dataset to provide the data in the fields of specific field groups.

LOOP AT *itab*
  [**INTO** *workarea*]
  [**FROM** *first*]
  [**TO** *last*]
  [**WHERE** *condition*]
  [**ASSIGNING** <*field symbol*>]
  [**TRANSPORTING NO FIELDS**].
    ABAP statements
ENDLOOP.

This loop uses an internal table to provide records either in the table's header row or in the work area you specify with INTO. Alternatively, the system sets a field symbol on the appropriate record in the table's memory area. In this case, you do not have to copy the data. However any modifications to the data are then carried out immediately in the table and not in a separate work area. You use the FROM or TO additions to restrict the loop run to the corresponding records. The system starts counting from 1. You can use WHERE and a logical condition to select the records you want to process in the loop. The TRANSPORTING NO FIELDS addition prevents the system from transporting the data out of the selected record into the work area.

LOOP AT SCREEN.
  ABAP statements ...
ENDLOOP.

You can only use this statement in the PBO module of a screen program. It displays the field descriptions of the fields in the current screen program one after the other in the predefined `SCREEN` header row. In this case, you can process `SCREEN` like an internal table. The system uses `MODIFY` to write any changes to the header row to the `SCREEN` internal table. These changes become effective when the screen program is output. The release status defines how the structure is created.

```
LOOP AT table.
  ABAP statements ...
ENDLOOP.
```

This statement is obsolete and is now only supported for reasons of compatibility. It was formerly used to process special database tables line by line.

```
MESSAGE tnnn[(class)]
  [WITH parameter_1 ... parameter_4]
  [RAISING exception]
  [INTO field].
```

You use this statement to output message nnn, which has message type t. In the message text, you can replace up to four of the placeholders shown with the & character with the `parameter_1` to `parameter_4` parameters. The message class is usually defined in the `REPORT` or `PROGRAM` statement. If you do not want to use the default settings, you must enter the message class in round brackets after the message number. The `RAISING` addition triggers an exception in the function module. If this happens, the system merely displays the message if the calling program does not process the exception. If you use the `INTO` addition, this also prevents you sending a message. This addition has the effect that the message text with the parameters you added is written to the field.

```
MESSAGE ID class TYPE typ NUMBER number
  [WITH parameter_1 ... parameter_4]
  [RAISING exception].
```

This statement corresponds to the previous statement. However, you must enter the three values used to identify message (class, type and number) individually. In this statement, they can also be set dynamically.

```
METHOD method.
```

You use this statement to implement a method within a class in ABAP Objects.

```
METHODS method
  [ IMPORTING ( [[VALUE | REFERENCE](parameter)] | parameter
      [ TYPE type | LIKE field ]
      [ OPTIONAL  | DEFAULT default ] ) . . . ]
  [ EXPORTING ( [[VALUE | REFERENCE](parameter)] | parameter
      [ TYPE type | LIKE field]
      [ OPTIONAL  | DEFAULT default ] ) . . . ]
  [ CHANGING  ( [[VALUE | REFERENCE](parameter)] | parameter
```

```
    [ TYPE type | LIKE field ]
    [ OPTIONAL | DEFAULT default ] ) . . . ]
[ RETURNING VALUE(parameter)
    [ TYPE type | LIKE field ] ]
[ EXCEPTIONS { exception } ]
[ FOR EVENT event OF class]
[ ABSTRACT ]
[ FINAL ]
[ REDEFINITION ].
```

You use this command to declare a method within a class or an interface in ABAP Objects. You only define the method's interface in the declaration. You use the IMPORTING, EXPORTING and CHANGING parameters to define the transfer parameters. You can use the RETURNING addition to specify one return code that the calling program can then evaluate in a special way. You use EXCEPTIONS to inform the calling program about exceptions to the method. Use ABSTRACT to mark the method as abstract, i.e. a method which does not function. You must overwrite this kind of method. The FINAL addition prevents a method from being overwritten. REDEFINITION means that an existing method should be overwritten. In this case, you cannot enter any more interface parameters because you cannot change the interface by overwriting it.

You use the FOR EVENT addition to declare a method that is to process an event.

```
MODIFY table | *table | (field_with_tablename)
  [FROM workarea]
  [CLIENT SPECIFIED].
```

You use this command to modify a record in a database table or to add a new record to it. You can enter this record's name either statically or dynamically. The system takes the data from the table's header row or from a specific work area that you have specified. The contents of the key fields are used to identify the record. You can use the CLIENT SPECIFIED addition to switch off automatic client field processing. This field, just like all the other fields, must contain a correct value. This ensures that you can process client-dependent tables for more than one client. The MODIFY command can identify whether an existing record is to be modified or if a new record is to be added. As this check can have a negative effect on performance, you should only use MODIFY if you cannot make a clear decision to use INSERT or UPDATE in the program.

```
MODIFY table | (field_with_tablename) FROM TABLE itab
  [CLIENT SPECIFIED].
```

This command works in the same way as the previous version of the MODIFY command. However, this one takes the data from an internal table so that you can modify several records with just one command.

```
MODIFY table | *table VERSION field_with_tablename.
```

This command is obsolete. It allows you to enter a table name dynamically. Otherwise, it works in the same way as the first version of the MODIFY command.

```
MODIFY itab [FROM workarea]
  [ INDEX index ]
  [ TRANSPORTING fieldlist | (field_with_fieldname)
    [ WHERE condition ]].
```

You use this statement to change the records of an internal standard-type table. You cannot add new records with this statement, unlike the MODIFY command for database tables. The system either takes the data from the table's header row or from a work area that you have specified with the FROM addition. You can use the TRANSPORTING addition to select the fields you want to transfer. The system does not transfer any fields from the table to the work area unless they are listed in the field list. You can specify the fields as constants or dynamically.

You can define the different ways in which a record or records are to be processed. If you do not use the INDEX or WHERE addition, the command can only be used within a LOOP through an internal table. In this case, only the current record is changed. Outside the LOOP, you can use INDEX to specify a record number to identify a specific record. This index can, for example, have been defined during a previous READ statement. You can use the WHERE addition to carry out a mass update of the data in an internal table. In all the records of the internal table that fulfil the conditions, you can set the fields named by TRANSPORTING to the current value of the corresponding fields in the work area or header row. Because this results in identical field contents in several records, it is essential that you use the TRANSPORTING option.

```
MODIFY TABLE itab
  [FROM workarea]
  [TRANSPORTING fieldlist | (field_with_fieldname)].
```

You use this generic command to modify records in an internal table. This command works with all three types of internal table.

```
MODIFY LINE line
  [INDEX level]
  [LINE FORMAT   { formats } ]
  [LINE VALUE FROM record]
  [FIELD VALUE   { target FROM source } ]
  [FIELD FORMAT { field formats } ].
```

You should only use this command when you process lists. It modifies the line line in the current list or the list in the level list level. You can use the LINE FORMAT addition to assign one or more new formats to the line. The formats correspond to those in the FORMAT command. You use FIELD VALUE to assign a new value to a field that was written to the list. You use LINE VALUE to change the entire line. The changes apply immediately in the list. You can use FIELD FORMAT to assign specific formats to a particular field.

```
MODIFY LINE i ( OF CURRENT PAGE | OF PAGE page )
  [LINE FORMAT   { formats } ]
  [LINE VALUE FROM record]
  [FIELD VALUE   { target FROM source} ]
  [FIELD FORMAT { field formats } ].
```

You use this command to change the line you enter in the current list. When you do this, the system's line-counting function is restricted to the page you specified with OF PAGE. To select the current page, use OF CURRENT PAGE instead of OF PAGE. You cannot change lines in other lists.

```
MODIFY CURRENT LINE
    [LINE FORMAT   { formats } ]
    [FIELD VALUE   { target FROM source} ]
    [LINE VALUE FROM record]
    [FIELD FORMAT { field formats } ].
```

You use this command to change the format of the current line (this is the last line read by the line selection function or by READ LINE). The additions correspond to those of both previous variants.

```
MODIFY SCREEN.
```

You use this command to write the modified attributes of a screen program's fields within a LOOP AT SCREEN loop to the screen program description.

```
MODULE modulname [ INPUT | OUTPUT ].
```

You use this command to define a module that you can call in the flow logic of a screen program. Use ENDMODULE to close the module. In the PBO phase of a screen program, the system only searches for and executes modules that have the OUTPUT addition. In the PAI phase, the only modules that are effective are those that do not have an addition or those with the INPUT addition.

```
MOVE source[+offset][(length)] | method() TO
    target[+offset][(length)]
    [PERCENTAGE percentage [LEFT | RIGHT]].
```

You use this statement to transfer the contents of the source field into the target field. When this happens, both the source and target can have static or dynamic entries defining an offset within the field and a length. You can also use this statement to copy complex data structures and tables. A point (not a comma) is always used as the decimal point. If you use the object-oriented extension to the SAP System, you can use the RETURNING parameter of a method as the source value.

The PERCENTAGE addition expects the source and target fields to be C-type fields. It transfers the subset of characters specified with percentage from the source field to the target field. If you have not defined any length or offset entries, the system accesses the source field no matter what its current contents, using the length defined. You can use the LEFT or RIGHT addition to define how the transferred character string is aligned in the target field. The default value is LEFT. You do not have to program this addition.

```
MOVE ref1 ?TO ref2.
```

You use this statement to assign one object or data reference to another.

```
MOVE-CORRESPONDING source TO target.
```

You use this statement to copy all the fields from the `source` structure into the fields with the same name in the `target` structure. The system ignores fields which are not present in both structures.

MULTIPLY *field* **BY** *factor*.

You use this statement to multiply the contents of `field` by `factor` and to store the result in `field`.

MULTIPLY-CORRESPONDING *record_1* **BY** *record_2*.

You use this command to generate a simple `MULTIPLY BY` statement for all fields, which are present in both `record_1` and `record_2`. You also use this command to execute this `MULTIPLY BY` statement. Here, the fields in `record_1` act as source and target fields. The system takes the factor from `record_2`.

NEW-LINE [**NO-SCROLLING**].

You should only use this statement when you are processing lists. It inserts a line feed. You use the `NO-SCROLLING` addition to define that the following output line cannot be scrolled horizontally. Its position does not change when you browse horizontally through the list. This setting only applies to the next output line and is then automatically deactivated. If you do not use an addition, the subsequent line can be moved.

NEW-PAGE [*primary_options* [*secondary_options*]].

You use the `NEW-PAGE` statement to start a new page in list processing. You cannot create empty pages, because this command only comes into effect when you generate some actual output in the list. There are many other additions that you can use to create the list or to control the printer when you create printouts. The additions for this command are listed in Table 9.6.

Table 9.6   Additions for the NEW-PAGE command

Addition	Description
NO-TITLE	Title lines not output from the next page onwards
WITH-TITLE	Output the title line
NO-HEADING	Stop output of column headings
WITH-HEADING	Output column headings
LINE-COUNT lines	New line count from the next page onwards
LINE-SIZE columns	New list width from the next page onwards
PRINT ON secondary options	Interpret all output that follows as printer instructions. There are 25 different secondary additions that can be used here
PRINT OFF	End the printer control that was introduced with PRINT ON

NODES *node* **TYPE** *type* .

This command is only suitable for use with logical databases. The nodes of a logical database can have different types. In a report you use the NODES command to declare the name of a node in the logical database. If you do this, you can now use the GET command to transfer data from the logical database. If the hierarchy nodes in the logical database consist of a Data Dictionary table, you can also use the TABLES command.

ON CHANGE OF *field* [**OR** *field_2*] .
  ABAP statements ...
ENDON .

You use this statement in SELECT loops or GET processing blocks. It has the effect that the system only executes statements which lie between the ON and ENDON statements if the contents of field have changed since the last time the command was executed. You can use the OR addition to define as many additional fields as you require that will also trigger statement processing.

OPEN CURSOR [**WITH HOLD**] *cursor* **FOR SELECT** *select_statement* .

You use this statement to open the database cursor for the table you specified in the SELECT statement. The cursor must be of the CURSOR type, and declared with TYPE CURSOR.

OPEN DATASET *filename*
  [**FOR OUTPUT** | **FOR INPUT** | **FOR APPENDING**]
  [**IN BINARY MODE** | **IN TEXT MODE**]
  [**AT POSITION** *pos*]
  [**TYPE** *attribut*]
  [**MESSAGE** *textfield*]
  [**FILTER** *statement*] .

You use this statement to open the specified file. This is a file which is present at operating system level on the application server. For this reason, the file name must meet the requirements of the particular operating system and, if necessary, contain disk drive and path details. You use one of the three FOR additions to define whether the system is to read data from the file, write data to the file or append data to the end of the file. You use the IN TEXT MODE addition to ensure that the system always reads a complete line when it reads data in the file. The line end is identified by an end-of-line end character. Different operating systems use different end-of-line end characters. Each time the system writes data to the file, an end-of-line character is automatically added after the data. You can use the IN BINARY MODE addition (default) to suppress any of the various data- processing actions. You use AT POSITION to set any position in the file as the start position. You use TYPE to transfer operating system-dependent attributes to the system. If you use the MESSAGE option, the operating system returns an error message in the field you specify if an error occurs when the file is opened. The statement field in the FILTER addition tells you which operating system command will process the data.

OVERLAY *field_1* **WITH** *field_2* [**ONLY** *field_3*].

You use this statement to transfer the contents of field_2 line by line to field_1. However, this only happens if the positions in field_1 have a blank in them. You can use ONLY to define a different quantity of characters, that are to be overwritten in field_1. The system processes all the relevant fields as character fields (type C), no matter what type they actually are.

PACK *source* **TO** *target*.

You use this statement to pack (compress) the contents of the source field and store them in the target field.

PARAMETERS *parameter* [*option*].

When you process a list, the system declares a parameter which is displayed on the selection screen. You can use a range of additions to set specific characteristics for a parameter. These additions are listed in Table 9.7.

Table 9.7   PARAMETERS statement additions

Addition	Description
DEFAULT value	The system fills the parameter with a default value before it displays the selection screen
TYPE type	The parameter field is assigned the specified data type
DECIMALS decimal_places	This shows the number of decimal places for P-type parameters
LIKE field	The system derives the characteristics of the parameter field from an existing field
LIKE (namefield)	The system derives the characteristics of the parameter field from an existing field, whose name is transferred dynamically
MEMORY ID G/S-parameter	The parameter field in the selection screen is linked to a Get/Set parameter
MATCHCODE OBJECT matchcode	A matchcode is linked to the parameter field of the selection screen
MODIF ID modification_group	The parameter field in the selection screen is given the modification group you specify as its attribute
NO-DISPLAY	The parameter does not appear in the selection screen. The system only transfers the parameter's value if you use SUBMIT
LOWER CASE	The system does not automatically convert the data to upper-case letters

Table 9.7   Continued

OBLIGATORY	You must make an entry in the selection screen for this parameter (mandatory entry)
AS CHECKBOX	The parameter is displayed as a check box
RADIOBUTTON GROUP group	The parameter is displayed as a radio button within the group you specify
FOR NODE node	The system assigns a database-specific parameter to a table (only in the access program of a logical database)
FOR TABLE table	The system assigns a database-specific parameter to a table (only in the access program of a logical database)
AS SEARCH PATTERN	The system uses a complex object to accept the data from a complex pattern
AS MATCHCODE STRUCTURE	This is a database-specific parameter that is used for selection using a matchcode
VALUE REQUEST	For database-specific parameters only. You can use the AT SELECTION SCREEN ON VALUE REQUEST event to assign an input help text to the parameter
HELP REQUEST	For database-specific parameters only. You can use the AT SELECTION SCREEN ON HELP REQUEST event to assign a specific help text to the parameter
VISIBLE LENGTH length	You use this addition to set the width of an input field on the selection screen
VALUE CHECK	The system checks the value you specify against a check table. However, before this happens, you must use LIKE to derive the parameter from a Data Dictionary field
USER-COMMAND command	Triggers command if the checkbox or radio button parameters are clicked on

```
PERFORM [subroutine | index]
  [ (program) |
    IN PROGRAM program   |
    OF { subroutine_n } |
    ON COMMIT [LEVEL index] ]
  [TABLES    { itab_n } ]
  [USING     { parameter_n } ]
  [CHANGING { parameter_n } ]
  [IF FOUND].
```

You use this statement to call the subroutine you defined with FORM. You use the TABLES, USING and CHANGING additions to transfer internal tables or field parameters as current parameters.

You can use the (`program`) or `IN PROGRAM` additions to call subroutines from other programs. You can also transfer the program and subroutine name dynamically, using `IN PROGRAM`. You can use `IF FOUND` to prevent any runtime errors that may occur if the external subroutine you called is not available. You use `OF` to use an index to address the subroutine you want to call. The subroutines concerned follow `OF`. After `PERFORM` there is a data field, that must contain a valid index, instead of a name.

If you are using `COMMIT WORK`, you can use the `ON COMMIT` addition to execute the subroutine. If you do this, you cannot transfer a parameter. For this reason, the data must be stored in internal fields in the program or in the global memory until it is updated. You can use an optional index to define the sequence in which the subroutines are called for a commit.

POSITION *column*.

You use this statement to set the column position for the next output when you output lists.

PRINT-CONTROL [*option*].

You use the following additions to make different settings for the print formats of subsequent output lines. The various additions, some of which can have more options, are listed in Table 9.8.

Table 9.8   PRINT-CONTROL command additions

Addition	Description
CPI	Sets the number of characters per inch
LPI	Sets the number of lines per inch
SIZE	Sets the font size
COLOR	Sets the output colour if you are using a colour printer (BLACK, RED, BLUE, GREEN, YELLOW or PINK)
LEFT MARGIN	Sets the left margin
FONT	Sets the font
FUNCTION	Addresses a function directly
LINE	Define the output line that is to be used for PRINT-CONTROL
POSITION	Define the column, in the output line that has been set with LINE, for which PRINT-CONTROL is to be effective

PRINT-CONTROL INDEX-LINE *field*.

You use this statement to output the contents `field` as an invisible index line. This index line is only required for optical archiving. The field must have a predefined structure and be filled with specially- prepared values.

PRIVATE SECTION.

You use this statement in ABAP Objects to introduce the private component section in a class definition. None of the elements declared in this section is visible outside the class.

PROGRAM.

You use this statement to introduce a new program. It is equivalent to the REPORT statement and can be used as an alternative. You can use the same additions as for REPORT. When the system generates program cores automatically, it uses REPORT for reports and PROGRAM for module pools.

PROTECTED SECTION.

You use this statement in ABAP Objects to introduce the protected component section in a class definition. You can only access the elements declared in this section from the current class and from all subclasses.

PROVIDE { {*field_x*} **FROM** *itab*} **BETWEEN** *first* **AND** *last*.
   ABAP statements ...
ENDPROVIDE.

You use this statement to provide the contents of the fields you set in the internal tables in ranges. The system then executes the statements between PROVIDE and ENDPROVIDE for each interval.

PUBLIC SECTION.

You use this statement in ABAP Objects to introduce the public component section in a class definition. There are no restrictions on accessing the elements declared in this section from outside the section.

PUT *node* | *<node>*.

You can only use this statement in a logical database access program. It triggers the GET event in the corresponding report. The system then executes all the PUT subroutines of all the subordinate nodes if there are GET events in the report for these nodes. If the node is a dynamic dictionary-type node, the system accesses a field symbol (<node>) instead of setting a node (node) statically.

RAISE exception.

You use this command to trigger an exception within a function module. If this exception is not processed in the calling program, the system generates a runtime error.

RAISE EVENT *event* [**EXPORTING** { *parameter* = *field* }].

You use this statement to trigger an event within ABAP Objects. You use special methods to receive and evaluate this event.

RANGES *selection_table* **FOR** *field* [**OCCURS** *n*].

You use this statement to define a selection table for the field structure you specify. This table has the same structure as the selection table created with SELECT-OPTIONS. In the program, you can use the table like a selection. However, the tables you define with RANGES, also known as *ranges tables*, do not appear in selection screens. Instead, you must enter the values for a valid selection manually in the program. If necessary, you can enter an OCCURS parameter, to modify the table's memory area to meet the actual requirements.

READ CURRENT LINE
  [FIELD VALUE {*source* **INTO** *target*}**]**
  [LINE VALUE INTO *record*]**.**

You use this statement to reread the current line in the list (selected through line selection or line READ LINE). You use FIELD VALUE to store the fields that have already been read in fields that are not the original fields. You use LINE VALUE to store entire lines that have already been read in fields that are not the original fields.

READ DATASET *filename* **INTO** *field* **[LENGTH** *length*]**.**

You use this statement to read a record from an operating system file that you have opened with OPEN and then make this data available in the field you specify. If you have opened the file in binary mode, the system reads the number of characters required to fill the target field. For this reason, the target field should have the same structure as the stored data. If you have opened the file in text mode, the command reads one line each time. This can lead to characters being lost if the target field is shorter than the line being read. You can use the LENGTH addition to return the number of characters that were actually read in the length field.

READ LINE *line_number*
  [INDEX *list*]
  [FIELD VALUE {*source* **INTO** *target*}**]**
  [LINE VALUE INTO *record*]
  [OF CURRENT PAGE | OF PAGE *page*]**.**

You use this statement to read a specific line (that you identify by its line number) from a list. If you do not use any additions the system counts all the lines. Both the PAGE additions ensure that the system only counts the lines on a particular page. This page is either the current page or one that you specify. If you do not use the INDEX addition to select a list level, the system reads the current list. If you use the FIELD VALUE addition, the system does not return the field contents of the list line to their original fields. Instead, it returns them to other internal fields in the program that you specify. You can use the LINE VALUE addition to do this for an entire line.

READ REPORT *program* **INTO** *itab*.

You use this statement to read the source code of a specific program in the itab internal table. In protected systems, this command only returns the source code of non-SAP programs.

READ TABLE *table*.

This command is obsolete. It has now been replaced by the SELECT statement, which performs the same function (reading a record in a database table).

```
READ TABLE itab [INTO record]
  [ WITH KEY {field = key} | = key | key [BINARY SEARCH] |
    INDEX index]
  [ASSIGNING <field_symbol>]
  [COMPARING fieldlist | ALL FIELDS]
  [TRANSPORTING fieldlist | NO field].
```

You use this statement to read a record from a standard-type internal table. The system returns the result either in the table's header row or in a work area that you specify with INTO. If you did not use TRANSPORTING to select specific fields, the system transfers all the fields. If you only want to find one record (check if it exists or find its index), you can save processing time by using TRANSPORTING NO FIELDS to prevent the system from transferring values.

You select the record you want to read in a variety of ways. You can use INDEX to specify the record number. You can use the various WITH KEY additions to define a search key, either field by field or by defining a work area with several key values. If you use WITH KEY, you can also use the BINARY SEARCH addition to speed up the search if the table has been presorted according to the key you are using. In this case, the statement carries out a binary search instead of a sequential search. The default setting of the READ command (without the WITH KEY addition) expects the key to be in the header row of the internal table. In this case, the key consists of all the header row fields that are not I-, F- or P-type fields and whose contents are not blank.

You use the COMPARING addition to carry out an additional comparison between the fields of the record that has been read and the header row. This comparison does not prevent the system transferring the record; it merely sets the SY-SUBRC system field. This comparison is useful if you are checking non-key fields.

If you use the ASSIGNING option to assign a field symbol, you do not have to copy the data into a work area or a header row. Instead, the system sets a field symbol directly on the record within the data area of the internal table. This means that any changes to the record made through the field symbol come into effect immediately.

This command is only still supported for reasons of compatibility. You can use any of the generic variants instead, without causing any problems.

```
READ TABLE itab
  [ [FROM record] |
    [WITH TABLE KEY {field = value}] |
    [WITH KEY {field = value} [BINARY SEARCH] ] |
    [INDEX index] ]
  [INTO record]
  [ASSIGNING <field_symbol>]
  [COMPARING fieldlist | ALL FIELDS]
  [TRANSPORTING fieldlist | NO FIELDS].
```

You can also use this command to read a record in an internal table. However, this command operates generically and can therefore process any table type. Because you have to define a key to access sorted or hash tables, you can use FROM to create a reference to a record that contains the required key. You can of course also use the WITH clause to transfer the key. If you do this, you must ensure that you use the entire key that has been defined using WITH TABLE KEY in the table definition. If you use WITH KEY, you can use any field in your search.

READ TEXTPOOL *program* **INTO** *itab* **LANGUAGE** *language.*

You use this statement to read the specified *program*'s text elements in the specified *language* in an internal table.

RECEIVE RESULTS FROM FUNCTION *function*
   [**KEEPING TASK**]
   [**IMPORTING**   { *parameter* = *field* }]
   [**TABLES**   { *parameter* = *itab* }]
   [**EXCEPTIONS** [{ *exception* = *value* }]
              [**OTHERS** = *value*]
              [**ERROR_MESSAGE** = *value*]].

You use this command to query the return values of an RFC function module that has been called asynchronously. If you use this command, you must also use a special program structure and ensure that you meet a few specific conditions.

REFRESH *itab.*

You use this statement to refresh the itab internal table. The system deletes all the records contained in this table. However, the header row remains unchanged.

REFRESH CONTROL *control* **FROM SCREEN** *screen.*

You use this statement to reset the control element, defined with the CONTROLS statement, in a specific screen program.

REFRESH SCREEN.

The REFRESH SCREEN command has become obsolete and you should use the SET USER-COMMAND instead. This command was used to refresh the current screen program after it had received an RFC event. This command has the same effect as when you press (Enter). You should only use this command together with the RECEIVE RESULTS FROM FUNCTION command. The REFRESH SCREEN command has become obsolete and you should use the SET USER-COMMAND instead.

REJECT [*table*].

You use this command to stop processing the current record in the current database table. The system continues processing with the next record. If you enter a specific file name, the system processes the next record in this table. This type of call is very useful, for example, as part of GET processing in logical databases. The table you specify must be present on the same (or higher) hierarchical level as the current table.

REPLACE *pattern_1* **WITH** *pattern_2* **INTO** *field* [**LENGTH** *length*].

You use this command to process character strings. The system treats all the fields involved as C-type fields, no matter what their actual type is. In the field target field, the first occurrence of `pattern_1` is replaced by `pattern_2`. The system also takes subsequent blanks into consideration. You can prevent this by using the `LENGTH` addition to define the appropriate length of the `pattern_1` search pattern.

REPORT *program*
  [**NO STANDARD PAGE HEADING**]
  [**LINE-SIZE** *number_of_columns*]
  [**LINE-COUNT** *number_of_lines*[(*number_of_footer_lines*)]]
  [**MESSAGE-ID** *message_class*]
  [**DEFINING DATABASE** *logical_database*].

You use this statement to introduce a report. You can use the optional additions to define some characteristics of the report. Use NO STANDARD PAGE HEADING to switch off output of the standard page header. Use the LINE-SIZE addition to define the list width in characters. The maximum number of characters is 255. If you do not use this addition, the system uses the current window size when it runs the report to define the page width. In some cases, this can affect the list's structure. You use LINE-COUNT to specify the page length and the area to be reserved for any footers. The default value for footers is 0. If you also do not define the page length, the NEW-PAGE command is the only way of triggering page breaks. If you want the system to output messages in the report, you can use MESSAGE-ID to set the name of the message class that is required for the simplified form of the MESSAGE command.

You only need to use the DEFINING DATABASE addition in the access programs of a logical database. As these programs are generated automatically, you do not usually have to program this addition manually.

RESERVE *number_of_lines* **LINES**.

You use this statement to trigger a page feed in list processing if the number of lines you specify is no longer available on the current page.

ROLLBACK WORK.

You use this statement to reverse all the changes made to the database since the last COMMIT WORK statement.

SCROLL LIST [**INDEX** *index*]
  [**LINE** *line*] **TO FIRST PAGE** |
  [**LINE** *line*] **TO LAST PAGE** |
  [**LINE** *line*] **TO PAGE** *page* |
  [**LINE** *line*] **TO COLUMN** *column* |
  [*page* **PAGES**] **FORWARD** |
  [*page* **PAGES**] **BACKWARD** |
  [**BY** *characters* **PLACES**] **LEFT** |
  [**BY** *characters* **PLACES**] **RIGHT**.

You use this command in list processing to execute program-controlled scrolling through the current list extract. The SCROLL command is only complete when used together with one of the additions (TO FIRST PAGE ... RIGHT). You can see what effect these additions have from their names.

In addition to the obligatory additions there are other optional additions. You can use the INDEX addition to define the list's number (list level). The other additions define the direction and range of scrolling. You use LINE to specify the line on the target page, to which you want to move. You use PAGES to define the number of pages through which the extract is to move when you use the FORWARD and BACKWARD additions. In the same way, you can use the BY PLACES addition to define the number of characters through which the extract is to move when you roll the data horizontally with LEFT or RIGHT.

```
SEARCH [ field | itab ] FOR string
   [ABBREVIATED]
   [STARTING AT first]
   [ENDING AT last]
   [AND MARK].
```

When you use this statement, the system searches through the field or internal table (the entire table, but not the header row) you have specified to see whether the character string you have entered is present. The character string can contain the sample character '*' as a placeholder for any character, either at the beginning or at the end. If you use the ABBREVIATED addition, the command finds the search pattern even if the characters you are looking for are separated from each other by other characters in the search field. You use STARTING or ENDING to restrict the search to the area you enter in the search field. These additions also show the lines to be searched for in internal tables. You use the AND MARK addition to convert the character string into upper-case letters when it is found in the search field or in the internal table.

The system handles all the fields involved, especially the records of the internal table, as C-type fields.

```
SELECT result [target]
   [INTO fieldlist]
   FROM source
   [WHERE condition]
   [GROUP BY fieldlist]
   [HAVING condition]
   [ORDER BY sortorder].
   [ ABAP statements ]
[ ENDSELECT. ]
```

You use the SELECT statement to read records from database tables. It consists of several clauses that define how the statement behaves. The functions of the SELECT statement are heavily dependent on the current release Releaselevel. In its basic form, the SELECT statement is a loop statement which must be closed with the ENDSELECT statement.

Because of the size of the statement, the individual clauses are described separately from each other. However, you cannot use a meta-description to fully describe the correct syntax of the SELECT statement, because there are strong dependencies between the clauses.

The SELECT clause

```
SELECT [[SINGLE [FOR UPDATE]] | [DISTINCT]] fieldlist | (itab)
```

These options of the SELECT clause specify the output data type (single record or data volume) as well as the fields that the system returns. If you use the SINGLE addition, the system returns a single record. If you use this addition, you do not use the ENDSELECT statement. You must use the WHERE clause to make the record uniquely identifiable. You use the optional FOR UPDATE addition to block the record from being processed by anyone else.

You use the DISTINCT addition to suppress identical output records. If you use the SELECT clause, you must enter a structure which contains all the fields that are to be returned. This structure can consist of one asterisk as a symbol for all the fields or a list of fields or aggregate expressions.

The INTO clause

```
INTO    record |
        (field [,field]) |
        [CORRESPONDING FIELDS OF] workarea |
        [CORRESPONDING FIELDS OF] TABLE itab
            [PACKAGE SIZE number_of_records ]]
        [APPENDING [CORRESPONDING FIELDS OF] TABLE itab
            [PACKAGE SIZE number_of_records ]]
```

You use the INTO clause to define the target for the records that have been read. Depending on the SELECT clause field list, this can be a work area (a structure), a list of individual fields or an internal table. The system deletes the target before it is overwritten. If you use internal tables, you must use the APPENDING clause instead of INTO. This allows the system to add data to the internal table. If you use the optional CORRESPONDING FIELDS additions, the system only transfers the contents of fields that have the same name.

You do not need ENDSELECT when you transfer the selection result, unless you have used the PACKAGE SIZE statement to predefine the maximum number of records that are to be written to the internal table. If you do this, the system carries out as many loops as necessary until all the records are read.

The FROM clause

```
FROM table [AS alias] |
    (field_with_tablename) |
    tab1 [INNER] JOIN tab2 ON condition |
    tab1 LEFT [OUTER] JOIN tab2 ON condition
    [CLIENT SPECIFIED] [BYPASSING BUFFER] [UP TO n ROWS]
```

The FROM clause like the SELECT clause is mandatory. It defines the table from which the system is to read data. You can enter the table name either statically or dynamically. You can also use three optional additions to define the details of the selection procedure. From a logical point of view, they do not entirely belong to the FROM clause. Their assignment to it is due to historical reasons. You use CLIENT SPECIFIED to switch off the automatic client-handling process. If you do this, you must evaluate the client field manually. You use the BYPASSING BUFFER addition to read the data directly from the database and ignore any buffers that may be present. You use UP TO n ROWS to define the number of records that are to be returned.

In the FROM clause you can also link several tables together. You do this by entering the keyword JOIN to define table links. You can also use what is known as an INNER JOIN to link two tables by means of a logical condition. The join result contains all the columns of the tables concerned. However the system only includes those records from tab1 for which a record exists in tab2 that fulfils the conditions you specified. If you use an OUTER JOIN, the join result contains all the records from tab1. If a suitable record is present, the system adds the data from tab2 to the records from tab1. If not, the rest of the fields are filled with zero.

The WHERE clause

`[FOR ALL ENTRIES IN` *itab_param* `] WHERE` *condition* `|`
`(`*itab_condition*`)`

The WHERE clause contains the logical condition that defines how records are selected from the table. You must either program the parameters directly in the logical condition or assign them through the contents of an internal table. You can either program the condition directly or transfer it through an internal table.

The GROUP BY clause

`GROUP BY` *fieldlist* `|` `(`*itab*`)`

You use GROUP BY to form groups of records that have identical attributes. The structure in this statement must correspond to the structure in the SELECT clause. You can also transfer the structure in an internal table.

The HAVING clause

`HAVING` *condition* `|` `(`*itab*`)`

The system applies the condition that was predefined with the HAVING clause to the records returned by the GROUP BY clause. You can also transfer the condition in an internal table.

The ORDER BY clause

`ORDER BY` *fieldlist* | `PRIMARY KEY`

The system uses the `ORDER BY` clause to sort the records that are to be output in accordance with the field list you specify or key if you have used the `PRIMARY KEY` addition instead of the field list.

`SELECT-OPTIONS` *selection* `FOR` *field* | *(namefield)*.

You should only use this statement in reports, to declare a selection table. Users can fill this table with values in a report's selection screen program. You can use a range of different parameters to modify the characteristics of the selection (see Table 9.9).

Table 9.9   SELECT-OPTIONS statement additions

Addition	Effect
DEFAULT ...	Set default value(s)
MEMORY ID	Set a global parameter as a default value
MATCHCODE OBJECT	Left-hand field in the selection program screen with matchcode
MODIF ID	Assign a modification group for attribute SCREEN-GROUP 1 to the screen fields of a selection
NO-DISPLAY	Selection does not appear on the selection screen
LOWER CASE	Distinguish between upper case and lower case
OBLIGATORY	The user must make an entry here
NO-EXTENSION	The user can only enter one line
NO INTERVALS	In the selection, the user can only enter single values. You cannot specify ranges
NO DATABASE SELECTION	The selection is not used in logical databases
VALUE REQUEST...	Permit value help that you have programmed yourself
HELP REQUEST...	Permit help that you have programmed yourself
VISIBLE LENGTH l en	Define the width of the input field in the input screen

`SELECTION-SCREEN BEGIN` | `END OF SCREEN` *screen*
    [`TITLE` *title*]
    [`AS WINDOW`].

You use this statement to define a selection screen that you can call using the `CALL SELECTION-SCREEN` statement. You can give the selection screen a title, which appears in the window's header row. You can use the AS WINDOW addition to call the selection screen as a modal dialog box.

SELECTION-SCREEN BEGIN | END OF SCREEN *screen* **AS SUBSCREEN**
   [*NESTING LEVEL level*]
   [*NO INTERVALS*] .

You use this statement to define a selection screen that can be included as a subscreen in other screen programs. You use the NESTING LEVEL addition to define the number of frames within a tabstrip. If you use NO INTERVALS, the fields for the HIGH parameter do not appear.

SELECTION-SCREEN *option.*

You use the SELECTION-SCREEN statement to structure the selection screen. For this reason, you should only use it in reports. If you use this statement, you must also use one of the options listed in Table 9.10.

Table 9.10   SELECTION-SCREEN command additions

Option	Effect
BEGIN OF LINE	All subsequently declared elements are arranged in one line
END OF LINE	Ends the declaration of a line
SKIP	Inserts blank lines
ULINE	Underscores a line
POSITION	Positions an element
COMMENT	Outputs a static text
PUSHBUTTON	Creates a pushbutton in the selection screen
BEGIN OF BLOCK	Beginning of a block, to which you can assign a frame
BEGIN OF TABBED BLOCK block FOR n LINES	Reserves a subscreen area for a tabstrip control
TAB (l en) register USER-COMMAND fcode	Creates tabs for a tabstrip control
END OF BLOCK	Ends the declaration of a block
FUNCTION KEY	Declares a pushbutton in the pushbutton line
BEGIN OF VERSION	Begins the declaration of a version of the selection screen
END OF VERSION	Ends a version declaration
EXCLUDE	Excludes elements from a version of a selection screen
DYNAMIC SELECTIONS FOR TABLE	NODE	Declares dynamic selections
FIELD SELECTION FOR TABLE	NODE	Selects the table fields used in field selections

SET BIT *n* **OF** *field* **TO** *value.*

You use this statement to set bit n in the field hexadecimal field (field type X or XSTRING). The system starts counting at 1. You use the TO addition to specify the value to which the bit is set (0 or 1).

SET BLANK LINES [**ON** | **OFF**].

You use this statement to define whether blank lines are to be output or not. The default setting is SET BLANK LINES OFF.

SET COUNTRY *country.*

You use this statement to change the country code. This affects the way decimal places and dates are displayed. The effect of this statement applies to more than one program.

SET CURSOR
    FIELD *field* [**OFFSET** *offset* | **LINE** *line*] |
    LINE *line* [**OFFSET** *offset*] | *column line.*

You use this statement to set the cursor to a particular position. The three possible additions specify the type of positioning. The FIELD addition requires a field as a parameter that contains the name of the field on which you want to place the cursor. If you use the OFFSET addition, you can enter a character position within the field. In lists or step loops, you must use the LINE addition to define the line you require, because field names have several meanings in this case.

As the primary addition, the LINE addition places the cursor on the specified line in a list or a step loop. You can also use OFFSET here to position the cursor within the line. In screen programs, you can set the cursor to any position by entering the line and column directly.

SET EXTENDED CHECK [**ON** | **OFF**].

This statement has no effect during program processing. It is merely evaluated by the editor's syntax check or by the SLIN check transaction. You use SET EXTENDED CHECK OFF to switch off the extended syntax check. Use SET EXTENDED CHECK ON to switch it on again.

SET HANDLER FOR [*ref*] [**ALL INSTANCES**] [ACTIVATION f].

You use this command in ABAP Objects to register the methods that will handle events.

SET HOLD DATA ON | **OFF**.

You use this command to switch special screen program characteristics on or off. If this function is switched on, the system saves the values entered in a screen program's fields and prompts them as default values when you next call this screen program.

SET LANGUAGE *language.*

You use this command to output language-specific elements in the new language. Its effect is restricted to the current program.

SET LEFT SCROLL-BOUNDARY [**COLUMN** *column*].

You use this statement to fix all columns to the left or to the right of the current position or the position on screen specified with COLUMN. Any columns you fix in this way are not affected when you scroll horizontally through the screen content.

SET LOCALE LANGUAGE *language*
  [**COUNTRY** *country*]
  [**MODIFIER** *modification*].

You use this statement to define the text environment for an application. The text environment affects the processing of language-specific special characters, for example how they are sorted. You can use both these additions to select different versions of the language.

SET MARGIN *column* [*line*].

You should only use this statement in reports. If you use this command, the system prints out data starting from the line and column you specified. This statement also creates an additional margin.

SET PARAMETER ID *parameter* **FIELD** *field*.

You use this command to fill the parameter global parameter with the content of field.

SET PF-STATUS *interface*
  [**EXCLUDING** *function_code* | *itab*]
  [**IMMEDIATELY**]
  [**OF PROGRAM** *program*].

You use this statement to set the status of the current interface. You can use the EXCLUDING addition to deactivate selected function codes from this status. You can transfer a single status that you want to deactivate as a direct value. If you want to deactivate several function codes, you must transfer them in the form of an internal table. You use the IMMEDIATELY addition to also set the new status for the previous list. This means that you can change the status of a list you want to call within a details list. If you enter OF PROGRAM, you can use another program's status.

SET PROPERTY OF *object attributes* = *field* [**NO FLUSH**].

You use this statement to process OLE objects. The system sets the characteristic of an object that you have created with DATA and initialized with CREATE to the value you specify. You use the NO FLUSH addition to collect OLE requests in a buffer. They are stored there until you clear the buffer with FREE.

SET RUN TIME ANALYZER ON | **OFF**.

You use this statement to switch runtime monitoring on or off.

SET RUN TIME CLOCK RESOLUTION LOW | **HIGH**.

You use this statement to toggle the resolution of runtime monitoring from milliseconds to microseconds and back again.

SET SCREEN *screen_number*.

You use this statement to specify the number of the screen program that is to be executed after you have finished processing the current screen program. To close the program, specify the value 0 for the next screen. You should only use this statement in dialog applications.

SET TITLEBAR *title* [**OF PROGRAM** *program*] [**WITH** { *parameter* }].

You use this statement to set the title of the current window. You maintain the title with a specific tool that operates independently of the source code and use a three-digit descriptor to identify it. The title can contain single or numbered placeholders (&, &1– &9), that can be replaced by the parameters of the WITH addition. You use the OF PROGRAM addition to use another program's title.

SET UPDATE TASK LOCAL.

You use this statement to switch on *local updates*. This means that update procedures are now carried out in the current process. After COMMIT WORK, the system then processes all update tasks, before continuing with the program.

SET USER-COMMAND *field*.

You should only use this statement in reporting. The field you enter contains a function code that is buffered. The next time you display a list, the system processes this function code, as if you had triggered it yourself.

SHIFT *string* [**BY** *n* **PLACES** | **UP TO** *pattern*]
   [**CIRCULAR** | **RIGHT** | **LEFT**] |
   [**LEFT DELETING LEADING** *pattern_2*] |
   [**RIGHT DELETING TRAILING** *pattern_2*].

You use this statement to process character strings. In its basic form, it moves the contents of the character string by one character to the left, thereby deleting the first character. You use the BY addition to offset the character string by more than one character. You use the UP TO addition to search for a pattern in the character string you want to process and move to this position if the pattern is found. All three variants can be used with more additions that influence the direction of rotation. The LEFT addition is the default setting and can therefore be omitted. If you use CIRCULAR, the contents are rotated. No characters are lost because they are added again on the right of the character string. If you use RIGHT, the contents are rotated to the right. Both the DELETING additions move the contents of the character string until a character from pattern_2 stands in the first or last place.

The system handles all the fields involved as character strings, no matter what their actual type.

SKIP [*lines*] | [**TO LINE** *line*].

You should only use this statement in list processing. In its basic form, this statement outputs a blank line. If required, you can also specify the number of blank lines to be added. You can also place the cursor on an absolute line.

```
SORT [DESCENDING | ASCENDING]
    [BY fieldlist | BY fieldgroup]
    [AS TEXT]
    [STABLE].
```

The basic form of this statement sorts the extract dataset in accordance with the fields in the HEADER field group. You can use additions to define both the sorting sequence (DESCENDING or ASCENDING) and to select another sort key (field list or field group). However, all the fields involved must be defined in the HEADER field group. The AS TEXT addition forces the system to sort the data in accordance with the specified text environment (language-specific sorting of special characters). The STABLE addition prevents the sequence of records that have the same sort key from being changed.

```
SORT itab
    [BY fieldlist]
    [DESCENDING | ASCENDING]
    [BY fieldlist]
    [AS TEXT]
    [STABLE].
```

You use this statement to sort an internal table. Here, all the fields that are not number fields or tables act as sort keys. If necessary, you can specify the sort key for each field list. You can also use ASCENDING or DESCENDING to define the sorting sequence. You use the AS TEXT addition to sort the data in accordance with the current text environment. You use the STABLE addition to ensure that the sequence of fields that have the same sort key is not changed. Unless you use this addition, there is no guarantee that this will happen.

```
SPLIT string AT separator_sequence
    INTO (TABLE itab) | (fieldlist).
```

You use this statement to split a character string in accordance with the separator sequence. The system uses the entire (defined) length of the separator sequence, including the concluding blank, if the separator sequence has not been filled with enough characters. The subfields are stored either in the structure's fields or in their own record in the internal table. When you split the character string, if more subfields are created than there are fields in the structure, all the subfields are included in the last field.

```
START-OF-SELECTION.
```

The system processes this list-processing event statement immediately before it accesses a table for the first time. In this way, it introduces the 'main program' of a report. This type of event is triggered automatically at the start of a report.

```
STATICS:
    declaration ...
    .
```

This command is a variant of the DATA statement. You use it to create what are known as *static variables* in subroutines (performs). You can use it with the same additions as for the DATA statement. The difference between fields created in this way and those created with the DATA statement is the duration of the declared data fields. Fields created with the STATICS statement are not destroyed when you leave the subroutine in which they were defined. They and their values are saved. However, the validity range is restricted to the subroutine in which they were created.

STOP.

You use this statement to end data selection and to then output the list. After STOP, the system processes the END-OF-SELECTION event.

SUBMIT *report* | *(namefield)* *[options]*.

You use this statement to start a report. You can use a further 24 options to set almost all the important parameters of the report you called. Table 9.11 contains a selection of the most important additions.

Table 9.11   Important additions of the SUBMIT command

Option	Effect
TO SAP-SPOOL OPTIONS	Output as a print spool
EXPORTING LIST TO MEMORY	Store the output list in RAM without outputting it on screen
VIA SELECTION-SCREEN	Display the selection screen of the called report
AND RETURN	Return to the calling report once processing is complete
USING SELECTION-SET	Execute the report with a variant
WITH	Fill parameters and selections

SUBTRACT *field_1* **FROM** *field_2*.

You use this statement to subtract the contents of field_1 from field_2. The result is stored in field_2.

SUBTRACT-CORRESPONDING *record_1* **FROM** *record_2*.

This statement only processes those fields whose names are present both in record_1 and in record_2. The contents of the fields from record_1 are subtracted from the fields that have the same name in record_2.

SUM.

In a LOOP (after processing a group) the system displays all the subtotals for all number fields (type F, I and P) in the header row of the internal table.

SUMMARY.

This statement triggers the same function as FORMAT INTENSIFIED ON.

SUMMING *field*.

You should only use this statement in reporting. For each field you enter, the system creates an internal summing field with the name SUM_field_name. Every time you use WRITE to output the original field, the current contents of the summing field are added to it. You can access the current total at any event, for example, even after END-OF-SELECTION.

SUPPLY { *parameter* = *value* } **TO CONTEXT** *context*.

You use this command to fill the key fields of a data context with values.

SUPPRESS DIALOG.

You should only use this statement in the PBO module of a screen program. It suppresses the output of the screen program on screen and therefore prevents anyone from entering data. However, the flow logic commands are still carried out.

TABLES *table*.

You use this statement to declare the table or view you specify in the program. If you do this, the system creates a structure with the same name as a work area (header row). The object you enter must be present and active in the Data Dictionary.

TOP-OF-PAGE [**DURING LINE-SELECTION**].

You use this event statement in reporting to start outputting a new page. In its basic form, the statement only applies to the basic list (first list level). The system processes the TOP-OF-PAGE DURING LINE-SELECTION statement for the page headers of all details lists.

TRANSFER *field* **TO** *filename* [**LENGTH** *length*].

You use this statement to write the contents of field to the field you specify. If this file does not yet exist, the TRANSFER command tries to create it. The output format depends on the mode in which the file was generated (see OPEN). You can also enter an output length to restrict the number of characters that are to be written.

TRANSLATE *string*
  TO UPPER CASE |
  TO LOWER CASE |
  USING *pattern* |
  FROM CODE PAGE *codepage_1* **TO CODE PAGE** *codepage_2* |
  FROM NUMBER FORMAT *format_1* **TO NUMBER FORMAT** *format_2*.

You use this statement to transform the contents of the character string. The result is then displayed again in string. In addition to converting the characters to upper or lower case, you can use USING to convert individual characters into other characters. The conversion is defined in pattern. In this parameter (field or direct value), the character to be replaced and the new character stand next to each other in pairs.

You use the FROM or TO CODEPAGE addition to transform the characters by means of a conversion table in which you can maintain the various fonts or code tables with the SPAD transaction. You use the FROM or TO NUMBER FORMAT additions to convert numbers from one system-specific format to another.

TYPES *type*.

You use the TYPES statement to define data types that are specific to a user. This statement uses the same parameters as the DATA statement. This means you can define fields, structures and internal tables. Before you can use the types defined by types, you must use DATA ... TYPE to create a data field.

TYPE-POOL *typ_pool*.

You use this statement to introduce a type pool. Usually you never have to program it manually, because the system automatically inserts it in a type pool.

TYPE-POOLS *typ_pool*.

You use this statement to include a type pool in an application. After this you can use the data types that are defined in the type pool.

ULINE [**AT** [*/position(length)*]].

In its basic form, this statement generates a continuous underline. You can enter a format to predefine both the starting position and the length of the line.

UNASSIGN *<fieldsymbol>*.

You use this statement to remove the assignment of a field symbol. This field symbol then no longer refers to any valid element.

UNPACK *source* **TO** *target*.

You use this statement to unpack (decompress) the packed contents of the source field and to place them in the target field. If you do this, depending on the length of the target field, it is either filled with leading blanks or the contents are truncated.

UPDATE *table* **SET** { *assignment* }
  [**WHERE** *condition*]
  [**CLIENT SPECIFIED**].

You use this statement to update individual fields in a table. The new value is assigned using the format table_field = value. In this case, the value can be a field or the result of an arithmetical expression. However, only addition or subtraction is possible in this expression. You can use the WHERE clause to restrict the number of records to be updated. If you do not use the WHERE clause, all records will be modified. You can use the CLIENT SPECIFIED addition to switch off automatic client-handling. If you do this, you must fill the client field manually with a correct search pattern. In an UPDATE statement you can link several substatements to each other by colon notation. If you do this, the WHERE and CLIENT additions only apply to one of the substatements.

UPDATE *table* | **table* | *(field_with_tablename)*
  [**FROM** *record*] | [**FROM TABLE** *itab*]
  [**CLIENT SPECIFIED**].

The basic form of this statement (without the FROM TABLE addition) modifies exactly one record in the database table. The system takes the new data, including the key fields that must clearly identify the record that is to be modified, from the header row or the work area you specify. You use the CLIENT SPECIFIED addition to switch off automatic client-handling.

The system can also take the new data from an internal table that has been included in the UPDATE statement by the FROM TABLE addition. In this case, the system carries out a mass update in the database table.

WAIT [**UNTIL** *condition*] **UP TO** *n* **SECONDS**.

You use this statement to interrupt program processing for n seconds. If you set a condition that is not fulfilled, RFCs will be received from a previously called asynchronous call, until the condition is fulfilled or there are no more asynchronous calls or the waiting time you specify has expired. You can choose not to use the UP TO addition when you set a condition.

WHILE *condition*
  [**VARY** *field* **FROM** *field_1* **NEXT** *field_2*].

The system executes the statements between WHILE and ENDWHILE if the evaluation of the logical expression returns the value TRUE. You can use the same statements in the logical expression as you do for IF.

You can use the VARY addition to assign a value to field in the WHILE loop. The first time the loop runs, the field receives the value from field_1. In the second run, it receives the value from field_2. In later runs the new field contents are taken from the field whose address is the result of adding the offset of field_1 and field_2 to the last field in each case.

WINDOW STARTING AT *x1 y1* [**ENDING AT** *x2 y2*].

You use this statement to display the current list in a dialog box. The x1 and y1 values show the upper left-hand corner of the dialog box within the current window. The lower right-hand corner is the same as that of the current window. Alternatively, you can use the ENDING AT addition to enter the lower right-hand corner.

WRITE [**AT** */position(output_length)*] *field*
  [*options*]
  [*format*]
  [**AS CHECKBOX**] |
  [**AS SYMBOL**]
  [**AS ICON**] |
  [**AS LINE**]
  [**QUICKINFO** *info*].

You should only use the WRITE statement in list processing. It writes the contents of a field to the output list. The output in this case uses the default output length for the type of field. You can use the AT addition to position the output within the line and restrict its length. You can use a wide variety of additions and parameters to modify the output screen. The formatting options affect how the value is displayed (see Table 9.12), and you can use the output formats to set the colour and intensity. These output formats match the parameters of the `format` command. You can use other additions to display special fields as checkboxes. Icons or symbols are identified in the system by special character strings, so they may not necessarily be recognized as icons (for example, if the character string is read and the reading program does not know where to find the symbol to convert the string to). If you use the AS ICON or AS SYMBOL additions, the system has to output the icon which matches the field content. Suitable constants are defined in the <ICON>, <SYMBOL> or <LIST> includes.

You can use the QUICKINFO addition to define an `info` text that can be up to 40 characters long. This `info` text is displayed in a special display when the cursor rests on the relevant field.

Table 9.12   WRITE command formatting options

Option	Effect
NO-ZERO	Suppress leading blanks
NO-SIGN	No prefix operator output
NO-GROUPING	Suppress the thousands delimiter
DD/MM/YY	Display date using this format
MM/DD/YY	Display date using this format
DD/MM/YYYY	Display date using this format
MM/DD/YYYY	Display date using this format
DDMMYY	Display date using this format
MMDDYY	Display date using this format
YYMMDD	Display date using this format
CURRENCY	Processing according to currency
DECIMALS	Number of decimal places to be output
ROUND	Round off a P field
UNIT	Processing according to unit of measurement
EXPONENT	Format for writing exponents with predefined exponents
USING EDIT MASK	Use formatting mask
USING NO EDIT MASK	Do not execute conversion routine from Data Dictionary
UNDER	Output exactly under another field
NO-GAP	Suppress delimiter (space) after output
LEFT-JUSTIFIED	Justify to the left in the output field
CENTERED	Centre in the output field
RIGHT-JUSTIFIED	Justify to the right in the output field

```
WRITE field | (field_name) TO target[+offset(length)]
  [options]
  [INDEX index].
```

The WRITE TO statement does not write its output to the screen list, but to another field instead. This means you can also specify an offset within the field and also the length of the area that is to be overwritten as the target. You can use some of the formatting options listed in Table 9.12 to process the characters you want to transfer. You can also write data directly to a record in an internal table. This table must be identified by a record number.

9.4   Flow logic command overview

In addition to the true ABAP commands, there are more ABAP commands for the flow logic of screen programs. The syntax of these commands resembles some of the ABAP commands, but their functionality is very different.

```
CALL SUBSCREEN subscreen
  [ INCLUDING program screen_number ].
```

You use this command to call the flow logic of a subscreen. You can also define the subscreen in another module pool. You can transfer the module pool name and the screen program number either as constants or dynamically in a data field. You only require the INCLUDING addition at the PBO event.

```
CALL CUSTOMER-SUBSCREEN subscreen
  [ INCLUDING program screen_number ].
```

You use this command to call a subscreen that can be created by customers. You must specify the program name and screen program number as constants. The subscreen must be located in a program that starts with the characters SAPLX and has been registered by the customer as a customer extension, using the CMOD transaction.

```
CHAIN.
  flow logic statements
ENDCHAIN.
```

Together, the CHAIN and ENDCHAIN statements combine statements into a block. All the FIELD statements in this block apply to all subsequent MODULE statements. When one of the modules triggers a message, all the fields in the block you selected with FIELD become ready for input.

```
FIELD fieldlist [:]
  [ MODULE modul ] |
  [ SELECT statement ] |
  [ VALUES value_list ].
```

You use the FIELD statement to name one or more screen program fields, to which you can apply various check routines. The check routines can either stand directly in the

FIELD statement or be combined with the check command by means of a CHAIN-ENDCHAIN bracket. In the first case, you may only enter one field each time. In the second case, you can count several fields by using colon notation (putting a colon after the FIELD *fieldlist* statement.

When one of the check routines triggers an E-type message, you can only make entries in those screen program fields that were listed in the structure.

LOOP [**WITH CONTROL** *control*].
   flow logic statements
ENDLOOP.

You use this statement to process all the blocks in a step loop or a table view, one after the other. When you use this statement in a table view, you must use the appropriate addition to enter a control.

LOOP AT *itab*
[[**FROM** *first*] [**TO** *last*]] |
[**CURSOR** *cursor*] |
[**WITH CONTROL** *control*] |
[**INTO** *work_area*].
   flow logic statements
ENDLOOP.

You use this statement to process the contents of the itab internal table in a step loop or a table view. In this case, the system automatically creates a scroll function. If you are using a table view, you must specify the appropriate control. You can use both the FROM and TO options to restrict the area of the table that is displayed. If you use the INTO option, you can use a separate work area instead of the table's header row. If you use the CURSOR option to name a field, this field fulfils two roles. If it was filled dynamically in the program, the data is displayed in the screen program, starting from the corresponding table line. This acts as a program-controlled scroll function. In the LOOP statement, the field contains the number of each current table line.

LOOP AT *table*.
   flow logic statements
ENDLOOP.

This variant of the LOOP statement is only still supported for reasons of compatibility, as you can use other tools to maintain tables from Release 3.0 onwards. You use this statement to transfer the contents of a database table into a step loop, record by record. If you want to write the changed values back to the table, you must use the MODIFY command at the PAI event. This command was specially designed to enable you to maintain standard-type tables (Transaction SM30).

MODIFY *dictionary_table*.

You use this command to update this table in a LOOP through a database table. This command also deals with some actions which occur when you maintain standard-type tables.

```
MODULE module_name
  [ON INPUT]
  [ON CHAIN-INPUT]
  [ON *-INPUT]
  [ON REQUEST]
  [ON CHAIN-REQUEST]
  [AT CURSOR-SELECTION]
  [AT EXIT-COMMAND].
```

In the flow logic of a screen program, you use the MODULE statement to call a module from the module pool. The various additions, which can only be used at the PAI event, make the way in which the module is executed dependent on a range of preconditions. Furthermore, you can only use any of the ON additions in conjunction with a field assignment (FIELD and/or CHAIN statements). Table 9.13 describes how the different additions work.

Table 9.13   Options for calling modules

Addition	Module executed, if
ON INPUT	The value in the assigned input field is not the same as the initial value
ON CHAIN-INPUT	At least one of the fields in the CHAIN brackets contains a value that is not the same as the initial value
ON *-INPUT	The field accepts * for a wildcard, and a user has entered *
ON REQUEST	You have made an entry in the assigned input field
ON CHAIN-REQUEST	You have made an entry in at least one of the fields in the CHAIN bracket
AT CURSOR-SELECTION	The user has selected an object either by double-clicking with the mouse or by pressing (F2)
AT EXIT-COMMAND	A function code (that has function type E, Exit code) has been triggered in the screen program. The system then executes this module before all other modules and before the automatic value check

```
PROCESS (
  BEFORE OUTPUT    |
  AFTER INPUT      |
  ON HELP-REQUEST  |
  ON VALUE-REQUEST ).
```

You use this statement to introduce a separate section into a screen program's flow logic. You must use one of the additions. Each section corresponds to a particular event during screen program processing. Table 9.14 describes the different events.

Table 9.14   Events in the flow logic

Event	Abbreviation	Event of execution
PROCESS BEFORE OUTPUT	PBO	Before the screen program is displayed
PROCESS AFTER INPUT	PAI	After data has been entered in the screen program
PROCESS ON HELP-REQUEST	POH	When you press (F1) to request general help in the screen program
PROCESS ON VALUE REQUEST	POV	When you press (F4) to request value help

```
SELECT * FROM table
  WHERE keyfield = screen_field
    [ AND keyfield = screen_field ...]
  [ INTO field]
  [ WHENEVER ( NOT FOUND | FOUND )
      SEND ( ERRORMESSAGE | WARNING )
      [ message_number ]
      [ WITH field ... ]].
```

You use this command to read a record from a database table. You can do this at the PBO event to initialize screen program fields or at the PAI event to check the values in the screen program fields. In the first case you use the INTO addition to transfer the value into the screen program field. You can use other additions to evaluate the results of the selection so that you can create error messages.

9.5   System fields

The system fills the system fields with current values at runtime. Some of these fields play a vital role within the applications because they provide information about the system status. Other fields are only used to allow various basic programs to communicate with each other and are of no interest to application developers. This subsection describes the most important system fields. The fields are grouped according to subject and notes on usage.

When you are debugging an application, you can either display the system fields individually, by entering their entire name, or together in a list. If you display them together, you must select debugger mode (GOTO -> FIELD). You enter SY or SYST as a field name. All the system fields appear after you press (Enter). They are managed internally as elements in the SY or SYST structure. The two names are synonyms.

9.5.1 General information

This group includes those fields that cannot clearly be assigned to another subject area. This does not mean that these fields are unimportant. Some of the fields in this group are the most frequently used of all the system fields.

SY-ABCDE

This field contains the alphabet that is used in upper-case letters. You can use it to check that entries are correct. However in practice you usually do this another way.

SY-DATAR

The system initializes this field before a screen program is executed. After processing but before the first PAI module is executed, this field is set to 'X' if data has been changed in the screen program. This means you can identify changes to data in exit modules and prompt the user to save changes if necessary.

SY-DBCNT

After a database operation, this field contains the number of elements that have been processed or found. You often use this field together with a SELECT statement, for example to define whether 0, 1 or several records are present for a particular search term. You can also use the COUNT addition in the SELECT statement to do this because it also places the result in this system variable.

SY-FDPOS

Various commands used in processing character strings and operators in logical statements (e.g. CP, CS, etc.) fill this field with the position of the character string they find. You can also use the field contents from SY-FDPOS to replace parts of the character string or to resolve a partial string.

SY-LANGU

This field is filled with the short code for the current language when a user is registered in the system. A range of internal system resources use this field to define the correct language-dependent texts and messages. You must evaluate this field in applications, if these applications create their own language-dependent tables. These might, for example, contain texts that describe a record.

SY-MANDT

When you use this field, it is filled with the current client number. You usually do not need to evaluate this, because the system deals with client fields automatically. However, during testing, for example, it may be a good idea to block or release special applications by querying this field in particular clients.

SY-SUBRC

This is the most frequently used system field. After many statements have been executed, it contains a value that tells you whether they have been executed correctly. It does so for example in the case of OPEN-SQL statements and function module calls.

SY-UNAME

When the user logs on in the system, the system enters their logon name in this field. This name is used by the authorization check, for example, to define the user's current authorization profile. In applications, the field is often used to store the name of the last person who made changes.

9.5.2 Flow control

SY-DYNGR

In a screen program's attributes, you can maintain a value for a *screen program group*. This attribute is optional and it is not used very often. When a screen program is being processed, the value of the screen program group attribute is displayed in the SY-DYNG field.

SY-DYNNR

When a screen program is being processed, this field contains the current screen program's number. This value is used quite frequently to execute statements that refer to a specific screen program in modules that are used by several screen programs. For example, it can be used to set a status or to deactivate function codes, depending on the screen program number.

SY-INDEX

The system counts loop runs (LOOP DO, SELECT . . .) in this field. The system displays this value when it creates a sequential number or when it counts the actions within a loop. This value only applies within a particular loop. The value is not defined outside the loop.

SY-LOOPC

This field contains the number of lines in a step loop that are visible in the screen program. The content is only valid within the validity range of a LOOP-ENDLOOP loop in the flow logic and therefore also within the modules and subroutines that are called from there.

SY-PFKEY

This field contains the name of the current interface status. You rarely need to evaluate it.

SY-REPID

The current program's name is stored in this field.

SY-STEPL

In a `LOOP-ENDLOOP` loop in the flow logic, the number of the step loop line that is currently being processed is stored in this field. Like the `SY-LOOPC` value, this value only applies within the loop.

SY-TCODE

When the system executes a transaction, the transaction code is displayed in this field. Because applications are often called with different transactions, this field is often used to select a specific action within an application (e.g. create, change, display) or to select a value range for the authorization check.

SY-UCOMM

When a function code is triggered, this function code is set in the `SY-UCOMM` field. Because the function code can also be evaluated through other fields such as the command field in a screen program, you do not have to access `SY-UCOMM` very often in order to read the data. However, you usually have to use `LIKE` to derive from `SY-UCOMM` the data fields in a program that are to include a function code.

9.5.3 Internal tables

Some system fields are also set when you process internal tables. The primary function of these fields is to provide information about the size and status of a table. Two of these fields are used more frequently than others:

SY-TABIX

This field contains the number of the current record in the table that was processed most recently. This field is updated, for example, when you use the `READ` statement to search for a record. If you want to write the record back to the table after you have changed it, you must use the `MODIFY` command to enter the record number. You will find the record number in `SY-TABIX`.

SY-TFILL

This field is only valid within a `LOOP` through an internal table. It contains the number of records in the internal table.

9.5.4 Texts and messages

You can access the texts or characteristics of messages through a range of special system fields. This does not happen very often in applications. However, these fields can sometimes be really useful when you are debugging an application.

SY-MSGID

This field contains the message ID of the most recently output message.

SY-MSGTY

This field contains the type (E, I, W, S, A) of the most recently output message.

SY-MSGNO

This field contains the number of the most recently output message.

SY-MSGV1-4

These four fields contain the character strings that were used to replace the placeholders in a message text.

SY-ULINE

The system stores the character it uses for underlining in this field.

SY-VLINE

The system stores the character it uses for vertical bars (pipes) in this field.

SY-TITLE

This field contains an application's title.

9.5.5 Times and dates

You have to enter the date and time quite often, for example to log the time at which records were changed. For this reason, some of these fields are used very frequently.

SY-TZONE

The difference in seconds between the current time and Greenwich Mean Time is stored in this field.

SY-DAYST

This field is set when Summer Time is in use.

SY-FDAYW

This field contains the number of the day of the week, according to the factory calendar.

SY-DATUM

This field contains the current date.

SY-UZEIT

The system stores the current time in this field.

9.5.6 Creating screens and lists

The tools the system provides are usually sufficient for you to create the output you require. However, in order to use these resources correctly, you require some information about the current status of the list or the screen program. These values are stored in system fields and can in some exceptional cases also be of interest for your own applications.

SY-COLNO

When you output a list, the column (position of a character within a line) is stored in this field.

SY-CPAGE

This field contains the current page number.

SY-CUCOL, SY-CUROW

This field contains the current cursor position.

SY-LINCT

The SY-LINCT field contains the number of lines in a list.

SY-LINNO

When you create an output list, this field contains the current line number.

SY-LINSZ

The system stores the usable line length of the list in this field. This value is derived either from the list width you set with LINE-SIZE or the current window size if no value has been defined for the page width. It is possible to modify the format of a list to fit the available space by restricting the output length of very wide fields or by hiding fields completely. However, this is only a good idea if the list is designed to be output on screen, because the format of lists that are to be printed is predefined in great detail.

SY-MACOL, SY- MAROW

You use the SET MARGIN statement to define a free area on the upper margin of the left page. This area is not printed. You can use either of these fields to set the measurements of this area (left-hand and top margin).

SY-PAGNO

When you output a list, this field contains the number of the current page.

SY-SCOLS, SY-SROWS

The system stores the window measurements in these two fields. These values are updated when the user changes the window's size. You can use these values to create a list that fits the screen size.

9.5.7 Windows

The fields in a window group contain information about the size and position of a window as well as about the position of the cursor.

SY-WINX1, SY-WINY1

These fields contain the co-ordinates of the upper left-hand corner of a window relative to the higher level window.

SY-WINX2, SY- WINY2

These fields contain the co-ordinates of the lower right-hand corner of a window. These values are relative to the higher level window.

SY-WINCO, SY-WINRO

These two fields contain the position of the cursor in the window.

9.5.8 Interactive reporting

During interactive reporting, the system not only transfers information using the hidden data area (see the `HIDE` command), but also uses a range of system fields. However, these fields merely supply additional information that should only be used in exceptional cases.

SY-LILLI

After the user selects a line, the system inserts the absolute number of that line in this field.

SY-LISEL

After the user selects a line, the system inserts the contents of that line in this field. As the link with the individual fields is lost, the contents of this field can only rarely be evaluated in a useful way.

SY-LSIND

This field is very important as it contains the list level. The base list has the value 0, the first list to which the user branches has the value 1, etc. This field is used at the various `AT` events to select the program option necessary for the list that is to be generated.

SY-STACO, SY-STARO

These two fields contain the co-ordinates of the first character displayed in the list. They consist of the number of the first line in the window and the number of the first display column. These fields initially have the value 1. The value changes when the user scrolls through the list. If the user jumps between lists, these fields contain the corresponding values for the last list displayed and not for the current list.

9.5.9 System-specific fields

These fields provide information about the current R/3 System. They are of no interest to most applications. Their contents only need to be evaluated in very special cases such as when Native SQL statements are used.

SY-DBSYS

This field contains the name of the database system.

SY-HOST

This field contains the name of the computer on which the R/3 System is running. This name is identical to the computer name which is displayed in the status bar.

SY-OPSYS

This field is used to store the name of the operating system.

SY-SAPRL

The `SY-SAPRL` field contains the current system Release.

SY-SYSID

This field contains the name of the R/3 System. This value is also displayed in the status bar.

10 Listings

In this chapter, you will find the listings mentioned in Chapter 7 for the second application example. In the second screen program, a table view is used to maintain index values. This requires less programming effort than step loops. To keep things simple, the menus are not very complex in this program. In the first screen program, you only have the default functions, Cancel, Quit and Back. All of these are exit functions. In the second screen program, you have an additional function for saving data.

10.1 Flow logic of the base screen

```
PROCESS BEFORE OUTPUT.
  MODULE status_9100.
*
PROCESS AFTER INPUT.
  MODULE exit_9100 AT EXIT-COMMAND.
  MODULE read_data_9100.
  MODULE user_command_9100.
```

10.2 Flow logic processing picture

```
PROCESS BEFORE OUTPUT.
  MODULE status_9200.
  LOOP AT i_price INTO f_price CURSOR cursor WITH CONTROL
  tc_price.
  ENDLOOP.
*
PROCESS AFTER INPUT.
  MODULE exit_9200 AT EXIT-COMMAND.
  LOOP AT i_price.
    FIELD f_price-price
      MODULE data_changed_9200 ON REQUEST.
    FIELD f_price-price
      MODULE modify_itab_9200.
  ENDLOOP.
  MODULE user_command_9200.
```

10.3 Global declarations

```
PROGRAM sapmyz3p MESSAGE-ID y3.
TABLES:
  yz3stock,
  yz3price
.                                            " tables


CONSTANTS:
  c_true        VALUE 'X',
  c_false       VALUE ' ',
  c_yes         VALUE 'J',
  c_no          VALUE 'N',
  c_cancel      VALUE 'A',
  c_on  TYPE i  VALUE 1,
  c_off TYPE i  VALUE 0
.                                            " constants


DATA:
  fcode          LIKE sy-ucomm,
  g_fcode        LIKE fcode,
  g_date         LIKE yz3price-curdate,
  cursor         TYPE i,
  g_changed      LIKE c_false VALUE c_false,
  g_save         LIKE c_false VALUE c_false,
  g_exit         LIKE c_false VALUE c_false,
  g_exit_module  LIKE c_false VALUE c_false,

  i_stock        LIKE yz3stock OCCURS 20,
  f_stock        LIKE LINE OF i_stock,

  i_price        LIKE yz3price OCCURS 20,
  f_price        LIKE LINE OF i_price
.                                            " data

CONTROLS:
  tc_price TYPE TABLEVIEW USING SCREEN 9200
.                                            "controls
```

10.4 PBO modules

```
MODULE status_9100 OUTPUT.
  SET PF-STATUS 'STAT_G'.
```

```
    yz3price-curdat = sy-datum.
ENDMODULE.                              " STATUS_9100 OUTPUT
MODULE status_9200 OUTPUT.
   SET PF-STATUS 'STAT_A'.

*...initialize global fields
   g_exit       = c_false.
   g_exit_module = c_false.
ENDMODULE.                              " STATUS_9200 OUTPUT
```

10.5 PAI modules

```
MODULE exit_9100 INPUT.
   LEAVE TO SCREEN 0.
ENDMODULE.                              " EXIT_9100 INPUT
MODULE read_data_9100 INPUT.
*... Fill Itab for index values
   PERFORM read_data_9100.
ENDMODULE.                              " READ_DATA_9100 INPUT

MODULE user_command_9100 INPUT.
   g_fcode = fcode.
   CLEAR fcode.


*...If user presses (ENTER), process data

   IF g_fcode = ' '.
     LEAVE TO SCREEN 9200.
   ENDIF.
ENDMODULE.                              " USER_COMMAND_9100 INPUT

MODULE exit_9200 INPUT.
   g_fcode = fcode.
   CLEAR fcode.
   g_exit_module = c_true.

*...If the data changes, prompt user to save
   IF   g_changed = c_true OR
        sy-datum  = c_true.

*... Set G_CHANGED to make correct evaluation possible
*... in the first run
*... g_changed = c_true.
```

```
*.....prompt user to save if required
*.....and set EXIT flag

PERFORM check_save_9200.

*.....If quit without saving is required,
*.....jump back directly to the EXIT module
    IF  g_exit = c_true AND
        g_save = c_false.
      g_changed = c_false.

*....unlock record, then jump back
      PERFORM dequeue_9200.
      PERFORM navigate_9200.
    ENDIF.
  ELSE.

*.....if no data has been changed,
*.....set G_EXIT for evaluation in NAVIGATE_9200
    g_exit = c_true.

*..... unlock record, then jump back as defined by function code
    PERFORM dequeue_9200.
    PERFORM navigate_9200.
  ENDIF.
ENDMODULE.                              " EXIT_9200 INPUT

MODULE D9200_DATA_CHANGED INPUT.
*...SY-DATAR is always reinitialized,
*...therefore it must always be saved

  IF SY-DATAR = TRUE.
    G_CHANGED = TRUE.
  ENDIF.
ENDMODULE.

MODULE data_changed_9200 INPUT.
*...SY-DATAR is always reinitialized,
*...therefore it must always be saved,
  IF sy-datar = c_true.
    g_changed = c_true.
  ENDIF.
ENDMODULE.                              " DATA_CHANGED_9200 INPUT
```

```
MODULE modify_itab_9200 INPUT.
  IF f_price-price < 0.
    MESSAGE e010.       " correct index value entries!
  ENDIF.

*... upgrade Itab
  MODIFY i_price INDEX cursor FROM f_price.
ENDMODULE.                              " MODIFY_ITAB_9200 INPUT

MODULE user_command_9200 INPUT.
*... FCODE is reset in the EXIT MODULE in the case of FT03 and FT15

  IF g_exit_module = c_false.
    g_fcode = fcode.
    CLEAR fcode.

*..... establish whether data has to be saved
*.....and whether screen program may be left. Prompt
*.....to save is only necessary if EXIT MODULE was
*.....not effective
    PERFORM check_save_9200.
  ENDIF.

  PERFORM save_9200.
  PERFORM navigate_9200.
ENDMODULE.                              " USER_COMMAND_9200 INPUT
```

10.6 Subroutines

```
FORM read_data_9100.
  RANGES r_wkz FOR yz3price-wkz.

*...Save data from screen program 9100, as changes
*... will be made to header line
  g_date = yz3price-curdate.
  CLEAR: i_stock, f_stock.
  REFRESH i_stock.

*... read all share index values and save them in a buffer
  SELECT * FROM yz3stock
  INTO TABLE i_stock.

*...build RANGES table
  r_wkz-sign = 'I'.
```

```
  r_wkz-option = 'EQ'.
  LOOP AT i_stock INTO f_stock.
    r_wkz-low = f_stock-wkz.
    APPEND r_wkz.
  ENDLOOP.

  CLEAR: i_price, f_price.
  REFRESH i_price.

*...read index values for all valid shares

SELECT * FROM yz3price
    INTO TABLE i_price
    WHERE curdate = g_date AND
          wkz IN r_wkz.

*...lock table for index values
  CALL FUNCTION 'ENQUEUE_EY3PRICE'
    EXPORTING
*     MODE_YZ3PRICE = 'X'
*     MANDT = SY-MANDT
      wkz = ' '
      curdate = g_date
*     X_WKZ = ' '
*     X_AKTDATE = ' '
*     _SCOPE = '2'
*     _WAIT = ' '
*     _COLLECT = ' '
    EXCEPTIONS
      foreign_lock = 1
      system_failure = 2
      OTHERS = 3.

  IF sy-subrc <> 0.
    MESSAGE e005. "Record cannot be locked!
  ENDIF.

  LOOP AT i_stock INTO f_stock.

*.....check whether, for all records from YZ3STOCK,
*.....there is also an entry in YZ3PRICE, if not,
*.....then add a record
    READ TABLE i_price INTO f_price
      WITH KEY wkz = f_stock-wkz.
```

```
      IF sy-subrc <> 0.
        CLEAR f_price.
        MOVE-CORRESPONDING f_stock TO f_price.
        f_price-curdate = g_date.
        APPEND f_price TO i_price.

      ELSE.
        f_price-curdate = g_date.
        MODIFY i_price INDEX sy-tabix FROM f_price.
      ENDIF.

   ENDLOOP.
ENDFORM.                              " READ_DATA_9100

FORM check_save_9200.
  CASE g_fcode.

*.....(ENTER) key -> only data check
  WHEN ' '.
    g_save = c_false.
    g_exit = c_false.

*.....F3 = Back
*......-> Provide user with means of saving when changing data

WHEN 'FT03'.
    PERFORM save_question_9200.

*.....F11 = SAVE
*......-> Save and end screen program
  WHEN 'FT11'.
    g_save = c_true.
    g_exit = c_true.

*.....F12 = Cancel
*......-> Only system warning of possible data loss
  WHEN 'FT12'.
    PERFORM cancel_question_9200.

*.....F15 = FINISH
*......-> Provide user with means of saving when changing data
  WHEN 'FT15'.
    PERFORM save_question_9200.

  ENDCASE.
ENDFORM.                              " CHECK_SAVE_9200
```

```
FORM dequeue_9200.
  CALL FUNCTION 'DEQUEUE_EY3PRICE'
    EXPORTING
*      MODE_YZ3PRICE = 'X'
*      MANDT         = SY-MANDT
       wkz           = ' '
       curdate       = g_date
*      X_WKZ         = ' '
*      X_AKTDATE     = ' '
*      _SCOPE        = '3'
*      _SYNCHRON     = ' '
*      _COLLECT      = ' '
  .
ENDFORM.                               " DEQUEUE_9200
FORM navigate_9200.
  IF g_exit = c_true.
    CASE g_fcode.

*.......F3 = Back
*.......-> Return to the previous screen program
      WHEN 'FT03'.
        LEAVE TO SCREEN 9100.

*.......F11 = SAVE
*.......-> Return to the previous screen program
      WHEN 'FT11'.
        LEAVE TO SCREEN 9100.

*.......F12 = Cancel
*.......-> Return to the previous screen program
      WHEN 'FT12'.
        LEAVE TO SCREEN 9100.

*.......F15 = FINISH
*.......-> Finish entire application
      WHEN 'FT15'.
        LEAVE PROGRAM.

    ENDCASE.
  ENDIF.
ENDFORM.                               " NAVIGATE_9200

SHAPE save_9200.
  IF g_save = c_true.
    MODIFY yz3price FROM TABLE i_price.
```

```
*.....Test the status of the database operation
    IF sy-subrc <> 0.
      ROLLBACK WORK.

*.......Text: Save error!
      MESSAGE e013.
    ELSE.

*.......Text: data for & saved
      MESSAGE s004 WITH g_date.
    ENDIF.

*.....cancel data record lock
    PERFORM dequeue_9200.

*..... Save changes permanently
    COMMIT WORK.

*.....reset data change flag
g_changed = c_false.
  ENDIF.
ENDFORM.                                    " SAVE_9200

SHAPE save_question_9200.
  DATA: l_answer.

*...query only necessary when data has been changed

  IF g_changed = c_true.
    CALL FUNCTION 'POPUP_TO_CONFIRM_STEP'
      EXPORTING
*       DEFAULTOPTION    = 'Y'

*..........text: data will be lost!
        textline1        = text-012

*..........text: save first?
        textline2        = text-013
        title            = text-010
*       START_COLUMN     = 25
*       START_ROW        = 6
      IMPORTING
        answer           = l_answer
      EXCEPTIONS
        OTHERS           = 1.
```

```
    CASE l_answer.
*.......Save and finish
      WHEN c_yes.
        g_save = c_true.
        g_exit = c_true.

*.......finish without saving
        WHEN c_no.
         g_save = c_false.
         g_exit = c_true.

*.......Cancel function -> screen program will not finish

        WHEN c_cancel.
          g_save = c_false.
          g_exit = c_false.
      ENDCASE.

*...when data is not changed, you can finish any time
  ELSE.
     g_save = c_false.
     g_exit = c_true.
  ENDIF.
ENDFORM.                              " SAVE_QUESTION_9200

FORM cancel_question_9200.
  DATA: l_answer.

  CALL FUNCTION 'POPUP_TO_CONFIRM_LOSS_OF_DATA'
    EXPORTING

*...........text: really cancel?
        textline1      = text-011
*         TEXTLINE2      = ' '



*...........text: warning

        title          = text-010
*         START_COLUMN   = 25
*         START_ROW      = 6
    IMPORTING
        answer         = l_answer
    EXCEPTIONS
        OTHERS         = 1.
```

```
*...if user really wants to cancel, then set EXIT flag
  IF l_answer = c_yes.
    g_exit = c_true.
    g_save = c_false.

*...or else, deselect EXIT flag
  ELSE.
    g_exit = c_false.
  ENDIF.
ENDFORM.                                  " CANCEL_QUESTION_9200
```

11 The CD

You will find the following things on the accompanying CD:

An HTML-based description of the syntax of ABAP, for Release 4.6, structured alphabetically and according to subject area.

The source text for all example programs used in the book, supplied as pure ASCII text. In addition to the source texts for the current, second edition you will also find the source texts for the first edition as an update to that edition.

Special files in SAP's own format (transport files), which contain almost all the development objects described in the book (programs, tables, data elements etc.).

An HTML file, which can be used to access both the HTML help and a Web page in which any necessary additions and corrections will be published.

The corresponding files are in an SAP-specific format, that allows you to import the objects into an SAP system. From a technical point of view, the files on the CD are like a draft update. This section contains tips on how to load the CD into your SAP System.

The programs presented in the book were created on an SAP AG development system that is used as the development system for Version 4.6B. This is why major or minor problems can occur when the programs are loaded into older systems. This is primarily because many of the programs simply cannot run on older systems, because of differences in syntax. In addition, the format of the import file depends on which version of the SAP system is being used. This is another cause of technical problems. To make your task easier, and to reduce the number of technical errors to a minimum, you will find three versions of the transport files. These were created by loading and exporting the original transport files step-by-step into systems with earlier versions numbers. Any objects that contained obvious errors were not included in the export. However, programs that contained version-specific syntax errors were exported to provide anyone who is interested in this with the source text.

Importing a draft update is a task which involves working closely with the system. If your SAP System is set up correctly, you simply need to copy a few files into existing directories at operating system level, and execute a few system commands. However, problems may arise if your system configuration varies even slightly from the standard configuration. Please read the following important notes carefully before you start loading the example programs into your system:

You import the examples into your system at your own risk. Neither the publisher nor the author take responsibility for any damages caused as a consequence.

Neither the author nor the publisher can guarantee that the CD can be loaded into your system without causing any problems. The author and the publisher cannot provide any help on this matter

The CD and the programs it contains are not products of SAP AG. For this reason, SAP AG will not provide you with support for handling problems that arise in connection with using this CD.

The objects on the CD are within the customer naming range. If objects of the same name are already present in your system, these will be overwritten! You will find an item list of import files on the CD. It is crucial that you check for possible naming conflicts before you import the objects!

A few requirements must be fulfilled before you can load a draft update into your system:

You must be able to log into your system as a system administrator. The system administrator works with the user name <sid>adm, where the system name is entered in lower case letters for the value <sid>.

The transport management system (correction and transport) must be set up correctly. This means, among other things, that the directory /usr/sap/trans with the sub-directories bin, buffer, data, cofiles, log, sapnames and tmp must be present at system level and that the RDDIMPDP program is planned as a periodic background job in the SAP System.

The target system should not contain any conversion jobs. This means that the TBATG table must be empty (use Transaction SM31 to check this).

The tp and R3trans programs are present at operating system level for each SAP System. Various versions of these programs are present. For an import into a R/3 System, the version of these programs present must be the same as the system version.

To import the examples, you must carry out actions at both operating system level and in the SAP System. You start at operating system level. All instructions refer to UNIX-compatible operating systems.

Mount the CD. The commands you need to do this are operating-system-specific.

You must carry out all the following tasks as User <sid>adm. If necessary, you should log in again!

Copy the file R.xxxxxx.<SID> from the CD to the /usr/sap/trans/data directory. Copy the file Kxxxxxx.<SID> to the /usr/sap/trans/cofiles directory.

Go the the /usr/sap/trans/bin directory.

Execute both the

```
tp addtobuffer Kxxxxxxxxx <SID> and
tp import Kxxxxxxxxx <SID> client=<your test client> u4
```

commands one after the other.

For <SID>, enter your SAP System's name in upper case letters.

For xxxxxxxx enter the transport job number, for example BCEK020394.

You should carry out the next tasks in the SAP System. Call Transaction SE01, the Transport Organizer. In the Initial Screen, select REQUEST -> DISPLAY INDIVIDUALLY from the menu. In the next dialog, enter the transport job name in the input field. Now select GOTO -> TRANSPORT LOGS from the menu to check the status of the import. Only entries with error status 0 and 4 should appear here. Higher error numbers indicate that more serious problems have arisen during the import. In this case you must sort out the error and carry out the import again. You can do this at operating system level by calling this command:

```
tp import Kxxxxxxxxx <SID> u14
```

You should only execute the next work steps if the import was successful.

Index